LET'S GO

PAGES PACKED WITH ESSENTIAL INFORMATION

"Value-packed, unbeatable, accurate, and comprehensive."

—*The Los Angeles Times*

"The guides are aimed not only at young budget travelers but at the independent traveler; a sort of streetwise cookbook for traveling alone."

—*The New York Times*

"Unbeatable; good sight-seeing advice; up-to-date info on restaurants, hotels, and inns; a commitment to money-saving travel; and a wry style that brightens nearly every page."

—*The Washington Post*

THE BEST TRAVEL BARGAINS IN YOUR BUDGET

"All the dirt, dirt cheap."

—*People*

"Let's Go follows the creed that you don't have to toss your life's savings to the wind to travel—unless you want to."

—*The Salt Lake Tribune*

REAL ADVICE FOR REAL EXPERIENCES

"The writers seem to have experienced every rooster-packed bus and lunar-surfaced mattress about which they write."

—*The New York Times*

"[Let's Go's] devoted updaters really walk the walk (and thumb the ride, and trek the trail). Learn how to fish, haggle, find work—anywhere."

—*Food & Wine*

"A world-wise traveling companion—always ready with friendly advice and helpful hints, all sprinkled with a bit of wit."

—*The Philadelphia Inquirer*

A GUIDE WITH A SPIRIT AND A SOCIAL CONSCIENCE

"Lighthearted and sophisticated, informative and fun to read. [Let's Go] helps the novice traveler navigate like a knowledgeable old hand."

—*Atlanta Journal-Constitution*

"The serious mission at the book's core reveals itself in exhortations to respect the culture and the environment—and, if possible, to visit as a volunteer, a student, or a teacher rather than a tourist."

—*San Francisco Chronicle*

LET'S GO PUBLICATIONS

TRAVEL GUIDES

Australia
Austria & Switzerland
Brazil
Britain
California
Central America
Chile
China
Costa Rica
Costa Rica, Nicaragua & Panama
Eastern Europe
Ecuador
Egypt
Europe
France
Germany
Greece
Guatemala & Belize
Hawaii
India & Nepal
Ireland
Israel
Italy
Japan
Mexico
New Zealand
Peru
Puerto Rico
Southeast Asia
Spain & Portugal with Morocco
Thailand
USA
Vietnam
Western Europe
Yucatan Peninsula

ROADTRIP GUIDE

Roadtripping USA

ADVENTURE GUIDES

Alaska
Pacific Northwest
Southwest USA

CITY GUIDES

Amsterdam
Barcelona
Berlin, Prague & Budapest
Boston
Buenos Aires
Florence
London
London, Oxford, Cambridge & Edinburgh
New York City
Paris
Rome
San Francisco
Washington, DC

POCKET CITY GUIDES

Amsterdam
Berlin
Boston
Chicago
London
New York City
Paris
San Francisco
Venice
Washington, DC

LET'S GO

GUATEMALA &
BELIZE

RESEARCHERS

ELIAS BERGER
DANIEL NORMANDIN
ALISON TARWATER

ASHLEY R. LAPORTE MANAGING EDITOR
JOSEPH MOLIMOCK RESEARCH MANAGER

EDITORS
COURTNEY A. FISKE
SARA PLANA
CHARLIE E. RIGGS
RUSSELL FORD RENNIE
OLGA I. ZHULINA

HOW TO USE THIS BOOK

COVERAGE LAYOUT. *Let's Go Guatemala & Belize* was created to make reliable information that you need easy to find. The two-country introductory section includes the **Discover** chapter, which offers regional highlights, tips on when to travel, and itineraries. **History** glances at the past of these two fascinating countries. The **Essentials** chapter details the nitty-gritty of passports, transportation, money, communications, and more—everything you'll need to start your trip and stay safe on the road. **Beyond Tourism** advises on long-term stays: study abroad, volunteering, and work opportunities are just the beginning. Next come the two individual countries, which will each be sub-divided into **regional chapters**. Guatemala and Belize each begin with **Life and Times**, detailing history and culture, followed by Essentials, including important travel info specific to the country. At the back of the book, you'll find an expanded **Appendix** and **Glossary**—a crash course on sayings and popular words to get you through both the airports and the bars. Finally, our thoroughly updated **index** will make quick-reference a breeze. Check out the map index at the back, accompanied by a key. The black tabs on the side of each page separate chapters and help you navigate the book.

TRANSPORTATION. Both arrival and departure cities list information on transportation connections. Trip duration, frequency, and price are noted in parentheses; unless otherwise noted, the price is for a one-way trip. Orientation sections in each city describe the basic layout and notable landmarks of the town. In general, 12/14 Av. Nte., 3/5 C. Pte. means the establishment is between *Avenidas* 12 and 14, and *Calles* 3 and 5 *Poniente*.

PRICE DIVERSITY. We list establishments in order of value, and our absolute favorites are denoted by the *Let's Go* thumbs-up (◕). Since the best value does not always mean the cheapest price, we have incorporated a system of **price ranges (❶❷❸❹❺)** into our coverage of accommodation and food listings. At a glance, you can compare the cost of a night's stay in towns a mile apart or halfway across the region. The price ranges for each country can be found in **Price Diversity tables** located at the beginning of the Guatemala and Belize chapters.

> **A NOTE TO OUR READERS.** The information for this book was gathered by Let's Go researchers from May through August of 2009. Each listing is based on one researcher's opinion, formed during his or her visit at a particular time. Those traveling at other times may have different experiences since prices, dates, hours, and conditions are always subject to change. You are urged to check the facts presented in this book beforehand to avoid inconvenience and surprises.

CONTENTS

RESEARCHERS

Elias Berger
Western, Central, and Southern Guatemala

Armed with a semester of Spanish, a love for geography, and a friendly disposition, Eli took on Guatemala's biggest cities and most isolated villages with equal good cheer. Tirelessly searching for the best deals and the tastiest mojitos, this first-time Let's Go Researcher won us over with his sharp wit and determination to overcome food poisoning and unreliable bus schedules alike. From the bars and clubs of Panajachel to the most ancient Mayan ruins to the smoggy streets of Guatemala City, Eli wrote with candor and honesty—charming his editors and adding characteristic pizzazz to his coverage throughout the book.

Daniel Normandin
Belize and Northern Guatemala

Apparently, there is nothing that Dan can't do. Overcoming early obstacles, this Let's Go veteran never complained, never missed a deadline, and never stopped impressing us with his incredible work ethic and passion for travel. Immersing himself in the Mayan and Garífuna cultures of Belize's Toledo district, he opened the door for our readers with an emphasis on responsible travel and opportunities to make a difference. Whether wading through waste-deep water on jungle treks, befriending local hostel owners, or traversing the hallowed grounds of a Mayan temple, Dan traveled–and researched–with the boundless enthusiasm that pervades his entertaining and informative coverage of Guatemala and Belize.

Alison Tarwater
Eastern Guatemala

Street gangs, active volcanoes, and giant spiders were no match for Alison as she trekked through Honduras, El Salvador, and Guatemala. Braving city bus routes, remote mountain hikes, and even a suburban mega-mall or two, this three-time Let's Go veteran embodied the spirit of independent travel throughout her journey. Intrepid and fearless, Alison is also a keen observer of people. Keeping her finger on the pulse of Central American culture, she injected her coverage with the insight and experience of a local. Fueled by ever elusive fresh garden salads, Alison consistently completed comprehensive and detailed work along the way

STAFF WRITERS

Megan Amram	Allison Averill	Dan Barbero
Billy Eck	Anna Kendrick	Colleen O'Brien
C. Harker Rhodes	Maria Vassileva	Sara Joe Wolansky

ACKNOWLEDGMENTS

JOSEPH: Ashley for letting me get her coffee and be her stay-at-home dad. But really for being an amazing boss and friend—never simma down. My pen-pals, Alison, Dan, and Eli, for making me want to get out of the office. The RM pod for making me want to stay. The Eds for their hard work/summer UnFun. The whole LG office for being quaint, Bohemian, and tasty. My friends for letting me stay in on the weekends and stay here for the summer. Florence, NJ for still being home, and my family most of all; you're my five best friends.

EDITORS: The Ed Team would first and foremost like to thank our lord (Jay-C) and savior (Starbucks, Terry's Chocolate Orange). We also owe gratitude to Barack Obama (peace be upon Him), the Oxford comma, the water cooler, bagel/payday Fridays, the HSA "SummerFun" team for being so inclusive, Rotio (wherefore art thou Rotio?), the real Robinson Crusoe, the Cambridge weather and defective umbrellas, BoltBus, Henry Louis Gates, Jr. (sorry 'bout the phone call), the office blog, gratuitous nudity, the 20-20-20 rule and bananas (no more eye twitches), the Portuguese flag, trips to the beach (ha!), sunbathing recently-married Mormon final club alums, non-existent free food in the square, dog-star puns, and last but not least, America. The local time in Tehran is 1:21am.

But seriously, to the MEs and RMs, our Researchers (and all their wisdom on tablecloths and hipsters), LGHQ, HSA, our significant others (future, Canadian, and otherwise), and families (thanks Mom).

Managing Editor
Ashley R. Laporte
Research Managers
Joseph Molimock
Editors
Courtney A. Fiske
Sara Plana
Charlie E. Riggs
Russell Ford Rennie
Olga I. Zhulina
Typesetter
C. Alexander Tremblay

Publishing Director
Laura M. Gordon
Editorial Director
Dwight Livingstone Curtis
Publicity and Marketing Director
Vanessa J. Dube
Production and Design Director
Rebecca Lieberman
Cartography Director
Anthony Rotio
Website Director
Lukáš Tóth
Managing Editors
Ashley R. Laporte, Iya Megre,
Mary Potter, Nathaniel Rakich
Technology Project Manager
C. Alexander Tremblay
Director of IT
David Fulton-Howard
Financial Associates
Catherine Humphreville, Jun Li

President
Daniel Lee
General Manager
Jim McKellar

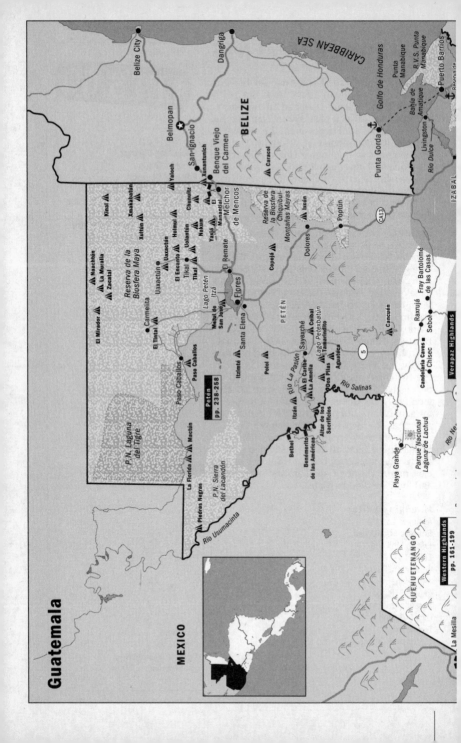

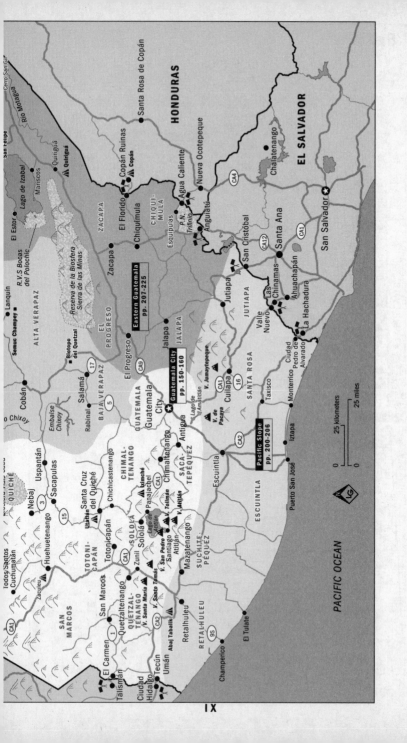

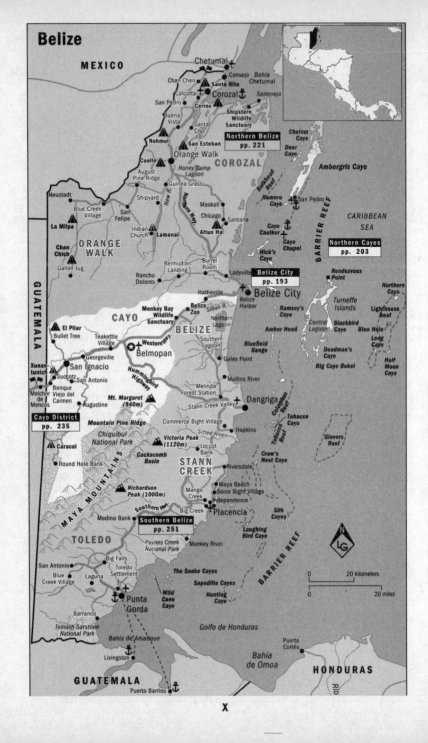

DISCOVER GUATEMALA AND BELIZE

Spider monkeys, camouflaged vine snakes, and lizards that walk on water. Lush jungles, thundering waterfalls, and tropical rainstorms. From their green mountains and white-sand beaches to expansive coffee fields and active volcanoes, Guatemala and Belize await. Grab your hiking shoes and go discover Tikal's 2000 year old ruins, or learn to speak Spanish in Xela. Tan on the Caribbean coast, explore ancient temples, or camp in the jungle. Give back by promoting fair trade practices in Quetzaltenango before jetting off to play drums with the Garífuna Maya. These two Central American countries are chock full of things to do and see.

Our Researchers have come up with excellent advice on how to get around, how to stay safe, what to eat, where to sleep, and how to plan your trip. Whatever your adventure, we've got you covered.

WHEN TO GO

The most important factor to consider when planning a trip to Central America is the **rainy season,** or *invierno* (winter). Central America's rainy season generally occurs between May and November. Predictably, the rest of the year is called the **dry season,** or *verano* (summer). The seasons are particularly distinct on the Pacific Coast, while on the Caribbean Coast, some rain should be expected regardless of the season. The temperature in Central America is determined by altitude rather than season; the highlands experience moderate highs and pleasantly cool nights, while the costal and jungle lowlands swelter. For a country-specific temperature chart, see the **Appendix (p. 280)**.

The dry season is the tourist "high season," meaning crazy crowds and elevated prices. Budget travelers should consider a rainy season trip. Even then, the sun generally shines all day, excluding furious but fleeting afternoon rainstorms. Dry season travel is for those in search or a tan or access to areas where roads and trains can be washed out for weeks during the rainy season. The region's best parties are using during **Semena Santa,** the week-long Easter holiday. For more destination-specific info, see the country introductions.

WHAT TO DO

⊠ UNDER THE SEA

If you're looking to explore the deep blue, these two countries are the place to be. With the Caribbean Sea to the east and the Pacific Ocean to the west, the region is literally surrounded by some of the best snorkeling and diving sites in the world. We know that jumping into Belize's Blue Hole takes more than just big *cajones*, so we've singled out some great budget options in a sea of tourist traps.

DISCOVER

DIVE RIGHT IN	SNORKEL SHMORKEL
THE BLUE HOLE (P. 208). This 400ft deep wonder is Belize's most famous attraction.	**AMBERGRIS CAYE (P. 210)** Spy on rays and sharks off the coast of this famous island.
CAYE CAULKER (P. 203). Amergris's sidekick, Caulker is a must-see.	**TOBACCO CAYE (P. 259).** Swimming, fishing, and snorkeling are this island's main attractions.
PLACENCIA (P. 265). This narrow peninsula is easy to access and great for almost all ocean exploration.	**HOL CHAN MARINE RESERVE (P. 216).** A hugely popular and convenient stop for snorkelers and divers.
TURNEFFE ATOLL (P. 216). Boasting beautiful coral reef formations, this is one of the most exhilarating places to dive in Belize.	**LAUGHING BIRD CAYE (P. 269).** More expensive than the rest, but if you have the cash, this little Belizean island is worth the splurge.

◪ HISTORICAL SITES

Over 2000 years ago, the inhabitants of Northern Guatemala begin hauling huge slabs of limestone out of the ground and thrusting them skyward, constructing temples and palaces more than 70m high. The structures embody the mystery and grandeur of the great Mayan cities, whose earliest remnants may date back more than 4000 years. The awesome temples, hieroglyphics, carvings, and statues that immortalize the ancients can be visited today at sites throughout Guatemala and Belize. Below are a few of the more incredible examples.

HISTORICAL SITES
ACTUN TUNICHIL MUKNAL (P. 246). An unforgettable trip to the underworld. Come see human skeletons in cathedral-like spaces 1km inside this enormous jungle cave in Belize.
TIKAL (P. 157). Camp beside soaring temples and catch a stunning sunset before the crowds come to attack this Guatemalan jewel.
ANTIGUA (P. 64). This well-preserved Colonial city with its cobblestone streets and grand architecture deserves its fame.
LAMANAI (P. 228). Check out towering Mayan temples and imposing, carved faces of rulers past.
UAXACTUN (P. 154). This secluded ruin is location in Guatemala's Petén Basic, just north of Tikal.
TOLEDO DISTRICT (P. 274). Free from hordes of tourists, Belize's "forgotten district" is known for its impressive Mayan ruins and vibrant Mayan villages.

▚ USE PROTECTION

Blessed with one of the most breathtaking and extensive park systems in the world, Central America is a nature-lover's paradise. The diversity of the region caters to every whim—whether you're looking to stroll along well-maintained trails or to machete you way through thousands of kilometers of jungle, Central America will not disappoint.

PROTECTED AREAS

⧉ RIO BRAVO CONSERVATION (P. 229). Nearly 206,000 acres of sub-tropical rainforest awaits the adventurous traveler at this Belizean treasure.	**⧉CROOKED TREE WILDLIFE SANCTUARY (P. 221).** Come see the 300 different bird species that flock to this sanctuary by the thousands.
⧉TURNEFFE ATOLL (P. 216). Boasting beautiful coral reef formations, this is one of the most exhilarating places to dive in Belize.	**⧉COCKSCOMB BASIN WILDLIFE SANCTUARY (P. 260).** This Belizean haven covers over 120,000 acres and is surrounded by the Maya Mountains.
⧉COMMUNITY BABOON SANCTUARY (P. 202). This farmer-run sanctuary is home to some 1000 howler monkeys.	**⧉RÍO BLANCO NATIONAL PARK (P. 277).** A 20 ft. high diving board, the Río Blanco Falls are some of the most impressive in the region.
⧉GALES POINT MANATEE SANCTUARY (P. 261). Help these sea cows out and learn a thing or two about the area while you're at it.	**⧉SHIPSTERN NATURE RESERVE (P. 229).** Bird-lovers flock to this reserve in Sarteneja.

⌑ WHAT'S SPANISH FOR HAGGLE?

MARKETS

⧉CHICHICASTENANGO (P. 83). If you can find some energy after trying to pronounce this town's name, use it to head out to the Thursday and Sunday textile markets Chichi is famous for.

⧉SAN IGNACIO (P. 239). Eat fresh produce and meet the local farmers who grew it at the Saturday market in the Savannah Plaza.

⧉SOLOLÁ (P. 80). Artisans and vendors flood this little city each Tuesday and Friday to sell their wares at the local market. They stick around for the Sunday parade; you should too.

⧉QUETZALTENANGO (P. 92). While most people head to Quetzaltenango for other reasons, the bustling market in the town center is worth a visit in and of itself.

⧉ BEACH BUMMING

Okay, so maybe ripping tasty waves isn't for you. Perhaps the idea of trekking through jungles makes you nauseous. Maybe you're one of those who gets claustrophobic when wearing a snorkel mask. Don't worry, we're not judging, and we've thought of you too. From the shores of the Caribbean Sea in Belize to the quiet coast of the Pacific in Guatemala, we've found the best places to lay out with a mixed drink in hand. All you have to do is bring the sunscreen.

BEACH IT

⧉HOPKINS (P. 262). Catch some rays by the sea, take in the incredible views, and visit the local Garifuna village while visiting this Belizean town.

⧉PLACENCIA (P. 265). You'll be among snorkelers and divers here, but no one will stop you from relaxing on the palm tree-lined beaches with a mojito in hand.

⧉LAGO DE IZABAL (P. 116). Guatemala's largest lake, Izabal provides a quiet break from the usual beach resort scene.

⧉MONTERRICO (P. 106). Colorful hammocks line the beach at this backpacker favorite in Guatemala.

DISCOVER

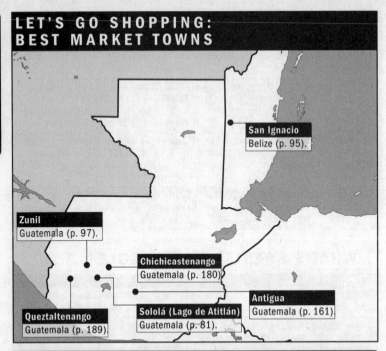

LET'S GO SHOPPING: BEST MARKET TOWNS

San Ignacio
Belize (p. 95).

Zunil
Guatemala (p. 97).

Chichicastenango
Guatemala (p. 180)

Antigua
Guatemala (p. 161)

Queztaltenango
Guatemala (p. 189).

Sololá (Lago de Atitlán)
Guatemala (p. 81).

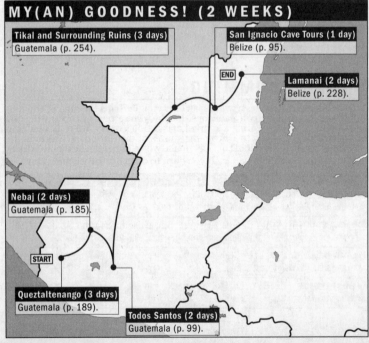

MY(AN) GOODNESS! (2 WEEKS)

Tikal and Surrounding Ruins (3 days)
Guatemala (p. 254).

San Ignacio Cave Tours (1 day)
Belize (p. 95).

END

Lamanai (2 days)
Belize (p. 228).

Nebaj (2 days)
Guatemala (p. 185).

START

Queztaltenango (3 days)
Guatemala (p. 189).

Todos Santos (2 days)
Guatemala (p. 99).

WHERE THE SALVAJE (WILD) THINGS ARE

Rio Bravo Conservation Area
Belize (p. 229).

Crooked Tree Wildlife Sanctuary
Belize (p. 221).

Bermudian Landing Baboon Sanctuary
Belize (p. 202).

Belize Zoo
Belize (p. 238).

Parque Nacional Tikal
Guatemala (p. 157).

Cockscomb Basin Wildlife Sanctuary
Belize (p. 260).

Belize Barrier Reef
Belize (p. 183).

Gales Point Wildlife Sanctuary
Belize (p. 261).

Parque Nacional Grutas de Lanquin
Guatemala (p. 137).

ESSENTIALS

PLANNING YOUR TRIP

EMBASSIES AND CONSULATES

For embassies and consulates in Belize see **Belize Intro,** p. 184. For embassies and consulates in Guatemala see **Guatemala Intro,** p. 39.

PASSPORTS

REQUIREMENTS

Citizens of Australia, Canada, Ireland, New Zealand, the UK, and the US need valid passports to enter both Guatemala and Belize and to re-enter their home countries. Guatemala and Belize do not allow entrance if the holder's passport expires in under three months; returning home with an expired passport is illegal and may result in a fine.

PASSPORT MAINTENANCE

Photocopy the page of your passport with your photo as well as your visa, traveler's check serial numbers, and any other important documents. Carry one set of copies in a safe place, apart from the originals, and leave another set at home. Carry an expired passport or an official copy of your birth certificate in a part of your baggage separate from other documents. If you lose your passport, immediately notify the local police and your home country's nearest embassy or consulate. To expedite your passport's replacement, you must show photo ID and proof of citizenship; it also helps to know all information previously recorded in your passport. In some cases, a replacement may take weeks to process, and may be valid only for a limited time. Any visas stamped in your old passport will be lost forever. Iny an emergency, ask for immediate temporary traveling papers that will permit you to re-enter your home country.

VISAS AND WORK PERMITS

See **Belize** (p. 183) and **Guatemala** (p. 39) for **visa** specific entrance information. US citizens can also consult http://travel.state.gov/travel. Admission as a visitor does not include the right to work, which is authorized only by a work permit.

IDENTIFICATION

When you travel, always carry at least two forms of identification on your person, including a photo ID. A passport and a driver's license will usually suffice. Never carry all of your IDs together; split them up in case of theft or loss and keep photocopies in your luggage and at home.

STUDENT AND YOUTH IDENTIFICATION

The **International Student Identity Card (ISIC)**, the most widely accepted form of student ID, provides discounts on some sights, accommodations, food, and transportation, access to a 24hr. emergency help line, and insurance benefits for US cardholders. In Central America, most discounts will be found in major cities, and usually apply at hotels or restaurants, with the odd sports store and boat cruise thrown in as well. Applicants must be full-time students, and at least 12 years old. Because of the proliferation of fake ISICs, some services (particularly airlines) require additional proof of student identity. For non-student travelers who are under 26 years old, the **International Youth Travel Card (IYTC)** also offers many of the same benefits as the ISIC.

Each of these identity cards costs US$22. ISICs and IYTCs are valid for one year from the date of issue. To learn more about ISICs and IYTCs, try www.myisic.com. Many student travel agencies issue the cards; for a list of issuing agencies, see the **International Student Travel Confederation (ISTC)** website (www.istc.org).

CUSTOMS

Both Guatemala and Belize require you to declare certain items from abroad and pay a duty on the value of those articles if they exceed the allowance established by the country's customs service. Note that goods and gifts purchased at duty-free shops abroad are not exempt from duty or sales tax; "duty-free" means that you won't pay tax in the country of purchase. Upon returning home, you must likewise declare all articles acquired abroad and pay a duty on the value of articles in excess of your home country's allowance. It's a good idea to keep receipts for all goods acquired abroad.

MONEY

CURRENCY AND EXCHANGE

As a general rule, it's cheaper to convert money in-country than at home. While currency exchange will probably be available in your destination airport, it's wise to bring enough foreign currency to last for at least 24-72hr. When changing money abroad, try to go only to banks or *casas de cambio* that have at most a 5% margin between their buy and sell prices. Since you lose money with every transaction, it makes sense to convert large sums at one time (unless the currency is depreciating rapidly).

If you use traveler's checks or bills, carry some in small denominations (the equivalent of US$50 or less) for times when you are forced to exchange money at poor rates. Bring a range of denominations since charges may be applied per check cashed. Also, keep in mind that traveler's checks are not readily accepted in both Guatemala and Belize. Store your money in a variety of forms; ideally, at any given time you will be carrying some cash, some traveler's checks, and an ATM or credit card. All travelers should also consider carrying some US dollars (about US$50), which are often preferred by local tellers.

CREDIT, DEBIT, AND ATM CARDS

Where accepted, credit cards often offer superior exchange rates—up to 5% better than the retail rate used by banks and other currency-exchange establishments. Credit cards may also offer services such as insurance or emergency help and are sometimes required to reserve hotel rooms or rental cars. **Master-Card** and **Visa** are the most frequently accepted; **American Express** cards work at

ESSENTIALS

some ATMs and at AmEx offices and major airports. **ATMs** are a viable option in urban and touristed areas in both Guatemala and Belize: give the same wholesale exchange rate as credit cards, but there is often a limit on the amount of money you can withdraw per day (usually around US$500). There is also typically a surcharge of US$1-5 per withdrawal, so it pays to be efficient. **Debit cards** are as convenient as credit cards but withdraw money directly from the holder's checking account. A debit card can be used wherever its associated credit card company (usually MasterCard or Visa) is accepted.

The two major international money networks are **MasterCard/Maestro/Cirrus** (for ATM locations call ☎+1-800-424-7787 or visit www.mastercard.com) and **Visa/PLUS** (for ATM locations visit http://visa.via.infonow.net/locator/global/). It is a good idea to contact your bank or credit card company before going abroad; frequent charges in a foreign country can sometimes prompt a fraud alert, which will freeze your account.

GETTING MONEY FROM HOME

If you run out of money while traveling, the easiest and cheapest solution is to have someone back home make a deposit to your bank account. Otherwise, consider one of the following options.

WIRING MONEY

It is possible to arrange a **bank money transfer,** which means asking a bank back home to wire money to a bank in Belize or Guatemala. This is the cheapest way to transfer cash, but it's also the slowest, usually taking several days or more. Note that some banks may only release your funds in local currency, potentially sticking you with a poor exchange rate; inquire about this option in advance. Money transfer services like **Western Union** are faster and more convenient than bank transfers—but also much pricier. Western Union has many locations worldwide. To find one, visit www.westernunion.com or call the appropriate number: in Australia ☎1800 173 833, in Canada and the US 800-325-6000, in the UK 0800 735 1815, in Belize 501 227 1225 and in Guatemala +502 22 564 741. To wire money using a credit card: in Canada and the US call ☎800-CALL-CASH (800-2255-2274), in the UK 0800 833 833.

US STATE DEPARTMENT (US CITIZENS ONLY)

In serious emergencies only, the US State Department will forward money within hours to the nearest consular office, which will then disburse it according to instructions for a US$30 fee. If you wish to use this service, you must contact the **Overseas Citizens Services** division of the US State Department (☎+1-202-501-4444, from US 888-407-4747).

TIPPING AND BARGAINING

When tipping and especially bargaining in both Guatemala and Belize, as in Central America more generally, tourists should adhere to several unspoken rules. In tourist and upscale restaurants, a 10% tip is common. In smaller restaurants frequented by locals, tipping is rare. Tour guides generally appreciate something extra, though taxi drivers do not expect to be tipped. At outdoor markets, handicraft markets, and some handicraft shops, bargaining is expected and essential. Prices at supermarkets and most indoor stores, on the other hand, are non-negotiable. Bargaining for hotel rooms and hostels is often a good idea, particularly in the low season (or if the hotel obviously has vacancies).

THE ART OF THE DEAL. Bargaining in Guatemala and Belize is a given: no price is set in stone, and vendors and drivers will automatically quote you a price that is several times too high. It's up to you to get them down to a reasonable rate. With the following tips and some finesse, you might be able to impress even the most hardened hawkers:

1. **Bargaining needn't be a fierce struggle laced with barbs.** Quite the opposite—good-natured, cheerful wrangling may prove your best weapon.
2. **Use your poker face.** The less your face betrays your interest in the item the better. If you touch an item to inspect it, the vendor will be sure to "encourage" you to name a price or make a purchase. Coming back again and again to admire a trinket is a good way of ensuring that you pay a ridiculously high price. Never get too enthusiastic about the object in question; point out flaws in workmanship and design. Be cool.
3. **Know when to bargain.** In most cases, it's quite clear when it's appropriate to bargain. Most private transportation fares and things for sale in outdoor markets are all fair game. Don't bargain on prepared or pre-packaged foods on the street or in restaurants. In some stores, signs will indicate whether "fixed prices" prevail. When in doubt, ask tactfully, "Is that your lowest price?" or whether discounts are given.
4. **Never underestimate the power of peer pressure.** Try having a friend make a show of discouraging you from your purchase—if you seem to be reluctant, the merchant will want to drop the price to interest you again.
5. **Know when to turn away.** Feel free to refuse any vendor or driver who bargains rudely and don't hesitate to move on to another vendor if one will not be reasonable about his final price. However, to start bargaining without an intention to buy is a major faux pas. Agreeing on a price and declining it is also poor form. Turn away slowly with a smile and "thank you" upon hearing a ridiculous price—it may plummet.
6. **Start low.** Never feel guilty offering a ludicrously low price. Your starting price should be no more than one third to one half of the asking price.

SAFETY AND HEALTH

GENERAL ADVICE

In any type of crisis, the most important thing to do is **stay calm.** Your home country's embassy abroad (Belize, p. 184; Guatemala, p. 39) is usually your best resource in an emergency; registering with that embassy upon arrival in the country is a good idea. The government offices listed in the **Travel Advisories** box (p. 11) can provide information on the services they offer their citizens in case of emergencies abroad.

Remember that you are subject to the laws of the country in which you travel, not those of your home country; it is your responsibility to familiarize yourself with foreign laws prior to your departure. Penalties and punishments in Guatemala and Belize may be more severe than for comparable crimes committed in the US.

DRUGS AND ALCOHOL

Illegal drug trafficking remains a pervasive problem in both Guatemala and Belize. In recent years, Guatemala has affirmed its status as Central America's foremost drug trafficking hub—authorities estimate that up to 90% of the Latin American cocaine that ends up in the US first passes through Guatemala. Such widespread narcotic activity makes traveling in **rural areas** of Guatemala and Belize more risky than sticking to the main roads. Pervasive drug smuggling makes the **Guatemalan border with Mexico**, specifically on the northwestern border of the Petén region (specifically around and within the Sierra de Lacandon and Laguna del Tigre National Parks) a region to avoid. The **Belize-Guatemala border** area is another region where travelers should take added precautions.

As a consequence of their intense narcotics problems, Guatemala and Belize impose severe penalties for **drug possession.** Your home country's embassies will provide little help if you get in trouble: offenders can expect harsh fines and long sentences. If you use **prescription drugs** when you travel, carry a copy of the prescriptions themselves and a note from your doctor. Lastly, avoid **public drunkenness:** in addition to being illegal in certain areas, it can jeopardize your safety and garner the disdain of locals.

SPECIFIC CONCERNS

SEISMIC ACTIVITY

Guatemala and Belize run along the boundary of several tectonic plates, making them the sights of frequent and unpredictable earthquakes. Tremors are more common, but large-scale earthquakes are still a threat. If an earthquake occurs, be sure to stay away from anything that could fall on you. If indoors, stand in a doorway or crouch under a desk. If you are driving, pull over to the side of the road until the quake passes. Guatemala is also the site of four **active volcanoes** which erupt infrequently.

HURRICANES AND FLOODING

The rainy season in both Guatemala and Belize runs from June to November. One can expect extensive flooding. Bridges and roads are often destroyed, making travel dangerous and impossible. Areas along the Pacific and Caribbean coasts and near rivers are most prone to flooding. **Mudslides** are a very real danger in Central America, and in recent years have led to deaths as well as the wholesale destruction of infrastructure. They occur most often in mountainous areas during the rain season.

CRIME

Crime rates are high in both Guatemala and Belize. Crime poses very real risks for travelers. Foreigners are assumed to have money, making them instant (and often easy) targets for thieves. Discretion is the best plan—never showcase valuables (such as cameras or expensive jewelry) or money, be conscious of what you are wearing, and avoid attracting unnecessary attention. To prevent falling victim to petty theft, women should securely hug their purses to their bodies, while men should hold their wallets in their front pockets. Refrain from traveling alone or in small groups, particularly as a female, and stay off the streets after dark, even when in a rural area. Due to pervasive drug smuggling activities, travel on rural roads at night is particularly dangerous. If you are held up, do not resist, since thieves will most likely not hesitate to shoot or stab. Know that when it comes to the police in both Guatemala and Belize, inefficiency, alongside a lack of resources, leaves many crimes against tourists unsolved. However, *Let's Go* still recommends that travelers report all crimes to the local police, in addition to the tourist police and the in-country embassy.

DEMONSTRATIONS AND POLITICAL GATHERINGS

Large demonstrations are a frequent sight in Guatemala and Belize, often due to labor problems or electoral results. While these demonstrations are usually nonviolent, they can occur with little notice and result in the blockage of airports, traffic, and public transportation. These areas are obviously better avoided during times of political unrest. Very rarely, tourists are taken hostage for short periods of time to bait the government, most recently during a 2001 demonstration in Tikal, Guatemala.

TERRORISM

While crime is a major problem, terrorism is limited in Central America. Drug and street gangs exist, especially in capital cities, but activity is generally local in nature. The box below lists offices to contact and websites to visit to get the most updated list of your government's travel advisories.

TRAVEL ADVISORIES. The following government offices provide travel information and advisories by telephone, by fax, or via the web:

Australian Department of Foreign Affairs and Trade: ☎+61 2 6261 1111; www.dfat.gov.au.

Canadian Department of Foreign Affairs and International Trade (DFAIT): ☎+1-800-267-8376; www.dfait-maeci.gc.ca. Call or visit the webside for the free booklet *Bon Voyage...But*.

New Zealand Ministry of Foreign Affairs: ☎+64 4 439 8000; www.mfat.govt.nz.

United Kingdom Foreign and Commonwealth Office: ☎+44 20 7008 1500; www.fco.gov.uk.

US Department of State: ☎+1-888-407-4747, 202-501-4444 from abroad; http://travel.state.gov.

PERSONAL SAFETY

EXPLORING AND TRAVELING

To avoid unwanted attention, try to blend in as much as possible. Respecting local customs (in many cases, dressing more conservatively than you would at home) may ward off would-be hecklers. Familiarize yourself with your surroundings before setting out and carry yourself with confidence. Check maps in shops and restaurants rather than on the street. If you are traveling alone, be sure someone at home knows your itinerary and **never tell anyone you meet that you're by yourself.** When walking at night, stick to busy, well-lit streets and avoid dark alleyways. If you ever feel uncomfortable, leave the area as quickly and directly as you can. There is no sure-fire way to avoid all the threatening situations that you might encounter while traveling, but a good **self-defense course** will give you concrete ways to react to unwanted advances. **Impact, Prepare,** and **Model Mugging** (www.modelmugging.org) can refer you to local self-defense courses in Australia, Canada, Switzerland, and the US.

For tips on how to drive safely in Guatemala and Belize, see **On the Road,** p. 20.

For tips on how to drive safely in Guatemala and Belize, see **On the Road,** p. 20.

E S S E N T I A L S

POSSESSIONS AND VALUABLES

Never leave your belongings unattended; crime can occur in even the most safe-looking hostel or hotel. Bring your own padlock for hostel lockers and don't ever store valuables in a locker. Be particularly careful on **buses and trains;** horror stories abound about determined thieves who wait for travelers to fall asleep. Carry your bag or purse in front of you where you can see it. When traveling with others, sleep in alternate shifts. When alone, be careful in selecting a train compartment: never stay in an empty one and always use a lock to secure your pack to the luggage rack. Use extra caution if traveling at night or on overnight trains. Try to sleep on top bunks with your luggage stored above you (if not in bed with you) and keep important documents and other valuables on you at all times.

Bring as little with you as possible. Buy a few combination **padlocks** to secure your belongings either in your pack or in a hostel or train-station locker. **Carry as little cash as possible.** Keep your traveler's checks and ATM/credit cards in a **money belt**—not a "fanny pack"—along with your passport and ID cards. Lastly, **keep a small cash reserve separate from your primary stash.** This should be about US$50 (US dollars or euro are best) sewn into or stored in the depths of your pack, along with your traveler's check numbers and photocopies of your important documents.

In large cities, **con artists** often work in groups and may involve children in their schemes. Beware of certain classics: sob stories that require money, rolls of bills "found" on the street, mustard spilled (or saliva spit) onto your shoulder to distract you while they snatch your bag. **Never let your passport or your bags out of your sight.** Hostel workers will sometimes stand at bus and train arrival points to recruit tired and disoriented travelers to their hostel; never believe strangers who tell you that theirs is the only hostel open. Beware of **pickpockets** in city crowds, especially on public transportation. Also, be alert in public telephone booths. If you must say your calling-card number, do so very quietly; if you punch it in, make sure no one can look over your shoulder.

PRE-DEPARTURE HEALTH

In your passport, write the names of any people you wish to be contacted in case of a medical emergency and list any allergies or medical conditions. Matching a prescription to a foreign equivalent is not always easy, safe, or possible, so, if you take **prescription drugs,** carry up-to-date prescriptions or a statement from your doctor stating the medications' trade names, manufacturers, chemical names, and dosages. While traveling, be sure to keep all medication with you in your carry-on luggage.

The names for common drugs in Guatemala and Belize are *aspirina* (aspirin), *paracetamol* or *acetaminofén* (acetaminophen), *penicilina* (penicillin), *ibuprofeno* (ibuprofen), and *antihistamínico* (antihistamine/allergy medicine). Brand names like Tylenol®, Advil®, and Pepto Bismol® are well known.

IMMUNIZATIONS AND PRECAUTIONS

Travelers over two years old should make sure that the following vaccines are up to date: **MMR** (for measles, mumps, and rubella); **DTaP** or **Td** (for diphtheria, tetanus, and pertussis); **IPV** (for polio); **Hib** (for *Haemophilus influenzae* B); and **HepB** (for Hepatitis B). Adults traveling to the developing world on trips longer than four weeks should consider the following additional immunizations: **Hepatitis A** vaccine and/or immune globulin (IG), **typhoid** and **cholera** vaccines (particularly if traveling off the beaten path), a **rabies** vaccine, and yearly influenza vaccines. While **yellow fever** is only endemic to parts of South America and sub-Saharan Africa, Guatemala and Belize require a **certificate of vaccination** from travelers arriving from these areas. For recommendations on immunizations and prevention, consult the **Centers for Disease Control and Prevention** (CDC; below) in the US or the equivalent in your home country and check with a doctor for guidance.

INSURANCE

Travel insurance covers four basic areas: medical and health problems, property loss, trip cancellation and interruption, and emergency evacuation. Though regular insurance policies may well extend to travel-related accidents, you may consider purchasing separate travel insurance if the cost of potential trip cancellation, interruption, or emergency medical evacuation is more than you can afford. Prices for travel insurance purchased separately generally run about US$50 per week for full coverage, while trip cancellation or interruption may be purchased separately at a rate of US$3-5 per day, depending on length of stay.

Medical insurance (especially university policies) often covers costs incurred abroad; check with your provider. **Homeowners' insurance** (or your family's coverage) often covers theft during travel and loss of travel documents (passport, plane ticket, railpass, etc.) up to US$500. **American Express** (☎+1-800-528-4800) grants most cardholders automatic collision and theft car-rental insurance on rentals made with the card.

USEFUL ORGANIZATIONS AND PUBLICATIONS

The American **Centers for Disease Control and Prevention** (**CDC;** ☎+1-800-CDC-INFO/232-4636; www.cdc.gov/travel) maintains an international travelers' hotline and an informative website. Consult the appropriate government agency of your home country for consular information sheets on health, entry requirements, and other country-specific issues (see the listings in the box on **Travel Advisories,** p. 11). For quick information on other travel warnings, call the **Overseas Citizens Services** (☎+1-202-647-5225) or contact a passport agency, embassy, or consulate abroad. For information on medical evacuation services and travel insurance firms, see the US government's website at http://travel.state.gov/travel/abroad_health.html or the **British Foreign and Commonwealth Office** (www.fco.gov.uk). For general health information, contact the **American Red Cross** (☎+1-202-303-5000; www.redcross.org).

STAYING HEALTHY

ONCE IN GUATEMALA AND BELIZE

INSECT-BORNE DISEASES

Many diseases are transmitted by insects—mainly mosquitoes, fleas, ticks, and lice. Be aware of insects in wet or forested areas, especially while hiking and camping. Wear long pants and long sleeves, tuck your pants into your socks, and use a mosquito net. Use insect repellents such as DEET and soak or spray your gear with permethrin (licensed in the US only for use on clothing). **Mosquitoes**—responsible for malaria and dengue fever—can be particularly abundant in low-lying rural areas of Guatemala and most areas in Belize; there is little

ESSENTIALS

risk, however, in Guatemala City, Antigua, Lake Atitlán and Belize City. **Yellow fever** is not a risk in Guatemala and Belize.

Dengue fever: An "urban viral infection" transmitted by *Aedes* mosquitoes that bite during the day. The incubation period is 3-14 days, usually 4-7 days. Early symptoms include a high fever, severe headaches, swollen lymph nodes, and muscle aches. Patients also suffer from nausea, vomiting, and rash. To reduce the risk of contracting dengue, use mosquito repellent and wear clothing that covers your arms and legs. See a doctor immediately upon noticing symptoms, drink plenty of liquids, and take a fever-reducing medication such as acetaminophen (Tylenol®).

Malaria: Transmitted by *Anopheles* mosquitoes that bite at night. The incubation period varies anywhere between 10 days and 4 weeks. Early symptoms include fever, chills, aches, and fatigue, followed by high fever and sweating, sometimes with vomiting and diarrhea. See a doctor for any flu-like sickness that occurs after travel in a risk area. To reduce the risk of contracting malaria, use mosquito repellent, particularly in the evenings and when visiting forested areas. See a doctor at least 4-6 weeks before a trip to a high-risk area to get up-to-date malaria prescriptions. A doctor may prescribe oral prophylactics, like mefloquine or doxycycline. Know that mefloquine can have serious side effects, including paranoia, psychosis, and nightmares. Halofantrine (often marketed as Halfan) is commonly prescribed overseas, but be aware that it has serious heart-related side effects.

Other insect-borne diseases: Lymphatic filariasis is a roundworm transmitted by mosquitoes. Infection causes lymphedema and enlargement of extremities. It has no vaccine, but can be prevented by avoiding mosquito bites through the use of protective clothing and sprays. **Leishmaniasis,** a parasite transmitted by sand flies, usually occurs in rural Central America. Symptoms include fever, weakness, swelling of the spleen, and skin sores weeks to months after the bite. There is a treatment, but no vaccine. **Chagas' disease (American trypanomiasis)** is a relatively common parasite transmitted by the cone nose or "kissing" bug, which infests mud, adobe, and thatch. Its immediate symptoms include fever, fatigue, headache, and nausea. If untreated in the long term, Chagas' can lead to fatal, debilitating conditions of the heart and intestines. There is no vaccine. Tropical specialists offer the only (limited) treatment available.

FOOD- AND WATER-BORNE DISEASES

Prevention is the best cure: be sure that your food is properly cooked and that the water you drink is clean. Watch out for food from markets or street vendors that may have been cooked in unhygienic conditions. Other culprits are raw shellfish, un-pasteurized milk, and sauces containing raw eggs. Buy bottled water or purify your own water by bringing it to a rolling boil or treating it with **iodine tablets**).

Hepatitis A: A viral infection of the liver acquired through contaminated water or shellfish from contaminated water. Symptoms include fatigue, fever, loss of appetite, nausea, dark urine, jaundice, vomiting, aches and pains, and light stools. The risk is highest in rural areas, but HepA is also present in urban areas. Ask your doctor about the Hepatitis A vaccine or an injection of immunoglobulin.

Traveler's diarrhea: Results from drinking fecally contaminated water or eating uncooked and contaminated foods. Symptoms include nausea, bloating, and a constant urge to urinate. Try non-sugary foods with protein and carbohydrates to keep your strength up. Over-the-counter anti-diarrheals (e.g., Imodium®) may counteract the problem. The most dangerous side effect is dehydration. Try un-caffeinated soft drinks, or eat salted crackers. If you develop a fever or your symptoms don't go away after 4-5 days, consult a doctor. Consult a doctor immediately for treatment of diarrhea in children.

Typhoid fever: Caused by salmonella bacteria; common in villages and rural areas. Mostly transmitted through contaminated food and water, typhoid may also be acquired by direct contact with another person. Early symptoms include high fever, headaches, fatigue, appetite loss, constipation, and a rash on the abdomen or chest. Antibiotics can treat typhoid, but a vaccination (70-90% effective) is recommended.

OTHER INFECTIOUS DISEASES

The following diseases exist all over the world. Travelers should know how to recognize them and what to do if they suspect they have been infected.

AIDS and HIV: For detailed information on Acquired Immune Deficiency Syndrome (AIDS) in Guatemala and Belize, call the CDC's 24hr. National AIDS Hotline at ☎+1-800-232-4636. Guatemala and Belize have no entrance restrictions on travelers with HIV/AIDs.

Hepatitis B: A viral liver infection transmitted via blood or other bodily fluids. Symptoms, which may not surface until years after infection, include jaundice, appetite loss, fever, and joint pain. HepB is transmitted through unprotected sex and unclean needles. A 3-shot vaccination sequence is recommended for anyone planning to seek medical treatment abroad; treatment must begin 6 months before traveling.

Sexually transmitted infections (STIs): Gonorrhea, Chlamydia, genital warts, syphilis, herpes, HPV, and other STIs are easier to catch than HIV and can be just as serious. Though condoms may protect you from some STIs, oral or even tactile contact can lead to transmission. If you think you may have contracted an STI, see a doctor immediately.

OTHER HEALTH CONCERNS

MEDICAL CARE ON THE ROAD

In general, medical facilities in Guatemala and Belize are fairly basic. In Guatemala City, you'll likely to find facilities equipped for advanced surgery or trauma treatment. Outside of the city, care is extremely limited, even non-existent. Similarly limited care exists in Belize. Most hospitals and doctors expect to be paid upfront in cash. In Guatemala, hospitals are wary to treat travelers who lack proof of medical insurance. Public hospitals in both Guatemala and Belize are often crowded, poorly equipped, unhygienic, and unable to provide appropriate care in many cases. Private hospitals are better and often staffed by U.S.-trained doctors, but are much more expensive. Ambulance services, available in cities, are often merely transportation to the hospital. It is important to let the driver know which kind of hospital you'd like to go to. While Guatemala have many English-speaking personnel, don't count on receiving good service unless you can communicate your needs in Spanish. Check with your embassy or consulate to see if they have a list of local doctors.

If you are concerned about obtaining medical assistance while traveling, you may wish to employ special support services. The **International Association for Medical Assistance to Travelers (IAMAT;** US ☎+1-716-754-4883, Canada +1-416-652-0137; www.iamat.org) has free membership, lists English-speaking doctors worldwide, and offers details on immunization requirements and sanitation.

Those with medical conditions (such as diabetes, allergies to antibiotics, epilepsy, or heart conditions) may want to obtain a **MedicAlert** membership (US$40 per year), which includes, among other things, a stainless-steel ID tag and a 24hr. collect-call number. Contact the **MedicAlert Foundation International** (from US ☎888-633-4298, outside US +1-209-668-3333; www.medicalert.org).

WOMEN'S HEALTH

Women traveling in unsanitary conditions are vulnerable to **urinary tract (including bladder and kidney) infections**. Over-the-counter medicines can sometimes alleviate symptoms, but if they persist, see a doctor. **Vaginal yeast infections** may flare up in hot and humid climates. Wearing loosely-fitting trousers or a skirt and cotton underwear will help, as will over-the-counter remedies like Monistat® and prescription drugs like Fluconazole®. Bring supplies from home if you are prone to infection, as they may be difficult to find on the road. And, since tampons, pads, and reliable contraceptive devices are sometimes hard to find when traveling, bring supplies with you. **Abortion** is not legal in Guatemala, except when the mother's life is endangered or fetal defects are present; abortion policy is mildly more liberal in Belize, but in most cases the procedure remains illegal.

SANITATION

It's best to avoid food from street vendors in both Guatemala and Belize, especially if you can't see it being prepared. Stick to bottled and boiled water, as local tap water is often unsafe. Be on the lookout for ice in your drinks and fresh vegetables and fruit that may have been washed in tap water. In general, staying away from raw, unpeeled, and uncooked food is the safest course. **Toilets** are often sub-par in Guatemala and Belize, especially outside of cities. Make sure to bring toilet paper with you everywhere, and remember that some plumbing systems are not equipped to handle paper waste.

GETTING TO BELIZE AND GUATEMALA

BY PLANE

When it comes to airfare, a little effort can save you a bundle. Check the websites of **Taca** (☎ 1-800-400-8222; www.taca.com) and **Copa** (www.copaair.com) for attractive fares. **STA** (www.statravel.com) and **StudentUniverse** (www.studentuniverse.com) provide quotes for student tickets, while **Orbitz** (www.orbitz.com), **Expedia** (www.expedia.com), and **Travelocity** (www.travelocity.com) offer full travel services. **Priceline** (www.priceline.com) lets you specify a price and obligates you to buy any ticket that meets or beats it; **Hotwire** (www.hotwire.com) offers bargain fares but won't reveal the airline or flight times until you buy. **Cheapflights** (www.cheapflights.co.uk) is another useful search engine for finding—you guessed it—cheap flights. Students, seniors, and those under 26 should never have to pay full price for a ticket.

AIRFARES

Airfares to Central America peak between December and April; holidays, especially Christmas and *Semana Santa* (the week before Easter), are also expensive. The cheapest times to travel are late spring and November. Midweek (M-Th morning) round-trip flights run cheaper than weekend flights, but they are generally more crowded and less likely to permit frequent-flier upgrades. Not fixing a return date ("open return") can be pricier than round-trip flights. Likewise, arriving in and departing from different cities ("open-jaw") will cost you. Patching one-way flights together is the most expensive way to travel. Flights between Central American capitals will tend to be cheaper.

Fares for round-trip flights to Guatemala City and Belize City from the US or Canadian east coast cost US$350-550 in the high season (Dec.-May), with comparable prices in the low, rainy season (June-Nov.); from the US or Canadian west coast US$500-800/400-600; from the UK, UK£1000-1200; from Australia AUS$2300-2600; from New Zealand NZ$1800-2200.

GETTING AROUND BELIZE AND GUATEMALA

BY PLANE

Taca (see p. 16) operates flights between all the capitals of Central America (Belize City to Guatemala City US$400-600).

> **AIRCRAFT SAFETY.** The airlines of developing-world nations do not always meet safety standards. The **Official Airline Guide** (www.oag.com) and many travel agencies can tell you the type and age of aircraft on a particular route. This can be especially useful in Guatemala and Belize, where less reliable equipment is often used for internal flights. The **International Airline Passengers Association** (www.iapa.com) provides region-specific safety information for its members. The **Federal Aviation Administration** (www.faa.gov/passengers/international_travel) reviews the airline authorities for countries whose airlines enter the US. **US State Department** travel advisories (www.travel.state.gov) sometimes involve foreign carriers, especially when terrorist bombings or hijackings may be a threat.

BY BUS

INTERNATIONAL BUSES

The cheapest way to shuttle between Guatemala and neighboring countries is **international coach bus**. There are two main lines that serve Central America; neither of these lines, unfortunately, offer routes through Belize. These buses feature amenities like air conditioning and reclining seats that you won't find on local buses. Note however that these perks come at a higher price.

King Quality (☎502 2369 7070; www.king-qualityca.com). Offers coach trips from Tapachula, Mexico through parts of Central America (excludes Belize and Panama). Also coordinates hotel stays in the destination countries. Mexico to Costa Rica US$98, round-trip $181.

Tica Bus (www.ticabus.com). Travels to multiple destinations all the way from Tapachula, Mexico to Panama City. Tickets allow you to hop on and off at different stops along the way—a nice way to see several countries. Mexico to Guatemala City US$15, round-trip $30.

LOCAL BUSES

Buses are the cheapest way to get from place to place in both Guatemala and Belize. Worn shocks help passengers feel every bump on rough and often unpaved roads. Most drivers have few qualms about putting it into high gear down hills. Snag a window seat (unless you're tall) to enjoy the view. Keep in mind those who chose to travel by bus in Guatemala and Belize occasionally fall prey to hijackers and roadside bandits, especially when traveling at night. Visitors to Guatemala are advised to avoid local public or "chicken" buses: in addition to being poorly maintained and dangerously driven, they are the frequent target of armed robbers—more than 200 bus drivers and passengers were killed in 2008 alone in such instances. Note that this mode of transportation is not the easiest: buses often seem to run on no schedule, even in the unlikely event that there is one posted. They often break down or run behind schedule; they are almost always hot and crowded. But all in all, they are generally cheap and reliable, and often the only way to get around.

CLUCK CLUCK. The chicken bus can be your best (dirtiest, least comfortable) friend, and as long as you know the name of where you're going, people will be more than happy to point you towards the bus you need to be on.

BY CAR

Driving in Guatemala and Belize frees you from cramped, overheated buses, but also promises bad roads and bad conditions. Getting around in Guatemala and Belize by car is a challenge—make sure to do your homework beforehand. Visit the **Association for Safe International Road Travel** (www.asirt. org) for more information.

DRIVING PERMITS AND CAR INSURANCE

INTERNATIONAL DRIVING PERMIT (IDP)

If you plan to drive a car while in Guatemala and Belize, you must be over 18 and have an **International Driving Permit (IDP)** or a valid American or Canadian driver's license (though the latter is only valid for a limited number of months). Even if you have an American or Canadian license, it may be a good idea to get an IDP anyway, in case you're in a situation (e.g., an accident or stranded in a small town) where the police do not understand English; information on the IDP is printed in 11 languages, including Spanish.

Your IDP, valid for one year, must be issued in your home country before you depart. An application for an IDP usually requires one or two photos, a current local license, an additional form of photo identification, and a fee. To apply, contact your home country's automobile association. Be vigilant when purchasing an IDP online or anywhere other than your home automobile association. Many vendors sell permits of questionable legitimacy for higher prices.

CAR INSURANCE

Most credit cards cover standard insurance. If you rent, lease, or borrow a car, you will need a **green card,** or **International Insurance Certificate,** to certify that you have liability insurance and that it applies abroad. Green cards can be obtained at car-rental agencies, car dealers (for those leasing cars), some travel agents, and some border crossings. Rental agencies may require you to purchase theft insurance in countries in which they believe there is a high risk of auto theft.

RENTING

While renting a car in Central America allows you to travel comfortably at your own pace, renting comes with its own set of hassles. The majority of rental cars have standard transmission; automatics can cost twice as much per day. In general, the cheaper the car is, the less reliable and more difficult it is to handle, which can pose problems on the road.

While regular cars might suffice during the dry season, four-wheel-drive vehicles are often essential during the rainy season, especially in rural areas. Note that less expensive four-wheel-drive vehicles tend to be more top heavy, and are more dangerous when navigating bumpy roads.

RENTAL AGENCIES

You can make reservations before you leave home by calling major international offices in your home country. It's a good idea to cross-check this information with local agencies as well. *Let's Go* includes local desk numbers in town listings.

To rent a car from most establishments in Guatemala and Belize, you must be at least 21 years old. Some agencies require renters to be 25, and most charge those aged 21-24 an additional insurance fee (around US$10 per day). Small local operations occasionally rent to people under 21, but be sure to ask about the insurance coverage and deductible. Always check the fine print.

Budget: ☎+1-800-472-3325; www.budgetcentroamerica.com. Rental cars available in Belize, (US$70 per day), El Salvador (US$30), Guatemala (US$25-45), and Honduras (US$25-40). Insurance costs an additional US$10/day. 24hr. roadside assistance in Belize, El Salvador, and Nicaragua.

National: ☎+1-877-222-9058; www.nationalcar.com. Rental cars available in El Salvador (US$20-25), Guatemala (US$20), and Honduras (US$20). US$25 surcharge for those under 25.

Thrifty: ☎+1-918-669-2168; www.thrifty.com. Rental cars available in El Salvador (US$25-30), Guatemala (US$20), and Honduras (US$40). Surcharges apply to drivers under 25.

COSTS AND INSURANCE

Rental-car prices start at around US$20 per day for national companies. Local agencies start around US$25. Expect to pay more for larger cars and for four-wheel-drive. Cars with **automatic transmission** can cost up to US$20 per day more than cars with manual transmission (stick shift), and, in some places, automatic transmission is nearly impossible to find. It is often difficult to find an automatic four-wheel-drive.

Remember that, if you are driving a conventional rental vehicle on an unpaved road in a rental car, you are almost never covered by insurance. Be aware that cars rented on an **American Express** or **Visa/MasterCard Gold** or **Platinum** credit card in Guatemala and Belize might not carry the automatic insurance that they would in some other countries; check with your credit card company before renting. Insurance plans from rental companies almost always come with an **deductible** (or excess) of around US$750-1000 for conventional vehicles; excess can reach US$1500 for younger drivers and for four-wheel-drive. This means that the insurance purchased from the rental company only applies to damages over the deductible; damages below that amount must be covered by your existing insurance plan. Some rental companies in Guatemala and Belize require you to buy a **collision damage waiver (CDW),** which will waive the deductible in the case of a collision. **Loss damage waivers (LDWs)** only do the same in the case of theft or vandalism. It is important to note that CDWs cover collisions with other cars, not "single-vehicle collisions", when the car hits a tree or jaguar.

National chains often allow one-way rentals (picking up in one city and dropping off in another). There is usually a minimum hire period and sometimes an extra drop-off charge of several hundred dollars.

ON THE ROAD

In Central America, **defensive driving** is imperative. The rules of the road are rarely enforced and rarely obeyed. Speed limits are not often posted, and thus somewhat discretionary. Passing on blind corners is common. In addition, roads outside of cities are unpaved, unlit, poorly maintained, and seasonally damaged by flooding and other natural disasters. Gasoline (petrol) prices vary, but they average around US$5 per gallon.

DANGERS

Urban roads and highways in Guatemala and Belize are by and large well-paved. Outside of these areas the roads are generally unpaved dirt tracks. In Belize, many streets, even in urban areas, lack lane markings: as a consequence, local drivers create as many lanes as they can fit on any given stretch of road. Be careful driving during the rainy season (May-Oct.), when roads can be in poor condition and landslides are common. When approaching a one-lane bridge, labeled *"puente angosto"* or *"solo carril,"* the first driver to flash her headlights has the right of way. Vehicles are often poorly maintained and many lack essential safety equipment, such as turn signals, flashers, and brake lights. Local driving practices may include passing on the right of a car attempting to make a right-hand turn; blocking traffic to talk to someone while stopped in the middle of the road; transporting passengers in the open beds of trucks; and high-speed tail-gaiting.

Carjacking and **armed vehicular robbery** are increasingly problematic in Guatemala and Belize. Robbers target tourists, often at night, on highways, small roads, crowded urban streets, and at traffic lights. Reports of violent criminal activity on Guatemala's central highways, such as the **Carretera,** have been on the rise in recent years: so much so that the US State Department warns against travel on certain highways (check http://travel.state.gov/travel/cis_pa_tw/cis/cis_1129.html for updated information). Foreign cars, sports cars, the visible use of cell phones—anything that will signal to a stranger that you are foreign or have money—should be avoided. Drunk driving is a common practice: a fact that makes driving at night even more dangerous.

To stay safe, learn local driving signals and wear a seat belt. Study route maps before you hit the road and, if you plan on spending a lot of time driving, consider bringing spare parts. Park your vehicle in a garage or well-traveled area and use a steering-wheel locking device in larger cities. Sleeping in your car is the most dangerous way to get your rest, and it's also illegal in many countries.

CAR ASSISTANCE

Some rental agencies offer 24hr. roadside assistance—ask about this when you're shopping around. Your best bet is to make sure your vehicle is ready for the road. Parts, gas, and service stations are hard to come by, so be prepared for every possible occurrence. Mechanically inclined drivers might want to bring tools for any problems that might arise. If in Guatemala, try contacting the 24-hour tourist security hotline manned by the country's **Tourist Institute** (p. 44).

If you are involved in an accident, wait until the police arrive to move your vehicle so that an officer can prepare a report. This must be done immediately and reported to insurers. Otherwise it is nearly impossible to file claims and receive coverage.

BY TAXI

Taxis are an inexpensive and easy way to travel. Potential passengers should take care to avoid unlicensed and illegal cabs. In Belize, official taxis are designated by green plates. All cabs lack meters so be sure to negotiate the fare before you buckle up. In Guatemala, official taxis are yellow (*Taxis Amarillo;* ☎502 2470 1515 in Guatemala City) and contain meters (*contadores*). They cannot be hailed on the street. You must call them to a specific address. Insist that your cab driver uses the meter before you enter the cab; if he protests that the meter is broken, call another cab. Bootleg taxis in Guatemala are white and do not contain meters. Visitors are advised to avoid traveling in these taxis. Lastly, do not to hail taxis on the street, especially in Guatemala City.

BY FOOT

Central America is not traditionally a hiking hotspot, but in recent years jungle trekking has become popular. Tours are most often arranged through small, local companies. Make sure to arrange prices and conditions beforehand. The **Great Outdoor Recreation Page** (www.gorp.com) has resources for planning hiking trips in Belize, Guatemala, Honduras, El Salvador, and Mexico. **Quetzaltrekkers** (www.quetzaltrekkers.com), which offers guided trips through Guatemala, donates all of its profits to help impoverished children. Trips cost around US$20 per day.

 LET'S NOT GO. *Let's Go* strongly urges you to consider the risks before you choose to hitch. We do not recommend hitch-hiking as a safe means of transportation, though it is common in certain areas of Guatemala and Belize.

CROSSING THE BORDER

An ongoing **border dispute** between Guatemala and Belize means that travelers must take added safety precautions when moving between the two neighboring countries. In the aftermath of a series of complicated treaties with European powers, Guatemala has laid claims on a large portion (more than 50%) of Belize's territory. Guatemala finally recognized Belize's independence in 1991, a full decade after Belize's official separation from Spain. The two countries established working, albeit strained, diplomatic ties. After an inflammatory proposal by the Guatemalan Foreign Ministry that involved the seizure of the majority of Belize's territory, the two countries entered into negotiations mediated by the Organization of American States. The dispute remains unresolved. Currently, there is an "adjacency zone" running between the neighbors, which extends one km on either side of the current border.

Coming from Belize, there is a single land crossing into Guatemala at **Benque Viejo del Carmen.** Buses run from San Ignacio, Belize, to Benque Viejo del Carmen every half-hour; from the bus station, its a 3 km walk, or US$5 taxi ride, to the border and the Belizean customs and immigration office. Coming from Guatemala, there is a single land crossing into Belize at **Melchor de Mencos.** For details on border crossings into Guatemala, see p. 44; into Belize, see p. 187.

ESSENTIALS

KEEPING IN TOUCH

BY EMAIL AND INTERNET

Internet access is widely available in Guatemala; less so in Belize. In the capitals and larger tourist areas of both countries, internet cafes are common and fairly cheap. In smaller cities and towns of Guatemala, internet access is slower and spottier but still available. In Belize, however, don't expect to find any access off the beaten path. In general, large hotels offer internet to their guests. Some larger restaurants, as well as American chains like McDonalds and Starbucks, and the Pollos Camperos chain in Guatemala, offer web access. Prices vary by region, but internet generally costs US$1-3 per hr. in Guatemala and around US$5 per hr. in Belize. Be aware that wireless hotspots pose security risks: as public, unencrypted, and unsecured connections, they often fall victim to hackers.

Although in some places it's possible to forge a remote link with your home server, in most cases this is a much slower (and thus more expensive) option than taking advantage of free **web-based email accounts** (e.g., ✉www.gmail.com). **Internet cafes** and the occasional free internet terminal at a public library are listed in the **Practical Information** sections of major cities. For lists of additional cybercafes in Guatemala and Belize, check out www.cybercaptive.com or www.travel-island.com/internet.cafes/CyberCafes.

BY TELEPHONE

CALLING HOME FROM GUATEMALA AND BELIZE

Prepaid phone cards are a common and relatively inexpensive means of calling from abroad. Each one comes with a Personal Identification Number (PIN) and a toll-free access number. Call the access number and then follow the directions for dialing your PIN. To purchase prepaid phone cards, check online for the best rates; www.callingcards.com is a good place to start. Online providers generally send your access number and PIN via email, with no actual "card" involved. You can also call home with prepaid phone cards purchased in Guatemala and Belize (see **Calling within Guatemala and Belize,** p. 23).

PLACING INTERNATIONAL CALLS. To call Guatemala and Belize from home or to call home from Guatemala and Belize, dial:

1. The **international dialing prefix.** To call from **Australia,** dial ☎0011; **Canada** or the **US,** ☎011; **Ireland, New Zealand,** the **UK** and **Belize,** ☎00; **Guatemala,** ☎00 or 130 + 00.

2. The **country code** of the country you want to call. To call **Australia,** dial ☎61; **Canada** or the **US,** ☎1; **Ireland,** ☎353; **New Zealand,** ☎64; the **UK,** ☎44; **Belize,** ☎501; **Guatemala,** ☎502.

3. The **city/area code.** Let's Go lists the city/area codes for cities and towns in Central America opposite the city or town name, next to a ☎, as well as in every phone number. If there's no number, then there's no area code.

4. The **local number.**

Another option is to purchase a **calling card,** linked to a major national telecommunications service in your home country. Cards generally come with instructions for dialing both domestically and internationally.

Placing a collect call through an international operator can be expensive but may be necessary in case of an emergency. You can frequently call collect without even possessing a company's calling card just by calling its access number and following the instructions.

CALLING WITHIN GUATEMALA AND BELIZE

The simplest way to call within the country is to use a card-based telephone, as coin-based phones are increasingly unavailable. Using prepaid phone cards, available at newspaper kiosks and convenience stores, usually saves time and money in the long run. Phone rates typically tend to be highest in the morning, lower in the evening, and lowest on Sundays and late at night.

 SEE YA SKYPE. Don't be surprised if efforts to use Skype yield confusing alerts that you're "offline." **BTL,** the major telecommunications company in Belize, has blocked Skype access throughout the country.

CELLULAR PHONES

Cell phone service is reliable and widely available in both Guatemala and Belize. The best option is to buy a cell phone when you arrive (US$20-30). It is cheapest to buy time in prepaid increments. The rates on the prepaid cards are comparable to payphone rates. If you need to make lots of calls or want people to be able to contact you more conveniently, prepaid cards are the best option. Local cellular rates for international calls can be prohibitively expensive. It is possible to bring your own cell phone, as long as it is not SIM-locked and operates on the same band. Be aware that expensive cell phones can be ostentatious and may attract unwanted attention or theft.

The international standard for cell phones is **Global System for Mobile Communication (GSM).** To make and receive calls in Guatemala and Belize, you will need a GSM-compatible phone and a **SIM (Subscriber Identity Module) card,** a country-specific, thumbnail-sized chip that gives you a local phone number and plugs you into the local network. Many SIM cards are prepaid, and incoming calls are frequently free. Belize operates at a GSM frequency of 1900 MHz; Guatemala operates at 850 MHz. Companies like **Cellular Abroad** (www.cellularabroad.com) rent cell phones that work in a variety of destinations around the world.

BY MAIL

SENDING MAIL HOME
FROM GUATEMALA AND BELIZE

Airmail is the best way to send mail home from Guatemala and Belize, though quality and timeliness of service varies. Belize's mail delivery is rather reliable and efficient while Guatemala's tends to be both temperamental and unreliable. **Aerogrammes,** most printed sheets that fold into envelopes and travel via airmail, are available at post offices. Write "airmail," *"par avion,"* or *"por avión"* on the front. Most post offices will charge exorbitant fees or simply refuse to send aerogrammes with enclosures.

ESSENTIALS

SENDING MAIL TO GUATEMALA AND BELIZE

To ensure timely delivery, mark envelopes "airmail," *"par avion,"* or *"por avión."* In addition to the standard postage system whose rates are listed below, **Federal Express** (☎+1-800-463-3339; www.fedex.com) handles express mail services from most countries to Guatemala and Belize. Sending a postcard within the country costs about US$0.20, while sending letters is around US$0.50. Mail theft is not uncommon, so avoid sending expensive items or money through the mail. In general, mail sent to and from cities has a better chance of arriving.

There are several ways to arrange pick-up of letters sent to you by friends and relatives while you are abroad. Mail can be sent via **Poste Restante** ("General Delivery" in Belize; *"Lista de Correos"* in Guatemala) to almost any city or town with a post office. Address these letters like so:

Emily Milam	**Jessica Erickson**
General Delivery	**Lista de Correos**
Belize City, Belize 78583	**Correo Central**
	Guatemala City, Guatemala 01005

The mail is delivered to a special desk in the central post office, unless you specify a post office by street address or postal code. It's best to use the largest post office in any given area, since mail may be sent there regardless. It is usually safer and quicker, though more expensive, to send mail express or registered. Bring a photo ID for pickup; you may be charged a small fee. If the clerks insist there is nothing for you, ask them to check under your first name as well. *Let's Go* lists post offices in the **Practical Information** section for each city and most towns.

ACCOMMODATIONS

HOTELS AND HOSPEDAJES

Hotels are the most common kind of accommodation in both Guatemala and Belize. It goes by many different names. *Hospedajes* or *casas de huéspedes* are usually the cheapest. *Hoteles*, *pensiones*, and *posadas* are slightly more expensive. Standards vary greatly, but generally speaking, for a basic room expect a bed, a light bulb, and perhaps a fan; other amenities are a bonus. Spending a little more gets you a room with a private bath and, if you're lucky, hot water. For a modest amount above that you might find a place with basic amenities, along with character and charm.

Lodging costs in Belize are significantly higher than those in Guatemala: a bare bones hotel single, with one bed, four walls, and a common bathroom will cost US$10; an upgrade to a private bathroom will cost around US$20, depending on the area. By contrast, hotels in Guatemala are among the most affordable in Central America, ranging from US$4 to US$5 for a budget single. Add in hot water, a private bathroom, and two meals, and you can still expect to pay only US$35 for a room. Prices are generally higher in both Guatemala and Belize in the high season and around holidays.

Hot water is a relative term in Central America, as "hot" can often be tepid at best. In rural areas and sometimes in cities, the water heating device is simply electric coils located in the shower head. Such devices work best at low water pressure. The electrical cord should be an easy reminder that water, electricity, and people do not mix well. **Toilets** in Central America often do not have seats and sewer systems cannot handle everything. Do not flush used toilet paper, tampons, or other waste products. Instead, use the receptacle (usually) provided.

HOSTELS

Many hostels are laid out dorm-style, often with large single-sex rooms and bunk beds. Private rooms that sleep from two to four are sometimes available. Hotels sometimes have kitchens and utensils for your use and will provide breakfast and other meals, storage areas, laundry facilities, internet, transportation to airports, and bike or moped rentals. Some hostels impose a maximum stay, close during certain daytime "lockout" hours, have a curfew, don't accept reservations, or, less frequently, require that you do chores. In Guatemala, a dorm bed in a hostel will average around US$3-5 and a private room will cost around US$10-20. Rooms and beds in Belize cost between twice and three times as much.

SPECIFIC CONCERNS

SUSTAINABLE TRAVEL

As the number of travelers on the road rises, the detrimental effect travelers can have on natural environments is an increasing concern. With this in mind, *Let's Go* promotes the philosophy of sustainable travel. Through sensitivity to issues of ecology and sustainability, today's travelers can be a powerful force in preserving and restoring the places they visit.

Ecotourism, a rising trend in sustainable travel, focuses on the conservation of natural habitats—mainly, on how to use them to build up the economy without exploitation or overdevelopment. Travelers can make a difference by doing advance research, by supporting organizations and establishments that pay attention to their carbon "footprint," and by patronizing establishments that strive to be environmentally friendly.

Deforestation and **biodiversity loss** are the greatest ecological problems facing Guatemala and Belize. It is estimated that these two countries have lost 20% of their forest cover in the past 20 years. Most of these forests have been converted into pasture to graze cattle for the North American beef market. Deforestation causes soil erosion, loss of wildlife, and greater carbon dioxide emissions. You can help by visiting the national parks and reserves. The admission fee and any donations you make will go toward the upkeep of the parks. You can also ensure that any tours you go on follow environmentally friendly practices. Some companies interested solely in profits and not in their negative impact on the environment may pretend to be eco-friendly in order to gain business. When on a tour, be sure that your tour guide is following the laws designed to protect the surrounding wildlife.

For opportunities to volunteer and work toward sustainable travel and conservation in Central America, see **Beyond Tourism,** p. 29.

ECOTOURISM RESOURCES. For more information on environmentally responsible tourism, contact one of the organizations below:

Conservation International, 2011 Crystal Dr., Ste. 500, Arlington, VA 22202, USA (☎+1-800-429-5660 or 703-341-2400; www.conservation.org).

Green Globe 21, Green Globe vof, Verbenalaan 1, 2111 ZL Aerdenhout, the Netherlands (☎+31 23 544 0306; www.greenglobe.com).

International Ecotourism Society, 1301 Clifton St. NW, Ste. 200, Washington, DC 20009, USA (☎+1-202-506-5033; www.ecotourism.org).

United Nations Environment Program (UNEP; www.unep.org).

WOMEN TRAVELERS

Due to the region's strong culture of *machismo*, women exploring on their own inevitably face some additional safety concerns. Women in Guatemala and Belize are accustomed to a steady stream of harassment from the opposite sex. Cat call and whistling are common. Foreign female travelers should expect similar treatment.

Single women should stay in hostels that offer single rooms that lock from the inside. It's a good idea to stick to centrally located accommodations and to avoid solitary late-night treks or bus rides. Always carry extra cash for a phone call, bus, or taxi. **Hitchhiking** is never safe. Look as if you know where you're going and approach older women or couples for directions if you're lost or feeling uncomfortable in your surroundings. If you are traveling with a male friend, it may help to pose as a couple; this will make it easier to share rooms and will also chill the blood of potential Romeos. Women in Guatemala and Belize seldom travel without the company of men; foreign women who do so often draw attention. Wearing a conspicuous **wedding band** sometimes helps to prevent unwanted advances. Generally, the less you look like a tourist, the better off you'll be.

The best answer to verbal harassment is no answer at all; feigning deafness, sitting motionless, and staring straight ahead at nothing in particular will usually do the trick. Don't hesitate to seek out a police officer, a store clerk, or a passerby if you are being harassed. Some countries have a *policía turística* (tourist police) specifically geared toward travelers. Memorize the emergency numbers in places you visit and consider carrying a whistle on your keychain. A self-defense course will both prepare you for a potential attack and raise your level of awareness of your surroundings. For more information, see **Personal Safety,** p. 11.

GLBT TRAVELERS

Homosexuality is illegal in Belize and punishable by a 10-year prison sentence. From a legal standpoint, Guatemala is considerably more liberal in its attitudes towards gays and lesbians. Homosexuality is legal. In Guatemala City, locals are relatively tolerant of alternative lifestyles and subtle displays of affection between same sex couples are permissible. Outside of the city however, and throughout Belize, homosexuality is considered to be socially unacceptable. Same sex partners are advised to keep their activities private.

Out and About (www.planetout.com) offers a comprehensive website and a weekly newsletter addressing gay travel concerns. The **International Lesbian**

and Gay Association (ILGA) (☎+32 2 502 2471; www.ilga.org) provides important political information for GLBT travelers, such as homosexuality laws of individual countries.

TRAVELERS WITH DISABILITIES

Traveling in Central America with disabilities can be very difficult, especially for travelers on a budget. Sidewalks are narrow and in disrepair and streets are busy and disorganized. Transportation is generally not wheelchair accessible, so planning with a tour group, though expensive, may be the best (or only) option.

Travelers with disabilities should inform airlines and hotels of their disabilities when making reservations, as some time may be needed to prepare special accommodations. Call ahead to restaurants, museums, and other facilities to find out if they are wheelchair accessible. Guide-dog owners should inquire as to the quarantine policies specific to Guatemala and Belize.

For those who wish to rent cars, some major car-rental agencies (e.g., Hertz) offer hand-controlled vehicles. The listings below are some organizations that can help plan your trip.

Accessible Journeys, 35 W. Sellers Ave., Ridley Park, PA 19078, USA (☎+1-800-846-4537; www.disabilitytravel.com). Designs tours for wheelchair users and slow walkers. The site has tips and forums for all travelers.

Mobility International USA (MIUSA), 132 E. Broadway, Ste. 343, Eugene, OR 97401, USA (☎+1-541-343-1284; www.miusa.org). Provides a variety of books and other publications containing information for travelers with disabilities.

Society for Accessible Travel and Hospitality (SATH), 347 5th Ave., Ste. 605, New York City, NY 10016, USA (☎+1-212-447-7284; www.sath.org). An advocacy group that publishes free online travel information. Annual membership US$49, students and seniors US$29.

MINORITY TRAVELERS

More likely than not, if you are a tourist in Belize or Guatemala, you are the minority, especially if you are white. No matter what you may try to do to disguise it, locals can spot a "*gringo*" from a mile away. This is not necessarily a bad thing; tourism is an important industry in many of the countries in the region and locals often go out of their way to help foreigners.

Tourists with dark skin should also be aware that they are an uncommon sight in Guatemala and Belize, and will attract curious stares and attention. Still, the chances of experiencing outright racism are slim. *Chinita*, *negra*, and *india* are terms that will be thrown out at minority travelers, though most are not intended to be insults. Understand that in Guatemala and Belize these are perceived as descriptive terms, and that these terms, along with other misperceptions, stem from unfamiliarity with people of different backgrounds. Reports of hostile racism and discrimination from minority travelers are not frequently reported.

DIETARY CONCERNS

Cuisine in Guatemala and Belize does not always cater to the traveler with specific eating concerns. **Vegetarian cuisine** is not hard to find in the more touristed, cosmopolitan cities, but in more remote areas, beans and rice may be the only option. Be aware that many eateries in Central America do not consider pork or chicken to be "meat." Make sure to ask for *vegetariano* food, not just a meal *sin carne* (without meat). If you are concerned about the specific ingredients dishes contain, be sure to ask very specific questions.

The travel section of **The Vegetarian Resource Group's** website, at www.vrg.org/travel, has a comprehensive list of organizations and websites geared toward helping vegetarians and vegans traveling abroad. Vegetarians will also find numerous resources on the web; try www.vegdining.com, www.happycow.net, and www.vegetariansabroad.com for starters.

Travelers who keep **kosher** should contact synagogues in larger cities for information on kosher restaurants, which are a rare sight in Central America. Your own synagogue or college Hillel should have access to lists of Jewish institutions across the nation. If you are strict in your observance, you may have to prepare your own food on the road. Travelers looking for **halal** restaurants may find www.zabihah.com a useful resource.

LET'S GO ONLINE. Plan your next trip on our newly redesigned website, **www.letsgo.com.** It features the latest travel info on your favorite destinations as well as tons of interactive features: make your own itinerary, read blogs from our trusty Researchers, browse our photo library, watch exclusive videos, check out our newsletter, find travel deals, and buy new guides. We're always updating and adding new features, so check back often!

BEYOND TOURISM

A PHILOSOPHY FOR TRAVELERS

> **HIGHLIGHTS OF BEYOND TOURISM IN GUATEMALA AND BELIZE**
>
> **WORK** with wildlife at the **Belize Zoo and Tropical Education Center** (p. 31).
>
> **VOLUNTEER** amid tropical forest & volcanoes at **Comunidad Nueva Alianza** (p. 30).
>
> **SPEAK** K'iche' Mayan like a local in one of Quetzaltenango's excellent full-immersion **language schools** (p. 35).
>
> **GO** to ☒ www.letsgo.com to find information on Beyond Tourism opportunities in other parts of Central America.

As a tourist, you are always a foreigner. Sure, hostel-hopping and sightseeing can be great fun, but connecting with a foreign country through studying, volunteering, or working can extend your travels beyond tourist traps. We don't like to brag, but this is what's different about a *Let's Go* traveler. Instead of feeling like a stranger in a strange land, you can understand Belize or Guatemala like a local. Instead of being that tourist asking for directions, you can be the one who gives them (and correctly!). All the while, you get the satisfaction of leaving these countries in better shape than you found them. It's not wishful thinking—it's Beyond Tourism.

As a volunteer in Belize or Guatemala, you can roll up your sleeves, cinch down your Captain Planet belt, and get your hands dirty doing anything from learning the language of the ancient Mayans to cleaning up after endangered jaguars. This chapter is chock-full of ideas to get involved, whether you're looking to pitch in for a day or run away from home for a whole new life in Latin American activism.

Ahh, to **study** abroad! It's a student's dream, and when you find yourself deciphering 2000 year old Mayan hieroglyphics, it actually makes you feel sorry for those poor tourists who don't get to do any homework while they're here. Not surprisingly, archaeology, zoology, Latin American studies, and urban development programs are common in the region.

Working abroad is one of the best ways to immerse yourself in a new culture, meet locals, and learn to appreciate a non-US currency. Yes, we know you're on vacation, but we're not talking about normal desk jobs. However, Let's Go strongly encourages those considering employment in developing countries to only pursue positions that do not involve competing for jobs with locals. Teaching English or helping to develop small businesses allow travelers to utilize their unique skills and aid development in Belize or Guatemala rather than hinder it.

 SHARE YOUR EXPERIENCE. Have you had a particularly enjoyable volunteer, study, or work experience that you'd like to share with other travelers? Post it to our website, www.letsgo.com!

VOLUNTEERING

Feel like saving the world this week? Volunteering can be a powerful and fulfilling experience, especially when combined with the thrill of traveling in a new place. Belize and Guatemala abound with chances to make a difference: in a school, a zoo, or a protected nature reserve. Social causes and ecological initiatives make up the bulk of volunteer opportunties in both countries so travelers interested in education, healthcare, and environmental issues are sure to find the perfect cause in Belize or Guatemala.

Some people who volunteer in Belize or Guatemala do so on a short-term basis at organizations that make use of drop-in or once-a-week volunteers. The best way to find opportunities that match your interests and schedule may be through intermediary organizations designed to connect volunteers with local NGO's and community service organizations. In Guatemala, **EntreMundos** (www.entremundos.org), with offices in Quetzaltenango (6a C., 7-31, Zona 1), partners with over 160 such organizations, mostly in the impoverished Western Highland region. In Belize, opportunities tend to be more localized, so directly contacting the organization for which you wish to volunteer may be more effective. Below are a few organizations that may accept short-term or drop-in volunteers.

SHORT-TERM OPPORTUNITIES

Belize YWCA, P.O. Box 158 Belize City, Belize, Central America (☎203 4971; www.cleuch.com/ywca). On the corner of St. Thomas Street. and Freetown Rd. The YWCA seeks weekly volunteers for swimming, after school, literacy, and other youth oriented programs.

The Fajina Craft Center, near the market in Punta Gorda, Belize. Sells authentic Mayan handicrafts (slate carvings and "jippy jappa" baskets) to support a local group of Mayan women develop economic empowerment. Drop-in volunteers are sometimes accepted to help with everyday operations.

SAGA Society (☎226 3266; www.sagahumanesociety.org). On Sea Star St., behind the Fairdale Plaza in San Pedro, Ambergris Caye, Belize. This local humane society works to monitor and protect the domestic animal populations of Ambergris Caye. Accepts volunteers for very short-term or even one-time service.

Comunidad Nueva Alianza, (☎+5729 9230; www.comunidadnuevaalianza.org), 45 minutes north of Retalhuleu, Guatemala. This organic coffee and macadamia plantation is owned and operated by a cooperative of forty Guatemalan families. Surrounded by tropical forest, waterfalls, and an active volcano, the plantation provides the unique opportunity to experience the life of a Guatemalan agricultural worker. No minimum time period to volunteer and no Spanish required. Volunteers stay in an on-site eco-hostel for between Q30 and Q40 per night. Meals Q15. Hostel and community service work also available.

LONG-TERM OPPORTUNITIES

Those looking for longer, more intensive volunteer opportunities often choose to go through a parent organization that takes care of logistical details and provides a group environment and support system—for a fee. There are two main types of organizations—religious and secular—although there are rarely restrictions on participation for either. Websites like **www.volunteerabroad.com**, **www.servenet.org**, and **www.idealist.org** allow you to search for volunteer openings both in your country and abroad.

I HAVE TO PAY TO VOLUNTEER? Many volunteers are surprised to learn that some organizations require large fees or "donations," but don't go calling them scams just yet. While such fees may seem ridiculous at first, they often keep the organization afloat, covering airfare, room, board, and administrative expenses for the volunteers. (Other organizations must rely on private donations and government subsidies.) If you're concerned about how a program spends its fees, request an annual report or finance account. A reputable organization won't refuse to inform you of how volunteer money is spent. Pay-to-volunteer programs might be a good idea for young travelers who are looking for more support and structure (such as pre-arranged transportation and housing) or anyone who would rather not deal with the uncertainty of creating a volunteer experience from scratch.

ENVIRONMENTAL AND WILDLIFE CONSERVATION

It isn't always easy being green, but volunteers in Guatemala and Belize help to make it a whole lot easier. In a region known for its natural beauty and biodiversity, environmental and wildlife conservation are essential to preserving the unique flora and fauna of Guatemala and Belize. These organizations are committed to doing just that and are always in need of volunteers.

Trekforce Expeditions, 530 Fulham Road London SW6 5NR, UK (☎+44 207-384 -3343; www.trekforce.org.uk). Combines adventure, conservation, and community service in treks through Guatemala and Belize. Treks range from one month (US$3300) to five months (US$6700). Longer itineraries include Spanish language training.

Belize Zoo and Tropical Education Centre, P.O. Box 1787 Belize City, Belize, Central America (☎220 8004; www.belizezoo.org). "The Best Little Zoo in the World" offers the chance to work closely with the zoo's animals, zoo officials, and the public through education initiatives. Minimum of two weeks. US$300 per week includes meals and accommodations. Application and guidelines available on the website.

Monkey Bay Wildlife Sanctuary, Mile 31 on the Western Highway (☎820 3032; www. monkeybaybelize.org). Offers internship and volunteer opportunities on its 3300 acre nature reserve. Homestay with community service also available.

Real Gap Experience (☎+1-866-939-9088; www.realgap.com). Offers a "Guatemala Wildlife Rescue And Rehabilitation" package ranging from 2 weeks (US$791) to 6 weeks (US$1421). Packages include a trip to the Tikal ruins.

Volunteer Petèn, Parque Ecològico Nueva Juventud San Andrès, Petèn, Guatemala (☎5711 0040 or 5160 9227; www.volunteerpeten.com). For US$120 per week (less for those staying more than 4 weeks, all meals included) volunteers live with a local family, work in an ecological park, and engage in local community service and education programs. Spanish language lessons also available for US$3 per hr.

Involvement Volunteers, P. O. Box 218 Port Melbourne, VIC 3207 Australia (☎+61 9646 9392; www.volunteering.org.au). Volunteer for 4 to 12 weeks on various conservation projects. Park maintenance, trail building, reforestation, helping in a tree nursery, and teaching about environmental conservation. Optional Spanish lessons. (US$5 per hr.) US$350 per month includes food and accommodations.

SOCIAL ACTIVISM, EDUCATION, AND RURAL DEVELOPMENT

What better way to make an impact on a country than to work directly with its people? Youth outreach initiatives, work in orphanages and domestic violence shelters, and non-profit organizations working to reduce poverty await do-gooders of all backgrounds in Guatemala and Belize. Whether you enjoy working with children, have an interest in gender-related issues, or prefer to make a difference from afar in an air-conditioned office, the listings below have something to offer every type of volunteer.

The King's Children Home (KCH), P.O. Box 144 38/40 Unity Blvd. Belmopan, Belize, Central America (☎822 2021; www.kingschildrenshome.org). Provides residential care and education for Belizean children in need. Teachers, teacher's assistants, counselors, and office assistants needed on a voluntary basis.

Help for Progress, P.O. Box 97. Belmopan, Belize, Central America (☎822 2543; www.progressbelize.org) on the corner of Slim Ln. & Forest Dr. This NGO focuses on development in the rural communities of southern Belize. Programs center around promoting gender equality, poverty reduction, and care for refugees and other displaced persons.

El Centro Experimental para el Desarrollo de la Pequeña y Mediana Empresa Rural Sociedad Civil (CEDEPEM), 20 av. 1-64, Zona 1, Quetzaltenango 09001, Guatemala (☎7761 3614; www.cedepem.org). Local non-profit that works with Western Highland indigenous communities on social and economic development. Past projects have focused on agriculture and forestry, craft development, and female empowerment.

Centro Pluricultural para la Democracia (CPD), C. A 23-84 Zona 1, Quetzaltenango, Guatemala (☎7761 0067; www.cpdguatemala.org). Focused on the largely indigenous Western Highland region, CPD works towards strengthening municipal government and promoting democratic participation among under-represetned groups.

Asociación Hogar Nuevos Horizontes (ANH), 3a C. 6-51, Zona 2, Quetzaltenango, Guatemala (☎7761 6140; www.ahnh.org). The ANH provides the opportunity to work in Central America's first domestic violence shelter. Alternatively, help out in the adjoining daycare that caters to working mothers. Minimum four week committment (at least three days of work per week). No fee to volunteer. Call Katrien (☎4543 4603) or Ariela (☎4607 5437) for information.

Café Conciencia, 12 Av. 3-35 Zona 1, Quetzaltenango, Guatemala. Another location at 18 Bleecker St. New York, NY 10012 (☎5346 9676 in Guatemala, 646-402-3049 in the US; www.cafeconciencia.org). International non-profit that works with worker-owned coffee cooperatives to promote fair trade practices, economic development, and social justice. They also run a women's empowerment project. Occasional volunteer or internship opportunities are posted to the website.

MEDICAL OUTREACH

Health-related concerns plague many areas of Guatemala and Belize, especially in impoverished rural areas and within indigenous communities. Volunteers in rural clinics and hospitals often provide the only medical care.

Cornerstone Foundations, P.O. Box 242 90 Burns Ave. San Ignacio, Belize, Central America (☎678 9909; www.cornerstonefoundationbelize.org). Broad community service organization geared towards improving the health and standard of living for the people of Belize. Long-term programs last a minimum of 3 months (US$385 per month) and include housing and lunch five days a week. Office volunteers contribute US$485 per month. Two-week natural healing ($899) and HIV/AIDS ($599) programs also available.

Global Crossroad, (☎+1-866-387-7816; www.globalcrossroad.com). Volunteer programs around the world, including a medical project in Guatemala. Participants assist at a clinic and hospital and engage in health related community education. Healthcare background and Spanish skills necessary. Application fee of US$350, prices vary depending on length of stay; room and board included with fee.

STUDYING

It's completely natural to want to play hookey on the first day of school when it's raining and first period Trigonometry is meeting in the old cafeteria, but when your campus is Antigua, Guatemala and your meal plan revolves around warm, hand-rolled burritos and a refreshing midday mojito, what could be better than the student life?

A growing number of students report that studying abroad is the highlight of their learning careers. If you've never studied in another country, you don't know what you're missing—and, if you have studied abroad, you do know what you're missing.

Study-abroad programs range from basic language and culture courses to university-level classes, often for college credit (sweet, right?). In order to choose a program that best fits your needs, research as much as you can before making your decision—determine costs and duration as well as what kinds of students participate in the program and what sorts of accommodations are provided. Don't forget to read up on the city or town where the program takes place too–rural Belizean villages aren't exactly known for the wild frat parties and all-night keggers that some students might be used to at home.

In programs that have large groups of students who speak English, there is a trade-off. You may feel more comfortable in the community, but you will not have the same opportunity to practice a foreign language or to befriend other international students. For accommodations, dorm life provides a better opportunity to mingle with fellow students, but there is less of a chance to experience the local scene. If you live with a family, you could potentially build lifelong friendships with natives and experience day-to-day life in more depth, but you might also get stuck sharing a room with their pet iguana. Conditions can vary greatly from family to family.

UNIVERSITIES

Many university-level study-abroad programs are conducted in Spanish, although many programs offer classes in English as well as lower-level language courses. Savvy linguists may find it cheaper to enroll directly in a university abroad, although getting college credit may be more difficult. You can search **www.studyabroad.com** for various semester-abroad programs that meet your criteria, including your desired location and focus of study. If you're a college student, your friendly neighborhood study-abroad office is often the best place to start. University study abroad programs in Guatemala and Belize tend to fall into three categories: Spanish language, archaeology (think uncovering Mayan ruins), and Environmental Science or Zoology (was that a jaguar?). Some universities will also offer classes in health related fields or urban development. Check individual curriculums and course offerings before paying application fees or a deposit.

AMERICAN PROGRAMS

AFS International Programs, 71 West 23rd St., 17th fl., New York, NY 10010-4102, USA (☎+1-800-237-4636 or 212-807-8668; www.afs.org). Runs study abroad and community service programs for high school and college students as well as educators around the world, including Guatemala. Volunteers live with host families and programs last from several months to one year. Cost varies based on the program type and duration.

Center for Global Education at Augsburg College, 2211 Riverside Ave., Minneapolis, MN 55454 USA (☎+1-800-299-8889 or 612-330-1159; www.augsburg.edu/global). Offers a semester-long program for called Sustainable Development and Social Change in Central America. College-age participants spend 5 weeks in Guatemala, 4 in El Salvador, and 4 in Nicaragua for the equivalent of 4 courses or 16 credits. Basic Spanish knowledge required. US$16,375 tuition and includes, room and board, medical and emergency insurance, travel within Central America, and in-country costs.

Where There Be Dragons, 3200 Carbon Place, Suite #1, Boulder, CO 80301, USA (☎+1-800-928-9203; www.wheretherebedragons.com). Runs summer and 4-week youth (ages 16-18) programs in Guatemala, focusing on language instruction, Mayan studies, and developmental issues. Also includes outdoor excursions. Cost of US$6200 does not include airfare.

Global Learning Semesters, P.O. Box 8458 Reston, VA 20195 USA (☎+1-877-300-7010 or 703-286-2641; www.globalsemesters.com). Coordinates summer and semester-long programs in Belize through Galen University in San Ignacio. Programs include classes in Environmental Science, Biology, Animal Science, and other fields of study. Summer programs range from US$3600-4500 while a full semester costs around US$8500.

UNIVERSITIES ABROAD

BELIZE

The small country of Belize has several junior colleges but only two Belizean universities within its borders. Both institutions, however, are eager to include visiting students looking to study abroad for a full semester or just the summer. Most campuses are located in Belmopan, Belize City, or San Ignacio.

University of Belize, P.O. Box 340 Belmopan, Cayo District, Belize, Central America (☎822 3680 or 1000; www.ub.edu.bz), on University Dr. With campuses throughout the country, UB offers Associate and Bachelor Associate degrees in a variety of fields, from Biology to Tourism Management. Visit their website for up-to-date information on study abroad or international student applications.

University of Galen, Study Abroad Office, P.O. Box 177 San Ignacio, Cayo District, Belize, Central America (☎824-3226; www.galen.edu.bz). Affiliated with the University of Indianapolis, U. of Galen has summer and semester programs with diverse coursework available in subjects like sustainable development, Mesoamerican civilizations, and advanced field archaeology. Summer programs range from US$3600-4500 while a full semester costs around US$8500.

GUATEMALA

Guatemala has one public university and nine private universities—some secular and some religiously affiliated. Most are located in Guatemala City, but several also operate smaller campuses in other parts of the country. **Universidad de San Carlos de Guatemala (USAC),** Ciudad Universitaria, Zona 12, Guatemala City, Guatemala (☎+502 276 0790; www.usac.edu.gt), located in Guatemala City, is one of the oldest universities in the Americas, dating back to the 17th century. Secular **Universidad Francisco Marroquín,** 6 C. Final, Zona 10 Guatemala,

Guatemala 01010 (☎+502-2338-7700; www.ufm.edu) is also located in Guatemala City and offers a broad curriculum. **Universidad Rafael Landívar,** Vista Hermosa III, Campus Central Zona 16, Guatemala City, Guatemala (☎+502 2426 2626; www.url.edu.gt) is a Jesuit-affiliated alternative.

LANGUAGE SCHOOLS

Old lady making snarky comments to you in the plaza? Imprudent cashier at the mercado? Cute moped girl that is totally into you? To communicate is to be human, and without the local language in your tool belt, you're up a creek without a *pala*]. Fear not! Language school is here to help--and Guatemala is chock full of them.

While language school courses rarely count for college credit, they do offer a unique way to get acquainted with Guatemalan culture and language. Schools can be independently run or university affiliated, local or international, youth-oriented or full of old people—the opportunities are endless. Many language school packages include meals, and accommodations in the form of a homestay with a local family. The packages usually include about five hours of instruction five or six days per week, and group activities or community service opportunities. From the bustling streets of Guatemala City to the quietest highland village, it seems that Spanish (and an occasional Mayan dialect) is being taught in every setting imaginable. Local language schools can be found under Beyond Tourism in the Practical Information sections of most cities and towns throughout the book. The US embassy website also offers an extensive list of Spanish language schools on their website, http://guatemala.usembassy. gov. Below are a couple places to begin your search.

BELIZE

123teachme, (www.123teachme.com). International language school database with links to online Spanish courses and general Spanish language resources, including a free test to determine your level of proficiency. Search language schools by country, city, cost, or ratings provided by past participants.

Amerispan, (www.amerispan.com). Language school travel agent that also provides information on volunteer, internship, and professional development opportunities in Latin America. Resource for specialized language instruction in fields like healthcare, education, and academics as well as a link to teen, college, and group deals.

GUATEMALA

In Guatemala, a few schools, particularly those in or around Quetzaltenango, offer language instruction in several Mayan dialects.

Casa Xelaju, Callejón 15, Diagonal 13-02, Zona 1, Quetzaltenango, Guatemala (☎+1-612-235-4347 in the US, in Guatemala 7761 5954; www.casaxelaju.com). For over 20 years, Casa Xelaju has offered one-on-one Spanish language lessons but now also offers the chance to learn the K'iche' dialect while living with K'iche' Mayan families. Accommodations and meals included in US$170-195 per week tuition. Weaving and other activities also available for an additional fee. College credits possible for Spanish program, contact your school's Spanish language department for approval.

Celas Maya, 6a C. 14-55 Zona 1 Quetzaltenango, Guatemala (☎7761 4342; www.celasmaya.edu.gt). Another quality language school in Quetzaltenango. Offers homestay accommodations and meals, 5 hours of one-on-one instruction 5 days per week, optional activities, and volunteer opportunities for US$150-180 per week. K'iche' Mayan classes also available. There is a US$33 online registration fee.

BEYOND TOURISM

DANCE, DRUM, COOK, WEAVE

Not all at the same time of course, but all four can be learned in Guatemala and Belize. Between volcano hikes and reef diving, learn to Salsa or Merengue in one of Quetzaltenango's many salsa clubs, play the Garifuna drums in Belize's Toledo district, weave a Mayan blanket in the highlands of Guatemala, or simply learn how to roll the perfect corn tortilla.

Xela Who, (www.xelawho.com). Quetzaltenango's self-proclaimed "leading culture & nightlife magazine" contains a plethora of cultural information for visitors and residents of Quetzaltenango (Xela). Local art galleries, live music, and listings for free salsa and merengue lessons.

La Salsa Dance Company, 5ta C. Poniente No. 6, Antigua, Guatemala (☎5400 0315; www.salsadancegt.com), inside of Centro Comercial La Canoa. One of the country's premier dance studios offers lessons starting at Q75 for one-on-one instruction or Q100 for couples. "Salsacrobics" group classes also available several times per week.

Maroon Creole Drum School (see p. 262). Dive into Belizean creole culture by learning to play the creole drums in Gales Point. You can also learn how to make them.

Maya Mountain Lodge, Cristo Rey Rd., San Ignacio, Cayo, Belzie (☎824 3019; www.mayamountain.com). Offers Mayan cooking classes on Thursdays and Thai cooking lessons on Fridays (both 8am-2pm, US$75 per person). Classes include visit to local market or garden tour and are available to guests and non-guests alike.

La Academia Culinaria de Guatemala, 10 Av. 15-88 Zona 10, Guatemal City, Guatemala (☎2368 2375; www.academiaculinaria.net). One of Central America's most prestigious culinary schools. Offers long-term programs (10 months) and a 10-week bartending course. Check website for occasional free courses and events.

Antigua Cooking School, 5a. Av. Nte. #25B Antigua, Guatemala (☎5944 8568 or 5990 3366; www.antiguacookingschool.com). Traditional Guatemalan cooking taught in English most days of the week for Q520 (US$65).

Art Workshops in Guatemala, Callejon Lopez #22 Antigua, Guatemala (☎7832 6403; www.artguat.org). Art school in Antigua offers traditional Mayan weaving classes (in Spanish, though class is taught by demonstration) in addition to drawing, Spanish language, and photography classes. Teaching positions occasionally available.

WORKING

Some travelers want **long-term** jobs that enable them to get to know another part of the world while immersing themselves in another culture and developing international connections. Most of these jobs are confined to the tourist industry or involve teaching English. Others seek **short-term** employment to finance their travel. However, Let's Go does not recommend competing for employment in developing countries where jobs for locals may already be scarce. Instead, English speakers and those with a particular area of expertise (education, healthcare, small business development) can use their unique skills to positively impact Belize or Guatemala through teaching or some other under-served field. **Transitions Abroad** (www.transitionsabroad.com) offers updated online listings for work over any time period.

BEYOND TOURISM

 MORE VISA INFORMATION. Work Permits are required for all foreigners planning to work in Guatemala and Belize. All those looking to work in Belize must reside in the country for at least 6 months prior to permit application. For more information, contact the **Immigration and Nationality Department** (☎011 501 822 2423).

LONG-TERM WORK

If you're planning on spending a substantial amount of time (more than 3 months) working in Belize or Guatemala, search for a job well in advance. International placement agencies are often the easiest way to find employment abroad, especially for those interested in teaching. Although they are often only available to college students, **internships** are a good way to ease into working abroad. Many students say the interning experience is well worth it, despite low pay (if you're lucky enough to get paid at all). Be wary of advertisements for companies offering to get you a job abroad for a fee—often times, these same listings are available online or in newspapers.

TEACHING ENGLISH

Suffice it to say that teaching jobs abroad pay more in personal satisfaction and emotional fulfillment than in actual cash. Nevertheless, even volunteer teachers often receive some sort of a daily stipend to help with living expenses. Salaries may be low for English teachers, but, considering the low cost of living in Guatemala and Belize, your Quetzals could go a long way. Most legitimate schools will only hire long-term teachers with a bachelor's degree or equivalent, although college undergraduates can sometimes get special summer positions teaching or tutoring. Many schools require teachers to have a **Teaching English as a Foreign Language (TEFL)** certificate. You may still be able to find a teaching job without one, but certified teachers often find higher-paying jobs.

The Spanish-impaired don't have to give up their dream of teaching, either. Private schools usually hire native English speakers for English-immersion classrooms where no Spanish is spoken. (Teachers in public schools will more likely work in both English and Spanish.) Placement agencies or university fellowship programs are the best resources for finding teaching jobs. The alternatives are to contact schools directly or try your luck once you arrive in Guatemala. In the latter case, the best time to look is several weeks before the start of the school year.

GUATEMALA

Guatemala contains Central America's most diverse landscape and the starkest class division in the region. Crisp mountain peaks, towering volcanic ridges, thick rainforest, and mellow Caribbean ports all coexist within Guatemala's borders. Home to the strongest modern Maya presence in Central America (around 46% of the population), Guatemala is also highly urbanized, with over 40% of the population living in cities. Nevertheless, a two hour bus ride from the frenzy of Guatemala City transports you to the rolling western highlands where Maya women in colorful traditional garb weave *huipiles* on the volcanic shores of Lake Atitlán. In many highland villages, travelers will find that Spanish can take them only so far—each of Guatemala's 23 Maya populations has its own language. Take it from the swarms of returning travelers: Guatemala is *the* place for culturally adventurous travel in Latin America.

ESSENTIALS

PLANNING YOUR TRIP

ENTRANCE REQUIREMENTS
Passport (p. 6). Required for all visitors.
Visa (p. 6). Not required for citizens of the US, UK, Australia, Canada, Ireland, and New Zealand for stays of up to 90 days. Extension of the 90-day period can be granted upon application by the **Guatemalan Immigration Office** (☎502 2411 2411)
Recommended Vaccinations (p. 12). Hepatitis A, Hepatitis B, Typhoid, and Rabies.
Required Vaccinations. None required.
Inoculations (p. 12). Travelers who have been to nations with endemic yellow fever must present proof of vaccination.
Other Health Concerns: Malaria pills are recommended for those traveling to areas at high risk for malaria. If your regular medical insurance policy (p. 13) does not cover travel abroad, you may wish to purchase additional coverage.
Work Permit. Required for all foreigners planning to work in Guatemala.
Departure Tax. US$30.

EMBASSIES AND CONSULATES

GUATEMALAN CONSULAR SERVICES ABROAD

Australia: 41 Blarney Av., Killarney Heights NSW 2087, (☎02 9451 3018).
Canada: 130 Albert St., Ottawa, Ontario K1P 5G4 (☎613-233-7188).
UK: 13 Fawcett St., London, SW10 (☎44 20 7351 3042).

US: 2220 R Street NW, Washington, DC 20008 (☎202-745-4953). **Consulates:** 1605 W. Olympic Bl., Suite 422, Los Angeles, CA 900105 (☎213-365-9251); 300 Sevilla Av., Suite 210, Coral Gables, FL 33134 (☎305-443-4828); 200 N. Michigan Av., Suite 610, Chicago, IL 60601 (☎312-332-1587); 57 Park Av., New York, NY 10016 (☎212-686-3837); 3600 S. Gessner Rd., Suite 200, Houston, TX 77063 (☎713-953-9531).

CONSULAR SERVICES IN GUATEMALA

Canada: 13 C. 8-44 Zone 10, Edificio Edyma Plaza (☎50 223 634 348; fax 50 223 651 216; www.guatemala.gc.ca).

UK: Edificio Torre Internacional, Nivel 11, 16 C. 0-55, Zona 10, Guatemala City (☎44 502 2380 7300).

US: Av. de la Reforma 7-01, Zona 10, Guatemala City (50 223 264 000; fax 50 223 348 477; http://usembassy.state.gov).

TOURIST OFFICES

Guatemala Tourist Institute (INGUAT): 17A. Av. 1-17, Zona 4, Apartado Postal 1020-A, Guatemala (☎50 224 212 810). 24hr. line for security information and advice. Service avaliable in English.

MONEY

CURRENCY AND EXCHANGE

The currency chart below was accurate as of August 2009. Check the currency converter on websites like www.xe.com or www.bloomberg.com for the latest exchange rates.

QUEZTAL (Q)		
AUS$1 = Q6.49	1Q = AUS$0.15
CDN$1 = Q7.44	1Q = CDN$0.13
EUR€1 = Q11.5	1Q = EUR€0.09
NZ$1 = Q5.19	1Q = NZ$0.19
UK£1 = Q13.1	1Q = UK£0.08
US$1 = Q8.11	1Q = US$0.12

The Guatemalan currency is the **quetzal** (Q). The US dollar is the only foreign currency freely exchangeable in Guatemala. Exchanging dollars for quetzals is straightforward enough at most banks, although making purchases with wads of Q100 can be difficult at small *tiendas*. Although **ATMs** are located in most locales, it is easy to find yourself in a town with no ATM and no place to change money. **Visa** and **Mastercard** are the most frequently accepted credit cards; **American Express** cards work at some ATMs and at AmEx offices and major airports. Some banks give cash advances on Visa cards and, less frequently, on Master-Card. **Traveler's checks** are not widely accepted in Guatemala.

COSTS

Guatemala makes budget travel look easy. A bare bones day will set you back US$15-20 without any substantial sacrifices. Add in hot water, a private bathroom, admission fees, and a few drinks, and you can expect to spend around US$60 per day.

PRICE DIVERSITY

Our Researchers list establishments in order of value from best to worst, honoring our favorites with the Let's Go thumbs-up (🖤). Because the best *value* is not always the cheapest *price*, we have incorporated a system of price ranges based on a rough expectation of what you will spend. For **accommodations,** we base our range on the cheapest price for which a single traveler can stay for one night. For **restaurants,** we estimate the average amount one traveler will spend in one sitting. The table below tells you what you'll *typically* find in Panama at the corresponding price range, but keep in mind that no system can allow for the quirks of individual establishments.

ACCOMMODATIONS	RANGE	WHAT YOU'RE *LIKELY* TO FIND
❶	Under Q41 Under US$5	Campgrounds and dorm rooms. Expect bunk beds and a communal bath. You may have to provide or rent towels and sheets. Found in most Guatemalan cities, with the possible exception of the capital.
❷	Q41-82 US$5-10	Upper-end hostels or lower-end hotels, sometimes with private bath. Most budget accommodations in Guatemala fall into this price range, and they're usually a good value.
❸	Q90-123 US$11-15	In Guatemala City, this will get you a comfortable dorm-style room. Anywhere else, you'll be in a hotel with small room and private bath. Decent amenities, like phone and TV. Breakfast is most likely included.
❹	Q131-148 US$16-18	Bigger rooms than a ❸, with more amenities or in a more convenient location. Breakfast probably included.
❺	Over Q18 Over US$18	Large hotels, upscale chains or intimate bed and breakfasts. If it's a ❺ and it doesn't have the perks you want, you've paid too much. You'll only find this price range in places like Guatemala City, Antigua, Reu, and Xela.

FOOD	RANGE	WHAT YOU'RE *LIKELY* TO FIND
❶	Under Q16 Under US$2	Probably street food or a low-end *comedor*-style restaurant. With food in this price range, you'll probably be eating on-the-go, and wish you would have remembered to pack Tums®.
❷	Q16-32 US$2-4	Sandwiches, pizza, appetizers at a bar, or low-priced entrees at a nicer *comedor*. Most Guatemalan eateries are a ❷. Either takeout or a sit-down meal, but only slightly more fashionable décor than a ❶.
❸	Q41-57 US$ 5-7	Some lower-end international restaurants. Fast-food restaurants in larger Guatemalan cities.
❹	Q-65-82 US$8-10	A somewhat fancy restaurant. Entrees tend to be heartier or more elaborate, but you're really paying for decor and ambience. Few restaurants in this range have a dress code, but some may look down on T-shirts and sandals.
❺	Over Q82 Over US$10	Your meal might cost more than your room, but there's a reason—it's something fabulous, famous, or both. Offers foreign-sounding food and a decent wine list.

Side tab: GUATEMALA

SAFETY AND HEALTH

Guatemala has one of the **highest violent crime rates** in Latin America—in 2008, an average of 40 murders per week were reported in Guatemala City alone. Tourists are directly targeted. Armed attacks are increasingly common in and around

Guatemala

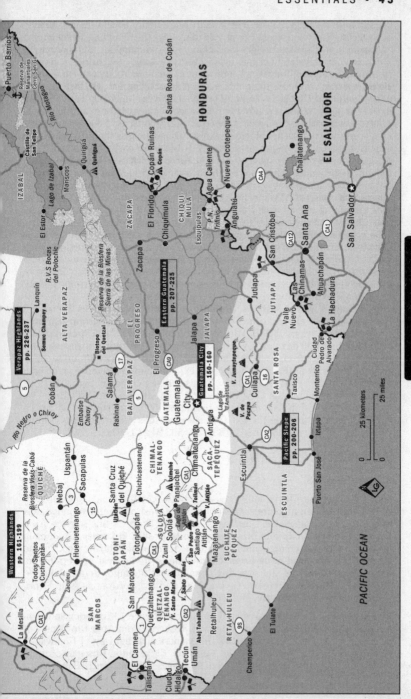

GUATEMALA

Western Highlands
pp. 161-199

Verapaz Highlands
pp. 226-237

Eastern Guatemala
pp. 207-225

Guatemala City
pp. 150-160

Pacific Slope
pp. 200-206

HONDURAS

EL SALVADOR

PACIFIC OCEAN

Puerto Barrios

Reserva de Manantiales Cerro San Gil

Castillo de San Felipe

Río Motagua

Quiriguá

Quiriguá

El Estor

Lago de Izabal

Mariscos

IZABAL

Santa Rosa de Copán

Copán Ruinas

Copán

El Florido

Chiquimula

CHIQUI-MULA

Agua Caliente

Nueva Ocotepeque

P.N. Trifinio

Anguiatú

Chalatenango

San Cristóbal

Santa Ana

CA4

CA1

San Salvador

ZACAPA

Zacapa

Esquipulas

San Cristóbal

CA12

Chinamas

Ahuachapán

Las

Lanquín

Semuc Champey

ALTA VERAPAZ

Reserva de la Biosfera Sierra de las Minas

R.V.S Bocas del Polochic

Reserva de la Biosfera Visís-Cabá

QUICHÉ

Biotopo del Quetzal

EL PROGRESO

JALAPA

Jalapa

Jutiapa

JUTIAPA

Valle Nuevo

La Hachadura

Ciudad Pedro de Alvarado

Cobán

Salamá

Rabinal

BAJA VERAPAZ

El Progreso

CA9

Guatemala City

V. de Pacaya

V. Jumaytepeque

Cuilapa

SANTA ROSA

16

Taxisco

Monterrico

Ciudad

Iztapa

Río Negro o Chixoy

Embalse Chixoy

5

5

17

Uspantán

Nebaj

Todos Santos Cuchumatán

Sacapulas

Santa Cruz del Quiché

Chichicastenango

Ixtahuacán

CHIMAL-TENANGO

CA1

Iximché

Antigua

SACA-TEPEQUEZ

Chimaltenango

Lago de Amatitlán

V. Agua

V. de Atitlán

Escuintla

Puerto San José

ESCUINTLA

CA2

3

15

La Mesilla

Huehuetenango

TOTONI-CAPÁN

Totonicapán

SOLOLÁ

Sololá

Panajachel

Lago de Atitlán

Santiago Atitlán

Toliman

V. San Pedro

SUCHITE-PÉQUEZ

Mazatenango

Zacúleu

San Marcos

SAN MARCOS

CA1

Zunil

Quetzaltenango

QUETZAL-TENANGO

V. Santa María

V. Santo Tomás

Abaj Takalik

RETALHULEU

Retalhuleu

El Tulate

1

Talismán

Ciudad Hidalgo

Tecún Umán

El Carmen

CA2

Champerico

95

Guatemala

0   25 kilometers

0   25 miles

places such as Antigua, Tikal, Peten, and Lake Atitlan. Local officials, already overwhelmed and underpaid, are unable to manage the mounting problem.

Assault, theft, armed robbery, carjacking, rape, kidnapping, and murder are the most common violent crimes against tourists. **Gangs,** well-armed and eager to employ force, are increasingly prevalent in Guatemala City and rural areas. **Violent robberies** are also commonplace, and **pick-pocketing** and **petty theft** are rampant. Guatemala City is a hotspot of criminal activity, especially in the central market area. Travelers are urged to refrain from staying in or near this region.

Attacks on vehicles, often when stopped at traffic lights, are frequent. In a common scenario, tourists are blockaded by an armed gang as their car leaves the airport; the assailants summarily proceed to slash the car's tires and steal any passports, cash, and luggage they can find. **Public and "chicken" buses**, in addition to being poorly maintained, are routinely attacked by armed robbers; private intra-city coach services are a much safer, and highly advisable, alternative. **Express kidnappings** at ATM machines, shopping centers, and around the airport area are on the rise as well. For short trips, your safest bet is to take official **taxis.** Do not hail cabs on the street or travel in bootleg vehicles.

Do not approach or take photographs of Guatemalan children without express permission from their guardians, particularly in more remote regions such as the Quiche, Peten, San Marcos, and Chiqmula provinces. Due to widespread fear of child kidnapping and organ harvesting, tourists who have failed to take this precaution have been met with violent reactions, including attempted and actual lynchings by local mobs.

Guatemala's **Tourist Institute (INGUAT)** staffs regional offices in tourist hotspots nationwide and offers security escorts for tourist groups through its **Assistance Office (ASISTUR).** With the purchase of an ASISTUR card policy (1 day, 15 days, 30 days, or 1 year; US$1 per day), visitors can access 24hr. telephone assistance for medical and legal issues, as well as obtain security escorts, roadside assistance, helicopter evacuation from remote areas, and assistance in the event of a robbery. Cards can be purchased at the INGUAT kiosks at the Guatemala City, Flores, and Tikal airports. ASISTUR can be reached from within Guatemala by dialing ☎1500. Call toll-free at ☎888-464-8281 from within the US. INGUAT also provides a 24hr. security hotline (☎502 24 212 810 or ☎502 55 789 836; fax 502 24 212 891).

BORDER CROSSINGS

BELIZE. See p. 187.

MEXICO. There are three land crossings between Guatemala and Mexico. In the Guatemalan highlands, **La Mesilla,** 90km west of Huehuetenango, has buses to San Cristóbal de las Casas, Mexico. There is bus service from **Huehue, Guatemala City,** and other towns to **La Mesilla. El Carmen,** Guatemala is west of Quetzaltenango and Retalhuleu, near Tapachula, Mexico. On the Pacific Coast, **Ciudad Tecun Umán,** Guatemala is 75km west of Retalhuleu. Buses head to this border crossing from Quetzaltenango, Retalhuleu, and Tapachula, Mexico. There are several land and river crossings from **Flores,** Guatemala toward **Palenque,** Mexico.

EL SALVADOR. There are three land crossings between El Salvador and Guatemala. **Valle Nuevo/Las Chinamas** (Highway 8) serves from Area 1 in Zone 4 of Guatemala City (p. 109). **San Cristóbal** (Interamericana Highway, or Highway 1) has buses from Guatemala City and **Santa Ana,** El Salvador. Buses also run to **Anguiatú,** Guatemala (Highway 10) from **Esquipulas** and **Metapán,** El Salvador.

HONDURAS. There are three land crossings between Honduras and Guatemala. **El Florido** is along a dirt road between **Chiquimula**, Guatemala and **Copán Ruinas**, Honduras. Buses run on the Guatemalan side (p. 110), and pickups run on the Honduran side. **Agua Caliente** is 10km east of Esquipulas, Guatemala near Nueva Ocotepeque, Honduras (p. 113). **Corinto**, near Puerto Barrios, Guatemala, has connections to **Omoa**, Honduras (p. 115).

LIFE AND TIMES

HISTORY

MAYA HAVE YOUR ATTENTION? (DAWN OF TIME-AD 1523). The first settlers of Guatemala were the ancestors of the great **Mayan civilization** that dominated the land until the Spanish arrived in the 16th century. The classic Mayan period lasted from AD 250-900, during which time the early villages became a mosaic of individual city-states, all constantly at war with one another. Each city-state built monumental stone temples, such as those at **Tikal** (p. 157) and **Uaxactun** (p. 154), to demonstrate power and to record victories through exquisite hieroglyphics. By the tenth century AD, the great Mayan cities had collapsed; remnants of the civilization continued to flourish until the Spanish conquest, but the days of giant stone temples were gone for good.

FROM CONQUEST TO UN-CONQUEST (AD 1523-1821). In 1523, Spanish conquistador **Pedro de Alvarado** headed to Guatemala with 120 cavalrymen, 300 footsoldiers, four cannons, and several hundred native auxiliaries, leading a cruel and bloodthirsty campaign to conquer the highlands. By 1527, the Spanish controlled enough of the region for Alvarado to be declared Governor of Guatemala. Still, it took another 170 years before the invaders destroyed the last Mayan stronghold in Guatemala—the island city of Tayasal in the Petén region. On the whole, the Spanish found Guatemala disappointing as it lacked the rich gold and silver deposits they yearned for. Nevertheless, the Spanish held on to the entire region between California and Costa Rica until the Mexican War of Independence.

INDEPENDENTE (1821-71). On September 15, 1821, Guatemala announced its official independence from Spain, and the country's incorporation into the new Mexican Empire. Two years later, Guatemala gave up on Mexico and joined the short-lived United Provinces of Central America, which collapsed during the civil war in 1838. Guatemala's independence from the Mexican Empire was engineered in part by **Rafael Carrera**. This savvy swineherd who turned politico became Guatemala's first conservative president in 1844. Backed by large landowners and the Catholic Church, Carrera declared himself president for life in 1854. Under his rule, Guatemala recognized the boundaries of British-controlled Belize in exchange for the promise of a road connecting the two countries. The road was never built, and Guatemala and Belize continue to argue about the logistics of their border. Unlike most Central American strongmen, Carrera managed to pull off his presidency-for-life, staying in control until he died peacefully in 1865.

ILLIBERAL LIBERALS (1871-1944). Starting as a revolt in western Guatemala, the Liberal Revolution of 1871 brought **Justo Rufino Barrios** to power, where he quickly became known as "the Reformer" for his rapid program of social and economic change. After establishing freedom of religion and press, Barrios oversaw the ratification of Guatemala's first constitution, maintaining dictatorial power. He also pushed for economic modernization by promoting the coffee industry and by promoting the construction of roads, railroads, and telephone lines. In 1898, **Manuel Estrada Cabrera** continued Barrios's policies of economic modernization and dictatorial rule. He made major land deals with the American-owned United Fruit Company and later even hired them to run the postal service. Bizarrely, he also attempted to promote the worship of Minerva, the Roman goddess of wisdom, through the construction of several Greco-Roman temples within the country. **Jorge Ubico**, the last of Guatemala's dictatorial liberals, also bolstered the country's infrastructure and economic ties with the United States. Ubico earned the nickname "Little Napoleon of the Tropics" for his peculiar fondness for the French emperor. Ubico even dressed his troops in an 18th-century French style of uniform, lending credence to **Tomás Borge Martínez's** description of him as "crazier than a half-dozen opium-smoking frogs." Ubico was finally ousted by a general strike in 1944, known as the **October Revolution.**

TEN YEARS OF SPRING (1945-54). The democratic election of **Juan José Arévalo** in 1944 ushered in the **Ten Years of Spring,** a new era of spiritual socialism. Drawing much of his support from organized labor, Arévalo enacted a new labor code, established a social security system, and worked towards agrarian reform. Arévalo's successor, **Jacobo Arbenz,** pursued the same radical program and even legalized the communist Guatemalan Labor Party in 1952. Most importantly, Arbenz finally carried out agrarian reform by expropriating and redistributing uncultivated lands that had been owned by the United Fruit Company and other wealthy elites. Unfortunately for Guatemala, United Fruit had powerful allies in Washington, and the United States government quickly retaliated. In 1954, a CIA-trained army invaded, deposing Arbenz's government and establishing a military junta under **Carlos Castilla Armas.**

OPPRESSION AND CIVIL WAR (1954-96). Military rule after the 1954 coup reversed the social reforms of the last decade and violently crushed any political opposition. These oppressive tactics aroused increasingly violent resistance, and many Guatemalans joined guerrilla groups demanding land reform and democracy. The 1960s saw a series of rigged elections and puppet presidents controlled by the US military. Meanwhile, right-wing paramilitary groups like the **White Hand** and the **Secret Anti-Communist Army (ESA)** attacked students, professionals, and the lower classes suspected of leftist activity. The period from the late 1970s to the early 1980s became known as *La Violencia*, as conflict spread throughout Guatemala. General **Efraín Ríos Montt** led the military's scorched-earth campaign from 1982-1983. Soon the violence turned genocidal when the general began targeting the indigenous Maya of Guatemala, destroying hundreds of Mayan villages, and torturing and killing over 10,000 indignuous inhabitants. After Ríos Montt was deposed, the conflict receded enough to allow peace negotiations brokered by the United Nations. Finally, in 1996, **Alvaro Arzú Irigoyen** won the presidency and signed peace accords with the guerillas in the same year.

TODAY

Guatemala has experienced rapid economic growth over the past few decades, consolidated by the country's ratification of the **Dominican Republic–Central America Free Trade Agreement (DR-CAFTA)** in 2006, which took effect in 2009 and formally opened the entire region to trade with the United States. This new, open movement of goods between north and south may reach levels achieved by the vast exodus of Guatemalans themselves: between 500,000 and 1 million Guatemalans have emigrated to the United States since the 1970s, mostly due to a mixture of civil war troubles and lackluster economic opportunities. While unemployment is low, about one-third of Guatemalans live below the poverty line, and the country remains among the 10 poorest of all Latin America. However, growth over the past decades, especially in the export sector, has been robust. General well-being has tentatively improved, with infant and general mortalities as well as inflation all decreasing.

Tourism, one of the nation's largest economic sectors, has grown with the country's stability. The traditional ebb and flow of travelers is now augmented by business tourism and large events such as the International Olympic Committee's 119th assembly held in Guatemala City. American visitors comprise the largest share of this tourism. The communities that survived the brutalities of the civil war have proved resilient in the face of commercialization.

Guatemala's salient illegal drug issue feeds into the larger problem of rampant crime. While rarely affecting foreigners, crime was the focus of the 2007 presidential elections for good reason: kidnappings are unsettlingly common and the murder rate reached 45 per 100,000 in 2007 (an even higher level of domestic homicide than was reported during the civil war). Apart from crime, natural disasters, such as the 2005 landslides (the result of the frequent hurricanes that strike Guatemala from June to November) have also plagued the country.

Guatemala's foreign relations are much less rocky than they were in the 1950s, when the acting president challenged the Mexican head of state to a duel to settle a dispute over fishing boundaries. Boundary disputes, rooted in the conflicts over Spanish and British colonial frontiers, remain a feature of Belize-Guatemala. In 1991, Guatemala recognized Belize and established formal, diplomatic ties. Eight years later, however, the Guatemalan Foreign Ministry changed course. In 1999, Guatemala proposed that Belize cede half of its territory; this was met with a peaceful refusal. Guatemala has smoother relations with its other neighbors. In a foreign relations oddity characteristic of several Central American nations, Guatemala recognizes the Republic of China as the legitimate representative of the Chinese people, rather than the People's Republic. Guatemala is the seat of **PARLACEN,** the Central American Parliament, one of the institutions of the **Central American Integration System** and the last in a long line of attempts to economically and politically integrate the region.

ECONOMY AND GOVERNMENT

Guatemala's economy, the largest in Central America, principally depends on subsistence agriculture with a primary focus on corn and squash. Guatemala's agriculture also consists of large-scale commercial farming on the Pacific slopes, where coffee, bananas, and sugar have been produced for mass export since the turn of the 20th century, replacing cocoa and dyes. The U.S. remains the principal export destination for Guatemalan goods, with neighboring countries such as Nicaragua coming in at a distant second. The Guatemalan economy witnessed slow growth of its industrial sector in the post-war era, but Latin America's **Lost Decade** (the misery-fraught 1980s) hit Guatemala as hard as any—GDP plummeted and inflation boomed. Since the 1990s and the decline of civil war violence, Guatemala has enjoyed marked economic growth, though poverty remains deeply entrenched in Guatemalan society and socioeconomic mobility is rare. Inflation has fallen from its previous heights, but corn prices have risen due to the global rise in food prices, a trend that threatens the well-being of a large segment of the population.

Guatemala has had a civilian government since 1985, though the early years of its democracy were marked by *autogolpe* (self-coup), intimidation, and corruption. Since the peace accords ended the 36-year civil war, power transitions have been stable and clean, and the legislative and judicial bodies have functioned coherently. The constitution provides for **22 departamentos**, each headed by a governor. Popular vote determines the election of presidents who serve four year terms, while a mix of department-based constituency elections choose the main legislative body, the **Congress of Deputies**. The current president, **Álvaro Colom**, of the social-democratic **National Unity of Hope (UNE)**, the largest party in the Congress, was elected in 2007. Other parties on the ever-changing Guatemalan political scene include the right-wing **Grand National Alliance (GANA)** and **Patriotic Party (PP)** and the **Guatemalan Republican Front (FRG)** of the 1930s-era Guatemalan dictator **Efraín Montt**.

PEOPLE

DEMOGRAPHICS

The composition of Guatemala's population is similar to those of many countries of Central America. A broad **Mestizo** population of mixed Spanish and indigenous descent forms a middle band, in Guatemala only about a fifth of the population. The vast majority of Guatemala, about 60% of the population, is of indigenous origin; in this case, some nation of the **Maya**. The largest of these are the **K'iche, Kaqchikel, Mam, and Q'eqchi** tribes. The K'iche are concentrated in the province of El Quiche, the Mam in western Guatemala, the Kaqchikel in the regions around Lake Atitlan and the Mid-western highlands, and the Q'eqchi in the Petén and more broadly across Guatemala. A small community of **Creole Guatemalans** of entirely Spanish descent makes up 5% of the population, mostly concentrated in the cities. The **Garífuna** people, a mixed ethnic group of Arawak, Carib, and African descent, have lived on the east coast of Guatemala for centuries.

LANGUAGE

The primary and official language of Guatemala is **Spanish,** spoken in the Central American style, which, much like Argentine and Uruguayan Spanish, makes use of the "vos" second person singular. However, this informality is safer to avoid for the traveler, who should stick with polite forms of address. Guatemala is also a country with an extraordinarily resilient Mayan culture; Spanish is spoken by 93% of the population, but a significant portion of that usage is as a second language. A full 23 languages, including most Maya tongues as well as Xinca and Garífuna, are recognized in the slightly lower category of National Languages that are entitled to some bilingual education and other cultural rights. The Peace Accords of 1996, which ended the epic civil war, included provision of voting materials and government proceedings in indigenous languages as an important part of the attempt to form a political order more inclusive of the Maya population.

RELIGION

In Guatemala, as in most of Latin America, the principal, and once official, religion is **Roman Catholicism,** and is evident in the omnipresent churches, missions, and cathedrals of the colonial era. About 60% of *guatemaltecos* are affiliated with Rome, under the two Archdioceses of Guatemala City and Los Altos Quetzaltenango-Totonicapán. Coexisting with the Church as it has for centuries is traditional **Mayan religion,** practiced by about 1% of the population, in part in the form of syncretism and in part as a surviving worship of the old Mayan gods, veneration of sacred places, and traditional practice of divination. Unlike its neighbors, however, Guatemala also has a very strong **Protestant** presence due to forceful evangelism, mostly from the United States, over the 20th century and the massive upheavals of the civil war. Mass conversion to various evangelical churches has resulted in about 40% of the population belonging to some sect, including, prominently, the Pentecostals. The Church of Latter-day Saints has a significant presence among the population as well. Tiny communities of Jews, Muslims, Buddhists, and the non-religious also exist in the country.

CULTURE

THE ARTS

On the topic of the arts, a traveler's thoughts tend to flit to the **Maya,** whether of the crafts and artisan's works that decorate the country, or the ancient reliefs, murals, and architecture of the Mayan past. Slightly more recent in pedigree, the **colonial period** left its imprint in the churches and religious infrastructure of Guatemala. Modern artistic endeavors have a small but important role in Guatemala's history. One of the best-known painters of Guatemala is **Carlos Mérida,** a mural painter who was born in 1891 and is often compared to Diego Rivera; another classical artist of Guatemala was **Alfred Jensen,** a painter and printmaker of Danish and German descent. In recent years, modern art in Guatemala has been carried forward by avant-garde performance artists, including **Regina José Galindo,** who work on an international scene.

LITERATURE

The most ancient Guatemalan literature is the mostly vanished corpus of **Mayan writing,** referenced in their artifacts and exemplified by the **Popul Vuh,** one of the main religious texts, and the traditional play, the **Rabinal Achi.** It was not until centuries after the Spanish conquest that another major literary tradition came about. These first stirrings included the poet and historian Francisco Antonio de Fuentes y Guzmán, who chronicled the recent conquest, and, later, the poet Rafael Landívar.

Early Guatemalan authors and intellectuals quickly became partisans of independence and **romantic nationalism;** many Guatemalan figures from the period of independence, the broad era comprising the end of the 18th century and the beginning of the 19th, traveled around Latin America and were significant figures in creating the new independent identity of the continent. **Antonio José de Irisarri Antonio** was a Guatemalan journalist and statesman who was deeply involved in the nascent republics of Guatemala, Chile, and El Salvador. **María Josefa García Granados** was an influential Spanish-Guatemalan socialite of this era who became renowned as a satirist, commentator, and woman of letters. More well-known was her friend, **José Batres Montúfar,** a poet and critic.

Later, Guatemalan literature began to leave behind the poetry and nation-building that had characterized it in decades past. The **novelistic tradition** began with **José ´Milla y Vidaurre,** a newspaper editor, international literary figure, conservative politician, and father of the Guatemalan novel, whose work mainly was in the field of historical fiction and the realistic portraiture of life in the colonial age. **Modernism,** and a heavy dose of Francophilia, began to reach Guatemala at the *fin de siècle*, with authors like **Domingo Estrada** and Máximo Soto Hall fostering a small but energetic hub of modern literature in Guatemala.

A new element of daring was injected into Guatemalan literature by the political strife of the 20th century, and the emergence of the **"dictator novel,"** a genre criticizing the authoritarianism of Latin America. **Miguel Ángel Asturias** received the 1967 Nobel Prize for his efforts in this genre, as well as the Soviet Union's Lenin Prize. In recent years, Guatemalan literature has diversified further, with a re-examination of the Mayan contribution to Guatemalan literature; a recent winner of the prize set up in Asturias's honor was **Humberto Ak'abal,** a K'iche Maya poet who declined the prize in protest. Guatemalan literature remains largely political, and focuses on the often turbulent question of Guatemalan national identity.

MUSIC

Guatemalan folk is the country's most widely exported musical genre; several distinct traditions make up this tradition. In one corner is **traditional Maya music,** reliant on wind instruments, drums, and, for the very authentic, the conch-shell trumpet. Coming from the African-derived culture of the Garífuna is the tradition of **Garífuna music,** which brought African rhythms and styles similar to those of the marimba, Guatemala's national instrument and the cornerstone of mainstream Guatemalan popular music. Classical music in Guatemala bears strong Spanish and Church influences, but became indigenous with **José Eulalio Samayoa,** who composed the first symphonies of the New World in the early years of the 19th century. The various strains of music in Guatemala have been unified in the 20th and 21st centuries by Guatemalan composers and conductors like Dieter Lehnhoff, who has brought together Mayan, African, and Western traditions to international acclaim.

FILM AND TELEVISION

The cinematic arts have had a checkered history in Guatemala. In 1905, the first film in Guatemala was produced, a documentary of a festival in Guatemala City. Detective films were soon to follow, and in the 1930s the government began to make use of film extensively. The first all-Guatemalan film with sound, **"El sombrerón,"** was produced in 1950 under director Eduardo Fleischman. The 1970s were an age of renewed work under directors like Rafael Lanuza. For much of the post war era, however, great parts of the country were too dangerous for film or documentary work, and many films with Guatemalan subjects were filmed in neighboring countries, including Mexico. Recently, however, both film and an indigenous television industry have taken off.

LAND

Guatemala lies between Mexico, Belize, El Salvador, and Honduras, with coasts on both the Gulf of Honduras in the east and the Pacific Ocean to the west. Divided into several areas by mountains and highlands, the landscape nevertheless retains broad similarities. Guatemala is a tropical, mostly mountainous country and a hothouse of biodiversity, ripe with forests and wetlands.

GEOGRAPHY AND GEOLOGY

Several large mountain chains split Guatemala. In the south, a string of 27 **volcanoes** reaches from Mexico to El Salvador, shielding a narrow, fertile plain huddled against the Pacific Ocean. The rectangular portion of Guatemala jutting into Mexico, the Petén region, features a thickly forested, isolated, **limestone plateau.** Part of its isolation is due to the mountains and highlands that wall it off to the south. These highlands represent the most densely populated areas of the country, including the capital of Guatemala City and other major cities, though some cities are also located in the **fertile Pacific plain.** The far east of Guatemala has high sierras and deeper valleys winding toward the tiny **Caribbean coast.**

WILDLIFE

Guatemala is internationally heralded as a wildlife hotspot. Over a third of Guatemala is under forest cover, with over half of that biosphere unlogged old-growth forest, much of it oak, pine, and otherwise coniferous. Additionally, a full 29% of the national territory is classified as protected from development, the highest ratio in Central America. In the northern lowlands of Petén, rainforest breaks into natural savanna grasslands, while in the southern lowlands of the Pacific plain most land has been cleared for agriculture.

The great forests of Guatemala host an immense variety of animal life, though some of the great mammals, including tapir, deer, ocelot, peccaries, and jaguars, are becoming rarer. The most flamboyant fauna include the birds of Guatemala. Chief among them is the vibrant emerald-and-red quetzal, the national bird, which reigns from its seat in the protected valleys of Copán.

WEATHER

The diversity of terrains in Guatemala is matched by a wide range of climates. Below 3,000ft., temperatures linger at the low end of tropical, between 21° and 27° C. The heaviest rains fall on the sierra slopes, at the Caribbean coastline, and on parts of the Pacific plain, especially during the wet season (March through December). The dry season grips the country between November and April. Severe tropical storms menace in September and October, as did Hurricane Stan in 2005.

FOOD AND DRINK

Corn is divine in Guatemala—literally. According to the sacred Quiché Maya text, the *Popol Vuh*, the gods unsuccessfully first tried to use mud, then wood, and finally corn in their attempts to create man. As man's original essence, it is hardly surprising that Guatemalan cuisine centers around **corn.** From **tortillas** and **tamales,** to the roasted cobs sold on street corners and the popular milky drink **atol,** visitors will find more than their typical earful of corn. Black beans, or **frijoles,** are another sure bet: while they may come refried (*volteado*) or whole (*parado*), they'll definitely be somewhere in most dishes.

Beyond the staples of corn, rice, eggs, and beans, Guatemalan cuisine features a wealth of traditional dishes and **stews** (*caldos*). In *restaurantes típicos*, thick, chili-based sauces spice up otherwise ordinary servings of vegetables, chicken, and turkey. Around Antigua, the rich sauce **pepián,** consisting of onions, tomatoes, and peppers, is particularly popular. Along the Caribbean coast, seafood reigns supreme. Savor a bowl of **tapado,** a rich, coconut-based soup in which an unlikely mix of shrimp, fish, tomatoes, and bananas are all mixed together. In the highlands, you'll find the distinct taste of indigenous Ki'iche cuisine with **Kak'ik,** a spicy turkey stew crafted by simmering cilantro, garlic, tomatoes and dried peppers in a wholly delicious culinary affair.

If you're searching for the basics, nearly every town has a market with stalls of fresh fruits and vegetables—look out for **guanábana** (soursop), a tropical fruit with a thorny exterior and pulpy, creamy, seed-studded flesh. Coffee is the **bebida preferida,** but with Guatemalan coffee in high demand by international coffee companies, locals are often peddling cheaper, weaker brews. Guatemala's temperate climate produces some of the world's best beans, along with exceptional crops of sugar, bananas, and cocoa. Fruit juice blends known as **licuados** are lifesavers on hot days. We suggest cooling off like a local by sipping on a homegrown beer like **Gallo, Mozo, or Dorado.**

CUSTOMS AND ETIQUETTE

Although etiquette is fairly universal throughout Central America, Guatemala has a few of its own customs. As in much of Latin America, **punctuality sometimes falls by the wayside**—no one seems to be in a rush, and lateness is both tolerated and expected. Between friends, it is customary to give a kiss on one cheek as a greeting, and handshakes are the norm among men. Gifts should always be accepted with emphatic gratitude, and visitors to a Guatemalan home should consider bringing a small offering like chocolate, flowers, or souvenirs from their home country.

Most Guatemalans have two surnames: their paternal name, followed by the maternal. When addressing Guatemalans, use only the first surname. To greet a stranger or authority figure, make sure to use the formal **usted** form, while the *tú* form should suffice for friends and informal acquaintances. A soft speaking voice is considered polite in Guatemala. Be aware of the volume and tone of the people around you, and notice how your voice sounds and travels—particularly when conversing in English. Approach conversations about politics and the recent violence in Guatemala with care, as you may hit upon a particularly painful or controversial subject. Feel free, however, to demonstrate your interest in Guatemalan history, culture, or geography with a well-posed question about Guatemala's 1967 Nobel Prize in Literature (to Miguel Asturias) or the *Liga Internacional de Fútbol*.

As a visitor to a highly touristed, developing country, **be sensitive about whom you photograph.** It is considered polite to ask permission of indigenous people and locals before you take their picture out of respect for their privacy. Don't be surprised, however, if you are asked for a few *quetzales* to seal the deal. **Machismo,** a chauvinistic attitude toward women, still colors gender relations in many communities across the country. While it is perfectly acceptable for women to dine alone, it is not advisable for them to go unaccompanied to bars or clubs or to walk alone at night. Women are encouraged to dress conservatively in order to stave off catcalls and unwanted advances, and all female travelers should be aware of the alarmingly high number of violent crimes targeted at Guatemalan women over the past decade. Public displays of affection are generally acceptable, but while Guatemala has no laws prohibiting homosexuality, same-sex relationships remain taboo. As always, rules of etiquette and codes of conduct tend to be more relaxed in cosmopolitan, urban areas.

GUATEMALA

GUATEMALA CITY

Guatemala City, or Guate (GUAH-te), is the largest urban area in Central America. Smog-belching buses and countless sidewalk vendors, together with the sheer number of people, noise, and the endless expanse of concrete, make the city center uncomfortably claustrophobic. Add to this a general concern for safety and it's easy to understand why many visitors flee Guatemala's capital for the surrounding highlands. Still, poking around Guate for a day or two does have its rewards. Fine architecture dating back to the 1700s and several worthwhile museums make for an engaging stay. After camping in the countryside and hiking through jungles, the city's modern conveniences and hot showers can be welcoming. While travelers may find comfort in Guate, many residents do not. Poverty is laid bare here, standing in harsh contrast to the antiseptic shopping malls and guarded, fortress-like mansions in the wealthiest neighborhoods. This disparity is particularly evident in Guatemala's large refugee population, mainly Maya who fled civil violence in their home villages.

Guatemala City was named the country's capital in 1775 after an earthquake in Antigua left the government scrambling for a safer center, though powerful tremors shook the new capital in 1917, 1918, and 1976. Despite the whims of Mother Nature, the city and its three million inhabitants persevere, expanding ceaselessly into the surrounding valleys.

⌐ INTERCITY TRANSPORTATION

FLIGHTS:

International Flights: La Aurora International Airport (☎2334 7680), 7km south of Zona 1 in Zona 13. Services the following airlines: **American** (☎2337 1177; www.aa.com); **Continental** (☎2331 2051; www.continental.com); **Delta** (☎2337 0642; www.delta.com); **Grupo Taca** (☎2470 8222; www.taca.com); **Iberia** (☎2332 0911; www.iberia.com); **KLM** (☎2367 6179; www.klm.com); **Mexicana** (☎2366 4543; www.mexicana.com); and **United** (☎2336 9923; www.united.com).

Domestic Flights: The most common domestic flight is from Guatemala City to **Flores,** near Tikal. Two airlines serve this route: **Grupo Taca** (see above) and **TAG** (☎2360 3038; www.tag.com.gt). Taca offers more frequent flights and larger aircraft. Round-trip Q700-950. Specials are often available. During peak season, Taca offers spotty (and pricey) domestic service via its regional affiliate, **Inter.** Destinations include **Huehuetenango, Puerto Barrios, Quetzaltenango,** and **Río Dulce. Rasca** can arrange charter flights, but these also tend to be expensive.

INTERNATIONAL BUSES

Domestic and international buses also leave from various locations across Guatemala City. Only one or two companies are listed here, but there are several others that offer bus service to Central America's largest cities.

San Salvador:

Melva Internacional and J.F. Pezarossi: 3a Av. 1-38, Zona 9 (☎2331 0874). 4hr., every hr. 5:15am-4:15pm, Q90.

Pullmantur: 1a Av. 13-22, Zona 10 (☎2337 2861). 4hr.; 7am, 1, and 3pm; Q254.

Belize City: Línea Dorada, 10a Av. and 16a C., Zona 1 (☎2415 8900). 2 days, Q330; stop-over in Flores.

Guatemala City

ACCOMODATIONS
Hotel Ajau, 19
Hotel Colonial, 20
Hotel Fénix, 18
Hotel Mi Casa, 8
Hotel Posada Belén, 22
Hotel Real InterContinental, 5
Hotel Spring, 23
Hotel Xamanek, 6
Otelito, 10

FOOD
Cafe León, 25
Long Wah, 27
Mexico Lindo, 3
Restaurante Altuna, 24
Sophos, 9
Tacontento, 4
Tamarindos, 11
Tasca El Rocío, 7

MUSEUMS AND SIGHTS
Casa MIMA, 21
Catedral Metropolitano, 26
Iglesia Yurrita, 15
Museo Ixchel, 12
Museo Nacional de
Arqueología y Etnología, 2
Museo de Los Niños, 1
Museo del Ferrocarril, 17
Palacio Nacional, 28
Popol Vuh Museum, 13
Torre del Reformador, 14

GUATEMALA CITY

Copán: Hedman Alas, 2a Av. 8-73, Zona 10 (☎2362 5072 or 2362 5075). 5hr., 5 and 9am, Q271.

Tegucigalpa:

Hedman Alas, 2a Av. 8-73, Zona 10 (☎2362 5072 or 2362 5075). 12hr., 5 and 9am, Q403.

King Quality y Confort Lines, 18a Av. 1-96, Zona 15 (☎2369 0404). 2 days; 6:30am, 8am, 2, 3:30pm; Q488; involves a stop-over in San Salvador.

Managua:

Cruceros del Golfo, 18a Av. 1-96, Zona 15 (☎2369 0456). 16hr., 4am, Q424.

Tica Bus, Blvd. Los Próceres 26-55, Zona 10 (☎2366 4234). 2 days; Q347; stop-over in San Salvador.

San José:

King Quality y Confort Lines, 18a Av. 1-96, Zona 15 (☎2369 0404). 2 days; 6:30, 8am, 2, and 6:30pm; Q568; involves stop-overs in San Salvador and Managua.

Tica Bus, Blvd. Los Próceres 26-55, Zona 10 (☎2366 4234). 3 days, one bus leaves at 1pm, Q521; involves stop-overs in San Salvador and Managua.

Panama City: Tica Bus, Blvd. Los Próceres 26-55, Zona 10 (☎2366 4234). 4 days, Q781; stop-overs in San Salvador and Managua.

Tapachula:

Linea Dorada, 10a Av. and 16a C., Zona 1 (☎2415 8900). 7hr., Q280.

Trans Galgos Inter, 7a Av. 19-44, Zona 1 (☎2253 9131). 7hr., 7:30am and noon, Q194.

DOMESTIC BUSES

The **bus terminal** is located in the southwest corner of **Zona 4,** framed by Av. 4, Av. de Ferrocarril, and C. 8. Many 2nd-class services depart from here; ask around to find an exact departure point. Departures are scattered throughout the blocks surrounding the main terminal. Domestic buses that do not depart from the Zona 4 terminal depart from various locations around a few of the Zonas. See **Orientation** (p. 56) for information on how to decipher addresses in Guatemala City. Be advised that none of these bus "stations" have ticket offices. Brace yourself for chaos: you pay for the trip on the road. Make sure to have your payment ready before you step on—you don't want to fumble with your wallet on a crowded bus.

Antigua: Multiple carriers. 23a Av. and 3a C., Zona 3. 1hr., every 15min. 7am-8pm, Q5.

Biotopo del Quetzal: Escobar y Monja Blanca, 8a Av. 15-16, Zona 1 (☎2238 1409). 3½hr., every 30min. 4am-5pm, Q50.

Chichicastenango: Veloz Quichelense, 41 C., between 6a and 7a Av., Zona 8. 3hr., every hr. 5am-6pm, Q12.

Cobán: Escobar y Monja Blanca, 8a Av. 15-16, Zona 1 (☎2238 1409). 4½hr., every hr. 4am-5pm, Q50.

Esquipulas: Rutas Orientales, 19a C. 8-18, Zona 1 (☎2253-7282). 4½hr., every 30min. 4:30am-6pm, Q40.

Flores:

Fuentes del Norte, 17a C. 8-46, Zona 1 (☎2238 3894). 9-10hr., every hr., Q100.

Línea Dorada, 10a Av. and 16a C., Zona 1 (☎2415 8900; 8hr., 10am and 9pm, Q145).

Huehuetenango:

Transportes Velásquez, Calzada Roosevelt 9-56, Zona 7 (☎2440 3316). 5hr., every 30min. 8am-3pm, Q60.

Los Halcones, Calzada Roosevelt 37-47, Zona 11 (☎2432 5364). 5hr.; 7am, 2, 5pm; Q60.

Puerto de Iztapa: Multiple Carriers. 4a C. between 7a and 8a Av., Zona 12. 1½hr., every 15min. 5am-4:45pm, Q15.

La Mesilla: Transportes Velásquez, Calzada Roosevelt 9-56, Zona 7 (☎2440 3316). 7hr., 6am-3pm, Q70.

Monterrico: Transportes Cubanita, 4a C. and 8a Av., Zona 12. 3hr.; 10:30am, 12:30, 2:20pm; Q40.

Panajachel: Transportes Rebulli, 41 C. between 6a and 7a Av., Zona 8 (☎2230 2748). 3hr., every hr. 5:30am-3:50pm, Q25. Alternatively, take any bus to the western highlands and change at Los Encuentros junction.

Puerto Barrios: Transportes Litegua, 15a C. 10-40, Zona 1 (☎2220 8840). 5hr., every hr. 4:30am-6pm, Q55.

Quetzaltenango:

Transportes Alamo, 12 Av. A 0-65, Zona 7 (☎2472 2355). 4hr.; 8, 10:15am, 12:30, 3, 4:15, 5:30pm; Q55.

Transportes Galgos, 7a Av. 19-44, Zona 1 (☎2220 0238). 4hr., 5:30am and 2:30pm, Q45.

Rabinal: Transporte Dulce María, 17 C. 11-32, Zona 1 (☎2253 4618). 3½hr., every 30min. 5am-5pm, Q27.

Retalhuleu: Transportes Fortaleza del Sur, 19a C. 8-70, Zona 1 (☎2230 3390). 3hr., every 30min. 6am-6pm, Q45.

Río Dulce: Transportes Litegua, 15a C. 10-40, Zona 1 (☎2220 8840). 5hr.; 6, 9, 11:30am, 1, 4:15pm; Q55.

Salamá: Transporte Dulce María, 17 C. 11-32, Zona 1 (☎2253 4618). 3hr., every hr. 5am-5pm, Q23.

Tecpán: Transportes Poaquileña, 1a Av. between 3a and 4a C., Zona 7. 2hr., every 15min. 5:30am-7pm, Q7.

✈ ORIENTATION

Upon Arrival Both international and domestic flights arrive at **La Aurora International Airport**, in Zona 13. The posh hotels of **Zona 10** are close, but the budget spots in **Zona 1** require a bit more of a trek. Bus #83 departs from outside the terminal and runs to Zona 1; watch your luggage carefully. Though more expensive, a taxi (Q50) is an easier and safer way of getting to your hotel.

If arriving by bus, prepare for some confusion. Many second-class services arrive in the **Zona 4** market area, referred to as the main bus terminal. Taxis are plentiful here; if you want to take a bus to Zona 1, walk to the corner of 2 C. and 4 Av. Other second-class buses arrive at scattered locations throughout the city. Most of these are in Zona 1, within walking distance or a short taxi ride from downtown hotels. Terminal addresses are listed under Transportation (p. 57). Avoid arriving by bus at night; if you do, take a taxi from the terminal.

LAYOUT. Although Guate is overwhelmingly large, sights and services are concentrated in Zonas 1, 2, 4, 9, 10, and 13. The major thoroughfare is **6 Av.**, beginning at the Plaza Mayor in the north and continuing south through Zonas 4 and 9. **Zona 1**, the city's oldest section and the true city center, houses budget hotels and restaurants. **Zona 4** lies immediately south of Zona 1. An industrial area, Zona 4 houses the INGUAT office, the second-class bus terminal, and the market area. **Zonas 9** and **10** house the boutiques, embassies, fancy restaurants, and five-star hotels. The two zones are divided by the north-south Av. de la Reforma: Zona 9 is to the west, and Zona 10 is to the east. Avenidas run parallel to Av. de la Reforma and the street numbers increase eastward. Calles run east-west and increase southward. The southern portion of Zona 10 is the **Zona Viva** (Lively Zone), home to the bulk of the city's most happening clubs. **Zona 13** is south of Zona 9. Its two notable features are the international airport and the **Parque La Aurora**, which contains museums, a market, and a zoo. Some possible causes for confusion: 1a Av. of Zona 1 is different from the 1a Av. of Zona 5. Also, some streets are nameless for a block, and some calles in Zona 1 have secondary names. Note that many streets—especially in Zona 1—do not have street signs, so it's best to ask for directions.

SAFETY. Personal safety is a definite concern in Guatemala City. Exploring the city on your own during the day is generally not a problem; be aware of your surroundings and carry yourself as if you always know where you are going, even if completely lost. Don't be afraid to step into an establishment if you are in need of help. Wandering alone at night is strongly discouraged by locals. The streets of Zona 1 are not safe after dark. If you must, travel by taxi and never alone. Nighttime bar and restaurant hopping in Zona 10 is reasonably safe, provided you stick with the crowds and have a companion. Pickpockets are ubiquitous, especially in bus terminal areas. Always keep your money and valuables close to your body and distribute bills among multiple pockets so that you don't lose everything if you are robbed. Thigh or waist money belts are recommended. Female travelers should expect cat calls and whistles all over the city. The best response is to remain quiet and move on.

▛ LOCAL TRANSPORTATION

Buses: Guate's city bus system is extensive and relatively efficient, but it takes a while to get the hang of it. The nicer and slightly more expensive buses, **preferenciales,** are large and red. Second-class buses are called **corrientes,** although they are not recommended for tourists due to safety concerns. Buses run from 7am until about 8pm, though you'll find the occasional bus running later. Buses have their destination clearly marked on the front; the best places to catch them in Zona 1 are 4 Av. or 10 Av. The latter is the place to go for buses headed towards the airport. Some major bus routes include:

82: Goes from the center of **Zona 1** into **Zona 4,** continuing down **Av. de la Reforma** through **Zona 9** and **Zona 10.**

83: Goes from **10a Av.** in **Zona 1** down to **La Aurora Airport** in **Zona 13,** passing through the sights of **Zona 13** and eventually returning to **9a Av.** in **Zona 1**.

101: Starts on **Av. de los Proceres** in **Zona 10,** continuing past the **INGUAT office** on its way through **Zona 4.**

Taxis: Taxis are relatively cheap in Guatemala City and necessary for travelers looking to go out after dark. A taxi ride is usually Q30-50, though prices vary depending on time of day and length of trip. If the cab is not metered, agree ahead of time on a price, as bargaining is sometimes necessary (and sometimes impossible). If there are no taxis around, you can call one of two taxi companies, named for the color of their vehicles: **Taxis Amarillos** (☎2470 1515) and **Taxis Verdes** (☎2475 9595).

Car Rental: There are about 12 car rental companies in Guatemala. Most have stations at La Aurora Airport; some have additional offices scattered throughout the city. Travelers will find both local and more expensive international options. **Avis,** 6a C. 7-64, Zona 9 (☎2339 3249; www.avis.com.gt), and at the La Aurora Airport, Zona 13 (☎2385 8781).

▛ PRACTICAL INFORMATION

TOURIST AND FINANCIAL SERVICES

Tourist Office

INGUAT 7a Av. 1-17, Zona 4 (☎2421 2800). The INGUAT headquarters are located in this building, right in the center of Guatemala City. Staff is helpful and bilingual. City maps are free. Open M-F 8am-4pm.

Tours:

Guatemalan Adventure 13a C. 3-40, Zona 10, Edificio Atlantis (☎2410 8260 or 2410 8261; www. guatemalanadventure.com), Offers tours around Guatemala City, as well as arranging excursions

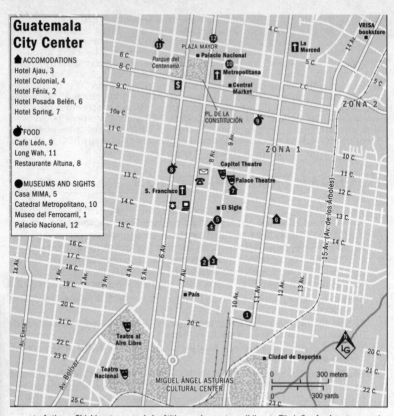

Guatemala City Center

🏠 ACCOMODATIONS
Hotel Ajau, 3
Hotel Colonial, 4
Hotel Fénix, 2
Hotel Posada Belén, 6
Hotel Spring, 7

🍎 FOOD
Cafe León, 9
Long Wah, 11
Restaurante Altuna, 8

⬤ MUSEUMS AND SIGHTS
Casa MIMA, 5
Catedral Metropolitano, 10
Museo del Ferrocarril, 1
Palacio Nacional, 12

to Antigua, Chichicastenango, Lake Atitlan, or longer tours/hikes to Tikal, Copán, Aguateca, and more. English spoken. Open Mon-Fri 9am-5pm.

GuateMaya (☎5852 7780 or 4581 6507; www.guatemayatour.com), Offers trip-packages to various countries throughout Central America, as well as transportation from the airport to hotels in Guatemala City. Open M-Sa 9am-5pm.

Embassies:

United States Embassy Av. de la Reforma 7-01, Zona 10 (☎2326 4000), Open M-Th 7:30am-5pm, Fri 7:30am-12:30am.

Canada Embassy 13 C. 8-44, Zona 10 (☎2333 6102), Edyma Plaza Niv. 8. Open M-F 8am-4:30pm.

UK Embassy Av. de la Reforma 16-00, Zona 10 (☎2367 5425), Torre Internacional, 11th fl. Open M-F 9am-noon and 2pm-4pm. Citizens of Australia or New Zealand can resolve any concerns within the UK embassy.

Currency Exchange and Banks: There are hundreds of banks in Guatemala City, and while all cards are served at various locations throughout the city, Visa card holders will have the least amount of trouble with banking needs. ATMs are also very common occurrences, though you should only use an ATM that is located in a safe zona or within a bank. Almost all of the main banks in the city (G&T Continental, Banrural, Banco Industrial, etc.) have Western Unions located within them. All require photo ID (most in the form of a passport) to exchange currency. The listings below are the central offices of the following banks, which have branches all over the city.

Banco Industrial 7a Av. 5-10, Zona 4 (☎2420 1737) Edificio Centro Financiero Torre I.

Banco Agromercantil 7 Av. 7-30, Zona 9 (☎2338 6565).

G&T Continental 6 Av. 9-08, Zona 9 (☎2338 6801) Plaza G&T Continental.

Citibank Metrocentro, Blvd. de los Heroes (☎2202 5610).

American Express: 7a Av. 6-26, Zona 9, Edificio Plaza el Roble (☎2361 0909).

Western Union: There are Western Unions located within many of the banks surrounding the plaza in Zona 1, as well as in banks throughout the other zonas.

LOCAL SERVICES

Bookstores: VRISA Bookshop 15a Av. 3-64, Zona 1 (☎7761 3237). Wide range of genres in both Spanish and English. Open M-Sa 9am-7pm.

Markets: Grocery stores include **Paiz** and **Super del Ahorro,** both on 7a Av. between 17 and 18 C. in Zona 1. There is also a large **Central Market** behind the main cathedral in an underground garage. Open M-Sa 6am-6pm, Su 8am-noon. Another **crafts market** is located in Zona 13 (see **Sights,** p. 61).

Laundromats: Many of the hotels in Zonas 9 and 10 offer laundry service. **Lavanderia Passarelli,** 4a C. A 0-20, Zona 1 (☎5896 0736), has ironing and dry-cleaning services.

EMERGENCY AND COMMUNICATIONS

Emergency: Fire ☎122. Ambulance ☎123 or 128.

Police: 6a Av. 13-71 (☎120).

Pharmacy: Farmacia Batres, 6a C. and 6a Av., Zona 10 (☎2332 7425). Open 24hr.

Medical Services: Hospital General San Juan de Dios, 1a Av. 10-50, Zona 1 (☎2253 0423). **Hospital Roosevelt,** Calzada Roosevelt, Zona 11 (☎2471 1441).

Telephones: TELGUA, 7a Av. in between 12a and 13a C., Zona 1 (☎2238 1098). Open M-F 8am-6pm, Sa 8am-1pm.

Internet Access: Cafe Internet Carambola, Carretera al Atlánt. (☎2258 3684). Internet Q20 per hr. Open daily 8:30am-8:30pm. **Cafe Internet Gamanet** 5a Av. 3-78, Zona 1 (☎2232 1569). Internet Q15 per hr. Open M-Sa 9am-8pm.

Post Office: 7a Av. and 12a C., Zona 1. Open M-F 8:30am-5:30pm, Su 9am-1pm. **Postal Code:** 01000.

▟ ACCOMMODATIONS

Almost all of Guate's budget hotels are located in Zona 1, the city's aging downtown area. Because robberies do occur here, prioritize safety when choosing a hotel: windows should be barred, balconies secure, locks functional, and the management should be conscientious. You may want to consider spending more than you would otherwise for accommodations here. Given nighttime safety concerns, a reservation or an early arrival is a good idea. Female travelers or those traveling alone may feel more comfortable paying slightly more for the safer surroundings in Zona 9 or 10.

ZONA 1

▨ **Hotel Posada Belén,** 13a C. A 10-30 (☎2253 4530; posadabelen.com). Loaded with charm and history, this hotel is as much of an experience as it is a place to stay. All rooms have private baths and hot water. Shuttle available for pick-up or drop-off at the airport. Breakfast C50. Laundry service available. Free Wi-Fi. Singles Q300; doubles Q400. AmEx/D/MC/V. ❺

Hotel Colonial, 7a Av. 14-19 (☎2232 6722; www.hotelcolonial.net). Gorgeous mahogany furniture fills this accommodation's spacious rooms, most with private baths, hot water, and cable TV. Singles Q100, with bath Q140. V. ❸

Hotel Spring, 8a Av. 12-65 (☎2232 2858, www.hotelspring.com). In a well-kept colonial home with an open air courtyard. Roomy and well-lit accommodations. Reserve in advance. Singles Q96, with bath Q136; doubles Q136/175. MC/V. ❸

Hotel Ajau, 8a Av. 15-62 (☎2232 0488). Slightly claustrophobic, windowless rooms, some with private baths. Singles Q64, with bath Q100; doubles Q75/115. Cash only. ❷

Hotel Fénix, 7a Av. 15-81 (☎2226 7343). One of the cheapest options in the city. Well-furnished rooms, some with private baths. A cafe is located downstairs. Singles Q43; doubles Q50. Cash only. ❷

OTHER ZONAS

Hotel Xamanek, 13a C. 3-57, Zona 10 (☎2360 8345; www.mayaworld.net). Backpacker-friendly hotel with dorm-style and private rooms. Ideal location in the heart of Zona Viva. Breakfast included. Free internet access and Wi-Fi. Dorms Q115; private rooms Q250. Cash only. ❸

Hotel Real Intercontinental, 14a C. 2-51, Zona 10 (☎2413 4444; www.intercontinental.com). Luxurious 4-star establishment in the heart of the Zona Viva. Japanese restaurant, **Tanoshii,** on the ground floor serves melt-in-your-mouth sushi. Free pool access. Continental breakfast included. Rooms from Q1130. AmEx/D/MC/V. ❻

Otelito, 12a C. 4-51, Zona 10 (☎2339 1811; www.otelito.com). Has the intimacy of a bed-and-breakfast with the amenities (and prices) of a luxury hotel chain. Impeccably executed decor. Ground-floor bar and lounge is a prime nightlife location. Rooms from Q700. AmEx/D/MC/V. ❺

Hotel Mi Casa, 5a Av. "A" 13-51, Zona 9 (☎2339 2246; www.hotelmicasa.com). Breakfast included. Free Wi-Fi. Free parking for guests. Airport shuttle service available. Singles with shared baths Q280, with private baths Q440; doubles Q400/520. Discounts for groups. V. ❺

⊡ FOOD

In Zona 1, sidewalk vendors offer the cheapest grub, though travelers have been known to experience stomach illness from these quick fixes. Local *comedores* are inexpensive, offering daily *típico* menus for Q10-20. There's also a fair amount of American fast food joints. The ever-developing Zonas 9 and 10 are featuring an increasing number of international options. Here, pad thai is just as common as *comida típica*.

ZONA 1

▨ **Restaurante Altuna,** 5a Av. 12-31 (www.restaurantealtuna.com). In a beautifully restored colonial home, old-fashioned, upscale Altuna has a long-standing reputation as the nicest restaurant in downtown Guate. Serves excellent Spanish food. Paella Q47. Desserts Q15-25. Open Tu-Sa noon-10pm, Su noon-4pm. Reservations recommended. AmEx/MC/V. ❹

Cafe León, 8a Av. 9-15. Join intellectuals and coffee enthusiasts at this smoke-filled cafe for an exquisite *café con leche.* Decent sandwich menu (Q30-40). Cash only. ❷

Long Wah, 6a C. 3-75 (☎2232 6611). Reasonably priced, authentic Chinese food in the heart of Zona 1. Entrees Q30-60. Take-out available. Open daily 9am-9pm. Cash only. ❷

ZONA 10

▨ **Tamarindos,** 11a C. 2-19A (☎2360 5630; www.tamarindos.com.gt). Extensive menu with irresistible dishes such as Pear and Ricotta Ravioli (Q85). Steak prepared any way you like it Q135. Impressive mixed drinks menu. Georgia Peach Q50. Restaurant open M-Sa noon-2:30pm and 7:30-10:30pm. Bar open until 1am most nights. AmEx/D/MC/V. ❺

▨ **Mexico Lindo,** 14a C. 2-56 (☎2337 3822 or 4132; www.mexlindo.com). This sports bar serves upscale Mexican cuisine in heaping portions. A well-stocked bar and savvy bar tender can mix you anything you want. The *tostidas Chiapanecas*, stacked with salsa, guacamole, goat cheese, shredded chicken, and a dollop of sour cream, are unreal. Open M-Sa 7am-1am, Su 7:30am-11pm. AmEx/D/MC/V. ❹

Sophos, 12a C. and 4a Av. (☎2419 7070), on the 2nd level of the Plaza Fontabella. Attached to a beautiful Spanish bookstore, this sophisticated restaurant has an extensive selection of coffees and a mouth-watering panini menu. Try the Ben Franklin (roast beef, carmelized onions, roasted red peppers and *camembert;* Q50). Pad Thai Q90. Ravioli Q60. Open M-Sa 9am-9pm, Su 10am-8pm. ❸

Tasca El Rocío, 4a Av. 12-59 (☎2366 1064 or 2336 6938), inside the Plaza Fontabella. Upscale Spanish cuisine in a refined atmosphere. Tapas from Q45. Paella from Q85. Mixed drinks Q35-Q45. Open M-Sa noon-10pm, Su noon-7pm. AmEx/D/MC/V. ❸

Tacontento, 14a C. 1-42 (☎2367 6044). Lower prices do not translate to lower quality. Tacos made on the spot in hefty portions. Burritos Q33. Wash it all down with a beer or a frozen mixed drink. Open daily noon-1am. AmEx/D/MC/V. ❷

◉ SIGHTS

ZONA 1

PLAZA MAYOR Surrounded by some of the finest architecture in the city, the Plaza Mayor has been stripped to its basic elements: a slab of concrete and a large fountain. Formerly known as "the center of all Guatemala," the space is now mostly filled with pigeons, shoeshines, and men playing card games. The exception to this rule comes on Sunday, when the plaza is flooded with indígenas selling textiles, families out for a stroll, and political protesters. *(Bounded on the west and east by 6a and 7a Av., and on the north and south by 6a and 8a C.)*

CATEDRAL METROPOLITANO The stately Catedral Metropolitana, reconstructed after the 1917 earthquake, rises dramatically against the Plaza. Inside the neoclassical structure are the usual saints and religious images—it is on the outer pillars where the magic lies. Etched into the twelve front columns are the names of all those who disappeared during the recent civil war, making the trip to the Catedral a pilgrimage for many families. It is perhaps the quietest spot in the city. Head through the building to a courtyard on the south side of the cathedral where you will see the entrance to the cathedral's museum; the museum houses some impressive religious relics and provides an interesting history of Guatemalan Christianity. *(Located on the east side of the Plaza Mayor. The Cathedral is open M-Sat 7:30am-1pm and 2pm-6pm, Su 7am-6:30pm. Free. The Cathedral's museum is open M-F 9am-1pm and 2pm-5pm, Sa 9am-1pm. Admission is Q10 for students with ID and Q30 for non-citizens.)*

PALACIO NACIONAL This grand palacio was built between 1928 and 1943 under the orders of President Jorge Ubico. Currently, the public is allowed to see only a few of the imposing palace's 350 rooms, but even the corridors are magnificent. La Sala de Recepción awes visitors with its massive Bohemian crystal chandelier, replete with graceful brass and gold quetzals. The Presidential Balcony offers commanding views of the plaza and the surrounding highlands. The second floor houses a fairly complete collection of modern Guatemalan art, including rotating exhibitions of the most renowned Guatemalan artists. In 1980, a car bomb shattered the stained glass windows of the central corridor which had depicted the 10 virtues of a good nation, and some have yet to be reconstructed. *(Located on the north side of the Plaza Mayor. Open daily 9am-11:45pm and 2-4:45pm. Free; tip expected for guided tours.)*

CASA MIMA A renovated 19th-century home, the Casa MIMA is a quirky look into the former glory of Guatemala. The house includes a fully furnished chapel and 1920s era kitchen. Relax with a cup of coffee (Q5) in the back courtyard of this truly picturesque and tranquil residence. *(8a Av. 14-12. ☎ 2253 4020, www.portalmuseosguatemala.net/m.casa.mima. Open M-Sat 10am-5pm. Admission is Q20, students Q15.)*

MUSEO DEL FERROCARRIL There was a time when Guatemala was connected by an expansive railroad system, stretching up and down the Pacific coast, across the country to the Atlantic, and even up into Petén. This museum, which also houses three trains that visitors can board and exlore, provides an extensive and interactive history of thse old railroads.*(9a Av. 18-03, ☎2238 0519. Located several blocks south east of the Plaza Mayor. Open M-F 9am-4:30pm, Sat-Sun 10am-4:30pm. Wheelchair accessible. Admission is Q2 for adults, Q1 for children.)*

ZONA 2

MAPA EN RELIEVE. Located in a park in the more quiet and suburban Zona 2, the Mapa en Relieve will satisfy any traveler trying to get their geographic bearings in Guatemala. Climb to the top of one of the two viewing towers to get a birds-eye view of this gigantic map of Guatemala, which features true-to-life topography (mountains, volcanoes, lakes, rivers, oceans, etc.), as well as countless little signs to indicate the locations of cities, towns, Mayan ruins, and more. *(Located in Zona 2. From the Plaza Mayor in Zona 1, ask a taxi driver to take you to and from the Mapa en Relieve for approximately Q40. Other than the viewing towers, this sight is wheelchair accessible. Open daily from 9am-5pm. Q25.)*

ZONA 4

IGLESIA YURRITA. Decked out in vermilion, this outlandish neo-Gothic curiosity was built in 1929. The color scheme inside the church, including an unusual window painted like the daytime sky, is nearly as blinding as the exterior. *(Ruta 6 and Via 8. Wheelchair accessible. Open Tues-Sun 7am-12pm and 4pm-6pm.)*

TORRE DEL REFORMADOR Check out this smaller (and considerably less polished) take on the Eiffel Tower, named in honor of forward-looking President Justo Rufino Barrios, who held office between 1871 and 1885. *(Located at the intersection of 7a Av. and 2a C.)*

ZONA 10

MUSEO IXCHEL DEL TRAJE INDÍGENA. A must see for any travelers interested in buying Guatemalan textiles. A detailed step-by-step of the traditional jaspee dye process and its use in indigenous garb informs those interested in purchasing items. The museum is on the campus of the Universidad Francisco Marroquín in a valley with well-landscaped picnic areas. The tranquil atmosphere here makes it a nice escape from the congested city center and an especially fine place to bring lunch. *(Take 6a C. Final east off Av. de la Reforma; the museum is located* *at the bottom of a large hill.* ☎ *2331 3622. Open M-F 9am-5pm, Sa 9am-1pm. Wheelchair accessible. Q35, students Q15. MC/V.)*

JARDÍN BOTÁNICO. Head over to the Jardín Botánico, where there are over 700 species of plants labeled in Spanish and Latin. Perfect for a quiet picnic, and great escape from the crowded and polluted urban scenery. *(1a C. off Av.enida de la Reforma.* ☎ *2333 0904. Open M-F 8am-3pm. Q5.)*

POPOL VUH MUSEUM. Named after the sacred Maya text, the museum has a first rate collection of pre-Columbian Maya pottery, as well as exhibits on colonial art and indigenous folklore. Visitors will leave this museum with a stronger understanding of a text that is extremely important to much of Guatemala's indigenous Mayan population. *(Next to the Museo Ixchel del Traje Indígena at the university; follow directions above.* ☎ *2361 2301. Open M-F 9am-5pm, Sa 9am-1pm. Wheelchair accessible. Q35, Q15 for students with university ID.)*

ZONA 13

The sights of Zona 13 are clustered within the vast Parque La Aurora, near the airport. Several government-run museums and an INGUAT-sponsored artisans' market reside here. The area can be reached by bus #83.

MUSEO NACIONAL DE ARQUEOLOGÍA Y ETNOLOGÍA. This museum traces eons of Mayan history with hundreds of artifacts and an excellent scale model of Tikal. The exhibits are strikingly similar to those of the Popol Vuh Museum. *(Located in the park at the corner of 7 Av., 5 and 6 C., Edificio #5.* ☎ *2472 0489. Open Tues-Fri 9am-4pm, Sa-Su 9am-noon and 1:30-4pm. Q60.)*

MERCADO DE ARTESANÍAS. La Aurora also holds an INGUAT-sponsored craft market. The traditional textiles, ceramics, and jewelry may make good gifts, but bargaining is off-limits. *(Open daily from 9am-6pm.)*

🔲🔳 NIGHTLIFE AND ENTERTAINMENT

Although the city's frenetic pace tends to die down after dark, there are several options for evening entertainment. The capital is a good place to catch an American flick. Two convenient Zona 1 theaters are the **Capitol**, 6 Av., 12 C., and **Palace**, across the street. **La Cúpula**, 7 Av 13-01, Zona 9, is a theater conveniently close to Zona 9 and 10 hotels. Theater and opera performances (all in Spanish) are staged at **Teatro IGA**, Ruta 1 4-05, Zona 4, and in the **Teatro Nacional** on Friday and Saturday nights. For a listing of cultural events, check *La Prensa Libre* or any other local newspaper.

Though it is generally unsafe to be out after dark in the capital, there are a few places worth checking out. Clubbers and bar-hoppers should be sure to take cabs to and from their nighttime destinations. The best places to get your dance on are in **Zona 4** and the **Zona Viva (Zona 10).**The pace picks up around 10pm and winds down around 2am. The hottest club is currently **Kahlua**, 1 Av. 15-06, Zona 10, which comes complete with two dance floors, a lounge room, and a pop music. (No cover.) **SUAE**, on Vía 5 (Cuatro Grados Norte) and the **Rec Lounge** 9 Av. 0-81, are two hot-pots in Zona 4 that are worth checking out for trendy atmospheres, electronic music, and lots of dancing. If you're looking for a bar with incredible live music and room to dance, visit local haunt **Bodeguita del Centro**, 12 C. 3-55, Zona 1 (Closed Sunday and Monday).

WESTERN HIGHLANDS

For many travelers, the Western Highlands are the reason to come to Guatemala. A vast expanse of rolling farmland rises up to dense jungle volcanoes and twisting roadways lead to stunning miradores. Meanwhile, the majority of Central America's indigenous population is packed into the region's untouched tiny hillside villages. Dialects of Mam, Ixil, and Cakchiquel echo in the vibrant markets; men stand outside churches swinging coffee-can censers filled with smoldering resin while chanting the cycles of the Mayan calendar.

The graceful colonial splendor of Antigua serves as a gateway to the altiplano. The unsurpassed beauty of Lago de Atitlán is ringed by traditional Mayan villages, while the colorful Mayan market of Chichicastenango is one of the country's most famous sights. Quetzaltenango, Guatemala's second-largest city, is home to increasingly popular language schools and provides easy access to hot springs. Two beautiful mountain towns offer a more serene highlands atmosphere: traditional Todos Santos, in the Cuchumatanes, and Nebaj, situated in northern Quiché.

ANTIGUA

After landing in Guatemala City, most people catch the first bus to the colonial city of Antigua, preferring to skip the country's capital in favor of a more historical and beautiful locale. From the cobblestone streets seemingly frozen in the 18th century to stunning courtyards concealed behind Mudéjar-influenced buildings, it is no wonder that Antigua remains one of the most popular destinations in Guatemala. If the colonial architecture fails to impress, Antigua's surroundings, featuring mountain ranges and three commanding volcanoes, certainly will.

Antigua was once the capital of Guatemala, but after a series of earthquakes destroyed the city, Guatemala City's solid ground seemed like a better fit. Today, Antigua is a city brimming with international influences thanks to the many tourists that flock here each year. These influences are particularly apparent in the diverse culinary scene, featuring everything from Japanese to French cuisine.

▐ TRANSPORTATION

Though its off the beaten path of the Interamericana, Antigua remains easy to reach by means of chicken bus routes and inexpensive shuttle services. Once in Antigua, the city is quite easy to navigate on foot; taxis and tuk tuks are only necessary for excursions to neighboring towns and villages. Many people rent cars, bikes, and motorcycles in order to explore the area around Antigua on their own.

Public Transportation:Buses: Station located behind Antigua's main market. While most people use private shuttles to travel from Antigua to cities throughout Guatemala (bookable through hotels, hostels, or travel agents), several chicken bus routes that originate in Antigua. **Chimaltenango** (40min., every 20min.); **Guatemala City** (1hr., every 30min.); **Panajachel** (3hr., daily, 7am); **San Antonio Aguas Calientes** (20min., every 30min.).

Taxis: Official cabs, labeled **"Antigua Guatemala,"** congregate around the Parque Central, but lack phone numbers or specific company names.

WESTERN HIGHLANDS

Western Highlands

Tuk Tuks: For less than Q10, Tuk Tuks—glorified motorcycles—will take you anywhere in Antigua. Some will even take you to neighboring towns and villages for a slightly steeper fee.

Car Rental:Tabarini, 6a Av. Sur 22 (☎7832 8107 or 7832 8108). Rates start at Q309 per day. AmEx/D/MC/V.

Bike and Motorcycle Rental: Mayan Bike Tours (☎7832 3383, 24hr. cell phone 4562 3103; www.guatemalaventures.com), on the corner of 1a Av. Sur and 6a C. Oriente. Open daily 9am-5pm. Prices vary based on length and nature of rental. AmEx/D/MC/V.

◼⚡🄶 ORIENTATION AND PRACTICAL INFORMATION

There are very few places in Guatemala that are as easy to navigate as this small city. With a few exceptions, Antigua's streets follow a grid where calles run east-west (*oriente-poniente*) and avenidas run north-south (*norte-sur*). The **parque central,** in the center of the city, is framed by 4/5 C. and 4/5 Av.. Providing a potential point of confusion, some street segments have reverted to their colonial names. Still, most businesses and residents refer to the numbered *calles* and *avenidas*. Many streets are also unmarked, so you may have to ask for directions.

Antigua's bus terminal is located behind the *mercado*, three blocks west of the *parque central*. Most visitors to Antigua arrive at the bus terminal; to get to the **parque central,** simply cross the tree-lined street, **Alameda Santa Lucía** (or C. Santa Lucía, depending on who you ask), and continue straight. It's hard to miss **Volcan de Agua,** the theatrical volcano looming to the south of the city. Be wary of following the INGUAT-authorized guides to your destination: they occasionally sometimes lead travelers astray. Instead, trust your instincts and take comfort in the fact that, given the relatively straightforward layout of the city, you will almost always be able to find your way around.

Tourist Office: INGUAT, 4a C. Oriente 10 (☎7832 5681; www.visitguatemala.com), inside the Casa Antigua El Jaulón courtyard. Head out of the *parque central* on 4A C. Oriente and the Casa Antigua El Jaulón is on your left; the INGUAT office is located in the back left corner of the courtyard. Helpful, English-speaking staff will answer any questions you might have. Open M-F 8am-5pm, Sa-Su 9am-5pm.

Tours: Adrenalina Tours, 5a Av. Norte 31 (☎7832 1108 or 5308 3523; www.adrenalinatours.com), just past the Arch on the right side of the street. Adrenalina Tours offers everything from jetting to Tikal (Q2,236) to excursions into Antigua and the surrounding area (Q406, 3 person minimum). If you want to hike the Pacaya Volcano, Adrenalina leads 2 tours per day, but be sure to book in advance, especially if you are banking on doing the morning tour. Flexible staff is willing to personalize any package. Offices in Antigua, Coban, Huehuetenango, Panajachel, and Quetzaltenango. AmEx/D/MC/V.

Currency Exchange and Bank: Banco Agromercantil, 4 C. Poniente (☎7832 0048). Open daily 9am-7pm.

Beyond Tourism:

Christian Spanish Academy, 6a Av. Norte 15 (☎7832 3922 or 7832 3924; www.learncsa.com). Take Spanish lessons for anywhere from 4 to 8 hours a day at this premier Spanish school in the heart of Antigua. Students stay with host families located within walking distance of the school. Open M-F. AmEx/MC/V.

Probigua, 6a Av. Norte 41B (☎7832 0860 or 7832 2998; www.probigua.org). One-on-one lessons with a local professor. Group classes avaliable for the more economically-minded. The dollars that you spend here will do more than just improve your Spanish: Probigua donates all of its profits go to the up-keep of libraries in rural villages of Guatemala.

Niños de Guatemala, 6a Av. Norte 45 (☎4379 1557; www.ninosdeguatemala.org). From the center of town, head North on 6a Av. Norte; just past La Merced on the right. Established in 2006, this non-profit organization works to endow educational projects in places where there is little to no

Antigua

🏠 ACCOMMODATIONS
Posada Asjemenou, **2**

📔 NIGHTLIFE
La Casbah, **1**
Mono Loco, **4**
Reilly's, **3**

opportunity for elementary education. Volunteers proficient in Spanish are always needed at Niños de Guatemala's newly opened school in Ciudad Vieja, a 20-min. bus ride from Antigua. Volunteers can also work in the Volunteer Center in Antigua, which focuses on fundraising and self-sustainability. Information session and tour of the school site departing from the main office W 2-4pm.

English-Language Bookstore: Rainbow Reading Room, 7a Av. Sur 8 (☎7832 1919; www.rainbowcafeantigua.com), on the northwest corner of the intersection between 7A Av. Sur and 6A C. Poniente. Tons of secondhand books that you can buy or rent for just Q2 per day. AmEx/D/MC/V.

Laundromat: Lavanderia Lily, 1a C. Poniente 12 (☎7832 2295). Walk down 2 blocks from La Merced, and the laundromat is on your right. Q12 per kg. Open daily 7am-7pm. Cash only.

Emergency: ☎1500 or 2421 2810.

Police:(☎7832 2266), on the corner of C. Santa Lucía and 4 C. Poniente. **Tourist Police:** (☎7832 7290), in the back of the *mercado* off of C. Santa Lucía.

24hr. Pharmacy: Ivori, at the intersection of 6A Av. Norte and 2A C. Pte. 19 (☎7832 1559).

Hospital: Santa Lucía Hospital, Calzada Santa Lucía Sur 7 (☎7832 0251).

Internet Access: Micronet, 3a C. Poniente 9 (☎7832 5081), between 5a Av. Norte and 6A Av. Norte. If you simply cannot decide whether to check your email or drink a beer, you can do both for the price of one at Micronet. Buying a beer snags you 15min. of free internet. 15 min. sans alcohol costs Q2, 1hr. Q6. Open M-Sa 8am-7:30pm, Su 10am-7:30pm. Cash only. **Cabaguil**, 5a C. Poniente 6 (☎7832 8316 or 5433 6671), in the Cabaguil Spanish School just down the road from the *parque central*. Internet Q4 per hr. Photocopies Q1 per page. Open daily 8am-8pm. Cash only.

Post Office: (☎7832 0485), at the intersection of 4a C. Poniente and Calzada Santa Luisa Esquina. Open M-F 8:30am-5:30pm, Sa 9am-1pm. **Postal Code:** 03001.

🏠 ACCOMMODATIONS

Antigua offers some of the nicest hotels and hostels in Guatemala. Even some of Antigua's cheapest hostels boast beautiful central courtyards and spotless communal bathrooms that would impress even the most highbrow traveler. The following establishments are all conveniently located in this small city.

🏅 **El Hostal** (☎7832 0442). This charming and tranquil hostel is the perfect place to stay. El Hostal manages to remain quiet and peaceful even with 2 bars across the street. Quaint courtyard with a fountain and hammock, and offers laundry service ($1.25 per kg), hot showers, free Wi-Fi, and reasonably priced shuttle service to several locations around Antigua. Delicious breakfast daily 7:30-10:30am. Reception 8am-8pm. Bunkbed Q73, single bed Q89; private single Q122; double Q211; triple Q301. AmEx/D/MC/V. ❸

Las Camelias Inn (☎7832 5483 or 7832 5176; www.cameliasinn.com) 3a C. Oriente #19, between 1a and 2a Av. Norte. Just down the street from the Convent of the Capuchinas, this charming inn will immediately enchant you. Each room has a private bath and cable TV. Second-floor rooms open onto a terrace with spectacular views of the surrounding volcanoes. Laundry included. Wi-Fi. Singles Q326; doubles with one bed Q407, with two beds Q489. AmEx/MC/V. ❺

Posada Asjemenou, C. del Arco 31 (☎7832 2670), located just north of the Arch on the right-hand side. The standard of cleanliness and unbeatable location of this hotel make its slightly pricey rooms worth it. Complimentary breakfast, private baths, safes, Wi-Fi, and a beautiful courtyard. Singles Q211; doubles Q285; triples Q326. AmEx/D/MC/V. ❺

Posada Juma Ocag (☎7832 3109), located directly across the street from the large *mercado*, between 3a and 4a C. Poniente. Hotel-like accommodations for hostel-prices. Clean and comfortable Posada Juma Ocag is a peaceful place to crash. Reserve rooms in advance. Singles Q122, doubles Q146. AmEx/MC/V. ❹

Kafka (☎5270 6865 or 4433 2414; www.kafkahostel.com), on the left on 6a Av. Norte, between 1a C. and 2a C. Poniente. Providing more than just clean, dormitory-style accommodations, the Kafka Hostel is also a great place to chill, with a bar and a hopping restaurant. Reservations accepted. All rooms Q57. AmEx/MC/V. ❷

Posada Don Diego, 6a Av. Norte #52 (☎7832 1401), on the left on 6a Av. Norte, between 1a C. and 2a C. Poniente. A convenient location and comfortable rooms make the Posada Don Diego another solid option in Antigua. Idyllic back garden. Free Wi-Fi. Singles Q114; doubles Q203. AmEx/D/MC/V. ❸

Jungle Party Hostal (☎7832 0463; www.junglepartyhostal.com), on the left on 6a Av. Norte, between 2a C. and 3a C. Poniente. As its witty moniker suggests, the Jungle Party Hostel is as much a social experience as it is a place to stay. Doors usually remain open as people wander in and out of rooms, opting to either smoke in the hammock area or check their email in the computer room. Cheap happy hours and complimentary breakfast seal the deal for most. Dorms Q61. Cash only. ❷

Hostal Pies Descalzos, 5a C. Poniente 8 (☎5754 6559), 2 blocks from the central plaza. Just half a block away from the *parque central*, this no-frills hostel offers decent rooms, a communal kitchen, and a great location. Reception 24hr. Dorms $7. Cash only. ❶

🌑 FOOD

Antigua's cosmopolitan flair is especially apparent in its vibrant food scene. It is just as easy to dine on budget-friendly rice and beans as it is to devour a delicious steak-frites for Q244 or more. More touristy areas like the *parque central* and the Arch offer some international fare; you'll need to duck down into less populated side streets to dine on authentic Guatemalan food. Snag some fresh produce from a local vendor. For groceries, visit **La Bodegona** on the corner of 5a C. Poniente and Av. Santa Lucía

Rainbow Cafe (☎7832 1919; www.rainbowcafeantigua.com), on the northwest corner of the intersection between 7a Av. Sur and 6a C. Poniente. Enter through a quaint secondhand bookstore to find yourself in a beautiful courtyard replete with live music and unparalleled ambience. If you can, snag one of the cushioned booths in the far corner and savor Rainbow Cafe's international cuisine while sipping on a delicious mixed drink. The chicken fajitas are incredible (Q49) and their mojito is one of the best in Antigua. AmEx/D/MC/V. ❹

Nokiate, 1a Av. Sur 7 (☎7821 2896; www.nokiate.com). This super-chic restaurant and bar in the southeast corner of Antigua serves up delicious Japanese cuisine alongside killer mixed drinks. Don't miss the *pollo teriyaki* (Q73). Tu and Th are martini nights; Q150 gets you a night of all-you-can-drink martinis. Open Tu-Th 6:30-10:30pm, F-Su 12:30-11pm. AmEx/D/MC/V. ❺

Y Tu Piña Tambien (☎5242 3574) Located at the corner of 6a C. Oriente and 1a Ave. Sur. One of the nicest cafes in town, Y Tu Piña Tambien is a perfect place to grab an omelette and some fresh juices (Q20). Espresso Q8. Free Wi-Fi. Breakfast served all day. Open M-F 7am-8pm, Sa-Su 8am-7pm. AmEx/D/MC/V. ❸

La Cuevita de Los Urquizú, 2a C. Oriente 9d (☎5656 6157 or 7832 2495). The slogan on La Cuevita's business card—"If you come to Antigua and don't eat here, it's like you never came!"—may be boastful, but it rings true. The highlight of this hole-in-the-wall is the 2 tables loaded with freshly made dishes, ranging from sumptuous guacamole to incredible sausages. Fill up a plate with whatever you're in the mood for; it's just Q65. AmEx/D/MC/V. ❹

Las Antorchas (☎7832 0806; www.lasantorchas.com), on 3a Av. Sur in between 5a C.and 6a C. Oriente. This classy restaurant offers everything from international cuisine to your standard rice and beans. Try the *churrasco típico antigüeño* (traditional Antiguan steak; Q97) accompanied by one of their delicious fresh juices (Q18). Boasts a wide selection of wines, beer, and tropical mixed drinks. AmEx/D/MC/V. ❺

The Bagel Barn (☎2454 4980), just off the *parque central* on 5a C. Poniente. A wonderful place to recharge. Order the afternoon special: a coffee and a bagel with cream cheese (Q16). Movie showings twice a day: one on their TV at 4:15pm, and another on their large projector screen at 7pm. Free Wi-Fi. Open daily 6am-9:30pm. AmEx/D/MC/V. ❷

Cafe Sky (☎7832 7300), at the intersection of 6a C. Oriente and 1a Av. Sur. In a city where most buildings do not venture above 2 stories, Café Sky's 3rd-fl. terrace offers the perfect location to enjoy dinner and a stunning sunset. Dishes like nachos seem overpriced (Q65), but that's because they're made for 2. Breakfast served all day (Q16-40), but most come to enjoy a cold beer (Q16) in the evenings. Open daily 8am-9pm. AmEx/D/MC/V. ❹

Gaia, 5a Av. Norte #35 (☎7832 3670), just north of the Arch, on the right. Gaia serves up tasty Mediterranean cuisine for lunch and dinner, but the place really comes alive in the late evenings as locals and tourists flock here to enjoy mixed drinks, beer, and hookah. A standard water pipe is Q61, but you can replace the water with vodka for Q69 or wine for Q97. Slightly pricey (entrees Q69-110). M-Th noon-midnight, F-Sa noon-1am, Sun noon-11pm. AmEx/D/MC/V. ❹

El Viejo Cafe, 6a Av. Norte 12 (☎7832 1576). El Viejo Cafe's colonial ambience does not disappoint. Coffee beans prepared on a machine that looks like a museum relic brew some of the best coffee in Antigua. A cappuccino (Q12) offers the perfect complement to one of the cafe's savory homemade sandwiches (Q36). M-Tu 7am-8pm, W-Sa 7am-10pm. AmEx/D/MC/V. ❸

Tapas y Tintos, 1a C. Poniente 2 (☎7882 4070), just down the road from Iglesia la Merced on the northeast side of town. Dine in the courtyard or grab a drink at the bar, both of which transforms in the evening hours into trendy hangout spots. Tapas Q32-40. Open M-Th and Su noon-10pm, F-Sa noon-10:30pm. AmEx/MC/V. ❸

🔵 SIGHTS

▨CONVENTO DE LAS CAPUCHINAS. This convent, founded by Spanish nuns in the 18th century, is one of Antigua's archictectural highlights. Though the convent has sustained significant damage from Antigua's many earthquakes, tasteful renovations have made it difficult to discern the old from the new. A beautiful museum on the second floor contextualizes the history of Christianity in Guatemala . The ruins and the underground catacombs are spectacular. *(On the corner of 2 Av. Norte and 2 C. Oriente. Open daily 9am-5pm. Q35, students Q16. Cash only.)*

CATEDRAL SAN JOSE. The Church of San Jose, located directly on the east side of the *parque central*, is certainly a sight to see, but it is the ruins of the Catedral San Jose, right behind the Church, that are truly remarkable. Inside, INGUAT guides await to debrief you on the rich history of the cathedral, which spans more than five centuries. Dominated by an angular archway juxtaposed with softer, rounded versions of the same. The cathedral's structural elements showcase the unique blend of Mayan and Spanish influences that mark much of Guatemala's architecture. Down into the catacombs, visitors learn that the region's history of discrimination is as old as the cathedral itself: the tombs of indigenous Maya are separated from those of the Spanish conquistadores. *(Entrance on 5a C. Oriente across from the Museo de Arte Colonial. Open daily 9am-5pm. Q4. Cash only)*

PALACIO DEL NOBLE AYUNTAMIENTO. On the north side of the *parque central*, the Ayuntamiento is home to two must-see museums: the **Museo del Libro Antiguo** and the **Museo de Santiago.** The Museo del Libro Antiguo—the Musuem of the Ancient Book—contains a wealth of information about the history of literature in Guatemala. This former Spanish colony was the fourth of its kind in the New World to boast its own printing press. In honor of this, the musuem houses an exact replica, in addition to the first book printed on this press and the announcement of the 1773 earthquake that leveled the city. Next door, in the Museo de Santiago, check out weapons and furniture from colonial Antigua. *(North side of the parque central. Open Tu-F 9am-4pm, Sa-Su 9am-noon and 2-4pm. Museo de Santiago is wheelchair-accessible; Museo del Libro Antiguo is not. Q32, Museo Santiago Q16. Cash only.)*

SAN FRANCISCO CHURCH. Built in 1579, the San Francisco Church is the burial place of the patron saint of Antigua, **Hermano Pedro,** a 17th-century Spanish missionary elevated to sacred status by Pope John Paul II. The church's stunning interior is definitely worth a peek. Its ruins, some of the most extensive and beautiful in town, are readily accessible to the general public. *(At the south end of 1a Av. Sur. Open daily 8am-6pm. Wheelchair-accessible. Dress appropriately: no shorts or bare shoulders. Ruins Q4.)*

CERRO DE LA CRUZ. You may be tempted to make fun of the fanny-pack wearing, Canon-toting tourists who scurry to Cerro de la Cruz, but they know what's up. A trip here provides a stunning panorama of Antigua and its surrounding volcanoes. Two tourist police permanently stationed on the road up the hill provide security; it is still advisable, however, to bring a friend along and to avoid nighttime excursions. *(Head north on 1a Av. Norte and follow signs. Tourist police lead group tours at 10am and 3pm.)*

MUSEO DE ARTE COLONIAL. Located in the former University of San Carlos Borromeo, this beautiful museum houses a hodgepodge of colonial art, religious artifacts, and paintings . Venture beyond the Moorish-inspired arches and check out the map of 17th century Antigua. Visitors with a knack for Where's Waldo will find a solid 10min. of fun in comparing the parts of the city that have changed to those that remain the same.*(Off of parque central on 5A C. Oriente, across from Catedral San Jose. Open Tu-F 9am-4pm, Sa-Su 9am-noon and 2-4pm. Q24.)*

IGLESIA LA MERCED. It's hard to miss this luxurious mustard yellow church just north of the Arch in the northwest corner of town. The recently repainted Baroque facade, replete with recessed statues and soaked in religious metaphor, is truly a masterpiece. Be sure to step inside to marvel at the cavernous interior.*(Located on the corner of 6A Av. Norte and 1A C. Poniente. Open daily from 8am-6pm. Wheelchair-accessible.)*

PARQUE CENTRAL. Many aspects of life in Antigua have changed since colonial times (the absence of Spanish imperial rule for starters), but one remains the same: everything revolves around the *parque central*. The park is perfect for a 15min. breather and the fountain at its center is stunning. Love-sick travelers be forewarned: the proliferation of couples locked in loving embraces may make the single more keenly aware of their solitude. *(Smack in the middle of town. Wheelchair accessible.)*

CASA POPENOE. This colonial mansion, formerly the residence of a wealthy Spaniard and his family, was renovated and restored to its former architectural glory in the early 20th century. Today, visitors can wander the house as it would have been in the 18th century, complete with a colonial-style kitchen, elegant artwork, and flowery paths through shady courtyards. *(On the corner of 5A C. Oriente and 1A Av. Sur. Open M-Sa 2-4pm. Q12.)*

🎵🎶 NIGHTLIFE AND ENTERTAINMENT

Though most bars in Guatemala close their doors at 1am, the nightlife scene in Antigua is known for pushing the envelope. Here you'll find everything from dive bars to trendy discotheques.

- 🏳 **Café No Sé,** 1 Av. Norte 11C (☎2552 2165), across from El Hostal. The perfect place to end a long day in Antigua. Friendly bartenders make this evening hangout one that every traveler should experience. Order a draft beer (Q18) or a tequila shot (Q16-89). Cash only.

- 🏳 **Bistrot Cinq,** 4A C. Oriente 7 (☎7832 5510; www.bistrotcinq.com). For sophisticated mixed drinks and unparalleled ambience, travelers should head to miss Bistrot Cinq, especially during happy hour (6pm-8pm). Guava Sling Q48. Open M-Th 6-10pm, F-Su, 2-11pm. AmEx/D/MC/V.

- **Reilly's,** 5A Av. Norte 31. Right in the thick of things, Reilly's is easily the city's most popular bar. Touted as Antigua's Irish tavern, this rowdy joint lives up to its motto, "come as strangers, leave as friends." Vodka tonic Q20. Su trivia night. Open until 1am daily. AmEx/D/MC/V.

- **Riki's Bar,** 4A Av. Norte, in the back of the La Escudilla restaurant (☎7832 1327; www.la-escudilla.com/en/rikis.htm). Peopled by foreigners and locals alike, Riki's Bar is the perfect place to start or end your night in Antigua. Happy hour 8:30pm-10pm. Open daily until 1am. AmEx/D/MC/V.

- **La Casbah,** 5A Av. Norte 30 (☎7832 2640; www.lacasbahantigua.com), just past the Arch. This happening discotheque blasts electronic and house music that can be heard from blocks away. There is a cover most nights, but that doesn't deter people

Start: Iglesia la Merced
End: Café No Sé
Total Distance: The equivalent of 13-14 blocks in Antigua.
Total Time: Between 3-4 hr. Begin around 3PM.

WALKING TOUR OF ANTIGUA

1. Iglesia la Merced: (Corner of 6a Av. Nte. and 1a C. Poniente.) This tour starts in the northeast corner of town at Iglesia la Merced. The stunning detail of the mustard-yellow and white facade (a color theme that travelers will find is a recurring one in Antigua) is only the beginning. Step inside and marvel at the beauty of this cavernous structure.

2. Nim Po't: (5a Av. Nte. #29.) Heading down 5a Av. Nte. with Iglesia la Merced at your back. Before you reach the Arch, you will see a huge **Mayan textile market** on your left-hand side. Aside from the many Mayan blankets and textiles that you can find here, there are plenty of Mayan-theme souvenirs at great prices. So, grab yourself a wicker basket and don't be afraid to fill it up! If you're at all hungry, there's also a little cafe in an open-air courtyard off of the back.

3. Ayuntamiento: (Northern side of the Parque Central.) Continue down 5a Av. until you reach the central plaza; the Ayuntamiento will be on your left. The Ayuntamiento is home to two museums: **Museo del Libro Antiguo** and **Museo de Santiago.** Even if museums aren't really your thing, at least glance through the great collections at each of these museums and learn about Antiguan colonial history. (Q15.)

4. Parque Central: (Smack dab in the middle of the city.) Once you step outside the Ayuntamiento, you will find yourself in the center of Antigua, known as the *Parque Central*. Stroll through the flower-lined paths, pass the beautiful fountain in the middle, and maybe even rest for a moment on one of the many benches. Fair warning, if you show up alone, you'll be judged. Everyone else in the park is a couple participating in various forms of PDA (public displays of affection); if you're alone, you'll undoubtedly stick out like a sore thumb.

5. Catedral San Jose: (5a C. Oriente, just off of the Parque Central.) Take the diagonal path through the park, toward the southeast corner. From there, it is just a few steps on 5a C. Oriente until you reach the ruins of Catedral San Jose (on your left). You should try and get a guide show you around. (Q3.)

6. Parque Union: (6a C. Oriente, in between 3a and 2a Av. Sur) Continue down 5a C. Oriente until you reach 3a Av. Sur (the first intersection), and make a right. One block down, you will bump right into the *Parque Union*, where two churches (**San Pedro** and **Santa Clara**) flank a beautiful palm tree-lined park where locals sit, chat, and play cards. Make your way down to the end of the *Parque Union* (you will now be on 2a Av. Sur), where you will see the arches of the pila, a place where local women sometimes scrub and rinse their laundry in the large stone basin.

7. San Francisco Church: (On the corner of 7a C. Oriente and C. de los Pasos) Head south on 2a Av. Sur and make your first left onto 7a C. Oriente; you will see San Francisco Church straight ahead of you. The church, which is the burial place of the patron saint of Antigua (Hermano Pedro) are well worth the visit. (Q3)

8. Café Sky: (1a Av. Sur #15) From the San Francisco Church, head up 1a Av. Sur, and you will see a bright blue, two-story building on your right (at the intersection with 6a C. Oriente). Head inside, and climb upstairs to the third floor, where you'll find a terrace with great views of the city. If you've timed it correctly, it should be just about time for the sunset. Order yourself a beer or a frozen cocktail and some nachos, and enjoy the beautiful surroundings.

9. Café No Sé: (1a Av. Nte. #11C) Once the sun has set, ditch the mellow crowd at Café Sky for more lively and exciting crew at Café No Sé, located just a few doors down from Café Sky. At Café No Sé, they offer a wide range of delicious Mexican food and ice cold draft beer. It's the perfect place to really get the night started, though you could very well end up staying here until last call.

from arriving en masse. Drinks are relatively expensive, but Antigua's main party spot comes at a price. W 80s night, Th ladies' night. Cover free-Q61, depending on night and gender. Open Tu-Sa 8pm-1am. AmEx/D/MC/V.

La Sala, 6A C. Poniente 9 (☎7832 9524). If you're after good dance music, head to La Sala. This bar and pizza joint is frequented by both locals and tourists. Electronic, reggae, and dance are just some of the musical offerings at this chic bar. Live music Th-Sa. Open until midnight. AmEx/D/MC/V.

Sangre, 5A Av. Norte 33A (☎5656 7618). Don't let the older, mostly tourist crowd scare you away. Located behind an art gallery, Sangre is a perfect place to down some delicious mixed drinks. Though drinks (Q48) are on the expensive side, the trendy ambience and back patio more than compensate. Open daily 11am-12am. AmEx/MC/V.

Mono Loco, 5A Av. Sur 6 (☎7832 4235), between 5A and 6A C. Poniente. Mono Loco is about as *gringo* as bars come. Drinks are well priced. Happy hour M-F 5-8pm. AmEx/D/MC/V.

Cine Lounge, 5A Av. Sur 8 (☎7832 0581), in the same building as La Sin Ventura hotel. Travelers looking to catch a movie while sipping on tasty drinks should make their way to the Cine Lounge. Open daily 5-11pm.

LAGO DE ATITLÁN

Lago de Atitlan has long been shrouded in a veil of mystery and enchantment, and it is hard to grasp the beauty of this place unless you see it for yourself. According to Quiché legend, Lago de Atitlán was one of the four lakes that marked the corners of the world. The towns surrounding the lake are inhabited mostly by indigenous Maya of Cakchiquel and Tz'utujil descent with deep ties to the region, and by foreigners who came for a visit, only to find themselves unwilling to leave. What has resulted is a mosaic of cultural and natural beauty that makes this a place unlike any other. The tourist mecca of Panajachel is the first stop for almost every visitor, and this is reflected in the diversity of the population. Several of the towns that ring Atitlán—bustling Santiago Atitlan, isulated Tzununa, and captivating San Antonio Palopó—are among the few in all of Guatemala in which the men wear traditional dress. San Pedro La Laguna has become a backpacker's paradise, while San Marcos, Santa Cruz, and Jaibalito are home to beautiful lakeside hotels and houses. Whether you are jetting across the lake's blue waters on a *lancha*, haggling with Mayan vendors over the price of a colorful hand-woven *tejido*, or enjoying the unparalleled view of the lake from the summit of the Volcan San Pedro, you are bound to eventually understand the magnetism of this magical lake.

 UMBRELLA ELLA ELLA. If you are traveling around Lake Atitlán during rainy season, never be deceived by brilliant morning sunshine. The weather is frequently unpredictable; you don't want to be caught unprotected in a Guatemalan downpour.

PANAJACHEL

Panajachel, located on the shore of the Lago de Atitlán, surrounded by volcanoes, teeters between staying true to its Mayan roots, and falling into a toruist trap. This town's unique past explains a lot. In the 1960s and 70s, Pana was a hippie hangout; today, the old-time peace-lovers sell goods and grub alongside

Lago de Atitlán

Lago de Atitlán

| Footpath |
| Finca |

0 ___ 5 kilometers

0 ___ 5 miles

traditional Mayans on the city's main thoroughfare, C. Santander. Given its status as Lake Atitlán's transportation hub, Panajachel has morphed a popular tourist destination. Though the town is more developed than other stops in the region, Pana's unique culture holds its own.

TRANSPORTATION

Panajachel is easy to access by chicken bus from any of Guatemala's major cities. Because of its small size, it's easy to get around as well. While some opt to make use of the **tuk tuks,** most people walk or bike. Panajachel is also a hub for boat travel on the lake, offering rides to almost every lakeside destination including Santiago Atitlán, San Marcos, Santa Cruz, and Tzunaná.

Buses: Chicken buses pick up and drop off passengers at the intersection of C. Principal and C. Santander. To: **Chichicastenango, Chimaltenango, Guatemala City,** and **Sololá** (15min., Q4). Aside from the trip to Sololá, prices and trip times vary by driver.

Boats: Panajachel has 2 docks, each servicing a different part of the lake. From the dock at the end of C. del Embarcadero, boats depart for cities on the northern part of the lake including **Santa Cruz** (10min., Q16), **San Marcos** (40min., Q24-32), and **Tzununá** (30min., Q24). From the 2nd dock at the end of C. Rancho Grande, boats leave for **Santiago Atitlán** (1 hr., Q32).

Panajachel

🏠 ACCOMMODATIONS
Hospedaje García, **3**
Mario's Rooms, **2**

🍎 FOOD
Deli Jasmin, **4**
Sunset Café, **5**

🍷 NIGHTLIFE
Circus Bar, **1**

Bike Rental: Emanuel, C. 14 de Febrero (☎7762 2790). Mountain bikes Q57 per day.

Tuk Tuk: For Q4, they'll take you anywhere in Panajachel.

🔥 ACCOMMODATIONS

Living up to its status as the "Gateway to the Lake," Panajachel has an impressive array of accomodations. Most establishments are conveniently located on or around the central street, C. Santander, though some are tucked away on quieter streets.

🏠 **Hospedaje Garcia** (☎7762 2187), follow the signs from C. Santander; once on C. de Chalí it's hard to miss. If the central location of Hospedaje Garcia isn't enough to seal the deal, its friendly staff, comfortable rooms, and great prices will do the trick. Rooms are spacious, secure, and well-kept, and the communal bathroom facilities are immaculate. Singles Q40; doubles Q81. Cash only. ❷

Hotel Dos Mundos (☎7762 2078, 7762 2140, or 7762 2865; www.hoteldosmundos.com). This resort-style hotel right on C. Santander is a pleasant, if relatively pricey, alternative to Panajchel's budget-friendly accommodations. Well-kept garden, pool, and ample outdoor seating. Singles Q325; doubles Q488. Reservations recommended. AmEx/D/MC/V. ❺

Mario's Rooms (☎7762 1313). Smack in the middle of town on C. Santander, Mario's Rooms offers a great budget alternative to some of the more expensive hotels in town, while furnishing many of the same amenities. Rooms are clean, spacious, and equipped with safes, private baths, and cable TV. Breakfast included. Free Wi-Fi. Checkout 1pm. Singles Q122, doubles Q162. Cash only. ❸

Larry's Place (☎7762 0767; hotellarrysplace.com), just off of C. Santander on C. de Chalí. Set back from the road and shrouded in lush greenery. Tastefully furnished rooms with private baths. Singles Q122; doubles Q154. Cash only. ❸

Casa Linda (☎7762 0386), in an alley off of C. Santander. A quiet, comfortable, and refreshingly simple accomodation with tidy rooms. Singles Q48; doubles Q89. Cash only. ❷

Hospedaje Montufar (☎7762 0406), off C. Santander. Clean, cozy, and quiet hostel with airy rooms and spotless communal baths. Friendly staff and reasonable rates make Montufar a hard deal to refuse. Singles Q40; doubles Q73. Cash only. ❶

✦ 🔋 ORIENTATION AND PRACTICAL INFORMATION

Panajachel is a small city that is very easy to navigate. **C. Santander** and **C. Principal** are the city's main thoroughfares and connect the old village in the north to the lake at the south end. C. Santander is well marked with signs directing travelers toward the town's amenities.

Tourist office: INGUAT, C. Santander 1-87, Zona 2, Centro Comercial San Rafael, L-No 11 (☎7762-1106; www.visitguatemala.com).

Tours: Atitrans, C. Santander, Anexo Hotel Regis (☎7762 0152 or 7762 0146; www.atitrans.com). Tours of the lake, 2 per day, Q285 per person. Offers 24hr. shuttle service to Antigua (Q98), Guatemala City (Q179), and Flores (Q489). Reservations required.

Bank: Banco Agromercantil, C. Principal (☎7762 1145), in the Edificio Mayan Palace. M-Sa 8:30am-6pm, Su 9am-1pm.

Beyond Tourism:

Jabel Tinamit, C. Santander (☎7762 6056 or 7762 6058; www.jabeltinamit.com). This Spanish school is owned and operated by local Maya. Cash only.

Jardín de America, C. del Chalí (☎7762 2637; www.jardindeamerica.com). Excellent Spanish language instruction with low teacher-to-student ratio. Cash only.

Habitat para la Humanidad (☎7762 0408), on the alley marked by signs for the Casa Linda and Hospedaje Montufar. Information on volunteer opportunities in the Atitlán region. Open M-F 8am-1pm and 2-4pm, Sa 8am-noon.

Laundromat: Lavanderia Santander, C. Santander (☎5756 8577). Open 7am-8pm. Cash only.

Emergency: ☎1500 or 2421 2810.

Police: ☎110. **Tourist Police (Asistur):** ☎2421 2810.

24hr. Pharmacy: Farmacia Batres, C. Principal 0-32, Zona 2 (☎7762 1485).

Medical Services: Pana Medic, C. Principal 0-72, Zona 2.

Internet Access: Mayanet, C. Santander, just north of C. 14 de Febrero. Q8 per hr. Open 8am-10:30pm. Cash only. **Tecnocompu,** C. Principal, just north of intersection with C. Santander. Scanner and international calls. Internet Q5 per hr. Open daily 9am-9:30pm. Cash only.

Post Office: Correo de Panajachel, A-3 C. Santander, Zona 2, Panajachel, Sololá (☎7762 2603). M-F 8:30am-5:30pm, Sa 9am-1pm. **Postal Code:** 07010

FOOD

Featuring everything from Malaysian dishes to Uruguayan delicacies, Panajachel's international culinary influence is truly impressive. For groceries, visit **Chalos** at the intersection of C. Santander and C. Principal.

- **Deli Jasmin** (☎7762 2585), at the south end of C. Santander, just up the road from the lake. Deli Jasmin is perfect any time of the day. Try their incredible banana pancakes (Q29) or pita pizzas (Q27). A Panajachel fixture since 1985, Deli Jasmine is not to be missed. Open M and W-Su 7am-6pm. Cash only. ❸

- **Las Chinitas** (☎7762 2612). From the traditional Chinese decor to the delicious food, it's difficult to pull yourself away from this fun and welcoming restaurant. Try the lunch special (dumplings, Malaysian fried rice, and fresh mango; Q57). Open daily 8am-10pm. Cash only. ❹

- **Crossroads Cafe,** 0-27 C. del Campanario (☎5292 8439; www.crossroadscafepana.com). There is no better way to start your day than with a perfectly crafted cup of coffee at the Crossroads Café. This café offers an unparalleled everybody-knows-your-name atmosphere. The cinnamon buns are out of this world. Open Tu-Sa 9am-1pm and 3-7pm. Cash only. ❷

- **Restaurante Guajimbos** (☎7762 0063), on C. Santander. Serving fresh Uruguayan dishes right on C. Santander. Its impossible to walk by the savory scents coming from this restaurant without stopping for a bite. Entrees around Q32. Open M-W 8am-10pm, F-Su 7am-10pm. AmEx/D/MC/V. ❸

- **Restaurante Ricasso Pizza** (☎7762 0686), next to the PanaRock Cafe on C. Santander. Come here for good Italian dishes and a never-ending happy hour. Spaghetti carbonara (Q30) will not disappoint. Open daily 7am-11pm. V. ❸

- **Cafeteria Panajachel** (☎5840 4304 or 5284 1341), on C. Principal just past its intersection with C. Santander. A no-frills restaurant that, in spite of its minimalist decor, does not disappoint. Wash down their *tortillas con pollo* (Q20) with a fresh strawberry *licuado,* and you'll have all the energy you need to brave the street vendors on C. Santander. Open M and W-Sa 7am-9pm, Tu and Su 7am-5pm. Cash only. ❷

⊙ SIGHTS

MUSEO LA CUSTRE ATITLÁN. This small museum provides a comprehensive history of the peoples and cities of Lake Atitlán. Museo La Custre also houses an interesting collection of Mayan artifacts found in and around the lake. *(At the south end of C. Santander. ☎ 7762 2326. Open M-F and Su 8am-6pm, Sa 8am-7pm. Parking availbale in the lot of the Hotel Posada de Don Rodrigo. Museum entry Q35, students Q20, under 12 free.)*

SAN FRANCISCO DE ASIS. Dominating a small plaza in the old village, this beautiful Catholic church definitely warrants a visit. *(At the intersection of Av. de los Árboles and C. del Campanario. No bathing suits.)*

⊠ NIGHTLIFE

Though the beginning of the week can be a bit slow, Panajachel's nightlife picks up as the weekend approaches.

- **PanaRock Café,** C. Santander 1-86 (☎7762 2194; www.panarockcafe.com). This place calls out to travelers once the sun sets. Live music, cheap happy hour, and great ambience make a night at the PanaRock Café too good to pass up. Open until 1am.

- **Circus Bar** (☎7762 0374 or 7762 2056; www.circus-bar.com), across the street from Chapiteau on C. de los Árboles. Known for its pizza (margarita; Q57), Circus Bar has been a fixture on the Panajachel nightlife scene for more than 20 years. Open noon-midnight. AmEx/D/MC/V over Q97.

Chapíteau (☎7762 0374 or 7762 2056), at the intersection of C. de los Árboles and C. Principal. Chapíteau has been a hallmark in Panajachel since 1988. Locals and tourists alike come to dance and play pool. Open W-Sa 7pm-1am. AmEx/D/MC/V.

Sunset Cafe, at the base of C. Santander, overlooking the lake. There's no better place to be when the sun sets. Perched right on the shores of Lake Atitlan, the cafe offers a great drink menu and hearty Mexican fare. Open daily 2-11pm. AmEx/D/MC/V.

Rumba, at the intersection of C. Santander and C. Principal. Rumba is home to a bar and a discotheque. Drinks are reasonably priced. Happy hour M-Sa noon-8pm. Open until 1am.

▶ DAYTRIPS FROM PANAJACHEL

SANTA CATARINA AND SAN ANTONIO

Minibuses depart from C. el Amante in Panajachel every 20min. Q30. Minibuses returning to Panajachel leave from Santa Catarina and San Antonio's main streets.

Visitors to Panajachel should be sure to check out Santa Catarina Palopó and San Antonio Palopó, two small towns built into the hillside southwest of Pana-jachel on the shores of Lake Atitlán. Both towns are known for their *tejidos* (knitting). The church in Santa Catarina, located right on the main road, is a good place to start exploring. Follow one of the many alleyways down to the stunning shore of the lake. At the edge of town is the local cemetery. Here, colorful tombstones watch over quiet Lake Atitlán.

San Antonio sits 2km down the lake's shore. This town is slightly larger than its neighbor and feels slightly more traditional. Alongside the terraced farmland that descends down the mountains enclosing this charming city, travelers can hardly avoid breathtaking lake views in the town's market-place. Head to the area around the main church (definitely worth a peek) where old women sell homespun ceramics, knittings, and often crafts. The Mayan influences in both towns are vibrant examples of the wider Mayan influence in the Lake Atitlán region.

If you want to extend your stay in Santa Catarina, **Hospedaje Santa Catarina ❶**, on the main road through town, is a solid budget choice. In San Antonio Palopó, the **Hotel Terrazas del Lago ❶** has reasonably priced rooms with great views of the lake.

SANTIAGO DE ATITLÁN

Though Santiago de Atitlan is accessible by road, most people arrive by lancha from Pana-jachel (20 min.; Q25). Once at the docks, the town is relatively easy to navigate. Santiago's main road originates at the dock, from which all of the city's sights are visible, and there is no shortage of locals willing to direct you. If a guide offers to show you around the city, which is unnecessary given how easy it is to get around, be prepared to pay a significant amount of money for his services. While taking pictures of people without their permission is never recommended, be particularly conscious of taking pictures of Santiago's inhabit-ants because some will charge. (Museo Cojolya open M-F 9am-4pm, Sa 9am-1pm; you can meet the weavers at 11am and 1pm.)

Santiago de Atitlán, Lake Atitlán's largest, and arguably most traditional, city is defined by its strong Tz'unujil Mayan culture. Nestled in a horseshoe-shaped bay in the southwest corner of Lake Atitlán, Santiago's sits between the San Pedro Volcano and the Tolimán Volcanoes. Accessible by road or by *lancha* (boat), most visitors arrive at the docks and make the 10min. walk up into the center of town. In the center of town stands a massive Catholic church, which, despite having undergone extensive renovations, still affords tourists glimpses of its original 16th-century construction. A powerful representation of Central

American Catholicism, the church's walls are populated by countless life-like statues of the country's indigenous people. Santiago's residents worship the folk saint, Maximón. A shrine devoted to Maximón is constructed each year and placed in a different spot in the city, where townspeople and tourists can come to pay homage. A trip to Maximón's dwelling typically costs Q2. In addition, expect to pay a small fee to the local who shows you where to find it. After paying their dues to this effigy, visitors should be sure to check out **Museo Cojolya,** located right on the main road. The musuem is devoted to the weaving culture of the Tz'unujil Maya and features exhibits that illustrate traditional dress and the intricate process of dying and weaving. (Offers explanations in both English and Spanish. Admission is free.)

On Fridays, just a few blocks from the church, Santiago de Atitlan plays host to a large market. Street vendors fill several streets and sell everything from vegetables to underwear and soap. At the docks, tourists can rent canoes to explore the bay. Those in need of more directed activity can find guides to take them to a scenic vantage point of the city and the surrounding volcanoes.

For a place to sleep, the centrally located **Hotel Chi-Nim-Ya ❶** (singles US$7, doubles US$10) and the **Hotel Tzan'juyú ❶** (rooms from US$13) are convenient choices. To soothe your grumbling stomach, the main street in town has plenty of restaurants that serve *comida típica* of Santiago and the surrounding region.

SANTA CRUZ

To get to Santa Cruz from Panajachel, head to the dock at the end of the C. del Embarcadero. Here, numerous lancha captains await. Boats make stops at Paxanax and other private homes before arriving at Santa Cruz. The ride takes no more than 15min. Once at Santa Cruz, most accommodations are located along the coast, and tuk-tuks can take you up into town for Q5.

Accessible only by foot or by boat, it is no wonder that once people arrive in Santa Cruz, they have trouble leaving (literally). The vibe here is a welcome change from the busier lakeside towns of San Pedro and Panajachel; chances are people are lounging and relaxing, rather than searching for their next big Guatemalan adventure. The town sits uphill from the more touristed coastline, and the difference between the two is quite pronounced. Other than Santa Cruz's main square, which features a white-washed church dating to the 16th century, there is not much to see in the town itself. The views on the way up are the real draw here. It's a steep climb to the village, but the views on foot are worthwhile. For the less physically inclined, *tuk-tuks* can transport you, but you'll miss out on some of the sights. Most visitors opt to spend the night at **La Iguana Perdida ❶,** the hostel located next to Santa Cruz's main dock. This fun and social hangout is full of travelers looking to enjoy a communal dinner and relaxed bar. **Isla Verde ❶,** a beautiful hotel with dorm-style housing, is another option, as is **Hotel Arca de Noé ❶,** (☎7848 1407; www.arcasantacruz.com). Food choices are limited, but **Jacaranda ❶,** a cafe located five to ten minutes east of the Santa Cruz dock, serves a delicious breakfast.

SAN MARCOS LA LAGUNA

San Marcos La Laguna can be accessed by minibus from San Pedro (20min.) or by lancha from either San Pedro (15min., Q10) or Panajachel (30min., Q15). Once you arrive at the San Marcos dock, most of the hotels and restaurants sit to the west; there are plenty of signs.

San Marcos features yoga studios doubling as massage parlors, charming cafes, and ambient music, all set against the halting background of Lake Atitlan and its attendant volcanoes. In fact, San Marcos is one of the only places that affords a view of all three at once. On this side of Lake Atitlán, the water is clean enough

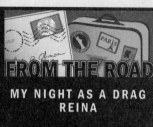

MY NIGHT AS A DRAG REINA

Exhausted from a day of exploring my eighth lakeside town of the week, San Pedro La Laguna, I returned to my hostel intending to take it easy until bedtime. Yeah, it was a Saturday night, but that doesn't mean anything when you're staying in the sleepy town of Santa Cruz, right? Wrong. When I arrived at the hostel, I was told that they hosted a party on Saturday nights. One detail caught me off guard: everyone was expected to cross-dress. I'm not one to get embarrassed or be a party-pooper, so I knew that I was going to be a full-fledged participant, but I didn't expect every attendee would heed to the gender-bending theme. Then again, the hostel did have a costume room dedicated to these Saturday night parties. That night, I walked down to the party, dressed in a purple lace dress, wondering what I was getting myself in to. I entered the room, and found myself surrounded by cross-dressed partiers. Apparently you don't even have to be staying at the Iguana to attend the party. You just have to tell them in advance that you're going to be there. The night included dancing, cat-walking on tables, brief moments of stopping to enjoy the stunning view of Lake Atitlán, and then more dancing.

-Elias Berger

for swimming, cliff jumping, and kayaking. As in Santa Cruz, nearly all of the tourist establishments are located on or close to the shore of the lake, while the town of San Marcos is set further back. **Posada Schumann ❶**, standing just off the western-most San Marcos dock, offers well-priced rooms and a restaurant with a decent menu. **Hotel Aaculaax ❶** (☎5473 9489), a five minute walk from the dock, is a stunning facility with reasonable rooms and a restaurant, **Las Mañanitas ❶**, that cooks up some of the best food in town (banana and nutella crepe, Q35). For lighter fare, the **Moonfish Café ❶**, another two minutes past Hotel Aaculaax, and the **Snack Shack ❶** serve some tasty options.

TZUNUNÁ AND EL JAIBALITO

Lanchas depart from San Pedro (30min.; Q15) and Panajachel (20min.; Q15)

Tzununá and Jaibilito are strong reminders of Lake Atitlán's strong Mayan culture and the huge socio-economic gap that exists between expatriates and the indigenous peoples. Not many tourists make it to these two small villages in between San Marcos La Laguna and Santa Cruz; as a result, locals are sometimes surprised to see *gringos* wandering around. While most visitors arrive at these two towns via *lancha*, it is also possible to hike along a beautiful lakeside path that connects San Marcos, Tzununá, Jaibalito, and Santa Cruz. In Jaibalito, charming hotels and villas grace the shoreline. The actual town of Jaibalito is much less glamorous, but its evident Mayan influence makes it well worth the visit. A short walk east of the Jaibalito dock is **Casa del Mundo ❶**, a gorgeous hotel with a hot tub, swimming holes, and garden that seems to hang off the cliffs over Lake Atitlán. (☎5218-5332; lacasadelmundo.com. Singles Q281, with private bath Q537. Cash only.) A trendy new restaurant, **Ven Acá ❶**, serves great food and creative mixed drinks like the *Granizada*, a mixture of cava, pink grapefruit juice, mint syrup, and frozen mango stick, for an entirely tourist crowd.

Tzununá, just a ten minute boat ride west of Jaibalito, is set back from the shore. This little town is one of Lake Atitlán's poorest communities. Aside from its two popular resorts—**Lomas de Tzununá ❶** and **Hotel Xocomil ❶** (rooms Q151, bungalow Q352)—there is not much to see.

SOLOLÁ. Though the city itself is nothing special, Sololá does have two draws: market days on Tuesday and Friday, and the parade of the *cofradías* on Sunday. On market days, Sololá is filled with artisans and vendors hailing from neighboring towns and villages. Though it can get a bit hectic (especially during the larger Friday market), meandering through the wealth of local fares is well-worth the experience. On Sunday, for the parade of the *cofradías*, elders of the community, wear colorful traditional dress on their way to late-morning mass. *(Chicken buses shuttle between Panajachel and Sololá every 10min. Be warned: the speed at which chicken bus drivers take the cliff-side curves will nauseate even the hardiest traveler.)*

SAN PEDRO

A dynamic city on the shores of Lake Atitlán, San Pedro never has trouble attracting visitors. Though plagued by drug problems, the town is an ideal base for those in search of outdoor adventures. From kayaking, snorkeling, and horseback-riding, to climbing the Volcán San Pedro, which looms above the city, San Pedro will not disappoint. Having become somewhat of a backpacker's paradise in recent years, San Pedro is an exciting and ever-changing place to visit.

▐ TRANSPORTATION

San Pedro La Laguna is easily accessible by **lancha, chicken bus,** or **minibus.** Most travelers make use of the convenient *lancha* service that connects San Pedro to the other towns on Lake Atitlán.

Buses: Chicken buses depart from the central plaza, across from the church, for **Quetzaltenango** (2½hr., every 30min., last bus 11am) and **Guatemala City** (3¼hr., every 30min., last bus 2pm).

Bike Rental: Excursion Big Foot (☎7721 8203), up from the Panajachel dock. Offers a variety of outdoor activities. Bike rental Q66 (US$8) per day.

Boats: Public *lanchas* depart from San Pedro every 20-30min. *Lanchas* to **Panajachel** (30min., Q25), **Santiago** (15 min., Q15), and **Santa Cruz** (20 min., Q20). Private *lancha* service is also available, though it is significantly more expensive and only marginally more convenient than the public service.

▟▐ ORIENTATION AND PRACTICAL INFORMATION

Visitors to San Pedro typically arrive at either the **Panajachel** or **Santiago dock,** which serve the north and south sides of the lake respectively. *Tuk-tuks* shuttle travelers between the docks (Q5). Most of the bars, restaurants, cafes, hotels, and hostels are located on or close to the shore of the lake, while the town itself is set further back. San Pedro is surprisingly hilly; if you want to explore beyond the tourist lakeside establishments but want to save your legs, have a *tuk-tuk* take you to the center of town (*"al centro"*). Winding roads and a lack of street names make San Pedro difficult to navigate, so don't be afraid to ask for directions.

Tours and Agencies: Asoantur (☎5423 7423 or 4379 4545), off the Panajachel dock. Volcano hikes Q200 (includes taxi ride to basecamp). Kayak rental Q20 per hr. **Rancho Moises** (☎5967 3235), on the trail between the 2 docks. Offers eco-tours of San Pedro and its surroundings on horseback (Q40 per hr.) **Atitlán Adventures** (☎4130 5205), on the trail between the 2 docks. Water activities like snorkeling and canoeing on Lake Atitlán are reasonably priced.

Bank: Banrural, 2 blocks down from the main square.

Laundry: Shampoo Laundry (☎5094 4230), to the right of the Panajachel dock. Q5 per lb.

Police: (☎5534 0256), just off the main square to the right of the church.

Internet access: D'Noz (☎5578 0201), just off the Panajachel dock. Also home to a restaurant, bar, and small library. Cash only.

Post Office: (☎2476 0202), next to the church. Open M-F 8:30am-12:30pm and 1:30-5:30pm, Sa 9am-1pm. **Postal Code:** 07018.

ACCOMMODATIONS

Hotel San Antonio (☎4423 1156). From Panajachel dock, head left through town; the hotel is on the right just before the road turns into a dirt path. Spacious well-kept rooms. Stunning lake views from the 3rd floor terrace. Laundry service available. Free Wi-Fi. Singles Q50; doubles Q80. Cash only. ❷

Hotel Gran Sueño (☎7721 8110), on the right as you head left from the Panajachel dock. A tranquil place to stay. Rooms have private baths and excellent views of the lake. Singles Q75; doubles Q120. Cash only. ❷

Hospedaje Casa Maria (☎4145 0307), on the dirt path between the 2 docks. Guests will enjoy escaping the bustle of San Pedro in this somewhat hidden *hospedaje*. Rooms are clean and spacious with private baths. Singles Q40. Cash only. ❶

Hotel Maria Elena (☎5864 4628), on the left side as you head left from the Panajachel dock. A new hotel with beautiful rooms. Singles Q100; doubles Q150. Cash only. ❸

FOOD

Covering everything from chop suey to homemade apple pie, the tourist industry has shaped Pana's restaurant business. While there are some solid local options concentrated in the center of town, travelers would be remiss not to take advantage of the great international restaurants that have sprung up here.

Zoola (☎5847 4857), on the path between the 2 docks. Guests dine Middle-Eastern style, seated on floor pillows and carpets. Delicious ethnic food and local fare. Small hotel on the premises with 8 rooms available. Open 9am-9pm. Cash only. ❷

Café La Puerta (☎5098 1272 or 5284 2406), on the path between the 2 docks. A wonderful cafe that offers guests the option of sitting lakeside or in a quaint garden. Sandwiches and heartier entrees for reasonable prices. Nachos and guacamole Q25. Open daily from 8am-5pm. Cash only. ❷

Fata Morgana, just up from the Panajachel dock, on the left. Fresh baked goods and delicious coffee. Entrees include sandwiches and pizza (Q30-Q40). Amazing smoothies (*Besa Fresa*, Q20). Open M-Tu and Th-Su 8am-2pm. Cash only. ❷

Nick's Place (☎7721 8065), on the Panajachel dock. Heaping portions; appetizers (Q20) are the size of entrees. Mixed drinks and beers (Q10-Q20) are some of the cheapest in town. Open daily 7am-11pm. Cash only. ❷

SIGHTS AND OUTDOOR ACTIVITIES

VOLCÁN SAN PEDRO. Many come to San Pedro in hopes of conquering the Volcan San Pedro, which dominates the landscape of this lakeside town. Though in recent times the hike has become safer for tourists to tackle without a guide, solo hikers should be cautious as robberies are still a concern. *(Several tour companies lead hikes up Volcan San Pedro (see Asoantur, p. 81). The hike to the summit takes 4hr. It's best to get an early start.)*

THERMAL POOLS. Visitors should not miss the thermal pools naturally heated by the Volcán San Pedro. To complete the experience, most thermal pool establishments serve food and drinks to their guests. *(Just off the path between the Pana-jachel and Santiago docks. Most charge Q20 per hr.)*

CHICHICASTENANGO

Chichicastenango's famous Thursday and Sunday markets draw people from across Guatemala to what is considered by many to be the country's greatest attraction. The tourist invasion has had both positive and negative effects: both cheap knock-offs of traditional textiles and the most well-crafted products that the Guatemalan countryside has to offer are for sale in the packed stalls. Despite of the tour groups that flood in from Antigua and Panajachel, "Chichi," with its nearly 50,000 inhabitants, remains very much an *indígena* town.

Like the town's bustling markets, Chichi's history is tumultuous. It was built by the Spanish in the 16th century as a home for refugees from Utatlán, the Quiché capital brutally leveled by the Spaniards. During the 19th century, the Guatemalan government used forced-labor laws written during the colonial era to pull Quiché workers from the mountains to work on coffee plantations. Tensions rose again in the late 1970s and early 80s, when guerilla activity disturbed the area. Despite these periods of persecution, the region's unique meld of indigenous and Catholic religious tradition continues to thrive.

▐ TRANSPORTATION

Located in the heart of the Western highlands, Chichicastenango is relatively easy to reach. A short jaunt to **Los Encuentros** (20 min. via microbus) allows travelers to connect to **chicken buses** heading to most major destinations in Guatemala.

Buses: Buses depart from the intersection of 5a Av. and 5a C. to **Guatemala City** (3hr., every 20min. 5am-4pm, Q20) and **Santa Cruz del Quiche** (30min., every 20min. 5am-4pm, Q5). **Microbuses,** stationed on 7a Av. between 8a C. and 9a C., shuttle passengers to **Los Encuentros,** where they can catch chicken buses heading to **Quetzaltenango, Chimaltenango,** and other popular destinations. Several local travel agencies (such as **Chichi Turkaj,** p. 83) offer shuttle services to several Guatemalan cities.

Tuk-tuks: In Chichi, as in most small Guatemala cities, *tuk-tuks* are the most commonly used alternative to walking.

▞ ▐ ORIENTATION AND PRACTICAL INFORMATION

Chichicastenango is centered around the **parque central.** The *parque* is bordered by 4 and 5 Av. to the west and east, and 7 and 8 C. to the north and south. Reading street signs gets a bit tricky during market days, when they are hardly discernible behind a slew of market stands. Tourist services are concentrated in the area surrounding the *parque central* and the **Centro Comercial,** located on the north side of the *parque central.*

Tours and Agencies: Chichi Turkaj, 5 Av. 5-24 (☎7756 1579), just off the main squre. Offers general information and shuttle service to many Guatemalan cities.

Bank: Banco Industrial, 6a C. between 5a and 6a Av. Open M-F and Su 9am-5pm, Sa 8am-noon. **Currency exchange** and **ATM.**

Beyond Tourism: Ut'z Bat'z, 5a Av. 5-24 (☎5008 5193; www.enmisalsa.com/english), just north of the central plaza. This Mayan handicraft collective works with the *En Mi Salsa* project to make environmentally friendly sustainable products and employ impoverished citizens. Open W 1-5pm, Th 9am-5pm, Sa 10am-5pm, and Su 9am-5pm.

Chichicastenango

🏠 ACCOMMODATIONS

Hotel Chugüila, **2**
Posada El Arco, **1**

🍴 FOOD

Casa San Juan, **3**
Restaurante La Parilla, **4**

Police: 4 blocks past the arch, next to the school.

Pharmacy: Farmacia Girón, 5a Av. 5-70 (☎7756 1226). Open daily 7:30am-12:30pm and 2-7:30pm.

Medical Services: El Buen Samaritano, 6a C. 6-30 (☎7756 1163).

Internet Access: Internet Café, 5a Av. 8-39 (☎7756 1215), just south of the central plaza. Internet Q8 per hr. Open daily 7am-9pm. Cash only.

Post Office: El Correo (☎2232 6101 or 2476 0202), on the corner of 4a Av. and 7a C. Open M-Sa 8:30am-5:30pm. **Postal Code:** 14006.

🏠 ACCOMMODATIONS

Most of Chichicastenango's hotels and hostels are located only a block or two from the center of town.

▨ **Hotel Chalet House,** 3a C. 7-44 (☎7756 1360; www.chalethotelguatemala.com). Three-floor hotel with a homey atmosphere. Spacious rooms have private baths. Breakfast included. Free Wi-Fi. Singles Q200. ❺

Posada El Arco, 4a C. 4-36 (☎7756 1255). Well-furnished rooms with private baths and large beds centered around a stunning courtyard. English-speaking owners are welcoming and a wonderful resource for information on Chichi and environs. Rooms Q225. MC/V. ❺

Hotel Chugüilá, 5a Av. 5-24 (☎7756 1134). Spacious rooms with private baths look out over a central courtyard. Singles Q80. AmEx/D/MC/V. ❷

Hotel Posada El Teléfono, 8a C. 1-64 (☎7756 1197), behind the El Calvario. A great budget option in a quiet part of town. No-frills, institutional-looking rooms, some with views of the colorful above-ground tombs in the city's large cemetery. Immaculate communal bathrooms. Singles Q30. Cash only. ❶

Hospedaje Girón, 6a C. 4-52 (☎7756 1156). Reasonably priced rooms with private baths and cable TV. Breakfast included. Internet Q6 per hr. Singles Q85; doubles Q145. Cash only. ❸

🍴 FOOD

While the many of the restaurants clustered around the *parque* are pricey, cheap and tasty options abound in the **market,** which plays host to a colorful labyrinth of food vendors.

⧉ Casa San Juan (☎7756 2086 or 5134 8852), in the main square, opposite Santo Tomás Church, on the 2nd floor. Upscale, by Chichi's standards. *Comida típica* Q60. Sandwiches with homemade bread Q20. Occassional live music. Open Tu-W and F-Sa 9am-9pm; Th and Su 7am-10pm. V. ❸

La Villa de Los Cofrades (☎7756 1643 or 7756 1678), on the 1st floor of the Centro Comercial, on the north side of the central plaza. *Comida típica* options are a safe bet. Club sandwich Q40. Open W and Sa 9am-8pm, Th and Su 7am-4pm. AmEx/D/MC/V. ❸

Restaurant Kieq Ik Wai'm Ja (☎7756 1013), off the central plaza. Outdoor balcony seating offers birds-eye views of the central plaza, which are especially impressive on market days. Specializes in steak dishes (Q50). Chile *rellenos* Q35. Impressive breakfast selection (banana pancakes Q27). Open M and W-Su 7am-8pm. AmEx/D/MC/V. ❸

Restaurante La Parrilla (☎7756 1321 or 7756 1497). Grilled entrees Q30-50. Hearty breakfast special (eggs, sausage, beans, cheese and tortilla) Q22. Open daily 7am-9pm. AmEx/D/MC/V. ❷

Tu Café, several doors down from the Santo Tomás Church on the main plaza. Great for a quick meal or a snack. Nachos and guacamole Q18. Sandwiches Q15-30. *Plato típico* Q45. Open daily 7:30am-9pm. Cash only. ❷

📷 SIGHTS

⧉MARKET DAY. Although a few stands remain open all week, the scheduled Thursday and Sunday markets are well worth a special visit. On these days, the otherwise calm, peaceful streets of Chichi undergo a drastic transformation: every inch of space is blanketed with vendors hawking their crafts and handiwork. The main **vegetable market** is inside the **Centro Comercial** on the north side of the plaza. If you're shopping for *artesanía*, remember that bargaining is expected (aim for 30% off the asking price). While prices in Chichi certainly aren't the lowest in the country, you can still find some good deals. Asking prices for wooden masks (Q20-100), hammocks (Q80-300), and big blankets (Q80-150) vary greatly depending on quality. Shop around before making a purchase. Tourist buses arrive at around 10am and leave at around 2pm; the best bargains are found before and after the crowds of tourists clog the streets and drive up the prices.*(The market usually lasts from about 8am to 5pm.)*

IGLESIA SANTO TOMÁS. Looming over the central market, this church provides a fascinating glimpse into the Catholicism of the Quiché Maya. The church is built on an ancient Quiché Maya holy site and is therefore sacred to local indigenous communities. *Indígenas* make an elaborate ritual of ascending the steps and repeatedly kneeling. An incense fire is kept burning at the base of the church's steps and, on market days, brightly dressed *indígena* women cover the stairs with hibiscus, lilies, roses, and gladiolas; churchgoers purchase the blooms to give as offerings. Inside the altars are surrounded by candles and petals dedicated to both Catholic saints and Quiché ancestors. Check out the former monastery, located to the right of the church. *(On the corner of 5a Av. and 8a C., on the parque central. Use the side entrance, to the right; the front entrance is reserved for senior church officials and cofradías. Dress modestly. No photography allowed. Free, but small donations appreciated.)*

PASCUAL ABAJ. This Mayan shrine, dating back to the Columbian era, consists of a ceremonial rock surrounded on three sides by a low stone wall. There's usually a small fire burning in front, as well as a profusion of flowers, liquor, and candles. The best time to go is Sunday mornings, when gatherings are larger and more frequent. Visitors should try to visit during a ceremony. *(Walk downhill 1 block from the Santo Tomás church on 5 Av. Turn right on 9 C. and follow it as it curves downhill and to the left. When the road crosses a small stream and then veers to the right, follow the large sign and proceed straight up the dirt path. Pass through a courtyard and a small museum of ceremonial masks and enter a forested area. The trail zigzags up the hillside until flattening out in a small meadow dotted with pines. The shrine is about 30km farther on the right.)*

MUSEO ROSSBACH. In addition to providing a detailed history of the region, this museum houses a collection of pre- and post-Classical Maya bowls, figurines, arrowheads, and necklaces. *(On the south side of the parque central. Open Tu-W and F-Sa 8am-12:30pm and 2-4:30pm, Th 8am-4pm, Su 8am-2pm. Q5.)*

EL CALVARIO. This chapel, which looks like a smaller version of the Iglesia Santo Tomás, is worth peeking inside. Incense-burning rituals are frequently held on the front steps. Perhaps more impressive than the chapel itself is the view of Chichi's colorful **cemetery,** to the left of El Calvario (8a C.). *(On the corner of 4a Av. and 8a C., on the southwest corner of the parque central. Dress modestly. No photography allowed.)*

SANTA CRUZ DEL QUICHÉ

Located about 18km north of Chichicastenango and 40km northeast of Quetzaltenango, Santa Cruz del Quiché (pop. 22,100) is the capital of the district and an important transportation hub for those heading to more remote parts of the highlands. The town is neither particularly attractive nor exciting, though some might take comfort in the big-city comforts that Santa Cruz provides, like western clothing stores and traffic lights set this city apart from the surrounding towns. The nearby Quiché Maya ruins are perfect for a brief escape from the city.

▐ TRANSPORTATION

Santa Cruz del Quiché is easily reached by **chicken bus, microbus,** or **shuttle.** Chicken buses connect Santa Cruz with Guatemala City, and microbuses connect Santa Cruz to Chichicastenango, Nebaj, and other nearby cities.

> **Buses:** Chicken buses arrive at and depart from the **bus station** at 1a Av. and 10a C. To reach the central plaza from there, head north for 4 blocks on 1 Av. and make a left on 6a C. Microbuses also leave from the bus terminal, but some (especially those headed to Nebaj) will drive through the central plaza to pick up more passengers. The times and prices listed below are for **chicken buses.** Microbuses take ¾ of the time and cost an additional Q5-10.

Guatemala City: (3hr., every 30min., Q20). Makes stops at **Chichicastenango, Los Encuentros,** and **Chimaltenango.**

Chichicastenango: (30 min., every 30min., Q3). Same bus as the Guatemala City bus.

Los Encuentros: (1hr., every 30min., Q6). Also the same bus as Guatemala City. At **Los Encuentros,** there are connections to **Quetzaltenango** or **Panajachel.**

Quetzaltenango: (3hr., every hr. from 5-7am, Q20).

Nebaj: (3hr.; 5am, noon, 6pm; Q15). Passes through Sacapulas, where transfers can be made for **Huehuetenango** and **Cobán.**

ORIENTATION AND PRACTICAL INFORMATION

Santa Cruz del Quiché is laid out on a grid, making it easy to navigate. The **central plaza** is bounded by **1a and 2a Av.** and **3a and 6a C.** The **bus terminal** is located a few blocks southeast of the plaza, though many microbuses will drop passengers right in front of the whitewashed **Catholic church** that stands on the east side of the main square.

Bank: Banrural, 2a Av. 3-22 (☎7755 1540), in Zona 1. Open M-F 8am-5pm, Sat-Sun 8am-12pm.

Police: 0 Av., 4 C. (☎7755 1106), in Zona 1.

24hr. Pharmacy: Farmacia Batres, 2a Av. 6-13, in Zona 1, right on the southwest corner of the main square.

Hospital: Hospital Nacional Santa Elena (☎7755 1782), just west of the city.

Internet Access: Hotel Acuario (☎7755 1878), on the 2nd floor. Q5 per hour. Cash only.

Post Office: 3a C., (☎7755 1085), between 0 and 1a Av. Open M-F 8:30am-5:30pm, Sa-Su 9am-1pm. **Postal Code:** 14001.

ACCOMMODATIONS

Not many people stay in Santa Cruz del Quiché, as it is more of a jumping off point than a destination in itself. If you are looking for a place to stay, don't stray too far from the center of this somewhat sprawling town. Budget accommodations tend to be rougher around the edges than in other Guatemalan destinations, so you might consider springing for some comfort and convenience.

Hotel Acuario 5a C. 2-44 (☎7755 1878). Just a ½-block west of the main square on 5a C., there's a staircase that leads up to the main entrance. Clean, secure, and spacious rooms with private bath and cable television. Internet Q5 per hr. Rooms Q100. V. ❸

Hotel Monte Bello (☎7755 3948 or 7755 3949), on 4a Av. between 9a and 10a C. Clean and comfortable rooms. All rooms have private bath, TV, and Wi-Fi. Singles Q125; doubles Q200. Cash only. ❺

Hotel Las Vegas (☎7755 1464), 3a Av. between 4a and 5a C. No-frills rooms for a good price. Singles Q60; doubles Q100. Cash only. ❷

FOOD

Santa Cruz del Quiché has plenty decent *comedores*. Santa Cruz is also home to many *panaderías* (bakeries), where you can get everything from a simple roll to an elaborate pastry—either way you can't go wrong. Try the *panadería* on the corner of 2a Av. and 5a C., right on the main square. Santa Cruz's **market** on Thursdays and Saturdays has delicious fresh produce.

El Portal de la Cruz, just west of the *parque central* on 4a C. The place to sample *comida típica*. Open daily 8am-7pm. Cash only. ❷

Pizza Argentina, 6a C. 3-31 (☎7755 0553), just west of the main square. Good slices for a good prices. Pizzas Q30-50. Delivery available. Open 9am-9pm. Cash only. ❷

📷 DAYTRIP FROM SANTA CRUZ DEL QUICHÉ

UTATLÁN

Just outside of Santa Cruz del Quiché lies Utatlán, capital of the Quiché Kingdom during AD 1250-1523. Under the rule of Q'uk'ab, the Quiché domain extended from the Pacific nearly all the way to the Atlantic. The capital also encompassed nine different nations, including Tzutuhil and Cakchiquel, two major indigenous groups. The official archaeological site of **K'umarkaaj** ("Houses of Old Reeds") covers an area of eight sq. km. The only discernible structures are located around a single *parque*. Once you enter the site, there is a **Visitors Center** that houses a **museum,** where you can check out a model of what Utatlán looked like in its heyday. To reach the ruins themselves, follow the path right from the Visitors Center. Standing in what was once the **central plaza,** you can make out the few of the structures that remain. One of the most interesting features of these ruins is the tunnel that runs under the plaza. This tunnel can be found by following the steep trail to the right of the plaza ruins. Follow the sign that reads "La dirección de la Cueva." Religious healing ceremonies have taken place in this tunnel for the last 500 years. If you're lucky, you may stumble across one. You need a flashlight to see into the cave; bring your own. *(To get to the ruins of Utatlán, follow C. 10 out of town (begin at the bus terminal), which eventually passes by La Colonia. At the sign for the SCEP, take a right up the hill to the park entrance. The walk from there is 3km (about 30min.). A tuk-tuk will take you from the main square in Santa Cruz (10 min.; Q50). Museum open daily 8am-4pm; gates close a little later. Q30.)*

NEBAJ

Though a mere 40km north of Santa Cruz del Quiché, winding dirt roads and imposing mountain passes make Nebaj (pop. 19,600) feel very isolated. Situated in a fertile, stream-fed valley high in the Cuchumatanes, Nebaj marks the southwest point of the Ixil Triangle. With Chajul to the north and Cotzal to the east, this is the homeland of the Ixil Maya. Nebaj is a beautiful, traditional town; the local clothing is striking. Women dress in deep-red *cortes* and adorn themselves with elegant, forest-green shoulder drapes with sewn golden birds and matching head wraps. Fires and landmines wrecked the land during Guatemala's civil war in the late 70s and early 80s. Today, the town's natural beauty makes it difficult to imagine its scarred past.

📷 TRANSPORTATION

The only way to get to Nebaj is via bus or microbus from Santa Cruz del Quiche (which goes through Sacapulas) or from Cobán.

Buses: The **bus station** is on 7a C., across from the market. The bus service is somewhat erratic, so it is best to check the schedules at the station. Buses run out of Nebaj to **Santa Cruz del Quiché** (2.5hr., every hr., Q20). These buses pass through **Sacapulas,** where passengers can connect to buses to **Huehuetenango,** and the intersection that heads to **Uspantán,** where passengers can connect to a bus to **Cobán.** Buses also head to **Cotzal** (30min., every hr., Q5) and **Chajul** (30min., every hr., Q5).

⚑ 🛈 ORIENTATION AND PRACTICAL INFORMATION

Arriving in the **parque central** of Nebaj, you'll see the large, whitewashed Catholic church towering over the south side of the plaza. For the most part, Nebaj's streets are organized on a grid (*calles* run east-west with *avenidas* going north-south), with the exception of **Calzada 15 de Septiembre,** which heads northeast (in the direction of Chajul and Cotzal) from the northeast corner of the *parque central.* Both the market and the bus terminal are located two blocks down from the southeast corner of the plaza.

Tourist Office: 3a C. between 5a and 6a Av. (☎4516 2059; www.nebaj.org), in the same building as El Descanso Café. Bilingual staff. Open M-Sa 8am-5pm, Su 8am-noon.

Tours and Agencies: Pablo's Tours, 3a C. between 5a and 6a Av. (☎4090 4924). Offers guided hikes to Acul (6hr., Q150) and other nearby towns. Also offers shuttle service to Santa Cruz del Quiche, Huehuetenango, Quetzaltenango, and other cities. Oddly enough, they also offer a **laundry service** for Q10 per lb. **Guías Ixiles,** 3a C. between 5a and 6a Av. (☎7756 0207 or 5847 4747), in the same building as El Descanso Café. Guided hikes to various locations around Nebaj, including Acul (5 hr.), Cocop (3-4 hr.) and the waterfalls (2 hr.). Cash only.

Bank: Banrural, on the 1st fl. of the Palacio Municipal, on the north side of the plaza. ATM. Open M-F 8am-4:30pm.

Beyond Tourism: Nebaj Spanish School, 3a C. between 5a and 6a Av. (☎7756 0207 or 5847 4747), in the same building as the El Descanso Cafe. Offers the unique opportunity to learn Spanish and Ixil. Offers a homestay program.

Police: (☎7756 0055), on the 1st fl. of the Palacio Municipal, on the north side of the main plaza.

Pharmacy: Farmacia Emanuel (☎5743 0798), on the northeast corner of the main square. Open daily 8am-9pm.

Hospital or Medical Services: Clínica Médica Familiar, 7a Av. between 5a and 6a C. (☎5784 8448). Open M-F 4:30am-8:30pm, Sa 9am-1pm.

Internet Access: El Descanso, 3a C. between 5a and 6a Av. (☎7756 0207 or 5847 4747). Internet Q10 per hr. Printing Q1 per page. Cash only.

Post Office: 4a C. 4-37 (☎7756 0239). Open M-F 8:30am-12:30pm and 1:30-5:30pm, Sa 9am-1pm. **Postal Code:** 14013.

⌂ ACCOMMODATIONS

Here, in Nebaj, a little luxury won't set you back a significant amount. As more and more travelers discover the amazing hiking and outdoor activities that this town has to offer, the number of hotels and hostels is increasing dramatically.

▨ **Hotel del Centro Naab'a,** 3a C. 3-18 (☎4145 6243 or 5722 6736), 2 blocks north of the main square. Friendly, quiet, and comfortable. All rooms have private bath and television. Singles Q65; doubles Q130. Cash only. ❷

Hotel Villa Nebaj, Calzada 15 de Septiembre 2-37 (☎7756 0005 or 7715 1651). Comfortable rooms at reasonable prices. Singles Q80, with private bath Q195; doubles Q150/275. ❷

Hotel Casa Shalom, Calzada 15 de Septiembre (☎7755 8028), across from G&T Bank. Clean and comfortable. All rooms with private baths and double beds. Singles Q75; doubles Q140. Cash only. ❷

Hotel Maya Ixil (☎7755 8168), on the north side of the main square. Right in the thick of things. Spacious and well-kept rooms all have private baths. Free Wi-Fi. Singles Q65; doubles Q120. Cash only. ❷

Popi's Hospedaje, 2 blocks west of the main square, down 5a C. A self-proclaimed "traveler's hangout." Dorms Q25. Cash only. ❶

Hospedaje Votzotz, 7a C. between 6a and 7a Av. (☎5715 1172), 2 blocks west of the church in the main square. Simple rooms with well-kept communal baths. Singles Q30; doubles Q60. Cash only. ❶

🍴 FOOD

Nebaj's food scene is continually expanding. Whether you're in the mood for pizza, tacos, or *comida típica*, you won't go hungry around here. Head to the **market,** two blocks east of the plaza on 2a Av. and 7a C., for food on-the-go.

🎖 **El Descanso,** 3a C. between 5a and 6a Av. (☎7756 0207 or 5847 4747). Founded by a Peace Corps volunteer in 2001, El Descanso is not to be missed. In addition to its menu of international breakfasts (French toast Q18), local dishes (traditional Ixil *boxboles* on Th) and great desserts, El Descanso has a bar, a Spanish school, an internet cafe, and a tourist office. Open daily from 6:30am-9:30pm. ❷

Café Restaurante Maya Ixil (☎7755 8168), on the north side of the main square. Grab a filling and well-prepared meal. Extensive breakfast selection. *Comida típica* offerings include *churrascos* (Guatemalan steak Q32). Open daily 7am-9:30pm. Cash only. ❷

Chévere (☎5765 0067). An abbreviated menu with *chévere* (Q7), hamburgers (Q12), and a few other grilled items. Open daily 8am-7pm. Cash only. ❶

Mi Taco Express, 3 C. 3-18. This eatery's authenticity is a friendly reminder that you're still in Central America. Great Mexican dishes for unbeatable prices (Q10-20). Open daily 8am-7pm. Cash only. ❶

Comedor Elsi'm, on the east side of the central plaza. One of the most popular spots in town. It's hard to get a table around lunch time. Come enjoy *comída tipica* with the largely Guatemalan crowd. Open daily 7am-9pm. Cash only. ❶

👁 🥾 SIGHTS AND OUTDOOR ACTIVITIES

Beyond taking in the scenery, there isn't much to do in Nebaj proper. Before heading off on the many hikes and daytrips for which Nebaj serves as an ideal starting point, make sure to head over to the bustling fruit and vegetable **market** (especially on Sundays). The colorful market sells everything from coffee beans to mangos and chili peppers.

ACUL. A challenging hike leads to the village of Acul and the cheese farm **Hacienda San Antonio.** From the police station on the *parque*, head north past Comedor Irene and down the hill. After 15min., continue over a small concrete bridge to a rougher, wider road. About 30-45min. after the bridge, turn right, leaving the smaller path. About an hour into the hike, the path flattens out and runs past a long, thin field. At the end of the field, take the well-worn path to the right (the left path will get you there, too; it's just longer). After 10-15min., you'll go around a bend and the village of Acul will come into sight. Follow the road through Acul with the fields on the left and the village on the right. About 10min. up the same road on the left is the Hacienda San Antonio.

Set in a picturesque pasture with a forested hillside rising behind it, the *finca* seems more like something out of the Swiss Alps. The farmers inside will show you a room filled with circular blocks of fine Swiss cheese they produce (Q30 per lb). The surrounding valley is perfect for a picnic. Small *tiendas* in the village sell drinks and snacks. Allow 3-5hr. for the whole trip and set out early in the morning when the air is cool and the skies are clear.

LA PISTA DE ATZUMAL. A hike to the old military airfield in the tiny town of Atzumal provides a peak into the area's violent history. Atzumal was built partly by foreign volunteers in the 80s. During the war, displaced Ixil families lived here after their homes were razed. The new homes contrast with the traditional lifestyle of their inhabitants. At the top of town is the old military airfield, a barren and silent strip of ground surrounded by a minefield. The minefield has been cleared, leaving the landscape awkwardly uneven. Watch out for barbed wire.

From the church in town, follow the road to Chajul until you reach the Quetzal gas station, where you should follow the left fork. When the paved road ends, take a quick left, and then immediately turn right onto the dirt road heading down the hill. After following this for about 30-45min., you'll come to the only junction (at the tall Feliz Viaje sign); take the right fork down the slope. After passing a couple of houses and *tiendas*, make a left onto the path just past a blue-painted *papelería*. At the end of the path, turn right, then left. You should now see La Pista in front of you.

LAS CASCADAS DE PLATA. Las Cascadas de Plata is a less rigorous hike than the others listed above. The largest *cascada* (1-1½hr. from Nebaj) is a jagged rock face carved out of a tree-lined hillside. The water here divides into many small cascades, making for a stunning display. The walk to the falls is a leisurely stroll through the pastures and valleys surrounding Nebaj. From the church in town, follow the road west to Chajul until you reach the first bridge. Take the road that veers left just before the bridge and stay on it for the rest of the walk. About ten minutes from the bridge, the valley narrows and the hillsides grow steeper. Less than one hour from the town, there's a small waterfall on the left and some small waterfalls on the right. Continuing on, the road soon curves sharply to the left and drops steeply downhill to the largest fall. Allow at least 2½hr. for the entire trip.

COCOP. A half-day of hiking will bring you to the remote, newly rebuilt village of Cocop. Like Atzumal and Acul, the village saw more than its fair share of activity during the war. Particularly harrowing were the massacres, when 98 villagers were brutally slaughtered. The few who were out in the fields working returned to find the village smoldering without a single survivor. After that, many left the village to avoid the 'poisonous' spirits lurking in the hills. Only recently have inhabitants begun to return.

To get to Cocop, start at the BanCafé on the market street in Nebaj and head east. At the end of the street, take a right, then a left down the hill. Cross over the small stream and continue on the well-worn path to a collection of wooden houses in the village of Xemamatzé. Take a left and follow the rutted road uphill for 2hr.

There is one shop in Cocop; the owners there will put you up in a room at the school for the night (Q15 per person). Otherwise, take the path towards Río Azul down the valley. Río Azul is on the road to Coatzal; from there you can walk the couple of hours back to Nebaj.

⚑ DAYTRIPS FROM NEBAJ

CHAJUL AND SAN JUAN COTZAL

Chajul's market days are on Tu and F; Cotzal's are on W and Sa. On these days, buses leave the Nebaj station around 6am. Regular microbuses now connect Nebaj to Cotzal and Chajul. In Nebaj, head to the corner of Calzada 15 de Septiembre and 3a C., where all microbuses to Chajul and Cotzal pass by. The destination of the microbus is usually painted on the bus; the driver's helper is usually screaming the destination as well. Buses to Chajul and Cotzal leave approximately every hr.; the same is true in the opposite direction. Once in Cotzal and Chajul, have the driver drop you off in the main square; here wait for a microbus back to Nebaj. Buses from Nebaj to Cotzal and Nebaj to Chajul (Q5); from Cotzal to Chajul (Q3).

Chajul and San Juan Cotzal, the towns that with Nebaj form the **Ixil Triangle,** are set in the stunning hills of the Cuchumatanes. Though out of the way, the strong sense of tradition and natural beauty in both of these towns make them worth a visit. New paved roads connect all three towns of the Ixil Triangle, making getting from one to another very easy.

CHAJUL

The most remote of the three towns, Chajul is composed mostly of smoke-filled, adobe homes. Women weave their fantastic *trajes* in front of these huts. In the plaza, the colonial church, **Iglesia de San Gaspar,** is relatively bare inside. Still, there are two notable elements: the trough of fire in the aisle, devoted to the assassinated Father José María Gran, and the gold-plated altar of Christ of the Golgotha, for whom a pilgrimage is made on the second Friday of Lent. Two angels stand guard on either side of the altar wearing the traditional Nebaj male dress. Many of the other religious figurines inside the church are also colorfully dressed in traditional Ixil garb. The artfully carved wood at the main entrance displays fine Mayan designs.

Market days are a sight to be seen, with people from all three villages meeting to buy and sell local wares in Chajul's plaza. Occasionally men will wear their white pants and blue sash *trajes:* women always wear their colorful blue *huipiles* and *pom-pom* head wraps.

If you are staying the night in Chajul, head to the **Posada Vetz K'aol** ❷ (☎7765 6114), a 5-10 minute walk south of the plaza (follow signs). Located in a converted clinic, this old building has comfortable rooms and a friendly staff (singles Q80). Alternatively, some travelers opt to stay with families who rent out beds in their houses.

SAN JUAN COTZAL

Along the road that branches away from to Chajul sits San Juan Cotzal. Larger, more developed, and closer to Nebaj, Cotzal remains a tranquil, traditional town set in a rolling green valley. The town's central plaza is picturesque, with flower-covered pergolas and fountains decorating the area in front of the whitewashed Catholic church on the east side of the plaza. Cotzal celebrates its patron saint with a festival the week of June 24. The festival features religious ceremonies and costumed dances in the afternoon.

For those who are spending the night in Cotzal, the **Hotel El Maguey** ❶ (☎5789 1009), across from the police station and up from the left side of the church, rents clean, basic rooms (singles Q45). Communal bathrooms are clean and have hot water; the *comedor* downstairs serves great *comida típica.* As in Chajul, some families offer the option of renting out a bed in their home.

QUETZALTENANGO

Quetzaltenango is more commonly known as Xela (SHAY-lah), meaning "under the 10" in reference to the ten mountain gods believed to inhabit the peaks surrounding the city. Xela is the largest and most important city in Guatemala's Western Highlands, lying at the intersection of major roads from the capital, the Pacific coast, and Mexico. Aside from the often bitter-cold evenings, it's a pleasant place, with polite locals, interesting architecture, and an increasingly cosmopolitan nightlife. There isn't a whole lot to see in town beyond the well-maintained *parque central*, but daytrips into the surrounding countryside promise hot springs, rugged volcanic peaks, and colorful markets.

TRANSPORTATION

Quetzaltenango is easily accessible from cities throughout Guatemala. In addition to being connected to various parts of the country via **chicken bus** and **microbus,** there are also many tourist agencies that provide **shuttles** to various destinations. The **Minerva Bus Terminal,** the main terminal located in the northwest corner of the city, sends chicken buses and microbuses to: **Chichicastenango** (2½hr., every hr., Q12); **Guatemala City** (4½hr., every 30min., Q25; stops in **Chimaltenango** (Q20), where buses connect to Antigua); **Huehuetenango** (2½hr., every 30min., Q15); **La Mesilla** (4hr., every hr., Q20); **Momostenango** (1½hr., every hr., Q8; stops in **San Francisco El Alto** (Q6) and **Cuatro Caminos** (Q5)); **Panajachel** (2½hr, every 2 hr., Q15); and **Retalhuleu** (1½hr., every 30min., Q10). Microbuses shuttle people from **Zona 1** (6a C. and 14 Av. A) to the Minerva Bus Terminal regularly for Q1.25. There are other intracity microbus routes, but most travelers stay within Zona 1 and the bus terminal.

ORIENTATION AND PRACTICAL INFORMATION

Quetzaltenango follows the mighty Guatemalan Grid. The **Parque Centroamérica,** the *parque central,* at the center of town in **Zona 1,** is bordered by 11 Av. on the east, 12 Av. on the west, 4 C. to the north, and 7 C. to the south. Walk a few blocks east or west of the *parque* and you'll find "diagonals" thrown into the mix. Most hotels, restaurants and services can be found in

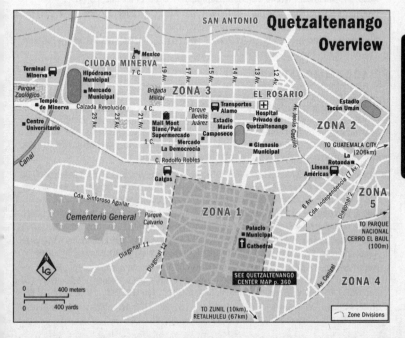

SAN ANTONIO **Quetzaltenango Overview**

Terminal Minerva
Parque Zoológico
Templo de Minerva
Centro Universitario

CIUDAD MINERVA
Mexico
Hipódromo Municipal
Mercado Municipal
Calzada Revolución
7 C.
ZONA 3
Brigada Militar
Mall Mont Blanc/Paiz Supermercado
Parque Benito Juárez
Mercado La Democrocía
1 C.
C. Rodolfo Robles

Transportes Alamo
Estadio Mario Camposeco

EL ROSARIO
Hospital Privado de Quetzaltenango
Gimnasio Municipal

Estadio Tecún Umán
ZONA 2

TO GUATEMALA CITY (206km)
La Rotonda
Líneas Américas

Galgos

Cda. Sinforoso Aguilar
Cementerio General
Parque Calvario

ZONA 1
Palacio Municipal
Cathedral

Diagonal 11
Diagonal 12

6 Av.
Cda. Independencia (7 Av.)
Diagonal 2

ZONA 5

TO PARQUE NACIONAL CERRO EL BAUL (100m)

Av. Central
ZONA 4

SEE QUETZALTENANGO CENTER MAP p. 360

0 400 meters
0 400 yards

TO ZUNIL (10km), RETALHULEU (67km)

Zone Divisions

SEE QUETZALTENANGO CENTER MAP p. 360

WESTERN HIGHLANDS

Zona 1 near the *parque*. The **Minerva Bus Terminal**, the second-class bus station, is in **Zona 3,** northwest of the city center. If you arrive here, walk straight through the bustling **market** and then across an empty lot to the street on the other side. Any of the city buses heading to the left will take you to the *parque central* (Q1.25; buses marked *parque*.)

Tourist Office: INGUAT, 11-35 C. de las Animas (☎7761 4931; www.visitguateamala. com), on the south side of the *parque central*. Open M-F 9am-4pm, Sa 9am-1pm. Many brochures and business cards for hotels and Spanish schools in Xela.

Tours and Agencies: Adrenalina Tours, 13 Av. 4-25 (☎7761 4509; www.adrenalina-tours.com), inside the Pasaje Enriquez. Shuttle services to many Guatemalan cities (Antigua Q210, Coban Q330, Panajachel Q125, Chichicastenango Q140). Twice daily round-trip shuttles to and from the Fuentes Georginas Q50. V.

Bank:Banrural, 12a Av. 5-2A, on the east side of the *parque central*. Open M-F 9am-7pm and Sa 9am-1pm.

Beyond Tourism: Miguel Angel Asturias Spanish School, 8a C. 16-23 (☎7765 3707; www.spanishschool.com). 1-on-1 instruction. Volunteer opportunities. **Sakribal Spanish School,** 6a C. 7-42 (☎7763 0717; www.sakribal.com), 3 blocks east of the *parque central*. Spanish instruction, homestays, and cultural activities such as field trips to local attractions.

Laundromat: Rapi-Servicio Laundromat, 7a C. 13-25a, less than 2 blocks from the *parque central*. Laundry Q22 per 4 kg. Cash only.

Police: 14a Av. (☎7765 4990 or 7761 0042), in the Hospital Antiguo.

24hr. Pharmacy: Farmacia Batres, 10a Av. and 6a C. (☎7761 4531). Open daily 8:30am-7:30pm. AmEx/D/MC/V.

Hospital: Hospital Privado Sagrada Familia, 13 Av. 5-38 (☎7763 2344).

Internet Access: The Buddha, 7a C. (☎4087 9751), between 12 and 13 Av., off the south end of the *parque central*. Q5 per hour. Cash only.

Post Office:El Correo, 4a C. 15-07 Zona 1 (☎7761 2671). Open M-F 8:30am-5:30pm, Sa 9am-1pm. **Postal Code:** 09001.

ACCOMMODATIONS

Hotels of all price ranges have cropped up around the city center, catering to the increasing number of students and travelers passing through Xela. Most are quite reasonable and are located within a few blocks of the *parque central*. Weekends tend to be busiest, when crowds of new Spanish language students wait for homestay assignments. Xela can be cool and damp at night; ask for hot water and extra blankets. All hotels listed are in Zona 1.

Black Cat Hostal, 13 Av. 3-33 (☎7765 8951; www.blckcathostels.net). Young travelers won't be disappointed by a stay at this very popular hostel. Dorms are social, comfortable, and cleaned daily. Laundry Q30. Breakfast included. Free Wi-Fi. Dorms Q60; private rooms Q120. ❷

Hostal Don Diego, 6a C. 15-12 (☎5308 5106 or 1489). Clean and comfortable rooms. Dorms feel a bit cramped when full. Breakfast included. Free Wi-Fi. Dorms Q40. Cash only. ❶

Villa de Don Andrés, 13 Av. 6-16 (☎7761 2014 or 5557 8313). Spacious rooms with private bath and cable TV. Rooms surround a beautiful courtyard. Singles Q80. AmEx/D/MC/V. ❷

Hotel Modelo, 14 Av. A 2-31 (☎7761 2529 or 7763 1376). An upscale option. Rooms are tastefully furnished with private bathrooms, cable TV, and closets. Picturesque courtyard and adjoining restaurant. Breakfast included. Singles Q318; doubles Q380. AmEx/D/MC/V. ❺

Hotel Altense, 9a C. 8-48 (☎7765 4648 or 7761 2811). Quiet rooms around a peaceful courtyard. Singles Q75; doubles Q120. AmEx/D/MC/V. ❷

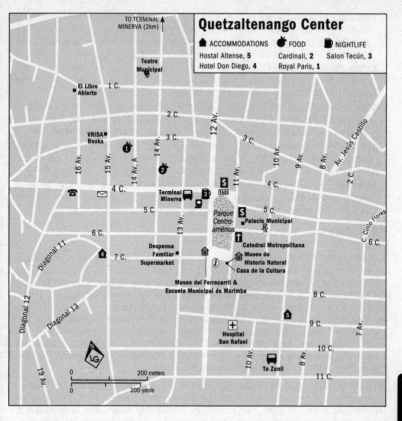

Quetzaltenango Center

🏠 ACCOMMODATIONS   🍎 FOOD   🍷 NIGHTLIFE

Hostal Altense, **5**   Cardinali, **2**   Salon Tecún, **3**
Hotel Don Diego, **4**   Royal Paris, **1**

TO TERMINAL
MINERVA (2km)

Teatro Municipal

El Libro Abierto   1 C.

2 C.

VRISA Books   3 C.

16 Av.   15 Av.   14 Av. A   14 Av.   12 Av.

❶

❷

4 C.

5 C.

Terminal Minerva

13 Av.   11 Av.

❸   TAXI

$

$

Parque Centro-américa

Palacio Municipal   ℞

Catedral Metropolitana

Despensa Familiar Supermarket   7 C.

❹   6 C.

Museo de Historia Natural
Casa de la Cultura

Museo del Ferrocarril &
Escuela Municipal de Marimba

3 C.   10 Av.   9 Av.   8 Av.   Av. Jesús Castillo

4 C.   2 C.

5 C.

C. Cirilo Flores   6 C.

Diagonal 11   Diagonal 12   Diagonal 13

8 C.

❺   9 C.

Hospital San Rafael

10 Av.   8 Av.   7 Av.

10 C.

To Zunil

11 C.

19 Av.

N

0   200 meters
0   200 yards

Guest Houses El Puente, 15 Av. 6-75 (☎7761 4292). No-frills rooms. Communal kitchen space. Singles Q40, with private bath Q50; doubles Q80/100. V. ❶

Hotel Occidental, 7a C. 12-23 (☎7765 4069). Simple rooms (some without windows) are clean and well-kept with private baths. Singles Q70; doubles Q120. Cash only. ❷

🍴 FOOD

Xela's affordable *típico* is supplemented by fast-food joints and a thriving cafe and bar scene that caters to the entire community. Most upscale places have both international and local offerings. All listed restaurants are in Zona 1.

▨ **Royal Paris,** 14 Av. A 3-06 (☎7761 1942). The menu of this elegant yet laid-back French restaurant quickly reveals its sophistication; try the *camembert* (Q43) or the house special trout *a la Florentine* (Q95). For a quick bite, the sandwiches (*croque monsieur* Q35) will satisfy. Quetzalteco special Q69. Live jazz on Sa night. Open M 6-11pm, Tu-Sa noon-11pm, Su noon-10pm. AmEx/D/MC/V. ❸

Pasaje El Mediterraneo, Pasaje Enriquez (☎5515 6724). Tapas dishes (Q35-60) make for good appetizers. Entrees Q80-120. Mixed drinks Q40. Open Tu-Su 4pm-midnight. AmEx/D/MC/V. ❹

Cardinali, 14 Av. 3-25 (☎7761 0924 or 7761 0922; www.restaurantecardinali.com). Walls covered in wine bottles and Italian flags attest to this restaurant's attempt create an authentic Italian experience. Diverse pizza toppings include mozzarella, walnuts, and asparagus. Small pizzas Q25-40, larges Q50-75. V. Open daily from noon-10pm. ❷

Coffee Company (☎2454 4330). Sophisticated sandwich menu, delicious crepes, and great ambience. Try their caramel latte (Q18) and pair it with a banana-Nutella crepe (Q20). Free Wi-Fi. Open M-Sa 7am-9pm and Su 3-9pm. Cash only.❷

Time, 12 Av. 4-52 (☎7768 3467). Sandwiches and hamburgers are a good bet at this restaurant and bar. The *desayuno típico* (Q37) makes for a satisfying morning meal. Mixed drinks Q20-30. F Ladies Night 8-10:30pm. Open M and Th-Su 8am-11pm, Tu-W 8am-8pm. V. ❸

The Buddha, 7a C. between 12 and 13 Av. (☎4087 9751). Strong coffee makes a delicious partner for fresh quiche (Q20). Free Wi-Fi. Internet Q5 per hour. Tu night 2-for-1 mojitos Q15. Th night Karaoke. Open M-Sa 10am-11:30pm, Su 10:30am-10:30pm. Cash only. ❷

Maya Cafe, 13 Av. 5-90 (☎7761 0606). *Comedor*-style restaurant with local cuisine at good prices. Breakfast available all day. Lunch of the day Q18. Open M-F 7am-7:30pm, Sa 7:30am-6pm, Su 8am-4pm. Cash only. ❷

👁 SIGHTS

PARQUE CENTROAMÉRICA. No matter how many central plazas you have seen on your trip to Guatemala, Xela's Parque Centroamérica does not fail to impress. With stunning Neo-classical architecture on all sides and beautiful landscaping and fountains throughout, this is the perfect place to relax and take in the surroundings. A three-sided sign on the west side of the *parque* gives a comprehensive description of this historical plaza. On the east side of the *parque* presides the **Municipalidad,** a stately structure built in 1897. There's a courtyard inside the main entrance. The first Sunday of each month explodes with the commotion of traditional clothing, outdoor concerts, and impromptu street performances.

MUSEO DE HISTORIA NATURAL. Located in the Casa de la Cultura, the collection includes a few Maya artifacts, ceramics, and a collection of soda bottles from throughout the ages. Don't miss the traditional **funeral urn.** Legend has it that a small donation to the urn can bring good luck. The strange collection of deceased animals (some with strange deformities) is entertaining, to say the least. Though the exhibits don't have the most polished displays, this charming museum is certainly worth checking out. *(On the southern side of the Parque Centroamérica. Open M-F 8am-noon and 2-6pm. Q6.)*

TEATRO MUNICIPAL. This beautiful Neo-classical structure hosts sporadic performances of traditional music and dance; call ahead or consult the tourist office for a show schedule. On a clear day, come enjoy the stunning views of the Volcán Santa Maria in the distance. *(1a C. in between 14 Av. and 14 Av. "A".)*

📷🎵 NIGHTLIFE AND ENTERTAINMENT

Unlike its neighbors in the Western Highlands, Xela will not fail to impress those seeking something to do after the sun sets. Many cafes are open late and play live music most nights. Travelers looking for a rowdier evening can choose from a wide selection of places where they can dance salsa all night.

Salon Tecun, inside Pasaje Enriquez, between 12 and 13 Av., just off the *parque central.* The perfect place to start an evening out in Xela. Bar food is cheap and tasty (*hamburguesa simple,* Q23). Beer Q35 per L. Cuba Libre Q14. Open daily from 8am-1pm. AmEx/D/MC/V.

La Parranda, 14 Av. 4-41 (☎5535 6163), down 7a C. to the west of the *parque central*. Devoted clientele flocks here for free salsa lessons (W 9pm). Reasonably priced drinks. Cover Sa-Su Q15-20. Open Tu-Sa 7pm-1am.

Ojalá, 15 Av. A 3-33 (☎7763 0206). Hookah and bean-bags make Ojalá a great place to start or end the night. Open Tu-Sa 5pm-1am, Su noon-10pm.

El Cuartito, 13 Av. 7-09 (☎7765 8835), 1 block from the *parque central*. Popular cafe during the day, happening bar with live music. Mango mojito Q18. Open M and W-Sa 11am-11pm, Su 11am-10pm. Cash only.

La Rumba, 13 Av. between 6a and 7a C. (☎4034 7431), next door to the Dispensa Familiar. The place to be for non-stop dancing F and Sa night. Drinks Q15-25. Th reggae and hip-hop night. Open Tu-Sa 7pm-1am.

Pool and Beer, 12 Av. 10-21 (☎4301 6560 or 7765 8916), 3 blocks south of the *parque central*. What you see is what you get at this happening bar. Drinks Q20. Open Tu-Sa 5pm-12am. Cash only.

▊ DAYTRIPS FROM QUETZALTENANGO

ZUNIL AND FUENTES GEORGINAS

Buses run to Zunil from 9 Av., 10 C., Zona 1 in Xela (20min., every 30min. until 6:30pm, Q2). To get to Fuentes Georginas from Zunil, hire one of the pickups that wait in the parque across from the church (20min., Q25-40 for up to 8 people). Adrenalina tours also offers trips to Fuentes Georginas (Q70). The tours begin at 9am and 2pm and tour guides are happy to stop in Zunil for some sight-seeing. Some opt to do the 8km uphill climb on foot. Fuentes (hot springs) open M-Sa 8am-5:30pm, Su 7am-5pm. In low season Q20, in high season Q25. Cooperative open M-Sa 8:30am-5pm, Su 2-5pm.

For a great daytrip from Xela, strike out to the picturesque town of Zunil. Tucked in a lush river valley about 8km southeast of the city, Zunil is just a short distance away from the nearby hot springs of Fuentes Georginas. Zunil's immense white church is delicately crafted both inside and out. The town is also noted for its idol **Maximón,** also known as San Simón. Just as in the town of Santiago Atitlán on Lake Atitlán (p. 73), the saint lives on through a life-sized icon who moves from house to house. His outfits are changed by the towns-people every two days—one of the trendiest includes a cowboy hat, red bandana, and sunglasses. The **Cooperative Tejedoras Santa Ana,** half a block down the steep hill to your left as you face the church, was founded in 1970 and employs more than 500 Quiché Mayan women as seamstresses. Near the square is an indoor market selling the locally produced woven goods (new headscarves Q350, used Q100).

A stunning 15min. ride (8km, or 1.5hr. walk) into the green hills overlooking Zunil brings you to the idyllic **Fuentes Georginas.** Shrouded in mist, the hot springs sit in a steep and narrow gorge with hanging tropical vegetation. Relax in one of five steaming pools, the largest of which features a pool-side restaurant and bar. Shelves and lockers for possessions are located near the main pool, but be sure to bring your own lock. It is possible to stay overnight in a *cabaña* (singles Q90; doubles Q120). The 30min. trek up to the steam vents, in the hills above the pools, makes for an interesting side-trip before or after your bath. The climb takes you through lush green arbor; at the top you can see huge vats of sulfur steaming up from the mountainside. The hike starts from the main road leading to the Fuentes, about 20m before the entrance on the left. The trail is unmarked, so it's best to ask one of the guards to show you where the hike begins. Rain gear is highly recommended. Robberies have occurred in the area; take a guide along for the hike.

VOLCÁN SANTA MARÍA

The hike starts from Llanos del Pinal, which is served by buses from Xela's Minerva terminal every hr. 5am-6pm. However, most tour agencies will pick you up from your hostel and guide you for the whole experience. Most tours leave very early (4am-5am). The hike up is 5hr., the descent about 3hr. Take note that most tour agencies have a minimum amount of people that they will lead, and the price adjusts accordingly. Ask around at your hostel if you need some fellow hikers.

Visible from downtown Quetzaltenango on a clear day, the inactive Volcán Santa María (3772m) forms a perfect cone 10km southwest of the city. The climb to the top is rigorous and sweaty, but well worth it for the view of the whole valley. As the unmarked trail is confusing at times, and is the site of occasional robberies, *Let's Go* does not recommend hiking here alone. Adrenalina Tours and Altiplano's Tours lead trips regularly (both Q100). It is possible to do it as a long daytrip from Xela, but watching the sun rise is well worth hauling along some camping gear. The weather tends to be cold and wet; arm yourself with lots of water, warm clothes, and rain gear.

TOTONICAPÁN

Buses and microbuses for Totonicapan leave Xela from the Minerva Bus Terminal (45min., every 30min., Q15). Return buses leave from the Toto bus terminal at the end of 3 C.

Totonicapan, or Toto for short, is a small district capital in the heart of one of the highlands' most heavily populated areas. Famous for its insurgent rebellions, the most recent in August 2001, the town is usually peaceful and quiet. Today it is a center of commercial weaving, producing much of the jasped clothing used in traditional dress. Workshops are scattered throughout the town and are open to the public, making Toto an excellent place to view weavers in action. Guides (Q50-100) and maps (Q5) are available at the **Casa de Cultura** near the bus terminal (☎7766 1517).

MOMOSTENANGO

An hour north of Xela, in the heart of Guatemala's wool-growing region, Momostenango's popular market sells—you guessed it—inexpensive woolen goods. Market days (Wednesdays and Sundays) are definitely the days to visit the otherwise unexciting city of Momostenango. The town is also famed for its natural open-air *riscos*, clay formations that usually only form in underground caves. Mayan tradition is particularly strong in Momo, as evidenced by the Mayan altar (often burning with incense) located just across the plaza from the Catholic church in the center of town. Many residents of Momo still abide by the *Tzolkin* calendar, which dates back to ancient times.

◨ TRANSPORTATION

Buses for Momostenango depart from **Cuatro Caminos** (1¼hr., every hr., Q6), **San Francisco El Alto** (1hr., every hr., Q5), and **Quetzaltenango** (1½hr., every hr., Q8).

◨▧ ORIENTATION AND PRACTICAL INFORMATION

All buses and microbuses arriving in Momostenango will let you off near the **parque central.** Most of what you will need is located in the center of town. Momo has two main plazas: the *parque* and the square in front of the

Catholic church, which fill to the brim on market days. The town is laid out on a typical grid of *calles* (east-west) and *avenidas* (north-south), making it easy to navigate.

Bank: Banco Reformador, 1a C. 1-73. (☎7733 6095), one block from the *parque central.* **ATM.** Open M-F 9am-5pm, Su 8am-noon.

Police (☎110), 4 blocks up 1a Av. from the *parque central.*

Pharmacy: Farmacias de la Comunidad, 1a C. 1-020 (☎4518 6141 or 5939 9341), across from the Banco Reformador. Open 24hr.

Internet Access: Cafe Net, 1a C., across from Banco Reformador. Internet Q6 per hr. Wi-Fi available. Open daily 9am-7pm.

▐ ACCOMMODATIONS

Few travelers opt to spend the night in Momo, but if you do find yourself in need of a place to sleep, these two budget options will get the job done.

▨ **Hospedaje Paglóm,** 1a C. (☎4257 8206), up the block from the central plaza. This centrally-located hotel is your best bet in Momostenango. Clean rooms and well-maintained communal bathrooms. Singles Q25. Cash only. ❶

Hospedaje Posada de Doña Pelagia (☎7736 5175). Signs for this hostel are visible from the plaza in front of the Catholic church. Very basic rooms. Showers Q10. Singles Q15. Cash only. ❶

▐ FOOD

▨ **Natalia's Cafe,** on the *parque central.* For a dose of gringo cuisine, head here. Hamburgers (Q20) and pizza (Q20-30) are decent and reasonably priced. Open daily 8am-7pm. Cash only. ❷

Comedor Paglóm, 1a C. and 2a Av. (☎4257 8206), on the ground floor of the Hospedaje Paglóm. Solid bet for *comida típica.* Open daily 8am-8pm. Cash only. ❶

HUEHUETENANGO

With fewer than 30,000 inhabitants, Huehue (WAY-way) is an inviting small city with welcome comforts like ice cream and real milk. Though there's not much to do here, it's a nice stopover on the way to or from the Mexican border. Huehue began as a suburb of Zaculeu, the capital of the Mam, an indigenous Mayan people. Since the Spanish conquest, Huehuetenango has witnessed a couple of minor silver rushes and a region-wide coffee boom. The mineral has since petered out, but coffee still holds its own here.

▐ TRANSPORTATION

Huehuetenango is an important transportation hub for the Western highlands. As such, it is easily accessible from cities as far as Antigua and Cobán. Most traveling to and from the city do so by **chicken bus** or **microbus.** Shuttles can be arranged by agencies such as Adrenalina Tours.

Buses: The **bus terminal** is 2km outside of town. From here, buses depart to **Guatemala City** (5hr., every hr., Q25). Use this bus to transfer to **Antigua** (4hr., transfer at Chimaltenango), **Chichicastenango** (3hr., transfer at Los Encuentros) or **Panajachel** (3hr., transfer at Los Encuentros). Buses also leave for **Quetzaltenango** (2hr., every hr., Q20) and **Todos Santos Cuchumatán** (2hr., every hr., Q25), although microbuses departing every 2hr. from El Calvario make the trip for the same price.

Taxis: in the *parque central* or at the intersection of 3a C. and 7a Av.

▓▓ ▓ ORIENTATION AND PRACTICAL INFORMATION

Huehue adheres to Guatemala's grid system. The **parque central** is in **Zona 1**, bounded by **2 C.** on the north, **3 C.** on the south, **4 Av.** on the east, and and **5 Av.** on the west. Most services, hotels, and restaurants are located within a few blocks of the *parque central*. Buses pull into the well laid-out station about 2km outside of town.

Tours and Agencies: Adrenalina Tours, 4 C. 6-54 (☎7768 1538; www.adrenalinatours. com), in Zone 1. Offers tours to Todos Santos Cuchumatanes and multi-day packages to places like Rio Chixoy and Laguna Braba. Horseback riding packages in the countryside around Huehuetenango. Shuttle service from Huehuetenango to Nebaj Q164 (US$20), Coban Q247 (US$30), Quetzaltenango Q164 (US$20), Antigua Q330 (US$40), Guatemala City Q410 (US$50), and other cities.

Bank: G&T Continental Bank, 2a C. 4-66, on the northwest corner of the *parque central*. Open M-F 8am-8pm, Sa 8am-1pm. **ATM** outside.

Beyond Tourism: Xinabajul Spanish School, 4a Av. 14-14 (☎7764 6631 or 5326 6525), in Zone 5. 1-on-1 teaching with homestay and volunteer opportunities.

Police (☎7764 1465).

Pharmacy: Farmacia Batres, 6a Av. 3-21 (☎7768 1354 or 7768 1499), in Zone 1. Open 24hr.

Hospital: Hospital de Especialidades, 5a Av. (☎7764 1414), in between 6a C. and 7a C.

Internet Access: Génesis Internet, 6a C. (☎7762 7820), across from Doña Estercita. Internet Q5 per hr. Open M-Sa 9am-7pm.

Post Office: 2a C. 3-51 (☎7764 1123). Open M-F 8:30am-5:30pm, Sa 9am-1pm.

▓ ACCOMMODATIONS

Huehuetenango has accommodations in all shapes and sizes, whether you're looking for a nice hotel or just a bed to crash on. Most places to stay in Huehue are centered around the **parque central** in Zona 1, though there are also budget accommodations located close to the bus terminal, 2km outside of the town center. Accommodations in Zona 1, though slightly more expensive, tend to be nicer and safer than those near the terminal.

▨ **Hotel Zaculeu** (☎7764 1086 or 1575), ½ block from the *parque central*. Spacious and beautifully furnished rooms with private bath and cable TV. Free Wi-Fi. Singles Q120; doubles Q225; triples Q300. V. ❸

Hotel La Sexta (☎7764 6612 or 7559), several blocks south of the *parque central*. Comfortable, if slightly underfurnished, rooms for reasonable prices. Rooms are clean and include private baths and cable TV. Singles Q60; doubles Q120. Cash only. ❷

Hotel Vasquez (☎7764 1338), 2 blocks west of the *parque central*. Singles Q100; doubles Q175. Cash only. ❸

Todos Santos Inn, 2a C. (☎5726 3301). An excellent budget option. Singles Q50, with private bath Q60; doubles Q80/100. Cash only. ❷

Hotel Gobernador (☎7769 0765), 1 block east of the *parque central*. Simple rooms with private bath and TV do the trick. Singles Q60; doubles Q100. Cash only. ❷

Hotel Imperial, 4a C. (☎5194 8295), a few doors down from the restaurant Mi Tierra. Comfortable, spacious rooms. Singles Q60; doubles Q80. Cash only. ❷

FOOD

Excellent local options abound in Huehue. Make sure to grab yourself a cup of joe when in town: the Huehue blend is one of Guatemala's finest. Market days on Thursday and Sunday are ideal for stocking up on fresh fruits and vegetables.

La Cabaña de Cafe, 2a C. 6-50 (☎7764 8903). Charming cafe modeled after a log cabin. Impressive selection of coffee and espresso drinks (Q6-15) alongside great sandwiches (Q20-30) and hard-to-pass-up crepes (Q10-15). Open M-Sa 8am-9pm. AmEx/MC/V. ❷

Doña Estercita, 2a C. 6-40 (☎7764 2212). This *cafeteria y pasteleria* is sure to satisfy your sweet tooth. Desserts range from apple pie (Q10) to cakes of all shapes and sizes. Quesadillas Q10. Open daily from 7am-9pm. Cash only. ❶

Mi Tierra, 4a C. 6-46 (☎7764 1473). A great place to take a break from the busy streets of Huehue. Try the Mexican-style fajitas (Q20) or the fries with your choice of toppings (Q15-25). Open M-Sa 7am-9pm, Su 2-9pm. Cash only. ❷

Le Kaf, 6a C. (☎7764 3202 or 7764 0598). The pizza-soda-mixed drink special (Q32) is perfect for travelers on a budget. Marimba Th and Sa-Su. Live music W and F. Pizza Q35-45. Mixed drinks Q18-30. Free Wi-Fi. Open daily 10am-11pm. V. ❸

Cafe Jardín, 3a C. and 6a Av. (☎7769 0769). For breakfast all day or some delicious *comida típica,* head to Cafe Jardín. *Plato típico huehueteco* Q44. Lunch specials M-Sa Q22. Open daily 6am-10:30pm. Cash only. ❸

SIGHTS

ZACULEU. About 3km west of Huehuetenango lies the ancient Maya site of Zaculeu. This was once the capital of the Mam people. Long ruled by the Quiché, the Mam became independent just as the Spanish rolled into town. When an army led by Gonzalo de Alvarado met the Mam on the battlefield, the Mam took one look at the fearsome Iberians, riding animals they had never seen, and retreated to their base. The temples, plaza, and ball court in Zaculeu were fortified on three side. Still the modern Spanish weapons proved to be too much; after a few months of battle the Mam were forced to surrender for lack of food. In 1946, the United Fruit Company sponsored the restoration of Zaculeu. As a result, Zaculeu is not what you'd expect from ancient ruins. Here, original stones are slathered in stucco, jungle vines are scarce, and the temples are free of rubble. Still, Zaculeu

ON THE MENU

FURTHER SOUTH OF THE BORDER

Cuisine from "south of the border" (Mexico) has become popular not only with the country's neighbor to the north, but around the world. From China to Finland, South Africa to New Zealand, words like "taco," "enchilada," and "tamale" evoke images of delectable, spicy Mexican fare. Try to order the same dishes in Guatemala and you'll get a quick reminder that you're south of a very different border.

Guatemalans and other Central Americans use many of the same culinary terms as Mexicans, but Guatemalans use different ingredients and methods of preparation. Guatemalan cooks typically cook with corn rather than flour tortillas and place less importance on "spicy;" they also favor rice, plantains, and potatoes more often than their Mexican counterparts.

Think you know what a taco is? Guess again; in Guatemala they are corn tortillas rolled with meat and vegetable filling, deep-fried, and served with steamed cabbage and Guatemalan cheese. Quesadillas are far from the Mexican variety; instead they're spongy, cheesy cupcakes served as a treat to deserving children. Eating a Guatemalan enchilada, you might be surprised to stumble across ingredients like hard-boiled egg, tomato sauce, and even pickled beets!

remains a beautiful place to visit, with the Cuchumatan Mountains looming in the background. *(Located 3km outside of Huehue. Microbuses to the ruins leave from the intersection of 3a C. and 7a Av.; they run approximately once every hr. (Q5). Alternatively, a taxi will take you roundtrip (from Q80). Ruins open daily 8am-4:30pm. Wheelchair-accessible. Limited parking is available outside of the ruins. Q50.)*

EL MIRADOR. If you have the time, be sure to head to El Mirador, a lookout point that provides stunning views of Huehue and the surrounding Cuchumatan Mountains. Though getting here takes a bit of time, El Mirador provides a great way to escape the bustle of the city. *(To get to El Mirador, head to El Calvario on 7a C. in the NE corner of the city, where all of the buses to the Cuchumatanes leave. Find a microbus heading to El Mirador (45min.; Q15) and hop on.)*

NIGHTLIFE AND ENTERTAINMENT

Kaktus Disco, 6a C. 6-38. Come to this Huehue staple to dance to latin, salsa, and electronic music. Open F-Sa 9pm-1am.

La Biblioteca, 6a C., next to the Kaktus Disco. This recently opened pub-sports bar is a great place to catch an afternoon game. Open Tu-Sa 2-11pm.

PACIFIC SLOPE

Guatemala's Pacific Slope is a sweltering plain that contrasts sharply with the mountain vistas of the highland region. Here, on fertile land divided into vast *fincas* (plantations), bountiful crops like sugarcane, bananas, and rubber make a vital contribution to the nation's economy. The Pacific Slope does not, however, usually make the tourist's hit list. The dusty inland trade towns tend to be busy but unappealing for visitors, and the black-sand coast is too often marred by trash and debris. There are exceptions: along the busy coastal highway between the Mexican border and Guatemala City, **Retalhuleu** is a pleasant town with the ruins of Abaj Takalik and a few beaches nearby. Farther east, as the coast makes its way toward the border, laid-back **Monterrico** captivates visitors with hammock-lined stretches of fine beach and a verdant nature reserve.

RETALHULEU

Reu (RAY-oo), as Retalhuleu (pop. 36,400) is concisely nicknamed, is a pleasant city on the Pacific slope. Buildings surrounding the *parque central* testify to Reu's colonial pretensions, from its stately neoclassical city hall to its snow-white church flanked by royal palms. Laid-back Reu is a logical stopover on the way to or from the Mexican border. Visit the Maya ruins of Abaj Tabalik, slide down fake ruins at the Xocomil water park, or take a trip to nearby Pacific beaches.

▐ TRANSPORTATION

Because Reu is just 5km southwest of El Zarco junction, where the coastal highway (CA2) meets the road to Quetzaltenango, there are plenty of buses heading toward the Mexican border and the Guatemalan highlands. Retalhuleu's main bus terminal, **La Galera,** is marked by food stands between 7 Av. and 8 on 10 C. To: **El Carmen** (2½hr., every hr., Q20); **Escuintla** (2½hr., every hr., Q20), transfer available to Antigua; **Guatemala City** (3½hr., every hr., Q25) via Escuintla; **Quetzaltenango** (1½hr., every hr., Q13) connections available to most destinations in the Western Highlands; **Tecún Umán** (1½hr., every 30 min., Q15). A second **bus terminal** a few blocks west of the *parque* serves **Champerico** and the coast. Grab a bus along 8 Av. and ask to be dropped off at the terminal (Q1) or take a taxi (Q10 from the main bus terminal). Walking from the park, follow 5 Av. until it runs into 2 C., turn left onto 6a Av., then right, and walk until you see parked buses.

▐ ▐ ORIENTATION AND PRACTICAL INFORMATION

Reu is organized on a grid with the *parque central* in the center. To reach the *parque central* from the main bus terminal, turn left on 7 Av., walk four blocks to 6 C., then turn right and go straight one block. The *parque* is bordered by 5 and 6 Av. and 5 and 6 C. Most services are near the *parque* or on 7 Av. between the bus stop and the center of town. Because the city is somewhat sprawling, you might want to hop in a *tuk-tuk*, which will take you wherever you need to go for Q5.

Tours and Agencies: REUXtreme and **REUXtours,** 4a C. 4-13 Zona 1 (☎7771 0443 or 5202 8180; www.reuxtreme.com or www.reuxtours.com), in the same facility as the

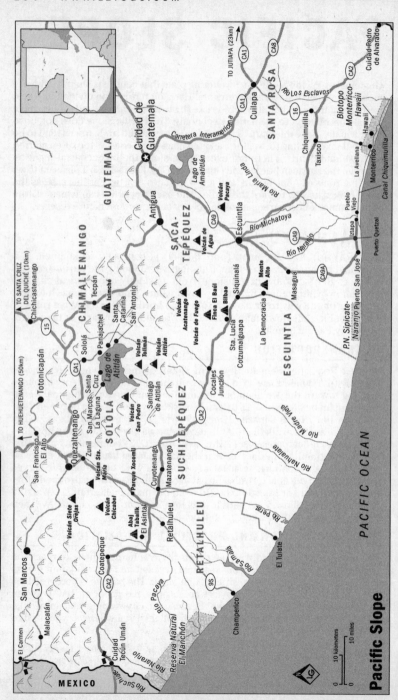

PACIFIC SLOPE

Pacific Slope

MEXICO

El Carmen
Malacatán
San Marcos
Cuidad Tecún Umán
Río Naranjo
Río Suchiate

1
Coatepeque
CA2
San Francisco El Alto
Quezaltenango
Zunil
Volcán Sta. María
Volcán Siete Orejas
Volcán Chicabel
Abaj Takalik
El Asintal
Parque Xocomil
Cuyotenango
Mazatenango
Retalhuleu
RETALHULEU

TO HUEHUETENANGO (50km)

Totonicapán
CA1
SOLOLÁ
San Marcos, Santa La Laguna
Santa Cruz
Lago de Atitlán
Volcán San Pedro
Santiago de Atitlán
Volcán Tolimán
Volcán Atitlán
Sololá
Panajachel
Santa Catarina
San Antonio

15
TO SANTA CRUZ DEL QUICHÉ (10km)
Chichicastenango
CHIMALTENANGO
Tecpán
Iximché

GUATEMALA
Antigua
Cuidad de Guatemala
Carretera Interamericana

SACA-TEPÉQUEZ
Volcán de Agua
CA9
Volcán Acatenango
Volcán de Fuego
Finca El Baúl
Bilbao
Siquinalá
Sta. Lucía Cotzumalguapa
La Democracia
Monte Alto
ESCUINTLA
Cocales Junction
CA2
SUCHITEPÉQUEZ

Champerico
El Tulate
Río Pacaya
Río Samalá
Río Icán
Reserva Natural El Manchón
95

Lago de Amatitlán
Volcán Pacaya
Escuintla
Río Michatoya
Río Naranjo
CA9
Masagua
CA9A
Puerto San José
P.N. Sipacate-Naranjo
Puerto Quetzal
Iztapa
Pueblo Viejo
Río Mate Vieja
Río Nahualate
Río Icán

PACIFIC OCEAN

SANTA ROSA
Cuilapa
CA1
CA8
TO JUTIAPA (23km)
Río Los Esclavos
Chiquimulilla
16
Taxisco
La Avellana
Monterrico
Pueblo Viejo
CA2
Ciudad Pedro de Alvarado
Biotopo Monterrico-Hawaii
Hawaii
Canal Chiquimulilla
Río María Linda

N
LG
0   10 kilometers
0   10 miles

Hostal Casa Santa Maria. Offers day tours of Abaj Takalik and Parque Xocomil, natural tours of the nearby mangrove reserves, kayaking and mountain biking, and shuttles to several Guatemalan cities, including Antigua, Chichi, Panajachel, and Xela.

Bank: Banco Agromercantil, 5a Av. on the *parque central*. Currency exchange inside. Open M-F 8:30am-7pm, Sa 9am-1pm. **ATM** outside.

Police: (☎7771 0120), on the *parque central*.

Pharmacy: Farmacia Las Palmas II, on the *parque central*. Open daily 8:30am-7:30pm.

Internet Access: Asys Computación (☎7771 5272), on the *parque central*. Q10 per hour. Open daily 8am-7pm. Cash only.

Post Office: El Correo, on the *parque central*. Open M-F 8:30am-5:30pm, Sa 9am-1pm.

ACCOMMODATIONS

Reu's tropical climate and proximity to the beach make it a prime vacation destination; its hotel offerings reflect this. Very few budget options exist, as the majority of hotels are nicer establishments geared towards families and older guests on vacation. Still, there are deals to be found, and some of the nicest places in town are quite reasonably priced.

Hostal Casa Santa Maria, 4a C.4-23 (☎7771 6136 or 5202 8180). Spacious and comfortable rooms, each with private bath, A/C, cable TV, and hot water. Free Wi-Fi. Parking available. Singles Q150; doubles Q225. V. ❺

Posada Don Jose, 5a C. 3-67 (☎7771 0180 or 7771 0841). Large rooms with private bath, hot water, A/C, and cable TV. Gym access and breakfast included. Free Wi-Fi. Singles Q332; doubles Q390. AmEx/D/MC/V. ❻

Hotel Modelo, 5a C. 4-53 (☎7771 0256). Well-priced alternative to the more upscale resort-style hotels nearby. Rooms are spacious with ceiling fans and private baths (though hot water is intermittent). Singles Q65; doubles Q90. Cash only. ❷

Hospedaje San Francisco, 6a C. 8-30. A budget option that might leave you wishing you hadn't opted for a budget option. Rooms are barebones, but they get the job done. Singles Q20, with fan Q30, with private bath Q50; doubles Q40/50/70. Cash only. ❶

FOOD

⌨Cafe Posada Don Jose, 5a C. 5-67 (☎7771 0180), in the Posada Don Jose. Excellent pasta dishes (Q60) and fresh seafood options (Q80-Q110) are only some of the diverse offerings at this lovely restaurant. Outdoor seating overlooks the beautiful hotel pool. Breakfast until 10:30am. Open 7:30am-10:30pm. AmEx/D/MC/V. ❹

Cafetería La Luna, 5 Av. and 5a C., on the *parque central*. Convenient spot to grab some *comida típica*. Always busy, in spite of the slew of *comedors* surrounding the *parque*. Lunch special Q20. Open daily 7:30am-10pm. Cash only. ❷

Restaurante El Patio, 5a C. If you're not immediately sold by the fact that the *almuerzo del día* is only Q12, then perhaps you'll be roped in by the hamburgers and sandwiches (Q10). The food won't disappoint, either. Open daily 7am-9:30pm. Cash only. ❶

SIGHTS

MUSEO DE ARQUEOLOGÍA Y ETNOLOGÍA. This musuem has a sizable collection of Mayan artifacts from the pre- to post-classical periods, and a rotating gallery with photographs of Reu's early history. *(On the parque central in the municipal building. Open Tu-Sa 8:30am-5:30pm, Su 9am-12:30pm.)*

NIGHTLIFE

Bar La Carreta, 5a C. 4-60 (☎7771 2559 or 0475), in the Hotel Astor. Sophisticated ambience with well-priced mixed drinks (Q30-40) and beer (Q20). A somewhat older crowd. Open Tu-Sa 5-10pm. AmEx/D/MC/V.

DAYTRIPS FROM RETALHULEU

ABAJ TAKALIK. Though only partially open and excavated, Abaj Takalik is one of the more interesting Mayan sites outside of Petén. The settlement, probably occupied between 800 BC and AD 900, once covered 9 sq. km. Today, you can see several temple platforms and a series of carved sculptures and stelae. *(From Reu, take a bus to El Asintal (45min., Q3) to the end of the line, which stops at the parque central. From there, it's a 4km walk continuing up the road, which will take you through a coffee plantation and to the ruins. Between 6am and 5pm there are pickups for hire near the parque that will take you to the site. Admission Q25, including guide. Tour companies offer round-trip shuttle service to and from the ruins, but at higher prices than the taxis at the parque.)*

PARQUE XOCOMIL. Sure, Abaj Takalik sounds kind of cool, but why bother with real ruins when you can dive into a "Maya-inspired" wave pool or speed slide? Parque Xocomil (pronounced SHOW-koh-meal) is a well-maintained, modern water park with theme slides and raft rides, food service, and locker rooms. This water park is the perfect way to cool down on one of Reu's hot, sticky days. *(15min. outside Reu; taxis will take you from the parque central. Alternatively, hop on a Xela-bound bus and ask the driver to drop you off. ☎7771 2673. Open daily 9am-5pm. Q75, children Q50.)*

THE COASTAL HIGHWAY. East of Retalhuleu, the highway passes Cuyotenango, where a side road runs 45km south to the nondescript beach of **El Tulate**. Further east on the highway are the towns of **Mazatenango** and **Cocales**. Buses from here run north to Santiago Atitlán and Panajachel. After another 23km, the coastal highway reaches **Santa Lucía Cotzumalguapa**, famous for its archaeological sites. Next up on the highway is run-down **Siquinalá**. A branch road serviced by a bus heads to the coast by way of La Democracia. The site of **Monte Alto** is east of La Democracia, but the town plaza houses its highlight: massive stone heads that may be as many as 4000 years old. Continuing all the way down to the coast from Siguinalá and La Democracia, you will arrive at **Sipacate**, located in the **Parque Natural Naranjo**. Sipacate is a more low-key, up-and-coming beach town with mangrove reserves and beautiful stretches of beach. Before winding its way to Guatemala City, the coastal highway from Retalhuleu runs though **Escuintla**, a transportation hub. From here, one road goes to **Taxisco**, a town en route to Monterrico and Guatemala's southernmost border with El Salvador. Another road runs to the large, scruffy beach "resort" of **Puerto San José** and the tiny beach town of **Iztapa**. Yet another road heads north to Antigua and Guatemala City.

MONTERRICO

If you have time to visit just one spot along the Pacific coast, this is the place to go. Separated from the mainland by the Chiquimulilla Canal and encircled by a mangrove swamp, Monterrico (pop. 1000) lives by the motto *"pura vida"* (literally, "pure life"). Its narrow stretch of black-sand beach and powerful surf are some of Guatemala's finest, drawing both fishermen and itinerant students. A sand shelf protects Monterrico from the rain, ensuring sunny, cloudless days.

The shelf also allows visitors to watch the frequent lightning storms a few kilometers offshore. So, grab a hammock and let the crashing waves of the Pacific lull you to sleep in relaxing Monterrico.

TRANSPORTATION

Getting to Monterrico by bus can be a bit tricky as it involves multiple transfers.

Buses: Buses from Guatemala City leave from the south-coast terminal at 8a Av. and 4a C. in Zona 12 (2½hr., 5 daily, Q20). Alternatively, you can take a bus bound for Iztapa or Puerto San Jose, and then transfer to a microbus heading to Monterrico. Buses depart from **Taxisco** (1 hr., every hr., Q10). These bus stop in **La Avellana,** where travelers can transfer to a ferry heading to Monterrico.

Ferries: Ferries connect Monterrico with **La Avellana** (40min., 8 per day, Q5). A ferry leaves Monterrico for La Avellana 30min. before each bus to Taxisco.

Microbuses: Most people opt to get to Monterrico on a microbus from Antigua. Travelers should book 1-2 days in advance, as these shuttles tend to fill up quickly. **Don Quijote Travel** (☎7832 7513), in Antigua, makes 2 trips to and from Monterrico each day. Departs from Antigua at 8am and 1pm; departs from Monterrico at 11am and 4pm; round-trip Q100.

ORIENTATION AND PRACTICAL INFORMATION

Monterrico has **one main road,** which begins at the *lancha* dock and ends at the beach. All of the town's hotels and restaurants are either on this street, along the beach, or set back one block from the beach. The higher-end hotels and restaurants tend to be located off of the main road. A street sign located where the main road hits the beach will point you in the direction of many hotels and restaurants. Though Monterrico is a fairly safe town, female travelers should exercise caution at night, particularly on the weekends. Check the town's website (www.monterrico-guatemala.com) for up-to-date information on lodging and tourist attractions.

Bank: There are no banks in Monterrico. **Super Monterrico,** just up from the beach on the main road, has an **ATM.** Open daily 8am-6pm.

Tourist Police: C. Principal (☎5551 4075).

Beyond Tourism: Proyecto Linguistico (www.monterrico-guatemala.com/spanish-school), on the main road, across the street from the internet cafe. One-on-one Spanish instruction. US$90 for 20 hr. AmEx/D/MC/V.

Post Office: C. Principal. Open M-F 8:30am-5:30pm, Sa 9am-1pm.

ACCOMMODATIONS

Hotels prices tend to rise dramatically on weekends, during the high season (July and August), and during Guatemalan holidays, especially *Semana Santa*. Make sure to get a room with mosquito netting, or bring your own. Most of the nicer accommodations in Monterrico are off the beaten path, so don't be afraid to explore a bit before settling down.

Hotel Brisas del Mar (☎5517 1142), 100m east of the main road. An unbeatable bargain for the amenities offered. Spotless rooms with private baths and fans are complemented by a beautiful pool and incredibly friendly staff. 2nd-floor restaurant and lounge area has hammocks and spectacular views of the ocean. Singles Q60. V. ❷

Hotel El Mangle (☎5514 6517 or 5490 1336). From the beach at the end of the main road, head to the left a few 100 meters. Beautiful hotel organized around a central courtyard. Rooms come with mosquito nets and fans. Pool and on-site restaurant. Singles Q200; doubles Q300. Discounts for groups. V. ⑤

Hotel Cafe del Sol (☎5810 0821), on the beach, 100m west of C. Principal. Breathtaking ocean views and comfortable rooms with private baths and fans. Singles Q200; doubles Q300. V. ⑥

Hotel El Delfin (☎5702 6701), on the beach, off of C. Principal. Popular with Guatemalans and backpackers. Simple accommodations with mosquito nets. Well-kept swimming pool and abundant hammocks. Decent *comedor* on-site. Singles M-F Q35, Sa-Su Q50. Cash only. ①

⬛ FOOD

If there's any place in Guatemala to order yourself a plate of fresh seafood, it's Monterrico. Though seafood dishes tend to be more expensive than the more common menu items, they are an incredible deal considering the freshness and the portion size offered at most places. *Comedor*-style restaurants line the main street; more upscale restaurants with international offerings grace the ocean-front. For groceries, visit **Super Monterrico**, located just up the main street from the beach (open daily 8am-6pm).

Taberna El Pelicano (☎5409 6775 or 4001 5885), 350m east of the C. Principal on the road that runs parallel to the beach. For a great meal at a reasonable price, dine under the huge thatched roof of Taberna El Pelicano in the company of the restaurant's impressive pet pelican. Fresh seafood dishes (fish filets Q75, jumbo shrimp entree Q110) are the main draw, but there are also delicious daily specials (Q65-Q75). Top off your meal with their homemade ice cream (Q20) or a frozen mixed drink (strawberry daiquiri Q28). Open W-Sa noon-2pm and 5:30-10pm, Su noon-3pm and 6-10pm. V. ④

Cafe del Sol (☎5810 0821; www.cafe-del-sol.com), in Hotel Cafe del Sol, 100m west of the main road. Stunning beachfront views and tasty entrees. Splurge on seafood (Q80-120) or feast on a hamburger with their special sauce (Q45, includes fries). Wash it down with a drink from their extensive mixed drink menu (Amaretto Sour, Q28). Open daily 7am-10pm. V. ③

Johnny's Place (☎5812 0409; www.johnnysplacehotel.com), across from El Pelicano. Johnny's Place, which doubles as a hotel, is a social and laid-back place to grab a tasty bite to eat. Hefty breakfast special Q35. Extensive panini selection (tuna panini Q35). Well-priced seafood entrees Q40-Q70. Mixed drink specials Q20-30. Open daily 7am-9:30pm. V. ③

⬛ NIGHTLIFE AND ENTERTAINMENT

El Animal Desconocido, on the beach. Beers and mixed drinks are well-priced (Q15). Try their signature drink, El Animal Desconocido, a sublime mixture of Malibu, milk, and cacao. Happy hour 8-10pm. Open daily 5pm-1am. Cash only.

El Punto Disco (☎4211 5201), next to Hotel El Marlin, 300m east of C. Principal. If a long day of lounging on the beach leaves you feeling energized, head to El Punto Disco to dance the night away. The DJ blasts Latin and electronic music. Reasonably-priced drink menu (beer Q15, mixed drinks Q15-Q25). Open Sa-Su 7pm-1am, later in summer. Cash only.

⬛ OUTDOOR ACTIVITIES AND BEACHES

Biotopo Monterrico-Hawaii. Established to protect three species of nesting sea turtles, Biotopo Monterrico-Hawaii encompasses 2800 hectares, including Monterrico and several smaller towns. In addition to housing thousands of birds, the Biotopo preserves one of Guatemala's last remaining mangrove swamps. Pole-pushed sunrise boat tours offer a chance to catch the animals in their natural habitat. Plus, you'll get to see a spectacular view of Volcán Tecuamburro. *(Iguanatours, off the main street and down the road across from the soccer field, arranges tours. 2hr. tour Q40.)*

Reserva Natural de Monterrico (CECON). This natural reserve offers an up close and personal view of iguanas, baby turtles, and caimans. The volunteers at the Reserva organize turtle races to the sea every Saturday morning during the hatching season (September and November). The lucky winner gets a free dinner for two at the local restaurant of their choice. *(Next to the Hotel Baule Beach. Open 8am-noon and 2-5pm. Q8, Guatemalans Q3.)*

BORDER WITH EL SALVADOR

Chiquimulilla and **Taxisco** are the best places to catch a ride to the border (45min., every hr. 5am-5pm, Q10). If you're entering Guatemala at this border crossing, **buses** head toward Guatemala City via Chiquimulilla and Taxisco. Pullman buses run (4hr., every 30min. 9am-4pm, Q30) as do 2nd-class buses (4½hr., every hr. 6am-3:30pm, Q15). Taxisco is the transfer point for Monterrico. On the El Salvador side, frequent buses run to Sonsonate. The **immigration office** is open daily 6am-10pm.

The bustling crossroad of **Ciudad Pedro de Alvarado** sits at Guatemala's southernmost border crossing with El Salvador, dominated by long-distance truckers on the Interamerican Highway and government officers. La Hachadura on the Salvadoran side provides easy access to Sonsonate, though it's not the most convenient way to reach San Salvador. Americans and Canadians must buy a US$10 tourist visa in El Salvador. At the border, street exchangers will change US dollars and quetzals. Keep a close eye on their calculations, as they are prone to dropping a zero here and there. (Open daily 6am-9pm.)

> **WHEN CROSSING.** Beware of shady men carrying thick wads of cash. Independent money changers on the border are convenient but tend to be unscrupulous—know your conversion rates and make sure you're getting a good deal. To avoid the haggling process, change your money beforehand at a bank with a fixed rate.

EASTERN GUATEMALA

Guatemala's short Caribbean coastline, squeezed between Belize and Honduras, is a world away from the jungles and highlands of the rest of the country. Populated mainly by people of African descent, the towns along the coast boast delicious seafood, numerous boating and hiking opportunities, and a distinct local culture. The region's two main attractions are laid-back Livingston, a well-known and tourist-friendly town, and the Río Dulce, which begins at the northeastern end of Lago Izabal and flows into Livingston.

There are two ways to get to the Caribbean coast. The first is to take the Atlantic Hwy. to its end in Puerto Barrios, where boats leave for Livingston. The highway passes numerous historically significant sites: the ruins of Quiriguá, home to some of the best preserved Maya stelae; a branch road to Esquipulas, one of the most important pilgrimage sites in all Central America; and Chiquimula, a gateway to the Mayan ruins of Copán in Honduras. The second option is to head to Fronteras, at the beginning of the Río Dulce on the Lago de Izabal, and boat down the river.

CHIQUIMULA

A transport hub for the Salvadoran and Honduran borders, Chiquimula is hot and bustling with a big market, lots of buses. This is also a great location for heading off to Honduras's Copán ruins.

E TRANSPORTATION. Buses enter Chiquimula on 2a C., turning right on 11a Av. and into the terminal on 10a Av. between 1 C. and 2 C. The bus station is hectic, and departing buses are often not in a specific spot but along the road shouting out destinations. Few buses are marked; tell your destination to anyone in the station and they will point you to the next departing bus. Pay on board. Buses go to: **Esquipulas** (1hr., every 10min. 5am-7pm, Q15); **Guatemala City** (3½hr., every 30min. 2am-4:30pm, Q40); **Puerto Barrios** (4hr., every hr. 4:30am-3:30pm, Q40); **El Florido/Frontera Honduras** (2½hr., every 30min 6:30am-4pm, Q25); **Zacapa** (30min., every 30min. 4:30am-5:30pm, Q10); **Flores**(8hr.; daily 6, 10am, 3pm; Q80) via **Rio Dulce** (Q35, 3hr.).

⬛🛈 ORIENTATION AND PRACTICAL INFORMATION. Hilltop Chiquimula is laid out in a grid. *Avenidas* run across the hill, while *calles* follow the slope down. As you head downhill, *avenida* numbers increase; *calle* numbers increase from left to right. The bus station is at 10 Av., 1/2 C. The *parque central* is at 7 Av., 3 C.

Currency exchange can be found at **Bancafé**, 2 C. 9-99 (☎7942 2335; open M-F 8am-4pm, Sa 8am-noon) where a **24 hr. ATM** also accepts international credit cards. Other services include: **police** (☎7942 0256), 8a Av. across from the station; **Farmacia Universal**, 8a Av. 3-61 (☎7943 8275; open 24hr.; delivery service available); **Hospital Centro Clínico de Especialidades**, 9 Ave., 4 C. (☎7942 4202; open 24hr.); **internet access** at **Enet Cafe**, 3 C. and 9/10 Av. (☎7942 4367; Q5 per hr.; open 9am-9pm); **post office**, 10 Av. and 2 C., across from the bus station (☎7942 0109; open M-F 8:30am-5pm, Sa 9am-1pm).

Eastern Guatemala

BELIZE

HONDURAS

EL SALVADOR

OCOTEPEQUE

CHIQUIMULA

ZACAPA

IZABAL

ALTA VERAPAZ

BAJA VERAPAZ

QUICHÉ

JALAPA

SANTA ROSA

EL PROGRESO

GUATEMALA

CHIMAL-TENANGO

Gulfo de Honduras

Bahía de Amatique

TO TEGUCIGALPA (100km)

TO POPTÚN (70km)

TO SAYAXCHÉ (50km)

SIERRA DE SANTA CRUZ

SIERRA DE CHAMÁ

SIERRA DE CHUACÚS

SIERRA DE LAS MINAS

SIERRA DEL MERENDÓN

SIERRA DEL ESPIRITU SANTO

SIERRA DEL GALLINERO

Montañas del Mico

Montañas del Gallinero

Montañas Rubelpec

Omoa
Puerto Cortés
San Pedro Sula
Tegucigalpita
Cuyamelito
El Cinchado
Finca Inca
Azacualpa
Quimistán
San Marcos
Petoa
La Entrada
Protección
Nueva Arcadia
Dulce Nombre de Copán
Sta. Rosa de Copán
Cucuyagua
Corquín
Guarita
Nueva Ocotepeque
El Poy
La Palma
Dulce Nombre de María
Macuelizo
Quiriguá
Copán Ruinas
Copán
Agua Caliente
La Unión
El Florido
Florida
Quiriguá
Las Minas
Concepción
Anguiatú
Lago de Güija
Las Moritas
Las Chinamas
Yupiltepeque
Jutiapa
Cuilapa
Sta. María Ixhuatán
Barberena
Pueblo Nuevo Viñas
Los Dolores
Esquintla
Chiquimula
Quetzaltepeque
Esquipulas
Agua Blanca
San Luis Jilotepeque
Jalapa
Montaña de Pinula
Volcán Jumay
Guastatoya
Sanarate
San Jerónimo
El Rancho Junction
Salamá
San Miguel Chicaj
Rabinal
Cubulco
Purulhá
Biotopo del Quetzal
La Tinta
Panzós
Cahabón
Lanquín
Semuc
Champey
Piedras Blancas
Sebol
Frey Bartolomé de las Casas
Chahal
Raxrujá
Chisec
Candelaria Caves
Lanquín Caves
Cobán
San Cristóbal Verapaz
San Pedro Carchá
Uspantán
Sacapulas
Nebaj
Santa Cruz del Quiché
Chichicastenango
Sololá
Totonicapán
Panajachel
Iximché
Lago de Atitlán
Playa Grande (Ixcán)
Parque Nacional Laguna de Lachuá
Modesto Méndez
Biotopo Chacón Machaca
Livingston
Fronteras (Río Dulce)
Finca Paraíso
Finca Tatín
El Estor
R.V.S. Bocas del Polochic
Mariscos
Amates
Zacapa
Río Hondo
Reserva de la Biósfera Sierra de las Minas
Castillo de San Felipe
Lago de Izabal
La Ruidosa
Bananera
Morales
Entre Ríos
San Francisco
Puerto Barrios
Biotopo Pinta de Manabique
Los Mixcos
Mataquescuintla
Ciudad de Guatemala
Mixco
Villa Nueva
Lago de Amatitlán
Amatitlán
Antigua
S. Vicente Pacaya
Volcán de Pacaya

BELIZE

HONDURAS

EL SALVADOR

LG

30 miles

30 kilometers

30 kilometers

0

0

CA13

CA9

CA14

CA1

CA12

CA1

ACCOMMODATIONS. Chiquimula has a fair number of budget options near the market; quieter rooms can be found on 2a C. before its intersection with 11a Av. **Hotel y Restaurante Grandorado ❷**, 2a C. 1-30, a few blocks from 11a Av., offers small, amenity-filled rooms. All rooms have fans, cable TV, and glistening private baths with color-coordinated decor. (☎7942 7644. Restaurant open 7am-9pm. Singles with fan Q60, with A/C Q85; doubles Q100/150. Cash only.) **Hotel Posada Perla de Oriente ❸**, 2a C. betwee 11/12 Av., with a massive walled-in complex, offers a large and relaxing setting to wait for your next bus. The hotel contains a pool for guest use, rooms with cable TV, private baths, restaurant on-site, balconies, and use of social space including billiards area. (☎7942 0014. Free parking. Rooms with fan Q80 per person, with A/C Q125 per person. AmEx/D/MC/V.) **Hotel La Palmera ❷**, 2a C. and 11a Av., on the corner, has second and third floor rooms with breezy balconies overlooking the street and perfect for people-watching. The complex is super secure, with a small side entrance watched day and night. All rooms have private cold water baths and cable TV. (☎7942 4647. Singles with fan Q70, with A/C Q95; doubles Q120/Q150; triples Q150 with fan. Cash only.)

FOOD. Chiquimula is filled with the standard selection of *comedores*, cafeterias, and low-key restaurants; for more refined dining, you'll have to go to a hotel or look elsewhere. For groceries, visit **Supermercado Paiz**, 3 C. and 7a Av., on the corner. (☎7942 6232. Open M-Sa 7am-8:30pm, Su 7am-7pm. Cash only.) **Anda Pícate ❶**, 8a Av. 2-60, provides cheap, tasty Mexican specialties in a chilled patio-area just blocks from the center and the bus station. (☎7942 7886. Platters of tacos Q10-20. Fajitas Q30. Burritos Q20. Nachos Q20-30. Open daily 10am-10pm. Cash only.) **Joe's Pizza ❷**, 11a Av., is a consistent winner for filling up any empty stomach, with its pizza-diner interior, quick delivery, and delicious menu including sandwiches, burgers, calzones (Q15-25), and huge pizzas (Q25-85). The service is friendly and fast, and the restaurant is a cool break from the heat of Chiquimula's busy streets. (☎7942 7530 and 7723 6118. Free delivery. Open daily 9am-11pm. Cash only.) **El Tesoro ❷**, 7a Av. and 4/5 C., draws in a consistent crowd of locals with its great prices and large portions of Guate-Chinese food and standard *típico*. (☎7942 3521. Chinese food Q20-37. *Típico* dishes Q20-45. Open daily 11am-9pm. Cash only.)

ESQUIPULAS

Home to Central America's most important Catholic shrine, breezy Esquipulas sits tucked in a small valley between the borders of El Salvador and Honduras. Pilgrims flock to the town throughout the year to receive blessings and benedictions at the magnificent white Basilica, which houses *El Cristo Negro*—the black Christ—reputed to have healing powers. The shrine's most famous devotee was Bishop of Guatemala Pardo de Figueroa, who was reportedly healed by the figure in 1737. Over a million Central American visitors still stream through each year, receiving blessings for themselves, their children, and their cars. The town of Esquipulas offers a unique chance to see large-scale tourism catering almost entirely to Central Americans; despite the abundance of hotels and restaurants, there's nary a gringo to be found.

TRANSPORTATION

Buses: Enter Esquipulas on 11a C./Doble Vía, dropping off and leaving from the section in front of the Basílica. Buses are usually unmarked; ask the driver for the destination. Buses from Esquipulas service: **Guatemala City** (4hr., every 30min. 2:30am-4pm, Q40); **Chiquimula** (1hr., every 10min. 5am-6pm, Q15); **Anguiatu/Frontera El Salvador** (1hr., every 30min. 6am-3pm, Q15); **Agua Caliente/Frontera Honduras** (20min., every 30min. 4:30am-5pm, Q10); **Las Flores** (8-10hr., hourly departures in front of gas station on Rutas Orientales from 7am-4pm and 2am, Q80).

Taxis: Mototaxis run between Q2-Q8. Most are on 3a Av. and 11a C.

ORIENTATION AND PRACTICAL INFORMATION

The town's two main streets are **11 C.** and **3a Av.**. Buses enter town on 11 C., the main east-west drag crossing in front of the Basilica and the *parque central*. 3a Av. runs perpendicular to 11 C. going north and downhill from in front of the Basilica. With your back to the church, *avenidas* increase in number as you go east and right; *calles* decrease as you go farther away and north of the Basilica.

Bank: Banco del Café, 3a Av. 6-68 (☎7943 1439). **24hr. ATM** accepts international credit cards. **Currency exchange.** Open M-F 8:30am-5pm, Sa 9am-1pm.

Police: 2 and 3 C. 6-10 (☎7943 2074).

Pharmacy: Farmacia Don Bosco II, 2a Av. and 11a C. (☎7943 1558). Open M-Sa 7am-9pm, Su 8am-5pm.

Medical Services: Hospital de Especialidades de Esquipulas, 8 C. 6-48 (☎7943 3919) Open 24hr.

Internet Access: Business Center Paraqui, 1a Av. (☎7943 1143), 50m from 11a C. Internet Q8 per hr. Open daily 7am-8pm.

Post Office: 2/3 C. and 6a Av. (☎7943 3627). Open M-F 8:30am-5:30pm, Sa 9am-1pm.

ACCOMMODATIONS

Accommodation options in Esquipulas are available from the Q823 (US$100) to smaller, more reasonably priced, amenity-filled hotels. The real cheap ones often show it in a lack of quality; spending a few more quetzals can provide a truly comfortable room with perks like a pool or internet use.

Hotel Payaqui, 2a Av. 11-56 (☎7943 1143 or 4447; www.hotelpayaqui.com). The nicest budget option in town, Payaqui has a big outdoor pool, on-site spa and salon, internet cafe and free Wi-Fi. Payaqui also has its own restaurant to accompany tastefully decorated rooms that come with cable TV, fans, and private hot water baths. Free parking. Singles with fan Q200; doubles Q300; triples Q400; quad Q450; A/C suites Q610-1020. AmEx/D/MC/V. ❺

Hotel Peregrino, 2a Av. (☎7943 1044), between Hotel Payaqui and Hotel Los Angeles. A seasoned veteran of Esquipulas' hotel competition, the Peregrino still has one of the best deals around, with standard amenities like a fan, cable TV, and private hot water bath in each room. Pool and Wi-Fi in the 2-block wide complex. Free on-site parking. Singles Q240; doubles Q300; triples Q420. AmEx/D/MC/V. ❺

Hotel Los Angeles, 2a Av. 11-94 (☎7943 1254 or 0607), next to Peregrino and across from the Basilica. Offers rooms comparable to its neighbors in a small courtyard behind the restaurant. Rooms have new and clean private hot water baths, fans, and cable TV. Restaurant open 7am-10pm. Singles Q250; doubles Q400; triples Q570. AmEx/D/MC/V. ⑤

Hotel Quirio Cataño, 11a Av. (☎4384 6590), 2 blocks before the Basilica. For those on a strict budget, the Quirio Cataño offers rooms with private hot water baths, cable TV, fans, and 24hr. security. Those interested in privacy may be turned off by the curtain lined glass walls on one side of each room. On-site cafeteria open 7am-8pm. Rooms Q50 per person. Cash only. ②

Hotel y Restaurante Aposento Altos, 3a Av. 10-66 (☎7943 1115). Rooms in a high tower overlooking the Basilica with cable TV, private hot water baths, and fans. There is an on-site restaurant serving breakfast (Q15-28), meat dishes (Q25-50), and beer and wine (Q12-17). Singles Q150; doubles Q200. Cash only. ⑤

FOOD

There are lots of restaurants on the blocks near the Basilica; unfortunately, the prices and menus are almost the same at all of them, making the variety a lot narrower than it seems. Most hotels have their own restaurants, offering, for the most part, the same dishes as other restaurants. For groceries, visit **Despensa Familiar**, 7 C. between 3/4 Av. (☎7943 3290. Open M-Sa 7am-7:30pm, Su 7am-7pm.)

Restaurante La Rotonda, 11a C. (☎7943 2038), at the entrance to town. With reasonable prices, delicious food, and one of the nicest dining spots in town, the Rotonda offers *típico* cuisine, Mexican specialties, and pizza in a 2-story dining area with modern Art Deco tables, sculpted light fixtures, and sparse decor overlooking the street. The *licuados* are delicious (Q12-18), as are the tacos (Q25-35). Pizzas Q38-125. Breakfast Q15-40. Entrees Q32-55. Open daily 7am-10pm. AmEx/D/MC/V. ②

Restaurante El Angel, 11a C. (☎7943 1372 or 5320 2500), in front of the Basilica. The most popular Chinese spot in town, El Angel serves up hearty if questionably authentic portions of Chinese standards including Wonton soup (Q40-45), chao mein (Q45-50), fried rice (Q15-50), meat entrees (Q50-60), and *"tacos chinos"* (Q45-50). It also has a vast repertoire of sugary *batidos* and *licuados* (Q10-18). Open daily 7am-10pm. AmEx/D/MC/V. ③

Comedor San Carlos, 3a Av., 50m from 11a C. The nicest *comedor* around. Standard breakfast dishes (Q20-40), entrees (Q40-50), and hamburgers (Q22-30) in a relaxed setting. Open M-F and Su 7:30am-9pm, Sa 7:30am-10pm. Cash only. ②

Restaurante Calle Real, 3a Av. 10-36 (☎7943 1194). One of the more pleasant dining options around, Calle Real has dark wood tables with plaid tableclothes, a big screen TV, and an extensive menu including breakfast dishes (Q20-40), meat entrees (Q40-50), seafood dishes (Q60-125), *licuados* (Q8-15), and a full bar. Open daily 7:30am-10pm. Cash only. ②

SIGHTS

BASÍLICA DE ESQUIPULAS. The main attraction in Esquipulas, the Basílica de Esquipulas attracts a huge crowd of Central American pilgrims seeking blessings and benedictions from monks and a glimpse of the famous *Cristo Negro*. The black Christ is behind the altar in the candle-lit auditorium, whose hallway is lined with small metal plaques of thanks and images of body parts that the Cristo has healed. On Sunday and religious holidays, you may wait hours for a 20-second glimpse of the statue. Remember to exit backwards down the ramp or else pilgrims will take offense (it is believed you are turning your back on the Lord if you do not comply). The grounds of the Basílica are open for visitors; the peaceful tree-lined gardens are particularly pleasant around sunset or in the morning, when clouds keep out the fairly intense daytime heat. *(Between 2/3 Av., on Doble Vía/11a C. Open daily from dawn to dusk. Free entry. Blessings are given to the left and right of the Basílica.)*

CUEVA DE LAS MINAS. If you are lucky, you may catch a religious ceremony at the Cueva de las Minas. Although there is significant evidence that Spanish sculptor Quirio Octavo fashioned the*Cristo Negro,*many still believe it was discovered in this cave. Located behind the Basílica's cemetery, the Cueva is part of a well-maintained park, with a restaurant, fishing pond, playground, and small zoo. Watch your head when walking through the tunnel and don't touch the walls unless you wish to emerge black with soot. *(To get to the Cueva, follow 2a Av. past the Basílica until you reach the highway and then take a left; there are signs marking the way. The ticket booth is 50m farther on the right; the park is another 15min. walk down the marked path. ☎ 7943 1628. Open M-Sa 7:30am-5pm.)*

CONVENTO FRANCISCANO. For a panoramic view of Esquipulas, climb up to the Franciscan convent on the opposite end of town. On the hillside, the **Cruz del Perdón** (Cross of Pardon) is surrounded by hundreds of plastic bags filled with small rocks and hanging from tree branches. Mayan pilgrims bring the rocks with them as a penance for their sins and leave them at the cross to gain forgiveness. *(Follow 3a Av. north away from the Basílica until it becomes a dirt road; turn left, and after 2 blocks you will approach a dead end. Walk 1km up the rocky road on the right until you reach the Cross of Pardon. Free.)*

DAYTRIPS FROM ESQUIPULAS

BORDER WITH HONDURAS: AGUA CALIENTE

From the center of Esquipulas, colectivo drivers can take you to Agua Caliente, the site of the border crossing (20min., every 30min. 4:30am-5pm, Q10). Another colectivo will whisk you to Honduran immigration 2km away (Q2).

The Honduran border at Agua Caliente is only 20min. from Esquipulas. US dollars and American Express traveler's checks can be changed at **Banco de Occidente** on the Honduran side (open M-Sa 8am-3pm, Su 8am-2pm). The immigration office is open 24hr. If you're driving across the border, go to the *transito* office around the corner from immigration. The forms that you have to fill out and the cost depend on your plans. Standard entrance tax is US$3. Keep in mind that Guatemalan immigration officials may try to ask for an unofficial exit fee, usually of about Q10. The best procedure in those situations is to follow their instructions. Once in Honduras, buses go to: **San Pedro Sula** (5hr., every hr. 4am-midnight, L100), **Tegucigalpa** (8hr.; 4, 6am, 4pm; L135), and **Ocotepeque** (every 30min. 4am-7:15pm, L10). The San Pedro Sula and Tegucigalpa buses crawl sluggishly over the misty hills and stop at **Santa Rosa de Copán** (2-3hr., L55) and **La Entrada** (3hr., L70), where you can catch buses to Copán Ruinas.

QUIRIGUÁ

Part of Guatemala's Ruta Maya, Quiriguá boasts a grand collection of *stelae*, altars, and human and animal-shaped zoomorphs. The site, in a hot field between the lowlands of Guatemala's Caribbean coast and the cooler hills of the Honduran-Salvadoran border, has been traced back to AD 300. Quiriguá developed into a major power after defeating Copán around AD 737. As the rest of the Mayan Empire slowly died out, Quiriguá lost its prominence and was completely abandoned by AD 900. The impressive carved sculptures that decorated the city during its successful years in the late-Mayan period now sit under tents in a visitor's center.

▣ TRANSPORTATION. There is no direct bus service to Quirigua or the ruins. The following buses service **Los Amayos,** on the highway: **Chiquimula** (2hr., every 30min. 6am-6pm, Q20); **Chiquimula** (2hr., every 30min. 6am-6pm, Q20); **Puerto Barrios** (2hr., every 30min. 5am-9pm, Q20). From Los Amayos, it is 1½km to Quirigua and another 2½km to the ruins. A regular bus service runs from the drop-off to the **ruins** (10min., every 30min. 7:30am-5:30pm, Q4), passing by the village of Quiriguá. For pickup, head to the village from Los Amayos; service is irregular (5min., Q1). You can walk to the Ruins from Los Amayos; it's about 4km down the road to Quiriguá. There is fairly frequent traffic and the road is safe to walk, though mosquitos and heat are a guarantee.

▚▨ ACCOMMODATIONS AND FOOD. There are several restaurants and hotels along the highway to and from Los Amatos, but only one option in town. **Hotel and Restaurante Royal ❶,** C. Principal, has a fairly large variety of rooms available, from basic singles (Q30) and doubles (Q60) with fairly-clean shared bathrooms, to tidy, en-suite singles (Q50) and doubles (Q90). The **restaurant** in front serves standard Guatemalan fare at reasonable prices. (☎7947 3639. Q15-Q35; vegetarian meals available. Open daily 7am-8pm. Cash only.)

◪ SIGHTS. The ruins' location in a hot field can be sweltering. Still, the ruins themselves are well organized. The main entrance has a bilingual guide to the site's history (Q10). There is also a free museum with photos and historical information. Past the museum and kiosk, the ruins are organized under thatched-roof huts connected by paved walking paths. The 22 *stelae* and zoomorphs (designated with letters of the alphabet) stand like sentinels in the site's central plaza. The plaza is an open field, making sunscreen and mosquito repellent a necessity. **Stela E,** a towering 12m, is the tallest in Central America and is on the Guatemalan 10-centavo coin. **Stela D** contains some of the most fantastically designed and best-preserved artwork in the region. Look for the **ball court** at the southwest end of the plaza (near the mango tree) and the **Acropolis,** the residence of the elite, to the south of the plaza. (*Entrance to the ruins Q25. Open daily 7:30am-5pm.*)

LAGO DE IZABAL AND FRONTERAS (RÍO DULCE)

The largest lake in Guatemala, Lago de Izabal is slowly becoming a major tourist attraction. The waterfront backpacker crowd in Rio Dulce is lured by calm, safe waters and beautiful scenery. The expansive lake to the west borders the marshes of Bocas del Polochic. Visitors have easy access to Castillo de San Felipe, the Spanish fortress turned beach destination. The swimming holes and waterfalls of Finca El Paraiso and El Boquerón are sandwiched between Rio Dulce and El Estor.

The land gateway to Río Dulce and Lago de Izabal, Fronteras—commonly referred to as Río Dulce—lies on the north side of a 1km bridge spanning the river. The peaceful waters of the river and lake are just fast enough to keep the mosquito population manageable, and the river's low-key atmosphere is a perfect contrast to Atitlán's gringo-party vibe. Most hotels are in isolated inlets along the river, and transportation by boat is more common than by bus. Yet, despite the influx of tourists and sailboats, Fronteras remains a humble town; upscale marinas are only blocks from worn-down playgrounds and small local fish-markets. The combination is both gritty and relaxing, making it a great option for an idyllic but budget-friendly hideaway.

▐ TRANSPORTATION

Buses: Stop on the north side of the bridge in front of the Litegua/Fuente del Norte offices. Each company services different destinations in their large, semi-luxury buses. Purchase tickets in the **Litegua** (☎7930 5251; open daily 3am-7pm) and **Fuente del Norte** (open daily 7:30am-5:30pm) offices.

Litegua Buses to **Antigua** (7hr., daily 8am and noon, Q100) and **Guatemala City** (5hr.; daily 3, 6, 8am, noon, 3:15pm; Q60).

Fuente Del Norte Buses to **Flores** (4hr., every hr. 7am-6:30pm, Q70), **Guatemala City** (5hr., 7:15am and every hr. 10:30am-4:30pm, Q60), **Jutiapa** (5hr., daily 9am and 9:30am, Q60), and **San Salvador** (7hr., daily 10am, Q125).

Local Buses departing two blocks north of the Puente service **El Castillo de San Felipe** (15min., every 30min. 6am-4pm, Q3) and **El Estor** (1hr., every hr. 7am-3pm, Q18-20).

Boats: Lanchas from **Trasportes Maritimo** (☎5561 9657), on the water underneath the north side of the bridge, can be hired for private trips. Daily departures for **Livingston** (1-3hr., 2 daily 9am and 1:30pm, Q130) leave from the dock as well. Buy tickets at the *colectivo's* ticket office on the dock. *Lanchas* to hotels in the area are mostly free; you can call or radio them at **Sundog Cafe** or **Restaurante Rio Bravo,** where the main dock is.

▟ ▐ ORIENTATION AND PRACTICAL INFORMATION

The town of Fronteras lies on the north side of the bridge that crosses the Rio Dulce. The highway stemming from the bridge doubles as the **C. Principal.** About 300m north of the bridge is the turnoff to the Castillo de San Felipe and El Estor; there are no other main streets. Most hotels and restaurants are on the water, either under the bridge or in secluded inlets accessible only by boat. *Lanchas* leave from Restaurante Río Bravo on the right just 50m past the bridge to most destinations.

Tourist Office: Tijax Express (☎7930 5196), on the north side of the bridge. Info about hotels and transportation in the area. Open Tu-Sa 9am-5pm. If Tijax is closed, **Restaurante Río Bravo** and **Sundog Café** are your best bets for info.

Bank: Banrural (☎7930 5161), 300m from the north side of the bridge on C. Principal. **Currency exchange. 24hr. ATM** accepts international cards. Open M-F 9am-5pm, Sa 9am-1pm.

Police: Km 277 (☎7930 5406), on the south side of the bridge. Open 24hr.

Medical Services: Centro de Salud, C. Principal (☎7930 5209), on the north side of the bridge. Open 24hr. for emergencies.

Internet Access: Bruno's Internet Cafe (☎7930 5721), under the bridge on the north side. Internet Q10 per hr. Open daily 7am-8pm.

Post Office: C. Principal, 500m north of the bridge. Open M-F 9am-5pm.

▐ ACCOMMODATIONS

Though there are a couple lodging options in Fronteras, the best options by far are along the water. Waterfront hotels cater to practically every budget. If you haven't already booked when you get in town, your best bet is to contact Restaurante Rio Bravo and Sundog Cafe. Both of these establishments can call a *lancha* for you. They also give basic information on the types of accommodations available.

Hacienda Tijax (☎7930 5505; www.tijax.com), on the water. *Lanchas* leave from the Río Bravo dock. Practically an institution in Río Dulce, Tijax does it all, with a restaurant, marina, and hotel on its lakeside property, and an information booth at the bus stop at the entrance to town. The hotel offers reasonably priced bungalows connected by wooden walkways to the pool area, and patio-style restaurant. Rooms have hot-water baths, mosquito nets, fans, and Wi-Fi. Single Q150, with private bath Q320, with bath and A/C Q560; double Q240/380/600; triple Q325/540/760. AmEx/D/MC/V. ❺

Casa Périco (☎7930 5666), accessible via *lancha* from Restaurante Río Bravo/Sundog Cafe. Though you'll need a fair supply of mosquito repellent for your stay, it is well worth the peace and budget-friendly rates at this Swiss-run backpacker favorite. Set back in the marshes along the Río, Casa Périco offers a secluded, swampy paradise. Thatched-roof dorms supplied with ample mosquito nets, a waterfront dining area, and free kayaks for guest use. Hot-water bathrooms and free safe for guests. Dorms Q40-45; private rooms with shared bath Q50-60 per person; 2-person bungalow with private hot water bath Q200. Restaurant open daily 7:30am-9pm. Cash or traveler's checks only. ❶

Hotel Backpackers (☎7930 5169), on the south side of the bridge; *lanchas* leave from the main dock in Rio Dulce. Though it's in a vintage, waterfront mansion on the south side of the Río, Hotel Backpackers manages to turn its old furnishings into authentic charm with one of the most relaxing atmospheres around. Run by the center for troubled youth, **Casa Guatemala,** Hotel Backpackers offers a communal kitchen, dorm rooms, private rooms, and space for hammocks. The outdoor bar and restaurant have reasonably priced food and is one of the best social spaces in town, especially if you like a little Latin music. Restaurant open daily 7am-9:30pm. Laundry Q20 per load. Bunks Q24-40; simple rooms Q80; private rooms with bath Q160-325. Cash only. ❶

Bruno's Hotel and Restaurant (☎7930 5174 or 5692 7294; www.mayaparadise.com), underneath the north side of the bridge. Another classic establishment, Bruno's has a popular waterfront restaurant and pool area in front of the hotel, along with its own internet cafe, huge library, and general store. Rooms have private hot water baths, A/C, cable TV, balconies, and Wi-Fi. Restaurant open daily 7am-10pm. Breakfast Q18-30. Seafood Q52-76. Meat entrees Q48. Mixed drinks Q18-32. Singles Q220; doubles Q300; triples Q430; 6-person apartment Q700. AmEx/D/MC/V. ❺

Hotel y Restaurante Vista Rio (☎7930 5665), under the north side of the bridge, across from the basketball courts. The 6 rooms at this waterfront enclave are some of the best deals in town; all have private hot water baths, cable TV, fans, Wi-Fi, and 2 queen beds. There's a private dock, breezy restaurant, internet cafe, and extensive book exchange as well. Restaurant open Tu-Su 7:30am-8pm. Breakfast Q20-35. Grill Q40-90. Pizza Q70-120. Double Q125, with water view Q150; A/C Q30 extra. Cash only. ❹

 FOOD

There are many restaurants in Río Dulce, though they're all about the same. Most restaurants serve the standard *típico* dishes with a few fresh seafood options thrown in for good measure; some of the hotel restaurants have slightly more extensive menus, but you'll have to shop around a bit if you're looking for anything out of the ordinary. For groceries, there is a **Despensa Familiar** on C. Principal, two blocks north of the bridge. (Open M-Sa 7am-8pm, Su 7am-7pm. Cash only.)

Sundog Cafe (☎5760 1844 or 4645 3192), in front of Restaurante Río Bravo just past the Tijax office. The best option in town for something outside the standard grilled dishes, Sundog serves up delicious sandwiches on homemade bread (Q24-38), smoothies and *licuados* (Q10-15), and daily specialties including fresh salads and curries. Open-air patio style dining, replete with lounging couches, a book exchange, and drink specials on W, Sa, and Su nights. Open M, Th-F, Su 10am-8pm; W and Sa 10am-midnight. Cash only. ❷

Pizzeria Rio Bravo (☎7930 5167), in front of the *lancha* dock. Right on the water, Rio Bravo gets the most traffic for its *lancha*-calling service, but it also serves up huge pizzas and standard Guatemalan fare in its restaurant internet cafe. Entrees Q30-55. Pizza Q12-115. Open daily 7am-10pm. AmEx/D/MC/V. ❷

Cafeteria Bendicion de Dios (☎7930 5421), next to the *colectivo* dock under the bridge. With its cavernous wood-plank interior and on-the-water porch area, this cafeteria feels more like an old ship than the standard cafeteria-*comedor*; the food is tasty and a bargain relative to other options in town. Great breakfast (Q10-23), seafood dishes (Q45-75), meat entrees (Q35), and sandwiches (Q15-35), served by friendly family members. Open daily 7am-7pm. Cash only. ❷

Restaurant Jocelyn (☎7930 5740), next to Cafeteria Bendicion de Dios, near the *colectivo* dock under the bridge. Dine on the water—literally—in this stucco and thatched-roof *cabana* on its self-contained dock, on the west side of the bridge. The restaurant specializes in seafood. Its location a bit outside of the marsh area means the mosquitos aren't quite as bad. Seafood Q55-115. Open daily 10am-10pm. Cash only. ❸

Restaurant Los Pinchos (☎7930 5185), behind Despensa Familiar, off the C. Principal. With its own dock between the marsh and the lake, Los Pinchos serves up a mixture of *típico*, Chinese dishes, and seafood on its thatched-roof hut with cobblestone floors and a jukebox. Breakfast Q20-30. Rice and pasta dishes Q40-55. Seafood Q75-100. Open daily 7am-midnight. Cash only. ❷

🔛 DAYTRIPS FROM FRONTERAS AND RÍO DULCE

EL CASTILLO DE SAN FELIPE

San Felipe and the castle are a 45min. walk from Fronteras. Heading away from the bridge, take the 1st left at Pollito Tienda; bear left at the fork. Boats coming from Livingston will drop you off in San Felipe if you ask, and Río Dulce boat tours often include a stop here. Direct lancha from Río Dulce Q37. Minibuses from Fronteras leave from the intersection of C. Principal and the road to El Estor (15min., every 30min. 6:30am-5pm, Q3). Open daily 8am-5pm. Grounds open daily 7am-6pm. Q30.

Resting on its original foundations, the Castillo de San Felipe is a reconstructed Spanish fortress turned tourist hotspot. Originally built in 1651 to stave off plundering pirates from looting warehouses on Lake Izabal, the *castillo* is now a stopping point on most Rio Dulce cruises. This is also a popular destination for tourists searching for the lake's elusive beaches. There is a special swimming area on the beach, equipped with underwater nets to keep pesky fish away. The truly fish-phobic can stay in the pristine pool area at the castle itself, replete with lounge chairs and a snack bar. There is an on-site picnic area as well.

FINCA EL PARAISO

The Finca is occasionally included on Río Dulce boat tours. It's also reachable on any bus traveling between Fronteras and El Estor. From Fronteras, you can get to Finca El Paraíso and Boquerón by hopping on a bus to El Estor (Q15). Otherwise, from El Estor grab a bus to Fronteras and tell the driver where you want to get off (Q4). From either city, it's no problem to see both the canyon and the waterfalls in a day. The last bus back to Fronteras passes the Finca at 4:30pm. Buses from Fronteras leave from the turnoff to El Castillo

EASTERN GUATEMALA

de San Felipe, 200m north of the bridge. Transportation and tours can also be arranged through Hacienda Tijax in Fronteras. ☎ 7949 7122. Entry Q10. Cash only.

Along the north side of the lake between San Felipe and El Estor, the beautiful Finca el Paraíso is a working ranch just a 10min. walk from a sauna and a fascinating hot waterfall that cascades into clear, cold pools perfect for swimming. Caves are nearby (bring a flashlight). Horse and rowboat rentals are available. (Horses Q50 per hr., boats Q25 per 30min.) The ranch has its own restaurant along with areas for camping (Q25, hammock rentals Q25) and more luxurious cabins with private baths (doubles Q240). A bit farther down the road to El Estor is El Boquerón. A 500m hike down a dirt path from the bus drop-off leads to an outhouse and a small collection of unmanned canoes. One of the guys around will paddle you (Q20) into the dramatic limestone canyon until a series of impassable river rapids and a rocky beach appear. You can also rent a canoe and paddle yourself (Q15). Across from the rapids is a series of stalactites hanging over the water and a large cave used for Mayan rituals. To get back, jump into the lime green waters and float down the lazy river.

▧BOCAS DEL POLOCHIN AND EL ESTOR

To get to Bocas del Polochin, take a minibus or bus from Río Dulce headed to El Estor (1½hr., daily 5:30am-3pm, Q18-20). Buses depart from the intersection of C. Principal and the road to El Castillo and El Estor; make sure to bring water. From El Estor, there are community lanchas serving Bocas del Polochic and Selempim (1hr.; M, W, Sa at noon; Q30). Return boats from Selempim (6am on M, W, Sa). Multi-day tours organized through Defensa de la Naturaleza usually provide transportation but must be arranged in advance.

Accessible only by boat and home to 250-plus animal species including the elusive manatee, Bocas del Polochin wildlife refuge is the crowning jewel of Lago de Izabal's undertouristed beauty. Often overlooked because of its remote location, the reserve offers hiking, boat trips, and visits to the nearby village of Selempim. The wetlands have the country's largest manatee populations and are also home to monkeys, birds, ocelots, and jaguars. The site is equipped with walking trails and guides giving visitors a chance to see wildlife up-close. The Selempim Research Station functions as a tourist and research center for the reserve, has its own restaurant, dorm rooms and cabins with shared bathrooms, solar-powered electricity, and a peaceful outdoor hammock lounge. Defensa de la Naturaleza, which runs the refuge, offers multi-day and custom packages and manages reservations for the Station. Visit their office in El Estor. (2a C. ☎7949 7237. Open M-F 9am-5pm.) It is also possible to see the wetlands on a 4hr. boat trip from El Estor; there are *lanchas* at the dock that can be hired for rental (Q250-400 per trip), though you'll have to bargain.

PUERTO BARRIOS

United Fruit Company exports once made Puerto Barrios (pop. 51,500) the nation's most crucial port. Commerce has since shifted to Pacific ports and the city's significance has faded. Today, the city's dusty, palm tree-lined streets function as a market and passageway for travelers and residents of Livingston, Belize, and Honduras. Walking the streets at night is not recommended.

▣ TRANSPORTATION

Buses: Bus traffic is centered around the railroad tracks and the market. **Litegua Buses** (☎7948 1172) leave from the west side of the railroad tracks at their intersection with

6a Av. To: **Guatemala City** (5-6hr.; every 30min. 1am-noon, every hr. noon-4pm; Q80), via **Quirigua** (2½hr., Q50) and **Rio Hondo** (3½hr., Q65) where you connect to buses headed to **Esquipulas** or **El Salvador**. Other buses leave from destination-specific stops, with service to **Chiquimula**, departing from the east side of the railroad tracks (4hr., every hr. 5am-5pm, Q45) and **Frontera Honduras**, departing from the north side of the market on 6a Av. (1hr., every 10min. 5am-5pm, Q15).

Boats: The dock is at the western end of 12 C. **Ferries** to **Livingston** (1½hr., 2 daily 10am and 7pm, Q20). **Lanchas** also make the trip to **Livingston** (30min., every hr. or when full 6:30am-5pm, Q30), and **Punta Gorda, BZE** (50min., Q100).

▰ ▰ ORIENTATION AND PRACTICAL INFORMATION

The center of Puerto Barrios is the **market,** between **8a/9a C.** and **6a/7a Av..** *Avenidas* increase in number from the western waterfront towards the eastern inland side of town. **1a C.** sits at the far north side of town; *calles* increase in number going south. The **railroad tracks** where most buses stop run diagonally through the intersection of **6a Av.** and **9a C.** before hitting the **Container Port,** where mercantile ships enter the city. The passenger port is several blocks south, at the **Muelle Municipal,** located at the western end of **12a C..**

Bank: Banco Internacional, 6a Av. and 8a C. (☎7948 2531). Open M-F 9am-6pm, Sa 9am-1pm. **Currency exchange** and has Western Union services. **24hr. ATM** accepts international cards.

Police: 5a C. and 6a Av. (☎7947 0484). Open 24hr.

24hr. Pharmacy: Farmacia 24 Horas, 13 C. and 5a Av. (☎7948 5518), on the corner.

Medical Services: Hosptial Nacional de la Amistad Japón (☎7948 3071 or 3073), at the turnoff to Santo Tomas de Castillo. Open 24hr.

Internet Access: Telgua, 10 C. and 8a Av. (☎7948 2198). Open M-F 8am-6pm. Internet, phones, and fax services. Internet Q10 per hr.

Post Office: 6a C. and 6a Av. (☎7948 7992). Open M-F 8:30am-5:30pm.

▰ ACCOMMODATIONS

There are many lodging options in Puerto Barrios. The city is not the safest at night so be sure to get a room you can spend some time in once it gets dark.

Hotel Miami, 3a Av. and 11/12 C. (☎7948 0537). Close to the dock, this hotel offers cheap and simple rooms with fans and basic private baths. Rooms are clean and secure. Singles Q45, with A/C Q100; doubles Q90, with A/C Q170. Cash only. ❷

Hotel Europa, 3a Av. and 11/12 C. (☎7948 1292), next to Hotel Miami. With a relaxing courtyard and friendly service, Europa offers a pleasant atmosphere and basic, clean rooms with fans and private baths. Q50 per person; Cash only. ❷

Hotel Lee, 5 Av. and 9/10 C. (☎7948 0830 or 0685). Though it's a walk from the port, Hotel Lee is quiet and offers rooms with fans, private baths, and cable TV within a few blocks of the center. Singles Q65; doubles Q115. Cash only. ❷

Hotel La Caribeña, 4a Av. between 10/11 C. (☎7948 0860). The amenities here make up for the lack of scenery. Rooms have private baths, TVs, and A/C. Free parking. There is an on-site restaurant that serves tropical food; entrees Q40-85. Singles Q120; doubles Q180. MC/V. ❸

Hotel El Reformador, 16 C. and 7a Av. #158 (☎7948 0533). Popular with large groups and conventions, Reformador makes up for its inconvenient location with pleasant rooms equipped with fans, private baths, phones, and TVs. Singles Q70, with A/C Q110; doubles Q100/150. Cash only. ❷

🍴 FOOD

Puerto Barrios has a suprising variety of food options, from the standard *tapado* and seafood dishes, to more exotic Portuguese and Chinese options. For groceries, visit **Despensa Familiar**, 8 C. and 7a Av. (☎7948 0462. Open M-Sa 7am-8pm, Su 7am-7pm.)

Pizza Luigi, 5a Av. and 13a C. (☎7948 0284). A local standard, Luigi's pies are some of the best in town. Pizzas Q45-125. Free delivery. Open Tu-Su 10am-1pm and 4-9pm. Cash only. ❸

Restaurante Safari, 1 C. and 5a Av. (☎7948 0563). On the prettier side of the water and out of sight of the port, this breezy spot is the most popular place around for seafood dishes (Q60-130). The open air-dining room is busy on weekends, but relaxing and quiet the rest of the week. Open daily 11am-11pm. AmEx/D/MC/V. ❹

Restaurante y Cafeteria Maxim, 6a Av. and 8a C. (☎7948 2258). A clean retreat from the dirty streets, Maxim offers big portions of Chinese-Guatemalan favorites, from the ubiquitous Chao Mein and Chop Sueys (Q30-55) to more exotic curry and sweet-and-sour meat dishes (Q45-65). Delivery available. Open daily 10:30am-midnight. Cash only. ❸

Café Vistalmar, 1a Av. and 9a C. (☎7948 1488), near the dock. Vistalmar lives up to its expectations, with sea views and great *tapado* (Q70) and seafood dishes in its open air dining area. Entrees Q45-110. Open daily 7am-1am. Cash only. ❸

El Cafecito Restaurante y Bar, 13 C. and 6a/7a Av. (☎7948 2810 or 7942 9121). While the other places in town serve the same chicken and seafood dishes, El Cafecito spices things up with delicious Portuguese specialties and rich coffee in a cafe-style dining area. Entrees Q30-85. Coffee Q10-25. Open M-Sa 7:30am-11pm. Cash only. ❷

⚔ BORDER CROSSING: HONDURAS

BORDER WITH HONDURAS

Minibuses run from Puerto Barrios, across from the Despensa Familiar on 8 C. and 6 Av., to the Honduran border (1 hr., about every 20min., Q15).

The minibus from Puerto Barrios drops you off across the border in no-man's land. From there, Honduran **pickup trucks** (L5) shuttle you 3km to their immigration office in **Corinto**, where money changers swarm outside. From Corinto, buses leave for Omoa and Puerto Cortés, Honduras on the Caribbean coast (every hour at about 20 past the hour). The trip from Puerto Barrios to Omoa takes about 4hr. in decent weather; rains sometimes close the road on the Honduran side. The jungle trail and boat crossings to Honduras are no longer used.

LIVINGSTON   007

Life is sweet in Livingston (pop. 11,300), where the Río Dulce meets the waves of the Atlantic and the Belizean Cayes are just minutes away. With a large Garífuna population, the descendants of African slaves and Carib Indians, the town has a unique language and culture, providing a taste of the laid-back Belizean lifestyle that waits just across the border. The Garífuna have a wandering history, having constantly been shuttled from island to island by Spanish and English invaders. Sizably cut down by disease, the Garífuna finally settled down in southern Belize

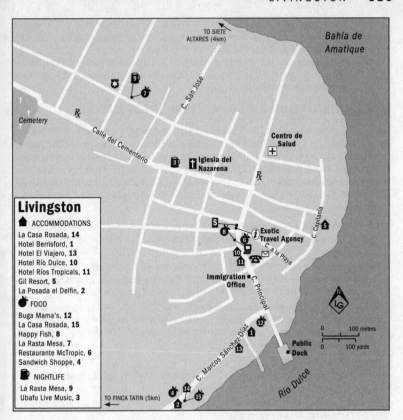

Livingston

🏠 ACCOMMODATIONS

La Casa Rosada, 14
Hotel Berrisford, 1
Hotel El Viajero, 13
Hotel Río Dulce, 10
Hotel Ríos Tropicals, 11
Gil Resort, 5
La Posada el Delfin, 2

🍅 FOOD

Buga Mama's, 12
La Casa Rosada, 15
Happy Fish, 8
La Rasta Mesa, 7
Restaurante McTropic, 6
Sandwich Shoppe, 4

🍺 NIGHTLIFE

La Rasta Mesa, 9
Ubafu Live Music, 3

at the beginning of the 19th century. Today's 6000 Guatemalan Garífuna seem to have departed from their highland compatriots; basketball is the chosen sport and reggae and rap the popular genres of music. Traditional *punta*-drumming music continues to play a significant role in Garífuna culture, though.

Once the largest port in Central America, Livingston now spends its days partying and transporting tourists to an array of breathtaking nearby sites, including the cascades of the Seven Altars and the effervescent *aguas calientes* (hot springs). The greatest tourist attraction is the beautiful Río Dulce boat ride, which starts in Livingston and heads to Lago de Izabal. In town, steady infusions of coconut bread, fresh fish, and reggae jams redefine *tranquilo*. Be aware that some crime (mainly drug-related) has found a way to disturb the peace.

◲ TRANSPORTATION

Livingston is accessible only by boat. There are two ferries per day arriving from and leaving for Puerto Barrios. Many quicker *lanchas* traveling around the gulf and the Rio Dulce. The town itself is small and walkable; because of its island location, most traffic is on foot or bike.

Ferries: Depart from the main dock, go to **Puerto Barrios** (1½hr., daily 5am and 2pm, Q20).

Lanchas: Depart from the main dock, offer quicker service to: **Puerto Barrios** (30min., every hr. 6:30am-5pm, Q30); **Rio Dulce** (1-2hr., 2 per day 9am and 1:30pm, Q85-125); **Punta Gorda, BLZ** (1hr., leaves when full, Q120); **Omoa and Puerto Cortés, HND** (3hr., minimum groups of 6, Q300 each). For international trips, remember to get your passport stamped at immigration.

ORIENTATION AND PRACTICAL INFORMATION

It's almost impossible to get lost in Livingston. The town's main street, **C. Principal,** leads directly up a hill from the **main dock** and hooks to the right at the public school painted with big, blue Pepsi signs. Most of the action occurs along C. Principal. **C. del Cementario** (a left turn off C. Principal) is similarly active. **C. Marcos Sánchez-Díaz** runs parallel to the **Río Dulce.** C. Marcos Sánchez-Díaz has a number of good budget hotels and restaurants. **C. del Capitánia** runs parallel to the beach on the gulf side.

Tours: Exotic Travel Agency (☎7947 0151), in Bahía Azul restaurant, halfway up C. Principal. Free maps and advice on border crossings, tours, and transportation. Little English spoken. Open daily 7am-midnight.

Bank: Bancafe (☎7947 0491), just above Bahia Azul on C. Principal. Changes travelers checks and gives cash advances on MC/V. **Currency exchange. 24hr. ATM** serves international credit cards. Open M-F 9am-5pm, Sa 9am-1pm.

Beyond Tourism: Livingston Spanish School (☎4151 0397; www.livingstonspanish-school.com), in Hotel Salvador Gaviota, 15 min. from the center in a taxi. Offers in residence 1-on-1 Spanish language tutoring. All-inclusive US$205 per week. For more **Beyond Tourism** opportunities, see p. 29.

Police: (☎7948 0120).

24hr. Pharmacy: Farmacia Sucey, on C. del Cementario, 400m past C. Principal. Open daily 8am-9pm.

Medical Services: Centro de Salud de Livingston (☎7947 0143), on C. Principal right after Restaurante Tiburón. Open 24hr.

Internet Access: Telgua (☎7947 0196), 20m right off C. Principal just before the Alcadia Municipal. Offers telephone service and 20min. free internet.

Post Office: (☎7947 0070), next to Telgua off C. Principal. Open M-F 8am-1pm and 3-5:30pm.

ACCOMMODATIONS

Budget rooms are around every corner, but the rush of visitors during the high season leaves only the nicest rooms available. Be sure to book in advance. The heat in Livingston can be sweltering, so it's worth it to check out rooms first and make sure you aren't buying yourself a night in a ventilation-free inferno.

Hotel Rios Tropicales (☎7947 0158), on C. Principal, 2 blocks north of the dock. In the center of town, Rios Tropicales provides affordable lodging with a little beach-flavor. The wooden building with a small courtyard, hammocks, lounging areas, and its own small cafe has great Wi-Fi and computers for guest use. Reasonably priced rooms with comfy beds, and fans. Cafe open 7am-6pm. Singles Q50, with bath Q150; doubles Q50/200. Cash only. ❷

Hotel Berrisford (☎7947 0471), on C. Diaz right before Buga Mama's. Though quiet is a hard to find here—between the ferries arriving at the dock and partiers arriving for the basement-level live concerts—Berrisford cranks up the amenities as well, with A/C, cable TV, and private baths for just Q100 per person. The rooms are by no means new, but the water views and blasting A/C are solid attempts to make the midday heat more bearable. Cash only. ❸

Gil Resort (☎7947 0039; www.gilresorthotel.com), in front of the beach on C. del Capitania. An upscale option that won't kill your budget, Gil Resort offers rooms with A/C, private hot water baths, and modern furnishings. Its beachside complex has a private dock, jacuzzi, Wi-Fi, kayaks, and its own section of the beach. Some rooms have ocean views; request in advance. On-site restaurant. Singles Q325; doubles Q410; triples Q490. AmEx/D/MC/V. ❺

La Casa Rosada, C. Diaz (☎7947 0303; www.hotelcasarosada.com), 400m. west of the main dock. Exotic furniture, peaceful gardens, hammocks on a gazebo over the water, a patio, and ocean views make this worth the extra quetzals. Bungalows are artfully simple, with mosquito netting, fans, and hand-painted furnishings. Clean, shared hot baths. English spoken. Excellent food and tours. Laundry Q2.50 per piece. Wi-Fi. 2-person bungalows Q150. MC/V. ❺

Hotel Rio Dulce (☎7947 0764), on C. Principal next to Hotel Rios Tropicales. The cool, cavernous downstairs lounge area of this main street mansion gives way to airy 2nd floor. A dorm for backpackers (Q40 per person), rooms with fans and shared baths (Q60 per person), and rooms with fans, private baths (Q75 per person). Cash only. ❷

Hotel El Viajero (☎5685 1635), 200m west from the dock on C. Marcos Sánchez-Díaz. The cheapest accommodation around. El Viajero offers simple, clean rooms with beds, fans, and private baths right on the water. At Q25 per person, it's hard to beat the price, though the rooms offer new meaning to the word basic. Cash only. ❶

La Posada el Delfin (☎7947 0303; www.posadaeldelfin.com), next to La Casa Rosada on C. Diaz. With its own dock on the water, along with a pool, cold jacuzzi, TV, and 2 restaurants, El Delfin has some of the best amenities around. Its rooming options are also expansive, from pricier 2nd floor rooms with A/C and private hot water baths (Q490-610), to simpler ground-level rooms with fans and private hot-water baths (Q150 per person, Q200 with A/C). English spoken. AmEx/D/MC/V. ❷

🗂 FOOD

Livingston's Garífuna population has blessed it with some of the best food in Guatemala. *Tapado,* seafood and plantains drenched in a spicy coconut broth is a delicious local favorite. Far superior to inland beans and rice, Caribbean rice and beans are stir-fried in coconut milk. Curries are common, and spice is popular, making for some flavorful hot and sweet delicacies. Because it's an island, expect Livingston's food to be a little more expensive.

La Casa Rosada, C. Diaz (☎7947 0303; www.hotelcasarosada.powerhost.be), 400m west of the main dock. Though it serves tasty and affordable breakfast and lunch (Q30-35), the real star here is the dinner. Orders must be put in by 6pm. The menu changes everyday to incorporate the freshest available seafood, meat, and vegetable entrees. All dinners (Q65-100) include fresh salad, coconut bread, and a dessert. Popular options include vegetarian pasta, *tapado,* lobster, and shrimp. Breakfast open from 6:30am to closing. Dinner open 7-9pm. Cash only. ❹

Buga Mama's, C. Diaz (☎7947 0891), 50m west of the dock. Run by non-profits dedicated to promoting job-training for young Maya, Buga Mama's offers one of the best locations and most varied menus around. Homemade pastas (Q45-55), breakfasts (Q15-25), seafood (Q70-100), curries (Q40-50), and pizzas (Q30-115) enjoyed on a waterfront patio overlooking the gulf. As a training restaurant, the service can be slower than normal, but the prices are some of the best around. Open daily 9am-9pm. AmEx/D/MC/V. ❷

Happy Fish (☎7947 0661), on C. Principal, 3 blocks from the dock. With large portions of the local seafood specialties (Q60-110), Happy Fish is the place to come for your fix of *tapado*, shrimp, fish, and lobster, all served up with rice and beans or french fries and salad. Popular with the weekend loungers, it also has a drinks menu and the ever popular *coco loco* (Q30). Open daily 7am-9pm. AmEx/D/MC/V. ❹

Restaurante McTropic (☎7947 0158), on C. Principal just past Hotel Rios Tropicales. A popular spot with wooden tables and lounge-style seating, McTropic serves up traditional rice and bean entrees (Q50-60) along with some of the best Thai chicken and vegetable curry in town (Q75). Its seafood is also reasonably priced (Q60-115). The service is friendly if a bit slow. Open daily 7am-10pm. Cash only. ❹

La Rasta Mesa, Barrio Nevago (☎4200 4371). Run by the Garífuna cultural center, this restaurant serves up local specialties with a dose of Garífuna culture and music. M and F reggae nights. Also arrange arts and cooking classes. Entrees Q20-75. Kitchen open daily 10am-10pm. Cash only. ❷

The Sandwich Shoppe (☎7947 0056), across from Posada del Delfín. For an affordable lunch or dinner, stop by this tiny hidden-away sandwich shop and diner for the best selections of salads (Q30-45) and sandwiches (Q20-35) in town. The Shoppe also has various types of sushi (prices vary according to season) and bakes its own bread daily. Specialties include the Philly Cheesesteak sub (Q35) and the home-made pastas (Q40-55), tested in the the owner's original Italian restaurant in New York. Open daily 7:30am-7pm. Cash only. ❷

🎵 NIGHTLIFE

A mellow village by day, Livingston apparently conserves its energy for nighttime partying. Most establishments are open until 3am but people stay out until dawn. Things are wild during the **Garífuna festival** from November 20 to 27. The cemetery has a happening party November 1 and 2 **(All Saints Day)** and **(All Souls Day).**

Ubafu Live Music, 50m down the C. del Cemeterio leg of the C. Principal. The Garífuna music scene and dance party begins and ends with Ubafu Live Music. The live music here never disappoints. *Coco loco* Q30. Open daily until 3am.

La Rasta Mesa, Barrio Nevago (☎4200 4371). With live reggae and Garífuna music every night, Rasta Mesa is your best bet for non-sketchy and creative nightlife in town. Music every night from 8pm until the last customer leaves. Cash only.

🎵 DAYTRIPS FROM LIVINGSTON

SIETE ALTARES

A 1½hr. walk down the narrow spit of beach. Note: there have been some reports of robberies. The arrival of tourist police along the walk has helped, but always use common sense: travel in groups and leave valuables behind. Head out early, both to avoid intense heat and to ensure an early return; around 5pm a rising tide makes travel difficult. At the end of C. Principal, make a left onto the beach. After about 40min., you'll reach the Quehueche River. Cross the bridge and keep walking until you reach the end of the beach. Continue up the hillside trail 5min. until you see the Balthazar family entrance stand and the cascades on your left. With your back to the sea, the trail on the right side of the pools leads to more cascades. Most hotels and travel companies in Livingston offer guided trips that include transport and lunch; expect to pay about Q100. Exotic Travel Agency's trip includes a mountain hike, canoeing, and lunch (Q100 per person). Happy Fish Restaurant

offers similar trips, guides, and prices. (Most leave at 9am. Sign up a day in advance.)
Some trips go to the pretty Playa Blanca, well worth a visit for those disappointed by the
drab beaches around Livingston proper. Entrance Q15.

Catching the waterfalls at their peak is a matter of delicate balance. If it
hasn't rained in a while, there won't be much to see; if it's been pouring,
access to the upper falls can be difficult and dangerous. Assuming reasonable conditions, the trip is well worth it—the crisp, clear pools glittering
with sunlight are lightyears better than Livingston's sub-par beaches. The
falls' big attraction is swimming; the water only crashes down a few feet.
The upper falls, although a slippery 10min. walk upriver, are well worth
the extra effort. A cool place to stop on the way back is **Larubella,** a Garífuna bar about 10min. before town. It entices patrons with *guífiti* (bitters);
aguardiente (strong liquor, literally translated "fire water") passed through
herbs and sticks is valued as a purgative and an aphrodisiac (Q5 per flask).
Some guided trips take you to the nearby **Playa Blanca,** easily the best beach
around. The white sand and pretty blue Caribbean waters are beautiful.

UP THE RÍO DULCE
Visits may be arranged in either Livingston or Fronteras/Río Dulce. Head to the docks to
arrange a trip with any of the boaters, or book at almost any of the hotels in Livingston or
Río Dulce for about the same price. (Q125 or round-trip Q200.) Trips last 2hr. and leave from
Livingston at 9:30am and 1pm; they leave from Río Dulce at 9am and 1:30pm. Lanchas will
deliver you to the dock of your hotel in Río Dulce; just tell the driver where you are staying.

The most enjoyable way to travel from Izabal to Livingston bypasses the
dirty, crowded streets of Puerto Barrios and heads down the scenic cliffs,
marshes, and islands of the Río Dulce on a 2hr. *lancha* ride. Boats travel
in both directions down the river, stopping at the sulfuric *aguas calientes*,
where the hot egg-smelling water mixes with cool river water. These trips
also pass by the **Isla de los Pajaros,** a tiny island swarming with *garzas*
(storks). The *lanchas* float passes by the bridge over the Río Dulce, considered the longest bridge in Central America, and gives riders a glimpse of
the **Castillo de San Felipe.** You'll also see the opening to the calm, blue **Lago
de Izabal**at the western end of the Río Dulce. The most impressive parts of
the trip are the sheer cliffs and intense greenery around the river as it spills
into the **Golfo de Honduras.** The stretch near Fronteras is peaceful, with lily
pads and magnificent sailboats around each turn.

The trips go rain or shine; it is a good idea to have a rain jacket and sunscreen available, as the weather can change rapidly and the sun shines brightly
in this part of Guatemala, regardless of the season. The boats usually make a
bathroom and refreshment stop, and then another at the hot springs. If you
want to visit Finca Tatín or the Biotopo, you should ask the driver in advance
and be prepared to wait for the next scheduled boat, which may be overnight.

FINCA TATÍN
The Finca offers its own transport in lancha from Livingston; call in advance to arrange. The
ranch is about 3km from town along the river. Tours along the Rio Dulce will drop you off at
the Finca, just tell the driver in advance that is where you're headed. ☎ *5902 0831; www.*
fincatatin.centroamerica.com.

A haven for weary backpackers, Finca Tatín lures in visitors with its jungle
paradise hidden deep in the swamps off the Río Dulce. Most end up sticking
around for the comfortable lodging, great food, and a relaxing atmosphere.

The *finca* offers an on-site Spanish school, kayak rentals, and is within swimming distance of the *biotopo*.

Accommodations are in **dorms** (Q45 per person) and beautiful hand-carved wood private **bungalows** with shared bath (singles Q60; doubles Q115). Some bungalows come with private baths (singles Q125; doubles Q160; triples Q220; quads Q280). Meals are served buffet-style, with ample vegetarian options. (Breakfast Q25-35. Lunch Q25-45. Dinner Q50.) Dinner is a full multi-course meal, with soup, salad, a main entree, and a side dish.

The Finca offers tours to its own Mayan **sauna** (Q10), nearby **caves** (Q35), and a **hike** that takes you all the way to Livingston (Q95). There are other trips up the river to the **Biotopo Chocón Machacas**, a manatee sanctuary. The shy sea cows, however, are often elusive. Giant tree ferns and butterflies are more abundant, but the highlight of the park may be the small and eclectic museum. The *biotopo* includes several scenic lagoons good for swimming. There is also a camping area with bathroom and kitchen facilities. (Tours Q120-180.)

VERAPAZ HIGHLANDS

No great geographic divide separates the Verapaces from the Western Highlands, though travelers will immediately sense the difference between Baja Verapaz's unique combination of near-desert and tropical forests and the densely-forested green hills of Alta Verapaz. Cobán, the capital of Alta Verapaz and the region's transportation hub, is a convenient base from which to explore the surrounding highlands, including Chisec, which is itself a wonderful jumping off point for numerous outdoor wonders.

The cloud-covered Alta Verapaz exists in sharp contrast with the highpines of the highlands. It consists of limestone pockmarked with sinkholes, humid tropical forest, and mammoth caves. When oil was discovered here, the region's first road—the Transversal del Norte—was built, and K'ekchi' from the war-torn highlands settled the area. Today, it remains a sparsely populated agricultural frontier criss-crossed by a baffling web of routes built by the oil and cardamon industry. If you're looking for an off-the-beaten-path adventure, a trip through the region is worth the hassle. Its magnificent natural sites, the Candelaria Caves and Parque Nacional Laguna de Lachuá, remain little touristed. Its reconstructed towns ring with K'ekchi' and are scented with caldo de chunto, and although the region may not boast the vibrant colors of the highlands, the Maya here remain undisturbed in their traditional lifestyle. The festive towns of Salamá and Rabinal are in Baja Verapaz, near the highway from Guatemala City to Cobán.

It was the area's long, successful resistance to the Spanish conquest that gave it the name Tuzuntohil, or "Land of War." Thanks to Fray Bartolomé de las Casas and the Franciscan friars, however, the region has earned its present Spanish name, Verapaz, or "True Peace." When the Fray organized a campaign in defense of the indígenas, the Spanish empire halted its military conquest and granted him five years for the "humane" conversion of the local people. The chiefs, assured that the friars were not interested in their gold and land, accepted them, and a peaceful conversion followed. By the end of the 19th century, however, the Guatemalan coffee boom had established large fincas in Verapaz, which strained available land and labor and disrupted many indigenous villages. Despite these tensions, the indígena presence in the region remains strong. Much of the native population speaks K'ekchi' and Pokomchí; a small population in the south of the region speaks Quiché. On a practical note, it takes a while to navigate this area. Transportation is like the quetzal: elusive, and most active in the early morning.

SALAMÁ

Despite being the capital of the Baja Verapaz region, Salamá is an intimate city whose isolated location wards off the tourist crowds. An added perk: Salamá makes a great hub for exploring the small villages of Cubulco or Rabinal.

⊏ TRANSPORTATION

Buses: All chicken buses departing from Salamá pass through the *parque central*. The bus to **Guatemala City** (3¼hr., every hr., Q25) passes through the La Cumbre junction, where connections are possible.

Microbuses: Microbuses also leave from the *parque central* and head to **Coban** (2hr., every hr., Q20), **Cubulco** (1hr., Q10), **La Cumbre** (via San Jeronimo; 45min., Q8), and **Rabinal** (30min., Q5).

Taxis: Try **Veliz y Amigos** taxi service (☎5616 5537; available 24hr.).

✈ 🛈 ORIENTATION AND PRACTICAL INFORMATION

For a regional capital, Salamá is a small city. If you are standing in the *parque central*, it is quite possible that you will be able to see the establishment that you're looking for. Banks, pharmacies, fast food restaurants, and the main cathedral are clustered around the **main plaza**, while most hotels and restaurants are only a block or two from the center of town.

Bank: Banrural (☎7954 0984 or 1110), on the west side of the *parque central*. **ATM.** Open M-F 8:30am-5pm, Sa 9am-1pm.

Police: 7a Av. 6-36, Zona 1 (☎7940 2240 or 0050).

Pharmacy: Farmacia Batres, 7a Av. 6-99, Zona 1 (☎7954 5175). Open 24hr.

Hospital or Medical Services: Hospital Nacional y Centro de Salud, 1a C. 1-01, Zona 4 (☎7940 0125).

Internet Access: Cafe Internet, 8a Av. 6-70, Zona 1, 1 block from the *parque central*. Q8 per hr. Open daily 8am-8pm.

🛏 ACCOMMODATIONS

Salamá does not play host to a large number of backpackers. As a result, the city lacks standard budget options.

Hotel Real Legendario, 8a Av. 3-57, Zona 1 (☎2833 0827 or 2709 8011), 2 blocks south of the *parque central*. A great value. All rooms have private baths, cable TVs, and hot showers. Free internet. Singles Q90; doubles Q160. Cash only. ❸

Hotel San Ignacio, 4a C. "A" 7-09, Zona 1 (☎2833 0827 or 2709 8011). Well-kept rooms with private baths. On-site restaurant. Parking available. Singles Q83; doubles Q150. Cash only. ❸

Hotel Posada de Don Maco, 3a C. 8-26, Zona 1 (☎2833 0827 or 2709 8011). Slightly more expensive than nearby options, despite the fact that it provides nearly identical amenities. All rooms have private baths, TVs, and hot water. Parking available. Singles Q100. V. ❸

🍴 FOOD

With a few exceptions, cuisine in Salamá is straightforward, with *comedores* on every street corner.

▨ **Deli Donas,** 5a C. 6-61, Zona 1 (☎7940 1121). Cafe-style restaurant offering delicious *comida típica* (enchiladas Q11) and a variety of sandwiches (Q16). Open daily from 7:30am-9pm. Cash only. ❶

La Cascada, 10a Av., 2 blocks southwest of the *parque*. Serves decent international entrees at reasonable prices (Q50-80). Open M-Sa for lunch and dinner. Cash only. ❸

📷 SIGHTS

▨ **COLONIAL BRIDGE.** Now only used by pedestrians, this crumbling colonial bridge was once the main way in and out of Salamá. *(Take any 8a Av. north from the parque central until you reach the river, from where you will see the colonial bridge.)*

🔲 DAYTRIP FROM SALAMA: RABINAL

About 1hr. west of Salamá, Rabinal (pop. 10,000) is famous for its impressive *artesanía* and the local dances showcased during the town's annual *fiesta* (January 19-25). If you can't make it to the *fiesta*, a visit to the Thursday and Sunday markets to see the town's renowned carvings and pottery is still worth the trip. Rabinal suffered a great deal during the country's nearly four-decade long civil war—hidden graves are still being uncovered—and a few sights in town memorialize the tragedy. By the altar of the *parque's* colonial church hang two striking murals, both painted in 1998. One depicts the town's troubled past, while the other illustrates Rabinal's rich culture, anticipating a bright future. There is a small community museum on 2 C. 4 Av., Zona 3, with exhibits ranging from drawings of an indigenous dance to over 300 photographs of local war victims. *(Minibuses regularly leave the main square of Salamá for Rabinal (30-45min., Q10). There are also some 2nd-class buses that go from Guatemala City to Rabinal, passing through Salamá; the entire trip from the capital to Rabinal takes 4¼hr. and costs Q30. Most of these buses will pass through Salamá's parque central; you can hop on one for the last leg to Rabinal for Q7. Taxis are also an option, although rates could be exorbitant.)*

COBÁN

Though touristed enough to be home to plenty of cosmopolitan pleasures, Cobán (pop. 51,100) gives the distinct impression that nature is never too far away. The lush green heart of the Alta Verapaz appears within arm's reach as the city's edges quickly fade into country terrain. Even though rain is common, the sun does show most days, and tourists use Cobán as an attractive base for exploring the natural wonders nearby, including the Biotopo del Quetzal, Rey Marcos, Semuc Champey, and the Grutas de Lanquín. When you need a break from the outdoors, Cobán is happy to oblige: sip a cup of the famous local coffee in a cafe and rest your head at one of several charming hotels.

▐ TRANSPORTATION

Buses: Unless otherwise noted, buses leave from the main terminal at 1/3 Av., 2/3 C. in Zona 4. Coming into town, some buses stop conveniently to the west of the *parque*, on 1 C. near the Telgua offices. Buses heading south also depart from this location. Make sure to get to the terminal at least 30min. early, especially for des-

FROM THE ROAD

CHICKEN BUSES

Of my past few months on the road, I would estimate about 1/6 of my time was spent in buses. Despite crowded, small space, bus rides can be one of the best parts of traveling.

While at the museums, or on hikes, or at the beach, I usually see people outside of their daily routines. I may occasionally see a local fisherman out on his boat while on water taxi, but the only people I see in their daily roles are service workers.

On a bus, I am doing the same thing as locals. It's a leveling ground that makes it easy to meet people.

At bus stops, cracking jokes with the other lone person waiting for that bus has led to some of the best conversations I've had on the road. A book, map, or article can bridge even more gaps; I've entertained 5 year olds with my meager Spanish music knowledge; I've discussed Latin American literature with old men.

Spending time on a bus isn't always fun. The smells can be ridiculous, the dust flying through the open window can leave you coated in dirt, and fitting 20 people into a 10-person vehicle has never ended comfortably. Still, it's a shared sense of discomfort, a sense that allows for training-camp-style bonding, because damn it, you might be suffering, but at least for these few hours, you're all suffering together.

-Alison Tarwater

VERAPAZ HIGHLANDS

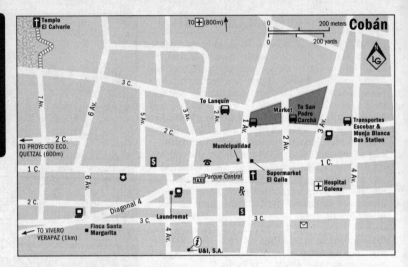

tinations toward Alta Verapaz and the Petén. Ask ahead for the latest info—services change frequently. Buses depart to:

Biotopo del Quetzal: 1hr., every 30min., Q6. Depart on any Guatemala City bound bus.

Chisec: 45min., every30 min., Q10.

Fray Bartolomé de las Casas: 7 hr., every hr., Q40.

Guatemala City: 5hr., every hr., Q30.

Lanquín: 3hr.; 5:30, 11:30am, 1:30, and 5:30pm; Q25.

Raxrujá: 1½hr., every hr., Q15.

Salamá: 1½hr., every hr., Q20. Take a bus to La Cumbre junction and transfer to a minibus.

Sayaxche: 3hr., every 2hr., Q25. Make sure to ask if it's a direct bus; some buses transfer at Raxrujá.

Taxis: Around the *parque central* and the bus terminal. *Parque central* to bus terminal Q5.

ORIENTATION AND PRACTICAL INFORMATION

The two main streets in Cobán, **1 Av.** and **1 C.**, adhere to the standard grid. They divide the city into **quadrants:** northwest Zona 1, southwest Zona 2, southeast Zona 3, and northeast Zona 4. The city's **cathedral** towers at 1 Av., 1 C. The neighboring **parque central** is directly west in Zona 2. The cathedral and *parque* rest atop a hill that encompasses Cobán. Numbered *avenidas* and *calles* continue through different zonas. Addresses on 1 Av. and 1 C. may be in any of the zonas they run through, depending which side of the street they lie on.

Tourist Office: There is no INGUAT office in Cobán, but both **Adrenalina Tours** and the staff at the **Hostal D'Acuña** will be able to provide any tourist services.

Tours: Adrenalina Tours (☎5356 8821), in the southwest corner of the *parque central*. Open M-F 8am-6pm. Offers tours to all surrounding attractions, including an excellent package for Semuc Champey (Q330 or US$40).

Bank: G&T Continental Bank, 1a C. 4-25, Zona 1 (☎7951 3939). Open M-F from 9am-7pm, Sa 9am-1pm.

Pharmacy: Farmacia Botica Central, 1a C. 3-23, Zona 1 (☎7951 2075 or 3721). Open daily 8am-9pm.

Hospital: Poliolínica Galeno, 3a Av. 1-47, Zona 3 (☎7951 3175). This well-equipped private clinic has emergency service, though not always 24hr. Walk-in hours M-Sa 10am-noon and 4-8pm.

Internet Access: Internet y Más L&M, 1a C., west of the *parque central* (☎7941 7371). Open daily 8:30am-9:30pm. Also offers tourist information.

Post Office: 3a C. 2-02, Zona 3. Open M-F 8:30am-5:30pm, Sat 9am-1pm. **Postal Code:** AV002.

ACCOMMODATIONS

Cobán has plenty of accommodation options, offering everything from hostel bunkbeds to king-sized beds in gorgeous boutique hotels. Most hotels and hostels are located wihthin one or two blocks of the *parque central*.

Casa D'Acuña, 4a C. 3-11, Zona 2 (☎7951 0482 or 0484), 2 blocks south of the *parque central*. With a colorful, inviting atmosphere, this is the best budget option and the center of tourist activity in Cobán. Bunkbeds are arranged in homey rooms for 2 or 4 people. Laundry Q35. Small courtyard garden and on-site restaurant. Hot water and dressers with padlocks. Dorms Q50 per person; private rooms Q150. AmEx/D/MC/V. ❷

Hotel La Posada, 1a C. 4-12, Zona 2 (☎7952 1495 or 7951 0588), on the west side of the *parque central*. This huge, beautiful hotel has impeccably furnished rooms, all spacious and with private baths. Sit in a chair outside your room and enjoy the views of the large, leafy courtyards within the walls of the hotel. Singles Q315; doubles Q395. AmEx/D/MC/V. ❺

Hotel Central, 1a C. 1-79, Zona 4 (☎7952 1442; www.hotelcentralcoban.com), 1 block east of the *parque central*. This bright and airy hotel has spacious rooms surrounding an attractive central courtyard. All rooms have private baths, TVs, and hot water. Free Wi-Fi. Singles Q98; doubles Q170. AmEx/D/MC/V. ❸

Casa Luna, 5a Av. 2-28, Zona 1 (☎7951 3528), northwest of the *parque central*. This is a great option for backpackers in Cobán. Staff couldn't be friendlier. Shuttle service available to many cities around Guatemala (Antigua Q164, Chichi Q290, Semuc Q65, Panajachel Q290). Dorms Q50; private rooms Q75 per person. V. ❷

Casa Blanca, 1a C. 3-25, Zona 1 (☎7951 4213), on the north side of the *parque central*. Clean rooms and well-kept communal baths in a convenient location. Dorms Q35 per person; private rooms Q45 per person. V. ❶

Posada de Don Pedro, 3a C. 3-12, Zona 2 (☎7951 0562 or 4509 3604), 1 block south of the *parque central*. Clean communal baths. Dorms Q50 per person; private rooms Q75 per person. AmEx/D/MC/V. ❷

Hospedaje Familiar, Diagonal 4 3-36, Zona 2 (☎7952 1750), on the southwest corner of the *parque central*. If a cheap room is the most important thing to you, then head to the Hospedaje Familiar. Rooms are dark and sparsely furnshed, but they do the trick. Communal baths lack showers but are otherwise clean. Singles Q25; doubles Q50. Cash only. ❶

FOOD

For groceries, visit the **Dispensa Familiar** one block east of the *parque central* on 1a C. (Open daily from 7am to 8pm.) Food prices are slightly higher than most Guatemalan cities because of the town's remote location.

Casa D'Acuña, 4a C. 3-11, Zona 2 (☎7951 0482 or 0484). This 1st-class restaurant offers European-style candlelit dining, good service, delicious home-cooked food, and plenty of *música tranquila*. Grab a table by the fire or on the terrace and enjoy a crepe with chicken and light parsley cream sauce (Q60), delicious ravioli (Q60), or a brownie (Q10). Open daily from 7am-10:30pm. AmEx/D/MC/V. ❹

Xkape Kob'an Diagonal, 4 5-13, Zona 2. This great option is a cultural center in a rebuilt colonial home. Legends and a Q'eqchi' dictionary are included on the menu. A wide array of Q'eqchi' books are scattered on the wooden tables. *Kaq-ik* (traditional duck soup) Q40. *Horchata* (milky cinnamon drink) Q6. Wide cappuccino selection starts at Q7. Open daily from 6am-7pm. ❸

La Posada Restaurante, 1a C.4-12, Zona 2 (☎7952 1495), within the walls of the Hotel La Posada. High-class Spanish-decor restaurant with both international and *típico* dishes. Chili rellenos with beef Q56. Delicous breakfast specials Q45. Try to get a table on the veranda overlooking the beautiful walled gardens of the hotel. Open daily from 7am-9:30pm. AmEx/D/MC/V. ❸

Cafe Cafeto, 2a C.1-36, Zona 2 (☎7951 2850). Head into this conveniently located cafe, right on the *parque central,* for a great cup of coffee (Q5-Q12) and a sandwich (Q30). There are magazines to peruse and usually some friendly people with whom to strike up a conversation. Open daily 7:30am-9pm. Cash only. ❷

Restaurante Cantonés, Diagonal 4 4-24, Zona 2 (☎7952 1592). Authentic Chinese food served in a typical Cobán house. The food is a great value considering the restaurant's generous portions. Try the *pollo con broccoli* (Q45) or some fried rice (Q40). Open daily 11am-10pm. MC/V. ❸

Cafetería Santa Rita (☎7952 1842), on the corner of the *parque central*. This typical *comedor*-style restaurant serves decent entrees (Q25-Q35). There is not much that distinguishes this *comedor* from others in Cobán except for its convenient location. Open daily 7am-9:30pm. Cash only. ❷

🄶 SIGHTS

TEMPLO EL CALVARIO. For a bird's eye view of Cobán, head out to Templo El Calvario. The hillside church dates back to 1559, but it's the expansive view from the church, reached by climbing 135 steps, that really makes the visit worthwhile. *(Follow 7a Av. north until you reach the stairs. Travel in a group, if possible.)*

VÍVERO VERAPAZ. Located within walking distance of the *parque central*, this orchid farm showcases thousands of different species, including the *monja blanca* (white nun), the national flower of Guatemala. *(Follow Diagonal 4 that begins at the end of the parque, to the left of Hotel la Posada. At the bottom of the hill turn left and continue for 15min. Open M-Sa 9am-noon and 2-5pm. Q5.)*

FINCA SANTA MARGARITA. Cobán's passion for coffee spills outside the town's cafes and into the surrounding *fincas*, many of which were once owned by wealthy Germans. For insight into the coffee culture, check out **Finca Santa Margarita,** 3 C. 4-12, Zona 2. Guided tours of the plantation explain the *finca's* history and give a detailed look at modern coffee production; some provide coffee samples for visitors to savor and compare. Spanish and English-speaking guides are available. *(3a C. 4-12, Zona . ☎7951 3067. Open M-F 8am-12:30pm and 1:30-5pm, Sa 8am-noon. Q20.)*

🄲 🄹 NIGHTLIFE AND ENTERTAINMENT

Milenio, 3a Av., half a block north of 1a C. in Zona 4. The front bar has a more upscale feel, but the atmosphere stays relaxed, with *fútbol* on the widescreen TV and a dance floor in back. There are 2 main lounges. Salsa is the music of choice. Pool tables. Open daily until 1am. Cash only.

Bok'atas (☎7952 2870), on 4a C., between 2a and 3a Av. This outdoor bar has a sports bar feel; there is often live music and a calm and sociable atmosphere. Drinks are reasonably priced. One of the few places that stays open late in Cobán. Open daily 7pm-midnight. Cash only.

◢ DAYTRIPS FROM COBÁN

BIOTOPO DEL QUETZAL

Buses on the route between Cobán and Guatemala City pass the biotopo. Buses also leave the biotopo to Guatemala City (3hr., every 30min. 3-7am, every hr. 7am-5pm) and Cobán (1hr., every hr. 7am-8pm, Q6). Open daily 7am-5:30pm; last entrance 4pm.

About 30km southeast of Cobán is the Biotopo Mario Dary Rivera, commonly known as the Biotopo del Quetzal (Quetzal Reserve), an expanse of rugged cloud forest home to Guatemala's national bird, the elusive quetzal. Two trails twist their way through the park: **Sendero los Helechos** (1hr., 2km) is the shorter trail, while **Sendero los Musgos** (2hr., 3½km) takes you deep into the dense forest. The longer route provides better vistas while the shorter leads to a waterfall, but both give excellent tours of the forest and an equally good chance of spotting the elusive quetzal. The road at the entrance to the reserve is actually one of the best places to catch a glimpse of the beautiful birds; they're seen most often in April and September in the early morning. Take time to look into the large leaves of the *aguacatillo;* its small green fruit is a favorite treat for elusive quetzals. But even if the bird eludes you (and odds are, it will), the beautiful forest canopy and a swim in the waterfalls are still worth a visit. You can stay the night at **Hospedaje Los Ranchitos ❶,** just down the road toward Cobán from the entrance to the reserve. It offers rustic accommodations and is a good place to look for the elusive quetzal. The *hospedaje* has its own patch of forest, complete with a private trail and a basic *comedor.* (Breakfast Q15-20. Lunch or dinner Q18-25. Singles Q30, with bath Q50; doubles Q60/80; triples Q90/100. Camping is also available inside the reserve for Q10 per person.)

GRUTAS DEL REY MARCOS AND BALNEARIO CECILINDA

To reach the Grutas from Cobán, take a bus to Chamelco from 5 Av., 5 C. in Zona 3 (20min., Q2), where you can find morning buses or pickups to Chamil. Ask to be dropped off at the road to Rey Marcos/Balneario Cecilinda, then walk about 500m to the entrance; follow the sign. Coming back, pickups to Chamelco are less frequent in the afternoon but still pass by. The last bus to Cobán departs in the late afternoon.

For adventure seekers who enjoy crawling and climbing through unlit caves, the Grutas del Rey Marcos are not to be missed. Listen to the roar of a sacred, underground Maya river, and splash around under gorgeous natural waterfalls. Discovered in May 1998 and open to the public since January 1999, the caves are believed to be the site of religious ceremonies that took place in pre-Columbian times; the Maya still hold the site sacred and ceremonies continue even today. The inner sanctuary of the cave is rumored to be the source of a large, mystic energy field, and Iván, the owner and occasional tour guide, warns that everyone who enters will leave carrying a blessing or a curse. Mysticism aside, a tour of Rey Marcos is an exhilarating experience and makes for a worthwhile daytrip from Cobán. After getting muddy exploring, cool off in the Balneario Cecilinda, the natural swimming area set into the mountainside below the caves. (Open daily 8am-5pm. Admission including guided tour, rubber boots, helmet, and flashlight. Q25.) For those adventurers who just can't get enough of Grutas, a pleasant farm and hostel has opened 500m from the entrance. **Don Jeronimo's ❺,** run by an American, is an all-inclusive resort. (For Q200 per day or Q360 for a couple, you get 3 full vegetarian meals and a pleasant *cabaña* next to a gurgling river.)

LANQUÍN

About 40km northeast of Cobán rests the village of Lanquín. Nearby are two natural wonders, the beautiful pools of Semuc Champey and the cave network known as the Grutas de Lanquín. Guided tours from Cobán are convenient and often a good deal for one or two travelers; the guides are excellent and will point out the sights' hidden marvels. Hostal D'Acuña in Cobán offers a "Semuc Special," which includes transportation, breakfast, lunch, and guides (Q280 per person, 4 person minimum). The Hostal can also organize transportation to Semuc Champey (Q205 per person, 4 person minimum; discounts for larger groups).

TRANSPORTATION

Many travelers make daytrips to Lanquín, catching the 6am bus from Cobán and returning on the 2:30pm bus. Buses from **Cobán** (2½hr., 6 per day 6am-3pm, Q10) and return buses from **Lanquín** (2½hr.; 6 per day 3:30am-2:30pm; Q10, minibus Q15) make several trips per day. Pickups also happen in the mornings, heading from Lanquín to Pujal and then on to Cobán. Go early and be prepared to wait.

ACCOMMODATIONS

While many travelers opt to visit Semuc Champey and Grutas de Lanquín in one day, there are options for those who want to spend the night in Lanquín. Below are some of the accommodation options that provide easy access to both the caves and Semuc Champey.

Casa Marbella (☎7983 0009), on the shore of the Lanquin River, 10min. east of town. This legendary hostel's laid-back style, beautiful setting, and terrific vegetarian food captures backpackers for weeks at a time. Arrive early as dorms fill up quickly. Free pickup is available at the bus stop. Dinner Q45. Dorms Q40; private bungalows Q80 per person, with bath Q100 per person. ❶

Hotel El Recreo (☎7983 0056), about 100m downhill from the town entrance. Spacious rooms, most with private baths. Decent budget bungalows with clean communal bath in forested grounds. Bungalows Q25 per person. Singles and doubles Q100 per person. Prices vary seasonally. MC/V. ❶

Hospedaje La Divina Providencia (☎7983 0041), uphill and to the right of the town entrance. All rooms have hot water. On-site *comedor* and pharmacy. Rooms Q25 per person. ❶

FOOD

Eating in Lanquín is straightforward—if you're not eating a home-cooked meal at the hostel or hotel that you are staying at, you'll be enjoying *comida típica* (local food) in a *comedor.*

DAYTRIPS FROM LANQUÍN

SEMUC CHAMPEY

If you are not on a tour and need to get to Semuc Champey on your own, make sure to leave early so that you can catch the 9am minibus that links Lanquín to Semuc Champey. There are also plenty of tour buses passing through that may be able to give you a ride for a small fee. The ride should not cost more than Q10. Open 8am-5pm daily. Q20 collected in the parking lot.

Semuc Champey is best reached by pickup, but you can do the 3hr. (8km) uphill hike by following the gravel road heading away from the river. Bring water. Pickups (Q10) pass by Café Semuc, most frequently on market days (M and Th), but the best bet is to take a round-trip pickup from El Retiro (daily 9am, Q30).

The 300m natural limestone bridge of Semuc Champey creates quite a show, with the mighty Cahabón River thundering into the depths below. The top of the bridge, in contrast to the chaos below, is pure tranquility. A descending series of clean pools, perfect for swimming, flow above the river. Framed by steep forested hillsides, the waters turn marvelous shades of blue and green as the sun moves across the sky. Alongside the pools is a covered rancho for camping and picnicking; the rancho also has bathrooms. To reach the departure point for the Cahabón River, start with the parking lot at your back and follow the trail that crosses over to the right side of the pools and continues past the picnic tables. Follow the slippery rocks carefully and don't get too close to the waterfalls. The trail which branches to the right before the changing rooms, continues steeply uphill for 30-45min. to a spot overlooking the entire series of pools.

If you don't want to bother with transportation and want to spend several days at the pools, the new **Posada Las Marias** (☎7861 2209) is the place to hang. Popular with travelers, the full service Las Marias is only 1km away from the Semuc Champey parking lot. The hostel has both dorm rooms and loft space. It can be a bit buggy, so bring a mosquito net or a strong bottle of DEET. Although it is isolated, Las Marias offers tasty *típico* grub so travel back and forth to Lanquín is not necessary. Minibus drivers from Cobán are more than happy to drop you off for a few extra quetzals.

GRUTAS DE LANQUÍN

See Transportation for Cobán, p. 131. Once in Lanquín, there are plenty of shuttles willing to take you to the caves (though the walk is also do-able).

Visitors to Grutas can explore the well-lit cave network, which extends more than 3km through five large "rooms." The Grutas de Lanquín are about 2km along the road toward Cobán and down a short drive that veers to the right off the main road. The path tends to be slippery, so sneakers are necessary. Some of the larger stalactites are named after famous people and animals like "La Virgen" and "El Sapo." The caves' thousands of bats pour out into the night sky around dusk. The spectacular sight is well worth the wait; since the park will be closed, this can only be done from outside the entrance. If you do stick around, bring a flashlight to find your way back to Lanquín. Wear clothes and shoes you don't mind getting dirty—especially if you venture out past the walkway. (Open daily 8am-5pm. Q20.)

CHISEC

Long a locals-only frontier territory, new roads have made Chisec (pop. 13,500) and its natural beauty accessible to all. Dominated by the K'ekchi' Maya, the area remained virtually unpopulated until 40 years ago when refugees entered en masse to escape the civil war. Unfortunately, the war found them. The town itself was burned and bulldozed twice during the 80's and is still recovering. Little Spanish is spoken; at times, creative hand motions are necessary. The main attractions are the turquoise rivers and limestone cave systems that dot the region, though they are well off the beaten track.

◤ TRANSPORTATION

Buses: Microbuses connect Chisec to the various other cities in the Alta Verapaz region. All microbuses leave from a parking lot on the south side of the *parque central.* To: **Cobán** (1½hr., every 30min., Q20); **Flores** (4hr., every 15min., Q50); and **Raxrujá** (40min., every 15 min., Q10), where connections to Sayaxche and Flores are possible.

ORIENTATION AND PRACTICAL INFORMATION

The main road, or **C. Principal,** runs directly through town and passes by the *parque central.*

Bank: Banco Agromercantil, on the north side of the *parque central.* Has **currency exchange** and **ATM.** Open M-F 9am-5pm, Sa 9am-1pm.

Police: (☎7983 2121), just south of the *parque central.* Open 24hr.

Pharmacy: Farmacia Arteaga, C. Principal (☎5325 7500), north of the *parque central.* Open daily 7am-8pm.

Internet Access: Restaurante Don Miguel, C. Principal (☎5156 7470 or 5439 8712), north of the *parque central.* Internet and Wi-Fi Q6 per hr. Open daily 7am-10pm.

Post Office: In Barrio El Centro. Open M-F 8am-12:30pm and 1:30-5:30pm. **Postal Code:** 16013.

ACCOMMODATIONS

All accommodations either border the *parque central* or line C. Principal.

Hotel La Estancia, C. Principal (☎7983 2010 or 5514 7444), north of the *parque central.* All rooms have private baths, A/C, and cable TVs. Outdoor hammocks and a beautiful pool with a theme-park-style waterslide. Restaurant in the lobby, as well as a small *tienda* selling everything from toothpaste to booze. Singles Q122; doubles Q150. V. ❹

Hotel Nopales (☎5514 0624), on the east side of the *parque central.* The best budget option in Chisec. Clean and simple rooms all have private baths and fans. Singles Q45; doubles Q86. Cash only. ❷

Hotel Elizabeth, on C. Principal, north of the *parque central,* across from Hotel La Estancia. No-frills, slightly shabby rooms. Singles Q44. Cash only. ❷

FOOD

Chisec's dining options are limited, but that doesn't mean there aren't a few places worth visiting. You'll find more exotic *comida típica* options than in larger villages (there might be deer on the menu), as well as a few international options limited mainly to burgers and pasta.

Restaurante Bonapek (☎5736 7699), on the north side of the *parque central.* Don't be intimidated by the stuffed animal decor: the creatures may prove helpful if you don't understand one of the entrees, as the waiter will point to the animal in the dish they are describing. Breakfast (eggs, beans, *plátanos,* cheese, and tortillas) Q30. *Lomito a la plancha* Q40. Open daily 7am-9pm. Cash only. ❸

Restaurante Hotel La Estancia (☎5514 7444 or 7983 2010), in the lobby of the Hotel La Estancia. Giant flatscreen TV plays a constant stream of soccer. *Comida tipica* Q30. Hamburgers Q25. Beer Q15. Open daily from 7am-9pm. V. ❷

Restaurante Don Miguel, C. Principal (☎5156 7470 or 5439 8712), north of the *parque central.* Half internet cafe, half restaurant. *Pollo frito* Q20. Free Wi-Fi. Open daily 7am-10pm. Cash only. ❷

DAYTRIPS FROM CHISEC

CANDELARIA CAVES

From Chisec, take any bus to Raxrujá and ask to be dropped at Candelaria Camposanto. Bring a flashlight. Tours are 2 hr. Dry tour Q30. Tubing tour Q40.

The beautiful and remote Candelaria Caves, located halfway between Chisec and Raxrujá, are part of an underground system more than 30km long. Now part of a national park, these caves are widely considered the most awe-inspiring in Central America. French spelunker Daniel Dreux discovered the caves in 1974, following a six-year search that began when he read about a sacred underground river in the *Popol Vuh*, the Quiché Maya holy book. Of particular note is the Ventana de Seguridad cave: a cathedral-sized vault with a large opening in the roof. Partially collapsed from a 1976 earthquake, the roof lets in a filtered column of light from the jungle above. Deeper in the cave are a series of unmarred stalactite, crystalline formations. Part of the caves are not open to tourists as they are still thought to be a sight sacred to the K'ekchi'.

LAGUNAS DE SEPALAU

To get to the lagunas, take a bus departing from the parque central or catch a pick up to Sepalau village (30min., Q2); otherwise it is a hot 7km walk to the village. Follow the road in front of the Chisec municipality out of town onto the dirt road and continue straight. Stop off in the office in town to pay the entrance fee (Q45) and get a guide to show you through the 40min. long jungle trail to the lakes. The 2nd of the 2 is for swimming. Admission includes guide and canoe ride.

Surrounded by wild primary jungle and towering limestone rocks, the turquoise Lagunas de Sepalau make a nice respite from the heat of the region. There are actually four lakes, but only two have the turquoise color that comes from mineral-laden underground springs. One of the lakes is sacred (and also supplies drinking water to the community) and swimming in that lake is prohibited. Long ago, legend has it, the sacred lake had quite a temper, turning violent and churning when approached by humans. Now the lakes have become accustomed to frequent visitors and have returned to their tranquil state—perfect for an afternoon of swimming and sunning.

B'OMB'IL PEK CAVES

Tubes are available for rent at the tourist office for Q20. A complete tour of the cave takes about 3hr., longer if tubing. Entrance Q30 includes guide and flashlight.

Just 2km from Chisec on the road towards Raxrujá, the B'omb'il Pek Caves ("painted rock") are home to the first Maya cave paintings discovered in Guatemala. Viewing the paintings and colorful rock flow formations requires technical assistance; guided tours are advisable. To enter the passage, descend the steep rope ladder or, for an extra rush, rappel into the darkened caves (don't forget your head lamp!). The 2km walk through the forest to the cave entrance is through lush jungle and fields of flowering cardamom, the spicy local crop. If rapelling wasn't enough excitement, a 15 min. float down fast flowing rapids of the San Simón River may get some more adrenaline pumping.

LAGUNA DE LACHUÁ AND PLAYA GRANDE

Microbuses or trucks from Cobán will drop you off in San Luis, a small settlement 5km from the park entrance—tell the driver you want to go to Lachuá. In San Luis, you can find a microbus or pickup heading east toward the park. From the park entrance it is 4.2km to the base camp. To return to Cobán, walk back to the Playa Grande-Cobán road (5km) and wait—departures are fairly frequent in the morning. The not-so-well-traveled road in front of the park runs east; a single bus passes by around 3:30am before taking the long road to Cobán via Chisec. To get to the Candalaria Caves, the bus will drop you off at a crossing where a pickup can take you farther. Open daily 7am-4pm. Q50.

Laguna de Lachuá, one of the least visited national parks in Central America, is a hidden gem. A new road from Cobán to Playa Grande has made accessing Lachuá much easier. Eons ago, a giant meteor landed on this remote stretch of rainforest, creating a clear, deep, limestone-ringed lagoon. A single river feeds the lagoon and two drain it. The park was established in 1975 to protect the area's humid tropical forest and the animals that live in it. Speedy lizards and colorful butterflies abound on the 4.2km trail leading to the lagoon and camping area. Other less visible fauna include jaguars, tapirs, wild boars, and hundreds of bird species, including parrots and toucans. The only trail in the 14 sq. km park is the one leading from the entrance to a tranquil lagoon. Bathe with fish and marvel at how this slice of the Caribbean became trapped in the wilderness. A building by the shore has rustic cooking facilities (bring your own food and water), solar-powered lighting, and bunk beds with mosquito netting (Q50). Latrines and a covered *rancho* for camping (Q25) are nearby.

Staying in nearby Playa Grande, which is neither a playa nor grande, is a more accommodating but less scenic option. Alternatively dusty and muddy, Playa Grande was constructed as a settlement for war refugees, and has all the grace and charm one would expect from the work of a military architect. If you stay the night, **Hotel España** offers rooms for a range of prices, some with private baths (☎ 7755 7645).

PETÉN

Guatemala's northernmost region once boasted one of the world's most advanced civilizations, but ever since the Maya mysteriously abandoned their power center at Tikal, humans have more or less avoided this foreboding area. The thick forest and thin soil here kept the Spanish settlers away, and today the Petén region contains a third of Guatemala's land mass but less than 3% of its population. Even so, nature's dominance is being threatened by new residents, slash-and-burn agriculture, and ranching. Conservation efforts have helped slow the destruction. With roads rolling over cleared grasslands dotted with banana trees, jaguars prowling, and stone pyramids hidden behind hanging jungle vines, Petén feels like something out of a movie.

The region's great attraction is Tikal, arguably the most beautiful of all Mayan sites. Flores and its sister city, Santa Elena, have the most visitor services in Petén and serve as pleasant bases from which to travel. El Remate, between Flores and Tikal, is a quiet lakeside village. Sayaxché provides river access to smaller Mayan sites, while the famous traveler's hangout of Finca Ixobel lies along the coastal highway to Guatemala City. North of Tikal are some isolated Mayan ruins, including Uaxactún and spectacular El Mirador.

POPTÚN

Formerly an important rest stop on the long, bumpy trek to Tikal, Poptún has diminished in importance with the advent of the Río Dulce bridge and the paved road through El Petén. In keeping with its rustic background, the area's biggest new attraction is the isolated Finca Ixobel, which offers idyllic woodland living surrounded by the natural wonders of the cave and hike-filled northern area.

▐ TRANSPORTATION

Buses enter and exit on Av. 15 de Septiembre.

Minibuses: To **Santa Elena** (2hr., every 15min. 6am-6pm, Q25).

Buses: To **Santa Elena/Flores** (2hr., every hr. 4am-midnight, Q20); **Fray Bartolomé de las Casas** (5hr., daily 10am, Q75); **Guatemala City** (6-7hr.; every 30min. 5am-midnight; regular Q85, especial Q170) via **Rio Dulce** (2hr.; regular Q35, especial Q55).

Taxis: Provide transportation around town and to nearby Finca Ixobel (Q15-35).

▐ ▐ ORIENTATION AND PRACTICAL INFORMATION

Poptun is laid out in the typical Guatemalan grid system. The main drag is **Av. 15 de Septiembre,** which runs north to south and serves as the de facto **bus stop.** *Avenidas* increase in number going west; *calles* increase to the south.

Bank: Banco de Desarrollo Rural, 6a Av. and 5a C. (☎7927 7553). Open M-F 8:30am-5pm, Sa 8:30am-noon. Western Union services. Visa cash advances. **Currency exchange.**

Police: 4a Av. 4-56 (☎7927 7330).

Pharmacy: Farmacia Popular, Av. 15 de Septiembre (☎7927 6255), in front of the hospital. Open M-F 7am-9pm, Sa-Su 8am-7pm.

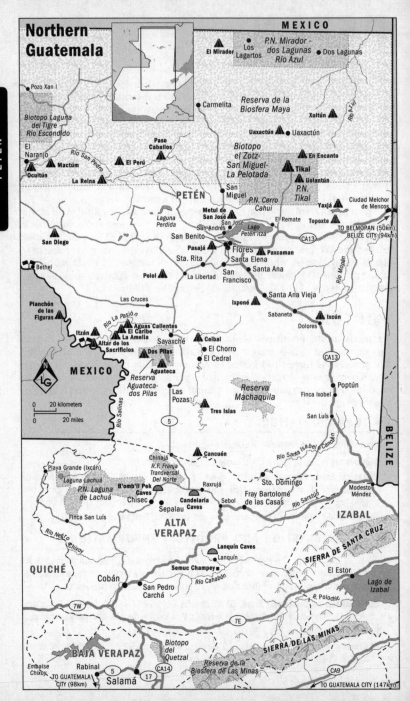

Northern Guatemala

MEXICO

El Mirador Los Lagartos P.N. Mirador-dos Lagunas Río Azul Dos Lagunas

Pozo Xan I

Carmelita Reserva de la Biosfera Maya Xultún Río Azul

Biotopo Laguna del Tigre Río Escondido

Uaxactún Uaxactún

El Naranjo Paso Caballos Biotopo el Zotz-San Miguel-La Pelotada En Encanto

Mactún El Perú Tikal Uolantán

Ocultún La Reina San Miguel P.N. Cerro Cahui P.N. Tikal Yaxjá Ciudad Melchor de Mencos

PETÉN

Metul de San José Laguna Perdida San Andrés Lago Petén Itzá El Remate Topoxte TO BELMOPAN (50km); BELIZE CITY (94km)

San José San Benito Pasajá Flores Paxcaman CA13

San Diego Sta. Rita Santa Elena Santa Ana

Bethel Polol La Libertad San Francisco Santa Ana Vieja

Las Cruces Ixponé Sabaneta Ixcún

Planchón de las Figuras Río La Pasión Aguas Callentes Dolores CA13

Itzán El Caribe La Amelia Sayaxché Ceibal Poptún

Altar de los Sacrificios Dos Pilas El Chorro Finca Ixobel

MEXICO Aguateca El Cedral San Luís

Reserva Aguateca-dos Pilas Las Pozas Reserva Machaquila

0 20 kilometers
0 20 miles

Tres Islas

Cancuén Río Santa Isabel Cancán BELIZE

Chinajá R.F. Franja Transversal Del Norte Sto. Domingo Modesto Méndez

Playa Grande (Ixcán) Raxrujá Fray Bartolomé de las Casas Río Sarstún

Laguna Lachuá B'omb'il Pek Caves Candelaria Caves Sebol IZABAL

P.N. Laguna de Lachuá Chisec SIERRA DE SANTA CRUZ

Finca San Luís Sepalau Caves ALTA VERAPAZ El Estor

QUICHÉ Lanquín Caves SIERRA DE LAS MINAS Lago de Izabal

Río Negro Chixoy Semuc Champey Lanquín R. Polochic

Cobán San Pedro Carchá Río Cahabón

7W

7E

BAJA VERAPAZ Biotopo del Quetzal

Embalse Chixoy Rabinal Reserva de la Biosfera de Las Minas

5 TO GUATEMALA CITY (98km) Salamá 17 CA14 CA9 TO GUATEMALA CITY (147km)

PETÉN

Medical Services: Centro De Salud de Poptún, Av. 15 de Septiembre 4-05 (☎7927 6248). Open 24hr.

Post Office: 4a Av. 4-70 (☎7927 6228). Open M-F 8:30am-5:30pm.

 ACCOMMODATIONS

Hotel Posada de los Castellanos 4a C. and 7a Av. (☎7927 7222), in front of the Mercado Municipal. The most popular spot in town for lodging. Basic but functional rooms with fans, private baths, and cable TV. Rooms arranged around a gated, green courtyard. Singles Q75; doubles Q125. Cash only. ❷

⬛ FOOD

Fonda De Ixobel, Av. 15 de Septiembre 0-94 (☎7927 8483), next to Shell Gas station. One of the only dining options around, Ixobel offers pastries (Q5-10), bread (Q3-15) and sandwiches (Q10-18) in its small shop off the main street. Open daily 6am-5pm. Cash only. ❶

⬛ SIGHTS

FINCA IXOBEL

All buses on the Guatemala City-Flores route pass by the turn-off to the Finca (from which it is a 15min. walk to the property). Microbuses from Flores will drop you right at the entrance. Taxis from Poptún will run you at least Q35. Buses passing by at night don't usually stop for travellers; you must arrange tickets in advance through the Finca if you wish to take a night bus without going into town. Finca Ixobel can also arrange minibuses, a cheaper option for large groups.

Finca Ixobel has become notorious for the spell it casts on travelers, who come with plans to stay a day and end up staying for weeks or months. Run by American Carole DeVine, the 400-acre *finca* set in pine-covered hills is a peaceful spot. Travelers frustrated by hordes of backpackers might be disappointed. Still, the homemade all-you-can-eat dinners, including fresh bread and garden salad, meat and vegetarian entrees, vegetables, juice, tea, and coffee (Q30-60), are nothing short of delicious. The staff also offers a range of excursions into the surrounding wilderness. (Horse treks 2hr. Q100; 1 day Q225; 2 days with camping Q500. Jungle treks 2-4 days Q200 per day. Inner-tubing trips, 1 day Q175. A popular river cave trip, full day, Q75.) Dinner is served at large benches where travelers tell stories before heading over to the private bar, open until the last guest stops drinking. Relaxing accommodations vary from sheltered camping and dorms to simple rooms with private bath. There are a few short-term volunteer opportunities available. (☎5410 4307; www.fincaixobel.com. Camping Q25 per person in huts, tents, or cars; blanket or hammock rental Q3. Dorms Q35; regular singles Q60-100; doubles Q90-175; Treehouse singles Q60; doubles Q90; triples Q110; quad Q120. Treehouse with balcony, hammock, and views Q110-300. Bungalows with private bath, veranda, and hammocks: single Q150; double Q275; triple Q325; quad Q375.)

SAYAXCHÉ

Sleepy Sayaxché (pop. 7800) sits on the Río de La Pasión about 50km southwest of Flores. Although there's little to do here, the town makes a great launching point for trips to El Ceibal, Aguateca, and other ruins in the southwest Petén. Sayaxché also makes for a good stop over before heading south toward Tikal or Cobán and the Verapaz Highlands. During the rainy season, however, the river often floods its banks, making travel through the area exciting but dangerous.

TRANSPORTATION

All buses and microbuses leave Sayaxché from the waterfront and pass through the *parque central*. To: **Cobán** (4¼hr.; 6, 11am, and 3pm; Q45); **Flores** (1½hr., every 20min., Q15); and **Raxrujá** (2hr., every 30min., Q25).

ORIENTATION AND PRACTICAL INFORMATION

Most travelers arrive to Sayaxché on microbuses which stop in the *parque central*, just three blocks from the river. Most hotels and restaurants line the streets that run along or parallel to the river.

Tourist Office: There is no tourist office in Sayaxche, but Cecilia at **Restaurante Yaxkín** (☎4144 7334) is a wealth of information on happenings in Sayaxché and environs.

Bank: Banrural: on a corner of the *parque central*. Open M-F 8:30am-5pm, Sa 9am-1pm. Has **ATM** and **currency exchange.**

Police: (☎7928 6144), 1 block from the waterfront, across from Restaurante Yaxkín.

Pharmacy: Farmacia Arteaga (☎7928 6104), 2 blocks from the *parque central* and 2 blocks up from the waterfront. Open daily 7am-9pm.

ACCOMMODATIONS

There are no luxury hotels in Sayaxche, but there are plenty of accommodations that make a perfect base for exploring the area around Sayaxche and Lake Petexbatun. Most accommodations are located in between the river and the *parque central*.

Hotel del Río (☎7928 6138 or 5150 1231). The nicest option in town. Spacious rooms have private baths and hot water. Rooms with fans Q150, with A/C Q225. Cash only. ❹

Hotel Guayacán (☎7928 6111), 1 block from the waterfront. Clean, secure rooms in a convenient location. All rooms have private baths and fans. Singles Q100; doubles Q150. Cash only. ❸

Hotel la Pasión (☎5170 7913), across the street from the Hotel Guayacán. Rooms with private baths, fans, and cable TVs. The staff couldn't be friendlier. Singles Q60; doubles Q80. Cash only. ❷

Hospedaje Sayaxché (☎4576 1905 or 5914 4454). Rooms made entirely of cement are dark, drab, and furnished with cruelly uncomfortable beds. Communal bathroom is clean enough. Singles Q30; doubles Q60. Cash only. ❶

FOOD

In this small town, *comedor*-style restaurants are impossible to escape.

Restaurante Yaxkín (☎4144 7334). *Comida típica* options abound. Try the *pollo frito* (Q25). Box lunch is perfect for daytrips (Q40). Open daily 7am-7pm. Cash only. ❷

NIGHTLIFE

El Botanero (☎4545 2229), 2 blocks up from the river, on the left. It's all about the attitude at this eatery and disco. The decor is log cabin meets discotheque. *Pollo a la plancha* Q34. Open daily 10am-8pm. ❷

🔳 DAYTRIPS FROM SAYAXCHÉ

CEIBAL

The best way to reach Ceibal from Sayaxché involves a 1hr. boat journey along the Río de la Pasión through pastures, hamlets, and the Parque Nacional Ceibal. The best service is provided by Don Pedro, whose office is to the right on the water (☎ 7928 6109. Q250-300 round trip for 1-5 people.) A slightly less expensive option is to hire a direct pickup truck (45min., Q150 round trip). The least expensive option is to take a collective pickup from the bus terminal across the river to Aldea Paraíso (10min., every 30 min., Q3) and then walk the dirt road veering left to the ruins (8km, 2hr.). Open daily 7:30am-5pm.

The grandest of the Mayan ruins near Sayaxché is Ceibal, 15km east of town. With only 3% of the ruins restored, the site is small but still impressive. The main attractions are the wonderfully preserved stelae. Unlike the limestone stelae of Tikal, these were carved out of hard stone found only in the small area surrounding the site; the monkey-faced "stelae 2" is particularly unique. Ceibal reached its peak around AD 900 with more than 10,000 residents and seems to have been strongly influenced by the Toltec dynasties of Mexico. Most of the site surrounds several plazas off to one side of the guard's quarters. A path heading in the opposite direction from the information center leads to the only other restored structure, the *pirámide circular*, a Toltec-influenced platform used for astronomy. Free camping is permitted, but bring a tent, mosquito netting, water, and enough food to share with the guards (no joke). For tours of the ruins, hire a guide at the entrance.

LAKE PETEXBATÚN

A 30-45min. speed boat ride will take you from Sayaxche to the northern tip of Lake Petexbatún.

From Sayaxché, a short ride down the southern branch of the Río de la Pasión leads to the secluded Lake Petexbatún (Peh-tesh-bah-TOON), surrounded by forest and teeming with wildlife. The area was once an important trading center for the Maya, and the ruins of Aguateca overlook the southern edges of the lake. Occupied until about AD 790, the site has plazas, unexcavated temples, well-preserved stelae, and the only known Mayan bridge. The ruins are undergoing restorations scheduled for completion in 2004. The guards will show you around and let you camp if you bring food and equipment. Rain gear, mosquito netting, and plenty of bug repellent are advisable. Nearby is the **Petexbatún Lodge** ❺, a well-maintained hotel on the shores of the lake. (☎ 7926 0501. Dorms Q80; singles Q285.) A second Maya site, **Dos Pilas**, is a 13km (3½hr.) hike west of the lake. Find guides at the Posada el Caribe (☎ 7928 6114). Built in a unique east-west linear pattern, these ruins include stelae and hieroglyphic stairways.

AGUATECA

Aguateca is a 1½hr. boat ride from Sayaxché. The walk to the path to Dos Pilas takes 45min.; the walk to Aguateca is another 3hr. from there. Servicio de Lanchas Don Pedro arranges trips to Aguateca and Dos Pilas. During the dry season (Jan.-May), a four-wheel-drive pickup sometimes runs to Dos Pilas, departing from Sayaxché at 7am.

One of the shortest-lived Maya sites in the Petén region, Aguateca has recently become one of the area's most heavily excavated and studied sites. Occupied between early AD 700 and AD 790, the city was thought to be closely aligned with nearby Dos Pilas. There have even been similar stelae found at both sites chronicling the defeat of El Ceibal. Set high on a limestone platform and protected on three sides by a large rock wall and gorge, Aguateca's geology is both unique and fascinating. A slippery two-hour walk around the edge of the site delves into the gorge and ventures deep into the surrounding jungle which monkeys, snakes, mosquitoes, and sloths call home. The city came to its surprising end during the construction of the palace dedicated to the fifth governor, when an enemy attack forced locals to flee. The massive pile of rocks waiting to be erected still sits in the center of the main plaza.

EL REMATE

Huddled on the eastern coast of Lake Peten Itza, the long village of El Remate (pop. 2000) is a welcome alternative to the tourist hustle of Flores and the clatter of Santa Elena. It's location on the road north to Tikal might explain the explosion of hotels and restaurants in an otherwise nondescript town. Head here if you want to camp and get closer to nature than is possible in its well-trafficked neighbors.

TRANSPORTATION

Minibuses from San Juan travel through town on their way to **Tikal** (45min., 7 per day 5:30am-2:30pm, Q60). **Minibuses** also leave for **Santa Elena** (50min., every 30min. 8:30am-6pm, Q25).

ACCOMMODATIONS AND CAMPING

The two main roads in El Remate are lined with hotels taking advantage of the hilltop and lakeside views. Thankfully, expensive resorts are not the only option here, and accommodations feature a surprising blend of culture and charm.

Hotel Sak Luk (☎5495 5925 or 5048 3982). The rooms at this hillside site are well worth the shady climb. Blue, thatched-roof cabañas with clean beds and hammocks, many with spectacular views. Best of all, though, are the grounds themselves, rich with plant life and decorated with the works of the sculptor-owner, Erwin (don't miss the giant carved face down by the roadside). The restaurant and bar afford gorgeous views of the lake. Dorms Q30; rooms with bath Q40-50. MC/V. ❷

El Paraiso Hostal Y Camping just off the southern edge of town. Family-run and perfectly perched on a hillside, this guesthouse and campsite offers rustic but intimate accommodations for some of the cheapest prices in town. All beds come with mosquito nets. You'll most likely be mingling with the host family; be sure to enjoy the homemade food. Camping Q20 per person; dorms Q30 per person. Cash only. ❷

Hostal Hermano Pedro (☎2261 4181 or 4419; www.hhpedro.com). Quiet and hugging a green courtyard. Its 2 wooden stories, veranda with hammocks, and low-key restaurant are made for chilling before or after climbing the temples at Tikal. Cabin-like rooms with wooden walls. All private rooms with bath. Breakfast included. Free Wi-Fi. Dorms Q96; singles Q152; doubles Q208; triples Q288. AmEx/MC/V. ❸

Hotel Mon Ami (☎7928 8413 or 8480; www.hotelmonami.com), 1km along the east-west road that leaves the main road about 1km into town. Another quiet, groovy place by the shore. The expansive grounds house thatched-roof dorms and stand-alone bungalows, with verandas, hammocks, and leafy footpaths. On-site restaurant serves delicious crepes among many other things. Tours to the Biotopo Cerro Cahui (Q160). Dorms Q57; *casas* Q81; singles (in bungalows) Q122; doubles Q203; triples Q245; quads Q325. MC/V. ❷

⬛ FOOD

Almost every hotel has a restaurant. Since there are many hotels, the lakeshore teems with open-air establishments. If you're looking for cheaper fare, smaller *comedores* (eateries) mingle next to the swankier places.

Restaurante Cahui, along the main road by the turnoff to the dirt east-west road. Enjoy the lake breezes from the covered veranda by the shore. Soups Q13-25. Salads Q22-25. Sandwiches and burgers Q20-25. There's a small bar for (early) night owls. Open daily 9am-10pm. MC/V. ❷

Restaurante El Muelle (☎5514 9785 or 5581 8087; www.hotelyrestauranteelmuelle.com), along the main road. Another lakeside restaurant in a hotel, but the menu here is unusually varied and expansive. Basic salads Q27-45. Meat dishes Q54-77. Chicken plates Q45-70. You can also grab some pasta (Q37-53) and crepes (Q12-15). Chill with the hotel's guests under the *palapa* (thatched roof, open-air house) at the end of the pier. Open daily 8am-9pm. MC/V. ❸

⬛ ⬛ SIGHTS AND OUTDOOR ACTIVITIES

Two miles west from the village, along the dirt road that leaves the main road, **Biotopo Cerro Cahui** provides hiking trails and a small swimming area by the entrance. The protected area covers 2½ sq. mi. of subtropical forest by the quiet lakeshore. Dozens of tree species, 180 bird species, and 20 mammal species live in the region. Hiking trails start at the guarded entrance and loop through the hilly terrain, affording views of nearby lakes. (Open daily from 7am-4pm. Q20.)

More than just a base for exploring Tikal, El Remate allows for plenty of independent exploration of the surrounding area. Arrangements can be made at most hotels. **Sport Lake Rental** (☎5052 0327), along the main road, is the first stop for those interested in exploring the area. (Single kayaks Q25 per hr.; double Q35 per hr. Bikes Q10 per hr., Q60 per day. 2½hr. horseback rides Q125. Open daily 7am-6pm.)

FLORES

Far more than a mere jumping off point for Tikal, Flores (pop. 2000) is an island world unto itself. Just a short causeway across from noisy Santa Elena, narrow cobblestone streets wind their way past bright pastel facades and up steep inclines. Beautiful Lago de Petén Itzá is never far from sight, encircled by lush jungle hills. Still, don't expect a peaceful oasis free of tourist bustle; Flores wears its charm on its sleeve. Every street seems to hold at least five hotels, signs in English are unavoidable, and travel agencies flaunt their tour and shuttle deals from every corner. But all that fades into irrelevance when you're enjoying dinner by the waterfront at dusk, watching the brilliant sunset ripple on the water.

⬛ TRANSPORTATION

Flores is Guatemala's northernmost destination for most travelers; there are plenty of options for journeying south into the rest of Guatemala or heading into nearby Mexico and Belize. If you're really wheelin' it, you can even catch direct but long bus rides into bordering El Salvador and Honduras.

Flights: Mundo Maya International Airport, on the Santa Elena side, southeast of the causeway. *Tuk-tuks* from Flores Q20-25. There is a Q20 airport tax for all flights.

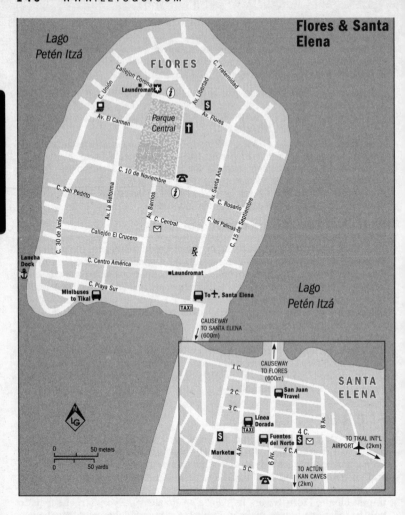

Flores & Santa Elena

Transportes Aeoreos Guatemaltecos (TAG) (☎2380 9494; www.tag.com.gt) flies
to **Guatemala City** (1hr., daily 4:30pm, Q915-1000). **Grupo TACA** (☎2470 8222;
www.taca.com) flies to **Guatemala City** (1hr.; 8:05am, 4:10, 7:20pm; Q915-1000),
Cancun, MEX (3hr., 11:25am, Q1900-2080), and **Belize City** (2hr., 12:30 and 1pm,
Q3080-3400). **Tropic Air** (☎1-800-422-3435; www.tropicair.com) flies to **Belize
City** (1hr., 9:45am and 4:15pm, Q950). **Continental Airlines** (www.continental.com)
flies to **Houston, Texas** W and Sa.

Tourist Buses: Seats on these buses must be reserved at least a day in advance;
you can usually book them at your accommodation and, in some cases, arrange to
be picked up there. **Aventuras Turisticas minibuses** go to: **Antigua** (10hr., 10pm,
Q245; 1st class 10hr., 9:30pm, Q285); **Coban** (5hr., 9am, Q150); **Guatemala City**
(8hr., 10 and 11pm, Q175; 1st class 8hr., 9 and 11pm, Q250); **Lanquin** (7hr.,

9am, Q150); **Panajachel** (12hr., 10pm, Q300); **Rio Dulce** (5hr., every 30min. 5:30-8:30am, Q125; 1st-class 5hr., 10am, Q210); **San Pedro Sula, HON** (12hr., 5:30am, Q300); **San Salvador, El Salvador** (12hr., 5:30am, Q300); **Semuc Champey** (7hr., 9am, Q150); **Tegucigalpa, HON** (14hr., 5:30am, Q330). San Juan buses go to **Belize City, Belize** (6hr., 5 and 7:30am, Q160), **Chetumal, MEX** via Belize City (8hr., 5am, Q225), and **Palenque, MEX** (8hr., 5am, Q265).

Public buses: Main bus station in Santa Elena, 1 mi. south of the bridge on 6a Av. *Tuk-tuk* ride from Flores Q5. Minibuses and buses also leave from inside the Santa Elena market along 5a C., but most of these rides start at the main station and are just trying to pick up more passengers among the crowds. **1st-class ADN** buses go to **Guatemala City** (8hr., 9 and 11pm, Q165). **AMCAS buses** go to: **Bethel** (3¼hr.; 11:30am, noon, 3:30pm; Q45); **La Tecnica** (3½hr., 8 and 9am, Q50); **San Andres** (25min., every 15min. 5am-6:30pm, Q9); **San Jose** (25min., every 15min. 5am-6:30pm, Q9). **ATIM minibuses** got to **El Remate** (45min., every 30min. 8am-6:30pm, Q25-30). **Fuente del Norte buses** go to **Guatemala City** (9hr., every 1½hr. 3:30am-10:30pm, Q110; 1st class 8hr.; 10am, 2, 9, 10pm; Q160), **Melchor de Mencos** (1½hr., Q30), and **San Salvador, El Salvador** (10hr., 6am, Q210). **1st-class Linea Dorada** buses go to **Guatemala City** (8hr., 9am and 8:45pm, Q150; luxury buses 8hr., 9:30pm, Q190). **Microbuses del Norte** go to **Sayaxche** (1hr. 20min., every 15min. 5:30am-6pm, Q20). **Rapidos del Sur buses** go to **Guatemala City** (7hr., 10 and 11pm, Q120). **Transportes Maria Elena** go to **Chiqimula** (7hr.; 6, 10am, 2pm; Q95), **Esquipulas** (8hr.; 6, 10am, 2pm; Q110), and **Rio Dulce** (4hr.; 6, 10am, 2pm; Q70). **Transportes Rosario** chicken buses go to **Guatemala City** (9hr., 7 and 8:30pm, Q95).

▟ ⁊ ORIENTATION AND PRACTICAL INFORMATION

Flores is connected to the mainland by a 1600 ft. causeway. **Playa Sur** (or **C. Sur**) heads left from the bridge; **Av. Santa Ana, Av. Barrios,** and **C. 30 de Junio** head north up the hill. At the hill's top is the **parque central,** with a basketball court, stone benches arranged in a circle, and a large cathedral (visible from Santa Elena). **C. Union** circles around the northern edge of the island, becoming **C. 15 de Septiembre** on the eastern side.

Tourist Office: There's a tourist information booth on Pl. Sur right by the causeway. Open M-Su 7am-11am and 2-6pm. **INGUAT,** Av. Santa Ana (☎7867 5334). Open M-F 8am-4pm.

Tours: Flores is littered with companies offering tour packages to various destinations in the Petén, many of them indistinguishable from or tied to the travel agencies in town. Most hostels and hotels will be able to arrange tours as well. Some companies have offices; with others it is best to simply contact in advance through phone or online (see **Sights Around Flores and Santa Elena,** p. 151, for details on trip destinations).

Martsam Tour and Travel, C. 30 de Junio (☎7867 5093; www.martsam.com). One of the best tour providers, offering a huge range of trips to the top destinations in Petén. Full-day trips to Tikal, Uaxactun, Yaxha, Nakum, Ceibal, and Aguateca; 3-day tours of El Zotz and Tikal; 5-day trips to El Mirador; 2- and 3-day trips to the Laguna del Tigre National Park. MC/V.

Quetzal Travel (☎4188 7883; www.mayanprincesstouroperator.com). Tours to Tikal, Uaxactun, Yaxha, El Mirador, El Zotz, and Ceibal.

Turismo Aventura (☎7926 0398 or 5510 2965; www.toursguatemala.com). Full-day and overnight tours of Tikal, full-day tours of Uaxactun, regular and sunset tours of Yaxha, 5-day trip to El Mirador, 3-day tours of El Zotz and Tikal.

Cafe Arqueologico Yaxha, C. 15 de Septiembre (☎5830 2060). Restaurant also offers tours to **La Blanca** and **Yaxha** (8am-5pm; 2 people Q620 per person, 3 people Q440 per person, 4 people Q350 per person, 5 people Q290 per person, plus Q80 park fee); **Topoxte** and **Yaxha** (8am-4pm; 2 people Q700 per person, 5 people Q500 per person, 4 people Q375 per person, 3 people Q315 per person); **Yaxha** and **Nakum** (2 days, 2 people Q1540 per person, 3 people Q1455 per person, 4 people Q1250 per person, plus Q80 park fee); **El Zotz** and **Tikal** (3 days, 1 person Q2200, 2 people Q1370 per person, 4 people Q1120 per person, + Q415 for English-speaking guide); **El Mirador** (5 days, 1 person Q3450, 2 people Q2450 per person, 4 people Q1800 per person, plus Q415 for English-speaking guide). MC/V.

Bank: Banrural, Av. Flores. Open M-Sa 8am-3pm. The only **ATM** in Flores is next to the Hotel Petén on C. 30 de Junio.

Laundromat: Mayan Princess Travel Agency, C. 30 de Junio. Wash and dry Q30. Open M-Sa 9am-6pm. **Lavafacil,** C. Jon el Crucero. Wash and dry Q35. Also has an internet cafe (Q8 per hr.). Open daily 9am-7pm.

Canoe Rental: La Villa del Chef, C. Union (see **Food,** p. 151). Rents canoes for Q40 per hr.

Police Station: In *parque central.*

Internet Access: Tikal Net, C. Centroamerica. Q10 per hr. Open daily 8am-9pm. **Peten Net,** C. Centroamerica, next to Tikal Net. Q10 per hr. Open daily 9m-10pm. **Maya Net,** corner of Av. La Reforma and C. Jon El Crucero. Q12 per hr. Book exchange and choco-late-dipped fruit. Open daily 9am-9pm.

Post Office: At the corner of C. Central and Av. Barrios. Open M-Sa 8am-5pm.

ACCOMMODATIONS AND CAMPING

Countless hotels running the full price gamut crowd the narrow streets, most of them with their own restaurants. Many allow guests to book tourist shuttles, which can pick you up at the hotel's door.

Los Amigos Hostel, C. Central (☎5584 8795; www.amigoshostel.com). Easily the best budget option in Flores, Los Amigos is always full of backpackers who flock to its groovy, jungle-like interior. It's a perfect example of controlled chaos—dogs and cats run through haphazardly placed plants, crowds of backpackers lounge in hammocks, and nonstop music provides eclectic background noise. There's also a restaurant that serves delicious vegetarian breakfasts (Q18-30), *tortas* (Q22-35), burritos (Q25-35; try the massive "Ay Caramba!"), pastas (Q30-35), and brownies (Q12). Internet Q10 per hr. Free Wi-Fi. You can also book bus and plane tickets here. Hammocks Q20; outdoor dorms with tin roofing Q25; indoor dorms Q30-40; singles with shared bath Q70; doubles with shared bath Q70, with private bath Q140; triples Q90/150; quads Q120/140. MC/V. ❶

Hospedaje Dona Gona 1 and 2, C. Union (☎7867 5513 or 7926 3538). Two buildings on C. Union form one of the most popular backpacker destinations in Flores. The 2nd building sports an interior waterfall and viewing hammocks under thatched roofs. Dorms Q25; singles Q60, with bath Q80; doubles Q80/100. MC/V. ❶

Inka Ti Jesh Maach Hostal, Pl. Sur (☎7867 5599 or 5818 3273). Basic rooms in a convenient location. Doubles as a travel agency. Free internet. Singles Q35; doubles Q70; triples Q105. Cash only. ❶

Hotel Mirador del Lago, C. 15 de Septiembre (☎7926 3276). Cheap lakeside lodging in appropriately blue rooms. The small, quiet garden area by the shore is perfect for unwinding. All rooms with private baths. Singles Q45; doubles Q60. MC/V. ❷

Hotel Santa Rita, C. 30 de Junio (☎7926 3224). Bare-bones rooms lack sea views, but are clean and comfortable. All rooms with private baths. Singles Q55; doubles Q105. MC/V. ❷

Hotel Petenchel, Pl. Sur (☎7926 3359). The location is the best part about this hotel: it's right across from the causeway, making picking up shuttles and buses easy. There's also a shady courtyard in the middle. Singles Q60; doubles Q110. MC/V. ❷

Hotel La Union, C. Union (☎7926 3584). On a quiet section of the shore on the island's north side, Hotel La Union offers clean and quiet rooms. Most have street views, but if you're willing to pony up, you can snag a great spot by the water. Internet in the lobby Q15 per hr. Singles Q62; doubles Q110, with lake view Q130. MC/V. ❷

FOOD

Flores's restaurants, like its hotels (sometimes they're the same thing), are numerous. Their menus feature an eclectic range of offerings, mixing local specialties (including Mayan dishes) with international fare. Many restaurants hug the waterfront, providing spectacular views and cool breezes.

Cool Beans, C.15 de Septiembre. "El Cafe Chilero" definitely lives up to its name, attempting eccentricities in every corner: a book exchange, board games, movies for sale, hammocks, and quirky decorations. If you don't want to stay for a meal, snatch up some homemade bread, muffins, and rolls (Q15-25). Breakfast served all day (Q25-32). Sandwiches Q18-35. Lunch and dinner options Q28-60. Drinks Q5-18. Open M-Sa 6am-9pm. V. ❷

Cafe Arqueologico Yaxha, C. 15 de Septiembre (☎5830 2060). The Cafe Yaxha proudly represents the Petén in more ways than one. With a small library of books, a handmade packet of information on the area, and a wide range of tours on offer, the cafe is an ideal base from which to plan explorations. The walls, lined with photographs of the region's archaeological treasures, are worth a close look. Check out the pictures from Tikal's earliest stages of excavation, when the ruins were still buried under moss and vegetation. Oh, and then there's the delicious food; a huge menu offering breakfast (Q20-30), beef, chicken, and pasta. Mayan specialties Q30-60. Entrees Q20-90. AmEx/MC/V. ❷

La Villa del Chef, C. Union. German expats offer fish dishes with fresh catches from the lake (Q110-120), lasagna and pasta (Q39-44), pizza (Q61-79), Guatemalan specialties (Q30-74), and Arabic food, including falafel and shish kebabs (Q34-64). La Villa is also the only place in town where you can puff on a hookah pipe (Q65). Come at sunset; the views from the waterfront seating are spectacular. Rents canoes for Q40 per hr. (maximum 2 people). Open daily 8am-10pm. AmEx/MC/V. ❷

Capitan Tortuga, C. 30 de Junio (☎7867 5089). A spacious restaurant and pizzeria with lakeside seating. Get after the burritos and tacos (Q30-45) or opt for the grill food (Q55-110), seafood (Q95-105), or pizzas (small Q39-44, grande Q79-87). Try Capitan Tortuga pizza, with mushrooms, eggplant, chicken, ham, and cheese. Open daily 11am-10pm. ❷

El Hacienda del Rey, corner of Pl. Sur and C. 30 de Junio. This open-air restaurant and bar throbs to a cosmopolitan beat. A variety of flags hang from the ceiling, while the menu showcases Argentinian and Mexican food. If you find yourself forgetting Guatemala, the beautiful lakeview will be sure to bring you back. Breakfast Q25-43. Lunch and dinner Q80-130. Open 5am-9pm. V. ❷

Suiche, C. Union. Because every town needs a sushi joint. Rolls are served in a small interior on the island's quiet northern shore. You can also enjoy chow mein and tempora. Sushi Q35-60. Open M-Sa 2-10pm. ❷

La Galeria del Zot'z, C.15 de Septiembre. The attention-grabbing interior sports striking blue walls with brightly painted stars and plenty of Mayan decor. Breakfast Q10-25. Seafood Q48-65. Chicken and beef dishes Q40-45. Small pizzas Q35-40, grande Q50-60. Open daily 7am-10pm. MC/V. ❷

Restaurante Las Brisas, C. Union. It may not have a lakeside setting like many of its neighbors, but Las Brisas attracts locals and tourists alike with some of the cheapest food in town. Breakfast Q10-20. Burritos Q15-25. Pasta Q25-35. Meat dishes Q35-45. Open daily 9am-10pm. Cash only. ❶

SIGHTS AROUND FLORES AND SANTA ELENA

So, you've seen Tikal. Maybe you've even made the grueling jungle trek to El Mirador. You think you've "done" the Petén and are ready to book it. Well don't. You'll be missing out on the region's smaller, more painlessly acces-

PETÉN

sible treasures: beautiful outlooks, thrilling parks, and quiet beaches all lie within navigable distance of Flores.

BOAT TRIPS. *Lancheros* (small boats) lurk along the island's coasts, offering service to all nearby points on the lake. The best place to find them is along Playa Sur right next to the causeway, but if you're heading to a northern point it will probably be cheaper to find a boat along the northern shore. These prices are general; hone your haggling chops by negotiating for a smaller fare. You can catch a ride to **Arcas** (one-way Q50, round-trip Q200), the **Petencito Zoo** (Q50/200), the lookout at **El Mirador** (one-way Q100), the **Playita beach** (one-way Q100), and the nearby lakeside towns of **San Jose** (Q250/350) and **San Andres** (Q200/300). You can also try to snag a relaxing **lake tour** (2hr., Q100-150).

PARQUE NATURAL IXPANPAJUL. Like a natural amusement park, this small nature preserve just south of Flores and Santa Elena provides a variety of thrilling ways to explore the rainforest. A network of high, hanging bridges is an ideal way to view the greenery. Or, to really give that fear of heights a workout, try the Tarzan Canopy Tour, where you can speed through the tree-tops on a zipline. Other opportunities here include horseback, bike tours, and night walks through the jungle. *(Take a Rio Dulce-bound bus or a minibus from the Santa Elena bus station and ask to be let off at Ixpanpajul (Q10-15).* ☎ *2336 0576 or 5619 0513; www. ixpanpajul.com. Q200. Open M-Sa 9am-5pm.)*

EL MIRADOR. Not to be confused with the large Mayan site on Guatemala's northern edge, the closer and humbler El Mirador is easily accessed—no five-day jungle treks here. High up on the sliver of land cutting into the lake north of Flores, a lookout provides a bird's-eye view of the island. Ask a *lanchero* (boatman) to take you to the village of San Miguel; from there, a trail climbs for 1 mi. up the lookout spot. Several small Mayan ruins dot the area, many of them under excavation—expect to meet a few archaeologists along the way. Relax on the walk back by stopping at the small beach near the trail, literally called "El Playita." *(One-way Q100.)*

ACTUN KAN CAVES. These small, mystic caves are decorated with old Mayan paintings and drawings—evidence of the beliefs that the caves were the entries into Xibalba, the underworld. *(The caves can be reached via a 10min. tuk-tuk ride (Q10) or by walking south from Santa Elena along 6a Av. Follow the signs for "Cuevas de Actun Kan." Be sure to bring your own flashlight. Q20.)*

MUSEO SANTA BARBARA. Located on a tiny island west of Flores, this small museum provides more chances to satiate your appetite for Mayan relics. The artifacts collected here, consisting mostly of bits of pottery and other ceramics, are small and local. *(A lanchero ride here costs about Q80-100. Museum Q12. Open M-Sa 8am-noon and 2-5pm.)*

THE ASOCIACION DE RESCATE Y CONSERVACION DE VIDA SILVESTRE (ARCAS). The Wildlife Rescue and Conservation Association was founded to aid animals abused in the illegal smuggling trade and to protect them before reintroduction into the wild. The NGO is based near the village of San Benito, on the shore northeast of Flores. The center offers a mile-long trail for visitors with opportunities for viewing some of the actual wildlife. *(A boat leaves for the center 7:30-8:30am by the arch in the middle of the causeway between Flores and Santa Elena. Free. A one-way lanchero Q50.* ☎ *2478 4096 or 2480 7270; www.arcasguatemala.com. Q10.)*

ENTERTAINMENT AND NIGHTLIFE

Flores is mostly quiet at night, with the few drinking establishments closing around 10pm. Most of the restaurants (see **Food,** p. 151) also have a bar with happy hours in the early evening, so if you want to have a few drinks and meander through the quaint streets you'll be able to do it. **C. Sur** on the island's southern edge is the best place to seek out rowdier restaurants and a few bars.

Cafe Bar El Tropico, C. Sur (☎5769 1281). There's a flatsceen TV above the bar and a small aquarium to entertain you if the view of Santa Elena across the lake gets boring. Beers Q15-20. Mixed drinks Q25-30. Try the *michelador* (Q25), a Guatemalan specialty aiming for a spicier Bloody Mary: salt, pepper, lime, hot sauce, and Gallo beer make for a delicious mix—if you can handle it. Open M-Sa 11am-10pm. Cash only.

HIKING

MAYAN RUINS

If Tikal didn't satiate your curiosity and you feel the old familiar tug of adventure, northern Guatemala hides many other Mayan ruins. Most are visited through a guided tour, and some require strenuous multi-day hikes through the most isolated of wildernesses. The romantic prospect of hidden ruins and beautiful views attracts the bold and willing, but don't expect comfort.

EL MIRADOR

El Mirador is only accessible via multi-day hiking and camping trips that last 5-6 days in total. Trips leave from Flores and begin walking from the northern village of La Carmelita, the last outpost of civilization before the jungle. You can book your trip at one of the tour companies in Flores (see Orientation and Practical Information, p. 149); a minimum of 4 people is usually required (though you can book solo trips at Cafe Yaxha for Q3450). With a group of 4, the cost per person runs between Q1750 and Q2080. All mules, equipment, and food are provided.

El Mirador is for the die-hards, those who either obsess over Mayan ruins or relish any chance for serious jungle adventure. "Getting there is half the fun" has never been so true—the long hiking and camping treks (5-6 days) are major tests of endurance (with 27-30hr. of rough walking). At the end of the journey lies one of the true hidden treasures of the Mayan civilization—a relic of the distant origins of the great civilization. El Mirador was one of the earliest cities in all of North America. Settled as early as 800 BC, it flourished during the late Pre-classic period, between 300 BC and AD 150. With over 80,000 inhabitants, El Mirador quickly became the first superpower of the Mayan world, lassoing all surrounding cities, including Tikal, into obedience. The excavated portion of the city covers 2 sq. km and includes the largest concentration of buildings ever found yet among Mayan ruins. The main structure here is **El Tigre,** a temple 55m high (180 ft.) and with a surface area six times that of **Templo IV,** the largest structure at Tikal. Enjoy a sunset from the top, with vistas of the unbroken jungle stretching as far as the eye can see. The **Danta Complex** consists of ascending platforms holding up three pyramids at the top. The structure is carefully laid out in an elegant geometric structure: the base is 7m high, the next platform 7m higher, the next platform is 21m higher, and the pyramids themselves are 21m high. All in all, it stands 70m tall, with each side of the base measuring 300m. Longer (6-day) trips circle around to visit the nearby ruins at **Nakbe,** another impressive site; by 800 BC a small city had been established there.

UAXACTUN

Uaxactun is located 23km down a road leading off from Tikal. A bus from Santa Elena's bus station heads to Uaxactun village (3hr., daily 1-3pm, Q50); ask at the bus station for the exact time, as it changes often. You'll have to wait a day to catch the return bus; it heads back to Santa Elena between 5 and 6am. If you want to visit straight from Tikal, you can catch this bus on its way through. San Juan Travel (☎5461 6010) runs a shuttle to Uaxactun at 6am (returning at noon), but they must be contacted in advance and require a minimum of 2 people (round-trip Q500). Otherwise, you can try to catch a ride from Tikal or (the easiest and most popular method) come on a tour (see Tours in Orientation and Practical Information, p. 149). Full-day tours Q415-580.

Uaxactun's original name was **Siaan K'aan**, "Born in Heaven"; the existing name was coined by the site's first excavator. Uaxactun is now contained within the grounds of the **Parque Nacional Tikal.** Its chronology roughly aligns with that of Tikal: primitive settlement in the Pre-classical Era, establishment of a flourishing, advanced civilization from about AD 500-800, and collapse by AD 1000. The city's subservient status frustrated any chance of growth comparative to that of Tikal, though, and travelers looking for the hidden grandeur like that of El Mirador will be disappointed. There is a village situated around the airstrip. Of most interest here is the **E group,** which provides evidence of the advanced state of Mayan science. Structures **E-1, E-2,** and **E-3** form an astronomical observatory. Structure **E-VII-B**, a truncated pyramid, with staircases on all four sides and decorated with stucco masks of sacred animals, is believed to have been a main point of observation, perfectly placed to record solstices and equinoxes. Groups **A** and **B,** about a 20min. walk away, have some comparatively unremarkable temple ruins. **Aldana's Lodge ❶** near the ruins has campsites (Q20) and rooms with shared baths (Q35).

YAXHA

Yaxha lies 14km north of the main Flores/Santa Elena-Belize road. There are 3 options for reaching it without a car. You can take a guided tour from Flores (full-day tours US$70-90; see Orientation and Practical Information, p. 149), take a taxi from Flores (Q500), or take a bus in the direction of Melchor de Mencos and the Belizean border and ask to be let off at the turnoff to Yaxha. Site Q80.

Just 30 km southeast of Tikal, the hilltop Mayan ruins at Yaxha give evidence of yet another powerful city in the region. With over 500 structures discovered—and excavation still ongoing (you're likely to see archaeologists at work)—Yaxha is the third-largest discovered city in Guatemala. Because of its inconvenient location, it usually lacks the teeming crowds of its neighbor to the northwest. So, a trip to these ruins, surrounded by rich flora and fauna ("Yaxha means "green water"), is likely to be a quiet one. Yaxha was even deemed remote enough to provide the setting for *Survivor: Guatemala* in 2005. Known mainly as a ceremonial center, Yaxha contained some 20,000 people during its eighth-century peak. Evidence points to a highly advanced culture: two astronomical observatories, three ball courts, and a well-established *sacbe* system connecting the city to the lake. Tikal's close presence was probably the greatest factor in establishing Yaxha's importance. Similarities between the two sites indicate that the larger city's protection and trade secured Yaxha, especially against the hostile Naranjo to the northeast. The *stelae* discovered at Yaxha seem to show that Naranjo finally defeated its rival. During the collapse of the Maya, it's believed that the city's elite fled to the nearby island of Topoxte. You can reach Topoxte via boat, which you can rent at El Sombrero.

Plaza F, distinguished by a pyramid affording great views of the other temples, is the first stop from the entrance. Just north is the **Grupo Mayer complex,** whose layout—twin temples separated by a plaza—is reminscent of Tikal's Gran Plaza. The temple-heavy **Acropolis Norte** features an unusual 22m structure with rounded edges. Southeast lies Yaxha's greatest pride, **Templo 216,** the tallest building here. Views of the lakes and lagoons make the tough climb worth it; go at sunset if you can, but check the park's closing times. Yaxha lies in the **Parque Nacional Yaxha-Nakum-Naranjo,** which covers over 91,000 acres and protects a huge range of wildlife, including over 22 species of fish that live in the region's lakes. For those who want to spend the night near the ruins, Campamento Ecologico El Sombrero (☎7861 1688 or 1691; www.ecosombrero.com) lies just off the road on the southern edge of the lake. Beautiful bungalows by the shore provide peace and views; there's also a restaurant on site. Singles Q140, with bath Q240; doubles Q240/312. Horseback riding tours available. Rent canoes and boats for trips around the lake, including the island ruins of Topoxte.

EL ZOTZ

Though a 25km road connects El Zotz with Uaxactun, the site is most easily visited as part of a guided tour. Hiking and camping trips usually last 3 days and include a visit to Tikal. (This grueling hike to see unrestored ruins will really separate the men from the boys among the Maya-obsessed.) Tours are Q2200 for 1 person, Q1370 for 2, and Q1120 for 3 (see Orientation and Practical Information, p. 149).

Thirty kilometers west of Tikal, El Zotz is an almost completely buried site just outside the Parque Nacional Tikal. The area was settled during the Classical era (AD 200-900) and was probably vassal to Tikal for most of its existence—wooden lintel carvings of Tikal's rulers were discovered here. On display are the careful tunnels of grave robbers who have looted the site for centuries. The tallest structure is the 148 ft. high **Devil's Pyramid,** which includes a large cave formation housing thousands of bats. Bats are the main residents here now—"Zotz" means "bat" in several Mayan languages—and those who camp nearby at night will most likely meet a few. The area around El Zotz is its own biotope and functions as a conservation protecting the bats and a variety of other wildlife, including jaguars, monkeys, and many bird species.

LAGUNA DE TIGRE NATIONAL PARK AND EL PERU RUINS

Trips to El Peru last 3 days and cost BZ$100-150 (US$200-300) per person. For tour companies, see Orientation and Practical Information, p. 149.

Guatemala's largest national park covers 335,080 hectares of lowland forest and wetlands. This is Central America's largest protected wetland. Unfortunately, the region is under attack from illegal immigrants, drug traffickers, ranchers, and oil drillers. Tourism in the area is strictly limited to the Waka'-Peru archaeological site and a few biological stations located in the park's southeastern corner. Trips to the ruins at El Peru start in Paso Cabelleros, a Kekchi Mayan village on the southeastern outskirts of the park. Tours continue on boat down the Rio San Pedro river. An hour-long hike leads to the small ruins, organized around four plazas. The highest structure is **El Mirador de los Monos** (the Monkeys' Lookout), a hilltop temple that provides expansive views of the jungle and Laguna El Peru. Hikes farther into the surrounding area offer sightings of local wildlife. The most fascinating are the threatened species of Scarlet Macaw (*Guacamaya*), who are unique to this area of Guatemala.

PETÉN

SANTA ELENA

Just a short causeway glide south of its better-known island neighbor, Santa Elena (pop. 25,000) is a world apart in atmopshere. No narrow, quaint, placid streets here; instead, angry cars snarl their way through crowded streets and loud vendors hawk their goods in the ceaseless cacophany of the large, tangled market. Those looking for a less touristed spot may prefer Santa Elena to Flores, but otherwise there's little reason (except for its bus station) to spend much time here.

TRANSPORTATION

See Flores **Transportation**, p. 147.

ORIENTATION AND PRACTICAL INFORMATION

Santa Elena is laid out in a rather lopsided grid pattern. The main north-south road is **6a Av.**, which goes down to the causeway leading into Flores. The **bus terminal** is about 1 mi. south of the bridge on 6a Av. **4a C.**, the main east-west road, which cuts across 6a Av. about ½ mi. south of the bridge. The **market** extends west of 6a Av. and south of 4a C.

Banks: Banco Agromercantil, corner of 4a C. and 6a Av. Open M-F 9am-6pm, Sa 9am-1pm. **Banco G&T Continental,** also at the corner of 4a C. and 6a Ave. Open M-F 9am-7pm, Sa 9am-1pm. Both banks have **ATMs.**

Pharmacy: 6a Av. and 4a C. are both lined with pharmacies.

Internet Access: Tikal Net, 4a C., just off 6a Av. Open M-Sa 8am-8pm, Su 9am-5pm.

Post Office: On the corner of 8a Av. and 4a C. Open M-Sa 8am-5pm.

ACCOMMODATIONS

Hotel Continental, 6a Ave. (☎7926 0095; www.hotelcontinentalpeten.com), 10min. walking distance from the bus station. A huge yellow facade conceals a spacious, bright courtyard at this convenient 3-story hotel. Clean rooms, each with TV, veranda, and private bath. Singles Q42; with A/C Q70; doubles Q70/90. MC/V. ❷

Hotel San Juan, 2a C. (☎7926 2146). It's not much to look at from the outside—a bare stone building in a relatively untrafficked part of town—but the rooms are adequate, with glimpses of the lake from some windows. Singles Q50, with bath Q74; doubles Q65/90. V. ❷

Hotel Posada Santander, 4a C. (☎7926 0574). You won't be far from the town's bustle at this basic and clean guesthouse, just a few blocks away from the teeming market. Get used to the noise. Singles Q50; doubles Q77. MC/V. ❷

FOOD

Restaurante Mijaro, 6a Ave. (☎7926 1615; www.restaurantemijaro.com), just south of the bridge. The perfect place to escape the noisy, dusty streets—a quiet, leafy courtyard extends back from the road and lets you enjoy the pasta and meat dishes in peace. Entrees Q25-50. Open daily 7am-9pm. MC/V. ❷

Restaurante Petenchel, (☎7926 1125), close to the bridge. Petenchel serves a wide range of local and international options. Get the usual Guatemalan meat dishes or try the seafood. If you're feeling really adventurous, go for Chinese. Entrees Q25-60. Open daily 9am-9pm. MC/V. ❷

TIKAL

The greatest reminder of the ancient Mayan world spreads over 10km in northern Guatemala—and that's just the excavated part, a mere fraction of the glorious city-empire that once dominated the region. The ruins proudly display their own kind of glory, an awesome majesty that transcends the defeated look characteristic of many other Mayan sites. High temples still reach above the jungle, in some cases visible from dozens of kilometers away. Meanwhile, in the surrounding 220km of wilderness that makes up the Parque Nacional Tikal, a bevy of exotic flora and fauna offer another brand of excitement. Go early and you'll catch howler monkeys swinging through the trees and countless bird species nesting among the ruins.

TRANSPORTATION. Almost every travel agency in Flores offers their own deal for heading to the site, and several bus companies operating from the Santa Elena station run buses there. But the easiest way to reach Tikal is with **San Juan Travel** (☎5461 6010), which runs **minibuses** leaving Flores (they can pick you up at your hotel) every hr. 5-10am and 2pm. Return trips head from Tikal back to Flores at 12:30pm and then every hr. 2-6pm. You can book by phone, at San Juan's offices along C. Sur in Flores, or in Santa Elena just south of the causeway. Round-trip cost is Q60. **Guided tours** of Tikal run between Q450 and Q600. If you're with a group, you can try to snag a guide at the park's entrance (about Q300).

ORIENTATION. The ruins lie 13 mi. inside the **Tikal National Park.** You'll pass the large arched **gate** about 30min. before reaching the site itself. Directly before reaching the **tourist information booth** and **ticket stand,** you'll pass the **Museo Litico** and the **Visitors' Center** on the left and a few *comedores* (eateries and restaurants) on the right. The **Museo Tikal** lies just ahead. The path to the ruins heads off to the left; you can buy your ticket (Q150) and a map (Q40) right at the trail's start. Any ticket bought after 3pm is valid for the next day. A 5min. walk toward the ruins will bring you to the **ticket control booth;** from there, it's about another 10-15min. to the **Gran Plaza.** The park is open daily from 6am to 6pm.

ACCOMMODATIONS AND FOOD. Watching the sunrise from a temple at Tikal is a legendary and elusive—given the mists that often descend at dawn— experience that can only be had by spending the night by the ruins. A few camping options exist for the budget traveler. The park's own **campsite** lies just south off the entrance road by the tourist information center. You can pitch your own tent for Q10 or rent one for Q60. **Jaguar Inn** ❷, to the right of the tourist information center, offers comfy and expensive bungalows with hammocks. You can also rent tents and put them in the backyard. (☎7926 0002; www.jaguartikal.com. Tent sites Q30; rented tent Q60; hammocks Q50; single bungalows; doubles Q470; triples Q590; quads Q710. MC/V.)

A small selection of restaurants provides relaxation and nourishment for the eager or exhausted explorer. A few small open-air eateries line the right side of the road as you approach Flores, serving cheap meals for Q20-60. They open as early as 6am, so you can enjoy a breakfast even if you're on the first morning shuttle.

MUSEUMS. The two on-site museums present a more detailed look at life in Tikal; they're perfect for either whetting your appetite or satiating the curiosity you've worked up while strolling the main ruins. A ticket to one museum buys access to both. **Museo Lítico** is to the left of the entrance road right before the ticket booth. *Stelae* depicting important historical and cultural information are housed here, along with pottery fragments and carvings. (Open daily 8am-4pm. Q10.) **Museo Tikal** is straight ahead as you enter the visiting center from the access road. Smaller than its definitive name suggests, this museum nevertheless attempts to convey the cultural weight of the site, displaying more small carved objects: *stelae*, pottery, tools, jewelry, and even bones. The spectacular **tomb** of Lord Chocolate uncovered in **Templo I** is reconstructed here in all its splendor, including over 150 carved jade objects. (Open M-F 9am-5pm and Sa-Su 9am-4pm. Q10.)

THE RUINS OF TIKAL

HISTORY

Tikal was already a small village by about 900 BC, though the oldest excavated buildings only date from 500-400 BC. By 200 BC a variety of ceremonial structures had been built, including the first buildings at what is now the **Acropolis**

del Norte. Over the centuries, Tikal developed, its art becoming more ornate and its political influence more widely felt, but with the domineering presence of the great city of El Mirador to the north, it never managed to attain super-state status. The collapse of El Mirador in the AD third century and the defeat of neighboring Uaxactun as a potential rival in AD 378 finally established the city as the region's main strongman. It was even able to apparently avoid an attempted takeover by Teotihuacan (today near Mexico City), assimilating the northern city's cultural styles but maintaining its own autonomy. During this time the city's population is believed to have been over 100,000.

In 562 AD, though, the city's growth was suddenly halted. *Stelae* reveal that Lord Water of Caracol (now in southern Belize), reacting against Tikal's attemped takeover of his kingdom, crushed the greater city, sacrificed its king Double Bird, destroyed temples, and forced it into subservience. Thus began what is known as Tikal's "hiatus" period—130 years during which no new building or development seems to have been attempted.

In the late seventh century, Hasaw Cha'an K'awil, sometimes known as Ah Cacau or "Lord Chocolate," came to power and defeated Caracol's ally Calak-mul in AD 711. Tikal's central, autonomous role was restored, and the city began a building spree that saw the construction of most of the existing struc-tures, including the five main temples. Lord Chocolate was buried in **Templo I,** while his wife was entombed across the Gran Plaza in **Templo II.** During the AD ninth and tenth centuries Tikal fell victim to the general and still mysterious collapse of the Mayan civilization. By AD 1000 the city was abandoned. Local peoples knew of the site for centuries, but its existence wasn't publicized until 1848, when a *chiclero* (street vendor) reported his find. Serious archaeological work commenced only in the 1950s, led by researchers from the University of Pennsylvania. Tikal was declared a UNESCO World Heritage Site in 1979.

THE MAIN SITE

THE GREAT PLAZA. A path leads about 1 mi. from the ticket booth to the first main sight, the Great Plaza. The cultural and ceremonial heart of city is surrounded by temples to its east and west and acropolises to its north and south. It's dominated by Tikal's most famous structure, emblazoned on Guatemalan license plates: **Templo I**—sometimes known as the **Jaguar Temple** after carvings in the structure's wood lintels—rising 144 ft. above the jungle canopy. Planned by Hasaw Cha'an K'awil and completed by his son to immor-talize and entomb his father, the temple was completed around the middle of the AD eighth century. The magnificent tomb was filled with beautiful arti-facts, including carved jade objects and bone carvings—you can see a recon-struction of the site in the **Museo Tikal** (p. 157). The steep structure is crowned with a distinctive three-room hollow building, or "roof comb," which was once brightly painted and lavishly decorated. Climbing the temple has been strictly forbidden after the deaths of several visitors.

TEMPLO II. Facing Templo I is Templo II, also called **Temple of the Masks,** shorn of its roof comb and now only 124 ft. high. Believed to have been built in honor of Hasan Cha'an K'awil's wife, the temple was actually begun before its more famous counterpart. Together, they form one of the most distinctive arrange-ments in the Mayan world. This one is accessible via a wooden stairway on the side. At the top, views of the plaza and the surrounding scenery await.

NORTH AND CENTRAL ACROPOLISES. The labyrinth of the **Acropolis del Norte** (North Acropolis), to the left as you face Templo I, is the result of centuries of building and deliberate rebuilding; the remains of about 12 temples exist today, but as many as 100 other structures are believed to have stood here. Two huge wall masks, once painted scarlet and green, stare out from beneath protective thatched roofs. Below the acropolis, a ruler's burial chamber was discovered, complete with the remains of nine servants and pottery. The **Acropolis Central** (Central Acropolis) across the plaza is even more complex, and its purpose still remains a mystery. Forty five rooms are organized around six small courtyards; they were used either as residences for the city's rulers and elite or as sites for sacred rituals. There is at least some certainty, though: the rectangular buildings at the complex's east end, structures **5D-45** and **5D-46,** are known to have served as royal homes for centuries.

CALZADA TOZZER AND TEMPLO IV. Behind Templo II stretch the remains of the Calzada Tozzer (the Tozzer Causeway), once a raised, paved road that connected parts of the city and served sacred, artistic, and astronomical purposes. To the right of the causeway behind the temple is the **Plaza Oueste** (West Plaza), with a late Classical temple; to the left is **Templo III,** still largely unexcavated and buried beneath mounds of earth. It was built around AD 810, very late in the city's history and unusually close to the Mayan collapse. On the left as you walk along the causeway, **Complejo N** (Complex N) features the distinctive twin-temple design, the Great Plaza in smaller form. A range of *stellae* honoring Hasan Cha'an K'awil lie around the site; he is believed to have built the complex to celebrate the completion of a *katun* (20-year cycle in the calendar). The causeway leads up to **Templo IV,** at 212 ft. the tallest of Tikal's buildings. Built in AD 741 by Hasaw's son, perhaps as his own burial tomb, the lower half of the temple is still covered in earth, the excavated top rising out of the ground. The views here are probably the most impressive, and the temple is popular among those looking to catch a good surise or sunset.

EL MUNDO PERDIDO AND PLAZA DE LOS SIETE TEMPLOS. A path leads southwest from Templo IV into the most evocatively named of Tikal's areas, **El Mundo Perdido** (The Lost World). The purpose of most of the 38 buildings here remains a mystery, though the large **pyramid** dominating the site and rising 105 ft. was believed to have served an astronomical function. The existing structure was built over four existing pyramids, the earliest of which, dating back to 500 BC, is the earliest discovered structure in Tikal. Just west is the **Plaza de los Siete Templos** (Plaza of the Seven Temples). The purpose of these temples, which date back to the Preclassical era, is also unclear. Aligned in a row, they offer a good example of the various states of repair and disrepair that can befall Mayan ruins; the central temple is almost fully restored, while the outlying ones are still mostly heaps of rubble. Excavation is noticeably ongoing here. A **triple ball court** lies to the north. The mostly unexcavated **Acropolis del Sur** (South Acropolis) lies to the west of the plaza, featuring structures built over a thousand years—some date from the Preclassical era, some from the late Classical.

TEMPLO V. The path continues on, circling around the back end of Templo V, whose restoration was completed only in 2004. Evidence suggests that the structure is the earliest of the six main temples here, built in a 50-year period between AD 600 and 700. The rounded edges are unusual for a Mayan temple. The temple is 190 ft. high, and you'll feel every foot as you stand at the rope-free top after a nearly vertical climb up a wooden staircase. The views are amazing, with the roof combs of Templos I and II jutting above the treetops. Just don't look down.

TEMPLO VI. Templo VI is the last discovered and most distant of Tikal's main structures, located about a 10min. walk (1km) down the Calzada Mendez from the Great Plaza (you can pick up the path while walking back from Templo V). It was completed in AD 766 by Hasaw's son Yik'in Chan K'awil, who also finished Templo I and built Templo IV. In fact, Yik'in is believed to be buried in either Templo IV or Templo VI. Also known as the **Temple of the Inscriptions,** it is famous for the long glyph text carved on the back of its roof comb. Almost 200 glyphs record the city's history, from a legendary founding date in 1139 BC to the overthrow of Caracol and the takeover of Calakmul in AD 711. The text is very faded, though, so you might want to practice your Mayan glyph-reading skills elsewhere.

OTHER STRUCTURES. From Templo VI, the path circles around and heads back to the ticket control booth, making for a pleasant nature walk and wildlife spotting. Smaller complexes and reservoirs (so effective that they were used by archaeologists excavating the site in the 19th and 20th centuries) lie to the north of the main site. In all, thousands of structures lie buried amidst the jungles, entombed remnants of a city far larger than the already expansive ruins suggest.

THE BAY ISLANDS, HONDURAS

LA CEIBA

Honduras's third largest city, La Ceiba is known especially for its nightlife—particularly appropriate because a stay in northern Honduras's transportation hub probably shouldn't last longer than a night anyway. Surprising for a city of its size, La Ceiba is for the most part a one street town—or, more precisely, a town of two or three streets running parallel past the central park toward the narrow, nondescript stretch of beach, where most everything the city offers can be found. As a gateway city to the Bay Islands and numerous nearby natural parks such as Pico Bonito and Cuero y Salado Reserve, La Ceiba attracts a multitude of different types of people. If it's not the weekend, though, they're most likely moving on toward bigger and better things.

▐ TRANSPORTATION

Flights: Aeropuerto Goloson is 6km west of town on the road to Tela. Snag any Tela-bound bus and ask to be let off at the airport (L10). Alternatively, take a taxi from where they line up west of the *parque* (L100). **Islena** and **SOSA** have offices to the east opposite the *parque*. Call ahead to make a reservation.

Islena/Taca (☎441 2390) to: **Grand Caymen** (2hr., Th and Su 6pm, round-trip L9,935); **Roatan** (15 min.; daily 6am, noon, 2:30, 4, 5:30pm; round-trip L1,900); **San Pedro Sula** (25min.; daily 7:40, 10am, 1, 4pm; round-trip L2,580); **Tegucigalpa** (40 min.; M-Sa 7:30am and 2pm, Su 2pm; round-trip L3,120). Taca flies daily to: **San Jose, Belize City, Panama City, Guatemala City, Managua,** and most other major Central American cities. Airport office open daily 6am-7pm; *parque* office open M-F 7am-5pm, Sa 7am-11am.

SOSA (☎443 1399; www.aerolineassosa.com) to: **Bros Laguna** (55min., M and F, L2268); **Guanaja** (26min., daily M-Sa, L1392); **Puerto Lempira** (75min., M-Sa 6am, L2470); **Roatan** (15min.; M-Su 6:15, 11:15am, 3:30pm; L1056); **San Pedro Sula** (25min.; M-Sa 7:30am and 1:30pm, Su 9:45am; L1392); **Utila** (10min.; M, W, F; L1056). Airport office open M-Sa 5am-5:30pm, Su 6:30am-4:30pm; park office open M-F 7am-5pm, Sa 7am-noon.

Buses: The **station** is about 3km from Av. San Isidro west on Blvd. 15 de Septiembre; accessible by taxi (L20). Buses to: **El Porvenir** (30min., every hr. 6:30am-5pm, L15); **La Union** (1¼hr., every hr. 6:30am-3pm, L17); **Olanchito** (2hr., every 30min. 6:30am-4:30pm, L60); **San Pedro Sula** (4hr., every 1½hr. 6am-5:30pm, L90); **Tegucigalpa** (6½hr., 7 per day 3:30am-3pm, L180); **Tela** (2hr., every 30min. 4:20am-6pm, L40); **Trujillo** (4hr., every hr. 5:30am-4:30pm, L90).

Ferries: Nuevo Muelle de Cabotaje serves as the departure point for boats to the Bay Islands. The harbor is 5km east of La Ceiba and takes 15min. by taxi (L50-100). The **Galaxy II** (☎445 1795) heads daily to **Roatan** (1½hr., daily 9:30am and 1:30pm, L524), landing near **Coxen Hole.** The **Utila Princess** (☎425 3390) heads daily to **Utila** (1hr., daily 9:30am and 1:30pm, L425). With a little luck and lots of patience, you can catch a cheaper, longer ride on a cargo boat or motorized *cayuco*—ask around at the dock.

Taxis: A queue forms on the southwest side of *parque*. Fares around town L20. To the harbor or airport L100. Remember to negotiate (or try).

Car Rental: Union (☎440 0439; www.unionrentacar.com) on Av. San Isidro next to Hotel Iberia. Open M-F 8am-12pm and 1:30-5:30pm, Sa 8am-12pm.

✦ 🛈 ORIENTATION AND PRACTICAL INFORMATION

La Ceiba uses the same old grid system; *avenidas*, (labeled by name as opposed to number) run north-south and *calles* run east-west. Extending from the east side of the *parque* toward the water is **Avenida San Isidro**, the main drag. One block to the east is **Avenida Atlantida;** another block east is **Avenida 14 de Julio. Calle 1** runs along the shore. The **cathedral** is opposite the southeast corner of the *parque*. Most nightclubs are along C. 1 east of the Estuary. The **bus station** is 1½km west down **Boulevard 15 de Septiembre** from where it crosses Av. San Isidro, two blocks south of the *parque*. The area between Av. San Isidro and Av. 14 de Julio from C. 1 to 11 is the safest part of town.

Tourist Office: (☎440 3045), 1 block east of the *parque's* northeast corner. Open M-F 8:30am-4pm.

Tours: Garifuna Tours (☎440 3252; www.garifunatours.com), on the corner of C. 1 and Av. San Isidro. Tours to Pico Bonito L655 per person; rafting on Rio Cangrejal L750 per person; trips to Cayos Cochinos L750 per person. Most tours 8am-3pm. Open M-Sa 7:30am-12:30pm and 2-6:30pm. **Jungle River** (☎440 1268; www.jungleriverlodge. com) operates out of the Banana Republic Guesthouse on Av. La Republica. See **Outdoor Activities,** p. 165 for more details.

Budget Travel: Agencia de Viajes Lafitte, Av. San Isidro (☎443 0115), next to Hotel Iberia, 4 blocks south of C. 1. English-speaking travel agents.

Banks: All along both sides of Av. San Isidrio toward the beach. **Banco Credomatic,** Av. San Isidro, by C. 5 and across the street from Hotel Iberia. Cash advances on AmEx/ MC/V. Open M-F 8am-12pm and 1:30-7pm, Sa 8am-2pm.

Police: Preventiva (☎441 0995), off Blvd. 15 de Septiembre, next to the bus station. **Tourist Police** (☎441 6288), in the same building. Both open 24hr.

Pharmacy: Farmacia Central (☎443 0075), on Av. San Isidro across from the *parque*. Open M-F 8am-11:30am and 1:30pm-5:30pm, Sa 8am-12pm.

Hospital: Centro Medico Ceiba, C. 8 (☎442 2195), 4 blocks east of the *parque*. 24hr. emergency service.

Internet Access: Video Planet, on Av. Atlantida, 4 blocks south of C. 1. Internet L28 per hr. International calls to US L1 per min. Open M-Sa 8:30am-6pm. **Internet San Isidro,** on Av. San Isidro, next to the Hotel Iberia, offers the same services at the same prices. The **Pizza Hut** across from the *parque* on Av. San Isidro has free Wi-Fi for customers. Open daily 7am-10pm.

Post Office: Av. Morazan, C. 13, in the southwest part of town. EMS Express Mail in the same building. Open M-F 8am-3pm, Sa 8am-noon. **Postal Code:** 31301.

🏠 ACCOMMODATIONS

Hotel Amsterdam 2001 (☎443 2311). just off C. 1, 7 blocks east of Av. San Isidro, on Av. Miguel Paz Barahoa. Located close to the beach and to the best nightlife spots, Hotel Amsterdam is the best deal in town. 24hr. reception at the adjacent Dutch Cafe (on the corner of C. 1). Dorms L100; singles and doubles with bath L200; triples L300. Cash only. ❷

Hotel Rotterdam (☎440 0321), next to the Hotel Amsterdam 2001, about 25m from the water. All rooms have private baths and overlook a garden courtyard. Singles and doubles L250; triples L350. Cash only. ❷

Hotel Azul Caribe (☎443 1857), on C. 5 between Av. San Isidro and Av. Atlantida. Large rooms all have private bathrooms. Reception 24hr. Singles and doubles L225; triples and quads with A/C and cable L350. Cash only. ❷

Hotel Iberia (☎443 0401), on Ave. San Isidro, 4 blocks south of C. 1. Hotel Iberia has a few more amenities and a little more comfort than most La Ceiba lodgings. Large rooms have private bath, cable, A/C and free Wi-Fi. Singles L580; doubles L696; triples L696. AmEx/MC/V. ❹

Hotel Granada (☎443 2451), on Av. Atlantida, 3 blocks south of C. 1. The cheapest option in the city center. Small, basic rooms with fans and private baths. Reception 24hr. Singles L150, with cable and A/C L350; doubles L250/400. Cash only. ❷

🍴 FOOD

You'll find a bunch of fast food joints in the city center and along Av. San Isidro. Head a few blocks south and east of the *parque* to find cheaper *comedors* and buffets serving *comida típica*. The **San Isidro Market** C. 6, a block east of Av. San Isidro, is one of the biggest markets in Honduras. Here, crowds and produce stalls fill an indoor space and spill out onto the street. (Open M-Sa 7am-7pm, Su 7am-noon.) For groceries, visit the supermarket **Super Ceibeno,** one block north of the *parque* on Av. La Republica, which runs along the *parque's* western edge. (Open M-Sa 7am-7pm, Su 7am-noon.)

Pupuseria Universitaria (☎440 1070), on C. 1, 2 blocks east of Av. San Isidro. Two-room eatery with bamboo paneling and polished wooden ornaments. *Pupusas* L15-80. Tacos L31. Beer L30. Open daily 10am-11pm. Cash only. ❷

Kabasa? on Av. Miguel Paz Barahona, 4 blocks south from C. 1. Specializes in seafood. Eat outdoors under a wooden canopy, or indoors where ocean-themed murals decorate the air-conditioned dining room. T-bone steak platter L65. Fried fish from L89. Panamanian-style octopus L189. Conch soup L159. Beer from L20. Open daily 11am-10pm. AmEx/MC/V. ❸

Comidas Rapidas Flipper (☎440 1796), on Av. Atlantida, 2 blocks south of C. 1. Offers a slightly different menu each day. *Plato economico* L45; stand at a buffet and point at what you want on your plate. All sorts of *comida típica* L60-L80. Open M-Sa 7am-8pm. Cash only. ❷

Cafeteria Cobel (☎442 2192), on C. 7 between Av. Atlantida and Av. 14 de Julio. Cheap Honduran food in a dining room that's become a *ceibaño* institution. Breakfast and lunch L52-65. Open M-Sa 6:30am-6pm. Cash only. ❷

Masapan: Comida Rapida (☎443 3458), 1 block north of the *parque* on C. 7, west of Av. San Isidro. A cafeteria-style eatery, with separate stations for sandwiches, *comida típica*, and drinks. Great for a large group of people with different tastes. *Baleadas* L18-24. *Platos típicos* L49-69. Open daily 6:30am-8pm. Cash only. ❷

🎊 👁 FESTIVALS AND SIGHTS

During **Carnaval,** in the second and third weeks of May, La Ceiba fills with over 100,000 visitors. They come to see the wild tangle of parades, costumes, and tributes to the local patron saint, San Isidro. The great *ceibaño* pride fills neighborhood parties as residents cheer on contestants in the numerous youth beauty pageants. When it's not Carnaval time, there's suprisingly little to see in the third largest city in Honduras.

GARÍFUNA VILLAGES. For clean, swimmable shores, head to the Garífuna villages of **Corozal** and **Sambo Creek,** both outside of La Ceiba. *(Buses leave every 35min. from 5am-6:10pm and cost L16. Garífuna meals L80-L150. Simple rooms L100-L150.)*

UFC BOTTANICAL GARDEN. The influential United Fruit Company has maintained a modest but beautiful botanical garden curiously combined with a **railroad museum.** A free stroll around the lush grounds will reveal a dozen engines, cabooses, and handcars. *(1 block northwest of the parque central between C. 7 and 8. Open daily 6am-6pm.)*

BUTTERFLY AND INSECT MUSEUM. This jam packed museum is a jaw-dropper, featuring 12,000 insects from 110 countries. Be sure to check out the moth with the world's largest mouth and the moth with the world's largest wingspan. Robert Lehman, primary provider of local specimens, is frequently in the office and loves to chat it up with visitors. *(In Colonia Sauce Etapal, C. 5, 2 blocks east and 3 blocks south of FUPNAPIB. ☎ 442 2874; www.hondurasbutterfly.com. Open M-Sa 8am-5pm. Captions in English and Spanish. Tours in English or Spanish. L40, children L25. Tours free.)*

SPORTS. Consider taking in some *fútbol* at the local **stadium;** cheap seats are around L50. *(Info available at the tourist office.)*

◣ NIGHTLIFE

All of La Ceiba's nightlife is concentrated in the **Zona Viva** section of the city. This zone stretches from C. 1 along the beach before heading south through C. 5. Large crowds on Thursday, Friday, and Saturday nights keep you safe. It is best to avoid the area around the estuary along C. 1, a few blocks east of Av. San Isidro. Most clubs hire private security to keep an eye on things on the weekend. Still, use common sense: **stay alert, take taxis, and leave valuables behind.** In La Ceiba, minors (under 18) aren't allowed in nightspots, so be sure to **bring your ID** with you. Some clubs have dress codes on Thursday-Saturday nights: no shorts, no sandals.

La Casona, 2 blocks east of Av. Miguel Paz Barahona and 3 blocks south of C. 1. Casona is a major club in Ceiba. The local's favorite spot. Cover Th-Sa L150 for men. Open W-Su 9pm-late.

Hibou, to the east on C. 1, past Le Pacha. Another beachside club option. Beer L30. Cover Th-Sa L150 for men.

Kahlua Sports Bar y Grill, on C. 4, just east of the estuary. An alternative option for those looking for something other than discos. *Fútbol* is usually projected on the large screen on the outdoor deck. The Canadian owner sometimes plays big sports games popular in the United States. The upstairs seating area becomes a lounge Th-Sa. Beers from L25; bucket of 6 L125. *Baleada familiar* for 3 or 4 L365. Cover M-Th L60 for men, includes drink. Open Tu-Su 6pm-3am. MC/V.

◤ OUTDOOR ACTIVITIES

La Cebia's proximity to nearby national parks and reserves has inspired several local tour companies to offer relatively similar outdoor excursions. Shop around and to find the best activities offered at the best price. All tours include lunch and transportation to and from the location; overnight tours include accommodations.

GARIFUNA TOURS. This company leads tours to a number of nearby outdoor attractions. At **Pico Bonito National Park** (8:30am-2:30pm, L655 per person), a hike up through the lush jungle leads to expansive views of the Caribbean coast, encounters with butterflies and many different types of birds. The grand finale is the Zacate Waterfall. This company also offers tours of **Cuero y Salado Wildlife Refuge** (7am-3pm, L945 per person), where after taking the old railway from La Union, you can explore the mangrove lagoons where monkeys, alligators, manatees, and tropical birds coexist. **Cayos Cuchinos** (7am-3pm, L750 per person), has snorkeling among 13, sparsely inhabited coral cayes. The tour includes a lunch of Garífuna-style fish. At **Río Cangrejal** (8:30am-2pm, L750 per person) you can raft through class IV and V rapids through the Pico Bonito tropical forest before hiking the Bejuco trail to a waterfall. (☎440 3252; www. garifunatours.com. MC/V.)

🏝 DAYTRIP FROM LA CEIBA

CUERO Y SALADO RESERVE

Take the direct bus to La Union (every hr. 6:30am-3pm, L17). The park entrance is 9km from La Union. The visitor center has trail maps and a cafeteria (to your right, at the end of the tracks in Saldo Burra). Guides for up to 7 people L150. Boat use L300-450 for up to 7 people, plus mandatory guide. The FUCSA office is to the left of the visitor center. Only 30 people may enter the refuge per day, so call ahead to reserve a spot. For more info, check www.cueroysalado.org. Entrance fee L200, children L100, students L100.

The Cuero y Saladao Wildlife Refuge, 33km west of La Ceiba, is one of the most biologically diverse regions of Honduras. Spilling out into the Caribbean Sea, the 13,225 hectares of freshwater wetlands, saltwater marshes, and coastline protect 350 different species of animals, including jaguars, ocelots, sloths, and boa constrictors. Two hundred species of birds—more than a quarter of all those in Honduras—can also be found here. Topping it off, 10% of all the manatees in the world live in the Refuge.

There are four designated trails through the park; three are aquatic and one is terrestrial. Of the aquatic trails, **El Espejo** is the most easily accessible. It follows the **Estero de Garcia** river that runs south to Rios Termita, Bujaja, and Monos. **El Olingo** breaks off from El Espejo and heads up the Rio Salado to the Rio Limon, and into Rio Cocodrillo (famous for its crocodile sightings) and Marinero. From the coast, **Boca Cerrada,** the longest trail, follows the Rio Cuero through the entire length of the park, starting near the visitor center and going past Barra Rio Cuero to **Lago Boca Cerrada**; the majority of the park's manatees reside in Lago Boca Cerrada. **El Coco** (9km), the park's only land trail, heads east from the visitor center and runs along the coast. For those staying overnight, FUSCA rents four-person **tents** (L200 per night). There are also newly built cabins; bring your own sheets. Camping on the beach is permitted (L35 per night), but bring your own food, water, and bug repellent.

BAY ISLANDS

Though the silky white-sand beaches and world-class diving off the Bay Islands are Honduras' biggest tourist attraction, the islands feel less commercialized than many other Caribbean destinations. Dive prices and certifications are among the cheapest in the world and jungle coastline still outnumbers beachfront estates. Bay Island reef diversity is unmatched, so if you don't want to bother with scuba certification, snorkeling in the crystal clear water is almost as fun. Utila, just 32km by boat from La Ceiba, is the most budget-friendly island and is famous for sightings of the rare whale shark, the biggest fish in the sea. Roatán is the most developed of the islands with gorgeous beaches and phenomenal snorkeling. Once ravaged by Hurrican Mitch, Guanaja is now a sparsely populated island, perfect for private romantic getaways. Cayos Cochinos, with their beautiful tropical vegetation, are a miniature version of the main islands.

UTILA

Local legend has it that the real-life Robinson Crusoe spent a lot of time in Utila in the 17th century. Today, travelers have an easier time finding boats to the mainland, but still find it hard to leave behind the excellent seafood, nightly beach parties, and the best budget diving on the planet. Locals joke about how the most frequent lie heard in Utila is, "I'm leaving tomorrow."

TRANSPORTATION

Flights: Morgan's Travel (☎425 3161), at the foot of the main dock, is the best place to buy plane tickets. Open M-Sa 8am-noon and 2:30-5:30pm. **Isleña** (☎425 3364) has an office across from the fire station west of the dock. Open M-F 8:30am-4pm. **SOSA** (☎425 3166) flies to **La Ceiba** (15min.; M-Sa 6am and 3:30pm, Su 3:30pm).

Ferries: Utila Princess (☎425 3390; open 8am-4:30pm), across from Morgan's Travel, runs to **La Ceiba** (1hr., 6:30am and 2:30pm, L400). **San Ramon Express** (☎425 3979) also runs a small boat to La Ceiba from the dock at the Mariposa Cafe, 50m to the east from the Municipal Dock (daily 7am, L350). Note that the immigration officer on the Main Dock must look at your passport before he will let you leave. **Captain Vern** (vfine@hotmail.com) runs a Catamaran most days from Utila to **Roatan** (4hr., daily 7am, L1060), leaving either from Driftwood Cafe's dock to the west, or the UDC dock to the east. Reserve in advance.

Taxis: (☎425 3311).

Rentals: Rental Roney (☎425 3931) to the west from the dock just past the Methodist church. Bicycles L100 per day. Motorscooters L575 per day. Motorcycles from L675 per day. ATVs L1155 per day.

ORIENTATION AND PRACTICAL INFORMATION

Utila Town clings to the **East Harbour** on the south side of the island. **Main Street** runs from the decommissioned airstrip on the eastern lip of the harbor and hugs the bay until it reaches **Crepes Beach** on the western tip of the bay. Ferries land at the **Municipal Dock** which is directly in the middle of main street. **Cola de Mico Road** leads inland from the dock to **Pumpkin Hill** and the **airport.** Most services on the island take US dollars but also accept lempiras.

Tourist Information: (www.aboututila.com). Most dive shops offer free maps of the island; the one at Alton's (p. 171) is particularly good. Many dive shop representatives meet new arrivals from the incoming ferries with maps and information; these locals are also helpful for answering other questions.

Banks and Financial Services: BGA (☎425 3257), the first building up from the dock on the eastern side of the main road, exchanges travelers' Visa checks and does cash advances. Open M-F 8:30am-3:30pm, Sa 8:30-11:30am. **Banco Atlántida** (☎425 3374), to the east from the dock. Open M-F 9am-4pm, Sa 8:30-11:30am. **Bush's Supermarket** (☎425 3147), three buildings east of Banco Atlántida, exchange traveler's checks and does currency exchange. **Reef Cinema,** further to the east, gives cash advances on AmEx/MC/V (with a 6% commission).

Laundry: Alice Laundry (☎425 3785), next to Caye Caulker. L65-90 per bag, depending on size. Open daily 7am-8pm. **Tropical Hotel,** to the west from the dock, charges L80 per load. Open 8am-9pm.

Bookstore: Funky Town Library, underneath the Reef Cinema. Sells books and rents them for L20 per week (L200 deposit). Also rents DVDs for L40 per day (L500 deposit). Special deals on Tu and F. Open M-F 9am-7:30pm.

Police: (☎425 3255), upstairs from the post office, by the Municipal Dock, in the municipal office. Open M-F 9am-noon and 2-5pm. For after-hour emergencies, call **Preventiva** (☎425 3145), next to the football field, up Mamey Lane. Open 24hr.

Medical Services: Community Medical Clinic (☎425 3137), to the west of the dock, across from the Methodist church. Open M-F 8am-3pm. **Medical Store Utila** (☎425 3154), next to Banco Atlántida. Open M-Sa 8am-8pm.

Pharmacy: Utila Pharmacy (☎425 3632), to the west from the dock. Open M-Sa 8am-noon and 2pm-7pm.

Telephones and Internet: Caye Caulker, across from Reef Cinema. Internet L40 per hr. Calls to the US L3 per min. Open daily 8am-8pm. **Mermaid's Fast Food** (p. 169) offers free Wi-Fi to customers.

Post Office: Beneath the municipal building, on the dock, marked by a yellow headboard. Open M-F 9am-noon and 2-5pm, Sa 9-11:30am. **Postal code:** 34201.

GUIDED TOURS

A number of agencies lead tours to attractions in the area around Utila.

Utila Tours. Behind Munchie's. Tours to water caye (L400) and the freshwater caves (L250). Open M-Sa 6:30am-9:30pm, Su 6:30am-1:30pm.

Bay Islands Conservation Association. A unique, historically apocryphal tour of the life of Daniel Defoe's Robinson Crusoe. Open M-F 9am-noon and 2-4pm.

Whale Shark Oceanic Research Center, to the west from the docks. Snorkling trips with whale sharks M, W, F 12:30-5:30pm. L1135 per person. Center open M-F and Su 9am-noon and 2-5pm.

Iguana Station. Walk up Mammy Ln. and turn left at the first intersection, just before Stuart's Hill. Offers tours to local bat caves (L150). Also houses a visitor's center with exhibits about Utila's iguana, known commonly as "swamper." Open M, W, F 2-5pm.

ACCOMMODATIONS

From the dock, lodging is available down all three roads. To the east after Cooper's Inn, all accommodations tend to be reserved for divers or for those looking to stay longer. Reservations are necessary during the high season (July-Sept. and Dec.-Apr.). Most dive centers include or discount lodging as part of diving deals.

Rubi's (☎425 3240), east of the main dock next to Reef Cinema. Cozy rooms with hot baths. Large coral courtyard. Communal kitchen and free Wi-Fi. Singles L345; doubles L480, with A/C L770. Cash only. ❹

Cooper's Inn (☎425 3184), east of the dock just past Zanzibar Cafe, and after Rubi's. A friendly spot with good-sized rooms. All rooms equipped with fans, a common room, a communal kitchen, and shared cold bath. Singles L200; doubles L250; apartments from L7,700 per month. Cash only. ❷

Mango Hotel (☎425 3335), up Cola de Mico Rd., at the 2nd intersection. Beautiful resort-style rooms with wooden floors. Amenities include cable TV, hot baths, and phones. Pool and sauna on site. Shared 3- to 4- person rooms are the real steal. Reception 6am-8pm. Shared rooms L200. Doubles L975, with A/C 1075. Cash only. ❸

Backpacker's Lodge (☎425 3350), across from Gunter's Dive Shop (p. 171), west of the dock, past the fire station. Clean private rooms with a double bed and shared cold bath, just minutes from Chepe's beach. Check in at Gunter's Dive shop. Dorms L50; private rooms L190. Cash only. ❶

Margaritaville (☎425 3366), just west of Gunter's Dive Shop (p. 171). Rooms with 2 double beds, hot baths, and charming porch seating overlooking the beach. Doubles L400, with A/C L760; cabins L1150. Cash only.❸

Hotel Utila (☎425 3140), to the west from the dock, just past Mamey Lane. A comfortable option for those looking for an accommodation without a dive course. All rooms feature private bath, cable TV, and access to a communal kitchen. Singles L290, with A/C L675; doubles L345/L960. Cash only. ❸

Seaside Hotel (☎425 3150), to the west from the dock, across from Gunther's Dive shop. Rooms have private bathrooms, fans, and access to a balcony, common kitchen, and free internet. Singles L230; doubles L290. Rooms with A/C L675. Cash only. ❷

🔲 FOOD

Heaping fruit salads and vegetarian entrees are refreshingly common among the assortment of local, European, and North American menu choices here in Utila. To cook your own food, purchase groceries at **Bush's Supermarket** (☎425 3147), a few houses east of the Banco Atlántida. (Open M-Sa 6:30am-7pm, Su 6:30am-10:30am.)

Ultra Light (☎425 3514), to the west from the dock, past the Methodist church. Get your Middle Eastern fix here with authentic Israeli food. Stuffed breakfast pitas L75-85. *Shakshurka* (tomatoes, onions, pepper, eggs, zalabia, with 2 salads) L140. Hummus L95. Falafel L95. Chicken curry L140. Open Su-F 7am-10pm. Cash only. ❸

Driftwood Cafe (☎408 5168), to the west of the dock, past Gunther's Dive Shop. Texas-style cuisine (meat, in large portions) on a shaded dock. Half-pound cheeseburger L130. BBQ Pork Ribs L195. Beer from L25. Cash only. ❹

Bundu Café, east of the dock, across from Banco Atlántida. A cozy place to lounge, with expansive open-air seating mercifully sheltered from the rains of the Monsoon season. Large book exchange. Backpacker breakfast L40. Super *baleadas* L50. Deep dish veggie pizza L158. Occassional all-you-can-eat M nights. Open M-Tu, Th, Sa-Su 9am-9:30pm. Cash only. ❷

Munchiés (☎425 3168), a few houses down from Bundu cafe, to the west of the dock, across from Deep Blue Divers. Serves up delicious veggie quesadillas (L70), grilled chicken in mushroom sauce (L120), and American breakfasts (L80). Open M-Sa 6:30am-9:30pm, Su 6:30am-1:30pm. Cash only. ❸

RJ's BBQ and Grill, east on the main road before Alton's. The island's most popular BBQ. Come early to avoid crowds drawn by grilled wahoo fish (L100), barracuda (L100), hamburgers (L65), and heaping portions of vegetables and rice. Open W, F, Su from 5pm. Cash only. ❸

Mango Cafe (☎425 3305), attached to the Mango Inn, up Cola de Mico Rd., at the 2nd intersection. Mouth-watering Italian can be ordered from the illustrated, multi-lingual menu. Pizza L138-220. Nightly specials. Open daily 6am-8pm. Cash only. ❸

Mermaid's Fast Food (☎425 3395), to the east from the dock. Buffet-style options for all meals. Spaghetti L35. Beans and rice L35. Fried chicken L48. Combos with side vegetables L75-90. Free Wi-Fi. Open M-Th and Sa 7am-10pm, F 7am-3pm. AmEx/MC/V. ❷

NIGHTLIFE AND ENTERTAINMENT

Utila seems to always find an excuse to party; locals celebrate the rising of the sun and moon. The annual Sun Jam (www.sunjamutila.com), typically held the first Saturday in August, draws a crowd second only to La Ceiba's carnaval (p. 164).

Coco Loco's, a thatched-roof bar on its own pier, to the west from the dock. A good place to start out the evening. Dip your feet in the ocean through the jacuzzi-like hole in the pier, laze in a hammock overlooking all the action, or dance to an eclectic mix of music. Beer L25. Happy hour 4-7pm. Open daily 4pm-midnight and later on weekends.

Tranquilo Bar, on the pier next to Coco Loco's. A relaxed scene (as the name implies). Beer L25. Open daily 3pm-midnight.

Bar in the Bush, at the 3rd intersection up Cola de Mico Rd. Popular for cheap drinks and late-night volleyball. W Techno Night draws a lot of expats; F reggaeton and hip-hop brings out more locals. Beer L25. Open W and F 9pm-3am.

Happy Hour Bar & Crazy Dawg (☎425 3851), to the west from the dock, between Deep Blue Shop and Gunther's Dive Shop. Discounts on different drinks each day of the week: Tu beers L20; W *flor de cana* L20; F shots L20. Also serves hot dogs, prepared in a variety of ways. 7 *chihuahua* (i.e., mini dogs) L125. Sloppy shepherd (served on a hamburger bun with Texas chili, cheese, and fries) L80. Open daily 11am-late. Kitchen closed Su. ❷

Reef Cinema (☎425 3254), to the east from the dock. Movies M-F and Su 7:30pm; Sa 6:30, 8:30pm. L65.

Whale Shark Oceanic Research Center, to the west from the dock. Gives a free presentation on whale sharks Su nights 7:30-8:30pm.

OUTDOOR ACTIVITIES

Divers come from around the world for a chance to spot the biggest fish in these seas: the bespeckled **Whale Shark,** which is frequently seen on Utila's north side during morning trips. The Whale Shark high season lasts from the end of February to the end of June. The south side has fewer big fish but compensates with greater coral diversity and unbelievable wall drops. In fact, some of the best diving can be found right outside the harbor on the east side, where eagle rays flap past in huge numbers. Divers also enjoy the open hull and pilot house of the submerged **Haliburton ship** (40m down). A little farther east, Utila's most popular dive site, **Black Hills,** is an underwater mountain that houses turtles, big schools of fish, and barracuda.

Because of steep competition among the various dive shops on the island, prices have been standardized for all open water activities. **Snorkel** equipment rental costs L95 per day for non-divers; **kayak** rentals cost L190 per day for non-divers. Both are free for those signed up for diving courses or other dives. A ride on a boat to various snorkel spots around the island costs L190. Receiving your **PADI certification** requires 3-4 days to complete the Open Water Divers course, costs L5,000, and always includes at least two free fun dives after certification. If you want to try **scuba diving,** take a half-day Discover Scuba Diving class (L1500), which can count towards your certification if you decide to continue. To become a Dive Master requires a one-month internship (for more information visit www.padi.com) and costs L14,450 (US$750); on Utila, all dive shops offer the added perk of free dives for life if you train with them. Fun dives cost L1,060, although with groups of eight people or more the price drops to around L480 per dive. Shops open daily 7am-6pm and accept AmEx/MC/V.

Captain Morgan's (☎425 3349; www.divingutila.com), directly across from the Municipal Dock. Captain Morgan's is the only dive shop based on the cayes to the southwest of Utila. If you take a course with them, you stay at their lodge on the islands and have greater access to less touristed dive sites on the north side of the island. For divers, transfer to the cayes is always free, but for those wishing to stay at the lodge without diving, each ride costs L100 per person.

Utila Dive Center (UDC), halfway to the airport beach, east of the dock that is next to Seven Seas. The most heavily publicized and one of the most popular dive shops on the island. Dive masters teach in 9 languages. The shop is also has a bar.

Alton's Dive Shop (☎425 3108; www.divealtons.com), to the east near UDC. One of the most popular dive shops on the island, featuring a very young, social crew and nightly parties during high season. Fast boats make daily trips to the north side (weather permitting). Underwater camera rentals, a water polo net, and waterfront accommodation included with courses.

Gunter's Dive Shop (☎425 3350), west from the dock near Crepe's beach. The oldest shop on the island. With a maximum class size of 4, Gunter's focuses on quality and personal attention. Daily northside trips (weather permitting). Divers are hosted in the Backpacker Lodge (p. 169).

ROATÁN

Roatan is Honduras's contribution to the Caribbean tropical paradise circuit, a destination at present still closer to "recently discovered" than "saturated" on the timeline of inevitable tourism decay. On the south side of the island are the ferry and cruiseship docks, the airport, and the small, bustling capital town, Coxen Hole. To the east past French Harbor, the terrain turns to green, rolling ridges offering expansive views across the island. Only a few exclusive resorts have opened and the villages remain largely untouched by tourism. The vast majority of the resorts lie to the west. The resort-village West Bay and the ex-pat rich West End also lie to the west; these are the only places on the island for budget travellers. Sandy Bay, on the highway between Coxen Hole and the West End, is near ecological foundations and parks, and sits on a sparsely utilized beach.

▐ TRANSPORTATION

Flights:Manuel Galvez International Airport (☎445 1880), 1½km east of Coxen Hole, is accessible by taxi and microbus. **Isleña** (☎445 1559; www.flyislena.com; open daily 5:30am-6pm) flies to: **La Ceiba** (15min.; 6:50, 9am, 1, 3pm; L1000); **San Pedro Sula** (40min.; 6:50, 9am, 1pm; L1385); **Tegucigalpa** (55min., 6:50am and 1pm, L1560). **Taca** (☎445 1918; www.taca.com) partners with Isleña to provide international service to: **Houston** (Sa 11am); **Miami** (Su 8:45am); and **San Salvador** (Su 3:30pm). **SOSA** (☎445 1154; www.aerolineassosa.com; open daily 5:30am-5pm) flies to: **La Ceiba** (15min.; 6:30, 9am, 2:30, 4pm; L1060); **San Pedro Sula** (40min.; 7, 9am, noon; L1350); and **Tegucigalpa** (45min., 7am and noon, L1560).

Ferries: The Galaxy II Ferry (☎445 1795), leaves from their dock east of Coxen Hole daily for La Ceiba (1½hr., 7am and 2pm, L500).

Car Rentals: A&G Rent a Car (☎445 0423), **Budget** (☎445 2290), **Best Car Rental** (☎445 1494), and **Caribbean Rent a Car** (☎445 6950) all have offices inside the airport.

Local Transportation: Microbuses run daily, every 15min. 6am-6pm. **Coxen Hole** to **West End** (L20); Coxen Hole to **Sandy Bay** (L13). Another set of microbuses run daily, every 2 hr. 6am-6pm. **Oak Ridge** to **French Harbor** (L20). Oak Ridge to **Coxen Hole** (L30). Oak Ridge to the **West End** (L40). Before the 2pm ferry, some microbuses run all the way to the **ferry** (L40).

Car Rental: Roatán Rentals (☎445 1171; www.roatansalesandrentals.com), across the street from Cannibal Cafe, south of the intersection on the main drag. Most rentals L1185-1885 per day. Open M-Sa 7:30am-6pm. AmEx/MC/V. **Best Car Rental** (☎445 4322), on the corner of the main intersection. The Beach House Information Office has various vehicles for L960-1250 per day.

Bike and Motorcycle Rental: Captain Van's (☎445 4076), south of the main intersection, just before Cannibal Cafe ,on the main road toward West Bay. Bikes L175 per day, L690 per week; scooters L750/3560; motorcycles L865/3850. All come with free treasure map and 10-point safety orientation. Open daily 9am-4pm. AmEx/MC/V.

Taxis: English Speaking Taxi Drivers (☎445 7478). **Colectivo taxis** between Coxen Hole and the West End, or French Harbor, should cost no more than L40. Hiring a taxi will cost L200.

▪ ORIENTATION

The **Manuel Galvez International Airport** is just to the east of Island capital **Coxen Hole;** Galaxy ferries and Carnival cruises arrive just east of the airport at **Dixon Cove,** while Royal Caribbean cruises arrive just west of Coxen Hole. The main highway passed **Sandy Bay** (6km) to the north; it then moves west to **West End** (11km) where you'll find the most tourist facilities, housing options, and dive shops. Roatán's best beach, **West Bay** (15km), is 2km south of the West End and features more expensive beachfront resorts and restaurants.

COXEN HOLE

Once a sleepy fishing village, Coxen Hole has been transformed in recents years, like much of the western half of the island, with the sudden influx of tourism dollars. These changes have manifested themselves equally in the construction of tourist villages like the West End, and in the traffic, noise, and confusion that now fill the small city. Coxen Hole does see its fair share of tourists, most of whom immediately move on to greener pastures and bluer waters.

▪ ▪ ORIENTATION AND PRACTICAL INFORMATION

From the cruiseship dock **Main Street** runs eastward along the coastline until it's junction with **Thicket Mouthe Road** (which marks the edge of the town center). Further on, the Main St. runs around a bend until it meets **Back Market Road**. Main St. continues east towards the airport where it meets the main Highway heading toward French Harbor and the ferry dock. Back Market Rd. runs around the north side of the town center, and swings around to form a T-intersection with Thicket Mouthe Rd. Thicket Mouthe Rd. runs north to the main highway and toward the West End.

Tourist Information: Bay Islands Conservation Association (☎445 1424), on the 2nd fl. of the green Cooper Building next to the (also green) Municipal Building. Open M-F 8am-5pm.

Banks: Banco Credomatic, along Main St. eastward from H.B. Warrens, gives cash advances and has a **24hr. ATM**. Open M-F 8:30am-4:30pm, Sa 9am-noon. **Banco**

Atlantida, 2 buildings to the west of H.B. Warren's, on the left. **24hr. ATM.** Open M-F 8:30am-4:30pm, Sa 8:30-11:30am.

Police: Preventiva (☎445 3449), up Thicket Rd. on the left, next to the hospital.

Hospital: Hospital Roatán (☎445 1499), on Thicket Rd., 2 blocks up from Front St. 24hr. emergency medical assistance. English spoken.

Pharmacies: Farmacia Roatán, 1 block up Thicket Rd. from Front St. Open M-F 8am-5pm, Sa 8am-noon.

Internet Access: Hondusoft Internet Cafe (☎445 1415), around back in the building next to H.B. Warren's. Internet L40 per hr. International phone calls L4 per min. Open M-Sa 8am-6pm. **Traveler's Internet Cafe** (☎445 1816), on the corner of Front St. and Thicket Rd. Internet L40 per min. International calls L4 per min. Open M-Sa 8am-9pm.

Post Office: On the Ocean side of Main St., just west of the bend. Receives but does not send packages. Open M-F 8am-5pm, Sa 8am-noon.

ACCOMMODATIONS

Hotel Sarita (☎445 1541), towards the east of town on Main St. The best option for budget travelers trying to make the best of Coxen Hole. Rooms feature private baths, TVs, and fans, while the hotel itself sits right on the edge of the harbor—some rooms offer rare panoramic views of the sea. Singles L350; doubles L400. Cash only. ❸

Hotel Coral (☎445 4714), on Main St., west of Hotel Sarita. Another budget option, with rooms on the 2nd floor of a small store. Fans, TVs, and shared bathrooms. Singles and doubles L300. Cash only. ❷

FOOD

Your best options for Food can be found along coastside **Main Street.** This road is just east from Thick Mouth road, the main access road for vehicles arriving from the West End. For groceries, an **H.B Warrens** supermarket, to the east of the intersection along Main St., is your best bet. (☎445 4208. Open M-Sa 7am-6pm. AmEx/MC/V.)

Tirza's Snacks, just across the street from H.B. Warrens on Main St. Typical Honduran food at prices that will make you, and your wallet, happy. Breakfast *tipico* L50. *Baleada* L25. Beer L20. Open 8am-9pm. Cash only. ❷

SANDY BAY

A small community (pop. 1100) 6km west of Coxen Hole and halfway to West End, Sandy Bay holds a

THE LOCAL STORY

ROCK ON

The 1970s were a guitar-riffing heyday for Rolling Stone magazine. From the breakup of The Beatles in 1970, to the Billboard domination of rock legends like Led Zeppelin and Aerosmith, there was no shortage of music news during this decade. While the rock revolution appeared to occur exclusively on either side of the Pond, Belizean musicians were having a notable jam session of their own along the sunny shores of the Caribbean.

The brainchild of Pen Cayetano and the Turtle Shell Band, punta rock started making waves in the late 1970s as a medium for social commentary. While the genre is built on the traditional punta rhythm of the Garífuna people, electric guitars, synthesizers, and catchy hooks contribute to the contemporary sound. Punta instrumentation—including bass and treble drums, maracas, and a set of turtle shells—is often accompanied by a performance of kuliao, a competitive fertility dance of West African origin. Punta rock has gained significant popularity throughout Latin America, but Belizean punta—often sung in the Kriol language—has established a unique following in its celebration of Belizean identity. Punta Rebels, Aziatic, and Super G are all great examples of modern punta.

few interesting diversions spread along the passing highway. The town boasts outstanding snorkeling in the well-protected **Sandy Bay Marine Reserve.** You can also visit the **Carambola Botanical Gardens,** across the highway from Anthony's Key Resort, where just about every kind of plant and lizard native to the tropics thrives. One of the best trails ascends to the summit of Carambola Mountain, from which you can see Roatán's reefs and Utila in the distance. (☎445 4117. Entrance L150, with tour L230. Open daily 7am-5pm.)

Make sure to check out the **Tropical Bird Park,** between Anthony's Key Resort and Coxen Hole. Tell the bus driver that you want to go there and he'll drop you off. The large collection of tropical birds includes birtds that have been reha-bilitated and saved from hunters. (☎444 4314. Open Tu-Sa 9am-4pm.) **Anthony's Key Resort** houses the **Roatán Museum** and the **Roatán Institute of Marine Sciences** (Anthony's Key ☎445 3003; www.anthonyskey.com). The museum has a small display on the history of the island, with exhibits in English. (L150. Open Th-Tu 8am-5pm.) The Institute features an enclosure with dolphin shows, as well as upclose tours that allow you to swim with the seafaring mammals. (L135. Swim with dolphins L1615. In open ocean L2385. Open M-F 10:30am and 4:30pm; Sa and Su 11:30am and 1:30pm. Call to arrange dolphin swims.)

Sandy Bay is a 2hr. walk from Coxen Hole; buses running between Coxen Hole and the West End stop regularly at the front of Anthony's Key Resort (every 10min. 6am-7pm, L13).

THE WEST END

The West End has by far the best concentration of resources useful to trav-elers on the island. Lodging options alternate with restaurants and dive shops. Many of the locals here were once travelers themselves, sidetracked by the beauty that is the Bay Islands. The spectacular views down the coast line, and the offshore presence of magnificent coral reefs do make a power-ful argument for lingering awhile.

◼✦⊠ ORIENTATION AND PRACTICAL INFORMATION

Almost all of West End surrounds one main drag which runs along the shore. To the north, this road passes **Half Moon Bay;** to south, towards **West Bay.** The road's main intersection is with the highway, a little north of the center of town where *colectivos* and buses wait to pick up passengers. The intersection faces Half Moon Bay, home to great snorkeling and a popular public beach. Most hotels, restaurants, bars and services are south, towards West Bay. While many prices are written in US dollars for tourists, items can be paid for with lempiras.

Tourist information: For up-to-date hotel, dive shop, resort, restaurant, and attrac-tion info, visit www.roatanet.com. At the airport, the **Island Information and Hotel Reservation Center** sells island maps (L20) and can help you get organized before you arrive in West End. Open daily 8am-6pm. **Beach House Information Center** (☎445 4260), located just north of the main intersection, is open daily 8am-5pm. **Roatan Tourist Information Center** (☎9815 4163) operates a tourist information kiosk about 50m south of the main intersection. Open M-Su 9am-5pm; the kiosk is occassionally unmanned, especially when a cruise ship has just arrived. Keep in mind, however, that each of these tourist information centers earns commission by selling tours. That said, prices aren't any higher to arrange tours with these centers. Plus, they provide useful information.

Banks: Banco Lafise (☎455 5643), 800m up the main highway toward Coxen Hole. Open M-F 9am-4pm, Sa 9am-12pm. **Unibank ATM,** south from the main intersection just past Vallerie's. Open 24hr.

Laundry: Bamboo Hut Laundry, next to Rudi's, south of the main intersection, past Eagle Ray's. Wash and dry L15 per lb.; minimum load L75. Open M-Sa 8am-4pm. Laundry service also available at Valerie's (p. 175) for L200 per load.

Police: (☎445 1199 or 1138). **Tourist Police** have an office to the north of the main intersection, next to Woody's Grocery. Open 24hr., but has no phone number.

Pharmacy: West End Farmacia (☎445 4173), just before West End Divers, south of the intersection on the main drag, toward West Bay Beach. Open M-Sa 8:30am-7:30pm.

Medical Services: Cornerstone Emergency Medical Service (☎ 445 3003), at Anthony's Key Resort, up the highway, toward Coxen Hole. Has a hyperbaric chamber; 2 doctors who speak English. **Fantasy Island Resort** on the south side of the island by French Harbor also has a hyperbaric chamber (☎455 7506).

Telephone and Internet Access: Barefoot Charlie's (☎445 4286; fax 445 4278) across from Fosters, south of the main intersection. Satellite internet service (L2 per min.), Skype, and fax. Two weeks of internet for L200 per person. Open daily 9am-9pm. **Paradise Computers** (☎445 4028), to the south of the main intersection between Dolfin Hotel and Capt Van's rental. Internet L2 per minute. Calls to the US L10 per minute. Open daily 8am-10pm.

ACCOMMODATIONS

Mid-priced hotels are far more common than budget accommodations. The few budget options that do exist are, for the most part, south of the main intersection. Many dive shops offer discounted lodging, especially for those taking their dive courses.

▨ **Valerie's Youth Hostel** (☎3263 2415; www.roatanonline.com/valleries), south of the main intersection, just past Cannibal Cafe, up a narrow boardwalk that's easy to miss. Stairs rise on all sides of the compound to rooms and patios on different levels, some with hammocks and ocean views. Communal kitchen. Longer-term apartment with A/C, balcony, private bath, cable TV, and kitchen available. Dorms L150; private rooms with shared bath L300; apartment price varies—ask for rates. Cash only. ❷

Tina's Backpackers (☎445 4144), far to the south of town, past Foster's Bar. Run by Barefeet Bar, Tina's offers a few beds in a small dorm room with a communal kitchen, fans, shared bath, living room, and cable TV. Lockers available. Dorms L135. Cash only. ❷

Chillie's (☎445 1214; www.nativesonsRoatan.com), north of the main junction, behind Native Sons Diving. Rooms accommodate up to 3 people. Guests have access to communal kitchen and courtyard. Most rooms have porches; all have private baths. Reception 8am-7pm. Quiet hours after 9pm. Doubles L385; triples L520; quads L615. Two-person cabin with kitchen L460, 3-person L580; 2-person hot water cabin L580, 3-person L675. AmEx/MC/V. ❸

Mariposa (☎445 4450; www.mariposa-lodge.com), to the south of the main intersection, up the dirt road just to the left of West End Divers. This hill estate offers clean and spacious rooms. Most come with full kitchens, hot private baths, and TVs. Good for families. Quiet hours after 9pm. Rooms with shared kitchen and bath L500-750, with private kitchen and bath L770-L1060, with A/C L865-1060. Cash only. ❹

Hotel Dolfin (☎445 4499), just to the south of the main intersection. Rising up in tiers from the street, the rooms at Hotel Dolfin boast expansive views of Half Moon Bay. No-frills exterior belies comfortable rooms with cable TV, A/C, and private hot water baths. Doubles L580, with balconies and sea views L865; triples L865/1060. AmEx/MC/V. ❹

Posada Arco Iris (☎445 1264; www.roatanposada.com), on the main street, north of the intersection behind the Argentinian Grill. Large wooden rooms with A/C, fridges, and tiled hot baths in the midst of a lush tropical garden with monkeys and parrots. Rooms have porches with hammocks. English spoken. Book exchange and kayak use. Free internet. High-season doubles L810, with full kitchen L925; triples L925/1040; quads L1040/1155. 10% discount for week-long stays. AmEx/MC/V. ❹

Sea Breeze Inn (☎445 4026), behind Cannibal Cafe, to the south of the main intersection. Rooms equipped with A/C, private hot water baths, and cable TV; some also have ocean views. Inquire about diving packages that might include accommodation discounts. Doubles L675. Cash only. ❹

◘ FOOD

A dizzying array of competing establishments line the main shore drag. Despite the competition, you'll be hard-pressed to find a meal that costs less than L100. Travelers on a budget might consider stopping by **Woody's Grocery Store** (☎445 4469) which lies to the north from the main intersection, near where the road curves away from the beach. (Open M-Th and Su 7am-6pm, F 7am-5pm. AmEx/MC/V.) Otherwise, the cheapest food you'll find are late night *baleadas* sold to the daring by street vendors for L25.

Lighthouse Restaurant (☎445 4201), south of the main intersection, across the street from Captain Van's. Enjoy glorious views of West Bay from the deck. Internet free until noon (with purchase of breakfast). Breakfast *típico* with choice of ham or bacon L80. Large fish tacos L120. Shrimp cooked in Lighthouse's famous coco sauce L265. Fruit smoothie L50. Fresh-squeezed juice L30. Beer L30. Open M-Sa 7am-10pm. AmEx/MC/V. ❹

Brick Oven Pizza (☎991 2690, delivery ☎8928 0066), to the south past West End Divers. Follow the signs up the path inland, take a right at the intersection, and follow the road around to the right and downhill again before taking another right—the most worthwhile 10min. walk you'll take on the island. Genuine brick-oven pizza prepared by Tony from Bologna. Mouth-watering 10 in. pizza L200-230. Focaccia L265. Rich homemade juices L37. Delivery 5-9pm. Open daily 5-10pm. Cash only. ❹

Cannibal Cafe (☎445 4026), south of the main intersection just after Captain Van's. This mainly Mexican restaurant serves rich feasts. Be sure to try the Big Kahuna Burrito (L150-225); if you can eat the entire thing on your own, you eat for free. The *Grande* quesadillas (L146), banana smoothies with a hint of chocolate (L55), and guacamole (L44) are all excellent. Vegetarian options available. Open M-Sa 7am-10pm. Cash only. ❹

Ali Baba's (☎445 4150), to the south of the main intersection, just before Rocket Burger, just after Nova. Middle Eastern cuisine like hummus (L115), falafel (L135), shawarma (L150), and chicken gyros (L135). *Shisha* pipe L150. Open M and W-Su 11am-10:30pm, Tu 5-10:30pm. Cash only. ❸

Rudy's (☎445 4205), just before Barefoot Charlie's, south of the main intersection. Rudy's offers delicious banana pancakes (L75), bulging omelettes (L95-120), cheeseburgers (L85), sandwiches (BLT L115, and thick whole fruit smoothies (L85-95). Open M-F and Su 6am-5pm. AmEx/MC/V. ❸

Argentinian Grill (☎445 1264; www.roatanposada.com), connected to the hotel Posada Arco Iris, just north of the main intersection on the main drag. Elegant and delicious dining overlooking Half Moon Bay. Vegetarian plate L280. Land & Sea (chicken and shrimp in chef's secret sauce) L315. Open M-Tu and Th-Su noon-10pm. AmEx/MC/V. ❹

Cream of the Trop (☎9870 1444). Homemade ice cream in over a dozen different flavors, made with local ingredients. Cup or cone L60. Crepe with chocolate or caramel L40. Fresh fruit smoothie L75. French toast L75. Free Wi-Fi with purchase. Open M-Sa 7:30am-9pm, Su 7:30am-8pm. ❸

♫ ♬ ENTERTAINMENT AND NIGHTLIFE

The Blue Channel, to the south of the main intersection near Cannibal Cafe, shows movies in English most nights at 8pm. (☎445 4133. L50.)

The Twisted Toucan, just past Barefoot Charlie's, to the south from the main intersection. Hard to miss—patrons inevitably spill out into the streets when stools run out. Grab a Jamaican-me-crazy (L80) or a chocolate-banana daiquiri (L60). Open M-Th 11am-midnight, F-Sa 11am-2am, Su 2-10pm. Happy hour M-Sa 4-7pm, Su 24hr.; 2-for-1 mixed drinks.

Sundowners (www.sundownersroatan.com), to the north from the main intersection next to the Beach House. A favorite for its Su quiz night. Bar menu L70-150. Mixed drinks from L50. Happy hour daily 5-7pm; beer L30. Open daily 4-10pm.

Good Vibrations, with a deck right over the water, just past Cannibal Cafe. Plays a solid soundtrack of reggae. Beer L25. Reggae-Punch L60. Open M-Th and Su 4-10pm, F and Sa noon-2am.

Foster's (☎403 8005; www.fostersroatan.com), to the south of town and out on its own pier. A good place to kick back and ponder the stars above. Beer and philosophy are standard weeknight pastimes, while Fridays feature a more lively atmosphere, occasional DJs, and live music. Beer L30. Mixed drinks from L95. Tu 2-for-1 beers. Th L100 beer buckets. Open M-Th and Su 11am-midnight, F-Sa 11am-2am.

Le Bistro (☎403 8854), to the south of the main intersection, above West End Divers. Beer L30. Karaoke Th 8pm—if you can't beat 'em, might as well join 'em. Open Tu-W 10am-10pm, Th-Sa 10am-midnight, Su 10am-8pm.

The Purple Turtle, formerly known as Mango Verde. A small place just to the south of town, about 50m from Sundowners. The Purple Turtle gets packed late at night, especially on the weekends. Beer L30. Open M-Th 8am-midnight, F-Sa 8am-2am, Su 8am-10pm.

Red Hot Chili Peppers, to the south of the main intersection, past Eagle Ray's. Offers deck patio and private lounge seating right on the beach. Beer L50. Red Hot Margherita L115. Appetizers L95-135. Chips and Salsa L95. Happy hour 4:30-6:30pm. Open M-Th noon-10pm, F-Sa noon-midnight, Su noon-8pm.

Eagle Rays (☎445 4283). 2nd fl. patio and a private pier that provides great views of the ocean. Tequila shots L30. Beer L35. Open daily 11am-11pm.

⚑ OUTDOOR ACTIVITIES

The West End Village is right next to spectacular coral reefs. You need only don snorkel gear and swim out a hundred feet into Half Moon Bay to witness stunning underwater environments. Dive shops and equipment rentals jostle for your services all the way down the shore drive. Tourist Information Centers sell watersports packages, many of which actually run out of Half Moon Bay; in the West End, these tours cost less and include transport to and from the beach 2km south.

DIVING

Half Moon Bay Wall, just a short swim out from the main intersection, remains one of the best in Roatán with spectacular wall drops and colorful marine life.
Mary's Place, the island's premier dive site, covers an impressive span of reef

along the south shore. **Peter's Place,** at the end of Marine Park, has tons of big fish, deep canyons, and vertical walls. **Pablo's Place,** boasts the island's highest and healthiest coral diversity. **West End Wall,** another wall densely packed with marine life, features terrific drift-diving. Nearby, **Overheat** and **Ulysess reefs** are great shallow dives. **Las Palmas** is an exhilarating dive while the famous **Hole in the Wall,** a sand-chute that swimmers can wriggle through, is suited for advanced divers. **Bear's Den,** with enclosed canyons, is also an unique experience for highly skilled divers. A popular tune-up for rusty divers, **Blue Channel** is a shallow dive (35ft.) through a natural channel packed with bright fish and the occasional octopus. The most popular wreck dive is massive **El Águila,** near Sandy Bay. Experienced divers find thrills at the deep and dark **Texas.** Recently sunk for recreational purposes, the **Odyssey** is drawing large crowds as the third largest wreck this side of the Caribbean.

Roatan's West End features a number of large dive shops, as well as several smaller, more personal establishments. Many resorts have their own equipment and guides for visitors. Similar to Utila, prices tend to be consistent between dive shops for individual dives, or dive courses. The shops differ in the deals they offer on multiple-dive packages; some include discounted lodging. **Open-water certification** costs L5390 ($280) plus PADI books, and **Discover Scuba courses** cost L1920 ($100). **Advanced certification** costs L5390 ($280) plus books. A single fun dive will cost L675 ($35). Experienced Roatan dive veteran William Welbourn maintains a website that divers should check out (www.bayislandsdiver.com).

Pura Vida Dive Center (☎445 4110; www.puravidaresort.com), to the south next to West End Divers. Pura Vida has earned PADI 5-star Gold Palm Resort distinction for its equipment, fast boats, and experienced instructors. Expert instructors lead dives to destinations for divers at all skill levels. Dives for guests L480. Underwater camera rental L385. Dive Master L17,312 ($900). Daily boats 9, 11:30am, 2:30pm. Open daily 8am-5pm. AmEx/MC/V.

Coconut Tree Divers (☎445 4081, in the US 813 964 7214, UK ☎0151 324 0701; www.coconuttreedivers.com), right at the main intersection. The only dive shop in the West End with an instructor development center that offers technical advanced dive training. Coconut Tree also has 4 daily dives on their 2 covered boats. Dive shop also an equipment retailer. Two-tank dives L1830 ($95). Dive Master including all materials L13,465 ($700), without materials L9620 ($500). Open M, W, F-Su 8am-5pm; Tu and Th 8am-8pm. AmEx/MC/V.

West End Divers (☎445 4289; www.westendivers.com), to the south, next to Pura Vida Dive Resort. One of the most frequented dive shops in the West End, with an experienced and friendly staff, and all female dive instructors. Dives conducted with covered boats. Special 2-tank trips include lunch L1830 ($95). Dive Master L13,465 ($700). Boats daily at 9am, 11:30, 2:30pm. Open daily 8am-5pm. AmEx/MC/V.

Happy Diver's (☎9898 7432), next to the Lighthouse Restaurant. Recently opened with new equipment on a private dock. Shop is small, so expect personal attention; the head dive instructor is a long-time local and knows all the island's best dive sites. Open water certification includes free fun dive afterwards. Dive Master Certification L12,500 ($650). AmEx/MC/V.

Native Sons Diving (☎445 1214; www.nativesonsRoatan.com), north of the main intersection, next to Chillie's. Dive Master L13,465 ($700). Boats daily at 9am and 2pm. Open daily 8am-5pm. AmEx/MC/V.

Cross Creek Dive Center (☎425 3326), across the street from UDC. Canal-side rooms with private showers.

SNORKELING

You don't have to blow a lot of cash to enjoy the remarkable reefs, considering two of the best dive spots are even easier to enjoy when snorkeling. All dive shops have snorkeling equipment (free for divers), L95-135 for non-divers (plus deposit). Half Moon Bay, at the north end of town, is nearly impossible to avoid—roll out of bed anytime you want and wade into its refreshing waters with your gear for a look around the coral megalopolis. Some of the best snorkeling on the island is in nearby West Bay.

On the Top of the Water Sports (☎445 0020). In West Bay, above the Cannibal Cafe, south of the main intersection. Rents snorkeling gear through the restaurant. L190 ($10) plus deposit. Open 9am-5pm. Cash only.

Roatan Tourist Info Center (☎9815 4163). In West Bay. Rents snorkel equipment. L95 ($5), plus L950 ($50) deposit; 6% commission from credit card transaction. Also hires snorkel boat trips for L940 ($49) per hr. (minimum of 2 people). Kiosk, south of main intersection, open daily 9am-5pm. AmEx/MC/V.

Beach House Info Center (☎445 4260; www.gumbalimbapark.com). In West Bay. Rents snorkel equipment for L95 ($5), plus deposit. Runs snorkel boat outings at nearby Gumbalimba Park for L675 ($35) per person, including transportation. Open 8am-5pm. AmEx/MC/V.

KAYAKING

Roatan Tourist Info Center. Rents 2-person kayaks. (L480 per 2 hr.) Clear 2-person kayak L675 per 2hr.

Beach House Info Center. Rents single kayaks. (L290 per 2 hr.) Doubles L480 per 2 hr.

HORSEBACK RIDING

Cayefites Ranch. Offers 1-1½hr. horseback rides along the beach, through the jungle, to destinations with incredible views. L1060 ($55) per person; sunset ride L1250 ($65). Organize ride through Roatan Tourist Info Center (p. 179).

Shirkie Bodden Ranch (☎9555 4880; www.barriodorcasranch.com). Offers 2hr. rides at reasonable prices. Daytime, sunset, and full moon tours for L770 ($40) per person.

SAILING/BOAT CHARTERS

Stray Cat Sailing Adventures (☎3385 7457). Offers 3 hr. sunset cruises for L1250 ($65) per person as well as more personalized excursions. Organize in the West End through the Beach House Info Center.

Roatan Tourist Information Center (☎9815 4163). 3hr. sunset tris L1250 ($65) per person. 5hr. trips L1710 ($89) per person, includes 1-2hr. ofsnorkeling, refreshments, lunch, and open bar. 8hr. cruises L2480 ($129) per person. Overnight cruises to Cayos Cuchinos, Utila, or Guanaja L5480 ($285). Trips leave from West Bay; transportation from West End included. AmEx/MC/V.

Action Sailing (☎916 7654) runs 5hr. sailing trips daily. Trips include snorkel rental and free beer. Leaves from Suenos de Mar, at the south end of the shore road, near Barefeet Bar. L865 ($45) per person plus tax. Organize trips with Action Sailing through the Beach House Info Center in the West End.

Glass Bottom Boat (☎3271 3873). Organized throught the Gumbalimiba Park Info Center; ask for Jimmy (☎8980 8216). Offers regular 1hr. tours (L480 per person), 1hr.

THE BAY ISLANDS

tours with snorkeling (L1250 per person), and 2-3hr. island tours (contact for rate; group rates available).

Captain Vern (☎3346 2600). Take a ride on the Captain's catamaran. Vern charters 4hr. trips from Roatan to Utila, Cayos Cochinos, or Guanaja for L1060 ($55) per person.

WATER SPORTS

On the Top of the Water Sports (☎445 0020). above the Cannibal Cafe, south of the main intersection. Rents wake board, inner tubes, knee boards and water skis. Each L1830 ($95) per hr. or L1250 ($65) per 30min.

Roatan Tourist Information Center (☎9815 4163). Wakeboarding, waterskiing, kneeboarding, and tubing outings L1830 ($95) per 2hr. This center also offers parasailing and rents jet skis. Transportation to and from West Bay included. Open daily 9am-5pm. AmEx/MC/V.

OTHER OUTDOOR ACTIVITIES

Happy Divers (☎9898 7452). Organizes sea fishing trips for up to 6 people. L1350 ($70) per hr.

Stanley Submersibles (www.stanleysubmarines.com), at their dock on Half Moon Bay. Submarine tours in their custom-built submarine "Idabel" to a depth of 2000 ft. Tours from 1½hr (L11,540 per person) up to 8hr. (L28,855 per person). The Roatan Tourist Information Center (p. 179) can arrange tours.

Gumbalimba Park (☎9914 9196; www.gumbalimbapark.com). A park built for tourists near West Bay has ropewalks, monkeys and tropical birds, and canopy zipline tours. Park admission L385 ($20 per person). Canopy Tours L865 ($45). Park & Canopy Tour L1060 ($55). Canopy tour, Park admission, and Glass Botton Boat Ride L1440 ($75), with scuba diving L2115 ($110). Organize at the Beach House in the West End for included transportation to and from the park. Open daily 7am-5am.

Dolphin Encounters are offered by Anthony's Key Resort (☎445 3003; www.anthonys-key.com; open daily 8am-5pm). Located between the West End and Coxen Hole. Organize tours in the West End at the Beach House Info Center (transportation included). Dolphin encounter L1615 ($84); in the open water L2310 ($120). Dolphin encounter, Canopy tour, and Park entrance combo offered through Gumbalimpa.

Roatan Butterfly Center (☎445 4481), about 500m up the main highway to Coxen Hole from the West End. Displays butterflies native to the Bay Islands as well as those that can be found in other areas of Honduras. Open M-Sa 9am-5pm. L95 ($5).

◣ DAYTRIP

EAST OF COXEN HOLE

French Harbour, the island's biggest fishing port, lies 10km east along a curvy paved road that traverses rolling green hills and great ocean views. Yachts stop here, but there is no beach. There are some inexpensive hotels. Try **Britos** or **Dixon's Plaza.** From French Harbour, the main road runs across the mountain ridge at the center of the island. Along the way, a side road branches out to **Oak Ridge,** a charming fishing village.

From Oak Ridge, boat tours hit the beautiful Jonesville mangroves and go through a mangrove tunnel. Stop and get a snack at the **Hole in the Wall** restaurant. A 1½hr. boat ride will cost around L375-L400. A good place to spend the night in Oak Ridge is the comfortable **San José Hotel ❺.** (☎435 2328. L220, with fan and bath L250.) The rustic and small **Reef House Resort ❺** may be too expensive for budget travelers, but its attached restaurant is a great place to grab a drink and watch the dolphins pass by. (All-inclusive package L1880.) **Buses** run to Oak Ridge from Coxen Hole (about 1hr., L15). Once in Oak Ridge, all transportation is by **water taxi** (L20).

Around 5km from Oak Ridge, the paved road ends at **Punta Gorda,** the oldest town on the island and the oldest Garífuna community in Honduras. The village celebrates its founding every year from April 8 to 12; Garífuna from all over come to join the celebration. **Ben's Restaurant,** along the coast south of the village, rents moderately-priced cabins. Beyond Punta Gorda a dirt road continues past new resorts to **Camp Bay,** a beach now partially closed. The road ends at **Port Royal,** site of the remains of a British fort. The fort is surrounded by the rather inaccessible **Port Royal Park and Wildlife Refuge.**

WEST BAY

West Bay is where tourists go to forget the stresses of everyday life. Opulent resorts line the length of the beach; these are at once enticing and appalling. There's no shortage of reclining chairs or reclining people. The boats for hire offer a comprehensive assortment of watersports; any ocean-related activity you wish to try is available. The beach here is long and sandy. The reefs offer spectacular snorkeling 20 yards from each end of the beach; especially nice is the southern section near the cliffs. If you want to keep your expenses down, consider bringing your own picnic supplies.

From West End, West Bay is a 45min. walk along the beach. You will need to navigate an awkwardly placed, tall, rusting metal bridge. Leave valuables at home, go in groups, and avoid walking after dark. You can also wave down a water taxi from any dock along the shore; you can also try the ones that regularly stop on the dock opposite West End Divers (5min., L50). Bring repellent to ward off sandflies.

GUANAJA

When Christopher Columbus first sighted Guanaja in 1502, he named it "island of the pines." He probably came up with this name partly because by his fourth expedition he was running out of names (there are only so many saints), but mainly because, unlike the other Bay Islands, Guanaja's forests are largely conifer. Similarly unique is the island's terrain—**Michael Rock Peak,** at 1350 ft., is the highest point on the Bay islands. The peak offers hikers expansive vistas across the small island's mountainous terrain. One dirt road connects Mangrove Bight (at the island's northeast corner) with Savannah Bight, (an hour and a half drive south and across the water from Barocca Town); this means that most travel around the island is done by boat. Resorts are spread along the coastline, far from each other. Here in Guanaia, peaceful seclusion is almost inevitable.

Reservations are a must for most Guanaja accommodations. Resorts are full-service, but tiny—with the full food and recreational options they offer, they can only afford to be operational if they know that there will be customers to serve. The cheapest rooms can be found at hotels in Bonacca Town. Savannah Bight, on a coral caye about 1km offshore, also has cheap rooms. One option is to simply inquire if anyone in these towns lets rooms.

All resorts offer pickup services from the airport or various small ports in Guanaja. On the sparsely settled northern side of Guanaja, **Island House,** run by Bo Bush has two guesthouses that can fit up to 12 people. The guest-houses have balconies and Spanish-tile floors. (☎9963 8551. L11,540 per week includes transfers and all meals. L13,465 per week includes 2 daily dives. Daily rates available upon request.) **The West Peak Inn,** on the western beach of the island, 3 mi. from its closest neighbor, runs on solar power and preaches sustainability—cool showers in the morning and sun-warmed showers in the afternoon. Rates include all meals and taxes. Unlimited access to kayaks, snorkel gear, hiking trails, and transportation. Cabins have private porches and private baths. (L11,930 per week per person, L1830 per night per person; singles extra L290 per day.)

Dive sights are plentiful around Guanaja. Explore reefs, volcanic caverns, and shipwrecks. Recently discovered **Mestizo Reef** features 16th-century Spanish artifacts under 65 feet of water.

Islena (☎453 4208; www.flyislena.com) and **Sosa Airlines** (☎443 1399; www.aerolineassosa.com) fly to Guanaja from **La Ceiba** (L1392). Additionally, a boat run by **Ocean Tour** leaves from the municipal dock of **Trujillo** (☎3285 2118; 2 per week, L720). From **Roatan** and **Utila,** Captain Vern will charter trips to Guanaja. (☎3346 2600; L1060 per person. Reservations required.)

BELIZE

The least inhabited country in Central America, tiny, English-speaking Belize is graced with nearly untouched natural beauty and stable politics, leading to one of the most developed tourist infrastructures in the region. With a diverse population of 300,000 and a predominantly Caribbean atmosphere, Belize is also the only country in Central America where reggae is more common than salsa. Though a bit pricier than its neighbors, Belize is extremely accessible; transportation is relatively easy, and few other places in the world offer such mind-boggling biological and geographic diversity in such a small space (23,000 sq. km). In fact, ecotourism has turned into the nation's leading money-maker; luckily, commercial development still remains modest, particularly in the south and the interior. While Belize has its share of Mayan ruins, they are less outstanding than their Guatemalan counterparts--the nation's most popular destinations are the dozens of coastal cayes and national parks, nearly twenty of which have been set aside for conservation.

In one day, an enthusiastic traveler could snorkel the second-largest barrier reef in the Northern and Western hemispheres, scale Mayan temples, and slide down waterfalls in a pine forest, stopping along the way at a jaguar or baboon reserve. After savoring inexpensive lobster and sipping smooth Belikin beers on one of the country's many idyllic beaches, many find they never want to go anywhere else. Thousands of travelers come each year to explore the country's wonders and affirm the tourist bureau's slogan: "You better Belize it."

ESSENTIALS

PLANNING YOUR TRIP

BEFORE YOU GO
Passport (p. 6). Required of all visitors.
Visa (p. 6). Not required for citizens of the US, UK, Australia, Canada, Costa Rica, Ireland, New Zealand, Mexico, and the European Union. Valid for 30 days. Extensions of up to 90 days granted by the Immigration Department.
Onward or Return Ticket. Required of all visitors.
Proof of Funds. If requesting to remain in country for more than 30 days, visitors must show proof of sufficient funds for the duration of the extension of their stay. Belize requires a minimum of US$50 per person per day.
Work Permit. Required for all foreigners planning to work in Belize. Must reside in Belize for at least 6 months prior to application. For more information, contact the **Immigration and Nationality Department** (☎011 501 822 2423).
Recommended Vaccinations (p. 12). Hepatitis A, Hepatitis B, Typhoid, and Rabies.
Required Vaccinations. None required.
Inoculations (p. 12). Travelers who have been to nations with endemic yellow fever must present proof of vaccination.
Other Health Concerns: Malaria pills are recommended for those traveling to Belize. If your regular medical insurance policy (p. 13) does not cover travel abroad, you may wish to purchase additional coverage.
Departure Tax. US$35 if leaving by air, US$19 if by land.

EMBASSIES AND CONSULATES

BELIZEAN CONSULAR SERVICES ABROAD

An updated list of Belizean embassies and consulates is available on the web at http://bz.embassyinformation.com/list.php.

Australia: 5/1 Oliver Road Roseville, NSW, Roseville (☎+61 298 807 160).

Canada: 1800 McGill College, Suite 2480, H3A 3J6, Montreal, Quebec (☎514-288-1687; fax 514-288-4998). **Consulates:** 2321 Trafalgar Street, V6K 3T1, British Colombia, Vancouver (☎604-730-1224); McMillan Binch, Suite 3800, South Tower, Royal Bank Plaza, Ontario, Toronto (☎416-865-7000; fax 416-864-7048); Suite 100, 1122-8th Avenue S.W. Calgary, Alberta (☎403-215-6072; fax 403-242-9907).

Ireland: Christchurch Square, Dublin (☎+35 314 544 333).

UK: Third Floor, 45 Crawford Place, W1H 4LP, London (☎+44 207 723 3603).

US: 2535 Massachusetts Ave. NW, Washington, D.C. 20008 (☎202-332-9636; fax 202-332-6888; www.embassyofbelize.org). **Consulates:** Korean Trade Center Park Mile Plaza 4801 Wilshire Blvd Suite #250, Los Angeles, CA 90010 (☎323-469-7343; fax 213-469-7346); 4173 S Le Jeune Rd., Coconut Grove, FL 33146 (☎305-666-1121); 4318 Ridgecrest Dr., Las Vegas, NV 89121 (☎702-451-8444); 7101 Breen, Houston, TX 77086 (☎281-999-4484; fax 281-999-0855); c/O Eztech Manufacturing, Inc. 1200 Howard Drive West Chicago, IL 60185 (☎630-293-0010; fax 630-293-0463).

CONSULAR SERVICES IN BELIZE

Australia: (☎+52 555 531 5225)

Canada: 80 Princess Margaret Drive, PO Box 610, Belize City (☎+501 231 060).

Ireland and the UK: P.O. Box 94, Belmopan (☎+501 822 2146; fax 501 822 2764).

US: 29 Gabourel Lane, P.O. Box 286, Belize City (☎+501 227 7161; fax 501 230 802).

UK: Embassy Squarew, P.O. Box 91, Belmopan (☎+44 207 723 3603).

TOURIST OFFICES

Belize Tourism Board, P.O. Box 325, 64 Regent St., Belize City (☎+011 501 227 2420; fax 011 501 227 2423; www.travelbelize.org).

MONEY

The currency chart below was accurate as of August 2009. Check websites like www.xe.com or www.bloomberg.com for the latest exchange rates.

BELIZEAN DOLLAR ($)		
AUS$1 = BZ$1.55		BZ$1 = AUS$0.64
CDN$1 = BZ$1.77		BZ$1 = CDN$0.56
EUR€1 = BZ$2.74		BZ$1= EUR€0.36
NZ$1 = BZ$1.23		BZ$1 = NZ$0.81
UK£1 = BZ$3.17		BZ$1 = UK£0.32
US$1 = BZ$2.00		BZ$1 = US$0.50

The **Belizean dollar** (BZ$) is locked in to the US dollar at a rate of two to one. American paper currency is accepted nearly everywhere, but US coins are not. As a result of this constant and straightforward exchange rate, US dollars are almost universally accepted; be careful, however, to specify which

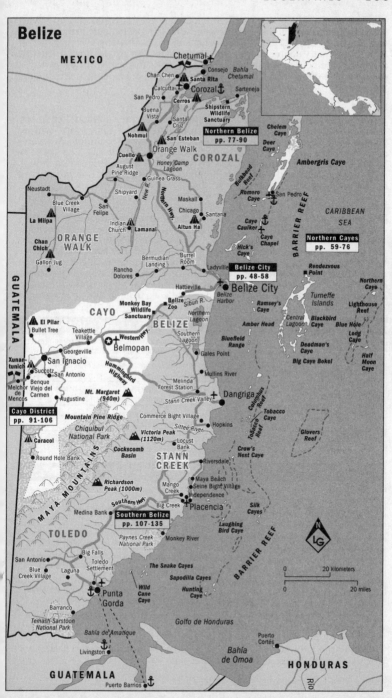

Belize

MEXICO

Chetumal
Chan Chen • Consejo
Santa Rita • Bahía
Calcutta • Chetumal
San Pedro • Cerros • Corozal • Sarteneja
Buena
Vista • Shipstern
Santa • Wildlife
Cruz • Sanctuary
Nohmul • San Esteban • **Northern Belize**
pp. 77-90
Cuello • Orange Walk • Chelem
Caye
August • Honey Camp • COROZAL
Pine Ridge • Lagoon • Deer
Guinea Grass • Caye • Ambergris Caye
Neustadt • Shipyard • New • Northern Hwy • Bulkhead
Reef
Blue Creek • San • Maskall • Romero • San Pedro
Village • Felipe • Caye
La Milpa • Indian • Chicago • CARIBBEAN
Chan • Church • Lamanai • Santana • Caye • SEA
Chich • ORANGE • Caulker
WALK • Caye
Gallon Jug • Altun Ha • Chapel • **Northern Cayes**
pp. 59-76
Bermudian • Burrel • Hick's
Rancho • Landing • Room • Caye
Dolores • Ladyville • Rendezvous
Hattieville • Point
Monkey Bay • Belize • Sibun R. • Belize City • **Belize City**
Wildlife • Zoo • **pp. 48-58**
CAYO • Sanctuary • Northern • Belize
Lagoon • Harbor • Ramsey's • Turneffe • Northern
El Pilar • BELIZE • Caye • Islands • Caye
Bullet Tree • Teakettle • Western Hwy • Southern • Amber Head • Central • Blackbird • Lighthouse
Village • Belmopan • Lagoon • Lagoon • Caye • Reef
Georgeville • Hummingbird • Bluefield • Blue Hole
Xunan- • San Ignacio • Highway • Gales Point • Range • Deadman's • Long
tunich • Succotz • Caye • Caye
San Antonio • Mullins River • Big Caye Bokel
Melchor • Benque • Melinda • Half
de • Viejo del • Forest Station • Moon
Mencos • Carmen • Mt. Margaret • Dangriga • Caye
Augustine • (940m) • Stann Creek Valley
Cayo District • Commerce Bight Village • Tobacco
pp. 91-106 • Mountain Pine Ridge • Sittee River • Caye
Chiquibul • Victoria Peak • Hopkins
Caracol • National Park • (1120m) • Locust • Glovers
Cockscomb • Bank • Crow's • Reef
Round Hole Bank • Basin • STANN • Nest Caye
CREEK • Riversdale
Richardson • Maya Beach • Silk
Peak (1000m) • Seine Bight Village • Cayes
Mango • Independence
Medina Bank • Creek • Big Creek • Placencia
Southern Belize • Laughing
TOLEDO • **pp. 107-135** • Paynes Creek • Bird Caye
National Park • Monkey River
San Antonio • Big Falls
Blue • Toledo • The Snake Cayes
Creek Village • Laguna • Settlement
Sapodilla Cayes
Wild • Hunting
Barranco • Punta • Cane • Caye
Gorda • Caye
Temash-Sarstoon
National Park • Golfo de Honduras
Bahía de Amatique • Puerto
Cortés
Livingston • Bahía
de Omoa • HONDURAS

GUATEMALA • GUATEMALA • Río
Puerto Barrios

GUATEMALA

CAYO

BELIZE

STANN CREEK

Northern
Cay

Rendezvous
Point

BARRIER REEF

0 _____ 20 kilometers
0 _____ 20 miles

BELIZE

"dollars" you are referring to when bargaining or you could end up paying twice as much. Internationally accessible **ATMs** are located only in major cities and tourist hotspots. Use ATMs as a backup measure while traveling, rather than as a primary source of funds. **MasterCard** and **Visa** are the most frequently accepted credit cards; **American Express** cards work at some ATMs and at AmEx offices and major airports. **Traveler's checks** are accepted at most hotels, but are not welcomed at many restaurants and stores.

COSTS

Belize is significantly more expensive than its Central American neighbors. A day without frills—a cheap hotel, transportation, and basic food—will set you back US$30-40. A stay in a nicer hotel, with a private bathroom, hot water showers, and a kitchenette raises costs to US$80-150 per day. The sky's the limit for spending in heavily touristed and resort areas. Prices rise in high season (Dec.-May) and holidays (Christmas, New Years, and *Semana Santa*), but are negotiable in low season.

PRICE DIVERSITY

Our Researchers list establishments in order of value from best to worst, honoring our favorites with the Let's Go thumbs-up (🖐). Because the best *value* is not always the cheapest *price*, we have incorporated a system of price ranges based on a rough expectation of what you will spend. For **accommodations**, we base our range on the cheapest price for which a single traveler can stay for one night. For **restaurants,** we estimate the average amount one traveler will spend in one sitting. The table below tells you what you'll *typically* find in Panama at the corresponding price range, but keep in mind that no system can allow for the quirks of individual establishments.

ACCOMMODATIONS	RANGE	WHAT YOU'RE *LIKELY* TO FIND
❶	Under US$10	Campgrounds and some cheaper dorm rooms. Expect bunk beds, a shared bath, and rustic conditions.
❷	US$10-15	Most hostels and lower-end hotels. Most likely a shared bathroom.
❸	US$16-22	A small room with a private bath. Should have decent amenities. If you're lucky, maybe even a TV.
❹	US$ 23-30	Should have bigger rooms than a ❸, with cable TV, A/C, and a private bath with hot water.
❺	Over US$30	Large hotels or resorts. If it's a ❺ and it doesn't have the perks you want, you've paid too much.

FOOD	RANGE	WHAT YOU'RE *LIKELY* TO FIND
❶	Under US$3	Market food and street stalls. Typically a take-out meal.
❷	US$3-5	Burgers, small salads, burritos, or fajitas. You may have the option to actually sit down at these places.
❸	US$6-8	Mid-priced entrees and pasta dishes. Since you'll have the luxury of a waiter, tip will set you back a little extra.
❹	US$9-15	Edging toward the fancier side of things, with heartier or more elaborate entrees. Most seafood dishes fall within this range.
❺	Over US$15	Your meal might cost more than your room, but there's a reason—it's something fabulous, famous, or both. Fancier dress might be expected.

SAFETY AND HEALTH

Violent crime is on the rise in Belize, especially in urban areas. Tourists at resorts or on the road are particularly vulnerable targets for sexual assault, theft, purse snatching, pick pocketing, and car jacking. The incidence of such crimes significantly increases during spring and winter breaks. Victims who resist when attacked run the risk of serious physical injuries.

BORDER CROSSINGS

GUATEMALA. See p. 44.

MEXICO. Buses cross at **Chetumal,** Mexico from **Belize City** and **Corozal,** Belize.

HONDURAS. Weekly boats run between **Placencia,** Belize and **Puerto Cortés,** Honduras and between **Dangriga,** Belize and Puerto Cortés.

LIFE AND TIMES

HISTORY

MAYAN TIMES. The roots of Belize are with the Maya, whose ruins still lie beneath the forests of the country. The oldest dated settlement is the city of Cahal Pech, built in 1200 BC, but the Maya people are estimated to have arrived centuries before. Other cities built in the very beginning include Altun Ha, Lubaantun, Lamanai, and Caracol, of which the latter two remain preserved to this day. In the centuries that followed, stone *sakbé* roads sprang up, crisscrossing the entire Maya civilization, of which Belize was one corner. The cities of Belize were built by the Mopan Maya, the tribe with the longest history in Belize, while the Yucatec would later migrate from the west and the Kekchi from the south. Several centers for the distant trade carried out amongst these tribes and cities were located in Belize; Moho Caye, Santa Rita, and Ambergris Caye. The Mayan culture began to decline at the end of the first millennium AD; in Belize, dramatic wars between the kings, or *ajaw,* of the city of Caracol and the kings of Tikal in Guatemala resulted in much bloodshed and an eventual victory for Water Lord, the ruler of Caracol. The cities were soon after abandoned in the mysterious decline of the entire Maya people.

ENTER THE EXPLORERS. In 1502, Columbus sailed along the coast of Belize, but it would be decades until Europeans entered in force. That venture, the 1540 invasion by a small force of conquistadors from the Yucatán, brought diseases that killed off 90% of the 250,000 Mayans living in the Belize. The Spanish, however, were never able to hold on to the trackless mountains and forests of the country, and soon left, leaving a scattered, depopulated Belize behind.

About a century later, the increase in European settlement and trade in the Caribbean brought more traffic, mostly of the pirating variety. British marauders in particular favored the region's coasts, and became known as the Baymen. Near the wealthy hubs of Havana, Mexico, and Panama, the seas presented an ungoverned wilderness. In 1638, the Scottish pirate captain Peter Wallace laid the crude foundations of what would become Belize City. The pirates also discovered other, more industrious work: the logging of the valuable forests of the countryside. Of course, much of this work was done by the forced labor of Africans and Creoles who also found their way to the colony.

By the 18th century, however, the British authorities had reined in the region, putting it under Britain's law and watchful eye. The Spanish came to envy the wealthy little colony, and mounted several assaults, both military and diplomatic.

Belize City was burned down in 1779, but a few years later, the Baymen bested the Spaniards in the Battle of St. George's Caye, pushing them out for good. September 10th, the day of the battle is now remembered as a holiday.

BRITISH HONDURAS. In 1840, after the tumult of the Napoleonic Wars and the growth of Britain's overseas empire, the unruly coast was officially named British Honduras, and more properly drawn into the imperial orbit. In 1862, it was elevated to the status of a crown colony, a multicultural, English-speaking enclave in the middle of the Caribbean. The tensions between Europeans, Africans, and Creoles deepened with the first British-Maya encounters in the middle of the 19th century, as logging operations and plantation clearings began to cut deeper into the forests. Initial strife was soon overshadowed by the massive Maya revolt against the Mexican elite in the Yucatán, known as the Caste War. Tens of thousands of refugees, many Yucatec Maya, fled to Belize over the course of the conflict. One futile uprising against the British, the Battle of Orange Walk, failed, consigning the Maya to marginalization for a century. Belize slowly modernized during the century, with roads finally linking its cities in the 1920s.

A PLACE IN THE SUN. The 1930s brought economic hardship that sparked mass resistance to British rule. The next economic blow, the devaluation of the British Honduras dollar in 1949, prompted the formation of the People's Committee, which became the powerful People's United Party (PUP). A few years later, Britain granted constitutional reforms, and in 1964 the PUP leader, George Price, became the colony's prime minister. Price held on to power in various forms for decades, becoming the head of government of a formally independent Belize in 1981, though British troops remained to guard against a Guatemala that claimed the whole region for itself. The opposition party, the United Democratic Party (UDP), took power for the second half of the 1980s, and has traded power with the PUP in recent decades as the country struggled to find peace with Guatemala, fight corruption, and foster growth. In 2005, Dean Barrow of the UDP became the country's first black prime minister.

TODAY

Current events in Belize are dominated by a few constants: scandals and corruption in the nation's small-scale politics, disputes with Guatemala and occasionally Mexico, and general economic ups and downs. Issues of local politics have had the highest profile in the last few years, with one hot-button issue: a proposed sweeping amendment to the Belizean constitution. Known as Amendment 7, it would make the international Caribbean Court of Justice the country's final court of appeal, allow dual citizens to sit in the National Assembly, and allow non-legislators to be appointed Attorney General. The United Democratic Party has taken criticism for these amendments, but with allegations of corruption still swirling around the People's United Party, no one is safe from attack. Ex-Prime Minister Said Musa of the People's United Party remains extremely controversial for his government's huge public spending and diversion of foreign aid into hospitals with undisclosed ownership. In February 2009, a lower court ruled that Musa could be tried in the Supreme Court of Belize. Similar scandals at the local level are epidemic, with recent news focusing on misdoings in the Treasury.

Robberies and violent crimes have become more pervasive in recent years in the capital and cities like San Pedro, Caye Caulker, and Placencia. One unusual case of property damage involved not a street ruffian but the Mexican billionaire Ricardo Salinas Pliego, whose careening yacht severely damaged Belize's tropical reefs—he was made to pay a huge fine and run Belize-promoting advertisements on his personal television networks.

In the still-poor country of Belize, the fate of the immigration industry is closely linked the country's future. Recently, Tropic Air, one of the main airlines serving Belize, opened a new $4.6 million dollar terminal in San Pedro to facilitate tourism and travel—but few tourists are coming as the global economic crisis resonates in the travel industry. In 2009, a drop in remittances from Belizeans working abroad, the fall in tourism, and an inflation rate above 12% combined to put the country in dire straits. Since 2007, the rise in global grain prices has put enormous pressure on the small country, and even before the last few years, the nation had received over $4 billion in international debt relief, which the government promised to continue spending on poverty alleviation. All the while, government salaries have drawn more and more from the public purse. As the government tries to cut costs, it has run into the powerful National Trade Union Congress of Belize, which accused it in July 2009 of amending the country's labor laws to squeeze the nation's workers.

Belize's foreign relations, on the other hand, have been mostly quiet, though the dispute with Guatemala has persisted in recent years. The failure of the Organization of American States to arbitrate the dispute led to both parties agreeing in December 2008 to go before the International Court of Justice in the Hague. The International Court of Justice is estimated to take six years to resolve the dispute, at least. Relations with Mexico have improved of late: a new bridge connecting the two countries was finished in the summer of 2009, and Mexico is on the verge of abolishing the visa requirement for Belizean citizens.

ECONOMY AND GOVERNMENT

Belize still bows to Queen Elizabeth, but is independent in every other regard. Its highest official is the **Prime Minister,** currently **Dean Barrow** of the United Democratic Party. His party swept into power in 2008 after years of rule by the People's United Party, the party that led the decades-long movement for independence and that was the main force in negotiations with Britain for autonomy. Only the third Prime Minister since that independence was achieved in 1981, Barrow is the first black Belizean to serve in the office. The **National Assembly of Belize** contains two familiar chambers: the lower, the House of Representatives, and the upper, the Senate. Party politics are particularly polarized in Belize, and American travelers will even recognize the dueling parties' colors: red and blue. Justice is administered through a British-style common law courts system, which, like most of Belize's institutions, comes off as a hothouse replica of the institutions of other English-speaking countries.

Real economic activity in Belize derives from tourism, agriculture, and a few small industries, like apparel production; yet the country remains the second poorest in Central America. Logging was once the lifeblood of the forested country, but valuable timber was exhausted decades ago, leaving the scarred forests to heal. Banana and citrus plantations blanket the arable land. But tourism, which has taken off in the last decades, employs over a quarter of Belizeans and has transformed Belize into a country heavily reliant on the traveler, as visitors will find out. The country's beautiful land and shorelines and diversity of flora and fauna have contributed to this transformation; the recent discovery of oil in the mountains has some worried about the continued survival of Belize's wilderness.

PEOPLE

DEMOGRAPHICS

Belize's diverse heritage draws upon the many nations that have come to the country by land or sea. Belize's largest ethnic group is the Spanish-speaking **mestizos.** The *mestizos* constitute 40% of the population and are of mixed Mayan and European heritage. Europeans, mostly of Spanish origins, are another 10% of the population. Large numbers of *mestizo* and Yucatec Maya were driven into Belize by the Caste War of the 1800s. Immigrants of similar backgrounds followed from Guatemala, Honduras, Nicaragua, and El Salvador in the last few decades. Maya natives still make up about 10% of the population, principally Kekchi-, Yucatec-, or Mopan-Mayan-speakers. The **Kriol** make up a third of Belize's population and are traditionally the largest group and one of the most culturally influential. The term Kriol encompasses those of mixed African and British descent. The **Garífuna** are another distinct group of mixed African and Carib Indian descent. They are located mostly in the south of the country, and have retained their indigenous language and lifestyle.

Adding to this mélange are the rural communities of **German Mennonite farmers** who emigrated from Mexico. These farmers are permitted a measure of autonomy, as they are free from the obligation of military service. They are, however, excluded from voting. Members of the South Asian, Arab, and Chinese communities also occupy key positions in the urban and commercial life of Belize. Very small American and British expatriate communities also exist.

LANGUAGE

The official language of Belize is **English,** although less than a tenth of the country speaks it in the home. **Kriol,** the day-to-day language of a good 40% of Belizeans, is a mishmash of English, West African languages, and Central American vernaculars like Miskito and Caliche slang. Another 40% of Belizeans (primarily *mestizos*) speak **Spanish** as their main language. The remainder of Belize speaks the various Mayan dialects (Kekchi, Yucatec, and Mopan), the Plautdietsch German of the Mennonites, and the Garifuna language, itself a mixture of Arawak, Carib, French, and English.

With such a profusion of languages, it has been estimated that over half of the population is either bilingual or trilingual. Anglophone travelers should take heart: approximately 80% of Belizeans have at least some knowledge of English and over half the population speaks it proficiently. English is spoken primarily in the cities, however, and it becomes less prevalent as one travels further into the countryside.

RELIGION

Belize is home to many faiths, but little religious polarization. *Mestizos*, Maya, and Central American transplants tend to identify themselves as **Roman Catholics** and exist in the fold of the Diocese of Belize City-Belmopan. These Belizeans make up about half of the population. Various strains of Protestantism account for another third of the population. Belize, like many of its neighbors, has been affected by the recent wave of evangelism from North American missionaries of the Assemblies of God, the Seventh-Day Adventists, the Jehovah's Witnesses, and the Church of Latter-day Saints. The numerous immigrants in the urban centers maintain the religious traditions of their homelands; communities of Hindus, Muslims, and Greek Orthodox, among others, thrive in the cities. Further out, among the Maya and Garifuna, old folk beliefs are mixed with elements of official Christianity.

BELIZE

LAND

The beautiful enclave that is Belize sits along 386km of marshy **Caribbean coast,** shielded by a string of **Caye Islands.** Behind this pleasant front rise the **Maya Mountains** in the south, which give way to the southern coastal plain and northern forested lowlands, which are crisscrossed by rivers and lagoons.

GEOGRAPHY AND GEOLOGY

Belize sits atop the limestone shelf of the Yucatán Peninsula. In the southwest, it shares a steep, mountainous border with Guatemala. The Maya Mountains dominate this region. These rugged karst hills and ridges give way to the fertile fields and gentle, rolling frontier of the north. Important rivers of Belize include the **Sibun,** the **New River,** and the Belize, or the **"Old River."** What may be Belize's greatest geographical feature is sunken offshore, in the form of the **Belize Barrier Reef,** the second-largest coral reef in the world. Around it rise hundreds of tiny islands called the **Cayes,** among which the most notable are **Ambergris** (p. 210) and **Caulker** (p. 203).

WILDLIFE

This tropical country features an unsurprisingly lush, not to mention profitable, array of flora and fauna. Logging was once the backbone of the Belizean economy, but much of the forest cover is no longer old-growth. All the same, over 700 tree species, including logwood, chicle, coconut, apple, mango, papaya, cashew, pineapple, guava, and mahogany (the country's national tree), shade the soil of Belize. An estimated 4000 species of native flowering plants, including 250 varieties of orchids, adorn the landscape, and as the wilderness is catalogued and categorized, many plants are finding medicinal use.

Animal life flourishes in this sparsely-populated domain, including the jaguar, the puma, the jaguarundi, and the three-toed sloth. Belize's national animal is the "mountain cow," or tapir. Hundreds of migratory birds winter in Belize, including wood storks, herons, white ibis, and keel-billed toucans.

WEATHER

Belize, as a **tropical country,** has only the **wet** and the **dry season,** though temperatures vary with elevation, proximity to the coast, and coastal trade winds. Average temperatures range from 24°C in January to 27°C in July and are higher further inland. Change in season entails less change in temperature than it does in humidity and rainfall, especially in the north and central regions of the country, which see practically no rain between January and May. This dry season is markedly shorter in the south.

BELIZE

BELIZE CITY

Blighted by crime, poverty, and drugs for years, Belize City (pop. 70,000) is nobody's idea of an ideal tourist stop. In fact, it's nobody's idea of Belize; travelers and Belizeans alike will agree that the nation's sole metropolis has little to do with the majestic beauty, natural wonders, and relaxed lifestyle that characterize the rest of the country. Most tourists pass through the city without a look back, taking advantage of its status as the country's main transit hub, but avoiding the crowded and claustrophobic streets themselves. The view from a taxi window isn't exactly a coastal getaway: canals filled with trash and sewage, seaside ghettos with dilapidated shacks, beggars sprawled on the hot, dusty streets, and aggressive hustlers looking to sell drugs or women.

Once upon a time, Belize City was a much quieter colonial capital. Settled in the 1700s, the city was reportedly founded on a pile of mahogany chips and rum bottles discarded by British lumberjacks. Soon it developed into the center of colonial rule in British Honduras, with a white ruling class mingling with a growing population of Creoles. In 1961, Hurricane Hattie virtually destroyed the city, killing hundreds. Belize's capital was forced to move to Belmopan. Since then, development in Belize City has stagnated, and drugs and crime are on the rise.

Caribbean paradise this isn't, but cautious travelers willing to brave an uncertain environment can escape the crowds in this decidedly untouristed area of the country. The city is the best place to see Belize's remarkable multiculturalism in action, with Creoles, Mestizos, Garinagu, East and South Asians, and the occasional Mennonite selling their wares. Their languages, foods, and music come together to create a unique city. Despite its problems, Belize City remains the country's commercial center. With its many teeming shops and tourist agencies, this city is also the best place to find quick supplies and prepare for further inland or aquatic adventures.

⌨ INTERCITY TRANSPORTATION

Since Belize City is the country's main transit hub, getting to or (more commonly) away from the city is a cinch. The city is the only international point of entry and departure from the air. Domestic service, though often rustic (prepare to relive your pre-teen years on school buses), is quick and usually painless.

Flights: The **Philip Goldson International Airport** (☎225 2045; www.pgiabelize.com), located 11 miles northwest of the city. Since no public transportation services the airport, you'll need to take a taxi from the airport exit (BZ$40-50).

Continental Airways (☎227 8309; www.continental.com), Belize offices at 80 Regent St. Flights to: **Houston** (3 daily); **Newark** (Sa).

US Airways (☎225 3589; www.usairways.com), offices in Belize Global Travel Services at 41 Albert St.. Flights to: **Charlotte** (daily).

American Airlines (☎225 4145; www.aa.com), offices in Sancas Plaza at Belcan Junction. Flights to: **Miami** (2 daily); **Dallas** (daily).

Delta Airlines (☎225 3423; www.delta.com), offices in the Goldson airport. Flights to: **Atlanta** (1 per day M-Tu and F-Su).

Grupo Taca (☎221 2163; www.taca.com), offices in Belize Global Travel Services at 41 Albert St.. Flights to **San Salvador, El Salvador** (daily); **Houston** (daily).

Belize City

ACCOMMODATIONS
Bagview Guest House, 9
Belcove Hotel, 5
Caribbean Salons Inn, 4
Coningsby Inn, 1
Hotel Mopán, 12
Seaside Guesthouse, 11

FOOD
Dit's Restaurant, 8
Jambel's Jerk Pit, 13
Macy's, 6
Nerie's, 3

NIGHTLIFE
Caesar's Palace, 14
MJ's Grand, 10
Planet Hollywood, 7
Princess Hotel, 2

BELIZE CITY

CARIBBEAN SEA

Maya Island Air (☎225 2219; www.mayaislandair.com), offices in the Goldson Airport. Flights to: **Flores, Guatemala** (2 daily).

Tropic Air (☎225 2302; www.tropicair.com), offices in the Goldson airport. Flights to: **Flores, Guatemala** (2 daily).

Domestic Flights: Maya Island Air and **Tropic Air,** both Belizean homegrown companies, offer flights to various cities within Belize. These flights are always more expensive than the bus or boat options, but travel time is considerably shortened. Both airlines leave both from the **Goldson Airport** and the **Municipal Airstrip,** located 2 mi. north of the city. Since flights leaving Goldson will stop at the airstrip en route anyway, it's a better bet to fly from the airstrip, where flights are less expensive.

Maya Island Air (airstrip office ☎223-1140; www.mayaislandair.com) flies from the airstirp to **San Pedro** (25min., every hr. 7:30am-5:30pm, one-way BZ$70, round-trip BZ$140);

Caye Caulker (25min., every 2 hr. 7:30am-3:30pm, BZ$70/BZ$140); **Dangriga** (30min., every hr. 8-10am and every 2hr. noon-4pm, BZ$86/BZ$166); **Placencia** (50min., every hr. 8-10am and every 2hr. noon-4pm, BZ$159/BZ$318); **Punta Gorda** (1hr. 20min., every 2hr. 8am-4pm, BZ$204/408).

Tropic Air (airstrip office ☎223-5671; www.tropicair.com) flies from the airstrip to **San Pedro** (25min.; every hr. 7:30am-5:30pm; one-way BZ$70, round-trip BZ$134); **Caye Caulker** (20min., every 2hr. 7:30am-4:30pm, BZ$70/134); **Dangriga** (15min., every 2hr. 8:30 am-4:30pm, BZ$83/159); **Placencia** (35min., every 2hr. 8:30am-4:30pm, BZ$159/310); **Punta Gorda** (1hr., every 2hr. 8:30am-4:30pm, BZ$204/401).

Intercity Buses: Belize City's main bus station is located next to the Collet Canal; just walk up King Street or Orange Street from downtown (be careful; the surrounding neighborhood is gritty). A dizzying array of bus companies now serve Belize after the meltdown of the former bus monopoly, Novelo's (whose name is still emblazoned on the colorful bus station). Since their prices, destinations, and durations are the same, don't worry about distinguishing between them. Just look for the cardboard destination sign in the front window and hop on.

Eastbound buses travel to **Belmopan** (1½hr., BZ$4); **San Ignacio** (2½hr., BZ$5); **Benque Viejo del Carmen** (3hr., BZ$7) every 30min. 5am-9:30pm.

Southbound buses travel to **Belmopan** (1½hr., BZ$4); **Dangriga** (2½hr., BZ$5); **Independence,** near Placencia (4½hr., BZ$7); **Punta Gorda** (6½hr., BZ$12) every 30min. 5:15am-6:15pm.

Northbound buses travel to **Orange Walk** (2hr., BZ$5); **Corozal** (3hr., BZ$6); **Chetumal, Mexico**(3½hr., BZ$7) every 30min. 9am-6pm.

Express Buses: These buses resemble charter or Greyhound buses rather than school buses, will cost a bit more, but won't stop as often at points in between. Buses to **Flores** (near Tikal) in Guatemala and other points in neighboring countries, including destinations in the **Yucatan,** leave from the front of the Caye Caulker Water Taxi Terminal. Just across the Swing Bridge on North Front St. BZ$50-110. Buy tickets at the **Mundo Maya Deli** desk inside the terminal (☎223 2923; mundomayatravels@yahoo.com).

Local Buses: Smaller and more specialized lines have their own bases in the city. Since these services are extremely informal, unpredictable and subject to change, ask locals for the details of departure. **Jex & Sons** buses to **Crooked Tree** (3 per day, 1hr., BZ$3.50) leave from the corner of Regent Street West and W Canal Street. **Russell buses** to **Bermudian Landing** (2 per day, 1hr., BZ$5) leave from the intersection of Cairo Street and Euphrates Avenue; to **Sarteneja** (3 per day, 2½hr., BZ$7) leave from the back of the Supreme Court building on the Southern Foreshore.

Boats: Belize City also offers the country's best and easiest access to the popular cayes off the coast.

Caye Caulker Water Taxi (☎203 1969, www.cayecaulkerwatertaxi.com) has its dock at 10 North Front Street, directly to the right after crossing the Swing Bridge. Boats leave for **Caye Caulker** (50min., one-way BZ$15, round-trip BZ$25) and **San Pedro** on Ambergris Caye (1½hr., one-way BZ$20, round-trip BZ$35) at 7:30, 8, 9, 10:30am, noon, 1:30, 3, 4:30, and 5:30pm. MC/V.

San Pedro-Belize Express (☎226 2194; www.sanpedrowatertaxi.com) has its dock just north, right next to the Fish Co-Op building, a 5min. walk along North Front St. from the Swing Bridge.

Boats leave for **Caye Caulker** (50min., one-way BZ$13, round-trip BZ$25) and **San Pedro** (1½hr., one-way BZ$25, round-trip BZ$45) at 8, 9, 10:30am, noon, 1:30, 3, 4, and 5:30pm (express to San Pedro). MC/V.

Triple J Express (☎207 7777 or 223 5752; www.triplejbelize.com), on the Southern Foreshore in front of the courthouse. Boats leave for **Caye Caulker** (one-way BZ$15, round-trip BZ$25) and **San Pedro** (one-way BZ$20, round trip BZ$35) at 7:30, 10am, 1, and 5:15pm. Cash only.

Car Rental: Driving yourself around Belize is the best (though certainly not the cheapest) way to avoid confusing and unreliable bus schedules and far-flung locales. You must be 25 to rent a car in Belize.

Crystal Auto Rental (☎223 1600; www.crystal-belize.com), offices at Mile 5 Northern Highway. BZ$107-270 per day; BZ$640-1700 per week. MC/V.

Budget Car Rental (☎223 2435; www.budget-belize.com), offices at Mile 2½ Northern Highway and at the Goldson airport. BZ$140-210 per day; BZ$840-1260 per week. MC/V.

Euphrates Auto Rental (☎227 5752; www.ears.bz), offices at 143 Euphrates Ave. in the city. BZ$130-150 per day. MC/V.

Avis (☎225 2629; www.avis.com.bz), offices at the Goldson airport and at 1 Poinsetta St. in Ladyville, a village near the airport. BZ$150-210 per day.

Hertz (☎223 0886, www.hertzbelize.com), offices at the Goldson airport and at 11A Cork St. in the city. BZ$140-220 per day.

BUSES GOT BACK. If you're carrying heavy luggage and trying to flag down a bus by the road, it might be a better—and more efficient—option to board the bus from the back. Don't worry about the door alarm; you're not in middle school anymore, and local riders jump on and off from this end all the time. Ask someone on the bus to hoist your bags up for you.

▣ ▮ ORIENTATION

Haulover Creek, emptying into the Caribbean Sea, neatly divides Belize City in two. To the south is the rough **Southside district** (between Collet and Southside Canals). Also to the south of the creek are the more affluent residential neighborhoods of **Fort George, Newtown Barracks,** and **Kings Park.** The **Swing Bridge,** spanning Haulover Creek, connect the two halves. **Albert Street,** the city's main road lined with banks, shops, and restaurants, extends south of the bridge. Two blocks south of the bridge on Albert St. is **Battlefield Park,** the city's center. Next to the Swing Bridge on the north side is the **water taxi terminal.** To the right along the seafront is **Tourist Village,** a shopping section closed off from the street and set aside for cruise-ship passengers. The main **bus station,** surrounded by fruit sellers and other vendors, is located on **Collet Canal** to the west of the Southside district. Twenty minutes north of the creek, a small cluster of restaurants, hotels, and clubs sits next to the **Newtown Barracks Green,** just north of the Princess Hotel & Casino (p. 200).

Travelers should take extra precautions when traveling through the Southside district at any time of day to reach the bus station. Taxis are available on Albert St. around Battlefield Park to get you there safely for a small fee. The same goes for traveling into the city from the bus station, where many taxis are also parked. Always take a taxi at night when going anywhere in the city; ask your hotel to call one if necessary. Khaki-shirted **tourist police** patrol the downtown area (☎227 6082).

▤ LOCAL TRANSPORTATION

Since the city does not have a public transportation system (given its size, it doesn't really need one), taxis are the best resource for traveling safely within the city. You'll most likely be offered a taxi before you find one, but the best places to get a ride are the main bus station and along Albert St. by Battlefield Park. Licensed taxis are marked by green license plates; make sure the cab is reputable before getting in. Most rides within the city cost around US$1.50-3.50. Unless you're in a large group, **always take a taxi at night.**

▤ ▨ PRACTICAL INFORMATION

TOURIST AND FINANCIAL SERVICES

Tourist Offices: Several throughout Belize City lead tours and distribute information.

Belize Tourism Board, 64 Regent St. (☎227 2420; www.travelbelize.org.), toward the south end of the city. Map and brochure selection especially helpful for those seeking to explore the country's interior as well as coastal hotspots. Open M-F 8am-5pm.

Belize Global Travel Services, 41 Albert St. (☎227 7185; www.belizeglobal.bz). Guided tours to Mayan ruins at Altun Ha (5hr., US$65), Xunantunich (6½hr., US$90), the Baboon (4hr., US$55), and Crooked Tree (4hr., US$55) Sanctuaries. The nautically inclined can sign up for dive tours (7hr., US$110) and snorkeling trips (6½hr., US$100) in the Barrier Reef. Open M-F 8am-noon and 1-5pm, Sa 8am-noon. AmEx/MC/V.

Discovery Expeditions (☎223 0748; www.discoverybelize.com), at the Philip Goldson International Airport. A substantial array of tours exploring remote areas of Belize and the Cayes. Office in San Pedro on Ambergris Caye.

Hugh Parkey Belize Dive Connection (☎223 4526; www.belizediving.com), in the Radisson Fort George Hotel. Specializes in diving (US$80-225) and snorkeling (US$60-130) expeditions. A sister company, **Hugh Parker's Jaguar Adventure Travel and Tours,** promises inland adventures.

S & L Travel and Tours, 91 North Front St. (☎227 7593 or 227 5145; www.sltravelbelize.com). This 30-year-old agency offers ½, full, and even multi-day tours in Belize's interior.

Sea Sports Belize, 83 North Front St. (☎223 5505; www.seasportsbelize.com). Diving US$120-220, snorkeling US$90-150, fishing US$400-700, and diving classes US$150-330.

Embassies and Consulates: See **Belmopan,** p. 236.

Banks: American travelers may not even need to exchange money; most businesses in Belize accept both US and Belize dollars. Most ATMs will dispense Belize dollars, but be sure to check at each bank or machine before withdrawing. All of the following banks have **24hr. ATMs:**

Belize Bank, 60 Market Sq. (☎227 7132). Open M-Th 8am-3pm, F 8am-4:30pm.

First Caribbean International Bank, 21 Albert St. (☎227 7211). Open M-Th 8am-2:30pm, F 8am-2:30pm.

Scotiabank, 4A Albert St. (☎227 7027). Open M-Th 8am-2:30pm, F 8:30am-4pm, Sa 9am-noon.

Atlantic Bank, 6 Albert St. (☎227 1225). Open M-Th 8am-3:30m, F 9am-3pm, Sa 9am-noon.

LOCAL SERVICES

Bookstore: The Book Center, 4 Church St. (☎227 7457). A tiny but well-stocked bookstore with magazines, newspapers, and paperbacks. Open M-Th and Sa 8am-5:30pm; F 8am-9pm. Cash only.

Laundry: G's Laundromat, 22 Dean St. (☎207 4461). Open 7:30am-5:30pm. US$6 per load.

EMERGENCY AND COMMUNICATIONS

Police: Raccoon St., at the intersection of Queen St. and New Rd. in the west side of the city. For **emergencies** call ☎911 or ☎90. **Tourist police** ☎227 6082.

Pharmacy: Central Drugstore (☎227 2138), Albert St., right next to Swing Bridge. Open daily 8am-9:30pm. AmEx/MC/V. **Brodie's** (see **Food,** p. 198) also has a pharmacy.

Hospitals: The public **Karl Heusner Memorial Hospital** (☎223 1548; www.khmh.bz.), Princess Margaret Dr. Belize's main referral hospital offers 24hr. emergency service. **Belize Medical Associates,** 5791 St Thomas St. (☎223 0302; www.belizemedical.com), a private hospital, also with 24hr. service.

Telephones: Several pay phones are located around the downtown area, but travelers seeking longer and cheaper conversations can head to **BTL,** 1 Church St. (☎227 7085). Booths for international calls. Open M-F 8am-6pm.

Internet Access: Many hostels have internet service, but several internet cafes also dot the city.

Angelus Press, 10 Queen St. (☎223 5777). US$3.50 per hr. Open M-F 7:30am-5:30pm, Sa 8am-noon. MC/V.

KGS Internet, 60 King St. (☎207 7130). US$2.50 per hr. In a gritty area, but well crowded and safe inside. Open M-F 8am-7pm, Sa 8am-6pm, Su 9:30am-2:30pm. Cash only.

Post Office: (☎223 2201), Paslow building at the intersection of North Front and Queen St. Open M-F 8am-noon and 1-4:30pm. Belize does not use a postal code.

▐ ACCOMMODATIONS

There's no shortage of hotels in Belize City, from backpacker meccas to luxury options for cruise-ship passengers. The city's status as a transportation hub translates into plenty of sleeping space. As always here, safety is of primary concern. Accommodations in downtown Belize City are generally more dangerous than those on the outskirts. Hotels in the northern **Fort George** and **Newtown Barracks** districts of the city are the quietest, while those closer to the center will likely offer more security.

▨ **Seaside Guest House,** 3 Prince St. (☎227 8339; www.seasideguesthouse.org). This old backpacker favorite is one of the best (and cheapest) options in the city. 19th-century coastal house lined with mahogany, quiet rooms provide a much-needed respite from the nervous bustle of the city. Common room, kitchen and dining room, and hammock-lined porches facing the

LOCAL LEGEND

PRINCE CHARLES

"I shall make you an ambassador of Belize!" Prince Charles intones knighting me. We're standing on Albert Street, Belize City's crowded main drag, where vendors, taxi drivers, and the homeless rub shoulders. Jacks-of-all-trades line Albert St. and Prince Charles is one of the more renowned. No, not the floppy-eared successor to the British throne, but a disheveled, middle-aged Belizean who offers personal tours of the city when he's not washing down cars and working the docks.

We head through the Fort George district, making a roundabout loop ending at the Bliss tomb and lighthouse. Prince Charles, his voice a mixture of stentorian authority and eccentric turns of phrases ("put a tack in that" instead of "remember that"), runs through his topics with the slight professionalism of the best tour guides. He talks about Belize's history, about its many people, about the Garínagu and their drum rhythms, about the Mennonites and their problems with inbreeding, about crippled Baron Bliss and the ancient Mayan princess-goddess who gave a form of her name to Belikin beer.

We come to the lighthouse. He completes the knighting ceremony, making me an official representative of Belizean culture, and commands me to spread the word.

-Dan Normandin

sea. Breakfast US$2-5. Free Wi-Fi. Dorms US$20; singles US$25, with bath US$35; doubles US$45, with bath US$55. MC/V. ❷

Caribbean Palms Inn, 26 Regent St. (☎227 0472). This converted house close to downtown has comfortable and clean rooms that vary in size. Enjoy the beautiful outdoor terrace facing away from the street. Dorm rooms US$18-23; single with bath US$20-30; double with bath US$30-50; rooms with A/C US$35-70. MC/V. ❶

Bayview Guest House, 58 Baymen Ave. (☎223 4179; www.belize-guesthouse-hotel.com). In the quiet, residential neighborhood that is Northern Barracks district, this guesthouse offers fantastically decorated rooms with quirky names to match. You can sleep in the Lavender Room, the Sunrise Room, the Blue Iris, or even the Pink Lady. All rooms with cable TVs and private baths. Free WiFi. Rooms with double bed and fan US$25; rooms with 1 double bed and A/C US$35-45; rooms with 2 double beds and A/C US$45. AmEx/MC/V. ❷

Belcove Hotel, 9 Regent St. (☎227 3054; www.belcove.com). Be warned, this hotel is located north of the Swing Bridge, in a somewhat dangerous neighborhood. Still, Belcove's convenient location on Haulover Creek is as scenic as budget accommodations get. A veranda provides a relaxing space from which to survey the center of town. The staff can arrange diving and fishing tours. Singles US$28, with bath US$35, with A/C, TV, and bath US$50; doubles US$35/40/52; triples US$59. Beware hidden fees: there's a US$5-6 tax per person. MC/V. ❷

Freddie's Guest House, 86 Eve St. (☎223 3851). 3 quiet, sizable, cozy rooms. Shared bath. US$25 each. Cash only. ❷

Hotel Mopan, 55 Regent St. (☎227 7351; www.hotelmopan.com), toward the western side of downtown, near the Government House and St. John's Cathedral. A sprawling mansion with elegant, clean rooms. Outdoor patios provide shade and views of the neighborhood. Some rooms with balconies and A/C. Rooms US$45-75. US$10 tax per person. MC/V. ❺

Coningsby Inn, 76 Regent St. (☎227 1566; www.coningsby-inn.com). Next to the Hotel Mopan, this colonial-era house offers serious old-school grandeur. 10 spotless rooms, each with a small patio space. All rooms have A/C, cable TVs, and baths. Doubles US$50; triples US$60. MC/V. ❹

◖ FOOD

Belizean food is as varied as its population, and Belize City is the best place to sample the whole shebang. Downtown, near Albert St., is a carnival of cuisines. Taco stands brush shoulders with Creole restaurants and fruit hawkers, old Mayan recipes are preserved in tiny food stalls, and sizable immigrant populations offer Chinese and Indian food. Seek out the cowfoot soup (trust us, it's better than it sounds). Try the food stands that pop up on Albert St. near the Swing Bridge at night. It's the best opportunity to enjoy Belizean hot dogs and spicy chicken burgers, tacos, and beans-rice-chicken mixtures on the cheap (US$1-2). For groceries, head to the ever-reliable **Brodie's** at 2 Albert St. (☎227 7070. Open M-F 8am-10pm, Sa-Su 8am-6pm; AmEx/MC/V).

Dit's Restaurant, 50 King St. (☎227 3350). Entering its 51st year, Dit's is the oldest restaurant in the city and is still owned by the founding family. Along with its wide selection of local pastries—johnny cakes, jam rolls, coconut tarts, meat, rice, and bread puddings (US$1-2.50)—you can get a good start on Belizean favorites like bean-and-rice stews (US$1.50). Desserts US$2-6; entrees US$2-5. Open M-Sa 7am-8pm, Su 8am-4pm. Cash only. ❷

Nerie's (☎223 4028), corner of Queen and Daly Streets in the Fort George district. A spacious, 2-floor local favorite serving an elaborate selection of Belizean dishes. For breakfast, try those beans, ham, and eggs, or try the ever-popular fry jacks (biscuits). For dinner, lap up some cowfoot soup and finish it off with one of Nerie's excellent puddings (rice, meat, or cassava). Entrees US$3-9. Drinks US$1-3. Open M-Sa 7am-9pm. Cash only. ❷

Macy's, 18 Bishop St. (☎207 3419). Macy's is the definition of Belizean cooking. Bravely order deer and boar (US$4.50-7). Their fish fillets—served, of course, with rice and beans (US$3)—are local favorites. There are only 5 tables, so hurry up for that cherished slab of game. Open M-Sa 8am-9pm. Cash only. ❷

Jambel's Jerk Pit, 164 Newtown Barracks Rd. (☎223 1966). Jambel's has gone through several chapters in its history: starting on Ambergris Caye, opening a branch on King St. in Belize City, and recently moving north to a safer neighborhood by the Princess Hotel. What hasn't changed is the popular Jamaican-style cuisine and welcoming staff. Try the jerk. Those willing to splurge can try the jerked lobster (US$15). Entrees US$8-15. Open M-Sa 11-3pm and 6-10pm. Cash only. ❸

◎ SIGHTS

Most travelers see Belize City only as a travel hub. For those interested in the country's culture and history, several sites are worth a quick look.

MUSEUM OF BELIZE. Built as Queen's Prison in 1857, rid of criminals in 1993, and refurbished as a museum in 2002, this stately brick building now houses exhibits on Belize's wildlife, landscape, culture, and history. The 3D model of the Great Western Barrier Reef will interest prospective divers. The Mayan exhibits include a replica of the gorgeous jade head uncovered in a tomb at Altun Ha in 1968. Prison aficionados will appreciate the preserved 19th-century cell, graffiti and all. *(Gabourel Lane in the Fort George District.* ☎*223 4524. Open M-F 8am-4pm. US$5.)*

SWING BRIDGE. Chances are, you'll be crossing this unique structure at some point during your stay. Currently the only manually operated "swinging" bridge in the world, this overpass has become a symbol for Belize City. M-Sa at 6am and 6pm, six to eight operators use cranks to rotate the bridge open, letting boats pass. An illustration of this procedure holds a proud place on the back of some Belizean banknotes.

GOVERNMENT HOUSE. This seaside two-story colonial mansion was built in 1814 and housed British governors until the end of colonial rule in 1981. Historical exhibits are juxtaposed with showcases of modern Belizean art. Stroll the finely tended grounds by the sea. *(Open M-F 8:30am-4:30pm, exhibit hours 9am-4pm. BZ$10.)*

ST. JOHN'S CATHEDRAL. This Anglican church, the oldest in Central America, stands directly across from the Government House. Built from 1812 to 1820, this church was constructed using bricks that functioned as ballast during a sea journey from Britain. Tombstones dating from the earliest years of settlement line the front of the church. *(Services M, W, and Sa 6:30am; Tu 9am; Th 7pm; F 6:30pm; Su 9:30am. Spanish mass Sa 6pm.)*

SUPREME COURT BUILDING AND BATTLEFIELD PARK. This graceful building, designed in 1926 by a New Orleans-based firm, replaced an older structure that burned to the ground in 1918. Apparently a burning flagpole fell on the head of the British governor, who died of his injuries a few days later. Battlefield Park occupies the area in front of the building. Several demonstrations for Belizean independence were held here throughout the 20th century. It's now common ground for street vendors, the homeless, hustling taxi drivers, tour guides, and unwitting tourists.

FORT GEORGE LIGHTHOUSE AND BARON BLISS TOMB. Henry Edward Ernest Victor Bliss (1869-1926) was a wealthy and polio-afflicted English petroleum speculator who spent his last years traversing the Caribbean in his luxury yacht, the *Sea King II*. He chose Belize Harbour as his final yachting place and fell in love with Belize's climate and people. Tragically, because of his condition, he never managed to step onto Belizean soil. Upon his death Mr. Henry Bliss willed some US$2 million to the country. Today, the Bliss Center for the Performing Arts and the Bliss School of Nursing mark the influence of the baron's generosity. Baron Bliss Day is celebrated nationwide on March 9. This slender lighthouse was built and is still maintained using Bliss's funds; appropriately, the generous baron lies beneath it, having finally reached the mainland.

IMAGE FACTORY. This exhibit space for Belizean contemporary art has been doing its best to enrich the city's cultural scene since 1995. Exhibits usually last for a month; check the website for up-to-date information. The building is located right on the harbor and includes a deck with a sea view. On your way out, stop by the museum's shop, which has a respected collection of local crafts, artwork, and a relatively wide selection of books. *(91 North Front St. ☎ 223 4093; www.imagefactory-bz. Open M-F 9am-5pm. Free.)*

NIGHTLIFE AND ENTERTAINMENT

There's no shortage of nightlife opportunities in the city, but travelers are warned to take extreme care when traveling around at night. Always take a taxi, even for short distances. Travel in groups, preferably of three or more. If you do go out, we suggest the area north of the Swing Bridge. And if you don't want to take the risk, don't worry; countless nocturnal adventures await you in the rest of Belize, most of them far safer than what's offered in this city. Plus, Belize City offers numerous other forums for entertainment. Some of them are listed below.

Bliss Center for the Performing Arts (☎227 2110; www.nichbelize.org), on the Southern Foreshore. Another offspring of the ever-generous Baron Bliss trust, this relatively new theater hosts a range of drama, music, and dance performances. It also houses the headquarters of the Institute of Creative Arts, which encourages local creative expression and holds shows and exhibits. The broad gray building, located right on the coast, is sure to capture your attention as you approach the city by boat. Check postings by the entrance for show dates and times. Cash only.

Princess Hotel & Casino (☎223 2670; www.princessbelize.com). While the rooms at this luxury hotel are well beyond the average backpacker's budget (US$110 per night, anyone?), the complex's entertainment center attempts to provide diversified nightlife. For starter's, there's the **Calypso Club**, a restaurant offering high-end Belizean seafood (US$15-30) and drinks (US$2.50-7.50). True nighthawks can chill at the **Vogue Bar & Lounge,** with its 40-person capacity, 4 TVs, DJs Th-Sa 9am-2pm, and an occasional live Mariachi band (drinks US$2-6; open M-W noon-midnight and Th-Sa noon-2am). The Princess also houses the city's only **movie theater,** with 2 screens usually showing standard blockbuster films (screenings 6-9pm, 3pm on weekends, "adult showings" on weekend nights; US$5). At this pace, why not throw in some bowling? The hotel's 8-lane alley and arcade are open daily 11am-11pm. Last, but certainly not least, is the **casino,** with over 400 machines alongside blackjack, Caribbean poker, and more. (open daily noon-4am, 18+).

Caesar's Palace, 190 Newtown Barracks Rd. (☎223 7624). Another name poached from an American nightlife institution, another unique establishment. Latin music and dancing reign in this small and packed club on the city's northern shore. Expect some familiar pop hits, too. Things get going around 11pm. Drinks US$2-3. Open Th-Sa 10pm-2am. Cash only.

MJ's Grand, 160 Newtown Barracks Rd. A local favorite blaring punta rock and reggae blare while pouring Belikin beer (US$1.50). Relax at the pool tables and on the outside veranda. Open M-F 7pm-1am and Sa-Su 5pm-2am. Cash only.

Planet Hollywood, at the corner of Queen and Handyside streets. No relation to the American brainchild of Arnold Schwarzenegger and Sylvester Stallone. Instead, this bustling, 2nd-floor dance hall hosts a largely Latin crowd and a handful of tourists. Groove to local punta rock, reggae, and salsa. The fun starts around 11:30pm. Open Th-Sa 10:30pm-2am. Drinks US$1-3. Cash only.

⚑ DAYTRIPS FROM BELIZE CITY

ALTUN HA

Getting to Altun Ha without a car is very difficult, as it's located along rarely traveled routes. It is difficult to travel back and forth in one day with the bus schedules being fairly unreliable. An overnight stay might be a better option. If driving from Belize City, head north along the Northern Highway. Turn right on the Old Northern Highway and head toward Maskall. Turn left at the sign for Altun Ha and continue for the 3km. Buses to Maskall from Belize City (Sa and M, 1pm, US$1.50) can drop you off at the junction with the road leading to site, but infrequent service makes this an inconvenient option. The easiest, though more expensive, option is to find a taxi driver in Belize City willing to drive you to Altun Ha, wait, then drive you back. This usually costs US$75-100. In a group of 3 or 4, the rate per person can drop to US$25. The bus station is the best place to find willing drivers. From Belize City, Belize Global Adventure Tours, Discovery Expeditions, and S & L Travel and Tours run guided tours to the site and back (4½hr., US65-75). Open daily 7am-4pm. US$5.

These beautifully preserved and recently refurbished ruins stood at the ceremonial plaza of a city of 8,000 to 10,000 people from about AD 300 to 1000. Once a trading point between inland and coastal settlements, now Altun Ha is almost entirely overgrown by jungle. The 13 structures are organized around two plazas (marked A and B) and date from the sixth and seventh centuries. Turn right from the entrance to reach plaza A; turn left for Plaza B. The highlight of Plaza A is the elegant **Temple of the Green Tomb** (A-1), where the tomb of a seventh-century king was uncovered alongside a variety of ceremonial artifacts. The most famous temple is found in plaza B and is called the **Temple of the Masonry Altars,** or the **Sun God Temple** (B-4). You might recognize the temple from Belikin beer bottle labels. Inside the box-like structure, excavators found another tomb containing the body of an elderly, highly-respected priest. Among the jade objects buried with him was a beautifully carved head of the Mayan sun god Kinich Ahau. A replica of this piece can be viewed at the **Museum of Belize** in Belize City (p. 199). The top of B-4 gives the best view of the site as a whole. Behind B-6, half a mile down a pleasant rain forest, is a small pond that served as the city's reservoir.

 MAKE NEW FRIENDS. Getting to Altun Ha by taxi can suck up a few days' worth of money—find a buddy to tag along with you to lower the price of transportation. A taxi to Altun Ha usually costs around US$75-100, so you'll be looking at saving at least US$37.

COMMUNITY BABOON SANCTUARY

If driving from Belize City, head up the Northern Highway and turn left at the turnoff for Burrell Boom. Turn right into Burrell Boom village and continue straight for 9 mi. to Bermudian Landing. Russell buses leave from Belize City for Bermudian Landing at the intersection of Euphrates Ave. and Cairo St., next to the school lot; buses run M-Sa at around noon and 4pm (US$1.50). They head through Bermudian Landing to Belize City 3 times M-Sa between 6am and 7am. From Belize City, Belize Global Adventure Tours, Discovery Expeditions, and S & L Travel and Tours run guided tours to the sanctuary and back (4hr., US$55-65).

Thirty miles west of Belize City, this unique sanctuary is the product of an entirely grassroots effort to combine wildlife preservation with local economic development. The effort began in 1985 when 12 landowners in several villages promised to conserve their land for local baboons. In return, they hoped, this new tourist attraction would supplement the cost of using their land, while encouraging local economic growth. Today, over 200 landowners in seven villages have made the pledge, creating a sanctuary of over 20 sq. mi. Rather than making the area an untouchable wilderness, the program lets villagers share space—in an environmentally friendly way, of course—with these neighborhood primates. The black howler population has expanded dramatically, with over 2000 living in the protected areas. The sanctuary also protects a wide range of wildlife and flora within its grounds and has established various educational programs aimed at local citizens. For more information on the sanctuary, visit www.howlermonkeys.org.

The monkeys at the center of this effort are known for their incredibly loud guttural growls. You'll hear them well before you see them. If you do see a baboon (and it's never guaranteed), you'll probably be surprised by the discrepancy between the baboon's mighty cry and tiny body.

The village of Bermudian Landing is the best point of access for visitors. The small **CBS visitor's center** (☎220 2181) has small exhibits on the monkeys and other wildlife. Included with the admission fee (US$5) is a 45-60min. guided walk through the jungle. The center also offers river tours (US$25 per hr.), horseback riding (US$23 per hr.), and crocodile night tours on the river (US$50 per hr.). The daring can try the night walks (US$12 per hr.) through the jungle.

The **Nature Resort** (☎610 1378), right behind the visitor's center, offers bare but clean cabanas with electricity, a fan, and a cold-water private bath (US$30-60). The family-run **Howler Monkey Lodge** (☎220 2158; www.howlermonkeylodge.org), 400 yards down the road after turning right from the visitor's center, has slightly more luxurious digs. The Lodge offers cabanas on the river (some with air-conditioning and a river view), and occasionally complimentary dinner and breakfast. In addition to local tours, the lodge also arranges longer expeditions to surrounding sites like Lamanai, Crooked Tree, and Altun Ha. *(Rooms with jungle view and fan: singles US$35; doubles US$4; triples US$65. Rooms with river view and A/C: BZ$87/114/147.)*

NORTHERN CAYES

Few travelers overlook Belize's exquisite Cayes (pronounced KEYS), strung along the second-largest barrier reef in the world. As Belize's number-one tourist destination, the Cayes feature some of the best diving in the world. Although there are several hundred cayes off Belize's aquamarine coast, visitors primarily concern themselves with Ambergris Caye, with its top-end resorts and dive shops. The more rugged Caye Caulker is also popular and is a budget traveler's haven. Regardless of which Caye suits your budget, you'll be able to visit the amazing Belizean reef and its 400 species of fish.

CAYE CAULKER

Caye Caulker (population 800) is Ambergris Caye's scruffy younger cousin: playing hooky, lounging in a hammock, most likely smoking a joint. The streets here are unpaved, the waterfront is uncluttered, and the pace of life matches the ubiquitous street sign and the island's unofficial motto: "Go slow."

Maya populated Caye Caulker thousands of years ago. Modern settlement began with *mestizo* refugees, fleeing the Yucatán Peninsula during the Caste War. A fishing community soon developed and continues to this day. In the 1970s, backpackers and hippies making their way from Tulum, Mexico, to Antigua, Guatemala made the island an established budget stop. Since then, possibilities for adventure on or below the seas have grown to rival those of Ambergris Caye's. So hit the water, groove to the reggae beat, settle into a hammock by the sea, and go slow.

⊏ TRANSPORTATION

Located directly along the Belize City-San Pedro boat route, Caye Caulker is easy to travel to and away from. Flying out from the island's airstrip is also possible, but it's an extremely costly option, especially considering the relatively cheap water taxi prices.

Flights: The **Caye Caulker Airstrip** is located well south of the village, about a 10-15min. walk from town along the coast or on Back Street. **Maya Island Air** (☎226 0012; www.mayaislandair.com) flies from the airstrip to **Belize City,** stopping at the Philip Goldson International Airport (10min.; one-way US$62, round-trip US$125) and at the **Municipal Airstrip** (15min., US$62/256) at 7:10, 9:10, 11:10am, 1:10, and 3:10pm. Flights to **San Pedro** (10min., US$35/70) leave at 7:45, 9:45am, 1:45, and 3:45pm. **Tropic Air** (☎226 0040; www.tropicair.com) flies from the airstrip to **Belize City,** stopping at the Goldson International Airport (10min.; one-way US$63, round-trip US$120) and the Municipal Airstrip (15min., US$35/65), at 7:10, 9:10, 11:10am, 1:10, 3:10, and 5:10pm. Flights to **San Pedro** (10min., US$35/65) leave at 7:50, 8:50, 9:50, 10:50, 11:50am, 12:50, 1:50, 2:50, 3:50, and 4:50pm.

Boats: Caye Caulker Water Taxis (☎223 5752; www.cayecaulkerwatertaxi.com) arrive at and leave from the **arrival pier** in the middle of the village. Boats leave for **Belize City** (50min.; one-way US$7.50, round-trip US$12.50) at 6:30, 7:30, 8:30, 10, 11am, noon, 1:30, 3, 4, and 5pm. Boats leave for **San Pedro** (30min., US$7.50/12.50) at 7, 8:20, 8:45, 9:50, 11:20am, 12:50, 2:20, 3:50, 5:20, and 6:15pm. You can buy tickets at the pier, the Tropical Paradise Restaurant, or Femi's Restaurant and Lounge. **San**

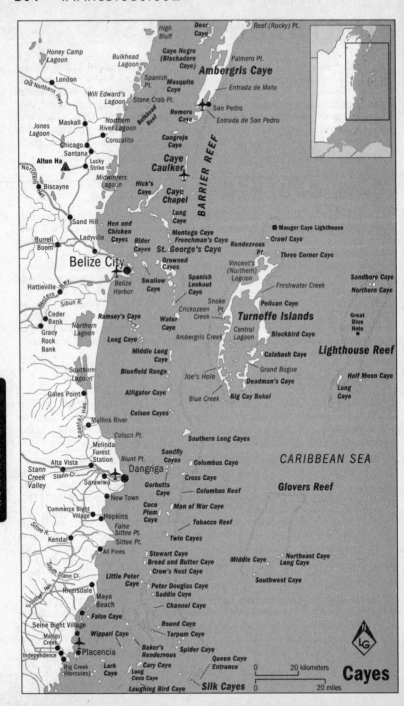

NORTHER CAYES

High
Bluff
Deer
Caye
Reef (Rocky) Pt.
Honey Camp
Lagoon
Bulkhead
Lagoon
Cayo Negro
(Blackadore
Caye)
Palmero Pt.
Ambergris Caye
London
Old Northern Hwy.
Spanish
Pt.
Mosquito
Caye
Entrada de Mato
Will Edward's
Lagoon
Stone Crab Pt.
Romero
Caye
San Pedro
Entrada de San Pedro
Jones
Lagoon
Maskall
Northern
River Lagoon
Corozalito
Altun Ha
Chicago
Santana
Lucky
Strike
Cangrejo
Caye
Biscayne
Midwinters
Lagoon
**Caye
Caulker**
BARRIER REEF
Hick's
Caye
Caye
Chapel
Long
Caye
Sand Hill
Ladyville
Hen and
Chicken
Cayes
Rider
Cayes
Montego Caye
Frenchman's Caye
St. George's Caye
Mauger Caye Lighthouse
Rendezvous
Pt.
Crawl Caye
Three Corner Caye
Burrell
Boom
Belize City
Drowned
Cayes
Vincent's
(Northern)
Lagoon
Freshwater Creek
Sandbore Caye
Northern Caye
Hattieville
Belize
Harbor
Swallow
Caye
Spanish
Lookout
Caye
Snake
Pt.
Pelican Caye
Great
Blue
Hole
Sibun R.
Ceder
Bank
Ramsey's Caye
Water
Caye
Crickozeen
Creek
Turneffe Islands
Blackbird Caye
Lighthouse Reef
Gracy
Rock
Bank
Northern
Lagoon
Long Caye
Ambergris Creek
Central
Lagoon
Calabash Caye
Southern
Lagoon
Middle Long
Caye
Bluefield Range
Joe's Hole
Grand Bogoe
Deadman's Caye
Half Moon Caye
Long
Caye
Gales Point
Alligator Caye
Blue Creek
Big Cay Bokel
Colson Cayes
Mullins River
Colson Pt.
Southern Long Cayes
CARIBBEAN SEA
Melinda
Forest
Station
Blunt Pt.
Sandfly
Cayes
Columbus Caye
Alta Vista
Stann
Creek
Valley
Stann-Cr.
Sarawiwa
Dangriga
Cross Caye
Columbus Reef
Glovers Reef
New Town
Gorbutts
Caye
Man of War Caye
Commerce Bight
Village
Hopkins
Faise
Coco
Plum
Caye
Tobacco Reef
Sittee R.
Sittee Pt.
Kendal
Sittee Pt.
Twin Cayes
All Pines
Stewart Caye
Bread and Butter Caye
Crow's Nest Caye
Middle Caye
Northeast Caye
Long Caye
Little Peter
Caye
Peter Douglas Caye
Southwest Caye
Riversdale
Maya
Beach
Saddle Caye
Channel Caye
False Caye
Round Caye
Tarpum Caye
Seine Bight Village
Wippari Caye
Spider Caye
Mango
Creek
Baker's
Rendezvous
Queen Caye
Entrance
0   20 kilometers
Independence
Big Creek
(Hercules)
Lark
Caye
Cary Caye
Long
Coco Caye
Silk Cayes
0   20 miles
Laughing Bird Caye
Cayes

Pedro-Belize Express boats (☎226 2194; www.sanpedrowatertaxi.com) arrive at and depart from the pier just north of the Caye Caulker Water Taxi arrival pier. Boats leave for **Belize City** (50min.; one-way US$3.50, round-trip US$6) at 7:30, 8:30, 10am, noon, 1:30, 3, 4, and 5pm. Boats leave for **San Pedro** (30min.; one-way US$6, round-trip US$10) at 8:40, 9:40, 11:10am, 12:40, 2:10, 3:40, and 4:40pm. Buy tickets at the **Xtreme Adventures office** on Front St. one minute north of the arrival pier. **Triple J Water Taxis** (☎207 7777; www.triplejbelize.com) arrive at and depart from the pier in front of the Rainbow Bar and Grill. Boats leave for **Belize City** (50min.; one-way US$5, round-trip US$12.50) at 7:30, 8:30, 11am, 1:30, 3, and 4pm. Boats leave for **San Pedro** (30min., US$7.50/12.50) at 8:45, 11:15am, 12:45, 2:15, 3:45, and 5:15pm.

Taxis: Golf cart taxis usually congregate around the **arrival pier,** but in most cases they're not necessary for getting around the small village.

TAKE A HIKE. For a small island, Caye Caulker is mysteriously teeming with taxi drivers who descend, vulture-like, on new arrivals from the water taxis. Unless you're a wimp, don't take them up on their offer—most destinations on the Caye are within 10 minutes' walking distance of one another.

⬥🔢 ORIENTATION AND PRACTICAL INFORMATION

Three main north-south drags constitute Caye Caulker's village. **Front Street** is closest to the eastern coast and the arrival piers. **Middle Street,** which begins farther south, and **Back Street** are the other main roads. Front St. is lined with hotels, restaurants, and tour companies. The more residential and less developed Middle St. and Back St. feature a few restaurants and services. More restaurants, beach bars, and hotels stretch along the eastern shore. At the very north of town, the **Split,** a water channel created by a hurricane, separates the village from the northern section of the island. Fifteen minutes south of town are the **Caye Caulker Forest Reserve** and the **airstrip.** Expensive resorts perch on the coasts to the north and south of town.

Tours and Agencies: See **Outdoor Activities,** p. 215.

Bank: Atlantic Bank, Middle St. (☎226 0207). Open M-F 8am-2pm, Sa 8:30am-noon.

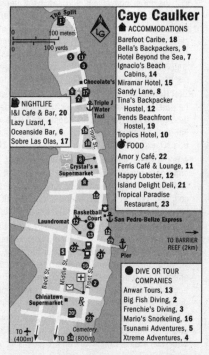

Caye Caulker

🏠 ACCOMMODATIONS
Barefoot Caribe, **18**
Bella's Backpackers, **9**
Hotel Beyond the Sea, **7**
Ignacio's Beach Cabins, **14**
Miramar Hotel, **15**
Sandy Lane, **8**
Tina's Backpacker Hostel, **12**
Trends Beachfront Hostel, **19**
Tropics Hotel, **10**

🍴 FOOD
Amor y Café, **22**
Ferris Café & Lounge, **11**
Happy Lobster, **12**
Island Delight Deli, **21**
Tropical Paradise Restaurant, **23**

NIGHTLIFE
I&I Cafe & Bar, **20**
Lazy Lizard, **1**
Oceanside Bar, **6**
Sobre Las Olas, **17**

● DIVE OR TOUR COMPANIES
Anwar Tours, **13**
Big Fish Diving, **2**
Frenchie's Diving, **3**
Mario's Snorkeling, **16**
Tsunami Adventures, **5**
Xtreme Adventures, **4**

NORTHERN CAYES

Laundromat: Coin Laundromat (☎226 0137), on the street leading in from the dock . Wash US$2; dry US$2. Open daily 7am-9pm. **Ruby's Coin Laundromat,** down the street and under the same owner (☎226 0137). Wash US$2; dry US$2.50. Open daily 8am-9pm.

Police Station, Front St. (☎206 0179). A large, yellow building, with a large, drug warning plastered on its front.

24hr. Pharmacy: R&M's Pharmacy (☎226 0190) next to the post office. Open M-Sa 8am-noon and 1:30-7pm, Su 9am-noon and 5-7pm. MC/V.

Internet Access: Cayeboard Connection, Front St. US$5 per hr. Printing and copying services. Selection of used books. Open daily 8am-7pm. **Cyber Cafe,** Front St. (☎226 0402). US$7 per hr. Open daily 7am-10pm.

Post Office: Just off Front St. at the southern end of the village. Open M-Th 8:45am-noon and 1-4pm.

▐▘ ACCOMMODATIONS

The budget traveler arriving at Caye Caulker from Ambergris Caye has reached the Promised Land. From luxury hotels, our weary pilgrim arrives at a backpacker's paradise of cheap hostels. Here, affordable views of the beach aren't just possible—they're the norm.

▨ **Tina's Backpacker Hostel** (☎226 0351; www.tinashostelbelize.com), on the beachfront. From the arrival pier, walk right on the beach for 1min. After 11 years, Tina's is still the most convenient and satisfying budget option on the island. An elaborately decorated 2-story building, with a garden full of palm trees, hammocks, and chairs, affording expansive ocean views. Deck with hammocks right on the shore. The rooms are clean, but you'll be spending most of your time chilling with other guests in the garden (parties are plentiful during the winter months). A new annex provides dorms with A/C, large common rooms, a kitchen, couch, and cable TV. Free Wi-Fi. Computer rental US$2 per hr. Dorms in main building US$11, in annexUS$15; doubles US$27. MC/V. ❷

Hotel Beyond the Sea, Front St. (☎624 9258; www.hotelbeyondthesea.com). Formerly the Taj Hotel, a new American owner has transformed the space into yet another Caye Caulker destination for backpackers. Rooms are bright and clean, but the highlight is the open-air bar on the ground-floor, which offers Internet access (US$1.25 per hr.) and Skype. Dorms US$10, extended stay US$9; singles US$20/18; doubles US$27/25. Cash only. ❷

Bella's Backpackers (☎226 0360), off Front St. at the northern end of the village. From the arrival pier, turn right onto Front St. and turn left at the sign for Bella's after 5min. You won't find much privacy in these rustic, airy halls stuffed with beds, but the digs are cheap. Central common room with cable TV and a kitchen with fridge. Free Wi-Fi and internet. Free canoe use. Dorms US$10; high loft with a double mattress US$13. Cash only. ❷

Ignacio's Beach Cabins (☎226 0175). From the arrival pier, turn left and walk along the coast for 15-20min. Cheap, blue-painted cabins on a beachfront space. The area itself isn't exactly picturesque—the water is murky, a destroyed palm tree blights any clean views of the water, and many of the cabins themselves are aging and rustic—but the effect of solitude is complete. Each cabin comes with 2 beds, a porch with a chair and hammock, a private bath, and a fan. Kayak rental US$8 per hr.; US$13 per 2hr.; US$15 per 3hr. Beachfront cabins US$20; back cabins US$15. MC/V. ❸

Hotel Miramar (☎206 0357), on the beachfront. Verandas with beachfront views are the strongest attraction of this centrally located hotel which lacks amenities. Bare-bones but clean rooms. Small cafe on the ground floor sells coffee and pastries. All rooms with fans. Singles with shared bath US$13, with private bath US$27; doubles US$27/25. Triples US$30. Cash only. ❷

Tropics Hotel, Front St. (☎226 0374; www.thetropicshotel.com). Sporting a pale orange facade to match the sandy streets, Tropics is a comfortable and clean place to spend the night. Veranda and yard both perfect for sunbathing and people-watching. All rooms with 2 double beds, private baths, and fans. You can also book tours through the affiliated Star Tours, whose offices are conveniently located in front of the hotel. Back rooms US$17; downstairs rooms US$23; ocean view rooms US$28. MC/V. ❸

Barefoot Caribe, Front St. (☎226 0161). Affiliated with the Sobre Las Olas restaurant across the street, this expansive, striking hotel features sparkling-clean, well-decorated rooms. All rooms with private bath and cable TV. Free Wi-Fi. Economy rooms with fan US$25; back rooms with A/C US$30; front rooms with sea view and A/C US$50. MC/V. ❹

Sandy Lane Guest House and Cabanas, Front St. (☎226 0117). 1min. walk north of the arrival pier. Expect comfortable accommodations at this homey collection of rooms and *cabañas* in the western, more residential part of the island. Guest rooms US$20; *cabañas* US$23-30. Cash only. ❸

Trends Beachfront Hotel (☎226 0094; www.trendsbze.com). Trends lies on the coast directly in front of the arrival pier. It's not a bad introduction: the 2-story hotel features 2 wide, hammock-filled verandas looking out over a spacious yard and beyond it, the clear-blue ocean. Rooms are bright and neat, each with 1 queen bed and 1 double bed, a mini-fridge, private bath, and ceiling fan. Rooms US$40-50. MC/V. ❺

◩ FOOD

Caye Caulker is the place to be for Caribbean and Belizean seafood specials. Waterfront views, great food, and friendly service more than compensate for the high prices. For groceries, try **Crystal's Supermarket** (Front St.; ☎226 0033; open daily 7am-11pm.) and **Chinatown Supermarket** (Middle St.; ☎226 4585; open daily 8am-10pm).

Femi's Cafe and Lounge, Front St. (☎226 8963), 5min. north of the arrival pier. With prime waterfront real estate, Femi's is the ideal spot to relax after a day at sea. Seafood dishes US$6-15. The famous "Nacho Blast" US$6. Coffee US$2-5; smoothies US$3-6. For a stronger beverage, try a rum or colada (US$4.50-7.50) during the long happy hour (3-9pm). Open daily 8am-10pm. AmEx/MC/V. ❸

Happy Lobster Restaurant and Bar, Front St. (☎226 0064), 1min. north of the arrival pier. Cheerfully serves a wide range of Mexican and Belizean breakfasts like *huevos rancheros,* eggs, bacon, beans, and fruit plates (US$4-8). Seafood US$7.50-15. Open 8am-10pm. MC/V. ❸

Island Delight Deli, Front St., just south of the arrival pier. A tiny eatery with a mighty menu. Mexican salutes US$1. Belizean rice and beans US$3.50. Fried dishes US$4.50-10. Burgers US$2-7.50. The deli is take-out only, so grab your food and chill on the beach. Open daily 9am-7pm. Cash only. ❶

Amor Y Cafe, Front St. (☎601 4458). A small cafe that's been the locals' go-to breakfast stop for years. Homemade bread, cakes, and brownies along with more filling fare like scrambled eggs with bacon and tomatoes and grilled sandwiches. A wide variety of smothies, milkshakes, and fresh natural juices. You can take it to go or, if there's room, sit outside on the porch and watch the village wake up. Entrees US$4-8; drinks US$2-5. Open daily M and W-Su 6am-11am. Cash only. ❷

Tropical Paradise Restaurant, Front St. (☎226 0124). Ostentatiously perched next to the village cemetery, Tropical Paradise's sunny decor and relaxed atmosphere will take your mind off the dearly departed near your table. Breakfast meals include the Stevie

Wonder Special (scrambled eggs with tomatoes served with fry jacks; US$5-6). Dinners include the Paradise Pasta and breaded conch steak (US$7.50-13). Happy hour 3-7pm; 2 local rum drinks US$3.50. Open daily 7am-9:30pm. MC/V. ❷

🎭 🎵 NIGHTLIFE AND ENTERTAINMENT

Caulker is as relaxed at night as it is during the day, preferring laid-back socializing to sweaty crowds. These are just a few options for the groove-happy.

I&I Reggae Bar (☎625 0344), just off the southern end of Front St. 3-story I&I features a dance floor on the ground level, swings hanging from the ceiling on the 2nd fl., and hammocks for lounging and drinking on the 3rd. Beer US$2; mixed drinks US$4.50-8.50. Open daily 6pm-midnight. Cash only.

Oceanside Nightclub, Front St. Locals congregate here for frenetic punta and reggae dancing after 10:30pm on the weekend. Don't miss the dance contests; check the front door for flyers announcing dates and times. Drinks US$2.50-7.50. Open daily 7am-midnight. Cash only.

Lazy Lizard Bar & Grill (☎226 0280), on the Split. Proclaiming itself "a sunny place for shady people," the Lizard is perfectly placed next to the public swimming area. Local rum US$2.50; Belikin beer US$2. Happy hour 5-7pm. Open daily 11am-10pm. Cash only.

Herbal Tribe, Front St. The first stop for authentic Rasta flavor. Unique masks, colorful local paintings, and drums make this exotic restaurant and bar a nightlife must. Healthy mix of locals and tourists. Happy hour 3-10pm. Rum and coladas US$4-7.50; mixed drinks US$4.50-9. Cash only.

Sobre Las Olas, Front St. (☎226 0161) Yet another beachfront restaurant and bar (the name translates to "on the waves"). Sobre distinguishes itself with its whimsical decor and free WiFi. Breakfast fruit plates and scrambled eggs with ham and bacon US$4.50-8. Grilled seafood US$10-15. At night, the restaurant is ideal for enjoying the stunning Caribbean twilight. "Happy Day" 11am-9:30pm; 2 for 1 mojitos. Open daily 7am-midnight. MC/V.

🏃 OUTDOOR ACTIVITIES

It may not have Ambergris's range of companies, but Caye Caulker still manages to offer access to Belize sea adventures. Most likely, the crowds won't be as stifling. Though trips visit many of the same sites accessed from Ambergris, Caulker also offers treasures of its own.

DIVING AND SNORKELING DESTINATIONS FROM CAYE CAULKER

CAYE CAULKER MARINE RESERVE (CCMR). Established in 1998, the CCMR covers the local section of the barrier reef as well as a turtle grass lagoon closer to shore. Angelfish, parrotfish, colorful sponges, Christmas tree worms, shrimps, crabs, and lobsters all call the reserve their home. The reserve boasts its own **Shark Ray Alley** (not to be confused with Hol Chan's) and a brilliant array of coral formations at **Coral Gardens.** *(Diving and snorkeling ½-day trips leave at 9am and 2pm. Diving US$80-90; snorkeling US$23-30.)*

SWALLOW CAYE WILDLIFE SANCTUARY. One of the best spots in the world to catch a glimpse of **manatees** (sea cows), the sanctuary stretches over 9,000 acres southwest of Caye Caulker. Swimming with the manatees is forbidden. The sanctuary was created after excessive disturbance damaged the population. Still, several tour companies allow snorkelers to watch and share space with these delicate sea creatures.

GOFF'S CAYE AND SERGEANT'S CAYE. It's hard to believe, but tiny **Goff's Caye** was once home to a colonial fishing settlement and cemetery. Today, snorkelers take advantage of its location in a particularly healthy section of the barrier reef. The area northwest of the caye is a foraging area for sea turtles. **Sergeant's Caye** is just a tiny scrap of sand, but the plentiful coral sites around it make the caye a popular snorkeling site. These cayes are most often visited in snorkeling trips, but Frenchie's Diving (see below) also offers diving trips around the area (US$95-100).

DIVING COMPANIES

Frenchie's Diving (☎226 0234; www.frenchiesdivingbelize.com), on a dock by the Split. Diving in the local reef, Hol Chan, Spanish Bay, St. George's Caye, Turneffe Atoll, and Blue Hole. The kicker is an overnight diving and camping trip to Half Moon Caye in the Lighthouse Reef (US$500). AmEx/MC/V.

Big Fish Dive Center, Front St. (☎226 0450; www.bigfishdivebelize.com). 5min. south of the arrival pier. Run by a Caye Caulker native, Big Fish offers diving tours to 7 locations, including the local reef, Hol Can, and Blue Hole. MC/V.

Xtreme Adventures, Front St. (☎206 0065 or 206 0225; xadventures@hotmail.com). 1min. north of the arrival pier. Dive trips to the local reef, Hol Chan, and Blue Hole. You can also buy tickets for the San Pedro-Belize Express Water Taxi here. AmEx/MC/V.

Mario's Snorkeling and Inland Tours, Front St. (☎226 0056). 5min. south of the arrival pier. Diving trips to Blue Hole. MC/V.

Tsunami Adventures, Front St. (☎226 0462; www.tsunamiadventures.com). 5min north of the arrival pier. Diving at Hol Chan, Blue Hole, and Turneffe North and South. MC/V.

SNORKELING COMPANIES

Raggamuffin Tours, Front St. (☎226 0348; www.raggamuffintours.com). Snorkeling trips to the local reef (US$23), Hol Chan (US$45) and Turneffe (US$75). Their most famous tour is a 3-day sailing trip down to Placencia, stopping for fishing, snorkeling, and camping on small, deserted cayes along the way (US$225-300). MC/V.

Tsunami Adventures, Front St. (☎226 0462; www.tsunamiadventures.com), 5min. north of the arrival pier. Snorkeling trips to the Caye Caulker Marine Reserve, Hol Chan, Blue Hole, and Turneffe. Night snorkeling US$33. MC/V.

Mario's Snorkeling and Inland Tours, Front St. (☎226 0056), 5min. south of the arrival pier. Snorkeling tours to the Caye Caulker Marine Reserve, Hol Chan, and Caye Chapel. MC/V.

Blackhawk Tours, Front St. (☎607 0323), 2min. north of the arrival pier, across the street from the merchandise booths. Snorkeling trips to the Caye Caulker Marine Reserve (US$23) and Hol Chan (US$37). MC/V.

Star Tours (☎226 0374; www.startoursbelize.com), offices in front of the Tropics Hotel on Front St. Local reef, manatee, and Hol Chan snorkeling trips. AmEx/MC/V.

Anwar Tours, Front St. (☎226 0327), in front of the Sandy Lanes Guest House. Snorkeling trips to the Caye Caulker Marine Reserve and Hol Chan. MC/V.

Hicaco Tours, Front St. (☎226 0174; www.hicacotour.com), south of the arrival pier. ½day Caye Caulker Marine Reserve and manatee watching snorkeling tours, full-day trips to Hol Chan. MC/V.

Xtreme Adventures, Front St. (☎206-0065 or 206-0225), 1min. north of the arrival pier. Snorkeling expeditions to the Caye Caulker Marine Reserve, Hol Chan, and Blue Hole. MC/V.

French Angel Expeditions, on the street leading in from the arrival pier. Snorkeling at the Caye Caulker Marine Reserve and Hol Chan. MC/V.

HANG WITH MANATEES

Chocolate's Manatee Tours, Front St. (☎226 0151). 5min. north of the arrival pier. One of the most renowned manatee tour services, founded by a pioneer of the manatee cause. Full-day tours to Swallow Caye and Sergeant's Caye (US$60-65). Also rents kayaks (single US$5 per hr.; double US$7.50 per hr.). Chocolate's gift store open M-Sa 9am-9:30pm. MC/V.

French Angel Expeditions. Occasionally runs trips to Goff's Caye with a barbeque on the tiny beach there (US$60). MC/V.

Mario's Snorkeling and Inland Tours (☎226 0056). Manatee watching trips to Swallow Caye (US$45). MC/V.

Tsunami Adventures, Front St. (☎226 0462; www.tsunamiadventures.com), 5min. north of the arrival pier. Full-day "Southern Reef Discovery Tour," including manatee watching at Swallow Caye, snorkeling at Gallow's Point, and lunch on St. George's Caye (US$60). MC/V.

WINDSURFING AND KITEBOARDING

Kitexplorer, Front St. (☎226 0303; www.kitexplorer.com), near the Split . 9hr. windsurfing and kiteboarding adventures, including instruction, lunch, and gear. MC/V.

FISHING

Shallow flats near the caye make for some of the best fishing in Belize. Many tour companies offering diving and snorkeling trips can also arrange fishing expeditions for a negotiated price.

Anglers Abroad (☎226 0303; www.anglersabroad.com), at the Sea Dreams Hotel. This fly fishing shop also offers fly fishing instruction and ½-day, full-day, and overnight trips. MC/V.

Tsunami Adventures, Front St. (☎226 0462; www.tsunamiadventures.com), 5min. north of the arrival pier. ½-day local fishing trips US$175; 4hr. fly fishing trips US$200, 6hr. US$300. MC/V.

INLAND TRIPS

Xtreme Adventures (☎206 0065 or 206 0225; xadventures@hotmail.com). Inland trips to Altun Ha and Lamanai.

Mario's Snorkeling and Inland Tours (☎226 0056). Offers inland trips to Lamanai and to the Belize Zoo with cave tubing. MC/V.

Tsunami Adventures, Front St. (☎226 0462; www.tsunamiadventures.com), 5min. north of the arrival pier. Inland trips to Altun Ha, Lamanai, cave tubing, zip lining, and the Xunantunich Mayan ruins with a tour of San Ignacio. MC/V.

AMBERGRIS CAYE

Ambergris has avoided Mexican rule thanks only to a narrow canal dug by the Maya 500 years ago, separating the peninsula from the mainland. Once a hideout for European pirates, the island developed into a coconut plantation and fishing center before the tourist boom hit in the 1960s. Now chock-full of resorts, Ambergris is hardly the best option for backpackers looking for chill island vibes. Still, the range of sea adventures offered here is unbeatable, and, at times, the island's strained attempt to resemble a tropical paradise works.

San Pedro (population 11,300), is the center of civilization on Ambergris Caye. Belize's main tourist destination is full of peddling, diving, snorkeling, and fishing expeditions crowding the beach and the docks. Watch out for golf carts flying along narrow cobblestone streets past countless flashy gift shops, restaurants, and hotels; get ready to encounter aging resort denizens in polo shirts and golf caps mingling with Rastafarians. You've landed on Belize's largest Caye.

⊏ TRANSPORTATION

You can't throw a diving tank without hitting a service renting out golf carts and bikes, though they're only good for exploring the areas lying well beyond San Pedro. Ambergris's popularity ensures that a steady stream of boats floats constantly to and from San Pedro's piers.

Flights: The **San Pedro Airstrip** is located directly south of town, beginning just south of Esmerelda St. **Maya Island Air** (☎225 2219; www.mayaislandair.com) and **Tropic Air** (☎225 2302; www.tropicair.com) fly from the airstrip to **Belize City** (25min.; one-way US$63, round-trip US$125); **Caye Caulker** (10min., US$350/70); and **Corozal** (20min., US$50/100).

Boats: Thunderbolt skiffs leave from the western shore of San Pedro at the end of Black Coral St. at 7am and 3pm for **Corozal** (1½hr.; one-way US$23, round-trip US$33), with a stop in **Sarteneja** if requested (1hr., one-way US$23). The **Triple J Water Taxi** (☎207 7777; www.triplejbelize.com) leaves for **Caye Caulker** (40min.; one-way US$5, round-trip US$10) and **Belize City** (1½hr.; one-way US$7.50, round-trip US$14) at 7, 8, 10:30am, 1, 2:30, and 3:30pm. The **Caye Caulker Water Taxi** (☎223 5752; www.cayecaulkerwatertaxi.com), dock in front of the Blue Tang Hotel, leaves for **Caye Caulker** (45min.; one-way US$7.50, round-trip US$13) and **Belize City** (1½hr.; US$10/15) at 6, 7, 8, 9:30, 10:30, 11:30am, 1, 2:30, 3:30, and 4:30pm. The **San Pedro-Belize Express** (☎226-2194; www.sanpedrowatertaxi.com) leaves for **Caye Caulker** (30-40min.; one-way US$4, round-trip US$6) and **Belize City** (1½hr.; US$6/11) at 7 (express to Belize City), 8, 9:30, 11:30am, 1, 2:30, 3:30, and 4:30pm.

Taxis: Cabs wait midway up Barrier Reef Drive, by the public seating area on the shore.

Golf Cart: Polo's Golf Cart Rentals (☎226 3542), at the northern end of Barrier Reef Dr. Rentals US$13 per hr., US$25 per 2hr., US$30 per 3hr., US$62 per day. Open daily 9am-6pm. **Castle Car Rentals** (☎226 2421; www.castlecarsbelize.com), on the corner of Barrier Reef Dr. and Tarpon St. Rentals US$40 per 3hr., US$55 per 8hr., US$65 per day, and US$270 per week. **Ultimate Golf Cart Rentals** (☎226 3326), on the corner of Pescador Dr. and Tarpon St. **4-seater rentals:** US$15 per hr., US$25 per 2hr., US$50 per 8hr., US$70 per day, and US$300 per week. **6-seater rentals:** US$24 per hr., US$40 per 2hr., US$70 per 8hr., US$100 per day, and US$500 per week.

Biking: Joe's Bike Rental (☎226 4371), on the corner of Pescador Dr. and Caribena St. Rental US$2.50 per hr., US$10 per day, US$40 per week. Open daily 8am-6pm. **Los Quapos Bicycle Rental,** Pelican St (☎621 2505). Bike rental US$2 per hr., US$3 per 2hr., US$4 per 3hr., US$10 per day, and US$40 per week. **Calvio's Bike Rental** (☎661 7143), southern end of Pescador Dr. Rentals BZ$5 per hr., US$10 per 5hr., US$6 per day.

✈ 🛈 ORIENTATION AND PRACTICAL INFORMATION

SAN PEDRO

San Pedro is nestled near the southern end of the Caye. Behind it, a lagoon stretches into the **Hol Chan Marine Reserve.** The more remote areas north and south of town are dotted with expensive resorts, but scenic biking opportunities are plentiful there. Within San Pedro itself, three drives stretch from north to south: **Barrier Reef Drive, Pescador Drive,** and **Angel Coral Drive.** Small streets intersect the drives. Below **Tarpon Street,** at the southern end of the town center, the **airstrip** stretches south; paralleling it, **Coconut Drive** leads into unpaved, more residential sections of town. The **eastern coast** is lined with restaurants, bars, hotels, and docks laden with tour companies and ferry terminals. The quieter **western shore,** meanwhile, is mostly full of fishing boats.

Tourist Office: The San Pedro offices of the **Belize Tourism Board** (☎226 4531; www.travelbelize.org or www.belizetourism.org) are located at the southern end of Barrier Reef Dr. Open M-Th 8am-noon and 1-5pm, F 8am-noon and 1-4pm. A small **Tourist Information** booth loaded with pamphlets and other information is midway up Barrier Reef Dr. next to the opening on the beach.

Tours and Agencies: See **Outdoors Activities,** p. 215.

Banks: Atlantic Bank (☎226 2195), at the intersection of Barrier Reef Dr. and Buccaneer St. Open M-F 8am-3pm, Sa 8am-noon. **First Caribbean International Bank,** at the intersection of Barrier Reef Dr. and Buccaneer St. Open M-Th 8am-2:30pm, F 8am-4:30pm. **Belize Bank** (☎226 2450), at the north end of Barrier Reef Dr. Open M-Th 8am-3pm, F 8am-4:30pm, Sa 9am-noon.

Bookstore: Pages, Tarpon St., toward the south end of town. Decent selection of new and used books. Open M-Sa 8am-5pm.

Laundromat: Candace's Laundromat (☎226 2052), toward the northern end of Barrier Reef Dr. US$10 per load with service, US$7.50 without. Open daily 9am-7pm. Cash only.

Police Station: Midway up Barrier Reef Dr., by the opening to the sea.

Pharmacy: Ambergris Hope's Pharmacy (☎226 2983), at the northern end of Pescador Dr. Open M-Th 8am-9:30pm, F 8am-5pm, Sa 6-9pm, Su 9am-1pm and 5-9pm.

Internet Access: The **"D" Surf Shop,** on the beach at the northern end of Barrier Reef Dr. Internet US$7.50 per hr.; international calls US$0.50 per

San Pedro

🏠 **ACCOMMODATIONS**
The Conch Shell, 4
Coral Beach Hotel, 13
Hotel San Pedrano, 5
Lily's Hotel, 3
Pedro's Inn, 2
Ruby's Hotel, 14
Spindrift Hotel, 16
Thomas Hotel, 7

🍴 **FOOD**
Blue Water Grill, 1
Caliente, 10
Coramba, 19
Elvis Kitchen, 20
Esther's Dive
  by the Sea, 17
Jambel's Jerk Pit, 15
Mannelly's Ice Cream, 8
My Secret Deli, 18
Ruby's, 12

🍸 **NIGHTLIFE**
Big Daddy's, 21
Fido's, 6
Pier Lounge, 20
The Jaguar Temple
  Club, 9
Shark's Bar, 11

NORTHER CAYES

min. Open daily 8am-9pm. **Pelican Internet,** on Barrier Reef Dr. between Pelican St. and Caribena St. Internet US$0.50 per 5min.; use for over 20min. and get free unlimited calls to the US and Canada. MC/V. **Caribbean Connection** (☎226 4664; www.sanpedrointernet.com), on the corner of Barrier Reef Dr. and Black Coral St. A deluxe internet cafe, featuring outdoor seating, actual coffee, and with jewelry for sale to boot. Internet US$5 per hr. International phone service also available.

Post Office: near the corner of Barrier Reef Dr. and Buccaneer St. Open M-Th 8am-noon and 1-4pm, F 8am-noon and 1-3:30pm.

ꞓ ACCOMMODATIONS

Hotels seem to breed like rabbits on Ambergris, but a satisfying range of back-packer options has yet to develop. Still, a stable subset of hostels and cheap hotels survive the suffocating presence of the more affluent establishments nearby.

Pedro's Inn, Sea Grape Dr. (☎226 3825; www.backpackersbelize.com). Despite its distance from the docks, this is the cheapest and best backpacker option in San Pedro. Spread over 3 white clapboard houses in a quiet, mostly untouristed area of town. High-ceilinged rooms and spotless beds. Pool, free kayaks, and golf cart rentals. Well-stocked, popular bar and pizza joint, decorated with Jagermeister bottles, complete with pool table and card room. Singles US$10; doubles US$12.50. Rooms with private baths, cable TVs, and A/C US$50. MC/V. ❷

Ruby's Hotel, Barrier Reef Dr. (☎226 2063; www.ambergriscaye.com/rubys). Ruby's convenient location and ample veranda space by the beach has made it a budget haven for years. Rooms with stark white walls, wooden floors, and fans are a bit dark (especially on the street side). Arranges snorkeling, diving, and inland tours. Singles with shared bath US$20; singles and doubles with private bath US$30. MC/V. ❸

Lily's Hotel (☎206 2059; www.ambergriscaye.com/lilys). This family-run hotel features large rooms by the ocean with shaded balconies. All rooms with A/C and private baths; some with cable TVs. Restaurant downstairs. Singles US$55-65; doubles US$65-75. Seaside singles US$45-55; doubles US$55-65. AmEx/MC/V. ❺

San Pedrano Hotel (☎226 2054), on corner of Barrier Reef Dr. and Caribena St. Family-run for over 30 years. Clean, comfortable, wood-floor rooms, each with a private bath. Ocean views are rare, but some glimpses can be caught from the veranda upstairs. Singles and doubles with fan US$32.50, with A/C BZ$43.50; triples BZ$37/49. MC./V. ❺

Thomas Hotel, Barrier Reef Dr. (☎226 2061), next to San Pedrano. Viewless, but with a genial atmosphere. Nicely completes a block of budget hotels by the beach. Spacious, well-lit rooms, each with a private bath, TV, and fridge. Singles with fan US$17.50; doubles with fan US$32.50, with A/C US$48. MC/V. ❸

Coral Beach Hotel (☎226 2013; www.coralbeachhotel.com), above Jambel's Jerk Pit (p. 214) on the corner of Barrier Reef Dr. and Black Coral St. Clean, conveniently-located rooms, most of them newly renovated in this sky-blue hotel. Each floor has a veranda looking out over Barrier Reef Dr. with views of the sea. All rooms with private baths and cable TVs. Singles with fan US$36-46, with AC US$46-57; doubles US$46-57/57-70. MC/V. ❺

Spindrift Hotel (☎226 2174 or 226 2018; www.ambergriscaye.com/spindrift), on Barrier Reef Dr. and Buccaneer St. Indulge with an extravagant stay at Spindrift. Rooms are huge and clean, each with a private bath; the seaside location ensures plenty of light. Courtyard includes the Caliente restaurant, the Pier Lounge bar, various shops, and a seating area overlooking the sea. Book tours at the hotel office. Economy rooms with garden or street view and fan US$53; patio-view rooms with A/C US$75-85; beachfront rooms with A/C US$93-110. AmEx/MC/V. ❺

◧ FOOD

Jam-packed with restaurants, Ambergris doesn't skimp on the grub; finding food that's affordable is another story. The many cafes and snack shops will offer sustenance to the budget traveler; there are also a few restaurants in town that are easy on the wallet. For groceries, try **Richie's Supermarket**, at the northern end of Pescador Dr. (open M-Sa 7am-10pm, Su 7am-9pm) or **San Pedro Supermarket Ltd.**, next to Richie's (☎226-3446; open M-Sa 7am-11pm and Su 7am-10pm).

▨ **Estel's Diner by the Sea** (☎226 2019), on the beach at the end of Pelican St. Floors lined with beach sand, walls decorated with Belizean and American memorabilia, ceiling covered in flags, and a corner piano outfitted with country albums make Estel's worth a visit. Large, delicious, and reasonably priced breakfasts and lunches. Extensive breakfast menu (US$7-8.50), loaded with the traditional Belizean egg-meat mixtures and gems like Estel's Special (Mayan eggs with fried tortillas; US$7.50). The lunch menu (US$6-15) is heavy on Mexican dishes with burritos (US$5.50-7) and Mexican platters (US$10.50). Open M and W-Su 6am-5pm. Cash only. ❸

Ruby's Cafe, Barrier Reef Dr. (☎226 2063), next to Ruby's Hotel toward the south end of town. A local favorite satisfying desires for pastries and Mexican food. Pick up cinnamon rolls, rum cake, and banana bread (US$2.50-5) in the morning and return for burritos and tostadas in the afternoon or evening (US$3-6). Open M-Tu and F-Sa 6am-7:30pm, W 6am-2pm, Su 6am-noon. Cash only. ❷

Jambel's Jerk Pit, Barrier Reef Dr. (☎226 3515), beneath the Coral Beach Hotel. An old-time San Pedro favorite that wears its Jamaican affiliation proudly on its sleeve. Come here for "jerked" (a Jamaican process of grilling and spicing) seafood and meat dishes (US$10-17.50). Stay for the reggae beats, sometimes live. W buffet nights. Open daily 10am-10pm. Another location in Belize City. MC/V. ❹

Mannelly's Ice Cream, Barrier Reef Dr. (☎226 2285). There's no shortage of ice cream shops in San Pedro, but Mannelly's rises above the rest with its range of Belizean homemade options like bubble gum, coconut, rum n' raisin, and piña colada flavors. Single cone US$1.50-2.50; double scoop US$3-5. Cash only. ❶

My Secret Deli, Cabanera St. (☎226 3223), between Pescador and Angel Coral Dr. This small hole-in-the-wall at the north end of town serves up a surprising range of cheap dishes from American burger-and-fries staples (US$4-6) to fish and chips (US$4.50), Belizean breakfasts (US$3-4.50), and rice and beans (US$4.50). Refresh with a smoothie (US$2). Open M-Sa 7am-3:30pm and 6-9pm. Cash only. ❷

Caramba Restaurant, Pescador Dr. and Caribena St. Mexican and Caribbean food, served in a colorfully decorated building lined with pillars dressed as palm trees. Sample cuisine from Belize's northern neighbor with large burritos (US$7-14), *frujitos* (US$8.50-14), and quesadillas (US$7-14), or splurge on the more expensive seafood options. Fish dishes US$10-14; conch US$14-15; shrimp US$15-18. Open M-Tu and Th-Su 11am-2pm and 5-10pm. MC/V. ❸

Elvi's Kitchen, Pescador Dr. (☎226 2176; www.elviskitchen.com). The family-run Elvi's may look formal, with its eager waiting staff and elegant halls, but the food is surprisingly affordable. Belizean coconut curry shrimp US$12; squid US$15; fish meals US$15. Cheaper options include appetizers like stuffed jalapeno peppers (US$6) and burgers (US$5-9). Open M-Sa 11am-10pm. AmEx/MC/V. ❹

Caliente (☎226 2170), in the Seadrift Hotel on Barrier Reef Dr. Mexican and Caribbean dishes in a beachside seating. Salads US$2-3.50; stuffed jalapenos US$6; conch fritters US$8. Splurge on full-blown seafood meals (US$14-20). Finish off with desserts like chocolate key lime pie (US$3-7.50). Open daily 10am-9pm. MC/V. ❸

Blue Water Grill (☎226 3347; www.bluewatergrillbelize.com), on the beach just south of town. Feel like a luxury guest at Blue Water's open-air seaside setting, removed from San Pedro's clamor. Many of the meals are surprisingly affordable. Belizean breakfasts US$2.50-9. Grilled shrimp on French bread US$8.50. Seafood lunches and dinners US$6-20. Open daily 7-10:30am, 11:30am-2:30pm, and 6-9:30pm. AmEx/MC/V. ❹

🔆 🎵 NIGHTLIFE AND ENTERTAINMENT

SAN PEDRO

San Pedro is full of night venues. Most of them are open-air bars, strung along the beachfront. San Pedro's compact layout makes bar and club-hopping easy: just walk along the beach beginning at around 9pm and follow the music. As with everything else in San Pedro, the scene is busier during the popular winter season.

Fido's Restaurant and Bar (☎226 2056; www.fidosbelize.com). At 10pm each night, this massive, beachside seafood restaurant turns into one of San Pedro's main nightspots. Come drink and dance to live music under a thatched roof. Extensive list of special shots—Buttery Nipple and Mayan Dragon among them (2 for US$5). The party often spills over onto the beach, where Fido's owns its own pier. Drinks US$2-7.50. Live music (reggae, punta, R&B, classic rock, and funk) begins around 8pm. Open daily 11am-2am. Cash only.

Jaguar's Temple Club (☎226 4077; www.jaguarstemple.com). One of the most recognizable buildings in town, proudly lording over Barrier Reef Dr., next to the beachfront park. This jungle and Mayan-inspired "temple" can fit hundreds within its exotic walls. Light shows and live DJs playing remixes of old R&B hits along with the newest Caribbean sounds. You can be pretty sure that this nightclub won't attract the older resort crowd. Open Th-Sa 10pm-midnight. MC/V.

Pier Lounge (☎226 2002), in the Spindrift Hotel. For the full San Pedro entertainment experience, a visit to the Pier Lounge on W evenings at 6pm to see the "World Famous Chicken Drop" is a must. The Drop is a 20-year-old tradition wherein tourists drop a well-fed chicken onto a board of squares and bet on which square the bird will inevitably take a crap. For those who want a night free of bird poop, the Lounge features a daily happy hour daily 4-6pm (2 for 1 rum shots; US$4) and live music F-Sa at 8pm. Open daily 11am-10pm. Cash only.

BC's (☎226 3289), on the beachfront just south of town. Thatched-roof, outdoor bar in a quiet location on the beach. A flatscreen TV broadcasts sports games while locals and tourists mingle at the square bar. The crowd occasionally spills out toward barbeques on the beach. Beer US$2-3.50; mixed drinks US$4.50-8.50. Open daily 9am-midnight. Cash only.

Big Daddy's (☎226 8828), on the beachfront at the end of Ambergris St. Another popular beachfront restaurant by day and nightclub after 10pm. Nautical-themed paintings on the wall, coupled with black florescent lighting, can make for a aquatically trippy experience. Drinks US$2.50-9. Cash only.

🏊 OUTDOOR ACTIVITIES

Ambergris Caye's location next to the Mesoamerican Barrier Reef System, the second-largest barrier reef in the world, has made the island a draw for divers, snorkelers, and other watersports enthusiasts who flock here by the thousands every year.

DIVING AND SNORKELING DESTINATIONS

BLUE HOLE NATURAL MONUMENT. Probably Belize's most famous and photographed site, this 1000-ft-diameter circle has become a diving mecca ever since Jacques Cousteau explored and publicized it in the early 1970s. The Hole, lying at the center of Lighthouse Reef, started its life as a limestone cave during the last glacial period. Rising waters put an end to its above-ground existence, flooding it and collapsing its roof. Now extending over 400ft. below water, the Hole is filled with huge stalactites. Divers winding their way through these odd shapes can also see an abundant display of wildlife, including hammerhead sharks and Caribbean reef sharks. Word on the diving street is that the Blue Hole, for all its popularity and iconic status, is not as captivating as dives on Turneffe and even some other sites in the Lighthouse Reefs. If you're only planning on one dive in the Cayes, make sure you consult veterans before hitting the poster-friendly monument. *(The Blue Hole is an all day trip from San Pedro, with 1 or 2 additional stops elsewhere in the Lighthouse Reef. Trips usually leave at 5-7am and return at dusk. Diving trips cost US$225-250, including the US$40 marine park fee entrance. Snorkelers can also head out to see the monument, but be prepared to share the ride home with divers who have had a better experience than you fpr US$125-150.)*

LIGHTHOUSE REEF. Besides the Blue Hole, the reef boasts many other attractions. Divers can visit the **Painted Wall,** which features a teeming sponge community. The **Aquarium** boasts a huge collection of small reef fish. The (aboveground) bird sanctuary at **Half Moon Caye** is well worth the visit (park fee US$10), as is the abundant coral spurs and grooves at **Pete's Palace.** These sites are usually visited as part of a trip to Blue Hole.

TURNEFFE ATOLL. Perhaps the best site for divers, this huge atoll—the largest and closest—is 30 mi. long, 10 mi. wide, and packed with over 200 cayes. Exotic marine life is especially attracted to the area due to the preponderance of mangroves. You'll usually see signs for specific destinations within the atoll, i.e. "Turneffe Elbow" or "Turneffe South." **The Elbow,** one of the most exciting dives in Belize, lies at the atoll's southernmost tip. Its location at the convergence point of several ocean currents makes it a boisterous breeding and feeding ground for underwater life (you'll have to glance rather than stare, though; predictably, drift diving is the only option here).Visitors flock to **Myrtle's Turtle** to catch a glimpse of its famous eponymous resident. Head to **Three Anchorsto** to see the remnants of an old shipwreck. **Rendezvous Point,** at the atoll's northern end, features 3,000-ft. wall dives, with turtles and groupers for company. *(The Turneffe is an all-day, 3-dive trip, with a common cost of US$160-180.)*

HOL CHAN MARINE RESERVE. Located around the southern end of Ambergris, just four miles southwest of San Pedro, Hol Chan is a hugely popular and convenient stop for divers and snorkelers alike. The **Hol Chan Cut,** at the center of the reserve, is a 75 ft wide, 30 ft deep break in the reef that hosts a enormous population of striking corals and small fish life. Other "zones" in the reserve include a collection of **mangrove cayes** and **Shark Ray Alley,** whose residents—predominately nurse sharks and southern sting rays—are acclimated to boats and human visitors; they'll most likely come to visit even before you hit the water. For more information, visit the **Hol Chan Visitor's Center** in San Pedro on the corner of Angel Coral Dr. and Caribena St. *(☎ 226 2247; www.holchanbelize.org. Open M-F 8am-5pm, Sa 1-5pm. Diving and snorkeling trips to Hol Chan are usually a ½ day from Ambergris, leaving at 9am and 2pm and lasting 3-4 hours. 1 dive US$45; 2 dives US$75; 3 dives US$105.*

Snorkeling trips are US$40-50. From Caye Caulker, trips last 9am-5pm, including a few hours for lunch and exploring in San Pedro. Diving trips US$190-200; snorkeling US$40-50. Be prepared to factor equipment into your total price. Diving gear US$15-17; snorkeling gear US$6-10.)

MEXICO ROCKS AND TRES COCOS. Often visited in tandem, these nearby snorkeling sites lie directly off the northern shore of Ambergris. Mexico Rocks is located between the caye and the reef. It is very shallow (only 6-12ft. deep), but water visibility can reach 50ft. at times. Large, rare corals house small but plentiful creatures like conch, hermit crabs, and stingrays. Tres Cocos sits nearby on the reef, sporting elaborate 50ft. coral heads and schools of snapper and spotted eagle rays. *(Trips to Mexico Rocks and Tres Cocos are ½ day, leaving at 9am and 2pm and lasting 3-4 hours. US$35-45.)*

COMPANIES OFFERING DIVING AND SNORKELING TRIPS

Bottom Time Dive Center (☎226 3788), on the dock behind Ruby's. Diving and snorkeling around the local reef, Hol Chan, Turneffe's, and Blue Hole. MC/V.

Amigos del Mar Dive Shop (☎226 2706; www.amigosdive.com), on the dock at the end of Caribena St. Diving only; trips to the local reef, Turneffe, and Blue Hole. MC/V.

Karibbean Water Sports (☎226 3205, www.karibbeanwatersports.com), on the dock at the end of Bucaneer St. Pontoon boats head on snorkeling trips to Hol Chan (US$40), Mexico Rocks (US$40), and Tres Cocos (US$35). You can explore on jet ski (single ridger US$150, double rider US$175). MC/V.

Extreme Adventures Belize (☎226 3513; www.belizeextremeadventure.com), on the Fido's dock. Snorkeling only; trips to Hol Chan, Shark Ray Alley, Mexico Rocks, and other local destinations. MC/V.

Reef Adventures (☎226 2538; www.reefadventures.net), on the dock behind the Blue Tang Inn. Diving at Blue Hole and Turneffe, snorkeling at Hol Chan and Mexico Rocks. Manatee-watching tours from US$45. MC/V.

Ecologic Divers (☎226 4118; www.ecologicdivers.com), on the dock by the end of Caribena St. Diving trips in the local reef, Turneffe, Blue Hole; snorkeling at Hol Chan, Mexico Rocks, and Tres Cocos. MC/V.

Inland and Sea Adventures (☎226 3088; www.inlandandsea.com), on the dock at the end of Black Coral St. Diving and snorkeling in the local reef, Hol Chan, Turneffe, and Blue Hole. MC/V.

Aquadives (☎226 3415; www.aquadives.com), on a dock south of town, behind the Blue Water Grill. Diving and snorkeling at the usual suspects. Night snorkeling BZ$70. MC/V.

Ambergris Divers (☎226 2634; www.ambergrisdivers.com), on the dock by the end of Black Coral St. Night diving (US$100) and snorkeling (US$50). MC/V.

Chuck and Robbie's Scuba Diving and Instruction (☎610 4424; www.ambergriscayediving.com), on the beach towards the north end of town. Exit to the beach at the northern end of Barrier Reef Dr. Diving only; local reef, Turneffe, and Blue Hole explorations. MC/V.

SEArious Adventures (☎226 4202), on the beach behind Ruby's. Snorkeling at Hol Chan, Mexico Rocks, and Tres Cocos. Full-day trips around Caye Caulker US$75. Try the full-day "Manatte Snorkeling Adventure" on Swallow and Goff's Island Cayes (US$105). MC/V.

DIVING INSTRUCTION

You can't dive without certification, but the classes offered on the Cayes are often cheaper than those offered elsewhere. For safety's sake, beware of slip-shod classes and make sure that your instructors are PADI-certified. "Resort" or "beginner" classes (for those who want the bare-bones minimum instruction) run around US$125-135. If you've been certified but need a once-over, refresher courses are also US$125-135. To go the whole nine yards, take the open-water or certification courses (US$350-375). Companies offering diving instruction are listed below.

Aquadives (☎226 3415; www.aquadives.com), on a dock south of town, behind the Blue Water Grill. MC/V.

Ambergris Divers (☎226 2634; www.ambergrisdivers.com), on the dock by the end of Black Coral St. MC/V.

Chuck and Robbie's Scuba Diving and Instruction (☎610 4424; www.amber-griscayediving.com), on a dock towards the north end of town. Exit to the beach at the northern end of Barrier Reef Dr. MC/V.

FISHING

The reef is a fishing paradise. The tarpon and coral palaces are home to barracuda, jacks, snappers, and groupers. The Big Kahuna of reef fishing in Belize is the famous **Grand Slam**. Some opt to go beyond the reef, where the pickings are slimmer but still include a healthy array of marlin and sailfish. Half-day fishing trips in the reef run for about BZ$350-400; full-day trips are BZ$550-600. Half-day deep-sea fishing expeditions cost between US$300 and US$400, while full-day trips beyond the reef are US$550-600.

Freedom Tours (☎226 3308; www.fishingunlimited.bz), dock on the western shore of the island near the end of Pelican St. Run by the expert "Hilly Boo," this company specializes in reef and deep sea fishing. Also offers snorkeling and inland trips. MC/V.

Bottom Time Dive Center (☎226 3788), on the dock behind Ruby's. Reef and deep sea fishing. MC/V.

Amigos del Mar Dive Shop (☎226 2706; www.amigosdive.com), on the dock at the end of Caribena St. Reef and deep sea fishing. MC/V.

Reef Adventures (☎226 2538; www.reefadventures.net), on the dock behind the Blue Tang Inn. Reef fishing only. MC/V.

Ecologic Divers (☎226 4118; www.ecologicdivers.com), on the dock by the end of Caribena St. Reef and deep sea fishing. MC/V.

Aquadives (☎226 3415; www.aquadives.com), on a dock south of town, behind the Blue Water Grill. Reef fishing only. MC/V.

Inland and Sea Adventures (☎226 3088; www.inlandandsea.com), on the dock at the end of Black Coral St. Reef and deep sea fishing. MC/V.

SEArious Adventures (☎226 4202), on the beach behind Ruby's. Reef and deep sea fishing. MC/V.

WIND SPORTS

Though diving and snorkeling rule the roost on the cayes, thrill-seekers have created a niche for faster-paced adventure on the water. Though winds here are not as strong as the most hardcore aficionados might hope—the reef creates a huge protected area, freeing the sea of passing boats and other nuisances that plague these sports. The best winds blow through between February and June at 12-20 knots. **Windsurfing** is still the most popular water adventure sport here. **Kiteboarding** is also a favorite here. In this sport, the boarder is rocketed across the water by a high sail. For those who want to experience the sea from a higher elevation, check out Ambergris's abundant **parasailing** opportunities.

Seasports Belize (☎226 4488; www.sailsportsbelize.com), on the beach a ten-minute walk south of town. The Ambergris mecca for windsurfing and kiteboarding. Windsurfing board rentals US$22-27 per hr.; US$50 per day. 1hr. windsurfing lessons US$50. Kiteboarding rental US$82 per day; US$142 per 3 days; US$330 per week. Kite control lessons (2½hr.) US$165; board skill lessons (2½hr.) US$165; supervised rentals for beginners (2hr.) US$166. MC/V.

Extreme Adventures Belize (☎226 3513; www.belizeextremeadventure.com), on the Fido's dock. Parasailing US$70 for 1; US$1300 for 2. MC/V.

SAILING AND CRUISES

Several companies rent out sailboats and provide instruction. If you don't want to man the boat yourself, small cruises—especially those that set off to watch the setting sun—are popular.

Bottom Time Dive Center (☎226 3788), on the dock behind Ruby's. Sunset cruises US$55; manatee watching expeditions US$105; tours around the Bacalar Chico Marine Reserve with snorkeling stops US$105. MC/V.

Karibbean Water Sports (☎226 3205, www.karibbeanwatersports.com), on the dock at the end of Bucaneer St. The center for jet-ski excitement. Watersport enthusiasts leisurely embark on tours around the island (US$150 for single, US$140 for two), or cut loose on raucous 1hr. thrill rides (US$175). Pontoon boat cruises US$40-50. "Booze cruise" around the various seaside pubs on the island US$45. MC/V.

Reef Adventures (☎226 2538; www.reefadventures.net), on the dock behind the Blue Tang Inn. Sunset cruises US$45. MC/V.

Seasports Belize (☎226 4488; www.sailsportsbelize.com), on the beach a 10min. walk south of town. Sailboat rentals US$22-100, depending on the make of the boat. Beginner sail course US$275; Catamaran course US$65; monohull course US$65. MC/V.

SEArious Adventures (☎226 4202), on the dock behind Ruby's. Catamaran sailing US$60. MC/V.

Seaduced by Belize (☎226 2254; www.seaducedbybelize.com), on the beach behind Ruby's. Also has an office in the Vilma Linda Plaza off Tarpon St. Catamaran day sailing to Caye Caulker with snorkeling stops US$75; sunset cruise US$50. Manatee watch and snorkeling US$105. MC/V.

INLAND TRIPS

Many companies run one-day or overnight trips to the best sites in inland Belize. You'll either boat or fly to Belize City and continue on river or road to the site. If you are spending any time on the mainland, it's a better idea to take the far cheaper tours run from nearby towns, where guides are often more knowledgeable. Common trips from the Cayes include tours of the Mayan ruins at **Altun Ha** (US$75-85) and **Lamanai** (US$125-150); these trips are often combined with cave tubing, raising the price to US$50. Trips to the **Belize Zoo** are also usually combined with cave tubing (US$150-160). If you want to skip the ruins and wildlife and cut to the adventurous chase, combined **cave tubing** and **zip lining** tours (US$205-230) are available.

Bottom Time Dive Center (☎226-3788), on the dock behind Ruby's. Trips to Altu Ha, Lamanai, Belize Zoo with cave tubing, and Tikal, Guatemala (US$402-420). MC/V.

Extreme Adventures Belize (☎226 3513; www.belizeextremeadventure.com), on the Fido's dock (p. 215). Cave tubing ½-day US$250; full-day with zip line and Mayan ruin trip US$450. MC/V.

Reef Adventures (☎226 2538; www.reefadventures.net). Altun Ha, Lamanai, and Belize Zoo with cave tubing. MC/V.

Ecologic Divers (☎226 4118; www.ecologicdivers.com), on the dock by the end of Caribena St. Altun Ha with cave tubing. Lamanai, cave tubing and zip line. MC/V.

SEArious Adventures (☎226 4202). The full gamut: Altun Ha, Lamanai, Belize Zoo with cave tubing. Optional zip line. MC/V.

Seaduced by Belize (☎226 2254; www.seaducedbybelize.com), on the beach behind Ruby's. Also has an office in the Vilma Linda Plaza off Tarpon St. River trips to Altun Ha, Lamanai, and Belize Zoo. Cave tubing; optional zip lining. MC/V.

NORTHER CAYES

NORTHERN BELIZE

Northern Belize is a low-lying area of pine savannas, swamps, jungles, and coastal lagoons. The region feels a lot more like its neighbor Mexico than other parts of the country do, and Spanish is prevalent in many areas. Given the long stretches of cane fields, smokestacks jutting up from refineries, and the abundance of cheap rum, it's easy to see that sugar is the basis of the northern economy. After reaching most of the region's landlocked Mayan ruins and nature reserves, the Northern Highway turns inland. It doesn't return to the coast until it reaches Corozal eight miles from the Mexican border. Highlights of the region include the impressive Mayan site of Lamanai, accessible from mellow Orange Walk. Look for the rare Jaribu stork at Crooked Tree Wildlife Sanctuary, and marvel the many different species at the Shipstern Nature Reserve.

CROOKED TREE WILDLIFE SANCTUARY

Birds are the star attraction in the tiny, lagoon-bound village of Crooked Tree (population 900), 33 miles northwest of Belize City. With 286 species spread over 16,400 acres, the sanctuary is one of the largest of its kind in Central America. Bird watchers with binoculars flood this relaxed farming community, eager to catch a glimpse of the famous Jaribu storks (with a 12-foot wingspan), ospreys, whistling ducks, and the many other of migrating ilk who flock to the lagoon between December and May. Those who aren't as passionate about double-crested cormorants will enjoy the calm peace and quiet dirt paths of the village. Subsistence farmers tend their small plots while horses, cows, and bulls have the run of the village roads. The tranquility belies a rich history. Mayas lived in the lagoon thousands of years ago; small, scattered ruins here mark their previous existence. One of the first inland European settlements was established here around 1750 by British loggers, who named the island for a gnarled cashew tree that grew by the shore. Today, the cashew business is booming in Crooked Tree. Check out the **Cashew Festival** in mid-May that offers cashew products, animal rides, shows, late-night music, and dancing devoted to the almighty nut.

▄ TRANSPORTATION

The 3 mi. dirt road to Crooked Tree begins at the Northern Highway 32 miles from Belize City. Despite its isolated lagoon position, the village is actually not too difficult to access with some advance planning.

Buses: Jex & Sons buses leave Belize City at the intersection of Regent St. West and West Canal St. at around 10:30am and 5pm, M-Sa (1hr., US$1.50). The buses leave from the bus yard in Crooked Tree next to the visitor's center for Belize City M-Sa at 5am and 7am.

Northbound buses leave Belize City for Orange Walk. Ask the driver to let you off at the Crooked Tree turnoff (45min., US$1). Arrange a day in advance with your accommodation to be picked up at the turnoff. Some travelers have found hitchhiking to Crooked Tree a convenient option. Let's Go never recommends hitchhiking as a safe means of transportation, and none of the information presented here is intended to do so. **Belize Global Adventure Tours, Discovery Expeditions,** and **S & L Travel and Tours** run guided tours from Belize City to the village and back (4hr., US$55-60).

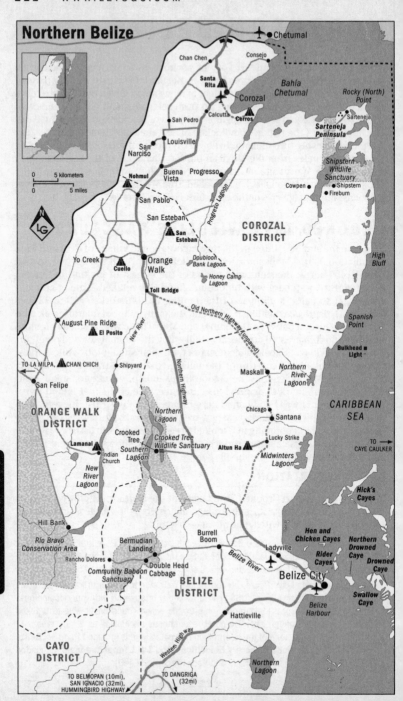

Northern Belize

NORTHERN BELIZE

✦ ☷ ORIENTATION AND PRACTICAL INFORMATION

The sanctuary's **visitor's center** (open daily 8am-4:30pm) is directly to the right as you enter the village. Pay the entrance fee of US$5 here, sign your name in the guestbook, and pick up a map of the sanctuary. A 5min. walk up the road from the center and through the bus yard will bring you to the village's **main road,** along which lies the village **police station,** cemetery, school, and a varied group of churches. Walking trails leave mostly from the eastern side of the village.

▚ ACCOMMODATIONS

The recent passing of Sam Tillett, a legendary bird-watcher who operated a lodge and tours around the sanctuary, has left a considerable lacuna in the village's tourist scene. Still, several excellent lodges provide comfortable accommodations and even tours for those who want to stay for more than a day.

Rhaburn's Rooms (☎225 7035). From the visitor's center, walk up to the main road and turn left. Cross the field next to the church on your right (you'll see a sign) and walk through the path that leads into the woods. The Rhaburns' house is through the first gate on your left. The cheapest find in Crooked Tree. The Rhaburns, a friendly Creole couple, offer 4 humble but comfortable rooms on the 2nd floor of their home. All rooms with fans and shared hot-water baths. Singles US$10; doubles US$15. Cash only. ❶

Crooked Tree Lodge (☎626 3820; crookedtreelodgebelize.com). Turn right along the main road, fork left just before the cemetery. Turn right at the sign for the lodge, and continue for 10 min. In a remote corner of the village, this fantastic new lodge is worth a stay just to soak up its breathtaking views. Positioned 11½ acres along the lagoon for maximum bird-spotting. Friendly owners Mick and Angie Webb keep 5 spotless *cabañas,* each with lovely decor, double beds, and private bath. Spacious dining hall, outdoor bar, deck on the lagoon shore, and manmade pools. The Webbs can also arrange tours of the sanctuary. Singles US$50; doubles US$70; family suite (fitting 7) US$100. The truly frugal can camp on the spacious front lawn for US$10 and have access to showers inside. MC/V. ❷

Bird's Eye View Lodge and Restaurant (☎203 2040 or 225 7027; www.birdseyeview-belize.com). From the visitor's center, take the path leading left along the shore and continue for 10 min. This grand hotel set along a lagoon is hardly a budget option, but it does offer the village's best range of tours around Crooked Tree and inland Belize. Stately, well-lit roms with fans and private bathrooms. 2nd floor patio with the best views of the lagoon in town. The restaurant below is pricey (US$10-18) but with an extensive menu. The lodge offers tours of the sanctuary (see **Activities and Tours,** p. 223) and explorations of sites throughout Belize. Singles US$50-60; doubles US$60-80; triples US$90-100. AmEx/MC/V. ❺

◖ FOOD

Don't expect any fine dining in Crooked Tree (unless you're willing to shell out at the **Bird's Eye View Lodge;** p. 223. The village includes a few small restaurants, but hours are very unpredictable. The few stands near the main road are your best bet if you want to venture out of your lodge for food. For easily accesible, down-home Belizean offerings, try **A & B's Fast Food Stand** ❷, next to the bus yard, 3 min. from the visitor's center. (Rice-bean-chicken stew US$3; drinks US$1-2).

▞ ☷ ACTIVITIES AND TOURS

Bird-watching is the name of the game here, so grab the visitor's center map, generously apply bug repellent, strap on your walking shoes, bring your binoculars, and head out into the lagoon. Spring is the best time to see birds, but satisfying sightings happen here year-round. A highlight is the large **viewing boardwalk** three miles north of town, accessible via the **Trogan Trail.** (Walk to the main street from the visitor's center, turn right, then head left at the sign for the trail.) Several trails, leaving directly from the visitor's center, wind along the shore and provide ample views of waterfowl.

Novices may want a guided tour of the sanctuary. The **Bird's Eye View Lodge and Restaurant** (p. 223) offers guided nature walks (US$7.50-10 per hr.), boat tours (US$35-75), and horseback riding (US$7.50 per hr.) around the area. From Belize City, **Belize Global Adventure Tours, Discovery Expeditions,** and **S & L Travel and Tours** run guided tours to the sanctuary and back (4hr., US$55-60).

ORANGE WALK

As the Northern Highway edges towards the Guatemalan and Mexican borders, the Creole presence gradually gives way to a predominantly Hispanic one. By the time you reach Orange Walk (population 16,000), the sounds of rapid Spanish dominate. Cries of fruit sellers mix with the constant hum of vehicles passing from Belize City to Mexico. The town was actually founded in the mid-19th century, when Mexicans fleeing the caste wars in the Yucatán peninsula poured into the area. Since then, Orange Walk, like any sizable town in Belize, has become a true melting pot of cultures. Chinese restaurants seem to populate every street, while straw-hatted Mennonites navigate the crowds of this relaxed riverside town. Sugarcane has long been the driving economical force in this "Sugar City." For Belizeans, Orange Walk is a trading center and transit point; for travelers, it's a natural starting point for river treks down to the Mayan ruins at Lamanai. But the bustling center and rich diversity of restaurants in the town itself merit a day's exploration. Be careful when walking at night, try to stay in groups of more than three people and always carry enough cash for a taxi.

▐ TRANSPORTATION

Getting to and from Orange Walk is a cinch. Buses traveling between Belize City and Corozal are constantly passing through, so you shouldn't have to wait any longer than 30 minutes to pick one up. **Southbound buses** heading to **Belize City** (1½hr., US$2) and **Belmopan** (2½hr., US$3) leave from the intersection of Queen Victoria Ave. and Albert St., right next to the post office, from 6am to 8:30pm. **Northbound buses** to **Corozal** (1½hr., US$1.75) and **Chetumal, Mexico** (2hr., US$2.50) leave directly across the street at the intersection of Queen Victoria Ave. with South Park St. **Local buses** traveling to the nearby villages of **San Jose** and **San Pablo** (45min., every hour 9am-7pm, US$1) leave from the lot next to the outdoor market by the Town Square. Buses to **Sarteneja** (1hr.; 3 per day at around noon, 2, and 5pm; US$1.75) leave from the corner of Main St. and Avilez Ln., near the bridge over the New River. **Tillett's buses** to **Indian Church** (a village near the Lamanai ruins) leave from the lot next to the market (2hr.; M, W, and F at 3pm; US$2). Three **taxi stands** with waiting drivers line Queen Victoria Ave. by the Town Square.

◢ ▐ ORIENTATION AND PRACTICAL INFORMATION

The Northern Highway passes through the center of town and becomes **Queen Victoria Ave.,** forming Orange Walk's main road and commercial center. Buses drop passengers off next to a small **clock tower** that stands in the center of the avenue. Bordering the street to the east is **Central Park,** a small space for playing and relaxing. Across the street and beyond the **Town Hall** is a broad, grassy expanse, the **Town Square.** An outdoor market is behind it. To the east, parallel to Queen Victoria Ave., **Main Street** is lined with banks and hotels. Further on, the town slopes down to meet the **New River.**

■ **Tours and Agencies: Jungle River Tours,** 20 Lovers' Ln. (☎302 2293). From the clock tower, walk down South Park St. along Central Park to Lovers' Lane. Offices are directly across the street. Easily the best option in Orange Walk for river tours to Lamanai. Provides 6-7hr. tours with expert guides who know their wildlife, nature, Mayan history, and Mayan glyphs. Open M-F 8am-5pm. Tours US$30, not including US$5 admission. Many hotels in Orange Walk can also arrange tours (see **Accommodations,** p. 223).

Banks: Belize Bank, at the corner of Main St. and Market Lane (☎322 2019). Open M-Th 8am-3pm, F 8:30am-4:30pm. **Atlantic Bank,** directly across the street from Belize Bank. Open M-F 8-3pm, Sa 8:30-noon. **Scotia Bank,** at the corner of Main St. and Park St. (☎322 2194). Open M-Th 8am-3pm, F 8am-4:30pm. All these banks have **24hr. ATMs.**

Laundromat: Mary's Laundry, Progresso St. (☎322 3454), behind the town square and market. Open daily 7am-5pm. US$1 per load.

Swimming Pool: D'Victoria Hotel (see **Accommodations,** p. 225) opens their pool to the public M-Sa 1-5pm. US$2.

Police Station: (☎322 2022), on the northern edge of town, up Queen Victoria St.

Pharmacy: Pharmacy Lucille (☎302 0346), at the intersection of Main St. and Slaughterhouse Rd. Open M-Sa 8am-5pm. There are several other pharmacies along Main St.

Hospital: Northern Regional Hospital (☎322 2072), 1 mi. north of town along the Northern Highway. 24hr. emergency service.

Internet Access: Kai & A Internet Café, on Queen Victoria Ave. just pass the intersection with Cemetery St., south of the Town Hall. US$2 per hr. Open 10am-9pm. MC/V. **Cyberwalk Computers** (☎322 3024), a 10min. walk north of town along Queen Victoria Ave. Internet US$2 per hr. Open M-Sa 9am-9pm. AmEx/MC/V.

Post Office (☎322 2345), at the intersection of Queen Victoria Ave. and Arthur St., right next to the bus stop. Open M-Th 8am-noon and 1-4:30pm, F 8am-noon and 1-4pm.

▌ ACCOMMODATIONS

Orange Walk is a way station for tourists, and it has the abundance of hotels to prove it. Budget options abound; luckily, most of them are in the heart of town.

■ **Akihito Hotel,** Queen Victoria Ave. (☎302 0185), 4min. south of the Town Square. This is a backpackers' heaven. Cheap and conveniently located rooms with cable TVs. Chinese restaurant and bar downstairs. Internet US$2 per hr. Free Wi-Fi. Check out 11am. Curfew 11pm. Dorms US$7.50-9 (only for groups of 3-5); rooms US$15-20, with bath BZ$23-27, with A/C US$30-32; jacuzzi room BZ$65. MC/V. ❶

Orchid Palm Inn, 22 Queen Victoria Ave. (☎322 0719; www.orchidpalmin.com). Walk north from the Town Square along Queen Victoria Ave. and turn right onto Bautista Ln. This spotless and well-decorated inn won the 2007 Best Small Hotel of the Year Award from the Belize Tourism Board. With a helpful staff and delightful cozy rooms near the center of town, it's not hard to see why. All rooms with bath and cable TV. The inn arranges tours to Lamanai and the Cayes. Free Wi-Fi. Check-in 2pm. Check-out 11am. Singles with fan US$23, with A/C US$33; doubles with fan US$35-55, with A/C US$40-60. Am/Ex/MC/V. ❹

D'Victoria Hotel, (☎322 2518; www.dvictoriabelize.com). 5min. walk south down Queen Victoria Ave. from the Town Square. From the street this gaudy pink building—with the unappealing remnants of a former bar in its front hall—may turn visitors off, but its rooms are clean and well-lit. Pool free for guests and open to the public daily 1-5pm

($4). Arranges tours to Lamanai, Crooked Tree, and Altun Ha (US$40-75). Free Wi-Fi. Singles US$23-40; doubles BZ$30-43; triples US$42-53. AmEx/MC/V. ❹

Lucia's Guesthouse, 68 San Antonio Rd. (☎322 2244). Walk south along Queen Victoria Ave., turn right at the fire station, and continue along San Antonio Rd. for 15min. It's a schlep to get to this well-advertised hotel on the western outskirts of town, but the rooms are cheap and generally clean, though bare. Swimming pool. Rooms with fan US$13; with TV US$15; with bath and TV US$17; with A/C US$33. MC/V. ❷

Hotel de la Fuente, 14 Main St. (☎322 2290; www.hoteldelafuente.com). Bare-bones but very comfortable rooms near the river, with a leafy second-floor patio. Arranges Lamanai, Baboon Sanctuary, and cave tours (BZ$80-120). Free internet and Wi-Fi. All rooms with private bath. Rooms with 1 double bed and fan US$27, with A/C US$35; rooms with 1 double bed and 1 single bed with fan US$40, with A/C US$50. AmEx/MC/V. ❺

Hotel St. Christopher, (☎322 2420 or 302 1064; www.stchristophershotelbze.com). Right next to the Hotel de La Fuente, this older hotel's linoleum-floored rooms are spacious and spotless. Offers tours to Lamanai, Altun Ha, Cerros, and the Rio Bravo area for groups of 2-4 people (US$40-75). Internet US$2 per hr. Free Wi-Fi. Rooms US$25-50. MC/V. ❺

Lamanai Riverside Retreat, Lamanai Alley (☎302 3955). Walk toward the river from the bus stop, turn right on Riverside St., and then left at the sign. Isolated and charming spot right on the river. 3 rooms with double beds, colorful decor, and sparkling private bathrooms. Fan and cable TV. Complementary coffee in the morning. A popular outdoor restaurant and bar sits in front; see if you notice anything strange about the pictures of the Beatles above the bar. Free Wi-Fi. All rooms US$40. AmEx/MC/V. ❺

▣ FOOD

Orange Walk may be small, but its culinary offerings are arguably some of Belize's best. As evening approaches, the downtown area, already packed with fruit stands, fills up with street vendors hawking Mexican standards (more prevalent here than anywhere else in the country) and Belizean favorites. With delicious tacos and enchiladas going for only US$1-2, this may be the best dinner option for the budget traveler. The outdoor market operates during daylight hours behind the grassy Town Square. Just walk up Arthur St. from the bus stop. The biggest supermarket is **The People's Store** on Main St (Open M-F 8am-9pm. Sa and Su 10am-6pm. MC/V).

Juanita's Restaurant, Santa Ana St. (☎302 2677). Walk south down Queen Victoria Ave. and turn right just before the Shell station. A local favorite specializing in delicious Belizean recipes. Breakfast (US$2-3) includes combos of eggs, chicken, and beans, while dinner (US$3-3.50) features local standards like the ubiquitous rice-beans-chicken combo and cowfoot soup. Open M-Sa 6am-2pm and 6-9pm. Cash only. ❷

Roechelle's Restaurant, 25 Cemetery St. (☎302 1535). Walk south along Queen Victoria Ave. and turn left onto Cemetery St. Proudly owned by a hospitable Belizean family. Traditional homemade Belizean food US$5-7. Fresh-squeezed juices US$1-1.50. Open daily 7am-2:30pm and 5:30-8pm. Cash only. ❸

Panificadora la Popular, Bethias Lane (☎322 3229). Walk north along Queen Victoria Ave. and turn right onto Bethias Ln. They don't call Orange Walk "Sugar City" for nothing. This bakery and confectionery is usually bustling with locals eager to satisfy their sweet tooth. Chocolate cakes US$17-28, caramel cakes US$9-18, and cheesecakes US$7.50. Pizza BZ$7-8.50. Open M-F 6:30am-8pm, Sa 6:30am-8:30pm, Su 7:30am-3pm. Cash only. ❸

OK Restaurant, (☎322 1489). Walk up Queen Victoria Rd. from the clock tower. Orange Walk teems with Chinese restaurants, but word on the street is that this is one is better than OK. If Chinese (US$2.50-10) doesn't suit you, grab some Belizean seafood (US$6-10), or even some Texan meat dishes (US$7.50-17.50). Open M-Su 10:30am-11pm, Tu 10:30am-3pm. MC/V. ❸

Nahil Mayab (☎302 3358), at the corner of Santa Ana and Guadalupe St. Walk south along Queen Victoria Ave. and turn right onto Santa Ana St. before the Shell station. This new addition to Orange Walk's culinary scene is easily one of the fanciest, but it's still affordable. Wide range of food, from Mexican standbys like chicken fajitas (US$7) to Belizean seafood (shrimp creole US$10) and Italian pasta (US$12.50-15). Eat outside within the plant-lined, stone fence that separates the restaurant from its less luxurious surroundings. Inside, admire the Mayan-style carvings on the walls and the fake stalactites that hang over the bar. Appetizers US$2.50-7; entrees US$6-10; drinks US$1.50-3. Open M-W 7am-3pm, Th-Sa 7am-2pm and 6-11:30pm. AmEx/MC/V. ❹

👁 SIGHTS

If you're sticking around town to sample the food, a (very quick) visit to some of these moderately interesting historical sites won't hurt either.

BANQUITAS HOUSE OF CULTURE. Interesting exhibits on Orange Walk's history and culture, including the Mayan era, British rule, and modern times. The building itself is the highlight of a riverside plaza that plays host to an outdoor restaurant and an amphitheater. *(In Banquitas Plaza. ☎322 0517. Walk north on Queen Victoria St. and turn right at the police station. Open T-F 10am-6pm, Sa 8am-noon. Free.)*

LA IMMACULADA CHURCH. Dating from the 1890s, the church boasts an attention-grabbing exterior and a sizable front lawn perfect for lounging. Tombs of local religious figures, many of them foreigners, line the front of the building. An adjacent two-building Catholic school surrounds the church. *(Bethias Lane. Turn right onto Bethias Lane from Queen Victoria Ave. by the Town Square. Open M-Sa 10am-3pm. Services Su 9:30am.)*

FORT MUNDY. A desolate volleyball court marks the former site of the British fort that helped stop attacks from 150 Icaiche Maya in 1872, during the last years of the Caste War. A gazebo showcases a map of the fort's layout, while a crudely sculpted British soldier stands at the court's other end. *(Independence Plaza, directly to the north of the bridge over the New River. Walk north on Queen Victoria Ave. and cross right behind the police station.)*

GODOY'S ORCHID FARM. It's at least a 20min. walk north of town, but this large, family-owned garden

ON THE MENU

COWFOOT SOUP

There are plenty of reasons to try cowfoot soup while in Belize. It is a local delicacy, it is wholesome and nourishing, it combines reassuringly familiar tastes (potatoes, onions, peas, carrots) with the curious new texture of cow hooves and tripe, and it gives you the pleasure of discovering that cooked hooves soften until they feel like Jell-O. Despite all the reasons to eat the soup, most foreigners chicken out when it comes time to put hoof to mouth. Be strong; with enough seasoning, the soup will taste like... well, it will takes like cow feet and intestines. But, we promise it's good! Plus, you'll have a great story to tell your friends when you get home.

Don't worry, the feet have been boiling for long enough to release all the stuff you don't want to ingest. The once hard extremities have been transformed into tender deliciousness. Wash it all down with some Belikin beer and enjoy the sweet aftertaste.

with over 250 species of orchids (including the Black Orchid, Belize's national flower) is a must-see for the botanically inclined. *(Northern Highway. ☎ 322 2969. Personal tour US$5. If you want a quick trip, step aboard a northbound bus and ask to be dropped off at the farm: 5min., US$0.25.)*

⮞ DAYTRIPS FROM ORANGE WALK

LAMANAI

For many, getting to Lamanai is half the adventure. Most travelers visit the site via the New River. From Orange Walk, Jungle River Tours (p. 225) is the go-to company, with experienced tours of both the ruins and the wildlife. Many hotels in Orange Walk also arrange tours (p. 225). The standard rate for a guided tour is US$40, not including the US$5 admission fee. Trips last 6-7hr.; lunch is usually included. For those who want to bypass the Sugar City, Belize Global Adventure Tours, Discovery Expeditions, and S & L Travels and Tours run tours from Belize City (8hr., US$105-110). Tillet's buses occasionally run from the market in Orange Walk to Indian Church, the closest village to the ruins (2hr.; M, W, and F 3pm; US$2). Open daily 8am-5pm.

One of the true highlights of Belize, a jewel nestled deep inside the northern jungles beside the New River Lagoon, Lamanai ("submerged crocodile," a reference to a Mayan creation myth) has enticed countless visitors by the boatload since its excavation in the early 1970s. Lamanai is famous for its ruins which date as far back as 1500 BC and nestled near 17th-century Spanish relics. Lamanai's location on the New River established the city as a major trading point between Belizes inland and the coast. Between 200 BC and AD 700, Lamanai became known as a major economic and religious center, with a population of about 35,000. When the Spanish arrived in the early 16th century, the Mayan population in the city was still quite active. The Spanish brought several fatal European diseases which devastated the community despite its successful efforts to destroy the Spanish mission in the 1600s. By the late 18th century Lamanai was a mere vestige of its former self.

A walk through Lamanai can take up to 2hr. give that the site is large and spread out. The first major ruin as you enter from the river is the **Jaguar Temple** (Structure N10-9), which dates from the AD sixth century. Two jaguar faces glare from the temple's base. The holes in these patterns were once used as small incense chambers. Across the plaza lie several royal bedrooms, with stone beds that are nearly 1000 years old. On your right, another temple, fronted by a stone tablet, is intricately carved with glyphs and a royal portrait. This is **Stela 9**, a replica dating from AD 625 that was used to commemorate the royal accession of Lord Smoking Shell. Moving to the west, walk through the ball court to the tallest structure, **N10-43,** which rises well above tree level and affords gorgeous views of the surrounding jungle and river. A six minute walk through the jungle brings you to the **Mask Temple,** whose lower-right-hand corner bears the huge facial relief of a proud ruler. Excavators found this relief under a staircase constructed by another ruler who had sought to erase the memory of his predecessor. If you have any energy left at the end of your visit, head 400 yards south from the docks to the remains of two Colonial churches. These structures were built by Mayan slave labor and later were destroyed in Mayan rebellion. There are gift stores and a small museum near the entrance by the docks.

CUELLO AND NOHMUL

Cuello is most easily accessed by simply walking the 2½ mi. from Orange Walk. Walk south along Queen Victoria Ave. and turn right after the fire station onto San Antonio Rd. Continue straight for about an hour until you see the Cuello Distillery on your right; the site is beyond the distillery grounds. Since the ruins stand on private property, call *ahead (☎ 320 9085) before you head out. A taxi can take you there and back (30min., every 1½hr., US$25). If you have a car, drive north on the Northern Highway to San Pablo, then follow the signs to Nohmul.*

Cuello, Lamanai's much older but much poorer cousin, features ruins from an ancient Mayan town dating back to 2400 BC. The town functioned as a small agricultural center. Only a small pyramid-shaped temple, now overgrown, survives as evidence of its existence. Pottery, farming tools, and even tombs have been uncovered here. Nohmul ("great mound") was a grander place in its heyday, housing 3000 people. Its history was, however, turbulent. Reaching importance between 350 BC and AD 250, Nohmul was virtually deserted for much of the Classic Period before its revitalization in the 800s and 900s, when it ruled the surrounding area. Like Cuello, Nohmul is now abandoned and quite untouristed, so much so that parts of it were accidentally bulldozed in the 1990s. For a good view of the vicinity, check out the top of Structure 2.

RIO BRAVO CONSERVATION AND MANAGEMENT AREA

The Rio Bravo Conservation and Management Area is accessible only by private vehicle. See the Intercity Transportation for Belize City (p. 192) for information on renting a car. Otherwise, contact the Programme for Belize (PFB) to arrange transit from Belize City. To reach the La Milpa Field Station, drive 1½hr. from Orange Walk through Yo Creek, San Felipe, and Blue Creek Village. To reach the Hill Bank field station, turn off the Northern Highway towards Burrell Boom Village and continue through Bermudian Landing and Rancho Dolores. The trip takes about 2hr. from Belize City. Lodging arrangements must be made in advance with the PFB. Contact them at 1 Eyre St. in Belize City (☎ 227 5616 or 227 5617; www.pfbelize.org).

A true isolated jungle experience awaits devoted travelers in Belize's northwestern corner. **The Rio Bravo Conservation and Management Area (RBCMA)** covers nearly 206,000 acres of sub-tropical rainforest, 4% of Belize's total land mass. Once the site of powerful Mayan cities, the area was ravaged by loggers in search of mahogany in the 19th and 20th centuries. Preservation began in the late 1980s and 1990s, when a group of companies and trusts, including Coca-Cola Foods, donated land to the nonprofit **Programme for Belize (PFB)**, founded specifically to preserve the area.

Today the goals of the PFB are several: to preserve the rainforest (with over 200 tree species), protect wildlife (392 bird and 72 mammal species, including 39 endangered species), and to promote safe ecotourism to the 60 Mayan ruins in the area. The most treasured among these ruins is **La Milpa**, Belize's third-largest Mayan ruin. Once a metropolis of 50,000, Milpa's five-acre Great Plaza dwarfs most others in Belize.

More than a day is necessary to fully explore the Rio Bravo. The PFB offers lodging in the area at two field stations. **La Milpa Field Station,** in the northwest, near the ruins and about a 1½hr. drive from Orange Walk, offers dormitories (US$100) and thatched-roof cabanas (US$125), all with private bath, hot water, fan, and veranda. A full slate of meals and a busy itinerary, including birding walks, guided tours of La Milpa, and visits to local *Mestizo* and Mennonite communities is included. **Hill Bank Field Station,** accessible by road through Bermudian Landing and Rancho Dolores, lies in the southeast corner, near the New River Lagoon and Lamanai. It rents similar dorms and cabanas at the same price, with tours including canoe trips on the lagoon and boat trips to Lamanai.

SARTENEJA AND THE SHIPSTERN NATURE RESERVE

A tiny fishing village perched on Belize's northeastern corner, Sarteneja serves as an entry point to the Shipstern Nature Reserve three and a half miles inland. Sarteneja is an ideal spot to observe the gentle rhythms of coastal life. Watch villagers paint or repair their wooden boats, while fishermen ply their trade in the waters nearby.

▣ TRANSPORTATION. The most convenient way to reach the village is by **Thunderbolt boat** (☎422 0026).Thunderbolts leave **Corozal** and **San Pedro** at 7am and 3pm. They only stop in Sarteneja by request, so be sure to tell the boat crew your plans before departure. If you're leaving from Sarteneja by water, call Thunderbolt (☎422-0026) well in advance of departure time so they can pick you up. Trips to Corozal are US$12.50; to San Pedro US$23.

There's also a select **bus** service that travels to and from Sarteneja, Orange Walk, and Belize City. To get a ride from the village, wake up early. Two to three buses leave Monday-Saturday from Sarteneja for Orange Walk and Belize City between 5am-7am. They'll circle the village to wake potential passengers up, but the most convenient point to grab one is by the road leading into and out of town.

▰▱ ORIENTATION AND PRACTICAL INFORMATION. Like Corozal, Sarteneja is arranged in a fairly straightforward grid pattern by the coast. Unlike Corozal, the streets aren't numbered. You probably won't get lost in this tiny village, though, so feel free to stroll the tranquil streets without worry. The **dirt entry and exit road** can be reached by walking one block into town from the coast and turning right. After 10-15min., you'll reach the "Welcome to Sartneja" sign and the turnoff to Backpacker's Paradise.

⌂ ACCOMMODATIONS. There are a few inns and guesthouses in the village, but the true backpacker will want to head a little out of town to find his ideal home at **Backpacker's Paradise ❶**. Walk down the entry road to the "Welcome to Sarteneja" sign (15min.) and turn left. The Paradise is a one minute walk further down. Not just any place to stay, Backpacker's Paradise stretches over 27 acres of Sarteneja's environs. The grounds are filled with jungles, orchards, and farmland. You can take several trails through the wilderness or, if you like, go by horse. The large screen windows in the *cabañas* will make you feel like you're in the midst of the jungle. When you wake up, pluck some fresh mangos from the trees overhead. The friendly young French couple who run the place operate a small restaurant serving crepes (US$2-7) and other French and Caribbean specialties. (☎403 2051; www.blueandgreen.org. *Cabañas* with shared bathroom US$10, with private bathroom BZ$35. Camping BZ$6. Restaurant open 8am-8pm. Cash only.)

❒ FOOD. Sarteneja has a few modest eateries, but nothing of particular note. If you find yourself yearning for a bite in the village, stroll around and select from the number of small fast food shacks selling cheap Belizean and Mexican snacks. If you're willing to take a short walk (or if you're staying there anyway), check out **Backpacker's Paradise** (p. 230). Chances are you'll meet a few colorful locals and some fellow travelers.

▰ DAYTRIPS FROM SARTENEJA: THE SHIPSTERN NATURE RESERVE. Covering 27,000 acres in the driest area in Belize, Shipstern includes a remarkable variety of climates, terrains, and wildlife. The Reserve is one of Belize's top destinations for birdwatchers, who gaze admirably at the more than 300 species who call Shipstern home, including the endangered American Woodstork. Other creatures, including the full gamut of Belize's large cat population (Ocelots, Margays, Pumas, Jaguars, and Jaguaroundis), countless bats and butterflies (over 270 species), and 70 reptile and amphibian species, reside in the protected zone. Baird's Tapir, another rare species, lives in and around the Xo-Pol pond region, one of the main attractions for visitors.

The Shipstern forest, devastated by Hurricane Janet in 1955, has been re-growing ever since and now holds dozens of tree species and ten different veg-etation types. The headquarters by the road includes a small visitor's **museum** with exhibits describing the Reserve's history, flora, and fauna, as well as a **butterfly garden** displaying local species. To fully explore the region beyond the botanical trail (with almost 100 tree species labeled), look into renting the reserve's vehicles. A 45min. drive will bring you to an overlook nestled in the trees, providing views of a remote pond with accompanying wildlife (deer, crocodiles, and a range of waterfowl like the Reddish Egret and Rose-ate Spoonbill). You can also take guided boat tours of the lagoon areas. The wetlands attract many mosquitoes and other pests, so dress accordingly (long sleeves and pants, closed-toe shoes) and bring plenty of bug spray.

The Reserve's remote location makes arrival difficult for those without cars. To reach it you can take a very early morning **bus** (a few 5-7am) from Sarteneja and ask to be dropped off at the entrance to the Reserve (you'll have to wait a bit for the 8am opening). Ask the visitor's center for a ride back to the village (though it's never guaranteed). Otherwise, ask your lodgings for rides in and out of the area. Many Sarteneja guesthouses are partners with the Reserve. *(Headquarters along the Orange Walk-Sarteneja road 3½ mi. from the village; www.shipstern.org. US$5. Open daily open 8am-5pm.)*

COROZAL   ☎04

A sleepy seaside town that has miraculously avoided the tourist plague, Corozal (population 9100) lies just nine miles south of the Mexican border. The place is perfect for relaxing: ocean breezes seem to have lulled the town into a languid state far removed from the market bustle of Orange Walk and the tourist frenzy of San Pedro. Most use Corozal as a transit point on the way to and from Mexico or the northern Cayes. Still, a stay of more than a few hours here can provide cool and uncrowded relaxation under the shaded *palapas* in the waterfront parks.

▐▀ TRANSPORTATION

Flights: Corozal's **airstrip** is located about 1 mi. south of the city. To avoid a walk, take a taxi (BZ$8-10) to and from the city. **Maya Island Air** (☎225 2219; www.mayaislandair.com) and **Tropic Air** (☎225 2302; www.tropicair.com) both fly to **San Pedro** (20-25min.; every 2hr. 7:30am-3:30pm; one-way US$45, round-trip US$45).

Buses: The **bus station** is on the corner of 7th Ave. and 1st St. South. **Southbound** buses leave for **Orange Walk** (1¼hr., US$1.50) and **Belize City** (2¾hr., US$2.50) every 30min. 3:45am-7:30pm. Additional buses head only to **Orange Walk** (1¼hr., US$1.50) every 30min. from noon-4pm. **Northbound** buses leave Santa Elena on the border with Mexico (15min., US$0.25) every 30min. between 8:30am and 10pm.

Taxis: Taxi stands are located on the corner of Park St. and 1st St. South and in Central Park at the corner of 5th Ave. and 1st St. South.

Water Taxis: **Thunderbolt water taxis** (☎422 0026) leave from the dock at the end of 2nd St South for **Sarteneja** (30min.; one-way US$12.50, round-trip US$25) and **San Pedro** (2hr.; US$23/43) daily at 7am and 3pm.

◼▧ ORIENTATION AND PRACTICAL INFORMATION

Corozal spreads out along the bay of the same name in a grid pattern (a vestige of the rebuilding done after Hurricane Janet devastated the town in 1955), so navigation is easier than in most Belizean towns. However, many street signs are missing, especially in areas farther from the center. **Avenues run parallel to the coast (north-south) and streets run east-west.** Directions are complicated by the duplication of streets—1st St. North, for example, has a southern counterpart. Buses drop passengers off at **7th Avenue** and **1st Street South.** Walking down **2nd Street South,** you'll pass the **Central Park,** with its sky-blue **clock tower.** The **pier** for Thunderbolt skiffs leaving for San Pedro lies at the coastal end of 2nd St. South.

Tours and Agencies: Vitalino Reyes (☎602 8975; www.cavetubing.bz) is a travel agent, offering cave tubing and other adventures around the country from his home base in Corozal. He'll also take you to the Belize Zoo. The **George and Esther Moralez Travel Service** (☎422 2485; www.gettransfers.com), based out of the Corozal Airstrip, 1 mi. to the south of town, arranges tours to Altun Ha, the Belize Zoo, Lamanai, Placencia, and more. Travel service to the Mexican border and to all points in Belize.

Banks: Scotiabank, 4th Ave. Open M-Th 8am-2pm, F 8am-3:30pm, Sa 9-11:30am. **Atlantic Bank,** corner of 3rd St. North and 4th Ave. Open M-Th 8am-3pm and F 8am-4pm. **Belize Bank,** 5th Ave. by Central Park. Open M-Th 8am-3pm, F 8am-4:30pm.

Police Station: (☎422 2022), corner of 5th Ave. and 1st St. North.

Pharmacy: Annie's Pharmacy, 7th Ave. near the bus station. Open M-F 8am-10pm, Su 8am-7pm.

Hospital: The **Corozal Hospital,** (☎422 2076), 1 mi. northwest of town on the way to Chetumal.

Internet Access: BluePC, corner of 1st St. South and 4th Ave. (☎422 2828). Above the Shun Li Fashion Shop. US$1.50 per hr. Open M-Sa 9am-8pm. **Stellar Links,** 4th Ave. and 3rd St. N. (☎402 2043). Internet US$2 per hr. International calls US$2.50 per 15min. Skype access. Open M-F 8am-7pm, Sa 8am-5pm. **Gamaa Computer Center,** 22 4th Ave (☎422 0225), on the corner of 4th Ave. and 4th St. North. US$2 per hr. Open M-Sa 7am-7:30pm.

Post Office: 5th Ave. by Central Park. Open M-Th 8:30am-noon and 1-4pm, F 8:30am-noon and 1-4:30pm.

⌂ ACCOMMODATIONS

Like Orange Walk, Corozal's location has given rise to a number of lodgings, from bare bones to luxury seacoast. Luckily, you can find quiet rooms on the coast with plenty of amenities for a small charge.

Sea Breeze Hotel, 23 1st Ave. (☎422 3051, www.theseabreezehotel.com). From the park, walk down to 1st Ave. by the sea and head left for 10min. Set on beautiful and isolated coastal real estate, the Sea Breeze is as luxurious as budget accommodations get. There may be a Welsh flag flying above (the owner's proud declaration of nationality), but the decor inside, with its fishing maps and aquatic blue walls, pledges allegiance only to the sea. Bar on 2nd floor (drinks US$1-4.50) and a veranda overlooking the bay. All rooms with double beds, cable TVs, and private baths. Free Wi-Fi. Budget rooms with fan US$17.50; economy rooms with fan US$20; premium rooms with A/C US$25-30. 9% tax for each guest. MC/V. ❺

Maya World Guest House, 16 2nd St. (☎666 3577), north between 6th and 7th Avenues (☎666 3577). From the bus station, walk right on 7th Ave. and turn left on 2nd St. North. This 2-story house near the bus station holds several spacious, breezy rooms with large windows. Hammocks strung up on the porch for lounging. Kitchen and cooking areas downstairs. All rooms with fans. Singles US$22.50; doubles US$25.50. Cash only. ❹

Corozal Guest House, 22 6th Ave (☎402 0634). From the bus station, turn right on 6th Ave. Convenient (if not spectacular coastal) location and a double bed, fan, and private bath in each spare, clean room. This cheap offering will appeal to those just passing through town. Rooms US$17.50. Cash only. ❸

Hok'ol K'in Guest House (☎422 3329; www.corozal.net). From the park turn right on 4th Ave. and continue for 3 blocks. Each spotless room at this large waterfront hotel comes with a patio with an ocean view. The Mayan name means "rising sun." All rooms with private baths and cable TVs. Restaurant downstairs serves Belizean dishes (US$3-5). Tours to Mayan ruins at Lamanai and Cerros. Free Wi-Fi. Singles US$21, with fan US$38, with A/C US$46; doubles US$34/52/60. MC/V. ❹

Mirador Hotel (☎422 0189; www.mirador.bz), corner of 4th Ave. and 3rd St. South. One of the most noticeable buildings in town, a 4-fl. behemoth with large rooms, many of them with ocean views. Terraces wind their way around the building, allowing for lounging in the breeze. The **Romantic Restaurant and Bar** is on the building's ground floor. Internet US$1 per hr. Free Wi-Fi. Singles with fan US$35, with A/C US$50; doubles US$45/60. AmEx/MC/V. ❺

Hotel Maya (☎422 2082; www.hotelmaya.net). Walk down to the sea from the park, turn right, and continue along the coast for 15min. This waterfront guesthouse is a bit out of the way, but the affordable, sumptuously decorated seaside rooms make the hike worth it. All rooms with cable TVs and private baths. Includes travel agency and restaurant. Free Wi-Fi. Singles with fan BZ$55, with A/C BZ$70; double BZ$60/75. Small but gorgeous apartments for rent BZ$700 a month. AmEx/MC/V. ❹

Caribbean Village (☎422 2725; www.belizetransfers.com). From town, turn right along the coast and continue by the shore for 20min. For the cheapest digs in Corozal, pitch your tent at this campground right by the ocean (though inconveniently distant from town). It's right by the main road leading into town, so expect the sweet sounds of passing cars to lull you to sleep. Showers and restrooms provided. US$5 per night. MC/V.

FOOD

The streets may be lazy, but the kitchens are busy preparing a teeming multitude of local and foreign fare. Nearly every block has a few eateries to satisfy the cravings of hungry travelers. For groceries, try **Gabrielle Hoare market,** with outdoor fruit stands and a two-story building with small restaurants on the upper level (right behind the bus station between 6th Ave. and 7th Ave. and 1st St. North and 1st St. South). Likewise, **Central Supermarket** (Park St.; ☎422-0096; open daily 7am-9pm). **Amelio Reyes & Sons Supermarket,** 4th Ave., 2 blocks away from Central Park. Open M-Sa 8am-7pm, Su 8am-noon.

Romantic Bar and Restaurant (☎422 0013), in the basement of the Mirador Hotel. A highlight of the countless Chinese restaurants that populate Corozal, this ground-floor component of the 4-story Mirador Hotel serves Chinese standards in a large, sparse room hung with Chinese lanterns and cooled by strategically placed fans. Order take out and eat by the shore. Meals US$3.50-7; salads US$5-8. Open daily 10am-10pm. Cash only. ❷

RD's Diner (☎422 3796), near the corner of 4th Ave. and 4th St. North. A spiffy, sit-down restaurant offering Belizean standards (rice, bean, and meat combos US$3.50-4.50) as well as international food and swankier nightly specials (US$7.50-10). Open daily 8am-8pm. AmEx/MC/V. ❸

Marcello's Pizza, corner of 4th Ave. and 3rd St. North. If you're feeling homesick for American cooking, Marcello's—promising "a taste of America"—is the ideal cure. Pizza US$3.50-5; BBQ chicken and ribs US$3-4.50; ice cream US$1-2. Open daily 11am-10pm. Cash only. ❷

H.L. Diner, on the 2nd floor of the Gabrielle Hoare building by the outdoor market. The "H.L" stands for "healthy living"; this diner promises nutritional Belizean and Mexican meals (US$2.50-5), all cooked in soybean. Enjoy the breezy view over the outdoor market and Corozal rooftops from the veranda. Open daily 8am-6pm. Cash only. ❷

Al's Cafe, 5th Ave. and 2nd St. South. The setting is cramped—you'll literally be eating on the sidewalk—but this small eatery shouldn't be missed. Ultra-cheap Belizean breakfasts of ham, bacon, and eggs with rice and beans US$2-3.50. Mexican lunch and dinner offerings of burritos, tortillas, and gamaches US$0.50-1. Open M-Sa 8am-2pm, W, F, and Sa 6-10pm. Cash only. ❶

La Casa Restaurant, 147 5th Ave. (☎605 0159), on the corner of 5th Ave. and 5th St. South. True to its name, this Mexican food joint is run out of the owner's house. Mexican standards like *escabeche, chilmole,* and *frijol con puerco* US$3.50-6. Open M-Th 11:30am-5:30pm, F-Sa 11:30am-2pm and 6:30-10pm, Su 11:30am-4:30pm. Cash only. ❷

◉ SIGHTS

A stroll along the waterfront parks may be the best thing to do in Corozal. If you're feeling adventurous, head inland to check out the town's very own Mayan ruins.

SANTA RITA. The "ancient Corozal" once occupied roughly the same area as the modern Corozal. Today, Santa Rita is a small ruin site mainly consisting of one pyramid. The structure itself is by no means the most remarkable find in Belize, but from the top you can catch a view of the turquoise waters lapping Corozal's shores. Enjoy the breeze and imagine the old glory of this town that once took advantage of the trade routes on the Rio Hondo and New River to carve out its place in the Mayan world. *(To reach the ruins, head north on Santa Rita Rd. (stretching north of the bus station) and turn left after about 15-20min. at the Super Santa Rita store. After 10min., you'll see a forested area on the right that houses the Santa Rita ruins. Free.)*

◉ NIGHTLIFE

Corozal nightlife isn't exactly a raucous thrill ride. Many places shut down before 10pm, with only a few establishments keeping the taps running into the wee hours. If you do go out, be careful; Corozal isn't reputed to be especially dangerous, but some assaults have been known to occur after dark.

Cactus Plaza, 6th St. South (☎422 0394), between 4th and 5th Ave. The building itself, an extravagant, Gaudi-inspired bric-à-brac, makes the trek out from town center worth it. Mexican food US$3.50-7.50. Karaoke F and Su. DJ Sa. Open F-Su 6pm-1am. MC/V.

Vamp's Chill and Grill, 1st Ave. (☎402 2141). From the park, walk to the shore, turn right at the coast, and continue for 10min. By day Vamp's ice cream shop (US$1-2), to the side of the main building, draws kids excited to consume scoops; by night, an older crowd arrives to party under thatched roofs, right by the ocean. Drinks US$2.50-5.

Purple Toucan (☎422 2727), on the corner of 4th Ave. and 3rd St. North. The Toucan looks like a small purple shack on the street, but its diverse nightlife draws the locals. Options include outdoor seating, an indoor bar, and a pool table. Drinks US$2-5. Open daily 7am-midnight. Cash only.

CAYO DISTRICT

The Western Highway bisects Belize horizontally, cutting across the Cayo District and offering an avenue to rugged jungle adventure for those tired of the sandy beaches. Far from the sea and the grassy savannas of northern Belize, and nestled within the lush greenery of the Maya Mountains, the Cayo District is Belize's only highland region. Along the Western Highway, Monkey Bay Wildlife Sanctuary and Guanacaste National Park tease travelers with hints of

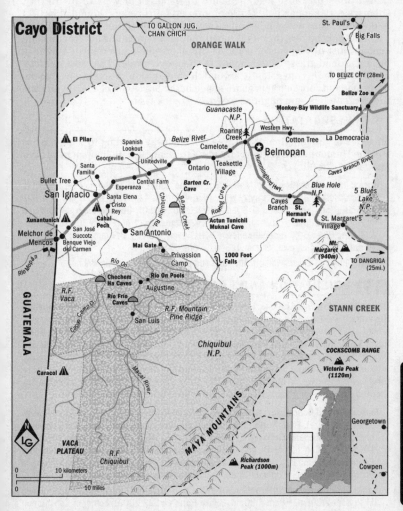

the tropical forests to come. From Mennonite farmland to the Maya village of San José Sucotz, this may be Belize's most culturally diverse district. Cayo is a mecca for outdoor adventure tourists, and San Ignacio makes a good base from which to explore the ruins, caves, and rivers of the region. Highlights include the Mountain Pine Ridge Reserve, with caves, waterfalls, refreshingly cool temperatures, and Caracol, the largest Mayan site in Belize.

BELMOPAN

Charmless Belmopan (pop. 17,500) is strategically placed at the junction of the Western and Hummingbird highways, making the city a convenient transit point for those heading south to Dangriga or west to Belize City. Otherwise, Belmopan holds little of interest for travelers. Founded in 1971 to provide Belize with a new capital after Hurricane Hattie wiped out Belize City ten years before, the city is mostly suburbia spreading out from a small center. Most of this center consists of unappealing government buildings placed around grassy plazas, many of them overgrown. The most interesting area by far is conveniently around the bus station, where shops, restaurants, and outdoor markets share space in the intriguing chaos. If you have to wait for a bus, you might as well pay a quick visit.

▐ TRANSPORTATION

Since it's at the junction of the Western Highway (leading to San Ignacio) and the Hummingbird Highway (leading to Dangriga), Belmopan is a major hub for bus traffic.

> **Buses:** The **bus station** is in Market Sq., at the corner of Constitution Dr. and Bliss Parade. Buses to: **Belize City** (1½hr., every 30 min. 4am-7:30 pm, US$1.50); **San Ignacio** (1hr., every 30min. 7:30am-midnight, US$1.50); **Benque Viejo del Carmen** (1½hr., every 30min. 7:30am-midnight, US$2); **Dangriga** (1¼hr., every 30min. 6:30am-7:30pm, US$1.50), **Independence** (2½hr., every 30min. 6:30am-5pm, US$2.50); **Punta Gorda** (4hr., every 30min. 6:30am-5pm, US$4).

> **Taxis:** Cabs and drivers wait outside (and sometimes inside) the bus station.

▐▌ ORIENTATION AND PRACTICAL INFORMATION

Belmopan is just southeast of the junction between the **Western** and **Hummingbird Highways;** two turnoffs connect the city with the Hummingbird. The heart of town—the government center and the market area—is surrounded by **North Road, South Road,** and **East Ring Road.** The western side is formed by **Constitution Drive.** The **bus station** is at the corner of Constitution Drive and **Bliss Parade,** which curves to meet **South Ring Road.** Around the bus station is a bustling shopping center known as **Market Square.** To the east, several **pedestrian walkways** cut through the grassy plazas, the largest of which is **Independence Plaza.**

> **Embassies and Consulates: US Embassy,** Floral Park Rd. (☎822 4011; www.usembassy. state.gov/belize). From North Ring Rd., turn left on Floriana Ave. Open M-F 8am-noon and 1-5pm. **Mexican Embassy,** Embassy Sq. (☎822 0406; www.sre.gob.mx/belice), at the corner of Constitution Dr. and North Ring Rd. Open M-F 9am-12:30pm. **British High Commission,** Embassy Sq. (☎822 2146; www.britishhighcommission.gov.uk), next to the Mexican Embassy. Open M-Th 8am-noon and 1-4pm, F 8am-2pm.

> **Bank: First Caribbean International Bank,** Courthouse Pl., off Melhado Parade. Open M-Th 8am-2:30pm, F 8am-4:30pm. **Belize Bank** (☎822 2303), corner of Constitution

Dr. and Melhado Parade. Open M-Th 8am-3pm, F 8am-4:30pm. **Scotiabank,** across from Belize Bank. Open M-Th 8am-2pm, F 8am-3:30pm, Sa 9am-11:30am.

Police Station: Off Bliss Parade, 5min. from the bus station.

Pharmacy: No less than 5 pharmacies dot the market area around the bus station. **Cardinal Pharmacy,** Constitution Dr. (☎822 3065). Open M-F 8:30am-7pm, Sa 9am-2pm. **Friendly Pharmacy** (☎822 2807), in Market Sq., across the street from the bus station. Open M-F 7:30am-6pm, Sa 8am-5pm.

Hospital: Belmopan Hospital (☎822 2264), enter at the corner of Constitution Dr. and North Ring Rd. 24hr. emergency service.

Internet Access: Angelus Press, Constitution Dr. (☎822 3866). US$1.50 per hr. Open M-F 7:30am-5:30pm, Sa 8am-noon. **Pross Computers,** Constitution Dr. (☎601 3529). Internet US$2.25 per hr. **PC.Com** (☎822 2449), in Market Square. Internet US$2 per hr. Open M-F 8am-7pm, Sa 8am-noon.

Post Office: Off Bliss Parade, 5min. from the bus station. Open M-Th 8am-noon and 1-5pm, F 8am-4:30pm.

▐ ACCOMMODATIONS

If you're forced to spend a night in Belmopan, be aware that true budget options are sorely lacking.

El-Rey Inn, 23 Moho St. (☎822 3438; www.belmopan hotels). From Constitution Dr., turn onto North Ring Rd., walk north for 15min., turn right on Nanche St., and turn right on Moho St. The cheapest rooms in Belmopan are bare, with white walls and linoleum floors. Despite its inconvenient location, the inn is clean and quiet. Rooms with fan US$22.20; family rooms US$37.50. MC/V. ❹

Hibiscus Hotel (☎822 1418; www.belmopanhotels.com), off Melhado Parade. Turn right on Melhado Pde. from Constitution Dr. Owned by the same family who runs El-Rey, the Hibiscus offers much more appealing digs: rooms are colorful, decorated, and spotless. They're also more expensive. Singles with fan US$32.50; doubles with A/C and TV US$47.50; triples US$55. MC/V. ❺

Belmopan Hotel, Bliss Parade (☎822 2340). The rooms here are a bit grungy for the price, with splotched carpets and bare walls. However, Belmopan's location next to the bus station and pool in the middle of the courtyard more than compensate. Free Wi-Fi. Doubles with A/C and cable TV US$60; triples US$65. MC/V. ❺

▐ FOOD

The area around the bus station, **Market Square,** is packed with small fast food restaurants. North of the station stretches a large **outdoor market** full of stands selling fruit, clothes, handicrafts, and bootlegged DVDs.

Caladium Restaurant, Market Sq. (☎822 2754), across from the bus station. A Belmopan favorite, this convenient restaurant serves Belizean specialties (rice and bean plates, US$4-6), grilled food (steak and pork, US$9-11), and Caribbean seafood (shrimp creole and fish fillet, US$7.50-15) in an immaculate and well-decorated setting cooled by fans. Burgers US$2-5.50. Salads US$-6. MC/V. ❷

Seri's Restaurant, Market Sq. (☎809 3970), across from the bus station. This 2nd-floor Chinese restaurant boasts better decor than most in Belize, with a large Chinese gate protecting the entrance to the restrooms. Curry dishes BZ$7.50-10; fried rice US$2.50-7.50; chow mein BZ$3-7.50. Open daily 9am-9pm. Cash only. ❸

◉ SIGHTS

GUANACASTE NATIONAL PARK

Catch any westbound bus (heading toward Benque Viejo del Carmen), and ask to be let off at the park, right along the Western Highway, at the turnoff to Belmopan (15min., BZ$1). Open daily 8am-4:30pm. BZ$5.

The smallest of Belize's many national parks (250,000 sq. yd.) provides a welcome and ready escape from the dullness of Belmopan. Named for the huge guanacaste tree that grows on its grounds, the park offers hiking trails with marked plants and trees. Though it's difficult to spend more than a few hours here, the park may be best used as a place to lounge and relax; the grounds are shady and there's a small pool for swimming open to visitors. On the weekends, local families from nearby towns and villages often have picnics on the park ground.

◉ NIGHTLIFE

One of Belmphan's few bar options is **Charishma,** across from the bus station. This small bar has a porch and pool tables in the back. Charishma's early closing hour makes it more of a place for day lounging than a nightspot, but it's an ideal place to rest up and grab a drink while waiting for buses. (Drinks US$1.50-5. Open daily 11am-8pm.)

◉ DAYTRIPS FROM BELMOPAN

BELIZE ZOO

29 mi. off the Western Highway, between Belize City and Belmopan. ☎ 220 8004; www. belizezoo.org. From Belmopan, take any Belize City-bound bus (or any Belmopan-bound bus from Belize City) and ask to be let off at the zoo. The grounds are a 2min. walk from the highway. On the way back, flag down a bus going in the direction you want. Open daily 8:30am-5pm. Night tours US$50 for 1-4 people; US$10 per person for groups of 5 or more. Guides can be hired during the day for US$25. Those who want or need to spend the night at the zoo can lodge at its Tropical Education Center (☎ 220 8003), just under a mile away. Camping US$5 per person; dorms US$31; forest cabañas US$66; VIP guesthouse US$71.50. Meals included.

The Belize Zoo is a worthwhile stop for anyone who wants an up-close look at the diversity of Belize's wildlife. The zoo had its start in 1983, when naturalist Sharon Matola was left with 17 animals she had been hired to care for during the filming of a documentary. From the start, the rules for acquiring new animals were strict and ensured a minimum of interference with the wild: only those injured, orphaned, bred in captivity, or seized from illegal owners were to be placed in the zoo. Today, after a renovation in 1991, the zoo's 29 acres house nearly 40 species native to Belize. Spider and howler monkeys swing from trees, huge jabiru storks flaunt their 12 ft. wingspan, jaguars and pumas prowl (or lounge), and tapirs (Belize's national animal, colloquially known as a "mountain cow") enjoy their fame. The birds here are the real stars: brown pelicans, great egrets, hawks, owls, eagles, and five species of parrot all call the zoo their home. Highlights are the massive harpy eagles, the largest in the world, and the beautifully colored (and rare) scarlet macaws, who can be found near the zoo entrance. The zoo itself still feels like a personal labor of love; each animal is introduced by a group of hand-painted signs describing it, much of the message warning against man's harmful effect on nature. The zoo is small and easily navigated. Those who want a unique and more personal look at the exhibits can take a night tour, led by a guide who's usually on a first-name basis with most of the animals.

MONKEY BAY WILDLIFE SANCTUARY

Any bus running between Belize City and Belmopan can drop you off here, 31 mi. along the Western Highway. The research headquarters are about 100m down the gravel road. On the way back, flag down a bus on the highway. Research Station ☎820 3032; www. monkeybaybelize.org. Free Wi-Fi. Camping US$3; dorms US$16.50; private rooms with shared bath US$22.50. Meals US$10.

Conveniently located just off the Western Highway, two miles west of the Belize Zoo, Monkey Bay is a fairly small (1.7 sq. mi.) but unique sanctuary along the Sibun River. The Sanctuary protects tropical forest and savannah regions, 300 species of birds, and a few howler monkeys who give the site its name. Founded by a Dutch-American conservationist couple, the sanctuary currently hosts a constant stream of student groups, from budding college biologists running field studies to lucky American fifth-graders on extended educational camp trips. It's also a tourist-friendly place, offering convenient, fairly inexpensive lodging and meals. A nature trail leads through the savannah, while a 30min. walk along the road to the river is a good introduction to the local flora and fauna. Those who want to explore the nearby **Sibun** can rent canoes. Across the river stretches the **Monkey Bay National Park,** much larger than the sanctuary and not so amenable to tourists; those who want to explore this region will need to inquire at the research station, which also arranges tours to many nearby destinations.

For those in search of a bite to eat, **Amigos Restaurant and Bar ❷** (☎822 3031), just west of Monkey Bay, serves delicious lunches and dinners (US$5-11.50), from burgers and sandwiches (US$5-9) to steamed chicken and beef (US$9) and Mexican dishes (US$9). Though the roof is thatched and the windows made of mosquito net, the campy bumper stickers lining the walls and American music blasting from the speakers will make you feel like you made a detour into the States. (Drinks US$1.50-3.50. Happy hour daily 5-7pm. Open 10am-9pm. MC/V.)

SAN IGNACIO

Sprawling over the hilly terrain of the western Cayo district, San Ignacio (population 19,000) is a picturesque Belizean town. Upper verandas open out on views of busy, winding streets and verdant hills dotted with houses. Ideally located near a plethora of outdoor activities, San Ignacio has become Belize's second most popular tourist destination. The wilds of Cayo are unforgettable destinations, but spend some time in town too—good restaurants are plentiful, the locals friendly, and the banks of the Macal River wonderful resting grounds.

▐ TRANSPORTATION

Intercity Buses: Arrive at and depart from an unmarked stand in the square in the town center, next to the Savannah Taxi Drivers' Co-Op building. Buses to: **Belmopan** (1hr., every 30min. 6:30am-8pm, US$1.50); **Belize City** (2hr., every 30min. 6:30am-8pm, US$2.50); **Benque Viejo del Carmen** (30min., every 30min. 7am-6:30pm, US$1). **Amigos Bus Service** (☎626 6795 or 804 4676), at the foot of the Hawkesworth Bridge on the Santa Elena side, still arranges pickups with the San Juan and Linea dorada bus lines. Express buses to: **Chetumal, Mexico** (4hr., daily 9am, US$25); **Flores, GUA** (3hr.,

CAYO DISTRICT

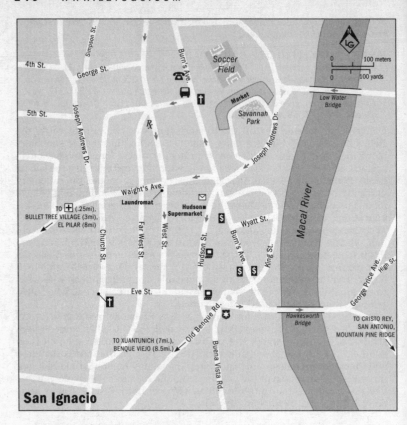

San Ignacio

daily 8am, US$17.50). You must register your name with the company at least a day in advance to have a seat on this bus.

Local buses: Depart from the sandy lot next to the grassy expanse by the river, just north of the main bus stop on Savannah St. Buses to: **Bullet Tree Falls** (15min.; daily 10:30am, 1, and 4:30pm; US$.50); **Spanish Lookout** (30min.; daily 10:30am, 1, and 4:30pm; US$1.50); **San Antonio** (50min., daily 11:30am, US$1.50). Be sure to check times with the bus drivers before boarding since these schedules are subject to change.

Taxis: Next to the bus stop. **The Savannah Taxi Drivers' Co-Op** (☎824 2155) is the main service provider. The **Bullet Tree Falls Taxi Association** runs **collectivos** to **Bullet Tree Falls** (15min., every 20min. 8am-9:30pm, US$1), leaving from the corner of Wyatt St. and Burns Ave., next to the Hot Summer Chinese restaurant.

◀ 7 ORIENTATION AND PRACTICAL INFORMATION

San Ignacio is actually one of the "twin towns" split by the Macal River; its sibling is the more residential **Santa Elena,** which lies on the river's eastern side. The web of roads in San Ignacio is confusing and difficult to navigate. Two bridges span the river: the small wooden **New Bridge,** which provides an entrance into town, and the large, suspended **Hawkesworth Bridge** (look for it on bank notes). From the New Bridge, **Savannah Street** leads past the outdoor market and the football field into the **town square** (sometimes known as **Savannah Plaza**), where buses pick up and drop off passengers, while taxis hunt for customers. The plaza is a tangled five-way intersection with no stop signs. **Burn's Avenue,** San Ignacio's main commercial strip (and tour company stomping ground), heads north, while **Waight's Avenue** curves west. South of the plaza, Burns Avenue leads uphill to the new, eye-grabbing **Town Hall** and the small columned park in front of it. From here, **Buena Vista Road** heads southwest.

Tours and Agencies: San Ignacio is packed to the brim with companies offering adventure tours around the Cayo district, it's never too hard to find a tour. Trips operate on a per-person basis rather than on a fixed schedule. Most tours need a minimum of 2 people, although the larger ones—**ATM, Caracol,** and **Tikal**—often require a minimum of 4. This can be frustrating for independent travelers, but if you spend a few days in San Ignacio and keep your schedule flexible, your desired tour is likely to attract members. Prices for the tours do not vary much between companies. All of the companies listed below offer tours to Caracol, cave tubing at Nohoch Che'en, Barton Creek Cave, and Mountain Pine Ridge. Pacz, Mayawalk, Eva's, K'Atun Ahaw, and Hun Chi'ik offer trips to Altun Tunichil Muknal. For details on the destinations themselves, see **Daytrips,** p. 246. In addition, nearly all companies offer full-day tours to Tikal in Guatemala; there's usually a change in vehicle and driver at the border. These tours leave at 7am and return at 5 or 6pm, running US$130-135.

Pacz Tours, Burns Ave. (☎822 0536; www.pacztours.com). Pacz is a San Ignacio stalwart, distinguishing itself from the crowded tour company crowd with its excellent personnel and wide variety of trips on offer. Their 8 guides are incredibly knowledgeable yet personal, offering some of the best, most comprehensive tours of ATM, Caracol, and the other usual destinations. MC/V.

Mayawalk Tours, Burns Ave (☎824 3070; www.mayawalktours.com). One of the original guide companies to set up shop in San Ignacio, Mayawalk is a sort of mothership: many of the guides have gone on to start their own companies in town. The parent company is still going strong, offering a huge variety of tours with professional and irreverent guides.

Eva's Daily Tours, Burns Ave. (☎625 4880 or 620 5616), in Eva's Restaurant. Max and Sergio, the affable owners of this company, also run all the tours, keeping it personal and professional. All the usual destinations are offered here.

K'Atun Ahaw, Burns Ave. (☎824 2080; www.belizeculturetours.com), in the Casa Blanca hotel. Friendly service headed by Elias Cambranes, one of the few Belizeans licensed to guide in Tikal, Guatemala. Also offers a full-day tour to nearby Mayan sites at Cahal Pech, El Pilar, and Xunantunich. MC/V.

Hun Chi'ik, Burns Ave. (☎824 2040; www.hunchiiktours.com), in the Plaza Hotel. In addition to the traditional tours, offers mountain biking trips to Che Chem Ha. MC/V.

David's Adventure Tours, Savannah St. (☎804 3674; www.mauricefield.net/belize/davidstour.html), 5min. back from the bus stop. David is a distinctive local Afro-Maya who's been offering a wide variety of tours for 15 years. He is highly conscious of the problems posed to the sites by tourism.

Easy Rider Tours, Burns Ave. (☎824 3734), in the Arts and Crafts of Central America store. Horseback riding tours around Cayo, including visits to such rare Mayan sites as Buena Vista del Cayo. ½-day US$30, full-day US$50. MC/V.

Bank: Scotiabank, Burns Ave. (☎824 4190), by the Town Hall. Open M-Th 8am-2pm, F 8am-3:30pm, Sa 9-11:30am. **Atlantic Bank,** across the street from Scotiabank. Open M-F 8am-3pm, Sa 8:30am-noon. **Belize Bank** (☎824 2031), corner of Waight Ave. and Hudson St., next to the town square. Open M-Th 8am-3pm, F 8am-4:30pm, Sa 9am-noon.

Laundromat: On Wyatt St. (☎824 2820). US$3 per load. Open M-Sa 8am-noon and 1-8pm, Su 9am-noon. **Martha's Guesthouse** (p. 243) also offers a public laundromat service. US$3.50 per load. Open 6am-9pm.

Police Station: In the Town Hall building next to the Hawkesworth Bridge.

Pharmacy: On West St. (☎824 0317). Open M-Sa 8am-noon, 1-5pm, 7-9pm; Su 9am-noon. MC/V.

Hospital: La Loma Luz Hospital, Western Highway
(☎804 2985), in Santa Elena. 24hr. service.

Internet Access: Tradewinds Internet Cafe, corner of
Waight Ave. and West St. Internet in an air-conditioned
setting. Grab a free cup of coffee while you surf.
US$2.50 per hr. Open M-Sa 7am-11pm, Su 10am-
10pm. **D+J Internet Cafe,** Burns Ave. (☎661 5712).
Open 9am-8pm. **Data Link Cafe,** in the town square.
US$2 per hr. Open M-Sa 8am-9pm.

Post Office: Hudson St. (☎824 2049), near the town
square. Open M-Th 8am-noon and 1-5pm, F 8-noon
and 1-4pm.

ACCOMMODATIONS

San Ignacio is full of lodgings of all conceivable
prices, from cheap guesthouses above family
homes near the town center to expansive lodges
perched on the tops of nearby hills. Backpackers
won't have to venture far; the guesthouses and
cheap hotels are intimate, affordable, and never
more than 5min. from the bus stop.

Mana Kai Camp and Cabins, Branch Mouth Rd.
(☎824 2317; www.manakaibelize.com), just north
of the outdoor market. The camp site and cabins
are right by the busy road leading into town, but the
rooms are clean and comfortable. Some, perched
high on stilts, offer decent views. Well-kept grounds.
Book well in advance. Camping US$5 per person;
cabins with shared baths US$12.50, with private
baths US$17.50-22.50. Cash only. ●

Cosmos Camping Branch Mouth Rd. (☎824 2116 or
669 0153), a 10min. walk from town. A beautiful, quiet
spot for camping. Well-maintained grounds with lots of
shade. You can pitch your tent behind the owners' home
or head across the street and sleep by the river. Camping US$5 per person. Showers provided. ●

Hi-Et Guest House, 12 West St. (☎824 2828). Spread
out over 2 buildings, this expansive house affords views
of town from the small, breezy verandas attached. You
have to walk through the living and dining rooms to
reach the rooms upstairs, but the friendly family is
used to it. Tiny rooms, each with fan. Beds remade
every day. Rooms with shared bath US$10-12.50, with
private bath US$20. Cash only. ●

Tropicool Hotel, 30 Burns Ave. (☎824 3052), behind
the Pacz Tours building. Conveniently located next to
several tour companies on Burns Ave. Rooms, situated around a back yard, are mostly sheltered from
street noise. Budget travelers snatch up the cheap,
spare rooms quickly, but Tropicool also rents spacious

rooms (resembling cabins) with private baths and TVs. Rooms with shared bath US$11.50, with private bath US$37.50. MC/V. ❷

Central Hotel, Burns Ave. (☎628 2361). The building shows its age, with rustic rooms and old wooden walls. The shared bathrooms could be cleaner, but these are some of the cheapest rooms in town, with a great location on one of San Ignacio's main streets. A massage room and a veranda with hammocks are pleasant surprises. Singles US$10; doubles US$12; triples US$15. Cash only. ❷

Elvira's Guest House, 6 Far West St. (☎804 0243). Elvira's rooms, directly above her cafe, are a bit dark, but comfy and colorful with high ceilings. All rooms with fans. Rooms with shared bath US$12.50, with private bath US$17.50. Cash only. ❷

J + R Guest House, Far West St. (☎824 2502 or 626 3604). A small, homey hotel tucked away in a quiet corner of town. We actually mean homey—you'll be staying at the friendly owners' home. All rooms with fan. Breakfast included. Singles with shared bath US$10, with private bath US$25; doubles US$12.50/22.50. Cash only. ❷

Casa Blanca, 10 Burns Ave. (☎824 2080; www.casablancaguesthouse.com). This beautiful hotel won the Best Small Hotel of the Year award from the Belize Tourism Board a few years back, and it's not hard to see why. From its stately column-lined facade, to the delightful communal kitchen and dining area, to the cleanliness of the 8 rooms, Casa Blanca is one of the best options in San Ignacio. Singles with fans US$24, with A/C US$30; doubles US$37.50/49. MC/V. ❹

Plaza Hotel, 5A Burns Ave (☎824 2040). Be prepared to get intimate: the large, brightly decorated guest rooms are near those of the couple who owns the place, and you'll be walking through their living room frequently. Singles with fans US$20, with A/C US$40; doubles BZ$27.50/40. ❸

Martha's Guesthouse, 140 West St. (☎804 3647; www.marthasbelize.com). Easily the best place in San Ignacio to splurge. Sumptuously decorated, this spacious, 3-story hotel has hallways with high ceilings. Large, well-adorned rooms with stuffed animals on the beds. Many with private balconies. All rooms with A/C and cable TVs. Downstairs, there's a restaurant serving pizza (US$6.50-10) and various local dishes, including the spicy *esabeche* soup (US$5-10). Free Wi-Fi. Economy rooms US$40; others US$45-75. MC/V. ❺

📷 FOOD

Several fruit stands cluster around Savannah Plaza, but the large **outdoor market** itself is located five minutes behind the bus stop along Savannah St.; you'll pass it on your way in. On Saturdays, farmers from near and far gather at 6am to sell produce and finger foods; it's your best chance to buy both Mennonite and Garifuna cuisine at the same place. For groceries, try **Hudson Supermarket,** on Hudson St (☎092 4623; open daily 7am-9pm), **Tai San Shop,** right across from the Hudson (☎824 3550; open daily 8am-9pm), or **Celina's Superstore,** on Burns Ave. (open M-Sa 8am-noon and 1-7pm).

Hannah's, 5 Burns Ave. (☎824 3014). The motto here is "Ko-Ox Hannah" ("Let's Go Eat"), and the diners heed the call. The menu is diverse, and the prices relatively cheap for food from local farms. You can go for the Belizean breakfasts, heavy with scrambled eggs (BZ$12-14), or stop in later for the smattering of lamb and steak (US$10-15). Sizable Indian and Asian food menu featuring a variety of curry meals (US$10-12.50). Lunch and dinner US$7-10. Open 6am-10pm; last orders at 9pm. MC/V. ❸

Pop's Restaurant, West St. (☎824 3366). One of the top breakfast spots in town, serving up delicious omelettes (US$6) along with small breakfast appetizers (US$2.50-4.50) in a diner-style setting. Breakfast meals US$5-6. Open M-Sa 6:30am-2pm. MC/V. ❷

Mickey's Fast Food, Burns Ave. This section of Burns Ave. is lined with snack stands, but Mickey's always seems to attract the largest crowds. Cheap, tasty, and quickly

ON THE MENU

CHICHAS FOR THE CHICAS: PANAMANIAN FRUIT ELIXIRS

Chichas, popular Central American juices, are often refered to as the "nectar of the gods." Drinking like a deity in Panama is cheap and easy, as street vendors in roadside snack shacks simply mash local fruits and add water and sugar. For about 25 cents, you can cool off with a healthy drink. While well-known flavors like pineapple, passion fruit, and guava are popular choices among tourists, **guanabana** (a sweet sherbety fruit also known as soursop), **naranjilla** (a tropical fruit with taste reminiscent of apple cider), and **tamarindo** (a pulpy fruit with a strong taste) are the local crowd's juices of choice. *Chichas* also include a variety of concoctions more complex than fruits mashed with sugar and water. *Chicha "de arroz con pina"* combines rice, pineapple, milk, and sugar to create a more filling elixir. While usually served as a nonalcoholic refresher, *chichas* can be kicked up a notch with rum or vodka to make a *chicha fuerte.*

While some like it hot, it turns out that in the Panamanian heat, most like it fruity and refreshing.

prepared Mexican standards: *tostades, garnaches,* and *salbutes* US\$.25-.50. Burritos US\$1.25. You can get a full breakfast plate (US\$3.25), or just go for a breakfast burrito or quesadilla (US\$1.75). Open daily 7am-3pm. Cash only. ❶

Eva's Restaurant, 22 Burns Ave. (☎804 2267). A restaurant, bar, tour company, and internet cafe rolled into one. Posters of popular Cayo trips line the walls of the dining space. The menu offers breakfast (US\$4.50-7.50), lunch, and dinner (US\$5-8), ranging from Mexican dishes to Belizean specials. Open daily 7am-10pm. MC/V. ❸

Serendib Restaurant, Burns Ave. (☎092 2302). A Sri Lankan restaurant in the midst of Belize's wild country. Elegant wooden interior. Sri Lankan curries US\$7-11; seafood US\$11-20. Desserts include *watalappan* (coconut custard), a Sri Lankan specialty. Open M-Sa 7am-3pm and 6-10pm. ❸

Hode's Place, Branch Mouth Rd. (☎824 2522). It's a 10min. hike from town, but if you've just taken a dip at Branch Mouth, or you're camping at one of the nearby sites, the large, open-air seating at this bar and grill is worth a visit. A playground and orchard provide the ideal backdrop for an afternoon meal. The menu focuses on grilled food (US\$10-15). Drinks US\$2-7.50. You can also refresh at the ice cream stand inside, serving dairy producuts from the nearby Mennonite community. Open daily 10am-11pm. MC/V. ❹

Eagle Landing Restaurant, Wyatt St. (☎824 0378). "Authentic Belizean dishes" (US\$4-7.50) as well as Mexican offerings like burritos and fajitas (US\$1.75-3.50), grilled food (US\$9-11), and seafood (US\$10-17.50). Eagle Landing's main claim to fame is daily 24hr. service, perfect for a substantial midnight snack. Cash only. ❸

Amore Mio, Market Sq. (☎602 8365), next to the bus stop. If you're looking for a break from the ubiquitous Sri Lankan restaurants, Amore Mio provides the escape: authentic Italian dishes prepared by authentic Italian chefs. It's pricey, but it may be one of your only chances to enjoy this kind of pasta (BZ\$6.50-11), pizza (US\$6.50-9), and *carni* (US\$8) in Belize. Open daily 5-9pm. MC/V. ❹

Erva's, 2 Far West St. (☎824 2821). Not to be confused with Eva's or Elvira's, Erva's provides large, cheap servings of down-home Belizean food. Appetizers US\$1.50-3; breakfast US\$4-5; lunch and dinner US\$4-7.50. Cash only. ❸

SIGHTS

> **TIP**
>
> **THANKS, BUT NO THANKS.** Don't be fooled into taking guided tours to nearby sites like Cahal Pech or Xunantunich. Both sites are easily accessible—Cahal Pech by walking from San Ignacio, Xunantunich by taking the bus to San Jose Succotz—so all you should be paying is the admission fee (US$5 each).

CAHAL PECH. A vist to a Mayan ruin doesn't get any easier: a 30min. walk up a steep hill or a quick taxi (US$2.50) gets you to this site named "Place of the Ticks" (a reminder of more cattle-pervasive and tick-plentiful times). Cahal Pech is the oldest site in area, with signs of settlement dating back to 1500 BC; the ruins here, though, all date from AD 400-850, when the area declined along with the rest of the Mayan civilization. The shaded grounds contain **seven plazas,** but the real attraction here are the **royal residences** at the rear of the site, some of the most extensive in the area. You can climb down narrow staircases and through small passages to visit the dark rooms that once were home to the town's elite. Caretakers sometimes give tours, and expect a tip. *(From the police station, take Buena Vista St. out of town. You will pass the San Ignacio Resort Hotel on your left, after the road curves to the right the sign for Cahal Pech will appear shortly. Follow it and take a left onto a gravel road; continue to the top. Entry to the ruins on your left. Taxi US$2.50. The ruins are also accessible by any bus bound for Benque Viejo; ask to get off by the ruins (US$.50). Open daily 6am-6pm. US$5.)*

BRANCH MOUTH. This popular swimming spot lies at the juncture of the Macal and the Mopan Rivers and the origin of the Belize River, just north of town. The swimming is nice enough to make the long, dusty walk worth it. A small bridge is perfect for jumping into the cool water. If you'd rather move than lounge, there are some gentle rapids nearby. Prepare to have company: plenty of locals, most of them under 20, gather here to hang out, barbeque, and swim. *(From town, walk along Savannah St. past the market and continue on Branch Mouth Rd. Continue walking for 25-30min.)*

NIGHTLIFE AND ENTERTAINMENT

San Ignacio is quiet most nights, with a limited nightlife scene focusing on a small handful of bars. Weekends are livelier, with the usual Belizean stew of beats animating the center and a few entertainment venues attracting crowds farther out from town.

Faya Wata, Burns Ave. (☎824 2660). Easily the best nightspot in town. Crowds of locals gather to drink, listen to live music shows, play darts and poker, shoot pool, or just chill by the open windows overlooking Market Sq. The wide mixed drink menu, scattered along the walls and including Faya Wata itself, runs US$4-10. Beer US$2. Open daily 5pm-midnight. Cash only.

Pitpan Tavern, Market Sq. This tiny drinking hole, distinguished by the large car sculpture above it, fills up very quickly. The bar can barely fit in the space, but the atmosphere is intimate and easy-going. Drinks US$2-7.50. Happy hour M-F 4-7pm. Open M-Sa 4pm-midnight. Cash only.

The Attic, Burns Ave. This huge 2nd fl. space, with its old name "Blue Angels" emblazoned on the windows, includes many seating areas and pool tables. Can be empty on weekdays, but a crowd gathers on weekends to enjoy the company of exotic dancers. Mixed drinks US$3.50-7.50. Beer US$2. Open M-Th 10am-midnight, F-Sa 10am-2am. Cash only.

Legends, Bullet Tree Rd., 5 mi. out of town. You'll need to take a taxi to reach it, but once you're there this popular nightclub will make you forget the logistics of getting home. Live DJs on occasional weekend nights spin punta, reggae, and reggaeton, while locals and a handful of tourists hang out at the bar. Drinks US$2.50-7.50. Cash only.

Princess Casino, 18 Buena Vista St. (☎824 2034), in the San Ignacio Resort Hotel. Quite a ways from town, the Princess is part of San Ignacio's fanciest hotel. Those who want to share a drink and test their luck alongside more well-to-do travelers would do well to make the trek (a taxi from the town center is the best option). Casino open M-Sa noon-midnight.

Movies 7, 38 West St. (☎804 2421). The Cayo district's only movie theater plays about 4 films each day; usually a range of American offerings from the past 10 years and the occasional new release. The place to be to relive that life-changing experience of seeing "Center Stage" on the big screen. Tickets US$2; the first show of the day (around 1pm) US$.50.

🔳 DAYTRIPS FROM SAN IGNACIO

An ideal starting point for exploring the natural wonders and thrills of the Cayo District, San Ignacio is Belize's second most popular destination after San Pedro. Tour companies loudly announce themselves at every corner, attempting to distinguish themselves from the guys next door, offering the same tours at the same prices. Unfortunately, most sites' remote locations make visiting them on your own nearly impossible, especially if you're without a car. It's an inevitable cost, but the guides themselves are usually excellent and multi-talented, as adept at explaining old Mayan rituals as they are at identifying the medicinal uses of plants. Plus, exploring the wilds of Belize with a group may be the best way to gain perspective on them.

🔳 ACTUN TUNICHIL MUKNAL

Actun Tunichil Muknal must be visited as part of a guided tour. Only certain specialized guides are licensed to give tours in the site, so there's not much selection to be had. The guides at Pacz Tours and Mayawalk (see Orientation and Practical Information, p. 240) are especially informative and respected. Trips to ATM usually cost US$75 and last all day, leaving San Ignacio at 8am and returning around 5pm. There's a lot of climbing and swimming involved, so be prepared for a strenuous and tiring adventure.

Remotely located in the **Tapir Mountain Reserve** at the end of a rocky 30min. drive from the Western Highway and a 45min. hike through jungle and across three rivers, the sacred Mayan site of Actun Tunichil Muknal (ATM) is one of the true highlights of any trip to Belize. The 5km long cave, rediscovered only in the late 1980s, is one of the most stunning in Central America, but it's the artifacts found within that make the visit unforgettable. From the base camp, the adventure begins with a plunge into a cold pool lying at the cave mouth. From there, groups are led through rocky, cavernous channels (most of them wet—be prepared to be soaked for hours) 500m into the cave, passing striking rock, crystal formations, and ledges of beautiful stalactites. The trip then leaves the water, ascending a ledge to the huge natural spaces that the Maya used as sacred temples. It's not hard to see why; these dark and silent caves are distinguished by stunning crystal and stalactite formations that to the Maya resembled the roots of the world tree. This was literally **Xibalba,** the underworld. Deliberately shattered pottery lies exactly where it was found, the ashes (used in ritual cooking ceremonies) still visible. Expanses of carefully planned burial grounds stretch out beneath vaulting cave ceilings. Most fascinating of all are the five human remains on display (14 in all have been discovered in the cave): buried skeletons, cracked skulls, and, at the very end

of the tour, the skeleton of a young woman, the **Crystal Maiden,** ritualistically positioned as if giving birth. Be careful when stepping amidst the artifacts; they are not protected from visiting feet, and several have been damaged by careless tourists. Many believe that the site won't be open to the public for much longer, so make a visit to this haunting site a top priority.

▩ CARACOL

Caracol lies at the end of a very rocky road leaving the Western Highway just before San Ignacio and passing through remote villages before entering the wilderness of Mountain Pine Ridge. If you're driving, follow the signs to the site. The last ten miles of the road are paved, but otherwise be prepared for a bumpy and dusty ride lasting over two hours. Since Guatemalan bandits had taken to robbing tourist vans heading to the site, a security system has been established. An armed convoy accompanies visitors from a base along the road at Douglas D'Silva to the ruins themselves. The van leaves Douglas D'Silva at 9:30am sharp and leaves Caracol at 2pm, so if you're on your own keep an eye on the time; leave San Ignacio by 7:30am to arrive at the the base on time. The easiest way to reach and explore the ruins is in a tour group. Tours leave San Ignacio 7:30-8am and return at 5pm. The return trip includes stops at the Rio Frio Cave and Rio On Pools (see Mountain Pine Ridge, p. 247). Trips US$75. www.caracol.org. Open daily 8am-4pm. US$7.50 (included in tour prices).

The mother of all Mayan sites in Belize, Caracol (Spanish for "snail," named either after the snail shells in the soil or the winding road leading up to the site) was once a mighty city-state inhabited by 150,000 people and covering 70 sq. mi. It reached its peak in the AD seventh century after defeating mighty Tikal, but was largely deserted by AD 900. The once vibrant, teeming city lay buried in the wilds near the Belize-Guatemala border until a logger happened upon the ruins in the 1930s. Since then, excavators have discovered over 4,000 structures and even 40 mi. of wide causeways that once served as thoroughfares connecting the city center with outlying areas. The highlight of the site is **Caana** (Sky Palace), which rises 141 ft. above Plaza B; Caana is still the tallest structure in Belize. About halfway up is a row of small rooms, complete with ledges that served as beds. At the top lies a small plaza featuring several tombs. Climb the final set of steps for a great view of the jungle spreading out in all directions from the site. The **Central Acropolis** south of the temple was an elite residential center—you can still see the beds— while **Plaza A** to the west includes the **Temple of the Wooden Lintels,** featuring wooden inserts above the doorway (one of which is original). You can also walk through two **ball courts** whose small stone altars have provided archaeologists with loads of historical information about the city

MOUNTAIN PINE RIDGE FOREST RESERVE

Chiquibul Rd., leaving the Western Highway from the village of Georgeville about 8 mi. west of San Ignacio, winds its rough way through the eastern side of the forest. Cristo Rey Rd. leaves the highway just before San Ignacio, passing through several villages before meeting up with Chiquibul. Public transportation does not reach the forest. For those without a car, most tour companies in San Ignacio offer combined driving and hiking tours in and around the area. They'll stop at the Thousand Foot Falls, the Big Rock Falls, the Five Sisters Falls, the Rio Frio Cave, and the Rio On Pools. Tours to Caracol will pass through the Reserve and usually stop at the Rio Frío Cave and the Rio On Pools. Tours last from 9am to 5pm and cost US$55-65.

The Mountain Pine Ridge covers 230 sq. mi. at the isolated center of the Cayo District, forming an environmental anomaly in the heart of Belize. The broadleaves of the jungle are abruptly replaced by tall, upright conifers, distinguishing a landscape that seems to have been exported straight from the American Pacific Northwest. The area is hilly and, due to the granite beneath the soil, unfit for agriculture; you won't see any human activity in these remote expanses. A severe pine beetle infestation destroyed over half the forest in the early 2000s, and vestiges of the devastation remain in noticeably depopulated sections. A combination of natural re-growth and human efforts is quickly restoring the growth. Waterfalls, pools, and caves dot the forest. The area is also full of expensive lodges, including the **Blancaneaux,** once Francis Ford Coppola's private retreat. Past the **Mai Gate** at the entrance of the Reserve (where vehicles are checked and information provided), **Chiquibul Road** provides the only main route through the Reserve, continuing all the way to Caracol. The turn-off to **Thousand Foot Falls** is a 25min. drive past the gate. The water actually plummets 1600 ft., forming the highest waterfall in Central America. One mile further down Chiquibul, you'll reach the turnoff (at the sign for the Blancaneaux Lodge) to the wide, beautiful **Big Rock Falls,** 1.6 mi. from the road. The area is open for swimming. Nearby is the **Five Sisters Lodge** with access (through a 45min. trail) to the **Five Sisters Falls,** where you can take shelter under the small but numerous falls. Several miles farther along Chiquibul are the **Rio On Pools,** where small waterfalls, giant granite boulders, streaming rapids, and small, cool pools form a natural swimming area. Another 10min. drive down Chiquibul takes you to the **Río Frío Cave,** a vast 65 ft. high tunnel with impressive stalactite formations; the sight of the forest through the other end of the cave is stunning. Nearby is a small nature trail with chicle-producing sapodilla trees.

BARTON CREEK CAVE

The turnoff to Barton Creek Cave leaves from Chiquibul Rd. about 5 mi. south of the Western Highway. From Chiquibul, it's a brutal 4 mi. drive to the cave. To actually enter the cave, though, you must have a guide. ½-day tours leave from San Ignacio at 9am and return around 2 or 3pm. Tours US$45-65.

For those who can't stomach a strenuous tour of Actun Tunichil Muknal, Barton Creek Cave provides a relaxing and rewarding alternative. Like ATM, the cave, with its high ceiling and intricate stalactite formations, was a sacred spot for the ancient Maya, who saw it as a segment of **Xibalba,** the underworld, and honored it with ritual ceremonies. The remnants of these ceremonies can be seen on the ledges above the water: shattered pottery shares space with the skeletal remains of 28 people, who were either used as human sacrifices or simply entombed in the holy site. Your tour will start off with a calm canoe trip along Barton Creek, continuing 750 ft. into the cave, where you'll disembark and explore the remains on foot.

NOHOCH CHE'EN CAVES BRANCH ARCHAEOLOGICAL RESERVE

The reserve lies at the end of a turnoff from the Western Highway east of Belmopan, about a 50min. drive from San Ignacio. From the Western Highway, turn at the sign for the Jaguar Paw Resort. If you're driving, you can hire a cave tubing guide at the reserve base (US$25 for two or three caves, US$35 for five caves). From San Ignacio, tour companies offer ½-day cave tubing trips for US$65-75, lasting from 9am to 2 or 3pm.

The Caves Branch River, passing through five expansive caves, seems tailor-made for a mobile, relaxing exploration. You could theoretically take a canoe through them, but shallow waters makes **tubing** the most popular option. It's an incredibly languid experience (though at high points you'll have to paddle yourself along). With your headlamps, you'll see stalactites, small cascades, beautiful crystal formations, and sleeping (sometimes flying) bats. In between caves, you can admire the nearby jungle and enjoy some slight rapids. Cave tubing is a popular activity; it'll be hard to avoid large crowds on the river—especially when cruise ship passengers decide to go for some strenuous exercise on the tubes. Tuesday, Wednesday, and Thursday are the most crowded days.

MACAL AND MOPAN RIVERS

Trips down the Macal start by the suspended Hawkesworth bridge in San Ignacio. The Mopan is a few miles outside of San Ignacio, so it's best to arrange a daytrip with one of the tour companies in the town. You can rent a canoe or kayak at Tony's Rental Service, right by the river on the Santa Elena side, across the wooden bridge leading into town (US$15 per day). David's Adventure Tours, next to the market, rents canoes and kayaks for US$20 per day. Mayawalk offers ½-day (US$30) and full-day (US$40) canoe tours along the Macal River. Pacz will take you to the Mopan as well (US$60).

San Ignacio is located near the north-south Macal and Mopan Rivers, which join just north of the town at Branch Mouth to form the Belize River. San Ignacio is a natural center for canoeing, kayaking, and tubing. The rivers wind through jungle, allowing for plenty of plant, tree, and wildlife spotting opportunities; keep a lookout for black vultures, iguanas, and even the deadly yellow-jaw snake. Take a trip towards evening, when animals come down to the banks for a drink and a cool-down. For some minor excitement, navigate the small white-water rapids on the otherwise peaceful Mopan.

XUNANTUNICH

The best way to get to Xunantunich is by colectivo, or Berque-based taxi which shuttle groups back and forth from San Ignacio (US$1.50 per person). Otherwise, take any west-bound bus and ask to be let off at the ferry in San José Succotz (US$.75). From Succotz take the small, cable-drawn ferry across the Mopan River to Xunantunich. Don't miss the last shuttle or you might get stranded. Shuttle M-F 7:30am-5:30pm, Sa-Su 7:30am-4:30pm. Free. From the river it is a steep 2km to the ruins. Guides are available at the ruins. US$20 per group. The visitor center next to the offices has enough info for you to guide yourself. Ruins open M-F 8am-5pm, Sa-Su 8am-4pm. US$5.

Xunantunich (Maiden of the Rock) was an important city in the Late Classical period (AD 700-900) and is one of the most accessible Mayan site in Belize. The aristocracy resided here, while workers lived in the more fertile Mopan River valley. Like many of Belize's Mayan ruins, Xunantunich is only partially excavated. The main temple, **El Castillo** (130 ft. high), is easy to climb. From the temple's roof, see every village, mountain, cloud, and buzzard in the kingdom. **Cahal Pech** is visible in the distance, along with the neighboring cities of **Benque Viejo del Carmen** and **Melchor de Mencos**. Leave the flip-flops and high heels at home, since the climb is steep and the staff has so far avoided the pesky guardrails found at Tikal. Climb the temple's lower portion to the first platform, where you'll see a fiberglass reproduction of the elaborate stucco friezes that once stood on the temple's eastern and western sides. Examine the stelae in the visitor center. A great place to grab lunch or dinner is **La Plaza ❷**, right across from the ferry.

▓ BORDER CROSSING: INTO GUATEMALA

The road from San Ignacio, Belize to Flores, Guatemala is a well-traveled one; using public transportation to make the popular trek can be complex. You're trip will be made much easier if you plan ahead and know what to expect.

First, take a **bus** bound for **Benque Viejo del Carmen** from San Ignacio (40min., every 30min., US$1.50). From there, take a taxi to the border—trust us, they're not hard to find (US$5 per taxi). **Independent money changers** gather at the border offering Guatemalan quetzals—the changers are handy, but if you're not careful you'll be given a bad exchange. Do the conversions beforehand or bring a calculator and know how much you should receive. For more information on conversions see **Money, p. 184**.

You'll have to cross the border on foot and pay a US$18.75 exit fee upon leaving the country; the money goes towards national park maintenance, so no need for outrage. You'll be offered taxi rides as soon as you cross, but they're not necessary if you're just trying to pick up a minibus.

Once in Guatemala, get your **passport stamped** in the large, open-air building to the left; beware of exorbitant fees (you shouldn't pay more than Q20 here). From here, continue straight across the bridge and into **Melchor de Mencos.** From the road in front of the gas station, **minibuses** leave for **Santa Elena** (the town right below Flores) every half-hour. The ride lasts 2½hr. and costs Q25-30. From Santa Elena's bus station, small, three-wheeled *tuk-tuks* can bring you to **Flores** (Q5).

SOUTHERN BELIZE

Southern Belize is a true smorgasbord of natural and cultural treasures. Here, you'll have your pick of near-impenetrable jungles, white beaches, imposing mountains, and vibrant coastal villages. This region hosts the country's best national parks and most beautiful terrain, as well as some of its most diverse people and vibrant culture.

South of the Hummingbird Highway—Belize's most stunning drive and a fitting introduction to the region—a patchwork of protected areas leaves huge swaths of the territory home only to wildlife. The coast, though, grooves to the percussive rhythms of the region's Garífuna culture. To the far south, where mountains give way to rolling hills, the resilient Maya continue their age-old traditions amidst reminders of a storied and ancient past.

HUMMINGBIRD HIGHWAY

Belize's most famous route, the Hummingbird cuts across the heart of the country from Belmopan to Dangriga, affording beautiful, postcard-worthy views of jungle hills and citrus orchards. Southbound buses that ply the route are usually packed, especially around late morning and early afternoon, so do your best to grab a window seat—it's worth the pushing. Several attractions along the way are worth a stop.

ST. HERMAN'S BLUE HOLE NATIONAL PARK

The Blue Hole National Park is located right alongside the Hummingbird Highway, 11 mi. from Belmopan; ask any bus traveling the route to drop you off here. The main visitors' center is by the highway in front of the trails giving access to St. Herman's Cave and the lookout tower; there's another ticket booth by the Blue Hole. This second entrance is most convenient for those staying at Ian Anderson's Cave Branch Jungle Lodge, whose turnoff is just 100 yd. north along the highway. Open daily 8am-4:30pm. Only 1 ticket is necessary for the whole park. US$5.

Blessedly accessible and tailor-made for individual exploration, this national park by the side of the Hummingbird offers a few hours worth of hiking, caving, and swimming. A small exhibit details the wildlife (including 268 bird species) and the unique geographic features that distinguish the 575-acre park. From the center, you can take either the **Highland Trail** (25min.), which is rough and steep but provides several breathtaking views of the orchard floor and jungle hills, or the **Lowland Trail** (15min.), a flat, easy trail that cuts across the valley floor. They meet at the entrance to **St. Herman's Cave,** which you can explore independently (rent a flashlight at the visitors' center for US$2.50). Extending 2500 ft. from entrance to exit, above the creek that runs beside the 300 yd. marked path, the cave features spectacular stalactite formations. Beyond the path's end lie some Mayan artifacts, leftovers from sacred rituals performed in the cave's depths; they aren't accessible without a guide. From the cave's entrance you can take a 1½ mi loop trail that culminates in a **lookout tower** perched on a hill. From here, you can get a bird's-eye view of the amazing terrain and the highway cutting through it. From the visitors' center, the **Dusky Antbird Trail** hugs the highway for about 45min. before reaching the **Blue Hole** itself. Not to be confused with the more famous collapsed cave formation far from Belize's coast, this inland site is still remarkable. The pool was created when water seeping into a limestone formation caused the rock to collapse into a tributary of the Sibun River, creating a 25 ft. deep *cenote* (or sinkhole). On good days the hole can be quite blue,

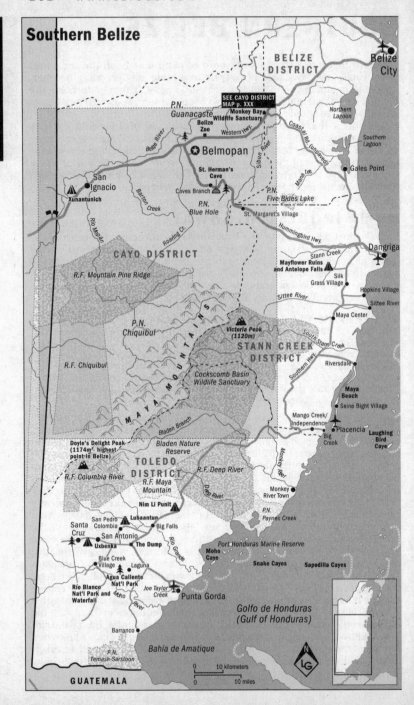

Southern Belize

BELIZE DISTRICT

Belize City

P.N. Guanacaste

SEE CAYO DISTRICT MAP p. XXX

Monkey Bay Wildlife Sanctuary

Belize Zoo

Western Hwy.

Northern Lagoon

Belize River

★ Belmopan

Sibun River

Southern Lagoon

Coastal Rd. (undaved)

San Ignacio

St. Herman's Cave

Manatee

Gales Point

Xunantunich

Caves Branch

P.N. Blue Hole

P.N. Five Blues Lake

Barton Creek

St. Margaret's Village

Río Mopán

Roaring Cr.

Hummingbird Hwy.

Dangriga

CAYO DISTRICT

Mayflower Ruins and Antelope Falls

Stann Creek

Silk Grass Village

R.F. Mountain Pine Ridge

Hopkins Village

Sittee River

Sittee River

P.N. Chiquibul

Victoria Peak (1120m)

Maya Center

M A Y A   M O U N T A I N S

STANN CREEK DISTRICT

R.F. Chiquibul

Cockscomb Basin Wildlife Sanctuary

South Stann Creek

Riversdale

Southern Hwy.

Maya Beach

Seine Bight Village

Bladen Branch

Doyle's Delight Peak (1174m², highest point in Belize)

Bladen Nature Reserve

Mango Creek/ Independence

Placencia

Laughing Bird Caye

R.F. Columbia River

TOLEDO DISTRICT

R.F. Deep River

R.F. Maya Mountain

Big Creek

Monkey River

Nim Li Punit

Deep River

Monkey River Town

San Pedro Colombia

Lubaantun

Big Falls

P.N. Paynes Creek

Santa Cruz

San Antonio

Uxbenka

The Dump

Río Grande

Port Honduras Marine Reserve

Moho Caye

Blue Creek Village

Laguna

Snake Cayes

Sapodilla Cayes

Agua Caliente Nat'l Park

Río Blanco Nat'l Park and Waterfall

Moho

Joe Taylor Creek

Punta Gorda

Golfo de Honduras (Gulf of Honduras)

Barranco

River

Bahía de Amatique

P.N. Temash-Sarstoon

GUATEMALA

0   10 kilometers
0   10 miles

N

LG

making a gorgeous ensemble with the limestone rock forming its high walls. After rain, though, the water turns murky. The pool is popular with swimmers who stop by during their trip down the Hummingbird. You can also buy a ticket for St. Herman's cave at the smaller visitors' center by the hole.

FIVE BLUES NATIONAL PARK

32 mi. of the Hummingbird Highway, 22 mi. from Belmopan. Ask any bus traveling along the Hummingbird to drop you off at St. Margaret's Village. From the turnoff, it's 4½ mi. to the park itself. The ticket office and visitors' center is right at the entrance to the village, 1min. from the highway. US$5.

This 4292 acre park centers on the unique and mysterious **Five Blues Lake.** Like its neighbor, the inland Blue Hole, the lake is essentially a large *cenote*, a karstic formation created by the erosion of soft limestone and the subsequent blockage of the stream that runs beneath it. In its healthiest years, the lake was thought to be 200 ft. deep at points (though official measurements have not been taken). The different forms of clay and stone on the lake bottom led to a shaded appearance on the water's surface. The park was a total grass-roots effort, created after pressure from inhabitants of nearby **St. Margaret's Village** (which you'll pass through on your way to the lake) in the early 1990s. It's still managed by a co-op of villagers. In 2006, the park suffered a huge blow when the lake's water levels began to fall drastically. It's believed that the materials causing the blockage that created the lake shifted, causing massive (in some areas complete) drainage and forever changing the appearance of the lake. The lake began to fill again in 2007, but the effect of the drainage is still noticeable in the lake's somewhat haggard appearance. A trail runs around the lake; several more of varying difficulty head off into the forest beyond. Limestone hills and cliffs line the lakeshore, many of them with small caves providing homes for the 20 bat species that inhabit the area. Ornithologists can keep busy, too; over 200 species of birds live here.

⌂ ACCOMMODATIONS. Ian Anderson's Caves Branch Adventure Co. and Jungle Lodge ❶, across from the entrance to the Blue Hole. Part high-class resort, part cheap wilderness spot, Ian Anderson's place provides an ideal base for exploring the sights along the Hummingbird Highway. Spotless thatched-roof *cabañas* come with bunk beds but without electricity. Bathing options include a "jungle shower" consisting of thatched walls and a bucket. Buffet-style breakfast US$12. Dinner US$24. Huge variety of tours, from Mayan ruins expeditions and canoeing trips, to ziplining and a "Black Hole Drop" (US$35-250). Most of them can be done for far less in San Ignacio. (☎822 2800; www. cavesbranch.com. Camping US$5, bunk beds US$15. MC/V.)

DANGRIGA

Dangriga (pop. 10,400) dances to its own rhythm, grounded in the unique history and culture of the Garífuna people. While it serves as the main transport hub for Southern Belize, the town's own vibrant energy (belied by a somewhat dilapidated appearance) makes a short stay worthwhile. This is one of the few towns in Belize that remains active after 9pm on weekdays, with locals congregating on St. Vincent Street to the muffled, frenzied beats of Garífuna drumming. And there is always the dominating presence of the sea—fishermen mingle with boat captains shepherding tourists out to nearby cayes, the outdoor market sells fresh catch, and small beaches hug the shore.

▣ TRANSPORTATION

Flights: Dangriga's **airstrip** is located to the north of town, about a 20min. walk from the center. **Maya Island Air** (☎223 1140; www.mayaislandair.com) and **Tropic Air** (☎226 2012; www.tropicair.com) both fly to **Belize City** (30min., 5 per day, US$41.50); **Placencia** (15min., 10 per day, US$46); and **Punta Gorda** (40min., 5 per day, US$75.50).

Buses: The main bus station is located at the south end of town at the corner of Havana St. and George Price Dr. Buses go to: **Belmopan** (1¼hr.; every 30min. 5-7am and 5-6:30pm, every hr. 7:30am-3:30pm; US$3); **Belize City** (3hr.; every 30min. 5-7am and 5-6:30pm, every hr. 7:30am-3:30pm; US$5); **Independence** (1½hr.; 5:30, 7:45am, and every hr. 9:15am-6:15pm; US$4); **Punta Gorda** (3½hr.; 5:30, 7:45am, and every hr. 9:15am-6:15pm; US$7.50); **Placencia** (1¾hr.; 9, 10:30, 11am, noon, 4:30, and 6pm; US$2); **Hopkins** (¾hr., 5:15am and 10:30am, US$1.50); **Sittee Point** (1¼hr., 5:15am and 10:30am, US$2).

Boats: To **Tobacco Caye** and other central cayes leave from just east of the bridge over North Stann Creek; you can usually find captains lounging in or near the Riverside Cafe (p. 256) on South Riverside Dr. Make arrangements with them personally; it's best to check a day in advance to make sure there's room on the boats (most of which can fit 15-20 people). Most boats leave for Tobacco Caye around 9-9:30am and return to Dangriga 3-4pm (US$17.50, round-trip US$35). **Nesymein Hardy Water Taxi** (☎522 0062, 604 4738, or 605 7336) heads intermittently to **Puerto Cortez, HON.** The boat leaves from North Riverside Dr. by the North Stann Creek bridge; you can buy a ticket at the offices just north of the bridge. Direct boats to **Puerto Cortez** (3hr., M and Sa 11am, US$50). Check-in time 8:30am. A boat leaves for **Puerto Cortez** on Th at 9am, though they stop to pick up passengers in **Placencia** and **Big Creek** (4½hr., US$42.50).

Taxis: Many wait at the bus station or along St. Vincent Street, the main road in town.

✈ ▢ ORIENTATION AND PRACTICAL INFORMATION

Dangriga hugs the Caribbean coast, extending almost three miles from north to south, but only about a mile inland. **George Price Drive** bounds the main part of town to the south (it becomes **Stann Creek Valley Road** as it heads west), while **Ecumenical Drive,** which leaves Stann Creek Valley Rd. about half a mile from town, provides a rough western boundary. The main road changes names a few times as it heads north. From its intersection with George Price Dr. (where you'll find the **bus station** and the **Drums of Our Fathers Monument** to **Havana Creek,** it's **Havana Street.** From Havana Creek to **North Stann Creek,** it's **St. Vincent Street**

Dangriga

▲ **ACCOMMODATIONS**
Bluefield Lodge, **8**
Chaleanor Hotel, **9**
Dangriga Central Hotel, **13**
Pal's Guest House, **10**
Riverside Hotel, **12**
Val's Backpacker Hostel, **11**
Weyohan Hotel, **4**

🍎 **FOOD**
J&N Restaurant, **2**
King Burger Restaurant, **5**

🍎 **FOOD (CON'T)**
Riverside Café, **6**
Roots Kitchen, **1**
Rosie's Tortilla Factory, **17**
A Taste of India, **3**
Yummy Yummy Fast Food, **14**

Garinagu Crafts and Art Gallery

Gulf of Honduras

■ **NIGHTLIFE**
Club Riviera, **7**
Coco Trop, **15**
Roxy Club, **16**

TO TOBACCO CAYE (16km)

TO SOUTHERN REGIONAL HOSPITAL (1mi.), GULISI GARIFUNA MUSEUM (2mi.), MARIE SHARP'S FACTORY (8mi.)

Havana Supermarket

Havana Bus Station

Stann Creek Valley Rd.

10th St.   TO ✈ (600m)

Boats to Tobacco Caye

(the busiest section, lined with shops, restaurants, and services). North of North Stann, it becomes **Commerce Street.** The area to the west of this road is more residential and can be dangerous at night. By the coast where North Stann Creek empties into the sea lies **Why-Not Island,** which is actually connected to the mainland by a slight sliver of land. A small and not-too-attractive **beach** spreads out along the coast north of the creek.

  Banks: Belize Bank, St. Vincent Street. Open M-Th 8am-3pm and F 8am-4:30pm. **Scotiabank,** St. Vincent Street, just south of the main bridge. Open M-Th 8am-2pm, F 8am-3:30pm, Sa 9am-11:30am. **First Caribbean International Bank,** Commerce St. Open M-Th 8am-2:30pm, F 8am-4:30pm.

  Laundromat: Val's Laundry, Mahogany Rd. (☎502 3324), in Val's Backpacker Hostel (p. 255). Wash and dry US$1 per lb. Open daily 9am-7pm.

  Police Station: On Commerce St., at the intersection with Court House Rd.

  Pharmacy: St. Vincent Drugstore, St. Vincent Street (☎522 3124). Open M-F 8am-noon and 1:30-8pm, Sa 8am-noon and 4-8pm. MC/V.

  Hospital: Southern Regional Hospital, Stann Creek Valley Rd. (☎522 2078). Follow George Price Dr. about 2 mi. north of town.

  Internet Access: Val's Internet, Mahogany Rd. (☎502 3324), in Val's Backpacker Hostel (p. 255). US$2 per hr. If you have a labtop, you can hook it up with an internet cable. Open daily 9am-7pm. **Griganet Cafe,** St. Vincent Street (☎522 2096). US$2 per hr. Printing and photocopying. Open M-F 8am-8pm, Sa noon-5pm.

  Post Office: Polack St. (☎522 2035), in the back of the low government office building. Open M-Th 8am-noon and 1-4:30pm, F 8am-noon and 1-4pm.

■ ACCOMMODATIONS

Hostels and cheap hotels abound in Dangriga, none of them too far from attractions or the shore.

  Val's Backpacker Hostel, Mahogany Rd. (☎502 3324). Walk down Mahogany Rd. to the coast. Don't let Val's grey concrete building with an unfinished 2nd fl. turn you off. Inside you'll find one of the most backpacker-friendly atmospheres in Belize. Two large, no-frills dorm rooms are lined with comfortable bunks. Communal area houses a book exchange, internet cafe, laundry room (see **Orientation and Practical Information,** p. 254), and a deli (delicious home-made ice cream, US$0.50 per scoop). A veranda catches all the right breezes from the ocean, which is just a playground away from the building. There's

BELIZEAN BREWS

  Anyone vacationing in a tropical climate knows the value of sitting back and enjoying a nice, cold beer. When in Belize, do as the Belizians do and gulp down a delicious Belikin, the leading domestically produced beer.

  First marketed in the late 1960s, the Belikin Beer brand proudly sports the tagline, "The Only Beer Worth Drinking." Belikin is created in the Belikin Brewery by 94 full time employees who produce 52,000 barrels of beer a year. Even though their production is not large scale, their product is perfect for quenching one's thirst on a sweltering Belizian day. The name "Belikin" comes from the Maya language and means "Road to the East." Their label, shamelessly marketed to tourists on T-shirts and glassware at the airport gift shop, features a drawing of a Pre-Columbian, Mayan temple-pyramid at Altun Ha.

  Their most popular product is a light lager beer; a premium lager and a stout beer are also brewed and sold under the Belikin name. The light lager has a golden color; it tastes soft and sweet, and is somewhat dry. So, what are you waiting for? Kick back, relax, and enjoy a Belkin.

little privacy, but that's the point; expect to meet other travelers on the porch. There is 1 fully stocked private double with bath and cable TV (US$30). Breakfast US$2.50. Reception 8am-7pm. Dorm beds US$11. Cash only. ❷

Bluefield Lodge, 6 Bluefield Rd. (☎522 2742). This well-established budget option was actually the childhood home of Louise, its owner. A clean, white-columned veranda introduces blue walls and large, tastefully decorated rooms inside. Knowledgeable staff will answer all your tourist questions. Singles US$13.50, with bath US$22; doubles US$19/27.50. MC/V. ❷

Chaleanor Hotel, 35 Magoon St. (☎522 2587). Chaleanor makes a striking first impression: a wide, 3-story building with columned verandas and paintings of Belize's wildlife. Regular rooms are spacious and bright, each with bath, fan, and cable TV. Budget rooms are cramped and rustic but clean and with a spotless shared bathroom. Budget singles US$11, regular singles US$31.50, with A/C US$46; doubles US$18/50/65; triples US$23.50/62.50/77. MC/V. ❷

Weyohan Hotel, Commerce St. (☎522 2278). This hotel is larger than it looks from the street. Plain but clean rooms with smooth tiled floors. Two ping-pong tables available for use. Small market downstairs run by the owners. Curfew 11pm. Singles US$10, with bath US$25, with A/C US$35; doubles US$17.50/32.50/45. MC/V. ❷

Dangriga Central Hotel, Commerce St. (☎522 2028). Conveniently located hotel with low ceilings, shared baths, and basic, unadorned rooms. Third floor rooms are cozier and more expensive, each with bath and cable TV. Large open space provides views over town to the water. Reception 24hr. Singles and doubles US$15, with cable TV US$17.50, with bath US$22.50, with A/C US$32.50; regular triples US$30. MC/V. ❷

Pal's Guest House, 868 Magoon St. (☎522 2095 or 522 2365). Walk to the coast right after crossing Havana Creek. Pal's has snagged quite the peaceful space for itself in busy Dangriga. Its 3 yellow buildings are fronted by a clean beach complete with seating and palm trees. Bare-bones rooms with tiled floors and painted walls. Verandas provide shade and views. Every room with fan, bath, and cable TV. Internet US$2 per hr. Free Wi-Fi. Singles US$32.50; doubles US$38. MC/V. ❺

Riverside Hotel (☎627 6505). Central creek-side hotel. Sparse rooms with peeling wallpaper and dim lighting. Clean and spacious dining area. Each room with bath and fan. Singles US$12.50; doubles US$25. Cash only. ❷

🔲 FOOD

While you're in Dangriga try some traditional Garífuna cuisine. *Hudut*, a plantain mash cooked in coconut milk, is the most common dish. The large, outdoor **Dangriga Central Market** is just north of North Stann Creek, by the coast; you can get all the fruits (and occasionally all the fish) you want there. Also try **Havana Supermarket,** on Havana St., across from the bus station (open M-Sa 8am-9pm and Su 8am-noon), **First Choice Supermarket,** on St. Vincent St. (open M-Sa 8am-9pm, Su 8am-noon), or **The Price Is Right Supermarket,** ironically right across the street from First Choice (open M-Sa 8am-8:30pm).

Riverside Cafe, South Riverside Dr. (☎502 3449). This small diner by the creek and the docks is populated by fishers, boat captains, and tourists about to head off to the Cayes. You can grab a hearty traditional Belizean breakfast in the mornings (US$3.50) and fish and meat dishes at lunch (US$4.50-6). Dinner is predictably dominated by seafood: lobster conch and a bevy of fish and shrimp plates (US$6-12.50) keep the small cafe busy all evening. Open M-Sa 8am-9pm. Cash only. ❸

Roots Kitchen, Ecumenical Dr. Walk 20min. up George Price Dr., turn right on Ecumenical Dr., and continue straight for 5min. This tiny restaurant on the outskirts of town is little more than a rustic shack, but the delicious specialties cooked inside have made it one of the most popular dinner spots in town. Breakfasts (US$2.50-3.50) are standard Belizean, but the highlight is the Garífuna cooking. It isn't prepared every day, though; come weekend nights for the best chances of sampling the coconut milk-drenched local cuisine. Entrees US$3.50-6. Open daily 6am-9pm. Cash only. ❷

King Burger Restaurant, Commerce St. (☎522 2476). Just barely avoiding major trademark infringement, King Burger keeps it real with standard breakfasts of omelettes and ham, egg, and meat combos (US$3.50-5). Meat-heavy dinner entrees features all things fried and grilled (US$5.50-8.50). Fresh natural juices US$1.50-3. Open M-Sa 7am-3pm and 6-10pm. Cash only. ❸

J&N Restaurant, Havana St. (☎600 9570). An unpretentious eatery right across from the bus station, J&N is one of the best places to try some standard Belizean cooking, including Gariguna cuisine. *Hudut* with BBQ, chicken, and fish dishes US$6-10. If you're arriving or heading out of town early, stop in for some large breakfasts featuring fry jacks and tortillas (US$3.50-5.50). Open M-Sa 6:30am-9pm. ❸

Rosalie's Tortilla Factory, Unity Zone (☎522 2397). Turn onto George Price Dr. from Havana St. and continue for 10min. It's somewhat out of town, but those looking for some fresh tortillas will want to make the trek; you can watch them be prepared amid the weighing of ground corn. Open M-Sa 9am-2:30pm. Fresh tortillas US$1; day-old tortillas US$0.75. Cash only. ❶

Taste of India Restaurant, St. Vincent St. (☎600 5675). Dangriga's only Indian restaurant serves healthy portions of spicy curry meals and other South Asian standards. Also serves tamer Belizean favorites like the reliable rice-beans-meat mix. Entrees US$6-12.50. Open M-Sa 9am-3pm and 5-9pm. Cash only. ❸

Yummy Yummy Fast Food, Commerce St. Yummy Yummy distinguishes itself from the other Chinese in Dangriga with its variety of cheap meals: curry dishes (US$3.50-5), chop suey (US$3.50-5), chow mein (US$3-5) and fried rice meals (US$3-5). The cooks don't skimp on the servings; expect some huge plates. With a bare-bones interior and minimal seating, this is more of a take-out place. Open M-Sa 9am-8pm. Cash only. ❷

🔆 SIGHTS

Two attractions on the outskirts of town allow for intimate looks at some of the basic ingredients of Belizean culture, while small stops in town bring you closer to the musical heart of Garífuna culture.

GULISI GARÍFUNA MUSEUM. The small museum is inconveniently located two miles from town, but is the best place to learn about the remarkable history and fascinating, unique culture of the Garífuna people. Colorful exhibits detail the story: the initial shipwreck, mixing with the native tribes, resistance to colonization, and arrival on the shores of Belize from Honduras. Music is the main focus. You can catch video footage of Dangriga's own **Pen Cayetano**, the founder of punta rock, inventor of the turtle shell as musical instrument, and noted painter. **Andy Palacios**, a more current punta legend, gets his fair share of attention as well. *(Stann Creek Valley Rd. A short bus ride (10min., US$0.50) is the quickest way to get to the museum. ☎669 0639; www.ngcbelize. org. Open M-F 10am-5pm, Sa 8am-noon. US$5.)*

MARIE SHARP'S FACTORY. In the early 1980s, a surplus of *habanero* peppers at her family farm prompted Mary Sharp to experiment and try out some new sauces. Nearly 30 years later, bottles of her hot sauce—from the elusive mild variety to the "Beware!" strain—adorn almost every restaurant table in Belize. This factory isn't the true home of the sauce (Marie moved here in the late 1990s), but it's close enough; you can take a tour of the creation process, sometimes with Marie herself as a guide. And, of course, a shop has the

full gamut of MS sauces. Just beware. *(1 mi. down Melinda Rd. off the Southern Highway, 8 mi. from Dangriga. Ask to be let off at the turnoff for Marie Sharp's. ☎520 2087; www. mariesharps-bz.com. Open M-F 7am-4pm.)*

GARINAGU CARFTS AND ART GALLERY. This small shop and gallery has Garífuna wood carvings and drums for sale (US$20-100). Pick up some turtle shells, a common punta instrument, or postcards (US$1) featuring the beautiful artwork of Pen Cayetano, originator of punta rock and noted painter of Garífuna scenes. *(Tubroose St. ☎522 2596. Open M-F 8:30am-6pm. Cash only.)*

AUSTIN RODRIGUEZ. Mr. Rodriguez is a local drum-making legend, whose workshop is one of the more noticeable structures in town: a huge seaside *palapa* (thatched-roofed open house) on Why-Not Island by the mouth of North Stann Creek. You can buy his handcrafted cedar and mahogany drums for US$50-125; he's also been known to offer drum-making lessons to groups. *(☎502 2380 or 665 3975. Open M-Sa 9am-7pm.)*

🎵 🎭 ENTERTAINMENT AND NIGHTLIFE

Be on the lookout for Garífuna drumming gatherings; they often take place in otherwise nondescript spots in the city's residential area (to the west of the main road) at night. It's best to roam these areas with a group.

Club Riviera, St. Vincent Street. Danriga's most happening night spot, no doubt because of the double promise of lubricated condoms and karaoke advertised on its front wall. On weekdays, Riviera is a popular karaoke bar; weeknights feature raucous dance parties and live performances by punta rockers and other local musicians. Drinks US$2-7. Open Tu, W, Th, and Su from 9pm-late; F and Sa from 10pm-late. Cash only.

Roxy Club, Commerce St., in Harlem Sq. The name conjures up ritz and glamor, but Dangriga's Roxy is as down-home and unassuming as they come. A small downstairs room fills up quickly with locals thirsting for cheap drinks (US$2-5). It's well north of town, so you might want to take a friend, as the area gets a little sketchy after dark. Game night Th. Open M-Sa 7-11pm. Cash only.

Coco Trop, Commerce St., right across from a church and convent. Coco Trop, serving stew dishes and Mexican snacks by day. But on Sa nights, this squat, blue eatery transforms into a club hosting dance parties with Latin, reggae, punta, and other Caribbean beats. Food US$1.50-5.50. Drinks US$1.50-5. Open M-F 7am-9pm, Sa 7am-2am. Cash only.

FESTIVALS

A small group of Garinagu landed in Dangriga from Honduras in a dug-out canoe on November 19, 1832. Now, the city erupts for the **Garífuna Resettlement Day** celebrations. It's easily the best time of year to see proud, joyous celebrations of traditional Garífuna culture. November 18 and 19 are filled with drum performances and dancing, while the streets fill with food vendors. The landing is reenacted on the morning of the 19th. Be sure to book accommodations at least a week ahead if you plan on traveling here in mid-November.

DAYTRIPS FROM DANGRIGA

TOBACCO CAYE

Boats leave from South Riverside Drive by the Riverside Cafe in Dangriga. Captains linger around the cafe during the day; check with them a day in advance to arrange a trip. Boats usually leave around 9-9:30am and can bring you back to Dangriga around 2-3pm. US$17.50, round-trip US$35.

Barely four and a half acres of sand and palm trees, surrounded by clear water and coral reefs, Tobacco Caye, 12 mi. from Dangriga, is Belize's most popular island south of Caye Caulker. Just over 20 inhabitants call the island home, but a steady influx of tourists who come to fish, snorkel, swim, and lounge in hammocks keep the pace at a lazy bustle. The caye is crammed with hotels, so finding a quiet spot can be difficult. Luckily, the accommodations themselves strive for an isolated atmosphere; your daytrip may turn into an extended stay (though it's best to call ahead to arrange a lodging). All of them include three meals in their price, so you don't have to fish to survive (though some have been known to make the valiant effort). Most can also rent out snorkeling and fishing gear. On the northern edge of the island, **Tobacco Caye Paradise** ❹ (☎520 5101) rents small but beautifully located *cabaña* (US$38.50) with porches extending over the shore. Rest on the porch hammocks. Plain, offshore rooms are also available (US$26, with bath US$33). The **Gaviota Lodge** ❺ (☎509 5032), in the middle of the island, has a few small rooms near its gift shop for US$35-40. **Lana's on the Reef** ❹ (☎520 5036) rents small, plain rooms (some without a sea view) for US$30. **Reef's End** ❺ (☎522 2419; www.reefsendlodge.com), a very noticeable bar and restaurant (and the caye's most expensive accommodation) perched on its own pier at the caye's southern end, is the only nightspot in town; the expansive ocean views are reason enough to make a stop there. Call ahead if you plan to take a meal. It's also the place to ask about diving near the site; scuba trips can be arranged to the nearby **Shark Hole.**

MAYFLOWER BOCAWINA NATIONAL PARK

North of Silk Grass village off the Southern Highway, about 30min. by bus from Dangriga (take any Punta Gorda-bound bus, US$2). From the highway turnoff, it's 4½ mi. to the visitors' center (just continue straight on the path). Passing buses are infrequent, so call the park ahead of time (☎668 0146 or 503 7309) to arrange for a pickup from the turnoff. Open daily 8am-4pm. US$5.

Since its founding in 2001, this small park has played second fiddle to the more popular **Cockscomb Basin Wildlife Sanctuary** to the south, but it contains many attractions and impressive scenery in its 7000-acre territory. Right across from the visitors' center, are the **Mayflower Ruins,** mostly overgrown but surrounding a well-kept grassy plaza. At least 11 structures have been uncovered at the site, believed to have been occupied in the ninth and tenth centuries. A small **birding trail** leaves from the plaza. The **Antelope Trail** (3km) heads to the right from the visitors' center. After five minutes you'll reach the **Mainzunum pyramid,** another overgrown Mayan structure resembling a hill. From there, the trail continues to very steep inclines (40min) until it reaches the **Antelope Falls,** a huge, spectacular cascade. You can continue (carefully) up a steep, damp path by the falls to reach a viewpoint with panoramic vistas (often closed if there are threats of mudslides). The flatter and easier **Bocawina Trail** continues straight from the path leading to the **visitors' center** and winds through the jungle for 2km before reaching the **Bocawina Falls.** At 40 ft., this cascade isn't nearly as tall as its neighbor, but it can be a lot more fun; a cool pool nestles at its foot, perfect for swimming and resting after a hike. There's a small **campground ❶** near the visitor's center (US$5 per person).

COCKSCOMB BASIN WILDLIFE SANCTUARY

At the end of a 6 mi. access road that leaves the Southern Highway at the village of Maya Centre, about 20 mi. south of Dangriga. Taxis (US$15, round-trip US$30) are available in Maya Centre and will bring you to the visitors' center; you can find one at Nu'uk Cheil Cottages in the village, 500 yd. down the access road, or at Tutzil Nah Cottages by the highway. Open daily 7:30am-4:30pm. US$5.

This massive reserve, Belize's largest and most popular, covers over 124,000 acres in the western part of the Stann Creek District. Although Cockscomb is known as a home to jaguars, spotting one in the park's vast territory is unlikely. However, it does happen, and excited notices by tourists in the sighting book at the visitors' center testify to the finds a patient wildlife observer can come across. The sanctuary dates back to the early 1980s, when the Belize Audubon Society, concerned about jaguar hunting in the country, asked Alan Rabinowitz of the New York Zoological Society to locate the best place for a big cat sanctuary. Using gentle traps to capture jaguars and attach radio collars to them, researchers found that the present-day sanctuary housed the most populous community of jaguars and four other species of big cats. The area was created as a forest reserve in 1984; in 1986, it was declared a wildlife sanctuary. The flood of excited tourists and dedicated wildlife enthusiasts began and continues to flow through the sanctuary. The reserve continues to grow; in 1999, Victoria Peak was added to its protected territory. Today, all five of Belize's big cats call the Sanctuary home, including an estimated 60 jaguars. Ornithologists also flock to the park drawn by the 290 bird species, including scarlet macaws, toucans, and curassows. Smaller animals, including the celebrated tapir (or "mountain cow"), are often seen.

TIP | **RISE AND SHINE.** If you want your name next to an amazing, ground-breaking wildlife sighting in the Cockscomb visitors' log, be prepared to get there early—most of the park's wildlife (especially the birds) are most active right after dawn. Your best bet is to spend a night within the park, either on a campsite or in their dorms.

Exhibits on the park, its history, geology, and wildlife, along with information on local Mayan culture, are on display in the small **museum** by the visitors' center. An extensive, 12 mi. network of trails restricts public access to a small but beautiful section of the sanctuary around the visitors' center. The easiest loop is formed by the **River Path** (500m), the **Rubber Tree Path** (500m), and the **Curassow Path** (0.4km). The River Path leaves the access road just before the visitors' center. From the Curassow, **Ben's Bluff Trail** (3.2km) crosses a creek and goes up a steep incline to a viewpoint looking out on the Maya Mountains, including mighty Victoria Peak and Outlier Mountain. On the way back, stop by the creek to enjoy a cool swimming pool at the foot of a small **cascade.** The **Wari Loop** heads for 2½km to **South Stann Creek,** where you can tube down the river to an established exit point and walk back on the Curassow path (rent tubes for US$2.50). Leaving the access road about 15min. before the visitors' center, the **Tiger Fern Trail** (2km) ends at the beautiful, 75ft. **Tiger Fern Waterfall,** which features another **swimming pool** at its base. Leaving the access road 25min. before the visitors' center, the 3½km **Antelope** or **Gibnut Loop** forms the sanctuary's largest regular trail, crossing several creeks and providing plenty of opportunities to spot wildlife (especially birds in the early morning hours). Much longer trails lead to the **Outlier Mountain** (6-7hr., 14km roundtrip), which is 1920 ft. high. Guides are not necessary, but you must travel in groups of two or more. The star attraction is **Victoria Peak**—at 3675ft, it is Belize's second highest mountain. A hike of three to four days is required to reach the summit, guides are required (US$40-45 per day), and the trek is only allowed between March and May. Those are some stringent limitations, but the mountain promises some of the most amazing views in Belize.

The best way to experience the full expanse of the sanctuary's available territory (and to spot wildlife during the crucial early morning hours) is to spend the night. You can choose between **"rustic cabins"** and newly built **dorm beds** near the visitors' center; each option is US$20 per person. **Camping** (US$10) is also available; the main campsite is not far off from the visitors' center. Other camps along the Tiger Fern trail and a very distant one near Victoria Peak are also available. It may be more convenient for transportation purposes to sleep near the highway; luckily, Maya Centre has some cheap options. **Nu'uk Cheil Cottages ❶** (☎520 3033 or 615 2091), 500 yd. down the access road (it's the last building before the park), is run by a former director of the Sanctuary and his friendly family. They rent clean bunk rooms for US$10, singles and doubles with shared bath for US$22.50, and triples with private bath for US$30. You can camp on their grounds for US$3.50. They also run a restaurant on site serving standard Belizean food and Mayan cuisine (entrees US$5-7.50; open 7am-8pm), and a gift shop. Right by the highway, the lodgings at **Tutzil Nah Cottages ❸** (☎520 3044; www.mayacentre.com) are a bit dingier, housed in squat concrete buildings. (Rooms US$18, with bath US$22.50.) The owner offers kayak trips (US$25 for 2, US$22.50 for 3 or more), day tours (US$22.50/20), and night tours (US$20/17.50) in the Sanctuary. Both offer taxi service to the sanctuary.

GALES POINT MANATEE

Perched precariously on a peninsula in the midst of the lagoons lining the coast between Belize City and Dangriga, Gales Point Manatee (pop. 450) is a unique and isolated destination. A visit here is really only suitable for those able to spend at least a few days. The village was founded around 1800 by a group of Nigerian slaves fleeing captivity in Belize City and seeking refuge in the tangle of swamps, jungle, and lagoons that make Gales Point one of the least settled areas in the region.

▐ TRANSPORTATION. The weekly bus from Dangriga to the village has been discontinued, leaving travelers without a car only a few options. There is a **shuttle** (☎663 9874; from US$20-30) that will pick you up if you call in advance. **Taxis** from Dangriga can take you to Gales Point for US$40 one-way. Otherwise, many travelers take any Belize City-bound **bus** from Dangriga, ask to be let off at the turnoff to the Coastal Highway, and hitchhike the rest of the way. *Let's Go* does not recommend hitchhiking. If you're coming from Belize City, ask to be let off at the turnoff for the Coastal Highway in La Democracia along the Western Highway.

ORIENTATION AND PRACTICAL INFORMATION. Gales Point is a one-street village that extends for the entire two mile-long peninsula. It's accessed by the **Coastal Highway,** an unpaved 36 mi. road connecting the Western and Hummingbird Highways. The turnoff to the village is 22 mi. from the Western Highway and 14 mi. from the Hummingbird Highway. The village's accommodations are conveniently clustered near each other, so getting around isn't very difficult. Beyond the village lies the expansive **Southern Lagoon.**

ACCOMMODATIONS AND FOOD. The village is tiny, but the accommodations here are surprisingly and refreshingly geared towards budget travelers. At **Gentle's Cool Spot** ❷ the rooms are simple; the on-site restaurant serving cheap Creole food and the owner—one of the most reputable tour guides in town—make the stay worth it. (☎609 4991. Singles and doubles US$15; triples US$25. Cash only.) **Sugar Shack** ❶, which is essentially an extension of the Maroon Creole Drum School, is a restaurant, shop, *cabaña* rental space, and campground all rolled into one. (☎603 6051. *Cabaña* on stilts US$15; camping US$5. Cash only.) **Ionie's Bed and Breakfast** ❸ is the closest thing to a hostel in Gales Point; the guesthouse (on stilts, like almost everything else here) features clean rooms and shared baths and ensures contact with like-minded intrepid travelers. (☎220 8066. Singles US$17.50; doubles US$20. Cash only.)

SIGHTS AND ENTERTAINMENT. Gales Point's location deep in the Southern Lagoon makes it a surprising tourist destination, appealing to hardcore bird, turtle, and manatee watchers. The lagoons around it are part of the 14 sq. mi. **Gales Point Wildlife Sanctuary,** protecting a large population of West Indian manatees who live in the **Manatee Hole,** some 150 hawksbill and loggerhead turtles who nest along the **Bar River** between May and October, and a variety of waterfowl who live in **Bird Caye** in the Northern Lagoon. Manatee watching tours cost US$50-60, bird-watching tours are US$60-65, and turtle-watching tours along the river are about US$100. Wildlife and nature tours can be arranged in the village, most easily through your accommodation. In Dangriga, and in the village you'll see many flyers for **John Moore** (☎608 3373 or 661 3094), a Gales Point local who leads fishing and bird-watching tours around the lagoon. The **Manatee Lodge,** at the end of the peninsula, also offers a wide variety of tours for guests and non-guests alike (☎220 8040; www.manateelodge.com). Visitors can try their lagoon tours, which explore the passages of the Northern and Southern Lagoons and include stops at popular crocodile and manatee spots (half-day US$137.50, full-day US$185). **Emmeth Young** is another familiar Gales Point name; one of Belize's leading Creole drummers (quite a different style than the more well-known Garífuna form to the south). Emmeth offers Creole drumming and drum-making lessons at the **Maroon Creole Drum School** (☎603 6051 or 668 7733; www.maroon-drumschool.com), behind the Sugar Shack (run by his wife).

HOPKINS

Miles away from Dangriga's noise and dust, Hopkins is just as proud of its vibrant Garífuna culture. The long village of Hopkins (pop. 1100) is a great off-the-beaten-path destination for those exploring southern Belize. Just two streets wide, Hopkins provides seaside tranquility for visitors looking to relax and enjoy some time by the shore. If you're looking to dive into the area's natural beauty and get right into the percussive heart of the Garínagu, Hopkins is just as fun as Dangriga. Here you'll find great snorkeling and diving opportunities, exhilarating watersports, and plenty of drumming. Hopkins isn't entirely undiscovered—there's a growing foreign population and plenty of hotels and craft shops catering to tourists.

TRANSPORTATION

Buses: Buses from **Sittee Point** pass through Hopkins on their way to **Dangria** (45min., 6:45am and 2pm, US$1.50) and will pick up passengers along the length of the village as far north as Lebeha Drumming Center.

Bike Rental: With long stretches of road by the beach, the Hopkins area is an ideal place for biking with or without a destination in mind. **Dolly's Bike Rentals,** half a mile south of the intersection just past the basketball court. US$2.50 per hr., US$10 per day. **Yugadah Cafe** (p. 264) rents bikes for US$1.50 per hr., US$5 per ½-day, and US$10 per full-day.

Kayak Rental: Tipple Tree Beya (p. 264). US$7.50 per hr., US$15 per ½-day.

ORIENTATION AND PRACTICAL INFORMATION

Hopkins is connected to the Southern Highway by a rugged, mostly unpaved, four-mile **access road.** The heart of town is at the intersection of this road with the village's **main street,** which continues south to the nearby settlement of **Sittee Point**; another street closer to the shore runs for about a mile.

Tourist Office: The **green shack** at the main intersection. Open M-Sa 9am-3pm.

Police Station: At the main intersection just past the mural.

Internet Access: Hopkins Internet, at **Windschief** (p. 264). US$4 per hr. Open M-Sa 1-9pm, Su 6-9pm.

ACCOMMODATIONS AND CAMPING

Tiny Hopkins is full of hotels catering to the ever-increasing tourist flood. Managers and owners of the hotels are some of the best people to ask for information about activities around the area. They may be able to provide a boat, kayak, or bike.

Lebeha Cabana and Drumming Center (☎666 6658; www.lebeha.com), half a mile north of the intersection. One of the coolest spots in town, Lebeha rents lodgings in a few plain but comfortable *cabañas*. Best of all, you get to be near frequent nightly drumming concerts. Doubles US$15 with bath US$25; beach doubles with bath US$49. MC/V. ❷

Tania's Guest House (☎523 7058), 1 mi. south of the intersection. The two ramshackle yellow buildings here don't have any sea views and stand next to a sanitation service center. Rooms are a little dingy but well-kept, with carpeted floors. Each room comes with bath, cable TV, and fan. Singles US$13; doubles and triples US$22.50. MC/V. ❷

Kismet Beach Apartments (☎523 7280), 1 mi. north of the intersection. A funky, earthy vibe prevails in these cheap apartments on the shore. It's technically an inn, but you have to sign a lease. Rustic rooms adorned with aquatic paintings and fishing gear. Organizes fishing and snorkeling tours for BZ$300 per boat. Homemade meals eaten in the upstairs kitchen; prices negotiable. Free bike use. Singles US$12.50; doubles US$25. Cash only. ❷

Glover's Hostel (☎509 7099 or 520 5016), in Sittee Point about 3 mi. south of the main intersection in Hopkins. Though difficult to reach, Glover's has more than enough activity on its grounds to keep you occupied. There's a restaurant, bike rental service, free canoe and kayak use, and river, fishing, birding, manatee-watching, snorkeling, and diving tours. Camping US$48 per person; dorms US$9; singles US$12; cabanas US$19. Stay 2 nights and get the 3rd night free. MC/V. ❶

Windschief Beach Cabanas (☎523 7249; www.windschief.com), half a mile south of the intersection. These large seaside *cabañas* catch plenty of wind from the shore. Ideally located next to a restaurant and bar, internet cafe, and windsurfing school. All *cabañas* with double beds. *Cabañas* US$25, with bath US$40. ❹

Tipple Tree Beya (☎520 7006 or 668 3604; www.tippletree.com), 1 mi. south of the intersection. A pricey option for budget travelers who aren't camping, but the rooms are well-kept, spotless, the location is perfectly peaceful that a splurge might be worth it. Kayak rentals US$7.50 per hr., US$15 per ½-day. Camping US$10 per person; rooms US$30, with bath US$40; *cabañas* US$50. MC/V.❺

🍴 FOOD

For information on Garífuna cooking see the Food section for Dangriga (p. 256). You'll most likely have to call ahead to get some real Garífuna meals. Hopkins also specializes in seafood and Belizean standards.

King Cassava Cultural Restaurant and Bar (☎503 7305), at the main intersection. Specializes in local food and seafood dishes. *Gial* (fried chicken) BZ$10. Garífuna shrimp sauteed in red onion sauce, pepper, and garlic US$12. Appetizers US$4-5. Breakfast US$5-8. Lunch US$6-10. Dinner US$8.50-12. Open Tu-Su 8:30am-9pm. MC/V. ❸

Thongs Cafe (☎602 0110), half a mile south of the intersection. Run by a German-Russian couple, Thongs is an anomalous bit of European polish in untidy Hopkins. Decorated with carved wooden masks, the cafe boasts a small book selection. Breakfast (omelets, rice and beans, cereal) US$6.50-7.50. Lunch and dinner (pastas, fajitas, eggplant) US$6-10. Delicious muffins and cinnamon rolls US$1.50. Open W-Sa 8am-1pm and 5:30-9pm, Su 8am-1pm. MC/V. ❸

Yugadah Cafe (☎503 7089), 1 mi. south of the intersection. A standard blend of seafood, Belizean basics, Mexican snacks, and friendly service. Garífuna food by order only. Breakfast US$5-6. Lunch US$3.50-6. Dinner US$9-12.50. Also rents bikes (see **Transportation,** p. 263). Open M-Tu and Th-Su 6am-2pm and 5-10pm. Cash only. ❸

The Octopus Garden (☎503 7346), 1 mi. north of the intersection. This small, laid-back, open-air restaurant serves specials like teriyaki shrimp and curry lobster with the usual burger, burrito, and rice-beans options. Appetizers US$2-3.50. Entrees US$6-7.50. Open M-Sa 10am-9pm. Cash only. ❸

🎭 ENTERTAINMENT

Lebeha Drumming Center (☎666 6658; www.lebeha.com), 1 mi. north of the intersection, is the best place in either Dangriga or Hopkins to see real and incredible Garífuna drumming in action. Informal jam sessions are held in the evenings on weeknights (usually around 7-7:30pm); you can watch these without an official fee, though donations are requested. Call or visit ahead to make sure there'll be drumming that night. Things get a bit more serious Friday and Saturday nights, when a mixture of locals and tourists come to see more polished concerts. Lebeha's drumming lessons, offered to individuals or groups, might be the best reason for an extended stay in Hopkins.

🏞 OUTDOOR ACTIVITIES

If simple relaxation was not the reason you came to Hopkins, there is diving, snorkeling, fishing, water sports, and even some drumming close at hand.

King Cassava Restaurant and Bar (☎503 7305 or 669 5499; see **Food,** p. 264) organizes tours to Mayflower Bocawina National Park (1-5:30pm, US$30 per person, 3 person minimum) and to the Cockscomb Basin Wildlife Sanctuary (8am-1pm, US$30 per person,

3 person minimum). Snorkeling tours around the nearby cayes and reef run to US$150 for up to 3 people, US$25 for each additional stop. Open Tu-Su 8:30am-9pm. MC/V.

AN's Snorkeling Gear Rentals/Noel's Fishing and Snorkeling Trips (☎523 7219 or 669 2407), 20min. south of the main intersection. Snorkeling equipment for US$5 per day. Organizes trips to the barrier reef (9am-3pm, 2 people US$75 per person, 4 people US$50 per person), including lunch on an island beach. MC/V.

Windschief Windsurfing School and Rental (☎523 7249; www.windschief.com). The multi-purpose Windschief offers 1hr. introductory windsurfing lessons for US$30. Rent equipment for US$10 for the 1st hr., US$5 each additional hr.

PLACENCIA

Crowded around the southern tip of a long peninsula which stretches into the Caribbean just south of Dangriga, Placencia village (pop. 600) enjoys its own beauty. White beaches leading to warm, clear water, and palm trees swaying in the ocean breeze—these views have transformed Placencia into a tourist village. At times the place can resemble Florida, especially toward the northern end where middle-aged North Americans and Europeans jog beside large, stately beach homes. But beneath the flashy veneer, Placencia's roots as a fishing village still exist. There are ample opportunities to mingle with the locals who catch and trap the seafood eaten in all the swanky restaurants. If relaxing in the village becomes a bore, offshore diving and snorkeling spots are readily available.

◧ TRANSPORTATION

Flights: Placencia's **airstrip** is located about 1 mi. north of the village along the main road. **Tropic Air** (☎226 2012; www.tropicair.com) and **Maya Island Air** (☎223 1140; www.mayaislandair.com) fly to the **Belize City Municipal Airstrip** (35min.; 7:25, 10:05am, noon, 2, 4:25 pm; US$79.50) and **Punta Gorda** (20min., every 2hr. 9:10am-3:10pm and 5:40pm, US$46.50).

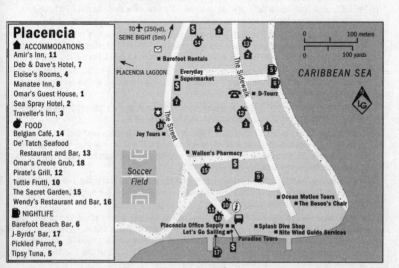

Placencia

⌂ ACCOMMODATIONS
Amir's Inn, **11**
Deb & Dave's Hotel, **7**
Eloise's Rooms, **4**
Manatee Inn, **8**
Omar's Guest House, **1**
Sea Spray Hotel, **2**
Traveller's Inn, **3**

◉ FOOD
Belgian Café, **14**
De' Tatch Seafood
  Restaurant and Bar, **13**
Omar's Creole Grub, **18**
Pirate's Grill, **12**
Tuttie Frutti, **10**
The Secret Garden, **15**
Wendy's Restaurant and Bar, **16**

◉ NIGHTLIFE
Barefoot Beach Bar, **6**
J-Byrds' Bar, **17**
Pickled Parrot, **9**
Tipsy Tuna, **5**

TO ✈ (250yd), SEINE BIGHT (5mi)

PLACENCIA LAGOON

Barefoot Rentals
Everyday Supermarket
D-Tourz
Joy Tours
Wallen's Pharmacy
Soccer Field
Ocean Motion Tours
The Boson's Chair
Placencia Office Supply
Let's Go Sailing
Paradise Tours
Splash Dive Shop
Nite Wind Guide Services

The Sidewalk

The Street

CARIBBEAN SEA

0   100 meters
0   100 yards

Buses: Stop at station at the southern end of the street by the piers. To **Dangriga** (1½hr.; 5:45, 6:15, 7am, 12:45, 2:15pm; US$2.50). Independence buses go to **Belize City** (every hr. 6-8am, every 2hr. 10am-4pm, 5, and 5:45pm) and **Punta Gorda** (9am, every hr. 10:45am-2:45pm, 4:45, 5:45, 7:45, and 8pm).

Boats: The **Hokey Pokey Water Taxi** (☎523 2376 or 601 0271) takes passengers between **Independence and Mango Creek** on the mainland and the western edge of Placencia village (20min., 8 per day, US$5). In Independence you can pick up buses traversing the Southern Highway, heading south to **Punta Gorda** or north to **Belize City**. The bus stops in front of Sherl's Restaurant, which is just off the main road, a 10min. walk from the docks. To reach the docks from the bus stop, walk to the Main Road from Sherl's, turn right, and continue straight for 10min.

Car Rental: Placencia Office Supply (☎523 3205), on the street. US$92.50 per day.

Kayak Rentals: Paradise Tours (☎642 1655 or 564 9400; www.belize123.com), on the street. US$5 per hr., US$30 per day.

⊁ ⁊ ORIENTATION AND PRACTICAL INFORMATION

Placencia Village lies at the southern tip of the **Placencia Peninsula.** Bordered by a wide **lagoon** to the west and the **Caribbean Sea** to the right, the village is only about half a mile wide at its broadest point. There are two thoroughfares: the **street** which runs the length of the peninsula and down through the west end of town, and a pedestrian **sidewalk** about 100 yd. east of it. Just east of the sidewalk is the long, clean **public beach.** A series of piers extend into the sea at the village's southern tip; **Placencia Caye** lies 200 yd. off the southern coastline.

Tourist Office: Placencia Tourist Center (☎523 3294; www.placencia.com), on the street. Plenty of brochures and a helpful staff. Open M-F 9am-11:30am and 1-5pm.

Tours: For mroe details on destinations and prices, see **Outdoor Activities,** p. 269.

Nite Wind Guide Services (☎523 3487), by the piers at the southern end of the village. Trips to Monkey River, snorkeling trips to Laughing Bird Caye and Silk Caye, ½-day snorkels, whale shark snorkel (US$105), manatee watching (US$35), fishing (US$330), and fly fishing (US$385). Inland trips to Cockscomb Basin Wildlife Sanctuary, Mayflower Bocawina National Park (US$80), and select southern Mayan ruins in the south. MC/V.

Splash Dive Shop (☎523 3058 or 620 6649; www.splashbelize.com), next to Nite Wind. Snorkeling trips to Laughing Bird Caye and to the reef, diving trips (US$100-175), Monkey River tours, trips to Cockscomb Basin, and tours of Mayan ruins. Scuba instruction classes US$150-350. MC/V.

Joy Tours (☎523 3325; www.belizewithjoy.com), on the street north of the football field. Diving and offshore snorkeling trips, fishing trips (fly, trolling, bottom, and casting), inland tours to Monkey River, Cockscomb Basin, and Mayan ruins. MC/V.

D-Tourz (☎523 3397 or 600 2318), on the sidewalk by the open beach expanse. Diving and snorkeling trips. Trips to Cockscomb, Xunantunich, and Blue Hole. MC/V.

Ocean Motion Tours (☎523 3162 or 523 3363; www.oceanmotionplacencia.com), on the sidewalk. ½-day snorkeling off the inner cayes, diving and snorkeling at the Silk Caye Marine Reserve and Ranguana Caye, and fishing trips. Inland trips to Monkey River with manatee watching, to Cockscomb Basin, and to Mayan ruins. AmEx/MC/V.

Let's Go Sailing (☎523 3138; www.belize-sailing-charters.com), on the street. Discover Sailing Special, a 1hr. intro class followed by a hands-on day sail (US$35 per person). Other sailing classes US$330-850. AmEx/MC/V.

Paradise Tours (☎642 1655 or 564 9400; www.belize123.com), on the street. Two-tank scuba diving trips (US$110), snorkeling, Monkey River tours with manatee watch, Mayan ruins and Blue Hole National Park (US$120), Cockscomb Basin, manatee watching (US$40), and fishing. Discover scuba course US$175; 3-day PADI certification US$410. Golf cart rental US$55 per day; kayak rental US$5 per hr., US$30 per day. MC/V.

Placencia Office Supply (☎523 3205), on the street. Trips to Monkey River, snorkeling around French Louis Caye (BZ$160), fishing trips, Cockscomb Basin, cave tubing (US$155), with zip-line (US$215), birding tours (US$65-125), southern Maya ruins. Auto rental US$92.50 per day. MC/V.

Banks: Belize Bank, at the southern end of the street by the piers. Open M-Th 8am-3pm, F 8am-4:30pm. **Scotiabank,** on the street just north of the Hokey Pokey docks. Open M-Th 8am-2pm, F 8am-3:30pm, Sa 9am-11:30am. **Atlantic Bank,** on the street at the north end of the village. Open M-Th 8am-3pm, F 8am-4pm.

Laundromat: The Boson's Chair (☎523 4063 or 622 3199), on the sidewalk near the southern piers. US$6 per load. Open M-Sa 6am-6pm, Su 6am-noon.

Police Station: On the street just north of the Hokey Pokey dock.

Pharmacy: Wallen's Pharmacy, on the street above Wallen's Market. Open M-Sa 8am-noon and 1:30-5:30pm.

Internet Access: Sea House Internet and Tours, on the sidewalk. Internet US$5 per hr. Open M-Sa 9am-noon and 2:30-7:30pm. **Placencia Office Supply** (☎523 3205), on the street. Internet US$4 per hr. Printing, copying, and faxing services. Open M-F 8:30am-7pm, Sa 8:30am-5pm.

Post Office: On the street at the north edge of the village. Open M-Th 8am-noon and 1-4:30pm, F 8am-noon and 1-4pm.

ACCOMMODATIONS AND CAMPING

There are plenty of cheap rooms for rent all over town, but most have bare, unattractive rooms that lack ocean views or breezes. With a long public beach a few minutes away, though, it hardly matters. After all, no one spends too much time indoors in Placencia. The prices in the following listings reflect summer rates; during the winter (November-April) they can go up by as much as BZ$20.

Deb & Dave's Last Resort (☎523 3207), on the street. Despite the name, you'll want to try this place first out of all the budget options in town. Communal atmosphere. Small, well-lit rooms in a house behind the owners' place. A shady, sandy yard provides a free pool for guests and relaxing space away from the tourist bustle. Deb and Dave also run tours through their Toadal Agency (www.toadaladventure.com). Singles US$19; doubles US$24.50. MC/V. ❸

Omar's Guest House (☎600 8421), on the sidewalk. It's hard to miss this well-advertised budget guesthouse. Rooms on the 2nd floor above Omar's private residence are spare and the shared bathroom at the hallway's end is cramped, but the veranda with chairs and hammock serves as a good resting spot. Dorms US$10; singles US$12.50-15; doubles US$20. Cash only. ❷

Traveller's Inn (☎523 3190). This unassuming budget inn's 2 green buildings hold a variety of cramped rooms. Don't expect breathtaking postcard views, unless sandy lots are your thing, but cheap prices make this a backpacker favorite. Singles US$12.50, with bath US$15; doubles US$15/20. Cash only. ❷

Eloise's Rooms (☎523 2399), between the sidewalk and the street. Accessible from either the street or the sidewalk, Eloise's sits in a quiet, mostly untrafficked sandy lot in the middle of the village. Both stories are fronted by shaded verandas with hammocks. Well-kept, comfortable rooms with baths. You can check in at Eliose's house behind the inn, closer to the street side. Singles US$15; doubles US$20. Cash only. ❷

Amir's Inn (☎523 3131 or 3202), on the street. Homey, clean rooms without sea views. Small restaurant and a private house in the same building. Singles US$12.50, with bath US$25; doubles US$17.50/25. Cash only. ❷

Sea Spray Hotel (☎523 3148; www.seasprayhotel.com), off the sidewalk on the beach. Its seaside location makes the Sea Spray one of the most popular stays in Placencia, though you'll have to forget about an ocean view if you want one of the cheap rooms. The rooms are well-lit and breezy. If you want to splurge, try the beach *cabañas*, complete with porches and hammocks. Economy rooms US$20-50; seaside rooms US$35-40; beach *cabañas* US$62.50-70. MC/V. ❸

Manatee Inn (☎523 4083 or 607 0202; www.manateeinn.com), between the street and the sidewalk on the northern edge of the village. Sizable, 2-story wooden exterior with gorgeous, spotless rooms. Tranquil atmosphere and easy comfort. Each room comes with bath and a fridge. A shaded veranda running around the 2nd floor is perfect for escaping the hot sun. Singles US$40; doubles US$45; triples US$50. MC/V. ❺

🗂 FOOD

Seafood rules in Placencia, and you can often enjoy it with a cheap, breezy ocean view. The influx of expats has created culinary diversity in the small village, so there are plenty of options other than the ubiquitous fish, shrimp, and ceviche dishes. For groceries, try **Everyday Supermarket,** on the street north of the Hokey Pokey dock (☎523 3230; open daily 7:30am-9pm).

🍴 **Tuttifruti Gelateria,** on the street. Some of the best ice cream in Belize is served at this Italian dessert shop. If you stay in town long enough you may find yourself addicted to the smooth, perfectly prepared creams which come in cappuccino, lime, and colada flavors. Cones US$1.75. Cups US$2.25-3.50. Milkshakes US$3. Open M-Tu and Th-Su 9:30am-9pm. Cash only. ❶

De' Tatch Seafood Restaurant (☎503 3385), on the beach off the sidewalk. It's worth eating at De' Tatch just for its beautiful beachside setting (grab a seat under the small *palapas* for full effect). Huge menu with stuffed fry jacks for breakfast, cheap seafood platters (US$6-7.50) for lunch, and beer batter shrimp for dinner. Breakfast US$3.25-5.50. Afternoon delights US$4.50-9. Dinner US$9-16. Internet available. MC/V. ❸

Pickled Parrot (☎604 0278 or 624 2651), between the street and sidewalk (accessible from either). Under a brightly colored tent. Some of the biggest crowds in town gather here all day. Pizzas US$17-21. Subs US$6-9.50. Burgers US$6-7.50. Fajitas US$7-9.50. Huge variety of mixed drinks after dark US$6-7.50. Brave souls can down the Parrot Piss, a large blend of juice and coconut rum (US$7.50). Lunch special (US$5) noon-2pm. Happy hour 5-6pm (US$2.50 appetizers). Open M-Sa noon-10pm, Su 5-9pm. MC/V. ❸

Omar's Creole Grub (☎600 8421 or 667 0651), on the street. This no-frills eatery, run by local fisherman and guesthouse owner Omar, serves fresh catch from the nearby sea. Seafood dishes (US$7-12.50) include baracuda steak, fish fillet, and shrimp dishes. You can also go for cheaper Mexican snacks like burritos and fajitas (US$3.50-7). W and F barbecue plates. Open M-F and Su 6am-8pm. Cash only. ❸

Pirates Grill (☎523 3119; www.piratesgrill.com), on the sidewalk. The menu here may well be the largest and most eclectic in Placencia. Shawarma grill wraps US$7.50. Baja Mexican snacks US$1.50-5.50. Jamaican, Ethiopian, Japanese, and Malaysian curries US$7.50. Austrian schnitzel US$7. Of course, the usual breakfast burritos (US$4-5) and fresh seafood dishes (US$7.50-15) keep things from getting too crazy. Appetizers US$1-5. Entrees US$6-15. Open M-Sa 8am-10pm. MC/V. ❸

Belgian Cafe (☎523 3519), on the street at the north edge of the village. Because nothing says waffles like a Caribbean getaway. This polished, out-of-the-way, upstairs cafe specializes in breakfasts you definitely can't get anywhere else in town. *Croques* (toasted sandwiches) US$2.50-6.50. Crepes US$5-9. And, of course, Belgium's most famous gift to the food world—waffles (US$5-9). Outdoor seating on the cafe's shaded porch. Open daily 8am-2pm. MC/V. ❷

The Secret Garden (☎523 3617), on the street. This restaurant and coffee house creates a romantic atmosphere with white curtains and soft lighting. Standard breakfasts BZ$13-20. Dinners featuring seafood and pasta options (low season US$12.50-13.50;

high season US$13.50-26.50) are the real highlight, changing every night as the chef desires. Free Wi-Fi. Open Tu-Su 7:30-11:30am and 5-9pm, Su 7:30-10pm. MC/V. ❹

Wendy's Restaurant and Bar (☎523 3335), on the street. Wendy's fuses Spanish and Belizean cuisine and sports a spotless interior. *Huevos rancheros* (Mexican breakfast) US$5-7.50. Pasta (US$11-12.50) and seafood (US$12.50-22.50). Grab a shaded seat on the sizable porch. Open daily 7am-9:30pm. MC/V. ❸

🎵 🎭 ENTERTAINMENT AND NIGHTLIFE

A range of beachside bars keeps things loud and lively at night, especially during the winter high season when tourists and locals really get to mingling. The clientele is a mostly middle-aged crowd, so expect more bars than DJs or dance parties. This is a compact village, so the stumble home shouldn't be too long or confusing.

Tipsy Tuna Sports Bar, on the beach next to the Barefoot Beach Bar. Keeps things ocean chill with sandy floors, pool tables, and high stools. Catch some soccer or basketball on the bar's TV. Drinks US$2.50-9. Open M-W 7pm-midnight, Th-Sa 7am-2am, and Su 7pm-midnight. MC/V.

J-Byrds' Bar (☎523 2412), on the waterfront by the docks at the village's southern end. Painted marine wildlife swims on windows and a giant jaguar wades through the sea above the bar. Karaoke and dancing nights F and Sa . A pool table, free darts, and a flatscreen TV keep things interesting during the weekdays. Drinks US$2.50-7.50. Open M-Th and Su 10am-midnight, F-Sa 10am-2am. MC/V.

Barefoot Beach Bar (☎523 3515), on the beach. The name explains it all: this open-air bar is as close to the shore as they come. A collection of American license plates on the walls almost rivals the collection of American tourists chatting with the bartenders. Drinks US$2.50-8. Open Tu-Th 10am-8pm, F 11am-9pm. Cash only.

🎉 FESTIVALS

Along with Caye Caulker, Placencia is the place to be to celebrate the opening of lobster season. During **Lobsterfest,** during the last weekend of June, the beach pulses to live reggae and punta, vendors hawk their wares along the shore, and fishing and lobster-catching competitions take place. Book ahead for this weekend—hotels fill up quickly.

🏞 OUTDOOR ACTIVITIES

Placencia is meant for relaxing, but a variety of tour companies offer daytrips and getaways to some of Belize's most exciting attractions, off-shore and inland. Unfortunately, prices for these trips range from dismaying to shocking. Skip the guided tours of Cockscomb Basin Wildlife Sanctuary (BZ$150-170) and nearby Mayan ruins (BZ$180-230), all of which can be visited privately. If you are going to trek from the village, head for the offshore sites, most of them inaccessible from the northern cayes and appealing to hardcore divers and snorkelers.

NEARBY CAYES. The nearest sizable island is **Laughing Bird Caye,** 12 mi. off the coast, which is at the center of its own national park but lies between the shore and the reef The **Silk Cayes Marine Reserve,** on the reef an hour boat ride from the village, features abundant tropical fish and coral species, making it a popular spot for both divers and snorkelers. Just south of the Silk Cayes, **Ranguana** and **Pompian Cayes** are similar underwater attractions; they can be visited as part of a trip to the Silk Cayes or independently. *(4hr. snorkeling trips BZ$90-100 per person, 6hr. BZ$120-130 per person; 6-7 hr. fishing trips BZ$140-160 per person).*

FISHING. If you've got interest and money to spare, the seas near Placencia are much less crowded than the areas near the northern cayes. *(½-day fishing trips to the reef BZ$450-500, full-day BZ$600-650.)*

MONKEY RIVER. The Creole fishing village of Monkey River lies about 15 mi. southwest of Placencia on the coast; after (or before) a lunch stop here, trips continue 4 mi. upriver in search of howler monkeys, crocs, and birds. The trip there may include some manatee watching among nearby mangrove estuaries. *(6-7hr., BZ$110-140 per person).*

RED BANK. Fourteen miles west of Placencia, this inland village attracts hundreds of birds species from November to March who come for the abundant fruits. Chief among them is Belize's national bird, the beautifully colored scarlet macaw. *(Full-day trips BZ$120-140 per person.)*

PUNTA GORDA

Belize's southernmost town (pop. 5100) lies well off the beaten track; for many it's simply a convenient crossing point to Guatemala after a stay in Placencia. But PG, as it's known here, is more than a transit hub. Though it was founded by Garinagu from Honduras in the early nineteenth century, the community has since opened up to a variety of cultures. Today, Garífuna, Creoles, Maya, East Indians, Chinese, and American expats mingle on the humid coastal streets. The town itself will probably get old after a few days, but the surrounding Toledo District is among the most beautiful in Belize, and PG serves as an ideal base for exploring.

⌐ TRANSPORTATION

Flights: Punta Gorda's **airstrip** is located about a ½-mile north of town along Prince, Queen, and King St. **Tropic Air** (☎226 2012; www.tropicair.com) and **Maya Island Air** (☎223 1140; www.mayaislandair.com) fly to **Placencia** (20min., BZ$84), **Dangriga** (40min., BZ$137), **Belize City Municipal Airstrip** (1hr., BZ$185), and the **Philip Goldson International Airport** in Belize City (1hr. 10min.; 7, 9:40, 11:35am, 1:35, and 4pm; BZ$218).

Buses: Punta Gorda is the home base of the **James Bus Line,** King St. (☎702 2049), which services most of southern Belize. Buses stop right in front of the offices; you can buy tickets inside or on the bus. Buses to: **Belize City** (6¼hr., BZ$23); **Belmopan** (5¼hr., BZ$20); **Dangriga** (3½hr., BZ$14); **Independence** (2hr., BZ$9) at 4, 5, 6, 8, 10am, noon, 2, 3, and 4pm. **Local buses** to Mayan villages in the Toledo district leave from Jose Maria Nunez St. between Prince, Queen, and King St. Buses for **San Antonio** (1hr., BZ$3), **Jalacte** (2hr., BZ$5), and all other villages along the route leave M-Sa between 6-7am, 11am-noon, and 4-5pm; check with the drivers for the exact time. Buses for **Silver Creek** (1hr., BZ$3) and **Indian Creek** (1½hr., BZ$5) leave between 11am-noon and 4-5pm.

Boats: Punta Gorda is a popular transportation hub for coastal towns in Guatemala. The **customs office,** Front St., answers questions about tickets and other procedures.

Marisol Boat Charters (☎702 0113). Leaves Punta Gorda daily at 4pm and arrives in Puerto Barrios at 5pm (BZ$44). Buy tickets at the **Dreamlight Computer Center** (p. 272).

Memo's Boat Service (☎625 0464 or 722 2622). Leaves Punta Gorda daily at 12:30pm and arrives in Livingston at 1:30pm (BZ$40) and in Puerto Barrios at 2pm (BZ$50).

Pichilingo (☎722 2870). Leaves Punta Gorda daily at 2pm and arrives in Puerto Barrios at 3pm (BZ$50).

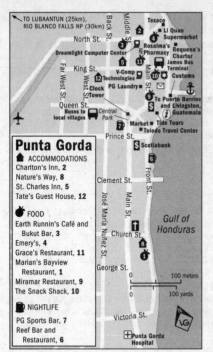

Punta Gorda

🏠 ACCOMMODATIONS

Charlton's Inn, 2
Nature's Way, 8
St. Charles Inn, 5
Tate's Guest House, 12

🍴 FOOD

Earth Runnin's Café and
  Bukut Bar, 3
Emery's, 4
Grace's Restaurant, 11
Marian's Bayview
  Restaurant, 1
Miramar Restaurant, 9
The Snack Shack, 10

🍸 NIGHTLIFE

PG Sports Bar, 7
Reef Bar and
  Restaurant, 6

Requena's Charter Services, Front. St. (☎722 2070 or 662 0042). Leaves Punta Gorda daily at 9am and arrives in Puerto Barrios at 10:30am (BZ$40).

Rigoberto James. Leaves Punta Gorda Tu and F at 10am and arrives in Livingston at 11am (BZ$40).

Kayak Rentals: Tide Tours, 41 Front St. (☎722 2129; www.tidetours.com). BZ$5 per hr., BZ$15 per ½-day, BZ$25 per day. Open M-F 8am-noon and 2-5pm, Sa 8am-noon.

🗺️🧭 ORIENTATION AND PRACTICAL INFORMATION

Punta Gorda is spread out on the shore next to the **Gulf of Honduras;** like many other coastal towns in Belize, it is longer than it is wide. Organized in a grid system, the town extends inland for about five blocks before meeting the local airstrip. **Front Street** hugs the shore while **Main, Jose Maria Nunez, West,** and **Far West Streets** march successively inland. From South to North, they are intersected by **Clements, Prince, Queen, King,** and **North Streets.** The **town park,** distinguished by its large, sky-blue **clock tower,** serves as the locus of market activity along Main St. between Prince and Queen St.

Tourist Office: BTIA Tourist Info, Front St. (☎722 2531), in the white hexagonal building. Has information on sights in the Toledo district; the **Toledo Ecotourism Association Program** (p. 275) has a stand here. Open Tu-F 8am-noon and 1-5pm, Sa 8am-noon.

Tours: Tide Tours, 41 Front St. (☎722 2129; www.tidetours.com). Offers a wide array of tours in southern Belize. Kayaking trips down Joe Taylor's Creek (3hrs., BZ$40 per person). Half-day trips to Rio Blanco park and Blue Creek Cave (BZ$140-170). Full-day trips to Barranco and the Sastoon-Temash National Park, Laguna and the Agua-Caliente Wildlife Sanctuary, and Nim Li Punit and Lubaantun (BZ$170). Proceeds go to development programs in the region. Open M-F 8am-noon and 2-5pm, Sa 8am-noon. **Toledo Travel Center** (☎614 2080 or 668 8811; www.suncreeklodge.com), on the corner of Front and Queen St. Leads trips in the Toledo District. Destinations include the Mayan ruins at Lubaantun and Uxbenka and the villages of Blue Creek and Laguna. Also leads multi-day hiking trips into the Maya Mountains, including a trek up Doyle's Delight, the highest point in Belize.

Banks: Belize Bank, on the corner of Main and Queen St. Open M-Th 8am-3pm, F 8am-4:30pm. **Scotiabank,** down Main St. just south of the park. Open M-Th 8am-2pm, F 8am-3:30pm, Sa 9-11:30am.

Luggage Storage: Toledo Travel Center (☎614 2080; www.suncreeklodge.com), on the corner of Front and Queen St. BZ$2 per day.

Laundromat: P.G. Laundry, Main St. BZ$1.75 per lb. Open M-Sa 8am-5pm.

Police Station: On the corner of Front and King St.

24hr. Pharmacy: Rosalma's Pharmacy, Main St. (☎722 2444). Open M-Sa 9am-noon and 2-5pm.

Hospital or Medical Services: Punta Gorda Hospital, Main St. (☎722 2026), 20min. west of town.

Internet Access: Dreamlight Computer Center (☎702 0113), on the corner of North and Main St. Internet BZ$6 per hr. Wi-Fi. Open M-Sa 8am-9pm, Su 9am-5pm. **Tide Tours,** 41 Front St. (☎722 2129; www.tidetours.com). Internet BZ$4 per hr. Wi-Fi. Open M-F 8am-noon and 2-5pm, Sa 8am-noon. .

Post Office: Front St. (☎722 2087). Open M-Th 8am-noon and 1-5pm, F 8am-noon and 1-4:30pm.

ACCOMMODATIONS

Nature's Way Guest House, 82 Front St. (☎702 2119), at the corner of Front and Church St. Peaceful and secluded, this family-run joint is the first choice of backpackers. Sizable rooms with huge windows. Common room with TV. Small book exchange. Chet Schmidt, the owner, provides information about the area and the Toledo Ecotourism Association program. Breakfast BZ$5-8. Internet access BZ$9 per hr. Singles BZ$26; doubles BZ$36; triples BZ$46. Cash only. ❷

St. Charles Inn, 23 King St. (☎722 2149; www.toucantrail.com/st.-charles-inn.html). Make yourself at home in this long-standing mid-range favorite. Rooms run the gamut from homey and well-decorated to rustic and cramped. All rooms come with cable TV. Shaded 2nd-floor veranda with hammock space. Singles BZ$40; doubles BZ$50, with A/C BZ$65. Cash only. ❷

Tate's Guest House, 34 Jose Maria Nunez St. (☎722 0147). Located in a residential part of town away from the center's activity. A beautiful house with all the comforts of home inside. Spotless and well-furnished rooms. Mr. Tate, a Punta Gorda expert, makes a genial host. All rooms with private baths and TVs. Singles with fan BZ$39, with A/C BZ$55; doubles BZ$55/76. Cash only. ❸

Charlton's Inn, 9 Main St. (☎722 2197; www.charltonsinn.com), at the corner of North and Main St. Large, 3-story inn on the north side of town with a plant-filled courtyard. All rooms with A/C; some with private baths and cable TV. Wi-Fi. Singles BZ$60; doubles BZ$70; triples BZ$80. AmEx/MC/V. ❹

FOOD

Front St. and the town park are filled with vendors from Toledo villages selling produce on Monday, Wednesday, Friday, and Saturday mornings. This market is the cheapest and best way to sample local food and grab some fresh fruit. For groceries, head to Main St., where you'll find **Mel's Enterprise** (open M and W 8am-12:30pm and 2-8:30pm, Tu and Th 8am-12:30pm and 2-6pm, and F-Sa 8am-12:30pm and 2-9pm), **SuPaul's Supermarket** (open M-Sa 8am-6:30pm), and **Li Quan Supermarket** (☎722 0097; open 7am-9pm).

▨ **Earth Runnins Cafe and Bukut Bar,** 13 Main Middle St. Rasta rhythm rules at Earth Runnins, easily the most distinctive restaurant in Punta Gorda. More of an experience than a mere eatery. Don't be surprised if the staff starts up a live reggae jam between taking orders and preparing meals. The menu is an amalgam of seafood, pasta, and Belizean dishes, all of them personally prepared by a dynamic chef (he's usually on vocals). Waits can be long, but they're worth it—just don't come if you're looking for a relaxing night out. Entrees BZ$12-25. Drinks BZ$4-10. Open daily M and W-Sa 9am-2pm and 5-11pm. ❸

Marian's Bayview Restaurant, Front St. (☎722 0129), across from Nature's Way Guest House. The ocean views from the high open-air deck are spectacular; the menu, with its blend of Belizean, East Indian, and vegetarian food, isn't bad either. All ingredients are organic and prepared in homemade soybean or coconut oil. Entrees from BZ$10. Open M-W and F-Sa 11am-2pm and 6-10pm, Th 11am-2pm, Su noon-2pm and 7-9pm. AmEx/MC/V. ❷

Grace's Restaurant (☎702 2414), on the corner of Main and King St. Seafood and Belizean food prepared grilled, fried, and stewed. Entrees BZ$7-12. Seafood BZ$9-34. Open daily 8am-10pm. MC/V. ❷

The Snack Shack (☎702 0020), off of Main St. The food is quick and cheap, but still tasty. Serves breakfast (BZ$6-10) and lunch (BZ$8-10) alongside a selection of snacks, cakes, and pastries. Seating is on an covered outdoor veranda. Open M-Sa 7am-4pm. Cash only. ❷

Emery Restaurant (☎722 2317), on the corner of Main and North Main St. Spacious outdoor seating area and stunning views of the ocean make Emery one of Punta Gorda's most popular spots. The menu is a mix of Belizean food (BZ$10-18) and seafood dishes (BZ$12-30). Open Tu-Sa 11:30am-2pm and 6-10pm. MC/V. ❷

Miramar Restaurant, Front St. (☎722 2033). The menu, saturated with standard Belizean recipes, will teach you to love rice and beans all over again. Eclectic decor combines posters, flags, and various mementos with Chinese-themed items. Entrees BZ$8-15. Open M-Sa 8:30am-8pm, Su 9am-3pm. Cash only. ❷

🎵 🎭 ENTERTAINMENT AND NIGHTLIFE

Front St. is the heart of nightlife in PG. Offerings range from dingy holes-in-the-wall overlooking the street, to breezy open-air spots with views of the sea.

Reef Bar and Restaurant, Front St. The Reef is a place to relax. The bar's hammocks are the best place to do it. Whether you're reclining or not, you can enjoy the breeze and views from this prime upper-floor, open-air location. Reggae and punta provide an undulating soundtrack. Drinks BZ$4-15. Open daily 11am-midnight. Cash only.

PG Sports Bar and Restaurant (☎722 2329), on the corner of Main and Prince St. Don't be alarmed by the *Space Jam* painting on the wall by the door. This popular spot draws locals with reasonably priced drinks and sports games on the bar's TV. Drinks BZ$4-10. Open Tu-Th 8pm-midnight, F-Sa 8pm-2am. Cash only.

🏕 OUTDOOR ACTIVITIES

Punta Gorda is an ideal base for inland day trips to the Toledo District. Travelers there will find fascinating parks, ruins, and living culture; see **Toledo District,** p. 274 for more details. Guided tours to the region are available through the tour companies listed in Orientation and Practical Information (p. 271). These tours, however, are uniformly expensive; the region is best explored independently over the course of a few days.

RIVERS. Nearby **Joe Taylor Creek,** which skirts Punta Gorda's northern border and empties into the Caribbean, is a popular and accessible spot for kayakers, birdwatchers, and wildlife enthusiasts. You can rent a kayak (see **Transportation,** p. 270) or take a half-day guided trip (BZ$30-40) with one of the tour companies in town (see **Orientation and Practical Info,** p. 271). You'll need a guide venture onto the **Moho River,** which snakes its way from Guatemala through the Toledo District and ends five miles south of Punta Gorda. Beware, excursions are costly (BZ$130-150).

CAYES. Though not nearly as popular as their neighbors to the north, Belize's southernmost cayes present ample opportunities for snorkeling, diving, and fishing. The **Port Honduras Marine Reserve** consists mostly of small, landless mangrove islands populated by manatees and dolphins. Fishing the waters there, still relatively undiscovered by tourists, is a popular activity. Forty miles from the shore, the fourteen **Sapodilla Cayes** consist of beautiful, unspoiled beaches and schools of jacks, spadefish, and angelfish. The **Halfmoon Beach** on Hunting Caye is a popular spot. Unfortunately, it's impossible to reach these islands at any reasonable price. Tours operating from Punta Gorda usually charge between BZ$300-500 dollars for snorkeling or diving trips; fishing will run you at least BZ$100 more.

TOLEDO DISTRICT

Belize's southernmost region is one of its most beautiful, yet also one of its most unexplored, likely due to the difficulty of traveling to and between its isolated rural villages. Those who don't make the effort, though, will miss out on a vibrant cultural experience. The population here is almost entirely Mopan and Q'eqchi' Maya. Though their ancestors have lived here for millennia, most of the modern settlements are no more than 150 years old. Refugees fleeing Guatemalan conscription and prejudice moved to neighboring Belize, retracing the paths of their forebears who fled inland from Spanish invaders centuries before. Today, most of the villages have Spanish names. Mopan, Q'eqchi', and through mandatory schooling, English and Spanish are the region's spoken tongues.

Toledo is often called the "forgotten district," neglected by the government and left to manage its lack of development and rural poverty on its own. Toledo is for serious independent travelers who aren't afraid of long walks, hitchhiking (though not recommended by *Let's Go*), and lack of amenities. But, the rewards are worth it. A range of fascinating natural and manmade sites, scenic views at every turn, and an inspiring, welcoming people meet those willing to strike out on their own.

⌨ TRANSPORTATION

Buses to the villages depart from Punta Gorda on Jose Maria Nunez St. For details, see Punta Gorda **Transportation,** p. 270. Buses back to **Punta Gorda** leave **Jalacte** (near the Guatemalan border) M-Sa between 6-7am, 11am-noon, and 4-5pm, and pass through all the villages along the main road before reaching the Southern Highway. Ask locals in each village for an estimate of the buses' arrival time.

Hitchhiking is a common method of getting around; in Toledo, it's practically an established form of public transportation. You might find yourself offered a ride even without asking for one. With infrequent and spotty public transportation, it's by far the most convenient way to travel. Of course, the dangers involved in hitchhiking anywhere also apply here. Although *Let's Go* does not endorse hitchhiking under any circumstances, it's generally agreed that the region is the safest place to hitchhike in Belize.

◼ ORIENTATION

The **main road** connecting a large number of villages in the region leaves the **Southern Highway** at the **Dump turnoff** (actually a gas station) about 15 miles from Punta Gorda. From here, the road, by and large unpaved, passes through the villages of **Mafredi, San Antonio, Santa Cruz, Santa Elena, Pueblo Viejo,** and **Jalacte** on the Guatemalan border. Another, smaller road leaves the main road about two miles from the Dump turnoff, running through **San Pedro Columbia** (known simply as Columbia), **San Miguel,** and **Silver Creek** before meeting up again with the Southern Highway. A road turns off at **Mafredi,** about five miles from the Dump, and leads to **Blue Creek** and **Aguacate. Laguna** and the Garífuna village of **Barranco** are located at the ends of their respective turnoffs, which branch off of the Southern Highway between the Dump turnoff and Punta Gorda.

ACCOMMODATIONS AND FOOD

Few hotels or guesthouses can be found in this rural area, though there are some pricey luxury lodges along the Southern Highway. Luckily, budget travelers can find lodgings—and much more—with the **Toledo Ecotourism Association (TEA),** (☎722 2096 or 722 2531; www.plenty.org/TEA/tea.htm), a unique program that attempts to introduce visitors to the region while boosting the local economy and aiding the environment. TEA runs a **guesthouse program** that allows visitors to stay nearby and eat with local families. All of the proceeds go towards the local economy; 80% of the money generated from the program remains in the village. Visitors are lodged in a guesthouse located next to or near the host family's own home; beds are dorm-style and most come with mosquito nets. There is no electricity in the guesthouses, so bring a flashlight or expect an early night. Outhouses and showers are next to the guesthouses. Price varies according to the village, but the cost per person usually runs between BZ$20 and BZ$26 each night.

Meals (BZ$6-8) can also be taken with the families. They're probably your best option from an economic standpoint, given that there are few kitchens for use and restaurants are very few and far between. The food is local (sometimes made with produce from the owners' farm); this is your chance to enjoy genuine, homemade Mayan food.

The program runs a range of activities. Some villages offer storytelling and dances; all offer guided tours of nearby wilderness and attractions, many of which lie well off the beaten bath. The cost for these varies, so it's best to ask the host or contact TEA with specific questions.

Participating villages include **San Pedro Columbia, San Miguel, San Antonio, San Jose, Santa Elena, Pueblo Viejo,** and **Laguna.** A different flavor of TEA is offered at the Garífuna coastal village of **Barranco,** where the culture is a world away from that of its neighbors, but the spirit of hospitality remains the same. To find a guesthouse, simply ask locals at each village. Most will be able to direct you to the right location. For more information, contact TEA or visit their stand at the **BTIA Tourist Booth** on Front St. in Punta Gorda (p. 271).

SIGHTS

NIM LI PUNIT

About 26 miles up the Southern Highway from Punta Gorda; a hilly ½-mile trail leads up to the site from the highway. Ask any bus traveling the route to be let off at the Nim Li Punit turnoff (1.5hr., BZ$4). Open 8am-4:30pm. BZ$10.

Perched on a hilltop affording spectacular views of the surrounding jungles, the ruins at Nim Li Punit are a true highlight of southern Belize. Throughout its history, the town's position between the mountains and seacoast has ensured its status as an important center of trade. At its peak during the Classic era, it was home to between 5000 and 7000 citizens and is believed to have been allied with mighty Copán in present-day Honduras.

The finds at the site's **South Group** constitute its main claim to fame. The **Plaza of the Stelae** once held 26 stone monuments dating from AD 700-900, seven of them carved with intricate historical and cultural details. Most of these monuments are now protected in the stelae room, but a few still stand under thatched-roof coverings in the plaza. To the east side of the plaza is the **E-Group,** a group of structures that may have functioned as an observatory; three stone markers, their positions based on solstices and equinoxes, still stand in front of Struture 1. To the west and raised slightly, the **Plaza of the Royal Tombs** was once the residence of the royal family. It was believed that this plaza also hosted their ancestors' spirits (hence the three excavated tombs there). No less than four members of the royal family, along with a huge assortment of jade figures and ceramic vessels, were found in **Tomb 1.**

A well-preserved **ballcourt** separates the South Group from the **East Group.** This ball court is centered around the **Ninki Pec ("Big Stones") Plaza,** so named because of the large stones placed in the ground at the foot of its well-preserved terraced platforms. Across a (usually dry) creek bed, the **West Group** is a mostly overgrown plaza, though the barely discernible pyramid there remains the highest structure at Nim Li Punit.

A stop at the **stelae room** next to the visitors' center is a must. Some of the largest and best-preserved stelae in Belize are on display here. The enormous **Stelae 14,** depicting a local ruler during a scattering or offering ritual, is the star of the collection. At nine meters, it's the tallest structure of its kind in Belize and the second-tallest in the Mayan world. The ruler's enormous headdress (think Marge Simpson) gives the stellae its height and the site its name—"Nim Li Punit" translates to "big hat" or "diadem" in Q'eqchi' Maya.

LUBAATUN

Near the village of San Pedro Columbia, about 3 miles from the main road running through the Toledo District. Reaching it is nearly impossible without hitchhiking (not recommended by Let's Go) or taking a guided tour, but there are a few buses that head to San Pedro Columbia from Punta Gorda (p. 270). From the village, turn right at the intersection by the convenience store, cross the river, and continue for 10min.; then turn left at the sign. Open 8am-4:30pm. BZ$10.

The "Place of Fallen Stones" (named by modern excavators, not its ancient residents) makes a strong first impression. Mountains of compact rubble rise up from clean, grassy plazas. Located in the foothills of the Maya Mountains in a drainage basin of the Río Grande, the town grew to become a site of great religious and economic importance during the eighth and ninth centuries, boasting a population of up to 11,000.

Early excavators, including Belize's chief medical officer, Thomas Gann, employed dubious methods, but over time, blasting temple tops with dynamite gave way to more accepted archaeological practices. Some believe that these new methods led to the discovery of the **crystal skull,** a product of advanced technology said to have been used by high priests to will death, by an excavator's teenage daughter in the 1950s. View the rigorous documentary *Indiana Jones and the Kingdom of the Crystal Skull* for more information.

The site is compact and easy to explore. Keep in mind that all the stones used to build the site were not found on the hilltop (as at Nim Li Punit) but carried or dragged up the hill from the riverbed three miles away. A system of interlocking stones was used to build the structures, lending the site its distinctive, disheveled look. To the north of the site, over the mound of rubble from the visitors' center, is the **Great Plaza (Plaza V),** backed by **Structure 62** and flanked by the east and west **ball courts.** This plaza affords decent views of the site. **Plaza IV** lies in the midst of ruined temples; climb down the stairs to reach **Plaza III** and the **Grand Ball Court,** one of the most impressive and best-preserved ball courts in Belize.

Lubaantun is known for the large number of small **figurines** found in its ruins. Most of these small objects depict animal heads, bodies, human heads or ball players. Many also double as whistles, with their tones corresponding to the figure. New figurines are constantly being found. In any case, the visitors' center has some of the best on display.

SAN ANTONIO

About five miles from the Dump turnoff along the region's main road. See Punta Gorda Transportation (p. 270) for details on reaching the village from Punta Gorda.

With a population of almost 2000, hilly San Antonio is both one of Toledo's largest villages and the largest Mopan Maya community in the country. Founded in the late 1880s by refugees fleeing forced conscription in the neighboring Peten region of Guatemala in the late 1800s, the village retains a communal feel despite its size and scattered layout. The village's large **stone church,** with stained glass windows and a heavy gray aesthetic, seems out of place here. Its lawn provides great views of the hills surrounding the village. Inside is a wooden statue of the church's namesake, San Luis, brought to the village from Guatemala. On the road 0.7 miles west of town, the **San Antonio Waterfall** is a quiet spot for a cool dip beneath the 20ft. cascade.

SANTA CRUZ, UXBENKA, AND RIO BLANCO NATIONAL PARK

Santa Cruz is 5 miles west of San Antonio along the main road and 10 miles from the Southern Highway. Uxbenka has no admission fee. Rio Blanco National Park is open daily 8:30am-4:30pm. Admission to Rio Blanco is BZ$10.

Far less developed than San Antonio, the mostly residential village of **Santa Cruz** is composed of scattered, thatched-roof houses. Development seems to have stalled here; natural diasters like Hurricane Iris in 2001 have caused significant damage, though the village rebounded after international aid organizations stepped in. Note that Santa Cruz does not have a TEA guesthouse, though **Santa Elena,** a few miles further west, does.

At the "Welcome to Santa Cruz" sign, opposite the water tower, an overgrown trail departs from the path and climbs over a hill after 0.3 miles. The weedy plaza at the hilltop, almost unrecognizable as such, forms the heart of **Uxbenka.** These were little-known ruins occupied by the Maya during the Early Classic period (250-500AD). Views from the hilltop plaza are obscured by trees, the temples are completely overrun, and the plaza itself seems to have been left untended for years. But fallen stelae, scattered rubble, a rock wall, and an excavated tomb make Uxbenka a quiet, undiscovered, and private spot for the Maya completist.

One mile west of town, the **Rio Blanco National Park** is the perfect spot for a few hours of relaxation. From the visitors' center by the road, the **Waterfall Trail** leads to a 20ft. cascade emptying into a cool, expansive pool. You can slide gently into the water or, if you're looking for a thrill, jump from a cliff by the trail. The **Cable Trail** leaves the Waterfall Trail just before the falls and crosses the Rio Blanco on a thin, wobbly cable bridge. From there, the **Jiffi Jaffa Trail** loops for 2km and returns you to the bridge.

BLUE CREEK VILLAGE AND CAVE

Three miles down a turnoff leaving the main road in the village of Mafredi. Admission to the cave is BZ$5; you can buy your ticket in the village at the trail entrance.

Blue Creek is one of the area's more beautiful villages. The views on the ride down are spectacular, as jungle hills slope down to grassy farmland (most of it owned by recent Mennonite arrivals from the US and Canada) by the road. The village is centered on the creek, which serves as a popular swimming and lounging destination for locals. The site was settled at the turn of the twentieth century by Guatemalan emigres. In the 1940s a hurricane devastated the community. In the 1950s, arrivals from nearby San Antonio founded the current village. Today, Blue Creek is one of the few communities with a mixed Mopan and Q'eqchi' Maya population.

The **Blue Creek Cave** (also called the **Hokeb Ha' Cave**) is accessed by a trail that departs from the village center, by the creek. The trail hugs the riverside for about 0.7 miles; at that point, it's necessary to clamber over the rocks in the river to reach the impressive mouth of the cave from which the creek flows. The sight is worth a few pictures and moments of rest. To explore further inside the watery interior (which includes two underground waterfalls), you'll need a guide. Tours run from Punta Gorda; usually the cave is combined with another destination in Toledo (BZ$140-180). Cheaper tours run from town.

LAGUNA AND AGUA CALIENTE NATIONAL PARK

Two miles down its own turnoff, which leaves the Southern Highway 1½ miles from the Dump turnoff as you head towards Punta Gorda. A few irregular buses serve the village, but the only reliable way of getting here is to walk from the highway. Ask any bus serving the route to let you off at the Laguna turnoff. BZ$10.

The small Q'eqchi Maya village of Laguna, nestled beneath scenic hills of thick jungle, is a gateway for tourists eager to visit one of Belize's premier wetland regions. The Agua Caliente National Park covers 8.6 square miles of wetlands and is home to hundreds of waterfowl, including ibis, herons, kingfishers, and the famous jabiru storks. Howler monkeys, tapirs, gibnuts, and jaguars have also been known to inhabit the park. In addition to wildlife, the park has three fresh water **lagoons** and two **hot springs.**

You can buy your ticket at the village center. Head down the grassy path leaving the road, which passes the TEA guesthouse. After 10min., a **boardwalk** juts out from the right; a 15min. walk brings you to the **visitor's center**— empty and gutted as of our last visit. From here, the boardwalk continues for 0.7 miles to the lagoon which forms the centerpiece of the park and gives the village its name. You can also try a 2km hiking trail that winds through the wetlands from the visitor's center, though it's often impassable during the wet summer months. For kayak trips through the lagoons, ask at the ticket office or at the TEA guesthouse.

BARRANCO AND SARSTOON-TEMASH NATIONAL PARK

Eight miles down a turnoff that leaves the Southern Highway 6 miles from the Dump turnoff. Ask a bus to let you off at the Barranco turnoff. There is no direct public transportation to the village. www.satiim.org.bz. Open daily 8:30am-4:30pm. Small areas of the park are accessible by walking trails. Land, kayak, and fishing tours leave from Punta Gorda (BZ$170-190; *see p. 271).* *For cheaper tours, inquire at the village's TEA Guesthouse. BZ$10.*

The southernmost village on Belize's coast is also one of its most unique. The Garinagu here struggle to hold fast to their traditions in this isolated location. Interestingly enough, Barranco is the oldest continuously inhabited community in the Toledo. The population now hovers at 150, and with a younger generation looking elsewhere for work, the future of this small fishing community remains uncertain.

Most tourists travel to Barranco to access the nearby **Sarstoon-Temash National Park,** Belize's southernmost nature and wildlife reserve. Encompassing over 41,000 acres and hugging the Guatemalan border, this reserve between the Temash and Sarstoon Rivers houses jaguars, tapirs, ocelots, and scarlet macaws. The Temash is lined by towering red mangrove trees, some of which rise over 100ft from the shoreline.

APPENDIX

CLIMATE

AVG. TEMP. (LOW/ HIGH), PRECIP.	JANUARY			APRIL			JULY			OCTOBER		
	°C	°F	mm	°C	°F	mm	°C	°F	mm	°C	°F	mm
Belize City, Belize	19-27	66-80	137	23-30	73-86	56	24-31	75-87	163	22-30	71-86	305
Guatemala City, Guatemala	12-23	53-73	8	14-28	57-82	31	16-26	60-78	203	16-24	60-75	173

MEASUREMENTS

Like the rest of the rational world, Mexico uses the metric system. The basic unit of length is the **meter (m)**, which is divided into 100 **centimeters (cm)** or 1000 **millimeters (mm)**. One thousand meters make up one **kilometer (km)**. Fluids are measured in **liters (L)**, each divided into 1000 **milliliters (mL)**. A liter of pure water weighs one **kilogram (kg)**, which is divided into 1000 **grams (g)**. One metric ton is **1000kg**.

MEASUREMENT CONVERSIONS	
1 inch (in.) = 25.4mm	1 millimeter (mm) = 0.039 in.
1 foot (ft.) = 0.305m	1 meter (m) = 3.28 ft.
1 yard (yd.) = 0.914m	1 meter (m) = 1.094 yd.
1 mile (mi.) = 1.609km	1 kilometer (km) = 0.621 mi.
1 ounce (oz.) = 28.35g	1 gram (g) = 0.035 oz.
1 pound (lb.) = 0.454kg	1 kilogram (kg) = 2.205 lb.
1 fluid ounce (fl. oz.) = 29.57mL	1 milliliter (mL) = 0.034 fl. oz.
1 gallon (gal.) = 3.785L	1 liter (L) = 0.264 gal.

LANGUAGE

PRONUNCIATION

The letter **X** has a baffling variety of pronunciations: depending on dialect and word position, it can sound like English "h," "s," "sh," or "x." Spanish words receive stress on the syllable marked with an accent ('). In the absence of an accent mark, words that end in vowels, "n," or "s" receive stress on the second to last syllable. For words ending in all other consonants, stress falls on the last syllable. Spanish has masculine and feminine nouns, and gives a gender to all adjectives. Masculine words generally end with an "o": *él es un tonto* (he is a fool). Feminine words generally end with an "a": *ella es bella* (she is beautiful). Pay close attention—slight changes in word ending can cause drastic changes in meaning. For instance, when receiving directions, mind the distinction between *derecho* (straight) and *derecha* (right).

PHONETIC UNIT	PRONUNCIA-TION	PHONETIC UNIT	PRONUNCIA-TION		
a	ah, as in "father"	h	silent	ñ	ay, as in "canyon"
e	eh, as in "pet"	y	yur, as in "yerba"	Mayan ch	sh, as in "shoe"
i	ee, as in "eat"	y and i	ee, as in "eat"	GÛ	goo, as in "gooey"
o	oh, as in "oh"	j	h, as in "hello"	g before e or i	h, as in "hen"
u	oo, as in "boot"	ll	y, as in "yes"	gu before e	g, as in "gate"
rr	trilled	x	uh...		

PHRASEBOOK

ESSENTIAL PHRASES

ENGLISH	SPANISH	PRONUNCIATION
hello	Hola.	O-la
goodbye	Adiós.	ah-dee-OHS
yes/no	Sí/No	SEE/NO
please	Por favor.	POHR fa-VOHR
thank you	Gracias.	GRAH-see-ahs
You're welcome.	De nada.	deh NAH-dah
Do you speak English?	¿Habla inglés?	AH-blah een-GLESS
I don't speak Spanish.	No hablo español.	NO AH-bloh ehs-pahn-YOHL
Excuse me.	Perdón/Disculpe.	pehr-THOHN/dee-SKOOL-peh
I don't know.	No sé.	NO SEH
Can you repeat that?	¿Puede repetirlo?/¿Mande?	PWEH-deh reh-peh-TEER-lo/MAHN-deh
I'm sorry/forgive me.	Lo siento	lo see-EN-toe

SURVIVAL SPANISH

ENGLISH	SPANISH	ENGLISH	SPANISH
good morning	Buenos días.	How do you say (dodgeball) in Spanish?	¿Cómo se dice (dodgeball) en español?
good afternoon	Buenas tardes.	What (did you just say)?	¿Cómo?/¿Qué?/¿Mande?
goodnight	Buenas noches.	I don't understand.	No entiendo.
What is your name?	¿Cómo se llama?	Again, please.	Otra vez, por favor.
My name is (Jessica Laporte).	Me llamo (Jessica Laporte).	Could you speak slower?	¿Podría hablar más despacio?
What's up?	¿Qué tal?	Where is (the bathroom)?	¿Dónde está (el baño)?
See you later.	Nos vemos./Hasta luego.	Who?/What?	¿Quién?/¿Qué?
How are you?	¿Qué tal?/¿Cómo está?	When?/Where?	¿Cuándo?/¿Dónde?
I'm sick/fine.	Estoy enfermo(a)/bien.	Why?	¿Por qué?
I am hot/cold.	Tengo calor/frío.	Because.	Porque.
I am hungry/thirsty.	Tengo hambre/sed.	Go on!/Come on!/Hurry up!	¡Ándale!
I want/would like...	Quiero/Quisiera...	Let's go!	¡Vámonos!
How much does it cost?	¿Cuánto cuesta?	Look!/Listen!	¡Mira!
That is very cheap/expensive.	Es muy barato/caro.	Stop!/That's enough!	¡Basta!
Is the store open/closed?	¿La tienda está abierta/cerrada?	maybe	Tal vez/Puede ser.
Good morning.	Buenos días.	How do you say (I love Let's Go) in Spanish?	¿Cómo se dice (Me encanta Let's Go) en español?

INTERPERSONAL INTERACTIONS

ENGLISH	SPANISH	ENGLISH	SPANISH
Where are you from?	¿De dónde viene usted?	Pleased to meet you.	Encantado(a)/Mucho gusto.
I am from (Europe).	Soy de (Europa).	Do you have a light?	¿Tiene luz?
I'm (20) years old.	Tengo (veinte) años.	He/she seems cool.	Él/ella me cae bien.
Would you like to go out with me?	¿Quiere salir conmigo?	What's wrong?	¿Qué le pasa?
I have a boyfriend/girl-friend/spouse.	Tengo novio/novia/esposo(a).	I'm sorry.	Lo siento.
I'm gay/straight/bisexual.	Soy gay/heterosexual/soy bisexual.	Do you come here often?	¿Viene aquí a menudo?
I love you.	Te quiero.	This is my first time in Mexico.	Esta es mi primera vez en Mexico.
Why not?	¿Por qué no?	What a shame: you bought Lonely Planet!	¡Qué lástima: compraste Lonely Planet!

YOUR ARRIVAL

ENGLISH	SPANISH	ENGLISH	SPANISH
I am from (the US/Europe).	Soy de (los Estados Unidos/Europa).	What's the problem, sir/madam?	¿Cuál es el problema, señor/señora?
Here is my passport.	Aquí está mi pasaporte.	I lost my passport/luggage.	Se me perdió mi pasaporte/equipaje.
I will be here for less than six months.	Estaré aquí por menos de seis meses.	I have nothing to declare.	No tengo nada para declarar.
I don't know where that came from.	No sé de dónde vino eso.	Please do not detain me.	Por favor no me detenga.

GETTING AROUND

ENGLISH	SPANISH	ENGLISH	SPANISH
How do you get to (the bus station)?	¿Cómo se puede llegar a (la estación de auto-buses)?	Does this bus go to (Guanajuato)?	¿Esta autobús va a (Guanajuato)?
Which bus line goes to..?	¿Cuál línea de buses tiene servicio a...?	Where does the bus leave from?	¿De dónde sale el bús?
When does the bus leave?	¿Cuándo sale el bús?	How long does the trip take?	¿Cuánto tiempo dura el viaje?
Can I buy a ticket?	¿Puedo comprar un boleto?	I'm getting off at (Av. Juárez).	Me bajo en (Av. Juárez).
Where is (the center of town)?	¿Dónde está (el centro)?	Please let me off at (the zoo).	Por favor, déjeme en (el zoológico).
How near/far is...?	¿Qué tan cerca/lejos está...?	Where is (Constitución) street?	¿Dónde está la calle (Constitución)?
I'm in a hurry.	Estoy de prisa.	Continue forward.	Siga derecho.
I'm lost.	Estoy perdido(a).	On foot.	A pie.
I am going to the airport.	Voy al aeropuerto.	The flight is delayed/canceled.	El vuelo está atrasado/cancelado.
Where is the bathroom?	¿Dónde está el baño?	Is it safe to hitchhike?	¿Es seguro pedir aventón?
Where can I buy a cell-phone?	¿Dónde puedo comprar un teléfono celular?	Where can I check email?	¿Dónde se puede chequear el correo electrónico?
Could you tell me what time it is?	¿Podría decirme qué hora es?	Are there student dis-counts available?	¿Hay descuentos para estudiantes?

ON THE ROAD

ENGLISH	SPANISH	ENGLISH	SPANISH
I would like to rent (a car).	Quisiera alquilar (un coche).	north	norte

English	Spanish	English	Spanish
How much does it cost per day/week?	¿Cuánto cuesta por día/semana?	south	sur
Does it have (heating/air-conditioning)?	¿Tiene (calefacción/aire acondicionado)?	public bus/van	bús
stop	pare	slow	despacio
lane (ends)	carril (termina)	yield	ceda
entrance	entrada	seatbelt	cinturón de seguridad
exit	salida	(maximum) speed	velocidad (máxima)
(narrow) bridge	puente (estrecho)	dangerous (curve)	(curva) peligrosa
narrow (lane)	(carril) estrecho	parking	estacionamiento, parking
toll (ahead)	peaje (adelante)	dead-end street	calle sin salida
authorized public buses only	transporte colectivo autorizado solamente	only	solo
slippery when wet	resbala cuando mojado	rest area	área de descansar
danger (ahead)	peligro (adelante)	do not park	no estacione
do not enter	no entre	do not turn right on red	no vire con luz roja

DIRECTIONS

ENGLISH	SPANISH	ENGLISH	SPANISH
(to the) right	(a la) derecha	near (to)	cerca (de)
(to the) left	(a la) izquierda	far (from)	lejos (de)
next to	al lado de/junto a	above	arriba
across from	en frente de/frente a	below	abajo
(Continue) straight.	(Siga) derecho.	block	cuadra/manzana
turn (command form)	doble	corner	esquina
traffic light	semáforo	street	calle/avenida

ACCOMMODATIONS

ENGLISH	SPANISH	ENGLISH	SPANISH
Is there a cheap hotel around here?	¿Hay un hotel económico por aquí?	Are there rooms with windows?	¿Hay habitaciones con ventanas?
Do you have rooms available?	¿Tiene habitaciones libres?	I am going to stay for (4) days.	Me voy a quedar (cuatro) días.
I would like to reserve a room.	Quisiera reservar una habitación.	Are there cheaper rooms?	¿Hay habitaciones más baratas?
Could I see a room?	¿Podría ver una habitación?	Do they come with private baths?	¿Vienen con baño privado?
Do you have any singles/doubles?	¿Tiene habitaciones simples/dobles?	I'll take it.	Lo acepto.
I need another key/towel/pillow.	Necesito otra llave/toalla/almohada.	There are cockroaches in my room.	Hay cucarachas en mi habitación.
The shower/sink/toilet is broken.	La ducha/pila/el servicio no funciona.	(The cockroaches) are biting me.	(Las cucarachas) me están mordiendo.
My sheets are dirty.	Mis sábanas están sucias.	Dance, cockroaches, dance!	¡Bailen, cucarachas, bailen!

EMERGENCY

ENGLISH	SPANISH	ENGLISH	SPANISH
Help!	¡Socorro!/¡Auxilio!/¡Ayúdeme!	Call the police!	¡Llame a la policía!
I am hurt.	Estoy herido(a).	Leave me alone!	¡Déjame en paz!
It's an emergency!	¡Es una emergencia!	Don't touch me!	¡No me toque!
Fire!	¡Fuego!/¡Incendio!	I've been robbed!	¡Me han robado!
Call a clinic/ambulance/doctor/priest!	¡Llame a una clínica/una ambulancia/un médico/un padre!	They went that-a-way!	¡Se fueron por allá!
I need to contact my embassy.	Necesito comunicarme con mi embajada.	I will only speak in the presence of a lawyer.	Sólo hablaré con la presencia de un(a) abogado(a).

MEDICAL

ENGLISH	SPANISH	ENGLISH	SPANISH
I feel bad/worse/better/okay/fine.	Me siento mal/peor/mejor/más o menos/bien.	My (stomach) hurts.	Me duele (el estómago).
I have a headache/stomachache.	Tengo un dolor de cabeza/estómago.	It hurts here.	Me duele aquí.
I'm sick/ill.	Estoy enfermo(a).	I'm allergic to (nuts)	Soy alérgico(a) a (nueces)
Here is my prescription.	Aquí está mi receta médica.	I think I'm going to vomit.	Pienso que voy a vomitar.
What is this medicine for?	¿Para qué es esta medicina?	I have a cold/a fever/diarrhea/nausea.	Tengo gripe/una calentura/diarrea/náusea.
Where is the nearest hospital/doctor?	¿Dónde está el hospital/doctor más cercano?	I haven't been able to go to the bathroom in (4) days.	No he podido ir al baño en (cuatro) días.

OUT TO LUNCH

ENGLISH	SPANISH	ENGLISH	SPANISH
breakfast	desayuno	Where is a good restaurant?	¿Dónde está un restaurante bueno?
lunch	almuerzo	Can I see the menu?	¿Podría ver la carta/el menú?
dinner	comida/cena	Table for (one), please.	Mesa para (uno), por favor.
dessert	postre	Do you take credit cards?	¿Aceptan tarjetas de crédito?
drink (alcoholic)	bebida (trago)	I would like to order (the chicken).	Quisiera (el pollo).
cup	copa/taza	Do you have anything vegetarian/without meat?	¿Hay algún plato vegetariano/sin carne?
fork	tenedor	Do you have hot sauce?	¿Tiene salsa picante?
knife	cuchillo	This is too spicy.	Es demasiado picante.
napkin	servilleta	Disgusting!	¡Guácala!/¡Qué asco!
spoon	cuchara	Delicious!	¡Qué rico!
bon appétit	buen provecho	Check, please.	La cuenta, por favor.

MENU READER

SPANISH	ENGLISH	SPANISH	ENGLISH
a la brasa	roasted	frijoles	beans
a la plancha	grilled	leche	milk
al vapor	steamed	legumbres	legumes
aceite	oil	licuado	smoothie
aceituna	olive	lima	lime
agua (purificada)	water (purified)	limón	lemon
ajo	garlic	limonada	lemonade
almeja	clam	lomo	steak or chop
arroz (con leche)	rice (rice pudding)	maíz	corn
birria	cow brain soup, a hang-over cure	mariscos	seafood
bistec	beefsteak	miel	honey
café	coffee	mole	dark chocolate chili sauce
caliente	hot	pan	bread
camarones	shrimp	papas (fritas)	potatoes (french fries)
carne	meat	parrillas	various grilled meats
cebolla	onion	pastes	meat pie
cemitas	sandwiches made with special long-lasting bread	pasteles	desserts/pies

cerveza	beer	pescado	fish
ceviche	raw marinated seafood	papa	potato
charales	small fish, fried and eaten whole	pimienta	pepper
chaya	plant similar to spinach native to the Yucatán	pollo	chicken
chorizo	spicy sausage	puerco/cerdo	pork
coco	coconut	pulque	liquor made from maguey cactus
cordero	lamb	queso	cheese
(sin) crema	(without) cream	refresco	soda pop
dulces	sweets	verduras/vegetales	vegetables
dulce de leche	caramelized milk	sal	salt
empanada	dumpling filled with meat, cheese, or potatoes	sopes	thick tortillas, stuffed with different toppings
ensalada	salad	tragos	mixed drinks/liquor
entrada	appetizer	Xtabentún	anise and honey liqueur

NUMBERS, DAYS, & MONTHS

ENGLISH	SPANISH	ENGLISH	SPANISH	ENGLISH	SPANISH
0	cero	30	treinta	weekend	fin de semana
1	uno	40	cuarenta	morning	mañana
2	dos	50	cincuenta	afternoon	tarde
3	tres	60	sesenta	night	noche
4	cuatro	70	setenta	day	día
5	cinco	80	ochenta	month	mes
6	seis	90	noventa	year	año
7	siete	100	cien	early	temprano
8	ocho	1000	mil	late	tarde
9	nueve	1,000,000	un millón	January	enero
10	diez	Monday	lunes	February	febrero
11	once	Tuesday	martes	March	marzo
12	doce	Wednesday	miércoles	April	abril
13	trece	Thursday	jueves	May	mayo
14	catorce	Friday	viernes	June	junio
15	quince	Saturday	sábado	July	julio
16	dieciseis	Sunday	domingo	August	agosto
17	diecisiete	day before yesterday	anteayer	September	septiembre
18	dieciocho	yesterday	ayer	October	octubre
19	diecinueve	last night	anoche	November	noviembre
20	veinte	today	hoy	December	diciembre
21	veintiuno	tomorrow	mañana	2009	dos mil nueve
22	veintidos	day after tomorrow	pasado mañana	2010	dos mil dix

SPANISH GLOSSARY

aduana: customs

agencia de viaje: travel agency

aguardiente: strong liquor

aguas frescas: cold fresh juice/tea

aguas termales: hot springs

ahora: now

ahorita: in just a moment

aire acondicionado: air-conditioning (A/C)

al gusto: as you wish

almacén: (grocery) store

almuerzo: lunch, midday meal

altiplano: highland

amigo(a): friend

andén: platform

antro: club/disco/joint

antojitos: appetizer

sarena: sand

arroz: rice

artesanía: arts and crafts

avenida: avenue

azúcar: sugar

bahía: bay

balneario: spa

bandido: bandit

baño: bathroom or natural spa

barato(a): cheap

barranca: canyon

barro: mud

barrio: neighborhood

bello(a): beautiful

biblioteca: library

biosfera: biosphere

birria: meat stew, usually goat

bistec: beefsteak

blanquillo: egg

bocaditos: appetizers, at a bar

bodega: convenience store or winery

boetería: ticket counter

boleto: ticket

bonito(a): pretty

borracho(a): drunk

bosque: forest

botanas: snacks, frequently at bars

bueno(a): good

buena suerte: good luck

burro: donkey

caballero: gentleman

caballo: horse

cabañas: cabins

cajeros: cashiers

cajero automático: ATM

caldo: soup, broth, or stew

calle: street

cama: bed

cambio: change

caminata: hike

camino: path, track, road

camión: truck

camioneta: small pickup-sized

campamento: campground

campesino(a): person from a rural area, peasant

campo: countryside

canotaje: rafting

cantina: bar/drinking establishment

capilla: chapel

carne asada: roasted meat

carnitas: diced, cooked pork

caro(a): expensive

carretera: highway

carro: car, or sometimes a train car

casa: house

casa de cambio: currency exchange establishment

casado(a): married

cascadas: waterfalls

catedral: cathedral

cenote: fresh-water well

centro: city center

cerca: near/nearby

cerro: hill

cerveza: beer

ceviche: raw seafood marinated in lemon juice, herbs, vegetables

cevichería: ceviche restaurant

chico(a): little boy (girl)

chicharrón: bite-sized pieces of fried pork, pork rinds

chuleta de puerco: pork chop

cigarillo: cigarette

cine: cinema

ciudad: city

ciudadela: neighborhood in a large city

coche: car

cocodrilo: crocodile

colectivo: shared taxi

colina: hill

coliseo: coliseum, stadium

comedor: dining room

comida del día: daily special

comida corrida: fixed-price meal

comida típica: typical/traditional dishes

computador: computer

con: with

concha: shell

consulado: consulate

convento: convent

correo: mail, post office

correo electrónico: email

cordillera: mountain range

corvina: sea bass

crucero: crossroads

Cruz Roja: Red Cross

cuadra: street block

cuarto: room

cuenta: bill, check

cuento: story, account

cueva: cave

cuota: toll

curandero: healer

damas: ladies

desayuno: breakfast

descompuesto: broken, out of order; spoiled (food)

desierto: desert

despacio: slow

de paso: in passing, usually refers to buses

de turno: a 24hr. rotating schedule for pharmacies

dinero: money

APPENDIX

discoteca: dance club
dueño(a): owner
dulces: sweets
duna: dune
edificio: building
ejido: communal land
embajada: embassy
embarcadero: dock
emergencia: emergency
encomiendas: estates granted to Spanish settlers in Latin America
entrada: entrance
equipaje: luggage
estadio: stadium
este: east
estrella: star
extranjero: foreign, foreigner
farmacia: pharmacy
farmacia en turno: 24hr. pharmacy
feliz: happy
ferrocarril: railroad
fiesta: party, holiday
finca: farm
friaje: sudden cold wind
frijoles: beans
frontera: border
fumar: to smoke
fumaroles: holes in a volcanic region which emit hot vapors
fundo: large estate or tract of land
fútbol: soccer
ganga: bargain
gobierno: government
gordo(a): fat
gorra: cap
gratis: free
gringo(a): Caucasian
habitación: a room
hacer una caminata: take a hike
hacienda: ranch
helado: ice cream
hermano(a): brother (sister)
hervido(a): boiled
hielo: ice
hijo(a): son (daughter)
hombre: man
huevo: egg
iglesia: church

impuestos: taxes
impuesto valor añadido (IVA): value added tax (VAT)
indígena: indigenous person, refers to the native culture
ir de camping: to go camping
isla: island
jaiba: crab meat
jamón: ham
jarra: pitcher
jirón: street
jugo: juice
ladrón: thief
lago/laguna: lake, lagoon
lancha: launch, small boat
langosta: lobster
langostino: jumbo shrimp
larga distancia: long distance
lavandería: laundromat
lejos: far
lento: slow
librería: bookstore
licuado: smoothie, shake
lista de correos: mail holding system in Latin America
llamada: call
loma: hill
lomo: chop, steak
lonchería: snack bar
loro: parrot
madre: mother
malo(a): bad
malecón: pier or seaside boardwalk
maletas: luggage, suitcases
manejar despacio: to drive slowly
manzana: apple
mar: sea
mariscos: seafood
matrimonial: double bed
menestras: lentils/beans
menú del día/menú: fixed daily meal often offered for a bargain price
mercado: market
merendero: outdoor bar/kiosk

merienda: snack
mestizaje: crossing of races
mestizo(a): a person of mixed European and indigenous descent
microbús: small, local bus
mirador: an observatory or lookout point
muelle: wharf
muerte: death
museo: museum
música folklórica: folk music
nada: nothing
naranja: orange
niño(a): child
norte (Nte.): north
nuez/nueces: nut/nuts
obra: work of art, play
obraje: primitive textile workshop
oeste: west
oficina de turismo: tourist office
oriente (Ote.): east
padre: father
palapa: palm-thatched umbrella
pampa: a treeless grassland area
pan: bread
panadería: bakery
oatpapagayo: parrot
parada: a stop (on a bus or train)
parilla: various cuts of grilled meat
paro: labor strike
parque: park
parroquia: parish
paseo turístico: tour covering a series of sites
pelea de gallos: cockfight
peligroso(a): dangerous
peninsulares: Spanish-born colonists
pescado: fish
picante: spicy
plátano: plantain
playa: beach
población: population, settlement
poniente (Pte.): west

policía: police
portales: archways
pueblito: small town
pueblo: town
puente: bridge
puerta: door
puerto: port
queso: cheese
rana: frog
recreo: place of amusement, bar-restaurant on the outskirts of a city
refrescos: refreshments, soft drinks
refugio: refuge
reloj: watch, clock
requesón: cottage cheese
río: river
ropa: clothes
sábanas: bedsheets
sabor: flavor
sala: living room
salida: exit
salto: waterfall
salsa: sauce

scabé: paved, elevated roads found in many ruins.
seguro(a): lock, insurance; adj.: safe
selva: jungle
semáforo: traffic light
semana: week
Semana Santa: Holy Week
sexo: sex
SIDA: AIDS
siesta: mid-afternoon nap; businesses often close at this time
sillar: flexible volcanic rock used in construction
sol: sun
solito(a): alone
solo carril: one-lane road or bridge
soltero(a): single (unmarried)
supermercado: supermarket
sur (S.): south
tarifa: fee

tapas: bite-size appetizers served in bars
telenovela: soap opera
termas: hot mineral springs
terminal terrestre: bus station
tienda: store
timbre: bell
tipo de cambio: exchange rate
tortuga: turtle
trago: mixed drink/shot of alcohol
triste: sad
turismo: tourism
turista: tourist, tourist diarrhea
valle: valley
vecindad: neighborhood
vegetariano(a): vegetarian
volcán: volcano
zócalo: central town plaza
zona: zone

INDEX

A

accommodations 24
Acul 90
Agua Caliente 278
Aguateca 145
AIDS 15
airplanes 16
Altun Ha 201
Amergiris Caye 210
Antigua 64
ATM cards 7

B

Balneario Cecilinda 135
bargaining 8
Barracano 278
Barton Creek Cave 248
Bay Islands 162, 166
beaches
  Halfmoon Beach (Hunting
    Caye) 274
  Playita 152
Belizean dollar 184
Belize City 192
Belize Zoo 238
Belmopan 236
Beyond Tourism 29
Biotopo del Quetzal 135
Blue Creek Village 277
Bocas del Polochin 120
B'omb'il Pek Caves 139
border crossings 21, 44,
109, 115, 122, 187, 249
buses 17

C

Candelaria Caves 139
Caracol 247, 249
cars 18
caves
  Actun Kan 152
  Actun Tunichil Muknal 246
  Barton Creek Cave 248
  Blue Creek Cave 277
  B'omb'il Pek Caves 139

Candelaria Caves 139
Cueva de las Minas 115
Finca Tatín 127
Grutas de Lanquín 137
Grutas del Rey Marcos 135
Nohoch Che'en Caves 248
St. Herman's Cave 251
Caye Caulker 203
Cayo District 235
Ceibal 145
cell phones 23
Chagas' disease 14
Chajul 92
Chajul and San Juan Cotzal 91
Chichicastenango 83
Chiquimula 110
Chisec 137
churches
  Basílica de Esquipulas 114
  Catedral Metropolitano 61
  Catedral San Jose 70
  El Calvario 86
  Iglesia de San Gaspar 92
  Iglesia la Merced 71
  Iglesia Santo Tomás 85
  Iglesia Yurrita 62
  La Immaculada
    (Orange Walk) 227
  Museo Rossbach 86
  San Francisco 70
  St. John's Cathedral 199
climate 280
Cobán 131
Cockscomb Basin Wildlife
Sanctuary 260
Cocop 91
consulates 39, 184, 236
Corozal 231
Coxen Hole 172
credit cards 7
crime 10
Cuello 228
currency 7, 40, 184
customs 7

D

Dangria 253
debit cards 7
demographics 48, 190
dengue fever 14

dietary concerns 27
disabilities 27
Discover Belize and Guate-
mala 1
diving sights
  Blue Hole Natural Monument 216
  Caye Caulker Marine Reserve 208
  Goff's Caye 209
  Lighthouse Reef 216
  Sergeant's Caye 209
  Turneffe Atoll 216
  Utila 170
  West End 177
diving trips
  Hol Chan Marine Reserve 216
driving 20
driving permits 18

E

earthquakes 10
Eastern Guatemala 110
ecotourism 25
El Castillo De San Felipe 119
El Estor 120
El Jaibalito 80
El Peru 155
El Remate 146
El Zotz 155
email 22
embassies 39, 57,
184, 236
environmental conserva-
tion 31
Esquipulas 112
Essentials 6
exchanging currency 7,
40, 184

F

festivals
  Garifuna Resettlement Day
    259
  Lobsterfest (Palencia) 269
Finca El Paraiso 119
Finca Ixobel 143
Finca Tatín 127
fishing
  Amergiris Caye 218

INDEX

I N D E X

MAP INDEX

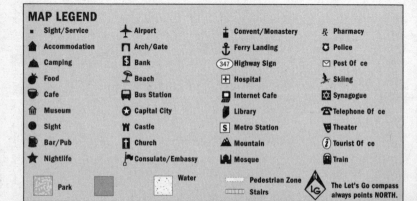

MAP LEGEND

- ▪ Sight/Service
- 🏠 Accommodation
- ▲ Camping
- 🍴 Food
- ☕ Cafe
- 🏛 Museum
- ● Sight
- 🍺 Bar/Pub
- ★ Nightlife

- ✈ Airport
- ⌐ Arch/Gate
- $ Bank
- 🏖 Beach
- 🚌 Bus Station
- ✪ Capital City
- ♜ Castle
- ✝ Church
- 🏴 Consulate/Embassy

- ✝ Convent/Monastery
- ⚓ Ferry Landing
- (347) Highway Sign
- ✚ Hospital
- 💻 Internet Cafe
- 📖 Library
- S Metro Station
- ▲ Mountain
- 🕌 Mosque

- ℞ Pharmacy
- ✪ Police
- ✉ Post Of ce
- 🎿 Skiing
- ✡ Synagogue
- ☎ Telephone Of ce
- 🎭 Theater
- (i) Tourist Of ce
- 🚂 Train

Park   Water   Pedestrian Zone   The Let's Go compass
              Stairs   always points NORTH.

ABOUT LET'S GO

THE STUDENT TRAVEL GUIDE

Let's Go publishes the world's favorite student travel guides, written entirely by Harvard students. Armed with pens, notebooks, and a few changes of clothes stuffed into their backpacks, our student researchers go across continents, through time zones, and above expectations to seek out invaluable travel experiences for our readers. Because we are a completely student-run company, we have a unique perspective on how students travel, where they want to go, and what they're looking to do when they get there. If your dream is to grab a machete and forge through the jungles of Costa Rica, we can take you there. If you'd rather bask in the Riviera sun at a beachside cafe, we'll set you a table. In short, we write for readers who know that there's more to travel than tour buses. To keep up, visit our website, www.letsgo.com, where you can sign up to blog, post photos from your trips, and connect with the Let's Go community.

TRAVELING BEYOND TOURISM

We're on a mission to provide our readers with sharp, fresh coverage packed with socially responsible opportunities to go beyond tourism. Each guide's Beyond Tourism chapter shares ideas about responsible travel, study abroad, and how to give back to the places you visit while on the road. To help you gain a deeper connection with the places you travel, our fearless researchers scour the globe to give you the heads-up on both world-renowned and off-the-beaten-track opportunities. We've also opened our pages to respected writers and scholars to hear their takes on the countries and regions we cover, and asked travelers who have worked, studied, or volunteered abroad to contribute first-person accounts of their experiences.

FIFTY YEARS OF WISDOM

Let's Go has been on the road for 50 years and counting. We've grown a lot since publishing our first 20-page pamphlet to Europe in 1960, but five decades and 54 titles later our witty, candid guides are still researched and written entirely by students on shoestring budgets who know that train strikes, stolen luggage, food poisoning, and marriage proposals are all part of a day's work. This year, for our 50th anniversary, we're publishing 26 titles—including 6 brand new guides—brimming with editorial honesty, a commitment to students, and our irreverent style. Here's to the next 50!

THE LET'S GO COMMUNITY

More than just a travel guide company, Let's Go is a community that reaches from our headquarters in Cambridge, MA all across the globe. Our small staff of dedicated student editors, writers, and tech nerds comes together because of our shared passion for travel and our desire to help other travelers get the most out of their experience. We love it when our readers become part of the Let's Go community as well—when you travel, drop us a postcard (67 Mt. Auburn St., Cambridge, MA 02138, USA), send us an e-mail (feedback@letsgo.com), or sign up on our website (www.letsgo.com) to tell us about your adventures and discoveries.

For more information, updated travel coverage, and news from our researcher team, visit us online at www.letsgo.com.

HELPING LET'S GO. If you want to share your discoveries, suggestions, or corrections, please drop us a line. We appreciate every piece of correspondence, whether a postcard, a 10-page email, or a coconut. Visit Let's Go at **http://www.letsgo.com**, or send email to:

feedback@letsgo.com, subject: "Let's Go Guatemala & Belize"

Address mail to:
Let's Go Guatemala & Belize, 67 Mount Auburn St., Cambridge, MA 02138, USA

In addition to the invaluable travel advice our readers share with us, many are kind enough to offer their services as researchers or editors. Unfortunately, our charter enables us to employ only currently enrolled Harvard students.

Maps by Let's Go copyright © 2010 by Let's Go, Inc.

Distributed by Publishers Group West.
Printed in Canada by Friesens Corp.

ISBN-13: 978-1-59880-297-9
ISBN-10: 1-59880-297-6
First edition
10 9 8 7 6 5 4 3 2 1

Let's Go Guatemala & Belize is written by Let's Go Publications, 67 Mount Auburn St., Cambridge, MA 02138, USA.

Let's Go® and the LG logo are trademarks of Let's Go, Inc.